ELIZABETH I

ELIZABETH I

COLLECTED

WORKS

Edited by
Leah S. Marcus, Janel Mueller,
and Mary Beth Rose

THE UNIVERSITY OF CHICAGO PRESS
Chicago & London

LEAH S. MARCUS is the Edwin Mims Professor of English at Vanderbilt University. Her books include *Childhood and Cultural Despair* (1978), *The Politics of Mirth* (University of Chicago Press, 1986), *Puzzling Shakespeare* (1988), and *Unediting the Renaissance* (1996).

JANEL MUELLER is professor of English and the William Rainey Harper Professor in the College at the University of Chicago and was recently made Dean of the Division of the Humanities. She has been the editor of the journal *Modern Philology* and is the author of *The Native Tongue and the Word* (University of Chicago Press, 1984).

MARY BETH ROSE is director of the Institute for the Humanities and professor of English at the University of Illinois at Chicago. She is the author of *The Expense of Spirit: Love and Sexuality in English Renaissance Drama* (1988) and is currently completing a study of gender and the transformations of heroism in early modern English literature.

The University of Chicago Press, Chicago 60637
The University of Chicago Press, Ltd., London
© 2000 by The University of Chicago
All rights reserved. Published 2000
Printed in the United States of America

09 08 07 06 05 04 03 02 01 00   1 2 3 4 5
ISBN 0-226-50464-6

Library of Congress Cataloging-in-Publication Data

Elizabeth I, Queen of England, 1533–1603.
    [Selections]
    Elizabeth I : collected works / edited by Leah S. Marcus, Janel Mueller, and Mary Beth Rose.
        p.   cm.
    Includes index.
    ISBN 0-226-50464-6 (cloth : alk. paper)
    1. Great Britain—History—Elizabeth, 1558–1603—Sources. 2. Elizabeth I, Queen of England, 1533–1603—Correspondence. I. Marcus, Leah S. II. Mueller, Janel M., 1938–   III. Rose, Mary Beth. IV. Title.
DA350.A25 2000
942.05'5'092—dc21   99-28794

CONTENTS

List of Illustrations *vii*
List of Abbreviations and Frequently Cited Works *ix*
Preface *xi*

I   1533–1558   3

    LETTERS 1–23 · 5
    POEMS 1–3 · 45
    PRAYERS 1–2 · 48

II   1558–1572   49

    SPEECHES 1–12 · 51
    LETTERS 24–33 · 111
    POEMS 4–5 · 132
    PRAYERS 3–28 · 135
    POEM 6 · 151

III   1572–1587   165

    SPEECHES 13–18 · 167
    LETTERS 34–77 · 205
    POEMS 7–12 · 299
    PRAYERS 29–35 · 310

IV 1588–1603   **323**

SPEECHES 19–24 · 325
LETTERS 78–103 · 355
POEMS 13–15 · 409
PRAYERS 36–39 · 423

List of Speeches, Letters, Poems, Prayers 429
Index of Names 439

ILLUSTRATIONS

1   Princess Elizabeth aged about thirteen, attributed to William Scrots, circa 1546–47 · 4

2   Letter 3, to Henry VIII, opening; BL, MS Royal 7.D.X., sig. 2r · 8

3   Letter 8; PRO, State Papers Domestic, Edward VI 10/2, fol. 84c · 18

4   Queen Elizabeth I in her coronation robes, by an unknown artist around 1600 · 50

5   Speech 6, Queen Elizabeth's draft version; BL, MS Lansdowne 94, fol. 30r · 78

6   Speech 9, version 1, fragmentary opening; PRO, State Papers Domestic, Elizabeth 12 /41 / 5 · 92

7   Speech 10, first page of Queen Elizabeth's draft version; BL, MS Cotton Charter IV.38 (2) · 104

8   Queen Elizabeth sitting in state, title page of Christopher Saxton, *Atlas of England and Wales*, 1579 · 166

9   Speech 17, version 2, first page of transcript with Queen Elizabeth's corrections; BL, MS Lansdowne 94, fol. 84r · 191

10 Speech 18, version 2, middle section of transcript with Queen Elizabeth's corrections; BL, MS Lansdowne 94, fol. 87v · 203

11 Letter 36 to George Talbot, earl of Shrewsbury, showing Queen Elizabeth's subscribed message; Lambeth Palace Library, MS 3197, fol. 41r · 213

12 Letter 41 to the earl and countess of Shrewsbury, showing Queen Elizabeth's superscription; Lambeth Palace Library, MS 3206, fol. 819r · 228

13 Miniature of the duke of Alençon from Queen Elizabeth's Prayer Book, BL, MS Facsimile 218, sig. 1v · 312

14   Miniature of Queen Elizabeth from her Prayer Book, BL, MS
       Facsimile 218, sig. 38r · 320

15   The Armada Portrait of Queen Elizabeth, by George Gower · 324

16   Letter 90 to King James VI of Scotland, second half; BL, MS
       Additional 23240, fol. 132v · 379

17   Poem 15, opening stanzas; Hatfield House, Cecil Papers 147, fol. 207r · 412

18   Prayer 36 on the defeat of the Spanish Armada; Hatfield House, Cecil
       Papers 147, fol. 214r · 422

ABBREVIATIONS
AND FREQUENTLY CITED
WORKS

ACFLO Janel Mueller and Leah S. Marcus, eds. *Elizabeth I: Autograph Composi-tions and Foreign Language Originals,* University of Chicago Press: forth-coming.

BL British Library. Items reproduced by permission.

BOOTY John E. Booty, ed. *The Book of Common Prayer, 1559: The Elizabethan Prayer Book.* Washington, D.C.: Folger Shakespeare Library, 1976.

BRADNER Leicester Bradner, ed. *The Poems of Elizabeth I.* Providence, R.I.: Brown University Press, 1963.

BRUCE John Bruce, ed. *Letters of Queen Elizabeth and King James VI of Scotland.* Camden Society No. 46. London: J. B. Nichols and Son, 1849.

D'EWES Sir Simonds D'Ewes. *The Journals of All the Parliaments during the Reign of Queen Elizabeth.* London: for John Starkey, 1682.

FOXE John Foxe. *Acts and Monuments of These Latter and Perilous Days.* London: John Day, 1563.

HARRISON G. B. Harrison, ed. *The Letters of Queen Elizabeth I.* 1935. Reprint, Westport, Conn.: Greenwood Press, 1981.

HARTLEY T. E. Hartley, ed. *Proceedings in the Parliaments of Elizabeth I.* 3 vols. Leicester: Leicester University Press, 1981–95.

HOLINSHED Raphael Holinshed. *The Third Volume of Chronicles.* London: Henry Denham et al., 1587.

HUGHES AND LARKIN Paul L. Hughes and James F. Larkin, eds. *Tudor Royal Proclamations*. New Haven: Yale University Press, 1964.

KNIGHTON C. S. Knighton, ed. *Calendar of State Papers, Domestic Series, of the Reign of Edward VI*. Rev. ed. London: Her Majesty's Stationers' Office, 1992.

MS Manuscript

NEALE Sir John Neale. *Elizabeth I and Her Parliaments*. 2 vols. New York: St. Martin's, 1958.

NICHOLS John Nichols, ed. *The Progresses and Public Processions of Queen Elizabeth*. 3 vols. 1823. Reprint, New York: AMS Press, n.d.

PRO Public Record Office. Crown copyright material in the Public Record Office, London, is reproduced by permission of the Comtroller of Her Britannic Majesty's Stationery Office.

STC *A Short-Title Catalogue of Books Printed in England, Scotland, and Ireland, and of English Books Printed Abroad, 1475–1640*. 2nd ed. Rev. and enlarged. Edited by W. A. Jackson, F. S. Ferguson, Katharine F. Pantzer, and Philip E. Rider. 3 vols. London: Bibliographical Society, 1986–91.

TANNER J. R. Tanner, ed. *Tudor Constitutional Documents, A.D. 1485–1603*. Cambridge: Cambridge University Press, 1951.

PREFACE

Elizabeth Tudor (1533–1603), best known as a ruler of England, was also an immensely productive writer. She received one of the finest humanist educations of her day; and from the age of eleven, if not earlier, she produced a steady flow of letters and translations in various languages. Beginning at least as early as her youthful imprisonment at Woodstock (1554–55), she also wrote verses and prayers. During her forty-five-year reign as queen of England, she continued to be a prolific letter writer and occasional poet; but her greatest literary achievement is a series of speeches that are often remarkable for their beauty and power.

Despite Elizabeth's historical importance, her production as a writer has been considered only piecemeal. Biographers describe her impressive education and stress instances of her unusual verbal and linguistic powers but seldom offer more than cursory attention to the content of her writings. Historians analyze her speeches and letters but usually as documents of policy—evidence charting the queen's relations with Parliament, the Privy Council, and other political bodies. Literary scholars and cultural historians focus on specific poems, letters, and speeches of widely acknowledged eloquence and force, in order to analyze the strategic gendering of Elizabeth's self-representation and the ways in which her subjects received and accommodated their powerful queen.

The compartmentalized particularity of such approaches has been to some extent dictated by the form in which Elizabeth's literary production has been made available to readers: until now, her writings have been published in undeniably valuable but small editions that concentrate on single genres (see, for example, Bradner and Harrison from the list of frequently cited works). In contrast, the present edition offers a sustained, varied presentation of Elizabeth's writings across generic boundaries in a single comprehensive scholarly edition.

Rapidly changing intellectual developments of the past twenty-five years have enabled a cultural moment when an edition like the present one can be produced. First, feminism and gender studies have brought increased attention to Renaissance women writers. Neglected texts by women in the medieval and early modern periods are being made accessible in new scholarly editions; gender studies have also successfully insisted upon new categories of analysis that make visible the multiple dimensions and complexities of these texts. Second, revised assumptions about literary value have enlarged and expanded the traditional canon, as boundaries between what previously were rigidly demarcated as literary and nonliterary texts have become more fluid. Then, too, in Renaissance studies a new privileging of the historically situated, local, and particular has broadened the range of texts that can be found worthy of study as literary and cultural documents. In the past, Elizabeth's reputation as a writer suffered both because of her gender and because her work did not seem to measure up to an idealized aesthetics of timeless literary greatness. Indeed, her writing is almost always occasional in nature: embedded in, and immediately responsive to, specific political situations. Different versions of a given speech, for example, would circulate independently for different purposes, and the precise historical context of each version is always an important part of its meaning. Like gender, this historical situatedness is now a central focus of analytic interest, not only for Elizabeth's speeches, but in the rest of her writings as well.

The vast and dispersed body of Elizabeth's written work presents a textually complicated situation, particularly since a significant portion of her writing was produced in collaboration or after consultation with officials of her government. Some of Elizabeth's writings offer an array of revisions that can be shown to form a complex coproduction, in which we are able to locate points at which others enter into the process of composition and at which Elizabeth responds to their interventions. But at other times, the participation of others in creating her writings cannot be systematically isolated or quantified. This is particularly true of Elizabeth's speeches before Parliament, which, we argue, usually began their lives not as written documents but as the queen's oral utterance, written down only after the fact by the queen's auditors rather than the queen herself, and sometimes then revised by Elizabeth and her ministers jointly for broader distribution. In such a situation, there is no single trustworthy text, but rather a range of materials representing various stages of evolution—from the lost oral performance that so bedazzled her contemporaries through to the finished public record of it.

As for the letters, Elizabeth dictated many of them, and signed many that were drafted by others. It is often impossible to separate the queen's "authentic" voice from an official style that she developed in conjunction with her secretaries and principal ministers and that was used with equal facility by all of them. The texts of Elizabeth's letters are usually more stable than the speeches, if only because a given letter would usually be sent out only once; but we reproduce some exceptions. The revised "official" version of Letter 41 to the earl of Shrewsbury about the earl of Leicester's visit presents one example: it weeds out the puckish details of an earlier draft. At whose behest was this interesting letter revised? Even the queen's most seemingly personal letters in her own hand—such as the love letters to the duke of Alençon—were often copied and incorporated into government archives.

Only two of Elizabeth's poems survive in her own hand: "No Crooked Leg" from the 1560s and her enigmatic "French Stanzaic Verses" of the late 1580s or early 1590s. The rest exist in manuscript copies whose variations may result from scribal intervention—in effect an ongoing process of cocreation. Similarly, the queen's prayers and devotional materials often so intersperse free composition with quotation from the Scriptures and liturgy of the English Church that they constitute yet another form of coproduction between an individual Christian and the collective voice of the Church, with its accumulated texts and traditions.

Clearly, Elizabeth's identity as princess and monarch cannot be separated from her identity as author. The complexities that surround her agency in creating her own texts are, however, no more vexing than the usual unanswered questions about early modern authorship. The writings of William Shakespeare and John Donne, to cite but two examples, are similarly beset with textual uncertainty—particularly given developments in textual studies of the past two decades, as editorial practices that artificially stabilized bodies of early modern work have lost credence with many scholars. Like Elizabeth's, the textual production of Shakespeare and Donne involved an irretrievable oral component—the plays as performed (and improvised?) in the playhouse; the sermons as uttered from notes or from memory in the pulpit before they were written down. Indeed, given the existence of a considerable body of material in Elizabeth's hand, along with meticulous contemporary records of (for example) the queen's delivery of many of her speeches, questions of authorship may actually be somewhat less intractable in her case than in many others of the same era. Her writings present an interesting and valuable example of the ways in which individual agency intersects with various cultural domains in the creation of literary texts.

Our edition presents all of Elizabeth's full-length speeches, prayers, and poems that we have been able to locate in texts we judge reliable. Our standards have been rigorous: most of our materials are newly transcribed from early manuscript sources that are very nearly contemporary with the act of composition itself; only rarely do we use sources that date from after Elizabeth's death, and those special cases are clearly indicated in the notes, along with a rationale for their selection. We also include a generous selection of Elizabeth's letters and a wide array of additional materials—depositions, parliamentary petitions, letters and verses responding to Elizabeth's, memoranda—that provide context for and dialogic engagement with Elizabeth's writings. Much though we might have wished to do so, we have not offered a full collection of Elizabeth's letters, including all of the official correspondence sent out over her formal signature or under her sign manual. That body of work in itself would run to several volumes. Nor do we include famous letters whose attribution is suspect. Most people's favorite among Elizabeth's missives is her abrupt ultimatum to the bishop of Ely:

> Proud prelate,
> You know what you were before I made you what you are now. If you do not immediately comply with my request, I will unfrock you, by God.
>
> *Elizabeth*

But this letter finds no place in the body of our collection because its provenance is uncertain: we have not located it in any early manuscript collections, and it sounds suspiciously like a later artifact modeled on her well-known upbraidings of bishops in her speeches (see in particular Speeches 15 and 16). Already in the early to mid-seventeenth century, Queen Elizabeth I had become such a powerful cultural symbol that her writings were freely adapted and transformed to meet emerging crises and occasions. In the present volume, we offer a generous selection of Elizabeth's best known and securely attributed letters, along with others that are less well-known but demonstrate the queen's epistolary range. We have omitted letters that are routine and formulaic in nature—detailed instructions for the conduct of diplomacy, military commissions, and the like—even if they bear Elizabeth's own signature. In selecting letters, however, we have occasionally violated our own policy against late versions, admitting seventeenth-century copies that we had reason to consider unusually trustworthy. One such case is the letters relating to Elizabeth's courtship deriving from Sir Francis Walsingham and preserved in Dudley Digges's "The Complete Ambassador," which exists in seventeenth-century manuscripts at the British Library and at the Houghton Library of Harvard University and which appeared in print in the mid-seventeenth century. The letters in Digges's collection are so similar to original letters from the same series preserved elsewhere that we have confidence in their basic accuracy. The same is true of some of James VI of Scotland's letters, which we have modernized from the reliable transcriptions in Bruce (see list of frequently cited works).

Elizabeth I was fluent in a number of modern as well as ancient languages, and an appreciable percentage of her writing was composed in languages other than English. This edition presents new translations of her Latin speeches, French and Latin poems, foreign language prayers, and some of the most important of her letters to the reigning families of France. Regrettably, however, we have elected to exclude the queen's translations from this edition, even though these often attracted as much attention during her lifetime as her own compositions. Elizabeth's known translations would constitute a large volume in themselves, and there are almost certainly other extant translations that have yet to be identified as hers. Moreover, several of Elizabeth's translations are already available to scholars in fairly convenient forms; had we reproduced them here, we would have had to omit less well-known and equally interesting materials that, we hope, will expand our readers' views of her authorial range. Our aim has been to bring together in a single volume a significant body of Elizabeth's writings in a form that will meet the demands of scholarship and at the same time be useful to the widest variety of readers.

In arranging materials, we have combined chronological and generic ordering in what we intend as a convenient format for readers. We could have adopted a strict chronological or a strict generic ordering of Elizabeth's writings, but either method in isolation has its disadvantages. To present items in strict chronological order would hinder close concentration on the individual genres in which she wrote, since the materials pertinent to such a perspective would be scattered throughout the volume. On the other hand, to group the materials solely by genre would make it difficult to locate texts in different genres relating to the same events and problems: a letter on the Northern Rebellion, for example, might be separated by several hundred pages from a poem composed in the aftermath of the same crisis. To facilitate use of the edition by readers with different interests and approaches, we have chosen to shape the collection by dividing Elizabeth's life and writings into four sections, each section arranged internally by genre and chronologically within each genre.

Section 1 presents materials produced while Elizabeth was still a princess. It includes her only known letter to her father, Henry VIII, and her letters to her stepmother Queen Katherine Parr, to her half-siblings Edward and Mary, and a little-known letter to Thomas Seymour written shortly after her mysteriously abrupt departure in 1548 from the household he shared with Katherine Parr. Additional documents in this section include a transcript of the testimony that Elizabeth's governess Katherine Ashley gave to the Privy Council regarding Elizabeth's relationship with Seymour. Section 1 also presents poems and prayers written during the dangerous months of Elizabeth's imprisonment under the reign of Mary Tudor.

Sections 2, 3, and 4 divide Elizabeth's reign into roughly equal fifteen-year segments. Section 2 begins with Elizabeth's accession to the throne in 1558 and ends in the aftermath of the Northern Rebellion in 1572. It includes her accession speech at Hatfield House, in which she applies the doctrine of the king's two bodies to her own situation as ruler, and her spirited speeches before Parliament during the tumultuous years when the Lords and Commons attempted to secure the nation's future by pressuring the queen into marrying and settling the succession to the throne. This section also features an early text of the queen's conversations with the Scottish ambassador William Maitland on the same subjects, along with her haunted likening of the naming of her succession to setting up a winding-sheet before her eyes; letters to and about Mary, Queen of Scots, and the Northern Rebellion, as well as Elizabeth's most famous poem, "The Doubt of Future Foes," relating to the same political crisis. In the final segment of section 2, we offer for the first time since the sixteenth century Elizabeth's devotional materials from two important printed collections of the 1560s. These texts—collectively authored though some of them may be—reveal the queen as a hitherto unrecognized cocreator of prayers for her own and her subjects' use.

Even though it spans the same number of years as section 2, section 3 (1572–1587) is much larger because of the far greater availability of important documents from this period. The speeches that begin this section show the queen in a later phase of her relationship with Parliament. The key issues are now ecclesiastical reform and the vexed matter of the execution of Mary, Queen of Scots. Section 3 also includes a number of letters chronicling Elizabeth's marriage negotiations with François Hercule, duke of Alençon, usually referred to as "Monsieur." In their range of subjects, the letters in this section also initiate the important and lively correspondence between Elizabeth I and James VI of Scotland. We have supplied a number of James's answers to Elizabeth's letters, as a way of indicating the interplay of sentiment and argument between them. Several poems in this section take the form of exchanges between Elizabeth and one or another of her subjects, showing her considerable range and accomplishment as an English and Latin poet. The section ends with the queen's miniature prayer book (circa 1579–82), which enclosed a cycle of the queen's prayers between exquisite miniature portraits of Alençon and Elizabeth.

Section 4 begins with a watershed event—the defeat of the Spanish Armada in 1588—and continues to the end of Elizabeth's reign. The speeches in this section are remarkably varied, beginning with the queen's address to the English troops encamped at Tilbury at the time of the Armada threat—a text which we have verified in a sufficiently early manuscript version to allay recent scholarly doubts that the queen's speech was indeed delivered, and in a form reasonably close to the later printed versions of it. Other high points of this section's speeches include Elizabeth's impromptu Latin response to the Polish ambassador, along with the responses of prominent courtiers, and her "Golden Speech" of 1601, which we offer in several different versions—probably all contemporary records of the speech as delivered—that demonstrate the differing recollections of auditors. The letters in this section continue to follow Elizabeth's relations with foreign monarchs and include early texts of some of the queen's most important missives to her final great favorite, the earl of Essex. This section also includes Elizabeth's recently discovered enigmatic French verses on the progress of the soul. The prayers of section 4 show the queen in a little-known public role as spiritual leader of the nation, composing prayers and thanksgivings for important campaigns and military victories.

All of the materials in this volume are reproduced with modernized spelling and punctuation and expanded abbreviations and contractions. To accommodate the range of readers that we envisage, we offer a separate volume that presents extant texts in Elizabeth's hand in her original spelling, as well as the originals of foreign language texts not in her own hand. Unlike the clean copy versions in the present volume, *Autograph Compositions and Foreign Language Originals (ACFLO)* indicates Elizabeth's insertions, deletions, and other revisions in her handwritten texts. Because of limitations of space, *ACFLO* does not include original-spelling versions of English language manuscripts not in the queen's hand. As any student of early modern culture recognizes, the copying of materials was a far from standardized process. The spelling, punctuation, and even wording in any given scribal copy can vary significantly from that of every other copy; such manuscripts consequently are less reliable transmitters of Elizabeth's meaning than her own handwritten texts. The original-spelling materials collected in *ACFLO* will also allow interested readers to assess our style of modernization and translation.

In general, although we have chosen to modernize, we have wanted to keep readers in contact with the irregularities and sometimes gritty intransigence of the manuscripts: we have retained archaic and foreign words and phrases where they occur in English language texts—unless the spelling of a word is quite close to its form in modern English, in which case we have silently modernized its spelling. Thus "sithence" and "sith" do not become "since" but retain their original forms. There are a number of borderline cases that we have regularized: for example, "farder" and "furder" become "farther" and "further"; Elizabeth's frequent spelling of "hit" becomes "it," "accompt" becomes "account," and "burthen" becomes "burden." We do not correct features of the original manuscripts that may appear grammatically incorrect to modern readers, such as lack of verb-subject agreement and "a" rather than "an" before a vowel. We have supplied or altered punctuation and paragraphing when we have judged necessary to make many texts more readable. As we are well aware, however, to modernize is to interpret: the spelling and punctuation that enable and clarify one possible interpretation of Elizabeth's often difficult writing may well obscure other possible readings, and we invite readers to interrogate our modernizations even while making use of them.

Although we have modernized spelling and punctuation in this volume to make these materials accessible to a wide range of readers, we have simultaneously preserved some of the flavor of the early modern documents. Interspersed illustrations allow readers to consult facsimiles of the originals while reading our modernized versions. Whereas most past editors of Elizabeth's writings have freely combined readings from different versions of a text in order to create a single "ideal" composite version, we have chosen instead to preserve the integrity of each manuscript version, recording—and where necessary, glossing—significant textual anomalies and variants in our notes. We do not silently emend apparent pen slips or repeated or dropped words; and we sometimes retain underscoring and other markings in a manuscript where those markings register emphasis. We preserve early manuscript headings as a guide to how the text was understood and classified, either by its scribe or by some other early reader. The words "Headed" and "Endorsed," enclosed in square brackets, signal these early interventions upon the manuscript text. Square brackets also enclose elements supplied where a given manuscript has been damaged. However, for manuscripts also included in *ACFLO*, the companion volume to the present edition, we include the brackets signaling supplied material only in the original-spelling texts reproduced there. Because we have aimed to insure accessibility while preserving the flavor of early modern documents, our policy has been to be fairly literal in translating foreign language texts, particularly by preserving where possible the syntax and phraseology of the Elizabethan originals. Our translations of Elizabeth's poems are, however, necessarily somewhat freer because we have also aimed to retain features of their verse design.

In response to the special circumstantial nature of the historical materials that constitute this edition, we have developed principles for handling introductory material and notes that differ from some standard practices in editing literary texts. We have kept interpretation to a minimum, preferring to let readers discover for themselves the materials as they unfold during the process of reading and in our notes, rather than supplying detailed or elaborate contextualization in headnotes. Such headnotes not only would tend to direct interpretation in ways that are unnecessarily restrictive, but for the most part would reduplicate the ample scholarship that already exists. For the same reasons, we have not glossed references that we judge to be either common knowledge or common usage; we have tried to be inclusive in glossing references that are less accessible. Full references to historical persons are given only the first time they are mentioned; but a very few names go unglossed altogether, usually because we have been unable to identify them. To facilitate identification of historical persons, we have supplied an Index of Names. Obviously, however, readers will differ in their appetite for contextual details: those readers who seek additional information are invited to consult the authorities cited in the notes and in our list of frequently cited works, which will provide useful starting points for further research.

One of the key ways in which our edition departs from standard editorial practice is in our choice not to provide comprehensive lists of textual variants. Indeed, given the lack of standardization from one manuscript to another, to supply such a list for Elizabeth's writings, particularly the poems and speeches, would be impossibly unwieldy. Instead we have chosen to record selectively those variants that create what we judge to be significant differences in the meaning of a phrase or passage, which we identify in the course of a single series of notes rather than in a separate section devoted solely to textual notes. By conjoining rather than separating notes about textual variants with notes identifying persons and events, we wish to call attention to the historicity of all elements of Elizabeth's text. Similarly, in our notes we list manuscript copies and offer variants only for texts that we judge to be early or significant for some other specified reason. To list all of the extant copies of a given speech or letter would be unnecessarily cumbersome.

In order to provide a sense of the variability of manuscript and early printed evidence, we have occasionally reproduced multiple versions of selected texts, rather than a single original. In the case of Elizabeth's letters, as already noted, differences among versions are typically fairly minimal. The poems are another story. There is recurrent evidence that Elizabeth made efforts to keep most of her verses out of general circulation: some copyists of Elizabeth's verses during the period registered the faintly transgressive nature of their activity by offering their attribution to the queen quite literally *"sous rature"*—written down and then struck through, as is several times indicated in our notes to the present edition. Occasionally we offer more than one version of a poetic text in order to indicate the variety of forms in which a poem circulated among the queen's contemporaries.

The case of Elizabeth's speeches is considerably more complex. The present edition develops and applies a new paradigm for understanding their production. Past editors have assumed that Elizabeth or a surrogate delivered her speeches from a text written out in advance—a version that scholars have imagined as arising from an originary moment of composition and have privileged for its authenticity on that ground. While Elizabeth may sometimes have spoken from a prepared written text and did occasionally prepare written speeches to be read out by her principal ministers, in a larger number of instances she spoke either extemporaneously or from memory, and only wrote the speech down afterward or had it transcribed from her dictation. Sometimes, the evidence clearly suggests, if she wanted a copy of a speech she had delivered, she acquired it from one of her auditors who had written down her words later from memory. Very frequently, those attempting to record Elizabeth's speeches after the fact vent their frustration at failing to capture the original speech in its full liveliness and pungency. And yet these recorded versions can produce, along with descriptions of the queen's gestures and inflections, more vivid and vigorous texts than other later manuscript and printed versions of the same speech, even when the later versions are written entirely in, or corrected in, the queen's own hand. Texts of speeches bearing the mark of Elizabeth's hand sometimes circulated as official versions that had been reshaped after oral delivery for the purpose of dissemination to a broader public than the original audience of members of Parliament. Speeches 17 and 18—in which Elizabeth replies impromptu to parliamentary petitions urging the execution of Mary, Queen of Scots—provide particularly vivid instances of such revision for broader circulation. Sometimes, then, there are compelling reasons for preferring memorial accounts by Elizabeth's auditors over her own manuscripts as records of the speeches as delivered.

This is not to suggest that later, and sometimes less vivid, versions of a given speech are without interest. Although we part company from earlier editors by ruling out the creation of "ideal" composite versions, we present some memorial versions of a given speech alongside printed or revised manuscript versions, so that readers can follow the interesting process by which the queen's more spontaneous rhetoric is reworked by herself and others into more considered—and often less inflammatory—language. In the case of speeches like those on Mary, Queen of Scots, already alluded to, variant versions can be understood as parts of a continuum from the queen's original utterance to the speech in process of revision by Elizabeth to the speech as it appeared later in print. However, in other instances, as in the case of the Golden Speech of 1601, the variant texts seem to preserve different memorial versions produced independently by several of Elizabeth's parliamentary auditors. By offering readers the opportunity to read and judge different versions of the speeches for themselves, we hope to leave the relations among these fascinating documents open to further study and discovery.

The present edition corrects the record of existing scholarship on Elizabeth's texts in a number of particulars. We have for the first time provided what we believe to be an accurate version of her much revised and nearly illegible manuscript of the 1567 speech dissolving Parliament (Speech 10). We present the first complete transcriptions of many of Elizabeth's lesser-known materials. Even for materials that are frequently anthologized, we offer texts based on more careful archival scholarship. Regarding Elizabeth poems, for example, we offer a corrected dating of the usual copy text of "On Monsieur's Departure" to the later seventeenth century, rather than to 1601, as stated in earlier editions. We identify and translate as Elizabeth's her polylingual devotions and prayers published in 1563 and 1569, and hope to stimulate debate about the authorship of these materials. However, we remain acutely aware that, even after all the months of checking and rechecking, our edition will inevitably contain omissions and errors of its own. The demons of mistranscription, as we have discovered time and again, are not easily exorcised. We would be most grateful if readers would bring errors of fact and transcription to our attention, so that they can be corrected in any subsequent editions.

The present collection has had an extended and interesting history. Leah Marcus and Mary Beth Rose envisaged it in 1988 as a small and compact volume that would include all of Elizabeth's known speeches and poems, but only a very selective array of her prayers and letters. However, in evaluating the wealth of manuscript sources, Marcus determined that the textual complexities of Elizabeth's writing demanded a more detailed presentation of materials, and in 1993 Janel Mueller joined the project as a coeditor to help with transcription and verification. During intermittent research visits to England from 1993–97, Mueller and Marcus transcribed all of the originally selected materials, along with many more of Elizabeth's writings that we found we could not bear to exclude from the volume. Mueller's entry into the project allowed us to expand the selection of letters and devotions and to offer translations of Elizabeth's foreign language originals. The division of tasks typically ran as follows: Marcus decided editorial policy, dated manuscript texts and determined the relationships among them, and produced the modernized versions; Mueller prepared most of the initial transcriptions and translations and wrote more than half of the notes; Rose helped conceptualize the volume in its initial phase, presided over the final stages of editorial decision making, and drafted the preface. In the spirit of collaboration that has defined every level of this project, however, the actual boundaries of our individual responsibilities have been far less clearly marked, and the product represents, we hope, a useful and well-blended synthesis of our differing areas of expertise.

Many individuals and institutions contributed to our work. The editors would like to acknowledge the financial support of the Newberry Library Center for Renaissance Studies, the University of Wisconsin, the Institute for the Humanities at the University of Illinois at Chicago, the University of Chicago, the University of Texas, the family of the late Jane and Roland Blumberg, and Vanderbilt University. For their permission to reprint documents, we acknowledge The Syndics of Cambridge University Library. In addition, we gratefully acknowledge the attention of the many librarians who have helped us with materials: Robin Harcourt Williams, librarian and archivist to the marquess of Salisbury, Hatfield House; Bridget White, royal librarian, Windsor Castle; Dr. Louise Yeoman of the National Library of Scotland; Alan Giddings and Clive Powell of Caird Library, National Maritime Museum, Greenwich; and the knowledgeable and efficient staffs of the Manuscript Readers' Room of the British Library; Duke Humphrey's Library of the Bodleian; the Manuscript Reading Room of Cambridge University Library; the Public Record Office, Kew; and the Scottish Record Office, Edinburgh; the Royal College of Arms, Library of the Inner Temple, and Lambeth Palace Library, all in London; and in the United States, the Folger Shakespeare Library, the Newberry Library, the Henry E. Huntington Library, the Harry Ransom Humanities Research Center of the University of Texas, the Houghton Library of Harvard University, and the J. Pierpont Morgan Library, New York.

So many friends and colleagues have contributed to this edition that it would be impossible to name them all, but Anne Prescott and David

Bevington stand out for their invaluable advice as readers for the University of Chicago Press. Steven May and Constance Jordan offered enormous and timely help. Thanks also to Mueller's students at the University of Chicago and the Folger Institute (fall 1995)—to Stephen Bennett, Christy Coch, Meiling Hazelton, Jeri McIntosh, Laurie Shannon, Jill Niemczyk Smith, and Alicia Tomasian, whose suggestions sparked a number of annotations and notes. Christy Coch and Meiling Hazleton helped in preparation of Mueller's initial transcriptions and notes. Several faculty colleagues helped with the translations: among Mueller's colleagues at the University of Chicago, warm thanks to Elizabeth Asmis for vetting Greek transcriptions and translations, to Joshua Scodel for vetting Latin transcriptions and translations, and to Elissa Weaver for vetting Italian transcriptions and translations; and among Marcus's former colleagues at the University of Texas, to Elizabeth Richmond-Garza, who also vetted Latin and Greek translations, and Dolora Chapelle-Wojciehowski, who helped in vetting Italian materials and offered many valuable suggestions. Finally, thanks to Marcus's present colleagues at Vanderbilt University, especially Barbara Bowen, and to Anne Prescott, Gérard Defaux, and Donald Stone, for help with the attribution of French verses in Queen Elizabeth's printed devotional materials from the 1560s. Regina Buccola of the English department at the University of Illinois at Chicago helped to secure permissions. Betsy Chambers, Shipeng Wang, and Paul Duncan, at the Institute for the Humanities at the University of Illinois at Chicago, assisted in the final preparation of the manuscript. Special thanks to Alan Thomas of the University of Chicago Press for his perseverance and his enthusiasm for this project from its beginnings. Erin DeWitt, copy editor extraordinaire, did a superb job of saving us from mistakes and inconsistencies, and deserves our warmest thanks. For errors that remain, the editors take full responsibility, asking only that our readers judge the collection in light of the magnitude of the task.

ELIZABETH I

I

LETTERS, POEMS, AND PRAYERS OF PRINCESS ELIZABETH

1533–1558

FIGURE 1 Princess Elizabeth aged about thirteen, attributed to William Scrots, circa 1546–47. Reproduced by permission of The Royal Collection © 1999 Her Majesty Queen Elizabeth II.

LETTERS 1–23

1 ❧ PRINCESS ELIZABETH TO QUEEN KATHERINE, JULY 31, 1544[1]

Inimical Fortune, envious of all good, she who revolves things human, has deprived me for a whole year of your most illustrious presence, and still not being content with that, has robbed me once again of the same good: the which would be intolerable to me if I did not think to enjoy it soon. And in this my exile[2] I know surely that your highness' clemency has had as much care and solicitude for my health as the king's majesty would have had. For which I am not only bound to serve you but also to revere you with daughterly love, since I understand that your most illustrious highness has not forgotten me every time that you have written to the king's majesty, which would have been for me to do. However, heretofore I have not dared to write to him, for which at present I humbly entreat your most excellent highness that in writing to his

1. *Source:* BL, MS Cotton Otho C.X., fol. 235r; in Italian, in the princess's fine italic hand, damaged by the fire of 1742 in Sir Robert Cotton's library. (For original Italian, see *ACFLO,* part 1.) The copy in the Bodleian (MS Smith 68, art. 49) is a poor transcript overall but was copied before the fire and has been used to supply portions of the letter destroyed in 1742. Queen Katherine Parr (ca. 1512–1548) was the sixth and last wife of Henry VIII.

2. Elizabeth's language of exile has frequently been read literally, with the implication that Henry had banished her from court. Here, however, since she anticipates a speedy reunion, she probably refers to the period of the regency (July–September 1544), during which Henry was on military campaign in France, Katherine and the privy councillors assigned to her were residing at Hampton Court, and Elizabeth herself was at Saint James Palace.

majesty you will deign to recommend me to him, entreating ever his sweet benediction and likewise entreating the Lord God to send him best success in gaining victory over his enemies so that your highness, and I together with you, may rejoice the sooner at his happy return. I entreat nothing else from God but that He may preserve your most illustrious highness, to whose grace, humbly kissing your hands, I offer and commend myself. From Saint James on the thirty-first of July.

Your most obedient daughter and
most faithful servant, *Elizabeth*

2 ⇋ PRINCESS ELIZABETH TO QUEEN KATHERINE, PREFACING HER NEW YEAR'S GIFT OF AN ENGLISH TRANSLATION OF MARGUERITE OF NAVARRE'S *MIROIR DE L'ÂME PÉCHERESSE*, DECEMBER 31, 1544[1]

To our most noble and virtuous Queen Katherine, Elizabeth, her humble daughter, wisheth perpetual felicity and everlasting joy.

Not only knowing the affectuous[2] will and fervent zeal the which your highness hath towards all godly learning, as also my duty towards you (most gracious and sovereign princess); but knowing also that pusillanimity and idleness are most repugnant unto a reasonable creature and that (as the philosopher[3] sayeth) even as an instrument of iron or of other metal waxeth soon rusty unless it be continually occupied, even

1. *Source:* Bodleian Library, University of Oxford, MS Cherry 36, fols. 2r–4v; in Elizabeth's hand, on parchment, with embellished embroidered cover that is also her work. (For original-spelling version, see *ACFLO,* part 1.) Queen Katherine was to become noted for her strong support of Protestantism. The most plausible date for her conversion is the summer of 1544, when as regent she consulted daily with Thomas Cranmer under the absent Henry's explicit instructions. The *Miroir* of Marguerite d'Angoulême (1492–1549), queen of Navarre—the freethinking sister of King Francis I of France—was first published in 1531. Marguerite had been an acquaintance of Elizabeth's mother, Anne Boleyn, beginning around 1516; indeed, in making her translation, Elizabeth may have used the 1533 edition of Marguerite's book that was in her mother's library. Elizabeth's translation, amended by the humanist John Bale, was published in Marburg (1548) and went through several Continental editions. For the full text of Elizabeth's translation and further information, see Marc Shell, ed., *Elizabeth's Glass* (Lincoln: University of Nebraska Press, 1993).

2. **affectuous** earnest, ardent.

3. **the philosopher** standard form of reference to Aristotle, but the saying was proverbial. See, for example, Ovid *Tristia,* bk. 5, poem 12, lines 21–22: "My wit, injured by long rusting, is dull, much inferior to what it was before."

so shall the wit of a man or a woman wax dull and unapt to do or understand anything perfectly unless it be always occupied upon some manner of study. Which things considered hath moved so small a portion as God hath lent me[4] to prove what I could do. And therefore have I (as for assay or beginning, following the right notable saying of the proverb aforesaid) translated this little book out of French rhyme into English prose, joining the sentences together as well as the capacity of my simple wit and small learning could extend themselves. The which book is entitled or named *The Mirror or Glass of the Sinful Soul*, wherein is contained how she (beholding and contempling[5] what she is) doth perceive how of herself and of her own strength she can do nothing that good is or prevaileth for her salvation, unless it be through the grace of God, whose mother, daughter, sister, and wife by the Scriptures she proveth herself to be. Trusting also that through His incomprehensible love, grace, and mercy, she (being called from sin to repentance) doth faithfully hope to be saved.

And although I know that, as for my part which I have wrought in it (as well spiritual as manual), there is nothing done as it should be, nor else worthy to come in your grace's hands, but rather all unperfect and uncorrect; yet do I trust also that, howbeit it is like a work which is but new begun and shapen, that the file of your excellent wit and godly learning in the reading of it, if so it vouchsafe your highness to do, shall rub out, polish, and mend (or else cause to mend) the words (or rather the order of my writing), the which I know in many places to be rude and nothing done as it should be. But I hope that after to have been in your grace's hands, there shall be nothing in it worthy of reprehension, and that in the meanwhile no other but your highness only shall read it or see it, less[6] my faults be known of many. Then shall they be better excused (as my confidence is in your grace's accustomed benevolence) than if I should bestow a whole year in writing or inventing ways for to excuse them. Praying God almighty, the Maker and Creator of all things, to grant unto your highness the same New Year's Day a lucky and a prosperous year, with prosperous issue and continuance of many years in good health and continual joy and all to His honor, praise, and glory. From Ashridge[7] the last day of the year of our Lord God, 1544.

4. **portion ... lent me** allusion to the parable of the talents (Matthew 25:14–30).
5. **contempling** contemplating.
6. **less** lest.
7. **Ashridge** one of the crown manors, located in Buckinghamshire.

ILLVSTRISSIMO. AC
potentissimo regi. Henrico octa
uo. Anglię, Francię. Hibernięq;
regi, fidei defensori. et secundum
christum. ecclesię anglicanę et hi
bernicę supremo capiti. Elizabeta
Maiest S humillima filia. omnē
foelicitatem precatur, et benedicti
onem suam suplex
petit.

Quemadmodum immortalis
animus immortali corpore prę
stat, ita sapiens quisque iudicat

3 ❦ PRINCESS ELIZABETH TO KING HENRY VIII, PREFACING HER
TRILINGUAL TRANSLATION OF QUEEN KATHERINE'S *PRAYERS OR
MEDITATIONS*, DECEMBER 30, 1545[1]

To the most illustrious and most mighty King Henry the Eighth, king of England, France, and Ireland, Defender of the Faith,[2] and second to Christ, supreme head of the English and Irish Church, Elizabeth, his majesty's most humble daughter, wishes all happiness, and begs his blessing.

As an immortal soul is superior to a mortal body, so whoever is wise judges things done[3] by the soul more to be esteemed and worthy of greater praise than any act of the body. And thus, as your majesty is of such excellence that none or few are to be compared with you in royal and ample marks of honor, and I am bound unto you as lord by the law of royal authority, as lord and father by the law of nature, and as greatest lord and matchless and most benevolent father by the divine law, and by all laws and duties I am bound unto your majesty in various and manifold ways, so I gladly asked (which it was my duty to do) by what means I might offer to your greatness the most excellent tribute that my capacity and diligence could discover. In the which I only fear lest slight and unfinished studies and childish ripeness of mind diminish the praise of this undertaking and the commendation which accomplished talents draw from a most divine subject. For nothing ought to be more acceptable to a king, whom philosophers regard as a god on earth, than this labor of the soul, which raises us up to heaven and on earth makes us heavenly and divine in the flesh; and while we may be enveloped by continual and infinite miseries, even then it renders us blessed and happy.

---

1. *Source:* BL, MS Royal 7.D.X., sigs. 2r–5r; translated from Latin. (For the original Latin, see *ACFLO,* part 1.) This New Year's gift for her father is in Elizabeth's youthful italic hand, on parchment, with an embroidered cover that is also her handiwork. It is not clear whether or not Elizabeth knew Katherine's source: the third book of Thomas à Kempis's *Imitatio Christi* in Richard Whitford's English translation (printed ca. 1530). This is Elizabeth's only known letter to Henry VIII.

2. Pope Leo X had given Henry VIII the title of "*Defensor fidei*" after he published his *Assertio septem sacramentorum adversus Martinum Lutherum* (1521), a tract vindicating the seven Roman Catholic sacraments against Luther's then reduction of them to three: baptism, penance, and holy communion.

3. **things done** The Latin phrase is *res gestae,* by the sixteenth century a standard phrase for the subject matter of historical writing. She implies that the soul, too, has the stuff of which history is made.

Which work, since it is so pious, and by the pious exertion and great diligence of a most illustrious queen has been composed in English, and on that account may be more desirable to all and held in greater value by your majesty, it was thought by me a most suitable thing that this work, which is most worthy because it was indeed a composition by a queen as a subject for her king, be translated into other languages by me, your daughter. May I, by this means, be indebted to you not as an imitator of your virtues but indeed as an inheritor of them. In the work, whatever is not mine is worthy of the greatest praise, as the whole book is at once pious in its subject, ingeniously composed, and arranged in the most appropriate order. Whatever is truly mine, if there is any mistake in it, deserves indulgence on account of ignorance, youth, short time of study, and goodwill. And if it is mediocre, even if it is worthy of no praise at all, nevertheless if it is well received, it will incite me earnestly so that, however much I grow in years, so much will I grow in knowledge and the fear of God and thus devote myself to Him more religiously and respect your majesty more dutifully. Wherefore I do not doubt that your fatherly goodness and royal prudence will esteem this inward labor of my soul not less than any other mark of honor and will regard this divine work as more to be esteemed because it has been composed by the most serene queen, your spouse, and is to be held in slightly greater worth because it has been translated by your daughter. May He who is King of kings, in whose hand are the hearts of kings, so govern your soul and protect your life that in true piety and religion we may live long under your majesty's dominion. From Hertford,[4] the 30 day of December 1545.

4 𝕖𝕤 PRINCESS ELIZABETH TO QUEEN KATHERINE, PREFACING HER ENGLISH TRANSLATION OF CHAPTER 1 OF JOHN CALVIN'S *INSTITUTION DE LA RELIGION CHRESTIENNE* (GENEVA, 1541), DECEMBER 30, 1545[1]

To the most high, most illustrious and magnanimous Princess Katherine, queen of England, France, and Ireland, Elizabeth, her most humble daughter, gives greeting and due obedience.

4. **Hertford** Castle in Hertfordshire that was used by the Tudors as a residence for the royal children.
1. *Source:* Edinburgh, Scottish Record Office, National Archives of Scotland, MS NAS RH

Of old, from great antiquity—most noble, most excellent and sovereign princess—the custom has always prevailed that to preserve the memory of notable things that were done in times past, and likewise to increase their renown, a number of ingenious men, both to apply their understanding and skill and to have it seen that in every way with their ingenious art they excelled the rest of all other animals, have in many places and in divers ways amused themselves by composing or putting into memoirs the things done in their time that seemed to them worthiest of commemoration or remembrance. And in order to do this (because the apt and requisite usage of letters and the way of writing were not yet invented), they were accustomed to draw out and bring forth their most memorable deeds with certain characters, figures, images, or effigies of men, beasts, birds, fish, trees, or plants, carved out crudely and grossly because they did not care how it was that they labored, provided that the memory of their intention was magnified, diffused, and noted by everyone. Now afterwards, since the creation of the world, we see that just as the days and months increase and multiply, so similarly, little by little, by succession of time the mind of man is more ingenious and inventive, more adorned and polished, than it formerly was. And therefore some have invented sculpting in the round, casting or engraving in gold, silver, copper, or other metals, yet others in stone, marble, wood, wax, clay, or other materials, statues of our predecessors—their size, height, breadth, proportions, body weight and volume, their physiognomy, complexion, color, and look, their bearing, gait, countenance, their exploits—in the doing of which, excellent painters do not deserve less praise. But all of these together never could and cannot yet represent or reveal by their works the mind or wit, the speech or understanding of any person.

And yet, especially among the aforesaid arts and sciences, the invention of letters seems to me the most clever, excellent, and ingenious. For through their ordering not only can the aforesaid bodily features be declared, but also (which is more) the image of the mind, wiles, and understanding, together with the speech and intention of the man, can be perfectly known—indeed, traced and portrayed so close to artless and natural that it actually seems that his words that were spoken and pro-

---

13/78, fols. 1r–7r; in French, in Elizabeth's youthful italic hand, on parchment. (For original French, see *ACFLO*, part 1.) This New Year's gift for her stepmother is a companion volume to that containing our Letter 3 to King Henry and has an elaborate embroidered cover featuring the intertwined initials *HR* and *KP*, which is also Elizabeth's handiwork.

nounced long ago still have the same vigor they had before.[2] Thus also we see that God by His Word and Scripture can be seen, heard, and known for who He is, inasmuch as it is permitted and necessary for our salvation—He who otherwise cannot be known or seen because in Himself He is invisible and impalpable and, for our part, He is impossible to see or touch. And yet there is no painter, engraver, sculptor, or other, however ingenious and subtle he may be, who could truly show or produce any image or likeness of His essential divinity, no more nor less than he could with the mind of any other creature. Thus the art of painting, engraving, or sculpting is the image and effigy of bodily, visible, and palpable things; and by contrast, the Scripture is the image and effigy of spiritual, invisible, and impalpable things.

And so, by a natural instinct, following our aforesaid predecessors, I have presumed and undertaken to translate into our mother tongue a little book whose argument or subject, as Saint Paul said, surpasses the capacity of every creature and yet is of such great vigor that there is no living creature of whatever sort that has not had within itself the feeling of it—which surely would require greater eloquence or adornment of words and sentences than I would know how to apply to it. But seeing the source from which this book came forth, the majesty of the matter surpasses all human eloquence, being privileged and having such force within it that a single sentence has power to ravish, inspire, and give knowledge to the most stupid and ignorant beings alive in what way God wishes to be known, seen, and heard: I yet think it is sufficient in itself and has no need for any human consent, support, or help.

Which when I considered (following principally the intention of my author), I was emboldened, and ventured to translate it word for word, and not that it might be a perfect work, but assuring myself that your highness will pay more regard to the zeal and the desire that I have of pleasing you than you will to the capacity of my simple ability and knowledge. And may you of your grace vouchsafe to judge it to proceed from a similar intention as theirs, the aforesaid, because they did not care how it was that they labored, provided that their intention was understood. By which I hope that in similar case your highness will excuse me, and with your gracious, accustomed welcome will receive it as tes-

---

2. Galileo Galilei makes the same point almost a century later in his *Dialogue Concerning the Two Chief World Systems.* He and Elizabeth may have had a common source that we have not uncovered. See his *Dialogue,* 2nd ed., trans. Stillman Drake (Berkeley: University of California Press, 1967), p. 105.

timony that not for anything in this world would I want to fall into any
arrears in my duty towards your grace, but rather, in my ability as the
least, hold the lamp and illumine so, and so that I may assist the fervent
zeal and perfect love that you bear towards the selfsame God who created all things. Whom I most ardently entreat to vouchsafe that you may
grow so very perfectly in the knowledge of Him that the organ of your
royal voice may be the true instrument of His Word, in order to serve as
a mirror and lamp to all true Christian men and women. From Hertford Castle this penultimate day of the year 1545.

5 &❧ PRINCESS ELIZABETH TO KING EDWARD VI, FEBRUARY 14, 1547[1]

[Addressed] To the most excellent and most noble King Edward the Sixth

That before this time I have sent no letters to your majesty, king most
serene and most illustrious, and have given no thanks for that singular
kindness and brotherly love that you have shown towards me, I beg you
not to account to the forgetting of benefits (which God forbid) nor think
it to follow from such forgetting, which is most unfitting, but rather that it
must be attributable to other, more just causes. For although I have often
endeavored to write to your majesty, the slight ill health of my body, especially, indeed, the pain in my head, held me back from beginning. On
which account I hope that your highness will be inclined to accept my
feelings towards you as a substitute for my letters. Which feelings, indeed, proceeding not so much from the mouth as from the heart, will
declare a certain due respect and faith towards your majesty. Truly I desire this to be known to you, and by deeds more than words. That this
might be so, I will strive with all my powers. Indeed, even as when gold
is melted down by fire and well purified from dross and not until then
deemed certainly worthy, so any man's works make his feelings very
surely known.

Henceforth, all that remains is for me to give your majesty the greatest thanks that I can because not only has he readily honored me with

1. *Source:* BL, MS Harley 6986, art. 11, fol. 19r; in Elizabeth's hand, in Latin. (For original
Latin, see *ACFLO,* part 1.) The year to which this letter is assigned here follows the BL
Harleian Catalogue. King Henry VIII had died in early 1547; his only legitimate son, Ed-
ward the "Boy King," succeeded him at the age of nine.

every human kindness in his presence, but also now, though absent, has made proof of his feelings towards me in my absence by sending a ring. From which, after it was sent, I could see that to refresh your majesty's memory of your promise was not the least bit necessary, not only because your highness commanded that I not do so, but also on account of your kindness (which I have not formerly doubted) shown to me. May God long keep your majesty safe and further advance (as He has begun to do) your growing virtues[2] to the utmost. From Enfield[3] the 14th of February.

Your majesty's most humble servant
and sister, *Elizabeth*

6 ⧉ PRINCESS ELIZABETH TO KING EDWARD VI UPON HIS
RECOVERY FROM SICKNESS, SEPTEMBER 20, 1547[1]

[Addressed] To the most illustrious and most noble King Edward the Sixth

Whereas in so long a space of time you have received so few letters from me, most illustrious king, in which I might have thanked you for favors or at least made testimony of my respect due to you, I hope easily to obtain your indulgence by asking for it: especially since my inaction has not proceeded from any forgetting of you, whom I never can nor should forget. Now in fact, as I understand that your majesty is staying in parts situated not far from London, I have decided that my silence must be broken, so that I might show that there has been no slackening of my due reverence to you nor is there anything more wished for by me than your health, which I understand to be firm and sound from certain people's reports. Indeed, when I call to mind the particular benefits of the most good and most great God, I judge this one to be the greatest of all: that He has quickly and mercifully restored you to London after your recent illness. Into which I think indeed that you fell by some spe-

---

2. **virtues** in Latin, *virtutes,* which could mean either "virtues" or "powers."
    3. **Enfield** a no longer extant crown manor in the county of Middlesex, north of London.
    1. *Source:* BL, MS Harley 6986, art. 15, fol. 21r; in Elizabeth's hand, in Latin. (For original Latin, see *ACFLO,* part 1.) Assignment of the year here follows BL Harleian Catalogue.

cial providence of God, just as I wrote in my recent letter to your majesty, so that once every occasion of illnesses has vanished, you may be preserved to hold the reins of this kingdom for the longest time possible. Nothing is so uncertain or less enduring than the life of man, who truly, by the testimony of Pindar, is nothing else than a dream of shadows.[2] And as Homer says, earth nurtures nothing more fragile than man.[3] Since then the life of every man is not only exposed to but overcome by so many and so great accidents, we judge that your past illness has been dispelled by the special mercy of divine providence, and that in those frequent changes of place and air (which I know have not been entirely immune to diseases) you have been preserved from all dangers of all illnesses. To which providence I commit the protection of your majesty, and at the same time ask that He keep you safe and sound for the longest possible time. From Ashridge, the 20th of September.

Your majesty's most humble sister, Elizabeth

7 ♥ PRINCESS ELIZABETH TO KING EDWARD VI, FEBRUARY 2, 1548[1]

[Addressed] To the most illustrious and most noble King Edward the Sixth

Of your love towards me no more numerous or illustrious proofs can be given, king most serene and illustrious, than when I recently enjoyed to the full the fruit of a most delightful familiarity with you. Which

---

2. Pindar *Pythian Ode* VIII, last two lines.

3. Homer *Iliad* XIV.446–47.

1. *Source:* Bodleian Library, University of Oxford, MS Arch. F.c.8; in Elizabeth's hand; formerly pasted onto the flyleaf of King James I's works in a MS that he himself presented to the Bodleian. (For Elizabeth's original Latin version, see *ACFLO*, part 1.) Assignment of the year is conjectural. The Rev. Dr. Giles—in *Whole Works of Roger Ascham* (London: John Russell Smith, 1865), vol. 1, pt. 2, p. 276—prints this letter among Ascham's compositions, following the precedent of William Elstob's edition, *Rogeri Aschami epistolarum libri quatuor* (Oxford: Henry Clements, 1703), pp. 380–81. However, both because this letter exists uniquely in Elizabeth's handwriting (a fact which Elstob records without comment) and because it does not appear in any of the first four English editions of Ascham's *Familiarum epistolarum libri tres* (London: Francis Coldock, 1576, 1578, 1581, and 1590) (*STC* 826–29) or in the three early seventeenth-century Continental editions, we find no reason to deny its authorship to Elizabeth, although Ascham may well have had a hand in its composition.

truly, when I recall (and I do recall it daily) I seem plainly, as it were, to be present with you and to be enjoying the humaneness of your conversations. What is more, when to my mind there come your innumerable favors to me, with which you received me on my arrival there and with which you sent me off on my departure, I cannot easily recount how much my mind is drawn in divers ways, bringing a double anxiety to my thinking. For while from the magnitude of your favors towards me, I perceive your brotherly love most greatly inclined towards me, by which I conceive no small joy and gladness; yet in return when I weigh in an even and fair balance the multitude of your deserts with regard to me, I grieve because I perceive I cannot reciprocate the force of these at any time, neither in thought, much less in returning thanks. Lest, however, your majesty should judge your so many and so great favors to me ill placed, or better (to use the words of Cicero taken from Ennius[2]), ill done; or, finally, lest it should appear that I am insufficiently mindful and grateful, I, although incapable of doing so, now desire to thank your majesty to some degree in words.

Which, indeed, I would have done more quickly, in sending either by letter or by messenger, if a small work that I desired to send to your majesty had not cheated me of my purpose. This, since because of the scarcity of time that I see flowing away from me more quickly than water, I myself could not bring to an end at all (as I supposed would be done), I now hope that this letter, however rude, will plead my cause with your majesty in my absence, and at the same time declare in some degree my feeling towards you. For that this can be done sufficiently fully or abundantly in these mute words, I judge to be impossible. Especially when it is (as your majesty is not unaware) rather characteristic of my nature not only not to say in words as much as I think in my mind, but also, indeed, not to say more than I think. The latter of which (I mean, saying more), as few detest it, so many make use of it everywhere, but mostly indeed in the courts of princes and kings, to whom this warning particularly pertains: not to appear to have more *kólakas* within their chambers than *kórakas*[3] outside their court. Of which matter enough for this place.

---

2. Cicero *De officiis* II.18, citing Ennius *Scenica* no. 24: "*nam praeclare Ennius, bene facta male locata malefacta arbitror.*"

3. *kólakas . . . kórakas* "flatterers . . . crows" (Greek words embedded within the Latin letter, yielding a pun).

This much I pray, that God may preserve your majesty in safety for the longest time possible, to the glory of His name and the advantage of the realm. From Hatfield, the second of February.

Your majesty's most humble sister
and servant, *Elizabeth*

8 ࣔ PRINCESS ELIZABETH TO DOWAGER QUEEN KATHERINE, CIRCA JUNE 1548[1]

[Addressed] To the queen's highness

Although I could not be plentiful in giving thanks for the manifold kindness receive[2] at your highness' hand at my departure,[3] yet I am something to be borne withal, for truly I was replete with sorrow to depart from your highness, especially leaving you undoubtful of health. And albeit I answered little, I weighed it more deeper when you said you would warn me of all evils that you should hear of me; for if your

---

1. *Source:* PRO, State Papers Domestic, Edward VI 10/2, fol. 84C; in Elizabeth's formal italic hand. (For original-spelling version, see *ACFLO*, part 1.) The PRO Calendar dates the letter circa December 1547; Harrison dates it circa June 1548 (7). The latter date is more probable as a more advanced point in Katherine Parr's pregnancy (note the references to her doubtful health and disquiet). Her only child, Mary Seymour, was born seven days before Katherine's death from puerperal fever on September 5, 1548.

2. **receive** received.

3. After Katherine Parr married Thomas Seymour—Baron Sudeley, lord high admiral, the younger uncle of Edward VI—her household included Elizabeth, but Elizabeth left precipitously sometime in 1548. According to Thomas Parry, Elizabeth's cofferer (treasurer), who testified before the Privy Council during the prosecution of Thomas Seymour on treason charges in January 1549, Katherine Ashley, Elizabeth's governess, had confided to him that "the admiral loved her [Princess Elizabeth] but too well, and had so done a good while; and that the queen was jealous on her and him, in so much that one time the queen, suspecting the often access of the admiral to the Lady Elizabeth's grace, came suddenly upon them, where they were all alone, he having her in his arms, wherefore the queen fell out, both with the lord admiral and with her grace also . . . and as I remember, this was the cause why she was sent from the queen, or else that her grace parted from the queen." Cited from Samuel Haynes, ed., *A Collection of State Papers Relating to Affairs in the Reigns of King Henry VIII, King Edward VI, Queen Mary, and Queen Elizabeth[.] Transcribed from Original Letters and Other Authentic Memorials, Never Before Published. Left by William Cecil Lord Burghley, and Now Remaining at Hatfield House* (London, 1740), p. 96. For Ashley's own testimony, see Letter 13, Additional Documents, pp. 25–30.

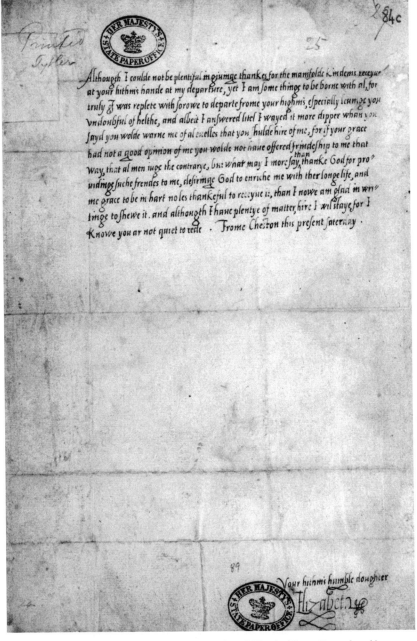

FIGURE 3 Letter 8; PRO, State Papers Domestic, Edward VI 10/2, fol. 84c. Reproduced by permission of the Public Record Office, the National Archives, England.

grace had not a good opinion of me, you would not have offered friendship to me that way that all men judge the contrary. But what may I
more say than thank God for providing such friends to me, desiring
God to enrich me with their long life, and me grace[4] to be in heart no
less thankful to receive it than I now am glad in writing to show it. And
although I have plenty of matter, here I will stay for I know you are not
quiet to read. From Cheston[5] this present Saturday.

Your highness' humble daughter, *Elizabeth*

9 ೬❧ PRINCESS ELIZABETH TO THOMAS SEYMOUR, LORD HIGH
ADMIRAL, SUMMER 1548[1]

[Addressed] To my lord admiral

My lord,

You needed not to send an excuse to me, for I could not mistrust
the not fulfilling of your promise to proceed for want of goodwill, but
only the opportunity serveth not; wherefore I shall desire you to think
that a greater matter than this could not make me impute any unkindness in you. For I am a friend not won with trifles, nor lost with the like.
This[2] I commit you and all your affairs in God's hand, who keep you from
all evil. I pray you make my humble commendations to the queen's
highness.

Your assured friend to my power, *Elizabeth*

4. **me grace** give me grace.

5. **Cheston** one of several contemporary spelling variants for Cheshunt, in Hertfordshire, where there was a royal residence (no longer extant).

1. *Source:* The Pierpont Morgan Library, New York, MS Rulers of England Box III (Elizabeth I), art. 6; a single sheet, approximately 6.5 by 5.4 inches, in Elizabeth's hand and decorated by Elizabeth with an embellished double-rule top and bottom in red ink. (For original-spelling version, see *ACFLO,* part 1.) Like Letter 8, this was written shortly after
Elizabeth's hasty departure from the Seymour household. The date is conjecturally supplied by the Morgan Library Catalogue.

2. **This** silently corrected to "Thus" in later copies.

10 ❧ PRINCESS ELIZABETH TO DOWAGER QUEEN KATHERINE,
JULY 31, 1548[1]

Although your highness' letters be most joyful to me in absence, yet
considering what pain it is to you to write, your grace being so great
with child and so sickly, your commendation were enough in my lord's
letter. I much rejoice at your health with the well-liking of the country,
with my humble thanks that your grace wished me with you till I were
weary of that country. Your highness were like to be cumbered[2] if I
should not depart till I were weary being with you: although it were in
the worst soil in the world, your presence would make it pleasant. I cannot reprove my lord for not doing your commendations in his letter, for
he did it. And although he had not, yet I will not complain on him, for
that he shall be diligent to give me knowledge from time to time how
his busy child doth, and if I were at his birth no doubt I would see him
beaten for the trouble he has put you to. Master Denny and my lady[3]
with humble thanks prayeth most entirely for your grace, praying the
almighty God to send you a lucky deliverance. And my mistress[4]
wisheth no less, giving your highness most humble thanks for her commendations. Written with very little leisure this last day of July.

Your humble daughter, *Elizabeth*

1. *Source:* BL, MS Cotton Otho C.X., fol. 236v; in Elizabeth's fine italic hand. (For original-spelling version, see *ACFLO,* part 1.) Like Letter 1, p. 5, shows damage from the 1742 fire.
Lost readings restored from the late copy in Bodleian Library, University of Oxford, MS
Smith 68, art. 49, fol. 50r. This is the last known communication between Princess Elizabeth and Dowager Queen Katherine.

2. **cumbered** encumbered.

3. **Master Denny and my lady** Sir Anthony Denny (1501–1549), a gentleman of King Edward's Privy Chamber and one of his tutors; his wife was appointed Elizabeth's governess
after Katherine Ashley had failed to prevent the familiarities taken by Thomas Seymour.

4. **my mistress** Katherine Ashley, whom Elizabeth had refused to see dismissed from
her service and still considered her "mistress."

11 & PRINCESS ELIZABETH TO KING EDWARD VI, SUMMER OR
FALL 1548[1]

[Addressed] To the most noble and most serene King Edward the Sixth

Although I have devoted myself, king most serene, to nothing so much
as escaping not only the mark but even the very least suspicion of ingratitude, I always fear nevertheless that I may seem to have fallen into
it; because being ever furnished with so many favors from your majesty,
I have in such a long interval sent no letters from which you might at
least discern the signs of a grateful heart. In the which case, as there are
urgent and necessary reasons, I hope and am at the same time confident
that your majesty will readily free me from every charge of ingratitude.
For an affliction of my head and eyes has come upon me, which has so
sorely troubled me since my coming to this house that, although I have
often tried to write to your majesty, I have until this day ever been restrained from my intention and undertaking. The which condition,
having somewhat abated with the power and help of the most good and
most great God, I have judged that my duty of writing is no longer to be
deferred, so that your majesty may understand that anything rather
than a heart grateful to you and mindful of your favors has thus far
been lacking in me. For although I have not been ignorant that the
magnitude of your favors to me is such that all hope is absolutely taken
away of repaying even the least part of them, I have nevertheless thought
that I should strain every sinew in this case to render just and merited
thanks with a goodwill and a remembering mind. In which, as nothing
indeed has as yet ever been allowed by me to remain forgotten, I hope
your majesty will not only accept in good part my (until now) delayed
duty of writing and giving thanks, but also be inclined to consider that
I have always maintained due gratitude towards you with my heart and
will. May the Lord Jesus, who preserves and watches over all things, perpetually enrich your excellency with this kingdom, with great virtues,
and with many years. From Enfield.

> Your majesty's most humble servant
> and sister, *Elizabeth*

1. *Source:* Bodleian Library, University of Oxford, MS Smith 19, art. 1, fol. 1; in Elizabeth's
formal italic hand, in Latin. (For original Latin, see *ACFLO*, part 1.) Dating is conjectural,
based on close similarity between the hand here and in the July 31, 1548, letter to Katherine
Parr. The sickness Elizabeth refers to may be the illness into which she fell, according to
Katherine Ashley's testimony, after Katherine Parr's death in September 1548.

**12 ෴ PRINCESS ELIZABETH TO EDWARD SEYMOUR, DUKE OF
SOMERSET, LORD PROTECTOR, SEPTEMBER 1548[1]**

[Addressed] To my lord protector's grace

My very good lord:

Many lines[2] will not serve to render the least part of the thanks that
your grace hath deserved of me, most especially for that you have been
careful for my health, and sending unto me not only your comfortable
letters but also physicians as Doctor Bill,[3] whose diligence and pain has
been a great part of my recovery. For whom I do most heartily thank
your grace, desiring you to give him thanks for me, who can ascertain
you of mine estate of health, wherefore I will not write it. And although
I be most bounden to you in this time of my sickness, yet I may not be
unthankful for that your grace hath made such[4] expedition for my
patent.[5] With my most hearty thanks and commendations to you and
to my good lady your wife,[6] most heartily fare you well. From Cheshunt
this present Friday.

Your assured friend to my power, *Elizabeth*

**13 ෴ PRINCESS ELIZABETH TO EDWARD SEYMOUR, LORD
PROTECTOR, JANUARY 28, 1549[1]**

My lord:

Your great gentleness and goodwill toward me, as well in this thing
as in other things, I do understand; for the which, even as I ought, so I

1. *Source:* PRO, State Papers Domestic, Edward VI 10/5/4; written in a clerk's hand and
signed by Elizabeth, with remnants of seal still attached. Dating is conjectural, proposed by
Knighton (65).
2. **lines** MS could read either "lynes" or "lyves."
3. **Bill** Dr. Thomas Bill, one of several court physicians to Henry VIII and Edward VI.
4. Right margin of the page has been torn away in MS after the letter **s** and again after the
initial letters of **thanks** in the next sentence. The missing letters are supplied conjecturally.
5. **patent** a letter or document from a sovereign or person in authority, used for various
purposes—for example, to convey some right, privilege, title, or property. The precise reference here is unclear, but see Letter 13 n. 4, p. 23.
6. **wife** Anne Stanhope Seymour (1497–1587), who became Edward Seymour's second
wife around 1535.
1. *Source:* Hatfield House, Cecil Papers 133/4/2; in Elizabeth's hand. (For original-spelling
version, see *ACFLO*, part 1.) Square brackets enclose editorially supplied identifications. As

do give you most humble thanks. And whereas your lordship willeth and counselleth me as a earnest friend to declare what I know in this matter and also to write what I have declared to Master Tyrwhit, I shall most willingly do it. I declared unto him first that after that the cofferer[2] had declared unto me what my lord admiral answered for Allen's matter and for Durham Place[3]—that it was appointed to be a mint—he [the cofferer] told me that my lord admiral did offer me his house for my time being with the king's majesty. And further said and asked me whether if the Council did consent that I should have my lord admiral, whether I would consent to it or no. I answered that I would not tell him what my mind was, and I inquired further of him what he meant to ask me that question or who bade him say so. He answered me and said nobody bade him say so, but that he perceived (as he thought) by my lord admiral's inquiring whether my patent[4] were sealed or no, and debating what he spent in his house, and inquiring what was spent in my house, that he was given that way rather than otherwise.

And as concerning Kat Ashley, she never advised me unto it but said always (when any talked of my marriage) that she would never have me marry—neither in England nor out of England—without the consent of the king's majesty, your grace's, and the Council's. And after the queen was departed[5] when I asked of her [Ashley] what news she heard from London, she answered merrily, "They say there that your grace shall have my lord admiral, and that he will come shortly to woo you." And moreover, I said unto him [Tyrwhit] that the cofferer sent a letter hither that my lord said that he would come this way as he went down to the country. Then I bade her write as she thought best, and bade her show it me when she had done; so she writ that she thought it not best

---

the proceedings in Lord Admiral Thomas Seymour's treason trial uncovered his familiar dealings with Elizabeth and evidence of his interest in marrying her, she fell under suspicion as a possible conspirator and was kept virtually under house arrest. Edward Seymour, duke of Somerset and Thomas's older brother, who presided over the investigation, dispatched Sir Robert Tyrwhit to interrogate Elizabeth and take down her testimony. She, however, chose to make her own representation in so delicate and dangerous a matter directly to the lord protector.

2. **cofferer** Thomas Parry, treasurer of her household.

3. **Durham Place** Elizabeth's London house. The reference to **Allen's matter** is obscure.

4. **patent** probably the patents for lands valued at £3000, provided for Elizabeth's maintenance in Henry VIII's will.

5. **departed** Dowager Queen Katherine, Thomas Seymour's wife, had died on September 5, 1548.

for fear of suspicion,[6] and so it went forth. And my lord admiral, after he heard that, asked of the cofferer why he might not come as well to me as to my sister.[7] And then I desired Kat Ashley to write again (lest my lord might think that she knew more in it than he) that she knew nothing in it but suspicion. And also I told Master Tyrwhit that to the effect of the matter, I never consented unto any such thing without the Council's consent thereunto. And as for Kat Ashley or the cofferer, they never told me that they would practice it.

These be the things which I both declared to Master Tyrwhit and also whereof my conscience beareth me witness, which I would not for all earthly things offend in anything, for I know I have a soul to save as well as other folks have, wherefore I will above all thing have respect unto this same. If there be any more things which I can remember I will either write it myself, or cause Master Tyrwhit to write it. Master Tyrwhit and others have told me that there goeth rumors abroad which be greatly both against mine honor and honesty, which above all other things I esteem, which be these: that I am in the Tower and with child by my lord admiral. My lord, these are shameful slanders, for the which, besides the great desire I have to see the king's majesty, I shall most heartily desire your lordship that I may come to the court after your first determination, that I may show myself there as I am. Written in haste from Hatfield[8] this 28 of January.

Your assured friend to my little power, Elizabeth

---

6. **suspicion** MS reads "iuspicion."

7. **sister** Princess Mary Tudor (b. 1516), daughter of Queen Catherine of Aragon, and Elizabeth's half-sister.

8. **Hatfield** royal residence in Hertfordshire where Elizabeth lived intermittently until she was called to the throne.

13 ᙓᗯ ADDITIONAL DOCUMENTS A–D

Examinations and Depositions of Katherine Ashley, Governess to Princess Elizabeth, Regarding Possibly Questionable Dealings with Thomas Seymour, Lord High Admiral, February 1549

LETTER 13, ADDITIONAL DOCUMENT A[1] *[Headed] February 2, 1548[9]. The answers of Mistress Ashley. What communication she hath had with my Lady Elizabeth's grace as touching the marriage with the lord admiral.*

She saith that incontinent[2] after the death of the queen,[3] at Cheshunt the said Lady Elizabeth was sick. She [Ashley] said unto her, "Your old husband, that was appointed unto you at the death of the king,[4] now is free again. You may have him if you will."

And she answered, "Nay."

Then said Mistress Ashley, "Iwis[5] you will not deny it if my lord protector and the Council were pleased thereunto."

And one there answered, "She cannot see who." [Addressing Elizabeth] "And why not him that was worthy to match a queen should not marry with you?"

And at divers other times when she [Elizabeth] hath been at play in drawing hands,[6] she hath seen my lord admiral and my lady of Suffolk[7] together. And when she hath chosen my lord admiral, she would laugh

---

1. *Source:* PRO, State Papers Domestic, Edward VI 10/6/19, fol. 51r–v (listed as no. 195 in Knighton). This sequence of legal documents is in two hands: the secretary's (whom Knighton identifies as Sir Thomas Smith, secretary of the Privy Council) and Ashley's own. As a group, the materials consist of Smith's transcripts of Ashley's testimony in two sessions, signed by Ashley at the foot of every page, and two further depositions in Ashley's hand. The notes identify only the major figures in Ashley's narrative; see also notes to Letters 10 and 13, pp. 20 and 22–24. Square brackets enclose identifications and other materials editorially supplied.

2. **incontinent** immediately.

3. **queen** Dowager Queen Katherine, who had died September 5, 1548.

4. **king** Henry VIII, who had died January 28, 1547, leaving Katherine as his widow. Although Thomas Seymour had shown interest in Elizabeth, which prompted rumors that he would marry her, he instead married Katherine in a clandestine ceremony that possibly took place as early as April 1547.

5. **Iwis** I know; certainly.

6. **drawing hands** choosing dancing partners.

7. **lady of Suffolk** Katherine Willoughby Brandon (ca. 1518–1580), dowager duchess of Suffolk, Dowager Queen Katherine's closest friend and, like her, a Protestant patroness.

and pale at it. And then this examinate [Ashley] would say, "Iwis you would not refuse him if the Council would be content thereunto." And then at the death of the queen, it was reported that my lord admiral was the heaviest man in the world, and this examinate would her [Elizabeth] to write, or cause her secretary to write to comfort him, and she to subscribe.[8] Her grace answered she would not, for then she should be thought to woo him.

ITEM: Upon Parry's letter, wherein he [Thomas Seymour] offered his house and household stuff and this examinate gave her counsel to refuse both except Mr. Denny would give advice unto it; whereupon she [Elizabeth] bade this examinate so to answer, and so she [Ashley] did [send] Thomas Parry[9] some word that the lord admiral would see her grace as he rode; whereupon this examinate wrote again that in no wise he should come there until the said lord admiral should come to that Parliament again, and then this examinate would come to London and tell him her mind.

Another time, about Allhallowtide,[10] she [Ashley] asked leave to go to London, and being demanded of her grace what she would do there, she answered she would speak with my lord admiral. Her grace said she should not, for it would be said that she [Elizabeth] did send her. This errand was to have begged the gatekeeper at Durham Place[11] for herself, for she had no good lodging nor house in London.

LETTER 13, ADDITIONAL DOCUMENT B[1] [Headed] February 24, 1548[9]. The Examination of Mistress Ashley.

She saith she came to London, as she thinketh, about three weeks or a month before Christmas. She spake with no person there but only with her husband Mr. Ashley, my lady of Berkeley, and my Lady Denny and Parry. There came home with her William, Mr. Ashley's servant and his horsekeeper, and one Hornby, Yeoman of the Chamber, and William

8. **subscribe** sign the letter.
9. **Thomas Parry** Elizabeth's cofferer (treasurer); **send** omitted in manuscript and supplied conjecturally.
10. **Allhallowtide** around All Saints' Day, November 1.
11. **Durham Place** Elizabeth's London house, which Somerset had requisitioned for use as a mint.
1. *Source:* PRO, State Papers Domestic, Edward VI 10/6/20, fols. 53r–54r (no. 196 in Knighton); in Secretary Smith's hand.

Russell, Gentleman of her grace's Chamber. And she [Ashley] went not out of Slayning's house till she went to take her house at my Lady Berkeley's in Fleet Street, with Slayning's wife, and thither came to her my Lady Denny. She came to London the Tuesday at noon and went away the next day at noon.

She had no sore arm indeed, but she had an ache in her arm; howbeit then she was not let blood for it. But she did pretend to my Lady Elizabeth's grace and to everybody that it was for that cause [that she had to go to London]. But indeed the very matter was because there had been a jar betwixt her husband and her, and he parted from her in a displeasure, as she thought, and therefore she could not be merry till she had spoken with him. For she had sent him a letter, but he had made no answer. And so she stayed for him, and he did tarry with her all that night. And her husband and Parry did break their fast with her that morning. And so she went, and Slayning's wife, to my Lady Berkeley's, and there she took horse. She did not go abroad into the town because she had but a russet nightgown, the which she hath on now in the Tower. Or else, she saith, she would have seen my lady of Somerset,[2] for she sent William Russell to her grace [Lady Somerset] with a token from my Lady Elizabeth, the which her grace [Elizabeth] gave her to carry. But because of her apparel, she would not be seen abroad. She remembereth more that Sir Gawin and Peter Carew and Henry Eliot came to her at Slayning's, and Archdeacon Carew. And she went away so soon because her errand was done when her husband and she were agreed. She saith she did not speak at that time neither with the lord admiral nor no one of his men. Nor was never one mile out of the Lady Elizabeth's house sith[3] she was first sick about Midsummer, and at that time she had no communication with Parry of any matter betwixt my Lady Elizabeth and my lord admiral.

What request or promise of secrecy was betwixt
Parry and her concerning these matters.

She saith that the same night that the lord great master[4] and Mr. Denny supped at Hatfield, my Lady Fortescue[5] and this examinate and Mr.

---

2. **Lady of Somerset** Anne Stanhope Seymour, wife of the lord protector.

3. **sith** since.

4. **lord great** [or grand] **master** title of the chief steward of the king's household; from 1545 to 1550 this was William Paulet, marquis of Winchester, Lord St. John.

5. **Lady Fortescue** Anne, widow of Sir Thomas Fortescue and married to Thomas Parry.

Controller's wife[6] supped with them. After supper Parry's wife looked upon her husband and wept and spake to this examinate and said, "Alas, I am afraid lest they will send my husband to the Tower, or what they will do with him."

Then said this examinate, "Nay, I warrant you, there is no such cause, but there was a certain private communication betwixt him and me. But I pray you, pray him that he will not meddle with that. For it doth not touch our examination." Then the said Parry sent his word again by the said Lady Fortescue, his wife, that he would be torn in pieces rather than he would open that matter.

She saith more: that what time she talked with Parry of speaking to my lord admiral, she forbade him to tell it to any person or to let any creature in the world know of the communication. The cause whereof was, she saith, she feared lest it should come to her husband's ear, whereupon she knew [he] would be displeased with it; for because he always did say to her that he feared the suitors of my lord admiral would once come to nought or to an evil end, and therefore forbade her to meddle in anything touching him.

LETTER 13, ADDITIONAL DOCUMENT C KATHERINE ASHLEY'S FIRST HANDWRITTEN DEPOSITION, LATE FEBRUARY 1549[1]

[Addressed in Sir Thomas Smith's hand] To my Lady Elizabeth's grace

Incontinent after the queen's coming to Hanworth, my lady's grace walking with the queen in the garden, my lord admiral did cut her gown in a hundred pieces, and I chid with her grace when she came up, that she was so trimmed. And she said the queen held her while my lord did so dress it. "Well," said I, "I would my lord would show more reverence to you, although he be homely[2] with the queen."

---

6. **Mr. Controller's wife** Philippa, wife of Sir John Gage, comptroller of the king's household and member of the Privy Council.

1. *Source:* PRO, State Papers Domestic, Edward VI 10/6/21, fol. 55r (no. 197 in Knighton); in Ashley's hand. Fols. 55v and 56 are blank.

2. **homely** familiar, intimate.

LETTER 13, ADDITIONAL DOCUMENT D KATHERINE ASHLEY'S
FINAL HANDWRITTEN DEPOSITION, LATE FEBRUARY 1549[1]

Again, I never went about secretly between[2] her and me to move her affection to him or any other, but always counsel her to keep her mind same and set it at my lords of the Council's appointment. Again, I never had letter nor token from my lord admiral to her grace nor to myself sithen[3] the queen died—in no matter. Nor but three commendations: one by Parry, John Seymour,[4] and Mary Cheke.[5] Nor her grace never sent to him, but the letter for Allen. Also, I told my lord [Thomas Seymour] in the park at Saint James that I heard ever said that he should have married my lady. "Nay," said he, "I have not to lose my life for a wife. For it has been spoken, but that cannot be. But I will prove to have the queen."

Said I, "It is past proof, as I hear you are married already."

[Addressed on verso in Smith's hand] To my Lady Elizabeth
To Mary Cheke
To Parry
per[6] *John Seymour*

This I have said to her grace: "Madam, now you may have your husband that was appointed you at the death of the king," she being sick in her bed. And she would say nay, by her troth. "Yes," said I, "if all the Council did agree, why not? For he is the noblest man unmarried in this land." And her grace would ever say nay, by her troth. And in like manner when she played at dances' hands, she chose my lord and chased him away. And I told her she would not refuse him if the lord protector and the Council did bid her. And she said yes, by her troth. And again I

1. *Source:* PRO, State Papers Domestic, Edward VI 10/6/22, fols. 57r–58v (no. 198 in Knighton); in Ashley's hand.

2. **between** MS reads "betowne."

3. **sithen** since.

4. **John Seymour** elder son of Edward Seymour, duke of Somerset, lord protector, and his first wife, Katherine.

5. **Mary Cheke** daughter of Richard Hill, Henry VIII's sergeant of the wine cellar; wife of Sir John Cheke, tutor to Edward VI and Elizabeth; and lady-in-waiting to Anne Seymour, duchess of Somerset.

6. *per* by; this deposition, or at least the portion of it that follows, was to be delivered to the addressees by John Seymour.

would have had her to write, or advised her secretary and she to put her hand to it, to comfort him in his sorrow at the death of the queen. And her grace said, "Nay, then they will think that I a-woo him." This I have talked at some certain time with her grace, that it was impossible for my lord admiral to have her grace till the king's majesty's grace came to his own rule, for I was sure that my lord protector's grace nor the Council would not suffer a subject to have her. But his grace [King Edward] at full age might do his pleasure. Also I think I had the same talk with Parry. At the delivery and reading of his letter, I think that this was my talk to her grace, for that purpose that she should not set her mind on it, seeing the unlikelihood of it.

I have no other thing that I can as now remember, but if I could I would not hide it, as the Lord knoweth, who move your hearts to have pity on me. And, good Master Secretary [Smith], speak that I may change my prison. For by my troth, it is so cold that I cannot sleep in it and so dark that I cannot in the day see, for I stop the window with straw; there is no glass. I must beseech you, good Master Secretary, to bear with my want of memory, which is never good when I am in best quiet, as my lady and all my fellows and husband can tell you. And this sorrow has made it much worse.

Thus I end. The Lord be with you, desiring you for the love of she so to move my lord's grace [Protector Somerset] to have pity on me and forgive this my great folly, that would either talk or speak of marriage to such a personage as she is, for punishment whereof I have suffered great sorrow and punishment and shame that never will out of my heart. But I do think myself worthy, trusting that my lord's grace, who has mercy on all, will not deny me for this, my first fault. For if it were possible that I might be with her grace again, which I look not for, never would I speak nor wis[7] of marriage—no, not to win all the world. And as touching my lord's [Thomas Seymour's] boldness in her chamber, the Lord I take to record I spake so ugly to him—yea, and said that it was complained on to my lords of the Council—but he would swear, "What do I? I would they all saw it!" that I could not make him leave it. At last I told the queen of it, who made a small matter of it to me, and said she would come with him herself, and so she did ever after.

Katherine Ashley

---

7. **wis** show the way, give information, know.

14 ?❧ PRINCESS ELIZABETH TO EDWARD SEYMOUR, LORD
PROTECTOR, FEBRUARY 6, 1549[1]

[Addressed] To my very good lord, my lord protector

My lord:

I have received your gentle letter and also your message by Master
Tyrwhit, for the which two things especially (although for many other
things) I cannot give your lordship sufficient thanks; and whereas your
grace doth will me to credit Master Tyrwhit, I have done so, and will do
so as long as he willeth me (as he doth[2]) to nothing but to that which is
for mine honor and honesty. And even as I said to him and did write to
your lordship, so I do write now again that when there doth any more
things happen in my mind which I have forgotten, I assure your grace I
will declare them most willingly. For I would not (as I trust you have
not) so evil a opinion of me that I would conceal anything that I knew,
for it were to no purpose. And surely forgetfulness may well cause me to
hide things, but undoubtedly else I will declare all that I know. From
Hatfield the 6 of February.

Your assured friend to my little power, *Elizabeth*

15 ?❧ PRINCESS ELIZABETH TO EDWARD SEYMOUR, LORD
PROTECTOR, FEBRUARY 21, 1549[1]

[Addressed] To my very good lord, my lord protector

My lord:

Having received your lordship's letters, I perceive in them your goodwill toward me because you declare to me plainly your mind in this

1. *Source:* Bodleian Library, University of Oxford, MS Ashmole 1729, art. 6, recatalogued
as Arch. F.c.39; in Elizabeth's hand, with remnants of seal attached. (For original-spelling
version, see *ACFLO*, part 1.) Reproduced in facsimile as no. 22 in *Humanistic Script of the
Fifteenth and Sixteenth Centuries* (Oxford: Bodleian Library, 1960). Although Tyrwhit suspected Elizabeth and her servants of collusion, complaining, "They all sing one song, and
so I think they would not do unless they had set the note before," all were exonerated of
treacherous activity by the Privy Council.

2. **doth** Elizabeth's MS reads "doth not," with "not" scored through.

1. *Source:* BL, MS Lansdowne 1236, fol. 33; in Elizabeth's hand, with traces of seals still visible. (For original-spelling version, see *ACFLO*, part 1.)

thing, and again for that you would not wish that I should do anything that should not seem good unto the Council, for the which thing I give you most hearty thanks. And whereas I do understand that you do take in evil part the letters that I did write unto your lordship, I am very sorry that you should take them so; for my mind was to declare unto you plainly as I thought in that thing, which I did also the more willingly because (as I write to you) you desired me to be plain with you in all things.

And as concerning that point that you write—that I seem to stand in mine own wit in being so well assured of mine own self—I did assure me of myself no more than I trust the truth shall try. And to say that which I knew of myself I did not think should have displeased the Council or your grace. And surely the cause why that I was sorry that there should be any such about me[2] was because that I thought the people will say that I deserved through my lewd demeanor to have such a one, and not that I mislike anything that your lordship or the Council shall think good (for I know that you and the Council are charged with me), or that I take upon me to rule myself. For I know they are most deceived that trusteth most in themselves,[3] wherefore I trust you shall never find that fault in me, to the which thing I do not see that your grace has made any direct answer at this time and, seeing they make so evil reports already, shall be but a increasing of their evil tongues. Howbeit you did write that if I would bring forth any that had reported it,[4] you and the Council would see it redressed. Which thing, though I can easily do it, I would be loath to do it for because it is mine own cause, and again that should be but a breeding of a evil name of me that I am glad to punish them, and so get the evil will of the people, which thing I would be loath to have.

But if it might so seem good unto your lordship and the rest of the Council to send forth a proclamation into the countries[5] that they refrain their tongues, declaring how the tales be but lies, it should make

2. **about me** Elizabeth refers to her vehement objections to being put under Lady Denny's formal custodianship; she claims that the measure makes her look both guilty and incapable of managing her own conduct.

3. Cf. 2 Corinthians 1:9: "Also we received an answer of death in ourselves, that we should not put our trust in ourselves, but in God, who raiseth the dead to life again" (Great Bible).

4. The unsayable **it** is the rumor that Elizabeth is pregnant by, or at least sexually involved with, Thomas Seymour.

5. **countries** that is, counties.

both the people think that you and the Council have great regard that no such rumors should be spread of any of the king's majesty's sisters (as I am, though unworthy). And also I should think myself to receive such friendship at your hands as you have promised me, although your lordship hath showed me great already. Howbeit I am ashamed to ask it any more, because I see you are not so well minded thereunto. And as concerning that you say—that I give folks occasion to think in refusing the good to uphold the evil—I am not of so simple understanding.[6] Nor I would that your grace should have so evil a opinion of me that I have so little respect to mine own honesty that I would maintain it if I had sufficient promise of the same, and so your grace shall prove me when it comes to the point. And thus I bid you farewell, desiring God always to assist you in all your affairs. Written in haste, from Hatfield, this 21 of February.

> Your assured friend to my little power, *Elizabeth*

16 ৫৬ PRINCESS ELIZABETH TO EDWARD SEYMOUR, LORD PROTECTOR, MARCH 7, 1549[1]

[Addressed] To my very good lord, my lord protector

My lord:

I have a request to make unto your grace which fear has made me omit till this time for two causes: the one, because I saw that my request for the rumors which were spread abroad of me took so little place. Which thing, when I considered, I thought I should little profit in any other suit. Howbeit now I understand that there is a proclamation[2] for

---

6. An apparent reference to Katherine Ashley's unauthorized discussion of a possible marriage between Elizabeth and Thomas Seymour: Elizabeth refuses to accept the argument that her failure to condemn Ashley's conduct proves that she condones it.

1. *Source:* BL, MS Lansdowne 1236, fol. 35; in Elizabeth's hand, with traces of seals still visible. (For original-spelling version, see *ACFLO*, part 1.) Although she has seen but meager results from her previous letters, Elizabeth continues to defend her longtime governess Katherine Ashley and herself.

2. **proclamation** Hughes and Larkin record no proclamation against rumor-mongering with a date that fits the date of this letter. The earliest known proclamation against rumor-mongering in Edward's reign (no. 352) is dated October 30, 1549. However, the government may have issued a more local order or declaration to the same effect.

them (for the which I give your grace and the rest of the Council most humble thanks), I am the bolder to speak for another thing. And the other was because peradventure your lordship and the rest of the Council will think that I favor her evildoing for whom I shall speak for, which is for Katherine Ashley, that it would please your grace and the rest of the Council to be good unto her. Which thing I do not to favor her in any evil (for that I would be sorry to do) but for these considerations which follow, the which hope doth teach me in saying that I ought not to doubt but that your grace and the rest of the Council will think that I do it for three other considerations.

First, because that she hath been with me a long time and many years, and hath taken great labor and pain in bringing of me up in learning and honesty. And therefore I ought of very duty speak for her, for Saint Gregory sayeth that we are more bound to them that bringeth us up well than to our parents, for our parents do that which is natural for them—that is, bringeth us into this world—but our bringers-up are a cause to make us live well in it.[3]

The second is because I think that whatsoever she hath done in my lord admiral's matter as concerning the marrying of me, she did it because, knowing him to be one of the Council, she thought he would not go about any such thing without[4] he had the Council's consent thereunto. For I have heard her many times say that she would never have me marry in any place without your grace's and the Council's consent.

The third cause is because that it shall and doth make men think that I am not clear of the deed myself, but that it is pardoned in me because of my youth, because that she I loved so well is in such a place.[5] Thus hope, prevailing more with me than fear, hath won the battle, and I have at this time gone forth with it. Which I pray God be taken no otherways that[6] it is meant. Written in haste from Hatfield this 7 day of March.

[Insert squeezed in between body of letter and signature]

3. Probable allusion to Saint Gregory of Nazianzus's famous funeral oration on Saint Basil the Great (Discourse 43, chaps. 12–13; J.-P. Migne, ed., *Patrologia Graeca* 36:509A–513A). Gregory compares the young Basil, whose father had just died, to a chick or calf that had only just learned to follow its parents around. But, adds Gregory, Basil received an outstanding education in rhetoric and philosophy from the teachers at the school to which his mother sent him.

4. **without** unless.

5. **place** the Tower of London.

6. **otherways that** otherwise than.

Also if I may be so bold, not offending, I beseech your grace and the rest of the Council to be good to Master Ashley, her husband, which because he is my kinsman I would be glad he should do.

Your assured friend to my little power, Elizabeth

17 ﷻ PRINCESS ELIZABETH TO KING EDWARD VI, WITH A PRESENT OF HER PORTRAIT, MAY 15, 1549[1]

Like as the rich man that daily gathereth riches to riches, and to one bag of money layeth a great sort till it come to infinite, so methinks your majesty, not being sufficed with many benefits and gentleness showed to me afore this time, doth now increase them in asking and desiring where you may bid and command, requiring a thing not worthy the desiring for itself but made worthy for your highness' request. My picture, I mean, in which if the inward good mind toward your grace might as well be declared as the outward face and countenance shall be seen, I would nor[2] have tarried the commandment but prevent[3] it, nor have been the last to grant but the first to offer it.

For the face, I grant, I might well blush to offer, but the mind I shall never be ashamed to present. For though from the grace of the picture the colors may fade by time, may give by weather, may be spotted by chance, yet the other nor time with her swift wings shall overtake, nor the misty clouds with their lowerings may darken, nor chance with her slippery foot may overthrow. Of this, although yet the proof could not be great because the occasions hath been but small, notwithstanding (as a dog hath a day) so may I perchance have time to declare it in deeds, where now I do write them but in words. And further, I shall most humbly beseech your majesty that when you shall look on my picture you will witsafe[4] to think that as you have but the outward shadow of the body afore you, so my inward mind wisheth that the body itself were oftener in your presence. Howbeit because both my so being (I think) could do your majesty little pleasure, though myself great good,

---

1. *Source:* BL, MS Cotton Vespasian F.III, fol. 48; in Elizabeth's hand. (For original-spelling version, see *ACFLO,* part 1.)
2. **nor** neither.
3. **prevent** anticipated.
4. **witsafe** vouchsafe.

and again because I see as yet not the time agreeing thereunto, I shall learn to follow this saying of Horace, *Feras non culpes quod vitari non potest.*[5]

And thus I will (troubling your majesty, I fear) end with my most humble thank,[6] beseeching God long to preserve you to His honor, to your comfort, to the realm's profit, and to my joy. From Hatfield, this 15 day of May.

Your majesty's most humbly, sister
and servant, *Elizabeth*

18 ౽❧ PRINCESS ELIZABETH TO KING EDWARD VI, APRIL 21, 1552[1]

[Addressed] To the most noble King Edward the Sixth

What cause I had of sorry when I heard first of your majesty's sickness all men might guess but none but myself could feel, which to declare were or might seem a point of flattery, and therefore to write it I omit. But as the sorrow could not be little, because the occasions were many, so is the joy great to hear of the good escape out of the perilous diseases. And that I am fully satisfied and well assured of the same by your grace's own hand, I must needs give you my most humble thanks, assuring your majesty that a precious jewel at another time could not so well have contented as your letter in this case hath comforted me. For now do I say with Saint Austin that a disease is to be counted no sickness that shall cause a better health when it is past than was assured afore it came.[2] For afore you had them, every man thought that that

---

5. "You must endure, not blame, what cannot be altered"; or, more colloquially, "What can't be cured must be endured." Presently ascribed not to Horace but to Publilius Syrus; see his *Sententiae*, ed. Wilhelm Meyer (Leipzig: B. G. Teubner, 1880), p. 30.

6. **thank** thanks.

1. *Source:* Department of Printing & Graphic Arts, The Houghton Library, Harvard University, pf MS Typ 686; in Elizabeth's hand with highly decorated capitals. (For original-spelling version, see *ACFLO*, part 1.) Dating is conjectural. In April 1552, Edward fell ill with an eruptive disease diagnosed as smallpox, followed by measles, but he made a surprisingly rapid recovery and wrote to Elizabeth that he was better; this letter is probably her response.

2. Close analogues to this idea occur in Saint Augustine (**Saint Austin**) *Confessions,* bk. 5, and his *Sermon on Psalm 37,* where he calls health in this life a sickness compared with the health of the life hereafter (*Enarratio in Psalmum XXXVII,* sec. 5, in Migne, ed., *PL,* 36:399).

should not be eschewed of you that was not scaped of many, but since you have had them, doubt of them is past and hope is given to all men that it was a purgation by these means for other worse diseases which might happen this year. Moreover, I consider that as a good father that loves his child dearly doth punish him sharply, so God, favoring your majesty greatly, hath chastened you straitly;[3] and as a father doth it for the further good of his child, so hath God prepared this for the better health of your grace. And in this hope I commit your majesty to His hands, most humbly craving pardon of your grace that I did write no sooner, desiring you to attribute the fault to my evil head and not to my slothful hand. From Hatfield this 21 of April.

Your majesty's most humble sister
to command, *Elizabeth*

19 ∾ PRINCESS ELIZABETH TO PRINCESS MARY, OCTOBER 27, 1552[1]

[Addressed] To my well-beloved sister Mary

Good sister,

As to hear of your sickness is unpleasant to me, so is it nothing fearful, for that I understand it is your old guest that is wont oft to visit you, whose coming, though it be oft, yet is it never welcome.[2] But notwithstanding it is comfortable[3] for that *jacula praevisa minus feriunt.*[4] And as I do understand your need of Jane Russell's[5] service, so am I sorry that it is by my man's occasion letted, which if I had known afore, I would have caused his will give place to need of her service. For as it is her duty to obey his commandment, so is it his part to attend your pleasure, and as I confess it were meeter for him to go to her, since she at-

---

3. Cf. Hebrews 12:6: "Whom the Lord loveth, him He chasteneth."

1. *Source:* BL, MS Lansdowne 1236, fol. 39; in Elizabeth's hand, with traces of seal still visible. (For original-spelling version, see *ACFLO*, part 1.) Assignment of the year is conjectural.

2. Probable reference to some menstrual complaint.

3. **comfortable** capable of being comforted.

4. "darts foreseen smite less" (proverbial).

5. **Jane Russell** probably a daughter of John Russell, first earl of Bedford, and Anne, the heiress of Sir Guy Sapcote.

tends upon you, so indeed he required the same, but for that divers of his fellows had business abroad that made his tarrying at home. Good sister, though I have good cause to thank you for your oft sending to me, yet I have more occasion to render you my hearty thanks for your gentle writing, which how painful it is to you, I may well guess by myself. And you may well see by my writing so oft, how pleasant it is to me. And thus I end to trouble you, desiring God to send you as well to do as you can think and wish or I desire or pray. From Ashridge, scribbled this 27th of October.

Your loving sister, *Elizabeth*

20 ❧ PRINCESS ELIZABETH TO KING EDWARD VI, CIRCA SPRING 1553[1]

[Addressed] To the king's most excellent majesty

Like as a shipman in stormy weather plucks down the sails, tarrying for better wind, so did I, most noble king, in my unfortunate chance a Thursday[2] pluck down the high sails of my joy and comfort, and do trust one day that as troublesome waves have repulsed me backward, so a gentle wind will bring me forward to my haven. Two chief occasions moved me much and grieved me greatly: the one for that I doubted your majesty's health, the other because for all my long tarrying I went without that I came for. Of the first I am relieved in a part, both that I understood of your health and also that your majesty's lodging is far from my lord marquess'[3] chamber. Of my other grief I am not eased, but the best is that whatsoever other folks will suspect, I intend not to

1. *Source:* BL, MS Harley 6986, art. 16, fol. 23; in Elizabeth's hand, with remnants of seal attached. (For original-spelling version, see *ACFLO,* part 1.) Dating is conjectural, based on the references to Edward's illness and to the anxiety that the lord marquis's presence poses. Though never robust, the young king's health suffered a severe decline after March 1553, probably from the onset of tuberculosis. He died on July 8, 1553, in his sixteenth year.

2. **a Thursday** on Thursday (colloquialism).

3. **lord marquess** most likely Henry Grey, third marquis of Dorset, father of Lady Jane Grey and member of the Privy Council of the second lord protector, John Dudley, earl of Warwick and duke of Northumberland. Dorset and Northumberland contrived the marriage of their respective offspring, Lady Jane Grey and Guildford Dudley, on May 21, 1553, as a prelude to setting the pair on the throne.

fear your grace's goodwill, which as I know that I never deserved to faint, so I trust will still stick by me.[4] For if your grace's advice that I should return (whose will is a commandment) had not been, I would not have made the half of my way the end of my journey. And thus as one desirous to hear of your majesty's health, though unfortunate[5] to see it, I shall pray God forever to preserve you. From Hatfield this present Saturday.

> Your majesty's humble sister to
> commandment,[6] *Elizabeth*

21 ᶔ PRINCESS ELIZABETH TO THE LORDS OF THE PRIVY COUNCIL, MAY 31, 1553[1]

If both apparent points touching mine honor and my necessity also constrained me not, good my lords, I should soon have served all your expectations touching Woburn and long sithence have appeased my lord of Bedford's mind therein. But since your wisdoms, informed of that other side, do affirm that it were mine honor and a point of common justice not to intromit[2] therewith, the matter being litigious, so, trusting in your goodwills towards me, do[3] for answer resolve with you in this manner. As knowing myself a long time to have great need of pastures for my provisions, the lack whereof hath been to my great charges, at Shrovetide[4] last and long time before my lord privy seal (to my knowledge) did intromit in such sort therewith, I contracted indeed

---

4. Elizabeth apparently fears that Edward's affections to her are being alienated; she was right in the event, for a "Device for the Succession," signed by Edward and endorsed by the Privy Council on June 21, 1553, disinherited both of his half-sisters and left his crown to Lady Jane Grey.

5. **unfortunate** not fortunate enough.

6. **commandment** command.

1. *Source:* BL, MS Cotton Vespasian F.XIII, art. 220, fol. 274 (formerly fol. 173); in the hand of a secretary with Elizabeth's signature and remnants of seal attached. Elizabeth had contracted with a man named Smith for pasturage rights at Woburn, Buckinghamshire, for the maintenance of her household. She held fast when her claim to these rights was challenged in court by John Russell (d. 1555), earl of Bedford, lord privy seal, a ranking magnate of the realm since her father's time.

2. **intromit** meddle, deal.

3. **do** that is, I do.

4. **Shrovetide** the three days preceding Ash Wednesday, the beginning of Lent.

with one Smith for his interest therein, being then (parcel thereof for a few years yet to come only excepted) clearly discharged of all former contracts and other things in his own hands and right. And he, upon such considerations of recompense as I took with him, to discharge the thing clearly at and until our Lady Day last;[5] and myself to bear the charges thenceforward. By force whereof I entered and am thereof, as ye may now well understand, by just order of the laws justly possessed; from the which to be now rejected were to my great dishonor, since all the country knoweth it.

And for your lordships' further satisfaction in this matter, since I heard of the controversy between my lord and Smith it is not unknown that I sent unto him my whole state and condition herein, with far larger and more benevolent offers than I received answer or, being evilly handled, can be contented to offer again. And therefore this I say, that if it be my right to hold it, I trust that ye will not mislike that I keep it; for I will not, God willing, forgo it until I may be better provided. And if my lord have better right thereunto than I have, then I will give it over with all my heart unto him without contention. And as I utterly deny to Smith any supportation[6] at my hands in any of his misdemeanors against my lord, and do and shall leave him to suffer that he hath most deserved at my lord's hands, so do I hope quietly to enjoy that that I this[7] justly have come by with my lord's goodwill: both because I have been such one towards my lord for the good service he did my father as, if ability served, I would not have failed to have given of mine own a far better thing; and again because it is not unknown to my lord nor to any of you all but that it is most requisite for me to seek some pastures for myself, which had never none out of lease appointed me by others. And thus I commit you all to God, desiring you to make my humble commendations to the king's majesty, for whose health I pray daily,[8] and daily and evermore shall so do during my life. At Hatfield, the last day of May 1553.

Your very loving friend, Elizabeth

---

5. **Lady Day** Feast of the Annunciation, March 25, legally the beginning of the New Year.
6. **supportation** support.
7. **this** that is, thus.
8. Edward VI was to die in fewer than six weeks (on July 8).

22 ❧ PRINCESS ELIZABETH TO QUEEN MARY, MARCH 16, 1554[1]

If any ever did try this old saying—that a king's word was more than
another man's oath—I most humbly beseech your majesty to verify it
in me, and to remember your last promise and my last demand: that I
be not condemned without answer and due proof. Which it seems that
now I am, for that, without cause proved, I am by your Council from
you commanded to go unto the Tower, a place more wonted for a false
traitor than a true subject. Which though I know I deserve it not, yet in
the face of all this realm appears that it is proved. Which I pray God I
may die the shamefullest death that ever any died afore I may mean any
such thing. And to this present hour I protest afore God (who shall
judge my truth, whatsoever malice shall devise) that I never practiced,
counseled, nor consented to anything that might be prejudicial to your
person any way or dangerous to the state by any mean. And therefore I
humbly beseech your majesty to let me answer afore yourself and not
suffer me to trust your councillors—yea, and that afore I go to the
Tower (if it be possible); if not, afore I be further condemned. Howbeit
I trust assuredly your highness will give me leave to do it afore I go, for
that thus shamefully I may not be cried out on as now I shall be—yea,
and without cause. Let conscience move your highness to take some
better way with me than to make me be condemned in all men's sight
afore my desert known.[2]

Also I most humbly beseech your highness to pardon this my boldness, which innocency procures me to do, together with hope of your
natural kindness, which I trust will not see me cast away without desert.
Which what it is, I would desire no more of God but that you truly
knew. Which thing I think and believe you shall never by report know
unless by yourself you hear. I have heard in my time of many cast away
for want of coming to the presence of their prince, and in late days I
heard my lord of Somerset say that if his brother had been suffered to
speak with him, he had never suffered. But the persuasions were made

1. *Source:* PRO, State Papers Domestic, Mary I 11/4/2, fol. 3; in Elizabeth's hand. (For original-spelling version, see *ACFLO*, part 1, where a photograph of fol. 3v is supplied.) Damaged; missing materials are supplied from an eighteenth-century copy among Dr. Thomas
Birch's papers in BL, MS Harley 7190, art. 2, fols. 125r–126r. After Elizabeth's Catholic half-
sister Mary Tudor became queen in 1553, Elizabeth found herself in serious jeopardy because she was a potential Protestant rival for the throne.

2. **desert known** that is, desert is known (a Latinism).

to him so great that he was brought in belief that he could not live safely if the admiral lived, and that made him give his consent to his death.[3] Though these persons are not to be compared to your majesty, yet I pray God as evil persuasions persuade not one sister against the other, and all for that they have heard false report and not hearken to the truth known. Therefore once again, with humbleness of my heart because I am not suffered to bow the knees of my body, I humbly crave to speak with your highness. Which I would not be so bold as to desire if I knew not myself most clear, as I know myself most true. And as for the traitor Wyatt,[4] he might peradventure write me a letter, but on my faith I never received any from him. And as for the copy of my letter sent to the French king,[5] I pray God confound me eternally if ever I sent him word, message, token, or letter by any means, and to this my truth I will stand in to my death.

[Diagonal lines fill the interval between the body of the letter and its ending to prevent unwanted insertions.]

I humbly crave but only one word of answer from yourself.

> Your highness' most faithful subject
> that hath been from the beginning and
> will be to my end, *Elizabeth*

3. **death** Edward Seymour, duke of Somerset, lord protector, had his younger brother, Thomas Seymour, lord high admiral, arrested, convicted, and beheaded on a charge of high treason in March 1549.

4. **Wyatt** Sir Thomas Wyatt the younger, convicted of treason against Mary on March 15, 1554, one day before the writing of the present letter, and executed April 11. Despite strenuous efforts on the part of the government, he did not implicate Elizabeth in the planning or execution of his rebellion.

5. On January 26, 1554, a courier employed by François de Noailles—a member of the French embassy to England—was arrested at Rochester on his way back to France; the courier was put in prison and his dispatches confiscated. One of the most mysterious items in his mailbag was a French translation of a letter purportedly written by Elizabeth to her sister Mary. Mary and her closest advisers took this letter as material evidence that Elizabeth and the French were conspiring against her, but no formal charges were ever brought.

23 &· PRINCESS ELIZABETH TO QUEEN MARY, AUGUST 2, 1556[1]

[Addressed] To the queen's most excellent majesty

When I revolve in mind (most noble queen) the old love of paynims[2] to their prince and the reverent fear of Romans to their Senate, I can but muse for my part and blush for theirs, to see the rebellious hearts and devilish intents of Christians in names, but Jews in deed,[3] toward their oincted[4] king. Which, methinks, if they had feared God though they could not have loved the state, they should for dread of their own plague have refrained that wickedness which their bounden duty to your majesty hath not restrained. But when I call to remembrance that the devil *tanquam leo rugiens circumit querens quem devorare potest*[5] I do the less marvel though he have gotten such novices into his professed house, as vessels (without God's grace) more apt to serve his palace than meet to inhabit English land. I am the bolder to call them his imps for that Saint Paul sayeth, *Seditiosi filii sunt diaboli,*[6] and since I have so good a buckler I fear the less to enter into their judgment. Of this I assure your majesty, though it be my part above the rest to bewail such things though my name had not been in them, yet it vexeth me too much than[7] the devil owen[8] me such a hate as to put me in any part of his mischievous instigations. Whom, as I profess him my foe that is all Christians' enemy, so wish I he had some other way invented to spite me. But since it hath pleased God thus to bewray[9] their malice afore they finish their purpose, I most humbly thank Him both that He hath ever thus preserved your majesty through His aid (much like a lamb from the horns of these Bashan bulls),[10] and also stirs up the hearts of

1. *Source:* BL, MS Lansdowne 1236, fol. 37; in Elizabeth's hand. (For original-spelling version, see *ACFLO,* part 1.)

2. **paynims** pagans.

3. **Jews in deed** Since medieval times, the Jews had been categorized as killers of their king and messiah, Jesus.

4. **oincted** anointed.

5. "as a roaring lion goes about, seeking whom he may devour"; except for *circumit* instead of *circuit,* an exact quotation of I Peter 5:8 in the Vulgate. Elizabeth carefully quotes the Catholic version of the Bible to her Catholic sister.

6. "The seditious are children of the devil" (loose paraphrase of Ephesians 2:2).

7. **than** that is, that.

8. **owen** owes.

9. **bewray** expose.

10. **Bashan bulls** cf. Psalm 22:12.

your loving subjects to resist them and deliver you, to His honor and their shame.

The intelligence of which, proceeding from your majesty, deserveth more humble thanks than with my pen I can render, which, as infinite, I will leave to number. And among earthly things I chiefly wish this one: that there were as good surgeons for making anatomies of hearts that might show my thoughts to your majesty as there are expert physicians of the bodies, able to express the inward griefs of their maladies to their patient. For then I doubt not but know well that whatsoever other should suggest by malice, yet your majesty should be sure by knowledge, so that the more such misty clouds obfuscates the clear light of my truth, the more my tried thoughts should glister to the dimming of their hidden malice. But since wishes are vain and desires oft fails, I must crave that my deeds may supply that my thoughts cannot declare, and they be not misdeemed there as the facts have been so well tried. And like as I have been your faithful subject from the beginning of your reign, so shall no wicked persons cause me to change to the end of my life. And thus I commit your majesty to God's tuition, whom I beseech long time to preserve, ending with the new remembrance of my old suit, more for that it should not be forgotten than for that I think it not remembered. From Hatfield this present Sunday, the second day of August.

Your majesty's obedient subject
and humble sister, *Elizabeth*

POEMS 1–3

1 &❧ WRITTEN ON A WINDOW FRAME AT WOODSTOCK[1]

O Fortune, thy wresting, wavering state
Hath fraught with cares my troubled wit,
Whose witness this present prison late
Could bear, where once was joy flown quite.
Thou causedst the guilty to be loosed

---

1. *Source:* The poem as copied in 1600 by the Moravian magnate Zdeněk Brtnický z Valdštejina, or Baron Waldstein, and reproduced in G. W. Groos, trans., *The Diary of Baron Waldstein: A Traveller in Elizabethan England* (London: Thames & Hudson, 1981), pp. [117, 119]. The poem was also copied in 1598 by Paul Hentzner, *Itinerarium* (Nuremberg, 1612), pp. 144–45; and in 1599 by Thomas Platter, as reproduced in Hans Hecht, ed., *Thomas Platters des Jüngeren Englandfahrt im Jahre 1599* (Leipzig: Max Niemeyer Verlag, 1929), pp. 121–22. Platter's and Hentzner's versions are so garbled that they can only be restored conjecturally, and modern versions of these texts derive from eighteenth-century attempts at reconstruction. Possibly authoritative variants in these reconstructed versions are recorded in the notes. Platter and Hentzner do not include the final line reproduced by Waldstein, which was probably originally a separate composition (see Poem 2, p. 46).

These verses almost certainly date from 1554–55, the period of Elizabeth's imprisonment at Woodstock. The three visitors to England who copied the poem more than forty years later describe it variously as written with charcoal (specified in Platter's account) on a shutter or window frame (literally *"fenestrae ligneae"* in Hentzner) or on a wall, as in Waldstein's slightly later rendition. The English during the sixteenth century made an inveterate practice of writing messages, proverbs, and "posies" on walls, shutters, and other public surfaces. We conjecture that by the time of Waldstein's visit in 1600, Elizabeth's original writing had faded to the point that both of her Woodstock poems may have been repro-

From lands[2] where innocents were enclosed,
And caused the guiltless to be reserved,
And freed those that death had well deserved.
But all herein can be naught[3] wrought,
So God grant to my foes as they have thought.[4]
   Finis. Elisabetha a prisoner, 1555
Much suspected by me, but nothing proved can be.

2 ℤ WRITTEN WITH A DIAMOND[1]

*In her imprisonment at Woodstock, these verses she wrote with her
diamond in a glass window:*

Much suspected by me,
Nothing proved can be.
   Quod[2] Elizabeth the prisoner

---

duced seriatim (and with some variations in wording) on a wall of her prison chamber for
the edification of the many visitors to Woodstock. Waldstein notes, "They say that she
wrote other things too with a diamond on one of the windows, but these inscriptions no
longer exist" ([119]).

 2. **lands** Waldstein's accompanying Latin translation reads "*vinculis*" (chains), confirm-
ing Platter's and Hentzner's variant reading of "bands."

 3. **naught** Platter and Hentzner read "nothing."

 4. Platter and Hentzner read (conjecturally) "So God send to my foes all they have
taught."

 1. *Source:* Foxe, 1714; the poem is identically worded in Holinshed (3:1158). Modern biographers date these verses to the period of Elizabeth's imprisonment at Woodstock in
1554–55, but John Foxe and Raphael Holinshed, for whom Elizabeth's sufferings under
Mary made her an exemplar of Protestant martyrdom, both attribute the verses to 1558, the
tumultuous final year of Mary's reign and the eve of Elizabeth's accession.

 2. *Quod* said.

3 ⇌ 'TWAS CHRIST THE WORD[1]

> *Hoc est corpus meum* [2]
> 'Twas Christ the Word that spake it.
> The same took bread and brake it,
> And as the Word did make it,
> So I believe and take it.
>   Queen Elizabeth

1. *Source:* Bodleian Library, University of Oxford, MS Rawlinson D.947, fol. 86v; a miscellany dated circa 1614. The poem is also attributed to Elizabeth in Sir R[ichard] Baker, *A Chronicle of the Kings of England* (London: for Daniel Frere, 1643), pp. 97–98, where she is said to have offered it as a reply to Roman Catholic priests who were examining her during Mary's reign; and in a marginal note in a hand of the period to a copy of Alexander Huish, *Lectures upon the Lord's Prayer* (London: William Turner, 1626), sig. Y2v of his 1625 sermon on "Give us this day our daily bread." Huish's version of what he terms a "vulgar rhyme" is

> Christ was the Word that spake it;
> Christ was the Bread that brake it:
> As Christ His word did make it,
> Do thou believe and take it.

The marginal commentator, who attributes the poem to "Elizabetha Regina," offers yet another version:

> 'Twas Christ the Lord that spake it:
> He took the bread and brake it,
> And what the Lord did make it,
> That I believe and take it.
> (*STC* 13927), transcribed from University Microfilms reel 1244.

The attribution to Elizabeth, though strengthened somewhat by the fairly early MS version reproduced here, is uncertain: a version of the poem is also included in the second (1635) ed. of John Donne's poems, along with several other poems not presently attributed to Donne. For arguments against Elizabeth's authorship, see Bradner (74 n.); and Sir John Neale, "The Sayings of Queen Elizabeth," *Essays in Elizabethan History* (London: Jonathan Cape, 1958), pp. 85–112, especially pp. 102–103. (Neale was, however, unaware of the MS version reproduced here.)

2. "This is my body"; cf. Matthew 26:26, Mark 14:22, and Luke 22:19. The phrase is uttered by the Roman Catholic priest when he consecrates and elevates the sacramental bread, ritually reenacting Christ's self-sacrifice on the cross in the celebration of the Mass.

PRAYERS 1-2

1, 2 ⟨℘⟩ PRINCESS ELIZABETH'S PRAYERS IN THE TOWER OF LONDON[1]

[Headed] The Christian prayers of our Sovereign Lady Queen Elizabeth, which her grace made in the time of her trouble, and imprisonment in the Tower...

Help me now, O God, for I have none other friends but Thee alone. And suffer me not (I beseech Thee) to build my foundation upon the sands, but upon the rock,[2] whereby all blasts of blustering weather may have no power against me, amen.

Another prayer made by her majesty, when she was in great fear and doubt of death by murder:

Grant, O God, that the wicked may have no power to hurt or betray me; neither suffer any such treason and wickedness to proceed against me. For Thou, O God, canst mollify all such tyrannous hearts and disappoint all such cruel purposes. And I beseech Thee to hear me, Thy creature, which am Thy servant and at Thy commandment, trusting by Thy grace ever so to remain, amen.

---

1. *Source:* Thomas Bentley, *The Monument of Matrons* (London: H. Denham, [1582]) (*STC* 1892), "The Second Lamp of Virginity," pp. 35–36. This source is quite late but potentially trustworthy. It also includes a copy of Queen Elizabeth's prayer on the occasion of her progress through London before her coronation that differs only slightly from the versions recorded in earlier printed sources (see Speech 2, pp. 54–55).

2. Cf. Jesus' parable in Matthew 7:24–27.

II

SPEECHES, LETTERS,

POEMS, AND PRAYERS OF

QUEEN ELIZABETH I

1558–1572

FIGURE 4 Queen Elizabeth I in her coronation robes, by an unknown artist around 1600. Reproduced by courtesy of the National Portrait Gallery, London.

SPEECHES 1–12

***

1 ❧ QUEEN ELIZABETH'S FIRST SPEECH, HATFIELD,
NOVEMBER 20, 1558[1]

*[Endorsed] Queen Elizabeth's speech to her secretary and other her lords
before her coronation.*

Words spoken by her majesty to Mr. Cecil:[2]

I give you this charge, that you shall be of my Privy Council and content
yourself to take pains for me and my realm. This judgment I have of
you: that you will not be corrupted with any manner of gift, and that
you will be faithful to the state, and that without respect of my private
will, you will give me that counsel that you think best, and if you shall
know anything necessary to be declared to me of secrecy, you shall
show it to myself only. And assure yourself I will not fail to keep taciturnity therein, and therefore herewith I charge you.

Words spoken by the queen to the lords:

My lords, the law of nature moveth me to sorrow for my sister; the burden that is fallen upon me maketh me amazed; and yet, considering I

---

1. *Source*: PRO, State Papers Domestic, Elizabeth 12/1/7; copy.

2. Then Sir William Cecil (1520–1598), Protestant humanist and graduate of Saint John's
College, Cambridge, who had served as secretary to Protector Edward Somerset, as secretary of state under Edward VI, and as Princess Elizabeth's own surveyor from 1550. He was
to serve Queen Elizabeth for forty years until his death.

am God's creature, ordained to obey His appointment, I will thereto yield, desiring from the bottom of my heart that I may have assistance of His grace to be the minister of His heavenly will in this office now committed to me. And as I am but one body naturally considered, though by His permission a body politic to govern,[3] so I shall desire you all, my lords (chiefly you of the nobility, everyone in his degree and power), to be assistant to me, that I with my ruling and you with your service may make a good account to almighty God and leave some comfort to our posterity in earth. I mean to direct all my actions by good advice and counsel. And therefore, considering that divers of you be of the ancient nobility,[4] having your beginnings and estates of my progenitors, kings of this realm, and thereby ought in honor to have the more natural care for maintaining of my estate and this commonwealth; some others have been of long experience in governance and enabled by my father of noble memory, my brother, and my late sister to bear office; the rest of you being upon special trust lately called to her service only and trust, for your service considered and rewarded; my meaning is to require of you all nothing more but faithful hearts in such service as from time to time shall be in your powers towards the preservation of me and this commonwealth. And for counsel and advice I shall accept you of my nobility, and such others of you the rest as in consultation I shall think meet and shortly appoint, to the which also, with their advice, I will join to their aid, and for ease of their burden, others meet for my service. And they which I shall not appoint, let them not think the same for any disability in them, but for that I do consider a multitude doth make rather discord and confusion than good counsel. And of my goodwill you shall not doubt, using yourselves as appertaineth to good and loving subjects.

3. The earliest of Elizabeth's references in her speeches to the doctrine of the "king's two bodies," by which the monarch is defined as composed of a mortal "body natural" and an immortal "body politic." See Ernest Kantorowicz, *The King's Two Bodies: A Study in Medieval Political Theology* (Princeton: Princeton University Press, 1957), pp. 7–14; and Marie Axton, *The Queen's Two Bodies: Drama and the Elizabethan Succession* (London: Royal Historical Society, 1977).

4. Here Elizabeth addresses the great landed magnates, who—whatever their religion and political alliances—she could not have removed from her Council because of their high rank.

2 ❧ RICHARD MULCASTER'S ACCOUNT OF QUEEN ELIZABETH'S SPEECH AND PRAYER DURING HER PASSAGE THROUGH LONDON TO WESTMINSTER THE DAY BEFORE HER CORONATION, JANUARY 14, 1559[1]

[Sig. Ai–Aii v] And on the other side, her grace, by holding up her hands and merry countenance to such as stood far off, and most tender and gentle language to those that stood nigh to her grace, did declare herself no less thankfully to receive her people's goodwill than they lovingly offered it unto her. To all that wished her grace well she gave hearty thanks, and to such as bade God save her grace she said again, God save them all, and thanked them with all her heart. So that on either side there was nothing but gladness, nothing but prayer, nothing but comfort. The queen's majesty rejoiced marvelously to see it so exceedingly showed toward her grace which all good princes have ever desired: I mean, so earnest love of subjects, so evidently declared even to her grace's own person being carried in the midst of them. The people, again, were wonderfully ravished with welcoming answers and gestures of their princess, like to the which they had before tried at her first coming to the Tower from Hatfield. This her grace's loving behavior, preconceived in the people's heads, upon these considerations was thoroughly confirmed, and indeed implanted a wonderful hope in them touching her worthy government in the rest of her reign. For in all her passage she did not only show her most gracious love toward the people in general, but also privately. If the baser personages had either offered her grace any flowers or such like as a signification of their goodwill, or moved to her any suit, she most gently, to the common rejoicing of all the lookers-on and private comfort of the party, stayed her chariot and heard their requests. So that if a man should say well, he could not better term the City of London that time than a stage wherein was showed the wonderful spectacle of a noble-hearted princess toward her most loving people and the people's exceeding comfort in beholding so worthy a sovereign and hearing so princelike a voice. . . .

[Sig Ciii] Out at the windows and penthouses of every house did hang a number of rich and costly banners and streamers, till her grace

---

1. *Source:* [Richard Mulcaster], *The Passage of Our Most Dread Sovereign Lady Queen Elizabeth through the City of London to Westminster the Day Before Her Coronation* (London: Richard Tottel, 1558[9]) (*STC* 7590), excerpts. Reprinted in Holinshed (3:1172–80).

came to the upper end of Cheap.[2] And there, by appointment, the right worshipful Master Ranulph Cholmley, recorder[3] of the City, presented to the queen's majesty a purse of crimson satin richly wrought with gold, wherein the City gave unto the queen's majesty a thousand marks[4] in gold, as Master Recorder did declare briefly unto the queen's majesty, whose words tended to this end: that the lord mayor, his brethren and commonality of the City, to declare their gladness and goodwill towards the queen's majesty, did present her grace with that gold, desiring her grace to continue their good and gracious queen and not to esteem the value of the gift, but the mind of the givers. The queen's majesty with both her hands took the purse and answered to him again marvelous pithily, and so pithily that the standers-by, as they embraced entirely her gracious answer, so they marveled at the couching thereof, which was in words truly reported these:

> I thank my lord mayor, his brethren, and you all. And whereas your request is that I should continue your good lady and queen, be ye ensured that I will be as good unto you as ever queen was to her people. No will in me can lack, neither do I trust shall there lack any power. And persuade yourselves that for the safety and quietness of you all I will not spare, if need be, to spend my blood. God thank you all.

Which answer of so noble an hearted princess, if it moved a marvelous shout and rejoicing, it is nothing to be marveled at, since both the heartiness thereof was so wonderful, and the words so jointly knit.

[Sig. Eiiii] But because princes be set in their seat by God's appointing and therefore they must first and chiefly tender the glory of Him from whom their glory issueth, it is to be noted in her grace that forsomuch as God hath so wonderfully placed her in the seat of government over this realm, she in all doings doth show herself most mindful of His goodness and mercy showed unto her. And amongst all other, two principal signs thereof were noted in this passage. First in the Tower, where her grace, before she entered her chariot, lifted up her eyes to heaven and said:

> O Lord, almighty and everlasting God, I give Thee most hearty thanks that Thou hast been so merciful unto me as to spare me to behold this joyful day.

2. **Cheap** Cheapside, a major London market street.
3. **recorder** magistrate having criminal and civil jurisdiction in a city or borough.
4. **marks** coins valued during the period at two-thirds pound sterling.

And I acknowledge that Thou hast dealt as wonderfully and as mercifully with me as Thou didst with Thy true and faithful servant Daniel, Thy prophet, whom Thou deliveredst out of the den from the cruelty of the greedy and raging lions.[5] Even so was I overwhelmed and only by Thee delivered. To Thee (therefore) only be thanks, honor, and praise forever, amen.[6]

The second was the receiving of the Bible at the Little Conduit[7] in Cheap. For when her grace had learned that the Bible in English should there be offered, she thanked the City therefore, promised the reading thereof most diligently, and incontinent[8] commanded that it should be brought. At the receipt whereof, how reverently did she with both her hands take it, kiss it, and lay it upon her breast, to the great comfort of the lookers-on! God will undoubtedly preserve so worthy a prince, which at His honor so reverently taketh her beginning. For this saying is true and written in the book of truth: he that first seeketh the kingdom of God shall have all other things cast unto him.[9]

Now, therefore, all English hearts and her natural people must needs praise God's mercy, which hath sent them so worthy a prince, and pray for her grace's long continuance amongst us.

---

5. Cf. Daniel 6:16–22.

6. Cf. Letters 22 and 23, pp. 41–44; and Foxe's "The Miraculous Preservation of the Lady Elizabeth, Now Queen of England, from Extreme Calamity and Danger of Life in the Time of Queen Mary, Her Sister" (1708–11). Sir John Hayward's later version of her speech at the Tower of London reads: "Some have fallen from being princes of this land to be prisoners in this place; I am raised from being a prisoner in this place to be prince of this land" (*The Life and Reign of King Edward the Sixth with the Beginning of the Reign of Queen Elizabeth* [London: for John Partridge, 1636], p. 458).

7. **Little Conduit** the smaller of two lead pipe outlets for fresh water supply at the west end of Cheap Street, situated close to Paul's Gate.

8. **incontinent** immediately.

9. Cf. Matthew 6:33 (in the Great Bible version presented to Elizabeth): "Seek ye first the kingdom of God and the righteousness thereof, and all these things shall be ministered unto you."

3 ᘒ QUEEN ELIZABETH'S FIRST SPEECH BEFORE PARLIAMENT,
FEBRUARY 10, 1559

SPEECH 3, VERSION 1[1] *[Headed] Friday the 10th of February. The answer
of the queen's highness to the petitions proponed[2] unto her by the lower
house concerning her marriage.*

As I have good cause, so do I give you all my hearty thanks for the good
zeal and loving care you seem to have, as well towards me as to the
whole state of your country. Your petition, I perceive, consisteth of three
parts, and mine answer to the same shall depend of two.

And to the first part, I may say unto you that from my years of understanding, sith[3] I first had consideration of myself to be born a servitor of almighty God, I happily[4] chose this kind of life in which I yet live,
which I assure you for mine own part hath hitherto best contented myself and I trust hath been most acceptable to God.[5] From the which if
either ambition of high estate offered to me in marriage by the pleasure
and appointment of my prince (whereof I have some records in this
presence, as you our lord treasurer well know);[6] or if the eschewing of
the danger of mine enemies; or the avoiding of the peril of death, whose
messenger or rather continual watchman, the prince's indignation,[7] was

1. *Source*: BL, MS Lansdowne 94, art. 14, fol. 29; copy. This speech exists in several contemporary MSS. What Hartley terms the "Duke of Portland" version is for the most part
similar in meaning to the Lansdowne version, though sometimes different in wording. The
most noteworthy differences are cited below from Cambridge University Library, MS
Gg.III.34, fols. 199–201, which has also been used to supply a few words illegible in the
Lansdowne MS as a result of damage. See Hartley (1:44) for a list of other copies of the
speech. The version printed by D'Ewes (46–47) is almost identical to the Lansdowne version. D'Ewes describes his text as copied from a printed copy "garnished with gilt letters,
given to the Honorable the Lady Stafford of her majesty's Privy Chamber and written out
by Alex. Evesham, 1590."

2. **proponed** put forth for consideration or adoption.

3. **sith** since.

4. **happily** or possibly "haply"; MS reads "happelie."

5. Cambridge MS reads: "Knowing myself to be born a servitor of almighty God, I did
choose this kind of life in the which I do yet live as a life most acceptable unto Him,
wherein I thought I could best serve Him and with most quietness do my duty to Him."

6. A probable allusion to the proposal to marry her to Philibert Emmanuel, prince of
Piedmont, which Philip advocated to Mary between 1554 and 1558. **lord treasurer** William
Paulet (1485?–1572), marquis of Winchester, lord treasurer since 1550.

7. Proverbial: "*indignatio principis mors est*"—"the prince's indignation is death." Although this loose quotation of Proverbs 16:14 in the Vulgate version was a byword about
Henry VIII's actions in the last decade of his reign, Elizabeth here uses it in reference to the
mortal danger she faced during and after Wyatt's Rebellion in 1554.

not little time daily before mine eyes, by whose means although I know, or justly may suspect, yet will not now utter; or if the whole cause were in my sister herself, I will not now burden her therewith, because I will not charge the dead. If any of these, I say, could have drawn or dissuaded me from this kind of life, I had not now remained in this estate wherein you see me; but constant have always continued in this determination. Although my youth and words may seem to some hardly to agree together, yet it is most true that at this day I stand free from any other meaning that either I have had in times past or have at this present. With which trade of life I am so thoroughly acquainted that I trust God, who hath hitherto therein preserved and led me by the hand, will not now of His goodness suffer me to go alone.[8]

For the other part, the manner of your petition I do well like of and take in good part, because that it is simple and containeth no limitation of place or person. If it had been otherwise, I must needs have misliked it very much and thought it in you a very great presumption, being unfitting and altogether unmeet for you to require them that may command, or those to appoint whose parts are to desire, or such to bind and limit whose duties are to obey, or to take upon you to draw my love to your liking or frame my will to your fantasies. For a guerdon constrained and a gift freely given can never agree together.

Nevertheless, if any of you be in suspect that, whensoever it may please God to incline my heart to another kind of life, ye may well assure yourselves my meaning is not to do or determine anything wherewith the realm may or shall have just cause to be discontented. And therefore put that clean out of your heads. For I assure you, what credit my assurance may have with you I cannot tell, but what credit it shall deserve to have, the sequel shall declare. I will never in that matter conclude anything that shall be prejudicial to the realm, for the weal, good, and safety whereof I will never shame to spend my life. And whomsoever my chance shall be to light upon, I trust he shall be as careful for the realm and you—I will not say as myself, because I cannot so cer-

---

8. The three preceding sentences in the Cambridge MS read: "If any of these, I say, could have drawn or dissuaded me, I had not now remained in this estate wherein you see me. But so constant have I continued always in this determination as albeit my youth and my words may seem to some hardly to agree together, yet it is true that to this day I stand free from any other meaning that either I have had in time past or have at this present. In which trade and state of living whereof I am so thoroughly acquainted, God hath ever hitherto so preserved me, and hath had so watchful an eye upon me, and hath so guided and led me by the hand, as my whole trust is He will not now suffer me to go alone."

tainly determine of any other—but at the leastways, by my goodwill and desire, he shall be such as shall be as careful for the preservation of the realm and you as myself.[9]

And albeit it might please almighty God to continue me still in this mind to live out of the state of marriage, yet it is not to be feared but He will so work in my heart and in your wisdoms as good provision by His help may be made in convenient time, whereby the realm shall not remain destitute of an heir that may be a fit governor, and peradventure more beneficial to the realm than such offspring as may come of me. For although I be never so careful of your well-doings, and mind ever so to be, yet may my issue grow out of kind and become, perhaps, ungracious. And in the end this shall be for me sufficient: that a marble stone shall declare that a queen, having reigned such a time, lived and died a virgin. And here I end, and take your coming unto me in good part, and give unto you all eftsoons[10] my hearty thanks, more yet for your zeal and good meaning than for your petition.[11]

SPEECH 3, VERSION 2[1] *1559. Her answer to [the Commons'] petition that she marry*

"In a thing which is not much pleasing unto me, the infallible testimony of your goodwill and all the rest of my people is most acceptable. As concerning your instant persuasion of me to marriage, I must tell you I

9. This and the preceding sentence vary significantly in the Cambridge MS, which reads: "I will never in that matter conclude anything that shall be prejudicial to the realm, for the weal and safety whereof, as a good mother of my country, will never shun to spend my life. And whosoever my choice may light upon, he shall be as careful for the preservation of the realm and you (I will not say as myself, for I cannot so certainly promise for another as I do surely know of myself) but as any other can be."

10. **eftsoons** soon after, in the next moment.

11. In the Cambridge MS this sentence reads: "To conclude, I take your coming to me in good part and give you my hearty thanks, more yet for your zeal, goodwill, and good meaning than for your message and petition."

1. *Source*: William Camden's printed Latin translation (1615) of Elizabeth's speech of February 10, 1559; English retranslation in *Annales: The True and Royal History of the Famous Empress Elizabeth* (London: for B. Fisher, 1625) (an unlisted variant of *STC* 4497), bk. 1, pp. 27–29. This is the form in which the speech has been best known to later ages, but it freely embroiders upon and condenses the speech as we have it from the early sources. As Camden himself states at a later juncture (bk. 1, p. 132), the queen spoke "in few words, which I will shut up in fewer."

have been ever persuaded that I was born by God to consider and, above all things, do those which appertain unto His glory. And therefore it is that I have made choice of this kind of life, which is most free and agreeable for such human affairs as may tend to His service only. From which, if either the marriages which have been offered me by divers puissant princes or the danger of attempts made against my life could no whit divert me, it is long since I had any joy in the honor of a husband; and this is that I thought, then that I was a private person. But when the public charge of governing the kingdom came upon me, it seemed unto me an inconsiderate folly to draw upon myself the cares which might proceed of marriage. To conclude, I am already bound unto an husband, which is the kingdom of England, and that may suffice you. And this," quoth she, "makes me wonder that you forget, yourselves, the pledge of this alliance which I have made with my kingdom." And therewithal, stretching out her hand, she showed them the ring[2] with which she was given in marriage and inaugurated to her kingdom in express and solemn terms. "And reproach me so no more," quoth she, "that I have no children: for every one of you, and as many as are English, are my children and kinsfolks, of whom, so long as I am not deprived and God shall preserve me, you cannot charge me, without offense, to be destitute.

"But in this I must commend you, that you have not appointed me an husband. For that were unworthy the majesty of an absolute princess, and the discretion of you that are born my subjects. Nevertheless, if God have ordained me to another course of life, I will promise you to do nothing to the prejudice of the commonwealth, but as far as possible I may, will marry such an husband as shall be no less careful for the common good, than myself. And if I persist in this which I have proposed unto myself, I assure myself, that God will so direct my counsels and yours that you shall have no cause to doubt of a successor which may be more profitable for the commonwealth than him which may proceed from me, sithence[3] the posterity of good princes doth oftentimes degenerate.

2. For the motif of the ring, see also Elizabeth's conversations with Maitland, Speech 4, p. 65.

3. **sithence** since.

"Lastly, this may be sufficient, both for my memory and honor of my name, if when I have expired my last breath, this may be inscribed upon my tomb:

> Here lies interred Elizabeth,
> A virgin pure until her death."

4 ❧ QUEEN ELIZABETH'S CONVERSATIONS WITH THE SCOTTISH AMBASSADOR, WILLIAM MAITLAND, LAIRD OF LETHINGTON, SEPTEMBER AND OCTOBER 1561[1]

[Headed] The discourse of the laird of Lethington's negotiation with the queen of England, etc.

After that he [Maitland] had declared the queen's majesty his sovereign's arrival,[2] good estate, and desire to continue and increase by good

---

1. *Source*: BL, MS Royal 18.B.VI, *Tractatus et Literae Regum Scotiae, 1448–1571*, which includes two partial copies, both incomplete. In making the present transcription, we have used the first copy (fols. 263r–265r) until the point at which the second, generally superior, copy begins (fols. 270r–271v); the second copy appears to lack only its first leaf. We have used the first copy to supply words that are no longer legible in the second copy because of rebinding and repair. Brackets enclose editorially supplied elements. This conversation is printed in *A Letter from Mary Queen of Scots to the Duke of Guise, January, 1562*, ed. with an appendix of original documents by John Hungerford Pollen, S. J., Scottish History Society, 43 (Edinburgh: University of Edinburgh Press, 1904), pp. 37–45. A third version from the Scottish Privy Council Register at the Scottish Record Office, Edinburgh (MS PC 5/2, fols. 12r–14v), is generally superior but unsuitable for use as copy text here because the upper fifth of each folio leaf is severely damaged. The most significant of its variant readings are recorded in the notes as SRO. A transcription of the SRO version is available in David Masson, ed., *Registers of the Privy Council of Scotland* (Edinburgh: Her Majesty's General Register House, 1898), addenda, vol. 14, pp. 172–78. Our modernized version preserves some Scots and French usages from the original.

William Maitland (1528?–1573), laird of Lethington, was a humanist graduate of Saint Andrews University employed as secretary and ambassador by Mary of Guise, queen regent of Scotland, and then by her daughter, Mary, Queen of Scots. Maitland may have written down his account of his conversations with Elizabeth as much as two months after the fact. A copy was enclosed in Mary, Queen of Scots' letter to the duke of Guise in January 1562. There is a much later Latin account in George Buchanan's *Rerum Scoticarum historia* (Edinburgh, 1583), which was translated and freely revised by Sir John Hayward for his *Annals of the First Four Years of the Reign of Queen Elizabeth*, written in the early decades of the seventeenth century but not published until John Bruce's edition for the Camden Society (London, 1840).

2. At the time of these negotiations, Mary, Queen of Scots, widowed by the death of Francis II of France in December 1560, had just arrived back in Edinburgh (August 1561).

means th'amity standing betwixt the realms, and had acquitted himself of the visitation and other good offices committed to his charge upon her majesty's [Mary's] behalf (tending to the conservation of friendship and good neighborhood and suchlike); had, upon the behalf of the nobility of Scotland, after some rehearsal of things past, desired her highness [Elizabeth] to use the queen their sovereign in all things concerning her or her estate so gently and favorably that she might thereby be provoked not only to be the more careful to entertain[3] but also to enter in a more strait[4] knot, if it were possible, whereof they from time to time would be bold to make overtures as occasion would serve, for the great desire they had to see intelligence betwixt the two realms to continue. He proposed the principal matter as the only moyen therein[5] whereby the principal difference might be honorably composed and taken away, with such good remonstrances and persuasions as he thought might best serve for furtherance of the purpose, and ample discourse of the commodities that thereby apparently should ensue to both the realms.

She answered at the first in this manner: "I looked for another message from the queen your sovereign, and marvels that she remembers not better her promise made to me before her departing from France, after many delays of that thing which she in honor is bound to do—to wit, the ratification of the treaty[6] wherein she promised to answer me directly at her homecoming. I have long enough been fed with fair words. It had been time I should ere now seen the effect of so many good words."

"Madame," said he, "her majesty was not fully fifteen days at home when I was dispatched toward your highness. In which time her majesty had not entered into the maniment[7] of any affairs, being fully occupied in receiving her nobility and people and admitting to her presence such as was convenient. And before all thing, it was expedient

3. SRO adds "th'amity."
4. **strait** tight.
5. **moyen** [means] **therein**; SRO adds "in their judgments."
6. **treaty** the Treaty of Edinburgh (1560), signed by France and England but as yet unratified by Scotland, which provided for the withdrawal of English troops from Scotland and called for Mary to recognize Elizabeth as the rightful ruler of England. By the terms of the treaty, Mary, Queen of Scots, was to give up her use of the arms of England, which she and her husband Francis II had adopted since the death of Mary Tudor as a way of asserting Mary, Queen of Scots' claim to the English throne.
7. **maniment** managing.

to take such stay in the difference standing for the matters of the religion, the weight whereof when your highness considers, and therewithal the short time before my direction, I doubt not but your majesty will perceive that her highness could not have the consultation and means[8] requisite in a matter of such importance. Besides that such noblemen as dwelt far from Edinburgh were not as yet arrived when I came thence, whose opinions nonetheless were necessary in so grave a purpose."

"What consultation," said she, "needs the queen to fulfill the thing whereunto she is obliged by her seal and handwriting?"

"Madame," said he, "I have no further answer to make in that behalf as a matter which her majesty looked not that your highness would lay to my charge, but that your own discretion would consider she has just cause of delay."

She,[9] after some words passed to and fro to this effect, she came to the principal matter thus: "I have noted as well that[10] you have said to me on the behalf of the queen your sovereign, as in the proposition made in name of the nobility, you put me in remembrance that she is of the blood of England, my cousin and next kinswoman, so that nature must bind me to love her duly,[11] all which I must confess to be true. And as my proceedings have made sufficient declaration to the world that I never meant evil toward her person nor her realm, so can they that knew most of my mind bear me accord[12] that in time of most offense, and when she by bearing my arms and acclaiming the title of my crown had given me just cause to be most angry with her; yet could I never find in my heart to hate her, imputing rather the fault to others than to herself. As for the title of my crown, for my time I think she will not attain[13] it, nor make impediment to my issue if any shall come of my body. For so long as I live there shall be no other queen in England but I, and failing thereof she cannot allege that ever I did anything which may hurt the right she may pretend. What it is I have not much considered, for the succession of the crown of England is a matter I will not mell[14] in; but as in the sacrament of the altar some thinks a thing, some other, whose judgment is best God knows. In the mean time *unus-*

8. **means** SRO reads "answer."   9. **She** SRO reads "So."
10. **that** SRO reads "in that."   11. **duly** SRO reads "dearly."
12. **accord** SRO reads "record."   13. **attain** SRO reads "acclaim."
14. **mell** meddle; SRO reads "I have nor will to mell of."

quisque in sensu suo abundent,[15] so leave I them to do with the succession of the crown of England. If her right be good she may be sure I will never hurt her, and I here protest to you in the presence of God I (for my part) know none better, nor that myself would prefer to her—or yet, to be plain with you, that case occurring that might debar her from it. You know them all, alas; what power or force has any of them, poor souls? It is true that some of them has made declaration to the world that they are more worthy of it than either she or I, by experience that they are not barren but able to have children," and there made a short digression upon my Lady Katherine's fact,[16] and therewithal dissembled not the inability of her and her sister to succeed to the crown by reason of their father's forfeiture.[17] In the end, "This is the first moyen," said she, "that ever was made to me in this purpose, wherethrough,[18] and that the matter is weighty, it is meet that I consider of it; and thereafter I will declare unto you more of my mind."

At the next audience she began thus: "I marvel what the nobility of Scotland should mean to send me such a message even at the first of their sovereign's homecoming, knowing that the principal offense betwixt us is not as yet taken away. They will, being injured and offended without any reparation, that I shall gratify her with so high a benefit. It seems to me to import some menacing. And if so be, I will they know I am puissant enough to defend my right and lack no friendship abroad, but has friends as their sovereign has."

"Madame," said he, "I have in the proposition sufficiently declared what has induced them to make your highness this overture, besides

15. "everyone abounds in his own feeling"; or, more colloquially, "is wise in his own conceit" (proverbial, but with echoes of Romans 11:25); SRO reads, more grammatically, "*abundet.*"

16. **Lady Katherine's fact** Lady Katherine Grey (1538?–1568), a younger sister of Lady Jane Grey; Lady Jane's right to the crown had been asserted briefly by some factions upon the death of Edward VI, and she was executed during the reign of Mary Tudor. At the time of the present conversations, Lady Katherine had contracted a secret marriage with Edward Seymour, earl of Hertford, and was as a result imprisoned in the Tower, since it was legally deemed treason for persons of royal blood to marry without the sovereign's consent. There she gave birth to a son on September 24, 1561; almost immediately thereafter she became pregnant with her second son.

17. **father's forfeiture** the forfeiture of lands, goods, and life that ensued when the Grey sisters' father, Henry Grey, duke of Suffolk, was convicted of high treason for conspiring to set up his eldest daughter as Queen Jane in place of Mary Tudor.

18. **wherethrough** for which reason.

the duty they owe to her majesty, whose honor, advancement, and surety they are bound to procure: the desire they have that her majesty may be in tender friendship with your highness, with whom they dare be bolder, for the experience they have had of your goodwill towards them, than they would be with any other prince; and partly their own surety whose lives for duty's sake must be hazarded in [prosecution][19] of this quarrel, if hereof[20] any impediment be made, by whatsoever party, to her right or break happen therefore betwixt the realms; and[21] whereupon they have just occasion to desire earnestly that in the meantime the matter may be made amicable[22] in good surety."

"Yea," said she, "if I meant to do anything to hurt her right, they have occasion to desire me to reform it, but this desire is without an example—to require me in my own life to set my winding-sheet before my eye![23] The like was never required of no prince."

That was answered: how many particular reports were to be considered in this case, and necessary it was for weal of both the realms that this matter were once cleared, and[24] of all doubt.

"In faith," said she, "I cannot take in evil part[25] the meaning of the noblemen, as proceeding of goodwill, but rather I heartily thank them for it, and do the more esteem them for good subjects, procuring the honor and advancement of their sovereign, and allow their wisdom in seeking their own surety and sparing of their blood I confess must be spent in that quarrel if any other party (the case occurring) would press to debar her. But in that, God knows, there is but little peril; for alas, who should or were able to do it? But present the case I were minded to do in effect the thing you required: think you that I will grant it upon motion made from the lords and not from herself?"

"For that, madame," said he, "though, be moyens[26] enough to be found, your mind being conformable, how the matter may be motionated[27] to the honor and reasonable contentment of both your majesties."

19. **prosecution** not in Royal MS and space left blank; word supplied from SRO.
20. **hereof** SRO adds "hereafter."   21. **and** omitted in SRO.
22. **made amicable** SRO reads "put amicably."
23. SRO version of this sentence reads: "Yea," said she, "if I meant to do anything that might hurt her right, they have reason to desire me to reform it; but this desire is without an example: to require me in my own time to set my own winding-sheet before my eye!"
24. **and** SRO adds "put out."
25. The second BL MS Royal of the Conversations begins here.
26. **though, be moyens** SRO reads "there be means."
27. **motionated** moved.

"No," said she, "there be many necessary considerations to draw me back from granting your request. First, *periculosum est tangere picem, ne forte inquiner ab ea.*[28] I have always abhorred to draw in question the title of the crown, so many disputes have been already touching it in the mouths of men. Some that this marriage was unlawfully,[29] some that someone was a bastard, some other, to and fro, as they favored or misliked. So many doubts of marriage in all hands that I stand awe[30] myself to enter in marriage, fearing the[31] controversy. Once I am[32] married already to the realm of England when I was crowned with this ring, which I bear continually in token thereof. Howsoever it be, so long as I live, I shall be queen of England; when I am dead, they shall succeed that has most right. If the queen your sovereign be that person, I shall never hurt her; if another have better right, it were not reasonable to require me to do a manifest injury. If there be any law against her (as I protest unto you I know none, for I am not curious to inquire of that purpose), but if any be, I am sworn when I was married to the realm not to alter the laws of it.

"Secondly, ye think that this device of yours should make friendship betwixt us, and I fear that rather it should produce the contrary effect. Think you that I could love my winding-sheet? Princes cannot like their own children, those that should succeed unto them.[33] Being witness, King Charles VII of France, how liked he his son Louis the XI, Louis the XI his son Charles the VIII, King Francis his son Henry?[34] How then

28. "it is dangerous to touch pitch lest perchance one be defiled by it"; a loose citation of Ecclesiasticus 13:1 in the Vulgate wording, "*qui tetigerit picem, inquinabitur ab ea.*"

29. **unlawfully** SRO reads "unlawful."

30. **awe** in awe.

31. **the** SRO reads "like."

32. **am** was.

33. In Hayward's later, freely revised version of the conversation, Elizabeth expresses precisely the opposite opinion: "It is natural, indeed, for parents to favor the succession of their children, to be careful for it, to provide for it, to assure it by all means unto them, because nature is of force to extinguish both the cause and the care of other respects."

34. Louis XI first rebelled against his father, King Charles VII, in 1439 and lived in open revolt from 1446 on, ruling his principality of Dauphiné like an independent sovereign. It was rumored that he used poison to hasten his father's death in 1461. When Louis himself became king, he kept his own son, the future Charles VIII, in virtual exile from his presence.

King Francis I sent his son Henry as a hostage to Spain in 1526, where Henry lived until the conclusion of the Peace of Cambrai in 1530. From the time of Henry's elevation to dauphin in 1536 until Francis I's death in 1547, father and son lived in open hostility.

shall I, think you, like my cousin, being once declared my heir apparent: as Charles liked Louis the XII[35] when he was duke of Orleans?

"But the third consideration is most weighty of all. I know the inconstancy of the people of England, how they ever mislike the present government and has their eyes fixed upon that person that is next to succeed; and naturally men be so disposed: *Plures adorant solem orientem quam occidentem.*[36] I have good experience of myself in my sister's[37] how desirous men were that I should be in place, and earnest to set me up. And if I would have consented, I know what enterprises would have been attempted to bring it to pass, and now perhaps affections of some are altered. As children dream in their sleep after apples, and in the morning when as they awake and find not the apples they weep, so ever[38] man that bare me goodwill when I was Lady Elizabeth, or to whom I show a good visage, imagineth with himself that immediately after my coming to the crown every man should be rewarded according to his own fantasy. And now finding the event answer not their expectation, it may be that some could be content of new change in hope to be then in better case. No prince's revenues be so great that they are able to satisfy the insatiable cupidity of men. And if we, either for not giving to men at their discretion or yet for any other cause, should miscontent any our subjects, it is to be feared that if they knew a certain successor of our crown they would have recourse thither. And what danger it were, she being a puissant princess and so near our neighbor, ye may judge; so that in assuring her of the succession we might put our present estate in doubt. I deal plainly with you, albeit my subjects, I think, love me as becomes them; yet is where so great perfection that all are content?"[39]

And there she of[40] entered upon my Lady Katherine's fact, with no obscure signification that she thought there was more hid matter in it than was yet uttered to the world, and that some of her nobility were partners in the making of that match. Albeit answer was made that, being a common accord, security might be provided that neither of their subjects should have recourse to the other prince but upon the

35. **Louis XII** SRO reads, more correctly, "Louis XI."
36. "More do adore the rising than the setting sun" (cf. Plutarch, *Life of Pompey*, 14f).
37. **sister's** SRO reads "sister's time."
38. **ever** SRO reads "every."
39. SRO makes this a statement: "yet is nowhere so great perfection that all are content."
40. **of** SRO adds "new."

knowledge and good leave of their own sovereign, nor yet the prince to have intelligence with the other's subjects; and no doubt the queen his sovereign would to that effect make what security could be devised whereby that peril might be fully avoided; yet would she not be satisfied, but still harped on that string, saying: "It is hard to bind princes by any security where hope is offered of a kingdom." And for her, if it were certainly known in the world who should succeed her, she would never think herself in sufficient surety.

This was the sum of her communication at that time, whereupon so far as he could collect by many words that passed, as also after in conference severally with Mr. Cecil her secretary and with my Lord Robert,[41] by their communication it appeared evidently that in her own judgment she liked better of the queen of Scotland's title next herself than of all others; and failing of her own issue, could best be content that she should succeed, and that none of all others who had any interest meet[42] for the crown or yet worthy of it; and that the third consideration was the only stay why she had no will to assure her title and succession by order of Parliament.

After, in new audience, when her highness was required what answer she would make to the noblemen anent[43] their motion, "I can," said she, "give no other answer but that I allow, as I said to you of[44] before, their duty and devotion to their sovereign in this behalf. Marry, the matter is such in itself and so great as I cannot for this present directly answer. When the queen has done to me that thing she is obliged anent the ratification, then were it time to require me to do her any pleasure; but before that time I cannot with honor gratify her in anything."

"Madame," said he, "as I said of before, I am instructed[45] to answer further to the demand of the ratification than I have said already, nor yet at any time entered in purpose with her majesty what she would do anent the ratification, so that if I either should say she would or she would[46] ratify it, I should transcend my bounds and speak further than I know. Marry, if your highness desire to know my own opinion, I will

---

41. **Lord Robert** Robert Dudley (1533–1588), earl of Leicester, Elizabeth's first and most enduring favorite, was the younger of the two surviving sons of John Dudley, duke of Northumberland, who had died a traitor's death for his part in Lady Jane Grey's (and his eldest son, Guildford's) pretensions to the English throne.

42. **meet** SRO reads "were meet."   43. **anent** concerning.

44. **said ... of** spoke of.

45. **instructed** SRO reads "not instructed."   46. **would** SRO reads "would not."

freely speak it: that I think that treaty so prejudicial to her majesty that she will never conform[47] it, and in such form conceived as her majesty is not in honor bound to do it, for such reasons as I upon the first sight and only inspection of the treaty collected; not doubting but men of greater judgment and that has more deeply weighed the effect of it (whose advice and consultations she has had in it), has been able to gather a great deal more, and more valuable.

"And sin[48] your majesty's pleasure is that I speak freely herein what I can, it is true that although your highness take yourself to be lawful, yet are ye not always so taken abroad in the world. First, all that follow in religion the Kirk of Rome, your highness knoweth, think the king your father's marriage with your mother unlawful, and consequently the issue of the marriage suchlike. The queen my sovereign's subjects must—and all other who are for any effect affectionate to her will—favorably think of her title. The impression of it belike is deeper rooted in her head than she will be easily persuaded to forgo it, and specially if perceive[49] that difficulty be made to assure her that title which not only in the judgment of foreign nations is without all controversy, but also your highness upon your conscience nor the wisest of your subjects can no wise disallow. It were for my opinion better to all respects that your two majesties come to such an accord as were apparent to continue, than to press her highness with that which could[50] no wise endure, although it were done. I am not privy to the proceedings, but I think assuredly, it being so prejudicial to her estate, when time served she would always seek occasion to break it, albeit it had been so far proceeded that in the confirmation she had followed the king her husband's commandment, by whose authority it was made. I enter not in dispute how that treaty was passed, nor by what authority, but this far I am assured: the commission was very slender to transfer from the queen my sovereign the title of a kingdom and debar her from it perpetually; and if she should once ratify the treaty, then were it[51] time to make this motion."

"Why," said she, "has the queen so long put me of[52] delays and has not rather answered me directly with a reason?"

"No," said he, "I know not that her majesty will yet answer thus. Nor yet speak I anything thereof as from her majesty, but rather to let

47. **conform** confirm.
48. **sin** since.
49. **perceive** SRO reads "she perceive."
50. **could** SRO reads "should."
51. SRO adds "not."
52. **of** SRO reads "off with."

your highness understand that the noblemen has reason to desire your majesty to come to some qualification for pursuing[53] of all controversies."

"Yes," said she, "if the treaty be prejudicial to her interest, she may acclaim;[54] afterwards I will content an[55] in her ratification she make this addition, that she shall not bear the arms of England, nor style herself queen of England and Ireland during my life and of the lawful issue of my body, reserving such title and interest as she thereafter may pretend or acclaim thereto." After some replies, she came to this point: that if the queen her sister would require that commissioners were appointed to review the treaty, she would be content thereof, and by them come to this qualification with the addition and reservation, and further oblige herself that either she nor the issue of her body during their reigns should do or procure to be done anything prejudicial or derogatory to the queen her sister's title.

This was all could be obtained at her hands, and therefore the matter was left *re integra*.[56] In the end she thought good, if it came to the naming of commissioners, that before they should meet, all matters they had to treat upon were first digested by letters betwixt their majesties' secretaries, whereunto their majesties should be privy; to the end that if any difficulty were in the conclusion, rather the meeting of the commissioners should be deferred than to meet and not agree fully, whereby the matter might come to the manifest break. Sir Peter Mewtas,[57] being sent direct from the queen his sovereign as ambassador to the queen majesty to congratulate with her for her safe arrival and prosperous estate, to visit her and do her other good offices as are accustomed to pass amongst princes, in the end did require the ratification of the treaty; whereunto her majesty's [answer][58] was that truth is, that same treaty was principally passed with the king her lord and husband in his time, the most part of the points and articles thereof chiefly concerned him, and but [none] of [them][59] which in any wise may appear to touch her or her realm; and was conceived in such form, as now, he being dead and thereby the marriage betwixt their majesties dissolved, it could not [be] formal to ratify the treaty of this same form. Nonetheless, for dec-

---

53. **pursuing** SRO reads "peasing" (appeasing).
54. **acclaim** make her claim.
55. **content an** be content if.   56. "a thing undecided."
57. **Sir Peter Mewtas** Elizabeth's ambassador to Mary, Queen of Scots.
58. **answer** Royal MS torn; word supplied from SRO, as is **be** later in the sentence.
59. **none ... them** Royal MS torn and words supplied conjecturally; SRO reads "few."

laration of the sincerity of her majesty's true meaning to continue in amity with her good sister, she would be content the commissioners were appointed on both sides to meet at such a day and place as convenient; and should be agreed upon to review the said treaty, treat upon the qualification thereof, and by a common consent come to such an accord as were apparent to endure forever and might stand with the honor of both the princes and commonwealths of the realms.

He desired her majesty to nominate such commissioners as for her part she would use for that effect. Her highness answered that if he had commission to require the nomination and to do the like of the part of his mistress, she was ready to nominate; but perceiving by his own declaration that neither was he specially instructed to receive the nomination nor yet to agree that commissioners should meet, the nomination was deferred unto the time her said good sister either by letter or other mean shall declare her contentation and pleasure therein.

This is the sum of the negotiation passed on both sides, so far as is it proceeded.

5 ࣻ QUEEN ELIZABETH'S ANSWER TO THE COMMONS' PETITION THAT SHE MARRY, JANUARY 28, 1563[1]

Williams, I have heard by you the common request of my Commons, which I may well term (methinketh) the whole realm because they give, as I have heard, in all these matters of Parliament their common consent to such as be here assembled. The weight and greatness of this matter might cause in me, being a woman wanting both wit and memory, some fear to speak and bashfulness besides, a thing appropriate to my sex. But yet the princely seat and kingly throne wherein God (though unworthy) hath constituted me, maketh these two causes to seem little in mine eyes, though grievous perhaps to your ears, and boldeneth me to say somewhat in this matter, which I mean only to touch but not presently to answer. For this so great a demand needeth both great and

1. *Source*: PRO, State Papers Domestic, Elizabeth 12/27/36, fols. 143r–144r; copy with marginal notation by William Cecil indicating Thomas **Williams** (line 1) as "the speaker of the Parliament" and the date as "1563." Part of the final paragraph is torn off in this manuscript version and supplied from a later copy, PRO, State Papers Domestic, Elizabeth 12/27/37, fols. 153r–154v. For the petition to which this speech responds, see Additional Document A, pp. 72–76.

grave advice. I read of a philosopher whose deeds upon this occasion I remember better than his name[2] who always when he was required to give answer in any hard question of school points would rehearse over his alphabet before he would proceed to any further answer therein, not for that he could not presently have answered, but have his wit the riper and better sharpened to answer the matter withal. If he, a common man, but in matters of school took such delay the better to show his eloquent tale, great cause may justly move me in this, so great a matter touching the benefits of this realm and the safety of you all, to defer mine answer till some other time, wherein I assure you the consideration of my own safety (although I thank you for the great care that you seem to have thereof) shall be little in comparison of that great regard that I mean to have of the safety and surety of you all. And although God of late seemed to touch me rather like one that He chastised than one that He punished, and though death possessed almost every joint of me,[3] so as I wished then that the feeble thread of life, which lasted (methought) all too long, might by Clotho's hand[4] have quietly been cut off, yet desired I not then life (as I have some witnesses here) so much for mine own safety, as for yours. For I know that in exchanging of this reign I should have enjoyed a better reign where residence is perpetual.

There needs no boding of my bane. I know now as well as I did before that I am mortal. I know also that I must seek to discharge myself of that great burden that God hath laid upon me; for of them to whom much is committed, much is required.[5] Think not that I, that in other matters have had convenient care of you all, will in this matter touching the safety of myself and you all be careless. For I know that this matter toucheth me much nearer than it doth you all, who if the worst happen can lose but your bodies. But if I take not that convenient care that it behoveth me to have therein, I hazard to lose both body and soul. And though I am determined in this so great and weighty a matter to defer

2. In her second speech on the question of executing Mary, Queen of Scots, November 24, 1586 (Speech 18, pp. 198, 204), Elizabeth uses this exemplum again and identifies the "philosopher" variously (depending on which copy one consults) as Augustus Caesar or Alcibiades. In Plutarch, the philosopher Athenodorus gives this advice to Augustus Caesar; see Plutarch, *Moralia,* ed. and trans. Frank Cole Babbitt (London: William Heinemann, 1931), 3:233.

3. A reference to Elizabeth's near-fatal smallpox of October 1562.

4. **Clotho** one of the three Fates; in most accounts it is Atropos who slits the thread of life.

5. Cf. Luke 12:48 (Great Bible): "For unto whomsoever much is given, of him shall be much required; and to whom men have committed much, of him will they ask the more."

mine answer till some other time because I will not in so deep a matter wade with so shallow a wit, yet have I thought good to use these few words, as well to show you that I am neither careless nor unmindful of your safety in this case, as I trust you likewise do not forget that by me you were delivered whilst you were hanging on the bough ready to fall into the mud—yea, to be drowned in the dung;[6] neither yet the promise which you have here made concerning your duties and due obedience, wherewith, I assure you, I mean to charge you as further to let you understand that I neither mislike any of your requests herein, nor the great care that you seem to have of the surety and safety of yourselves in this matter.

Lastly, because I will discharge some restless heads in whose brains the needless hammers beat with vain judgment that I should mislike this their petition, I say that of the matter and sum thereof I like and allow very well. As to the circumstances, if any be, I mean upon further advice further to answer. And so I assure you all that though after my death you may have many stepdames, yet shall you never have any a more mother[7] than I mean to be unto you all.

SPEECH 5, ADDITIONAL DOCUMENT A   THE COMMONS' PETITION TO THE QUEEN AT WHITEHALL, JANUARY 28, 1563[1]

1563. Your Commons in this your majesty's present Parliament assembled, most high and mighty princess and our most dread sovereign lady, as they do daily to their commodity and comfort feel and receive the inestimable benefits of your most gracious government of this your realm in peace and surety, so do also most thankfully acknowledge the same, beseeching almighty God long to bless and continue your most prosperous reign over them. And among all those benefits which they daily receive of your highness, they have willed me at this time in their names to recognize unto your highness that they account as not the

6. **dung** Catholicism and papal jurisdiction under Mary Tudor.

7. Another good MS (BL, MS Additional 33271, fol. 13r) reads "more natural mother," but there is no reason to assume, as most editors have done, that the present version is defective.

1. *Source*: PRO, State Papers Domestic, Elizabeth 12/27/35[B], fols. 139r–142r; copy with Cecil's marginalia and emphasis marks indicated here by underscoring. This is the petition, delivered to the queen both orally and in writing by Thomas Williams, speaker of the House, to which Speech 5 responds.

least, but rather among the greatest of them all, that your majesty hath at this time assembled your Parliament for supplying and redressing the greatest wants and defaults in this your commonweal and for th'establishing the surety of the same; which your majesty's most gracious meaning hath been at your commandment signified unto us by the right honorable the lord keeper.[2] Namely in this: that he, willed first to have consideration of the greatest matters that nearest touched the estate of our realm and the preservation thereof (seeming therein to express unto us the conformity of your majesty's mind in having principal respect to the matters of the greatest weight), for that respect assembled this our Parliament.

And forasmuch as your said subjects see nothing in this whole estate of so great importance to your majesty and the whole realm, nor so necessary at this time to be reduced into a certainty, as the sure continuance of the governance and th'imperial crown thereof in your majesty's person and the most honorable issue of your body, which almighty *Issue* God send us to our highest comfort, and for want thereof, in some certain limitation to guide the obedience of our posterity; and where almighty God to our great terror and dreadful warning lately touched your highness with some danger of your most noble person by sick- *the queen's* ness, from which so soon as your grace was by God's favor and mercy to *late sickness* us recovered, your highness sent out your writs of Parliament, by force whereof your subjects are at this present assembled; your said subjects are, both by the necessity and importance of the matter and by the convenience of the time (calling them immediately upon the recovery), enforced together. And confess your majesty, of your most gracious and motherly care for them and their posterity, have summoned this Parliament principally for stablishing some certain limitation of th'imperial crown of your realm, for preservation of your subjects from certain and utter destruction if the same should not be provided for in your life, which God long continue. They cannot (I say) but acknowledge how your majesty hath most graciously considered the great dangers, the unspeakable miseries of civil wars: the perilous intermeddlings of foreign princes with seditions, ambitions, and factious subjects at home; the waste of noble houses; the slaughter of people; subversion of towns;

---

2. **lord keeper** Sir Nicholas Bacon (1509–1579), Cecil's brother-in-law; appointed to his position by Elizabeth, he held the highest legal office in the realm before she appointed a lord chancellor.

intermission of all things pertaining to the maintenance of the realm; unsurety of all men's possessions, lives, and estates; daily interchange of attainders and treasons.

All these mischiefs, and infinite other, most like and evident if your majesty should be taken away from us without known heir (which God forbid), to fall upon your subjects to the utter subversion of the whole realm whereof you have charge under God, if good provision shall not be had in this behalf. Your majesty hath weighed the examples of for-

Alexander died without children.

eign nations, as what ensued the death of great <u>Alexander</u>, when for want of certain heirs by him begotten or appointed, the varieties of ti- tles, the diversity of dispositions in them that had titles, the ambitions of them that had color of doubtfulness of titles, forsook all obedience of titles, destroyed the dividers of his dominions, and wasted their poster- ity with mutual wars and slaughters. In what miserable case also was this your realm itself when the title of the crown was tossed in question

Lancaster York

between two royal houses of <u>Lancaster</u> and <u>York</u>, till your most noble progenitors King Henry VII and the Lady Elizabeth his wife restored it to settled unity and left the crown in certain course of succession.[3] These things, as your majesty hath upon your own danger most gra- ciously considered for our comfort and safety, so we your most humble subjects, knowing the preservation of ourselves and all our posterity to depend upon the safety of your majesty's most royal person, have most carefully and diligently considered how the want of heirs of your body, and of certain limitation of succession after you, is most perilous to your highness, whom God long preserve among us.

We have been admonished of the great malice of your foreign ene- mies, which even in your lifetime have sought to transfer the right and dignity of your crown to a stranger.[4] We have noted their daily most dangerous practices against your life and your reign. We have heard of some subjects of this land—most unnaturally against their country, most madly against their own safety, and most traitorously against your highness—not only hope of the woeful day of your death, but also lay in wait to advance some title under which they may renew their late un- speakable cruelty to the destruction of goods, possessions, and bodies,

3. **succession** The Tudor line succeeded to the English throne upon the defeat of Richard III at Bosworth Field in 1485, ending the Wars of the Roses between the rival houses of York and Lancaster. Henry Tudor (Henry VII) married Elizabeth of York.

4. **stranger** evidently an allusion to Mary, Queen of Scots' bearing of the arms of England in her coat of arms while she was queen of France (see Speech 4 n. 6, p. 61).

and thralldom of the souls and consciences of your faithful and Christian subjects.[5] We see nothing to withstand their desire but only your life. Their unkindness and cruelty we have tasted; we fear much to what attempt the hope of this opportunity, nothing withstanding them but your life, will move them. We find how necessary it is for our preservation that there may be more set and known between your majesty's life and their desire.

We see, on the other side, how there can be no such danger to your majesty by ambition of any apparent heir established by your benefit and advancement for want of issue of your majesty's royal body, as you are now subject unto by reason of the desire and hope we know not of how many that pretend titles and trust to succeed you. Whose secret desire we so much more fear because neither their number, force, nor likelihood of disposition is known unto us, and so we can the less beware of them for your preservation. We find also by good proof that the certain limitation of the reign of France hath in that realm procured so great quiet as neither the person of the prince in possession hath been endangered by secret or open practice, nor the commonwealth molested by civil dissension through any quarrel attempted for the title of that crown. And somewhat nearer home, we have also remembered the miserable estate of Scotland after the death of King Alexander[6] without any *Alexander* certain heir or limitation to whom the crown of Scotland should re- *of Scotland* main, by reason whereof the whole estate of that realm was left open to *without child* the ambition of many competitors, and most grievous desolation and spoil that grew upon such division, which afterward gave occasion to King James V[7] to limit the crown of Scotland to certain noble families of that realm, whereby they at this present enjoy that quiet surety which we do want. And all your majesty's progenitors, kings of the realm, hath in this behalf been so careful that from the Conquest to this present day the realm was never left as now it is, without a certain heir, living and known, to whom the crown after the death of the prince should apper-

5. Heresy trials—with consequent executions by burning at the stake and confiscations of property—were conducted by Queen Mary's Catholic bishops from 1555 to 1558.

6. **King Alexander** Alexander III of Scotland (1241–1286) who outlived several sons and whose death was followed by disputes over the succession and wars with England. He was succeeded by his infant granddaughter, Margaret, who died only four years later, ending that royal line.

7. **James V** of Scotland (1512–1542) had married the French noblewoman Marie de Guise in 1538 and died in 1542, shortly after his defeat at the battle of Solway Moss. He left as his sole heir his week-old daughter, the future Mary, Queen of Scots.

tain, so as your majesty of your singular care for us and our posterity
hath at this time assembled us for establishment of this great and only
stay of our safeties.

    We again (O most gracious sovereign lady) acknowledge ourselves
and all that we have to depend upon your preservation, being according
to our bounden duty most careful for the same, are in most humble

the speaker   manner come to your majesty's presence. And I̲ the mouth[8] appointed
for them together, which and in the name of all your most loving, natural, and obedient subjects do present unto you our most lowly suit and
petition. That forasmuch as your majesty's person should come to most
undoubted and best heirs of your crown, such as in time to come we
would most comfortably see and our posterity shall most joyfully obey,

that the   it may please your most excellent majesty for our sakes, for our preser-
queen will   vation and comforts, and at our most humble suit, to take yourself
accept any to be   some <u>honorable husband whom</u> it shall please you to join to you in
her husband   marriage. Whomsoever it be that your majesty shall choose, we protest
and promise with all humility and reverence to honor, love, and serve as
to our most bounden duty shall appertain. And where by the statute
which your most noble father assented unto, of his most princely and
fatherly zeal to his most loving subjects, for limitation of succession of
the imperial crown of this realm, your majesty is last expressly named
within the body of the same act.[9] And for that your subjects cannot
judge nor know anything of the form or validity of any further limitations set in certainty for want of heirs of your body, whereby some
great, dangerous doubt remaineth in their hearts to their great grief,
peril, and unquietness, it may please your majesty by publication of
certainty already provided, if any such be, or else by limitation of certainty, if none be, to provide most gracious remedy in this great necessity which by your most honorable and motherly carefulness for them
hath occasioned this assembly, that in this convenient time of Parliament upon your late danger most graciously called by you for that
cause, your grace may now extend to us the greatest benefit, which otherwise or at other times perhaps shall never be able to be done again. So
not only we, but also all ours hereafter and forever, shall owe no less but

---

    8. **mouth** standard term of reference for the speaker of the House of Commons.
    9. Henry VIII's Third Act of Succession, restoring Mary and Elizabeth to the succession
after Edward, was passed by Parliament in 1544. For pertinent excerpts, see Tanner
(397–400).

as to your majesty's propagation of succession that we do already owe to your most noble grandfather King Henry VII his uniting of division.

And your subjects in their behalfs for your majesty's further assurance, whereupon their own preservation wholly dependeth, shall employ their whole endeavors, wits, and powers, to revive, devise, and establish the most strong and beneficial acts and laws for the preservation and surety of your majesty and your issue in the imperial crown of this realm; and the most penal, sharp, and terrible statutes to all that shall but once practice, attempt, or convey against your safety. That by any possible means they may invent and stablish with such limitations of conditions and restraints to all in remainders[10] such grievous pains and narrow animadversions to all that shall enterprise or imagine anything in prejudice of your highness and your issue, as your majesty shall not have any just cause of suspicion, but most assured confidence in all your faithful subjects' continually watching and warding[11] for your preservation. Which God long continue, that you see your children's children to His honor and our comfort, and incline your gracious heart to our most humble petition.

---

10. **remainders** persons having an interest or estate in property that follows and depends on the termination of a prior possessory estate—in this case, the termination of Elizabeth's possession of the crown.

11. **warding** guarding.

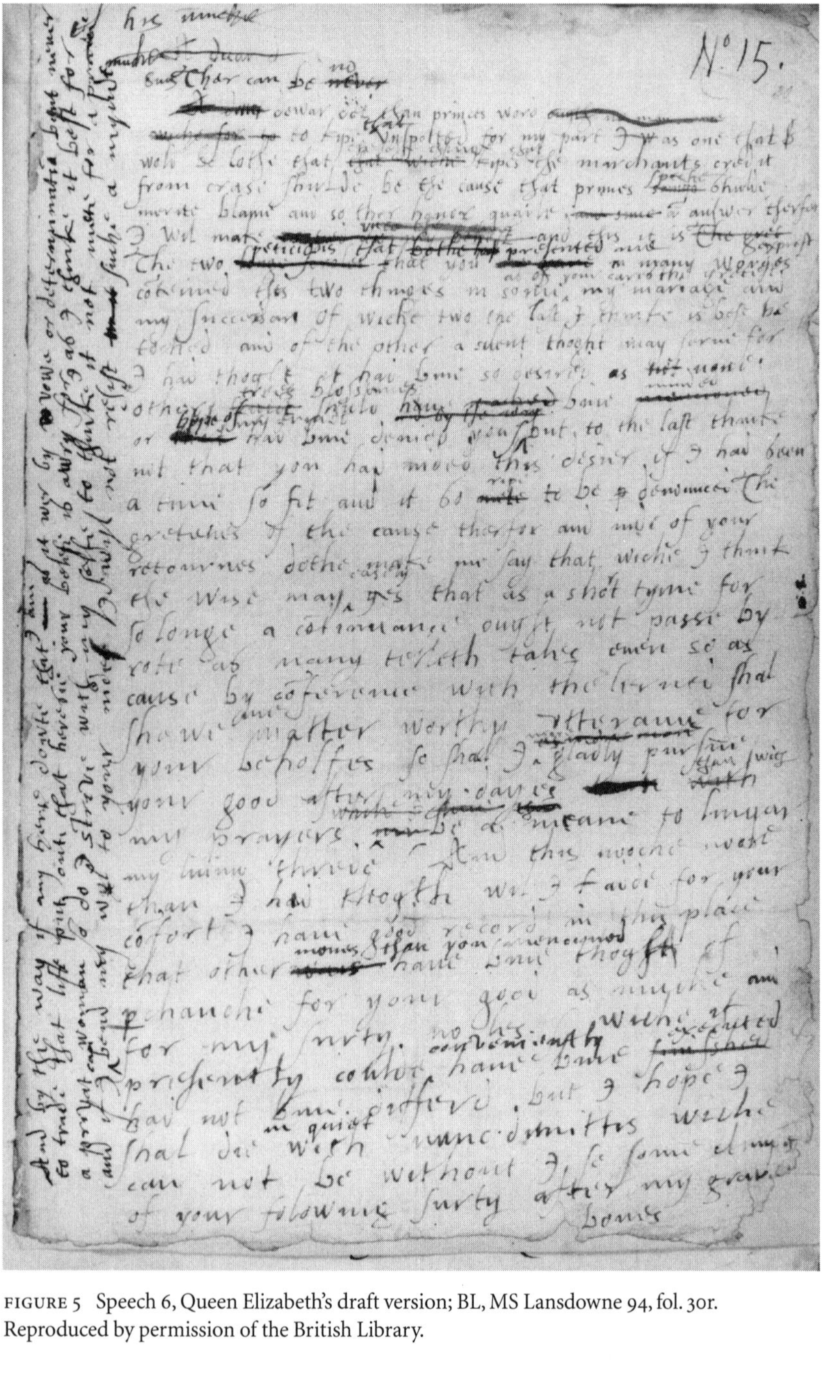

FIGURE 5 Speech 6, Queen Elizabeth's draft version; BL, MS Lansdowne 94, fol. 30r. Reproduced by permission of the British Library.

6 ᶤᴥ QUEEN ELIZABETH'S ANSWER TO THE LORDS' PETITION THAT SHE MARRY, APRIL 10, 1563, DELIVERED BY LORD KEEPER NICHOLAS BACON[1]

[Endorsed] The queen's majesty's answer to the petitions exhibited

Since there can be no duer debt than princes' word, to keep that unspotted for my part I would be loath that the self[2] thing which keepeth the merchants' credit from craft[3] should be the cause that princes' speech should merit blame, and so their honor quail. Therefore, I will an answer give, and this it is. The two petitions that you presented me,[4] expressed in many words, contained[5] in sum as of your cares the greatest: my marriage and my successor, of which two I think best the last be touched, and of the other a silent thought may serve. For I had thought it had been so desired as none other tree's blossoms should have been minded or ever hoped if my fruit[6] had been denied you. And yet, by the way of one due doubt[7]—that I am, as it were, by vow or determination bent never to trade that kind of life[8]—pull out that heresy, for your belief is there awry. For though I can think it best for a private woman, yet do I strive with myself to think it not meet for a prince. And if I can bend my liking to your need[9] I will not resist such a mind.

1. *Source*: BL, MS Additional 32379, "Discourses of Sir N. Bacon," fol. 21. This speech was not delivered by the queen herself, although she was present. It exists in two important early versions: BL, MS Lansdowne 94, art. 15B, fol. 30, a much-corrected text in the queen's own hand, reproduced here as Figure 5 and transcribed in *ACFLO*, part 1; and Nicholas Bacon's fair copy of the queen's text, which is our copytext for the present version and which probably represents the speech much as Bacon delivered it. Significant variants between the two texts are indicated in the notes below. The speech was followed by the customary reading of the acts and the prorogation of Parliament. For other MS versions, see Hartley (1:114–15). D'Ewes (75–76, 107–108) places a condensed version of the speech under 1563 and a much fuller version erroneously under 1566. For the Lords' petition to which this speech responds, see Additional Document A, which follows.

2. **self** Elizabeth's MS reads "least."

3. **craft** Elizabeth's MS reads "craze"—damage, breaking; D'Ewes also reads "craze" (107).

4. **two petitions** that of the Commons, to which she had responded in her speech of January 28, and the petition of the Lords, to which the present speech responds.

5. **contained** Elizabeth's MS reads "contained these two things."

6. **or . . . fruit** Elizabeth's MS reads "ere hope of my fruit."

7. **And yet, by the way of one due doubt** Elizabeth's MS reads "And by the way if any here doubt."

8. **that kind of life** Elizabeth's MS reads "that life."

9. **my liking to your need** Elizabeth's MS reads "my will to your need."

But to the last,[10] think not that you had needed this desire if I had seen a time so fit and it so ripe to be denounced. The greatness of the cause thereof and need of your returns doth make me say that which I think the wise may easily guess: that as short time for so long continuance ought not pass by rote (as many tell their tales) even so as cause by conference with the learned shall show me matter worthy utterance for your behoofs, so shall I more gladly pursue your good after my days than with my prayers whilst I live to linger my living thread.[11] And thus much more than I had thought will I add for your comfort. I have good record in this place that other means than you mentioned have been thought of—perchance for your good as much, and for my surety no less—which if presently and conveniently could have been executed had not now been deferred or overslipped.[12] But I hope I shall die in quiet with *Nunc dimittis*,[13] which cannot be without I see some glimpse[14] of your following surely after my graved bones.[15]

10. **last** the issue of the succession.

11. **than with my prayers whilst I live to linger my living thread** Elizabeth's MS reads "than with my prayers be a mean to linger my living thread."

12. **deferred or overslipped** Elizabeth's MS reads "deferred."

13. *Nunc dimittis* "Now lettest Thou Thy servant depart in peace," the opening words of the aged Simeon's prayer upon seeing the Christ child (Luke 2:29). This prayer, in English, follows the New Testament lesson in the Order for Evening Prayer (Booty, 63).

14. **glimpse** Elizabeth's MS reads "chances."

15. **surely after my graved bones** Elizabeth's MS reads "surety," as do some later MSS (e.g., BL, MS Harley 5176, fol. 9r, which is generally close to Bacon's version). D'Ewes's condensed printed version of the speech offers the following final paragraph: "For the second, the greatness thereof maketh me to say and pray that I may longer live in this vale of misery for your comfort, wherein I have witness of my study and travail for your surety. And I cannot with *Nunc dimittis* end my life without I see some foundation of your surety after my gravestone" (76). D'Ewes's fuller version (107–108) follows MS Harley 5176.

SPEECH 6, ADDITIONAL DOCUMENT A THE LORDS' PETITION TO
THE QUEEN, CIRCA FEBRUARY 1, 1563[1]

[Headed] 1563. An humble suit and petition made by all the Lords spiritual and temporal unto the queen's most excellent majesty, our most gracious sovereign lady.

Most humbly beseecheth your excellent majesty your faithful, loving, and obedient subjects—all your Lords both spiritual and temporal assembled in Parliament in your Upper House—to be so much their good lady and sovereign as, according to your accustomed benignity, to grant a gracious and favorable hearing to their petitions and suits, which with all humbleness and obeisance they are come hither to present to your majesty by my mouth[2] in matters nearly and dearly touching your most royal person, th'imperial crown of this your realm, and th'universal weal of the same. Which suits, for that they do tend to the surety and preservation of these two things—your person, crown, and realm, the dearest jewels that my lords have in the earth—therefore they think themselves for divers respects greatly bound to make these petitions. And first by their duty towards God, then by their allegiance to your highness, and lastly by their faith they ought to bear to their natural country.

   And like as, most gracious sovereign lady, by those bonds they should have been bold to have made the like petitions upon like occasion to any prince that it should have pleased God to have appointed to reign over them, so they think themselves double bounden to make the same to your majesty, considering that besides the bonds before remembered, they stand also bound so to do by the great and manifold benefits that they have and daily do receive at your highness' hands, which (shortly to speak) be as great as the fruits of peace and common quiet, mercy, and justice can give, and this with great care to yourself. And thus my lords, bound as your majesty hath heard, are now to open to your majesty their humble petitions and suits consisting in two points, which not sunderly nor th'one without the other, but both jointly they humbly desire your highness to assent unto. The former is that it would please your majesty to dispose yourself to marry where it

1. A petition to marry where, with whom, and

1. *Source*: PRO, State Papers Domestic, Elizabeth 12/27/35[A], fols. 135r–138v; a clerk's copy with Cecil's emphasis marks and marginalia indicated here by underscoring. This is the petition to which Speech 6 responds.
   2. **mouth** William Paulet, marquis of Winchester, speaker of the House of Lords.

as soon as

shall please

2. For the

succession

shall please you, with whom it shall please you, and as soon as it shall please you. The second, that some certain limitation might be made how th'imperial crown of this realm should remain if God call your highness without any heir of your body (which our Lord defend), as those your lords and nobles and other your subjects then living might sufficiently understand to whom they should owe their allegiances and duties due to be done by subjects, and that they might by your majesty's license and by your favor commune, treat, and confer together this Parliament time for the well doing of this.

1. Marriage

2. Succession

The former of these two, which is your marriage, they do in their hearts most earnestly wish and pray for as a thing that must needs breed and bring great and singular comfort to yourself, and unspeakable joy and gladness to all true English hearts. But the second carrieth with it such necessity that without it they cannot see how the safety of your royal person, the preservation of your imperial crown and realm, shall or can be sufficiently provided for. Most gracious sovereign lady, the lamentable and pitiful state and condition wherein all your nobles and councillors of late were when it pleased God to lay His heavy hand over you, and the amazedness by the bruits[3] that grew of your sickness that brought most men of understanding unto, is one cause of this petition.

the

queen's

majesty's

sickness

The second, the aptness and opportunity of the time by reason of this Parliament, whereby both such advice, consideration, and consent as is requisite in so great and weighty a cause may be better had and used now than at any other time, when no Parliament is.

3. The third, for that th'assenting to and performing of those petitions cannot (as they think) but breed terror to your enemies, and therefore must of necessity bring private surety to your person, and specially by addition of such laws as may be joined to this limitation for the certain and sure observing of it and preserving of your majesty against all practices and chances.

4. The fourth cause, for that the like (as is supposed) hath been done by divers of your noble progenitors, both of old times and late days, and also by other princes your neighbors of the greatest states of Europe. And for that experience hath taught that goodness hath come of it.

5. The fifth, for that it appeareth by histories how in times past, persons inheritable to crowns being votaries and religious, to avoid such

---

3. **bruits** noises, news.

dangers as might have happened for want of succession to kingdoms, *Constantia. 50*
have left their vows and monasteries and taken themselves to marriage. *annorum*[4]
<u>Constantia</u>, a nun and heir to the kingdom Sicil,[5] married after fifty *H. 6——Const.*
years of age to <u>Henry the Sixth</u> emperor of that name,[6] and had issue
Frederick the Second.[7] And likewise, <u>Peter of Aragon</u>,[8] being a monk,
married the better to establish and pacify that kingdom. Again, <u>Anto-
ninus</u> Pius is as much commended, for that not two days before his
death, he said to his Council, *Laeto animo morior, quia filium vobis re-
linquo.*[9] As <u>Pyrrhus</u> is of all godly men detested for saying he would
leave his realm to him that had the sharpest sword.[10] What but want of a
successor known made so short an end of so great an empire as Alexander the Great did leave at his death?

6. <u>The sixth cause</u> is for that my lords' doing[11] the performing of this
will breed such an universal and inward contentation, satisfaction, joy,
and gladness in the hearts of all your true and loving subjects, that is
likely and probably[12] you shall find them in all commandments ready
and glad to adventure their goods, lands, and lives in your highness' service according to their bounden duties, which of necessity must breed
great surety also to your majesty.

7. <u>The seventh</u> because the not doing of this (if God should call your
highness without heir of your body, which God grant be never seen if it
be His will, and yet your majesty right well knoweth that princes and

---

4. *annorum* years of age.   5. **kingdom Sicil** Sicily.

6. **name** Henry Hohenstaufen (1165–1197), king of Germany and Sicily, who advanced
his power by marrying Constance I, posthumous daughter of the Sicilian king Roger II.

7. **Frederick the Second** (1194–1250) Hohenstaufen king of Germany and Sicily and
Holy Roman Emperor from 1220.

8. **Peter of Aragon** (1174–1213) king of Aragon, who was crowned by Pope Innocent II in
Rome in April 1196 and declared his kingdom a feudatory of the Holy See.

9. "I die with a glad heart because I leave you a son." Reference is to Pius Antoninus,
Hadrian's adopted heir and Roman emperor (138–161), who died with equanimity after
committing the empire and care of his daughter Faustina to his son-in-law and adopted
son, Marcus Aurelius. See Julius Capitolinus, *Life of Antoninus,* chap. 12, sec. 6, and *Life of
Marcus Aurelius Antoninus,* chap. 7, sec. 4, in *Scriptores Historiae Augustae,* trans. David
Magie (London: William Heinemann, 1930), 1:131, 148.

10. **Pyrrhus** Reputed the most fearless military leader of antiquity after Alexander the
Great, Pyrrhus of Epirus (319–272 B.C.E.), king of the Molossians, gave this answer to his
young sons when they asked to whom he would leave his kingdom (Plutarch *Moralia,* bk.
3, sec. 185C).

11. **doing** BL, MS Additional 32379 reads "judge."

12. **probably** probable.

their offspring—be they never so great, never so strong, never so like to live—be yet mortal and subject every day, yea every hour, to God's call), my lords think this happening, no limitation made, cannot by their judgment but be the occasion of our evident and great danger and peril to all states and sorts of men of this realm by the factions, seditions, and intestine war that will grow through want of understanding to whom they should yield their allegiances and duties, whereby much innocent blood is like to be shed, and many of those to lose their lives that would now gladly bestow them for your sake in your majesty's service.

[8.] The eighth, which is the greatest danger that can hap to any kingdom, for every prince is *anima legis,*[13] and so reputed in law. And therefore upon the death of the prince, the law dieth, all the officers of justice whereby laws are to be executed do cease, all writs and commandments to all parties for the execution of justice do hang in suspense, all commissions for keeping of common peace and for the punishment of offenders do determine and lose their force, whereby it followeth consequently that strength and will must rule. And neither law nor reason, during such vacation and inter-reign within such an uncertainty of succession, is like to last so long as it is to be feared, if God's mercy be not the greater, that the realm may thereby become a prey to strangers (which our Lord defend), or at the least lose the great honor and estimation that long time have appertained unto it.

And like as, most gracious sovereign, my lords have been moved for the worldly respects aforesaid to make these their humble petitions to your majesty, so by the examples, counsels, and commandments that they have heard out of the sacred Scriptures, and for conscience' sake, they feel themselves constrained and forced to do the like. God (your highness knoweth) by the course of the Scriptures hath declared succession and having of children to be one of His principal benedictions in this life; and of the contrary He hath pronounced otherwise. And therefore Abraham prayed to God for issue, fearing that Eleazar his steward should have been his heir, and had promise that kings should proceed of his body.[14] Anna, the mother of Samuel, prayed to God with tears for issue;[15] and Elizabeth (whose name your majesty beareth),

13. "the soul of the law" (a concept from Roman law used during Elizabeth's reign and after to justify royal prerogative powers).

14. Cf. Genesis 17:6.

15. Cf. 1 Samuel 1:10–11.

mother to John Baptist, was joyful when God had blessed her with fruit, accounting herself delivered thereby of a reproach.[16]

And this is a blessing of private houses; so it is much more in kingdoms, as it plainly appeareth by two kingdoms of Israel and Judah.[17] Unto the kingdom of Judah, containing but two tribes or thereabouts, God gave lineal succession by descent of kings, and therefore it continued a long time. The kingdom of Israel, containing ten tribes or thereabout, often destitute of lawful heirs, the one half of the people following one and the other half another, by wars and seditions weakened came soon to ruin, as plainly appeareth by the third and fourth Book of Kings. Again in the time of the Judges, because there was no ordinary succession, the people were oftentimes overrun and carried to captivity.[18] Besides it is plain by the Scriptures that godly governors and princes, as fathers of their countries, have always been careful to avoid the great evil that might ensue through want of a certain limitation of succession. And therefore Moses did assign Joshua to be his successor, and David his son Solomon, whereby a great sedition was appeased, begun by Adonias.[19] Of these there be many examples. Further, seeing it may easily be gathered by experience of all ages past that civil wars, effusion of Christian blood, and consequently ruin of kingdoms do follow where realms be left without a certainty of succession, and that your majesty is also informed of the same, and sued unto here for redress; if therefore no sufficient remedy should be by your highness provided, that then it should be a dangerous burden before God to your majesty, and[20] you were to yield a strait account to God for the same, considering you are placed as the prophet Ezekiel sayeth, *in altissima specula*[21] of this commonwealth, and seeth the sword coming and provideth no remedy for it.

Lastly the Spirit of God promiseth by the mouth of Saint Paul to Timothy that whosoever maketh not due provision for his family is in danger to Godward.[22] And also by the mouth of Saint John, that whosoever seeth but our brother in necessity and doth shut up the bowels of

16. Cf. Luke 1:24–25.   17. 1 Kings 12:17–20.

18. Cf. Judges 3:8, 14; 4:2; 6:1; 10:7.

19. **Adonais** Adonijah; cf. 1 Kings 1 and Deuteronomy 31:23.

20. **and** if.

21. "in the highest watchtower" (cf. Ezekiel 33: the watchman who sees the sword coming and does not warn the people is held accountable to God).

22. **to Godward** toward God (an allusion to 1 Timothy 5:7).

pity and compassion from him, hath not the love of God remaining in him.[23] Whereby it is plain and manifest how fearful a thing it were of[24] this realm containing so many families were not in this perilous case upon their suit provided for, or if the bowels of mercy should be shut up from so many thousands, which every way were like to fall into extreme miseries if God should call your highness without certainty of succession, which we pray to God may never happen. Most excellent princess, the places of the Scriptures containing the said threatenings be set forth with much more sharp words than be here expressed.

Thus, most gracious sovereign, your lords and nobles both spiritual and temporal have, as briefly as they can, first showed to your majesty how diversly they take themselves bound to make these their humble petitions unto you; and then what their petitions be; and after that what reason for worldly respects, and what by the Scriptures and for conscience' sake have moved them thus to do. Which here upon their knees according to their bounden duties they most humbly and earnestly pray your majesty to have good consideration of—in time, most gracious sovereign, in time, in time—and to give them such favorable and comfortable answer to the same, as some good effect and conclusion may grow thereof before the end of the session of this Parliament, the uttermost day of the greatest hope. Whereby this commonweal, which your highness found to be *laetericia,* as Augustus did his, and by your great providence is now become *marmorea,*[25] shall not for want of reforming thus, if God shall call your highness without heir of your body, be in more dangerous state and condition than ever it was that any man can remember. True it is that suit is made by my lords, not without great hope of good success by reason of experience that they have had of your bountiful goodness showed to them and the rest of your loving subjects diverse and sundry ways since the beginning of your reign, which they pray to God long to continue to His honor with all felicity. God bless and save your majesty.

---

23. Echoes 1 John 3:17.

24. **of** if.

25. Suetonius' *Lives of the Caesars,* chap. 28, records of Augustus Caesar that he found Rome made of sun-dried brick (*laetericia*) but left it marble (*marmorea*).

7 ༂྅ QUEEN ELIZABETH'S LATIN ORATION AT CAMBRIDGE UNIVERSITY, AUGUST 7, 1564[1]

"Although feminine modesty, most faithful subjects and most celebrated university, prohibits the delivery of a rude and uncultivated speech in such a gathering of most learned men, yet the intercession of my nobles and my own goodwill toward the university incite me to produce one. Two stimuli prompt me to this, of which the first is the propagation of good letters, which I much desire and most ardently hope for; second, your expectation of all these things. Regarding what pertains to propa-

---

1. *Source*: BL, MS Sloane 401, fol. 38 (Rudolph Wilkinson's commonplace book). (For original Latin, see *ACFLO*, part 2.) No autograph of this speech is known to exist and there may never have been one. Elizabeth could well have spoken extemporaneously. Every known manuscript version of this speech is different, and frequently the Latin is made more formal and grammatically complex by the copyist. (For examples, see notes to Latin text, *ACFLO*, part 2.)The version used for translation here is early and preserves the oral, anglicized quality of the Latin speech as Elizabeth may well have delivered it.

In *Desiderata Curiosa: or, A Collection of Divers Scarce and Curious Pieces Relating Chiefly to Matters of English History*, vol. 2 (London, 1735), bk. VII, arts. 10–20, Francis Peck gives an account of the queen's Cambridge reception and the context in which she spoke:

"Her highness was advertised that the university by their orator would speak unto her majesty, whereupon she inquired for the orator and willed him to begin. Then Mr. William Master, of the King's College, orator, making his three curtsies, kneeled down upon the first grece or step of the west door (which was, on the walls outward, covered with verses), and made his oration, of length almost half an hour, containing in effect these things.

"First he praised and commended many and singular virtues set and planted in her majesty, which her highness, not acknowledging of, shaked her head, bit her lips and her fingers, and sometimes broke forth into passion and these words, '*Non est veritas, et uti-nam*—' ['It is not true; would that it were—'].

"[When he praised virginity] she said to the orator, 'God's blessing of thine heart: there continue.' After he showed what joy the university received of her presence . . . last of all he . . . humbly required of her grace that it would please her to hear them all in such things as the university should intend or purpose for her majesty's entertainment. When he had done, she much commended him, and much marveled that his memory did so well serve him, repeating such diverse and sundry matters, saying that she would answer him again in Latin but for fear she should speak false Latin, and then they would laugh at her. But in fine, in token of her contentation, she called him unto her presence and offered him her hand to kiss, requiring his name.

"[At the conclusion of her entertainment at Saint Mary's Church] the lords, and especially the duke of Norfolk and the Lord Robert [high steward of Cambridge University since 1562 and created earl of Leicester in September 1564], kneeling down, humbly desired her majesty to speak somewhat to the university, and in Latin. Her highness at the first refused, saying that if she might speak her mind in English, she would not stick at the matter. But understanding by Mr. Secretary [William Cecil, also chancellor of Cambridge Univer-

gation, the words of superiors, as Demosthenes said, are as the books of their inferiors, and the example of a prince has the force of law.[2] If this was true in those city-states, how much more so in a kingdom? No path is more direct, either to gain good fortune or to procure my grace, than diligently, in your studies which you have begun, to stick to your work; and that you do this, I pray and beseech you all.

"I come now to the second stimulus. This forenoon I have seen your sumptuous edifices erected by most noble kings who have perished before me, and in seeing them I breathed forth a sigh, not otherwise than did Alexander, who when he had read of the many monuments erected by princes, turned to his intimate, or rather to his counselor, and said, 'I have done no such thing.'[3] So do I no less. But if my grief is not removed, it can certainly be lessened by that saying of the people: Rome was not built in a day. For my age is not yet senile, nor have I reigned for such a long time; so may I, before I pay my debt to nature (if Atropos[4] does not sever the thread of life more quickly than I hope), do some famous and noteworthy work. Nor, for as long as the impulse guides my mind, will anything deflect[5] me from the purpose. And if it should

---

sity] that nothing might be said openly to the university in English, she required him the rather to speak because he was chancellor, and the chancellor is the queen's mouth. Whereunto he answered that he was chancellor of the university and not hers. Then the bishop of Ely [Richard Cox, a former chancellor of Oxford University], kneeling, said that three words of her mouth were enough. So, being moved on every side, she spake at length as followeth."

2. For the sense if not the wording of this sentiment, see the exhortation to the Athenians ascribed to Demosthenes' *On Military Organization,* secs. 21–22: "You need not go abroad for examples to teach you what you should do. Take Themistocles, who was your general in the sea-fight at Salamis, and Miltiades, who commanded at Marathon. . . . No one would dream of speaking of Themistocles' fight at Salamis, but of the Athenians' fight, nor of Miltiades' battle at Marathon, but of the Athenians' battle" (*Demosthenes,* trans. J. H. Vince [London: William Heinemann, 1930], I:366, 367).

3. An apparent reference to Julius Caesar, who burst into tears upon reading the history of Alexander the Great, explaining, "Do you not think it is matter for sorrow that while Alexander, at my age, was already king of so many peoples, I have as yet achieved no brilliant success?" (*Plutarch's Lives,* trans. Bernadotte Perrin [London: William Heinemann, 1949], 7:468–69). According to Valerius Maximus, Alexander the Great wept on hearing of the philosopher Democritus' theory of the plurality of worlds, for, said Alexander, he had not yet conquered his own (*Liber Factarum et Dictorum Memorabilium,* bk. 8, chap. 14, sec. 2).

4. **Atropos** the third Fate, who cuts the thread of life.

5. **deflect** We translate the MS reading, *"defaelcam,"* as *"deflectam,"* the reading in Bodleian, MS Rawlinson Poetical 85, fol. 38r.

come to pass (which clearly I do not know how soon it might) that I
have to die before I am able to complete that which I promise, yet will I
leave an exceptional work after my death, by which not only may my
memory be renowned in the future, but others may be inspired by my
example, and I may make you all more eager for your studies. But now
you see how much separates choice learning from instruction retained
by the mind: of the former, there are here more than sufficient witnesses; of the latter, I myself, too inconsiderately indeed, have today
made you witnesses because I have detained your most learned ears so
long with my barbarousness."

And thereafter [she said] these [words in English]: "I would to
God you had all drunk this night of the river of Lethe, that you might
forget all."

8 ⁀ QUEEN ELIZABETH'S LATIN ORATION AT OXFORD
UNIVERSITY, SEPTEMBER 5, 1566[1]

Those who do bad things hate the light, and therefore, because I am
aware that I myself am about to manage badly my opportunity in your
presence, I think that a time of shadows will be fittest for me. (I used

1. *Source*: Bodleian Library, University of Oxford, MS Additional A.63, fols. 16v–17r; copy in
the hand of John Bereblock, fellow of Exeter College, Oxford, and made dean in 1566. (For
original Latin, see *ACFLO*, part 2.) The same caveats apply to this speech as to the queen's
Latin speech at Cambridge: it is quite likely that she spoke impromptu or from notes. The
version presented here appears to be among the earliest but may show some of the same "im-
provement" of the queen's Latin as later versions of her Cambridge speech. For another later
version that circulated more widely than this one, see Bodleian, MS Rawlinson D.273, fol.
111r; its Latin endorsement records: "From Lawrence Humphreys' *Life and Death of Jewel*."

Anthony à Wood provides an account of the occasion of this speech in *Historia et Anti-
quitates Universitatis Oxoniensis* (Oxford, 1674), bk. 1, pp. 286ff. We cite from the translation
in [Samuel Jebb], *The Life of Robert Earl of Leicester, the Favorite of Queen Elizabeth* (London: for Woodman and Lyon, 1727), pp. 40–44: "Towards evening, as her majesty approached, she was met at Wolvercote, where the jurisdiction of the university ends, by the
chancellor the earl of Leicester, by four doctors—Dr. [John] Kennal [canon of Christ
Church], the vice chancellor, Dr. Lawrence Humphreys, Dr. Thomas Godwin, and Dr.
Thomas White, in their scarlet robes and hoods—and by eight Masters of Arts who were
heads of colleges or halls. . . . Mr. Roger Marbeck, the late orator of the university and now
canon of Christ Church, made an elegant speech to her majesty upon the occasion. She
then held out her hand to the orator and the doctors, and as Dr. Humphreys drew near to
kiss it, 'Mr. Doctor,' says the queen smiling, 'that loose gown becomes you mighty well; I

this opening because it was night, when all most secret things were hidden from sight and enveloped in dense shadows.) For a long time, truly, a great doubt has held me: Should I be silent or should I speak? If indeed I should speak, I would make evident to you how uncultivated I am in letters; however, if I remain silent my incapacity may appear to be contempt. From the time I came to this university, the things that I have seen or heard were, in my judgment, all very distinguished. Because the time that remains is truly short, I have ordered what I will say to you into two kinds, of which the one is praise and the other is blame.

Indeed, the praise belongs to you. For I am unable not to praise both you and the things you have said, and not to approve all these things as very distinguished and excellent. There were certain others that in themselves were more imperfect, which you yourselves excused in your prologues,[2] and to which, since I am a queen, I cannot extend approval. Nevertheless, because you always exhibited caution in your opening

---

wonder your notions should be so narrow.' This Humphreys, it seems, was at the head of the Puritan party and had opposed the ecclesiastical habits with great warmth of zeal. [Humphreys, who had been a Marian exile, was a moderate nonconformist cited before Archbishop Matthew Parker for his failure to wear the prescribed clerical vestments. Protected at first by Leicester, Humphreys was eventually made to conform.]

"As she entered the town, the streets were lined with scholars from Bocardo to Quatervois, who, as her majesty passed along, fell down upon their knees and with one voice cried out, 'Long live the queen!' At Quatervois the Greek professor, Mr. [Giles] Lawrence, addressed her majesty in a Greek oration and the queen answered him in the same language and commended his performance. From hence she was conveyed with the like pomp to Christ Church, where she was received by Mr. Kingsmill, the public orator, who in the name of the university congratulated her majesty's arrival among them.... For seven days together the queen was magnificently entertained by the university, and expressed an extreme delight in the lectures, disputations, public exercises and shows which she constantly heard and saw. On the sixth day she declared her satisfaction in a Latin speech, and assured them of her favor and protection. The day after, she took her leave, and was conducted by the Heads as far as Shotover Hill, when the earl of Leicester gave her notice that they had accompanied her to the limits of their jurisdiction. Mr. Roger Marbeck then made an oration to her majesty, and having laid open the difficulties under which learning had formerly labored, he applied himself to the encouragements it had lately received and the prospect of its arising to the height of splendor under her majesty's most gracious administration. The queen heard him with pleasure and returned a most favorable answer; and casting her eyes back upon Oxford with all possible marks of tenderness and affection, she bade them farewell."

2. **prologues** the prologues to the display of scholarly disputation that had preceded her speech. The debates in divinity centered on a highly inflammatory question: whether it is lawful for a private man to take up arms against an unjust prince ("*An privato homini liceat arma sumere contra malum principem?*") (Nichols, 1:241).

words, truly I did not disapprove of such things as were very perfectly done and disputed. But the other, that is, blame, belongs properly to me because, let everyone note, I have applied my effort for some time to good disciplines and even longer in learning; however, my teachers have put their effort into barren and unfruitful ground, so that I am not able to do what I wish most, to show fruit worthy either of my worth or of their labors or of your expectation. Wherefore when you praise me beyond measure, I who know myself best easily recognize that I am worthy of no praise at all. Therefore I will make an end to this my speech full of barbarisms, if I may first add two wishes[3] I have in mind: that while I live you may be most prosperous, and when I die you may be most blessed. I have spoken.

3. **wishes** the Latin *vota* can mean either "wishes" or "prayers."

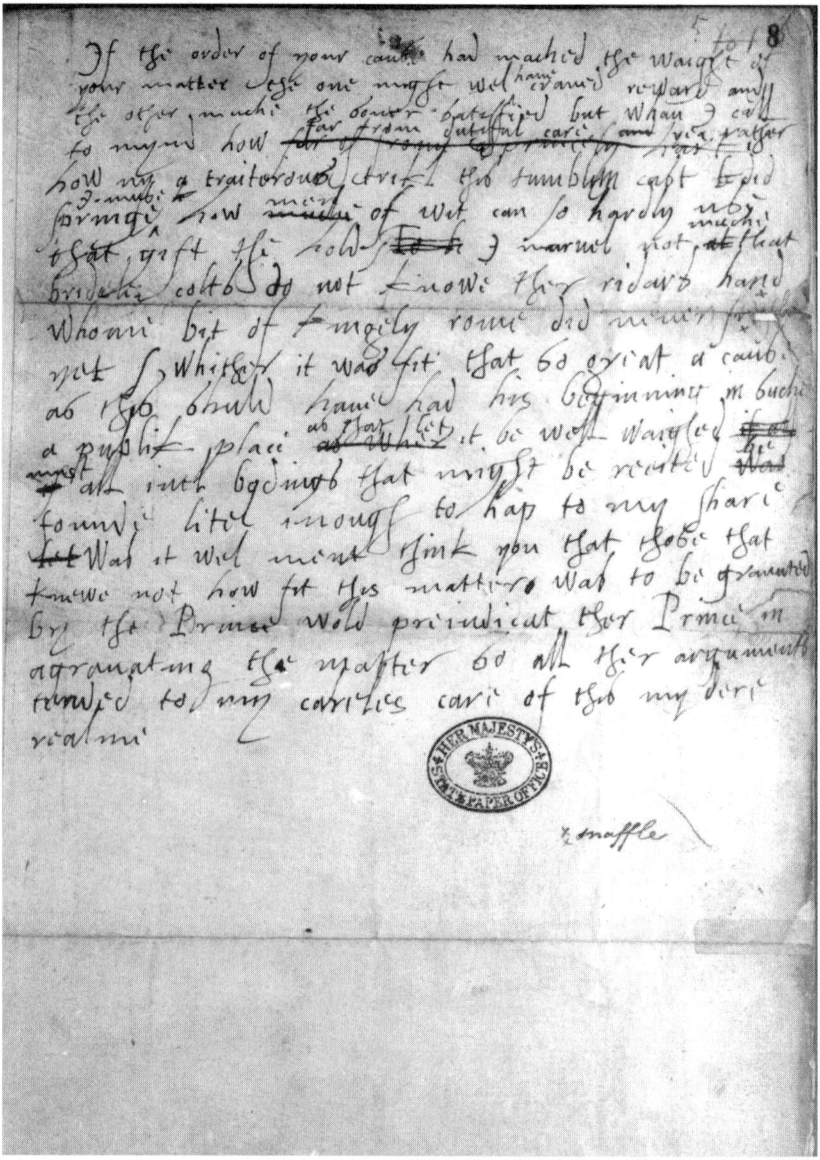

FIGURE 6 Speech 9, version 1, fragmentary opening; PRO, State Papers Domestic, Elizabeth 12/41/5. Reproduced by permission of the Public Record Office, the National Archives, England.

9 ᔅ QUEEN ELIZABETH'S SPEECH TO A JOINT DELEGATION OF
LORDS AND COMMONS, NOVEMBER 5, 1566

SPEECH 9, VERSION 1[1] *[Endorsed in Cecil's hand] A part of the beginning of the queen's majesty's speech to the thirty Lords and thirty Commons on Tuesday the 5th of November, 1566. Anno regni 8.*[2] *The queen's own hand.*

If the order of your causes had matched the weight of your matter, the one might well have craved reward and the other much the sooner satisfied. But when I call to mind how far from dutiful care, yea, rather how nigh a traitorous trick this tumbling cast did spring, I muse how men of wit can so hardly use that gift they hold. I marvel not much that bridleless colts do not know their rider's hand, whom bit of kingly rein[3] did never snaffle yet.[4] Whether it was fit that so great a cause as this should have had his beginning in such a public place as that, let it be well weighed. Must all evil bodings that might be recited be found little enough to hap to my share? Was it well meant, think you, that those that knew not how fit this matter was to be granted by the prince would

1. *Source*: PRO, State Papers Domestic, Elizabeth 12/41/5, fol. 8; a fragment in Elizabeth's own hand. (For original-spelling version, see *ACFLO*, part 1.) This speech was first delivered to a delegation of sixty Lords and Commoners who met with the queen to urge her marriage and limitation of the succession, then reported to the full Parliament. Since Elizabeth is likely to have spoken impromptu on this occasion, all MSS were probably created after the fact. Allison Heisch has presented the fragmentary version (Version 1) as Elizabeth's first thoughts, later tempered into the more moderate language of the speech as written down in advance and represented in the opening from the Cambridge Library version, our Version 2 (see Heisch, "Queen Elizabeth I: Parliamentary Rhetoric and the Exercise of Power," *Signs* 1 [1975]: 31–55). But it is equally or perhaps more likely that the fragment represents her angry afterthoughts as she attempted to record her spoken words in writing after the fact, and the full version (our Version 2), a more measured rendition that comes closer to the speech as she delivered it. In this instance, uncharacteristically, the queen's written version of the speech is more vehement than the speech as she is likely to have delivered it.

The queen was seriously angry with both Houses of Parliament for pressing the marriage and succession issues, and seeming, as in their document of later in November (Additional Document D, pp. 102–3), to tie their granting of subsidies to her acquiescence in the matter of the succession. The birth of Prince James (later James I of England) to Mary, Queen of Scots, on June 19, 1566, had only made the matter more pressing, since it was then assumed that the Scottish heir apparent would be raised as a Catholic.

2. "In the eighth year of the reign" (a standard method for dating documents during the period).

3. **rein** or "reign" (a pun).

4. **yet.** correct reading may be "yet so." It is unclear in the MS whether **yet** is followed by a slash and comma, or by "so," written with a long *s*.

prejudicate[5] their prince in aggravating the matter, so all their arguments tended to my careless care of this my dear realm?

SPEECH 9, VERSION 2[1] *[Headed] The speech of the queen's majesty had the next Parliament following, the Tuesday after All Hallow Day to the duke of Norfolk, the archbishop of York, and twenty-eight mo[2] of marquesses, earls, bishops, viscounts, and barons, and to thirty knights and esquires of the Lower House as followeth as I could carry away by remembrance.*

"If that order had been observed in the beginning of the matter and such consideration had in the prosecuting of the same as the gravity of the cause had required, the success thereof might have been otherwise than now it is. But those unbridled persons whose heads were never snaffled by the rider did rashly enter into it in the Common House, a public place, where Mr. Bell with his complices[3] alleged that they were natural Englishmen and were bound to their country, which they saw must needs perish and come to confusion unless some order were taken for the limitation of the succession of the crown. And further to help the matter, must needs proffer their speeches to the Upper House to have you, my lords, consent with them, whereby you were seduced and of simplicity did assent unto it, which you would not have done if you had foreseen before considerately the importance of the matter. So that there was no malice in you, and so I do ascribe it. For we think and know you have just cause to love us, considering our mercifulness showed to all our subjects since our reign.

5. **prejudicate** judge in advance, affect prejudicially.

1. *Source*: The Syndics of Cambridge University Library, MS Gg.III.34, fols. 208–12; copy based on a memorial account by one of the MPs in attendance. We omit the list of MPs present that follows the heading in this copy.

2. **mo** more (here and below).

3. **Mr. Bell with his** [ac]**complices** Robert Bell of King's Lynn, later Speaker Bell, was among the MPs who negotiated with the Lords' committee over the written joint petition they planned to submit to the queen. Her speech of November 5 anticipated them. Elizabeth was so incensed by their freedom in discussing the succession in the House of Commons that she and some other members of the Privy Council attempted to stifle debate on the matter. Eventually, after much protest by the House about the infringement of their traditional liberties, Elizabeth revoked the previous orders, arguing that they were no longer necessary as Parliament had not sought to resume its suit for a settled succession (see Additional Documents B and C, pp. 100–2).

"But there, two bishops[4] with their long orations sought to persuade you also with solemn matter, as though you, my lords, had not known that when my breath did fail me I had been dead unto you and that then, dying without issue, what a danger it were to the whole state. Which you had not known before they told it you. And so it was easily to be seen *quo oratio tendit,*[5] for those that should be stops and stays of the great good and avoiding of so many dangers and perils, how evil might they seem to be and so to aggravate the cause against me!

"Was I not born in the realm? Were my parents born in any foreign country? Is there any cause I should alienate myself from being careful over this country? Is not my kingdom here? Whom have I oppressed? Whom have I enriched to others' harm? What turmoil have I made in this commonwealth, that I should be suspected to have no regard to the same? How have I governed since my reign? I will be tried by envy itself. I need not to use many words, for my deeds do try me.

"Well, the matter whereof they would have made their petition, as I am informed, consisteth in two points: in my marriage and in the limitation of the succession of the crown, wherein my marriage was first placed as for manner[6] sake. I did send them answer by my Council I would marry, although of mine own disposition I was not inclined thereunto. But that was not accepted nor credited, although spoken by their prince. And yet I used so many words that I could say no more. And were it not now I had spoken those words, I would never speak them again. I will never break the word of a prince spoken in public place for my honor[7] sake. And therefore I say again I will marry as soon as I can conveniently, if God take not him away with whom I mind to marry, or myself, or else some other great let[8] happen. I can say no more except the party were present. And I hope to have children; otherwise I would never marry. A strange order of petitioners that will make a request and cannot be otherwise ascertained but by the prince's word, and yet will not believe it when it is spoken! But they, I think, that moveth the same will be as ready to mislike him with whom I shall marry as they are now to move it, and then it will appear they nothing meant it. I thought they would have been rather ready to have given me

4. **bishops** see n. 14, p. 97.   5. "where the speech was tending."
6. **manner** manners'.   7. **honor** honor's.
8. **let** hindrance; Elizabeth was then negotiating with Archduke Charles of Austria, but some members of the Privy Council were opposed to the match.

thanks than to have made any new request for the same. There hath been some that have, ere this, said unto me they never required more than that they might once hear me say I would marry. Well, there was never so great a treason but might be covered under as fair a pretense.

"The second point was the limitation of the succession of the crown, wherein was nothing said for my safety, but only for themselves. A strange thing that the foot should direct the head in so weighty a cause, which cause hath been so diligently weighed by us for that it toucheth us more than them. I am sure there was not one of them that ever was a second person,[9] as I have been, and have tasted of the practices against my sister, who I would to God were alive again. I had great occasions to hearken to their motions, of whom some of them are of the Common House. But when friends fall out truth doth appear, according to the old proverb, and were it not for my honor, their knavery should be known. There were occasions in me at that time: I stood in danger of my life, my sister was so incensed against me. I did differ from her in religion and I was sought for divers ways, and so shall never be my successor.

"I have conferred before this time with those that are well learned and have asked their opinions touching the limitation of succession, who have been silent—not that by their silence after lawlike manner they have seemed to assent to it, but that indeed they could not tell what to say considering the great peril to the realm and most danger to myself. But now the matter must needs go trimly and pleasantly, when the bowl runneth all on the one side. And alas, not one amongst them all would answer for us, but all their speeches was for the surety of their country. They would have twelve or fourteen limited in succession and the mo the better. And those shall be of such uprightness and so divine as in them shall be divinity itself. Kings were wont to honor philosophers, but if I had such I would honor them as angels, that should have such piety in them that they would not seek where they are the second to be the first, and where the third to be the second, and so forth.

"It is said I am no divine. Indeed, I studied nothing else but divinity till I came to the crown,[10] and then I gave myself to the study of that which was meet for government, and am not ignorant of stories wherein

9. **second person** second in line to the throne, as Elizabeth was under Mary Tudor.

10. Elizabeth's claim to have studied nothing but divinity in her youth is supported by her translations of religious works—Marguerite of Navarre's *Mirror of the Sinful Soul*, Queen Katherine's *Prayers or Meditations*, Ochino's *Sermo de Christo*, and bk. 1, chap. 1, of the French version of Calvin's *Institutes* (under the title "How We Ought to Know God").

appeareth what hath fallen out for ambition of kingdoms, as in Spain, Naples, Portingal,[11] and at home. And what cocking[12] hath been between the father and the son for the same! You would have a limitation of succession. Truly if reason did not subdue will in me, I would cause you to deal in it, so pleasant a thing it should be unto me. But I stay it for your benefit; for if you should have liberty to treat of it, there be so many competitors—some kinsfolk, some servants, and some tenants; some would speak for their master, and some for their mistress, and every man for his friend—that it would be an occasion of a greater charge than a subsidy.[13] And if my will did not yield to reason, it should be that thing I would gladly desire, to see you deal in it.

"Well, there hath been error—I say not errors, for there were too many in the proceeding in this matter. But we will not judge that these attempts were done of any hatred to our person, but even for lack of good foresight. I do not marvel though *Domini Doctores*[14] with you, my lords, did so use themselves therein, since after my brother's death they openly preached and set forth that my sister and I were bastards. Well, I wish not the death of any man, but only this I desire: that they which have been the practitioners herein may before their deaths repent the same and show some open confession of their faults, whereby the scabbed sheep may be known from the whole. As for my own part, I care not for death, for all men are mortal; and though I be a woman, yet I have as good a courage answerable to my place as ever my father had. I am your anointed queen. I will never be by violence constrained to do anything. I thank God I am indeed endued with such qualities that if I were turned out of the realm in my petticoat, I were able to live in any place of Christendom.

"Your petition is to deal in the limitation of the succession. At this present, it is not convenient, nor never shall be without some peril unto you and certain danger unto me. But were it not for your peril, at this time I would give place notwithstanding my danger. Your perils are

11. **Portingal** Portugal.   12. **cocking** fighting, contention.

13. **subsidy** taxes granted by Parliament to the sovereign to aid in meeting the expenses of government.

14. ***Domini Doctores*** literally "Doctors of the Lord"—her derisive term for bishops who either spoke for the petition in the House of Lords or attended as members of the Lords' delegation on the occasion of the present speech. Among the latter were the archbishop of York (Dr. Thomas Young) and, according to D'Ewes, the bishops of London (Edmund Grindal) and Durham (James Pilkington).

sundry ways, for some may be touched who resteth now in such terms with us as is not meet to be disclosed either in the Common House or in the Upper House. But as soon as there may be a convenient time and that it may be done with least peril unto you, although never without great danger unto me, I will deal therein for your safety and offer it unto you as your prince and head, without request. For it is monstrous that the feet should direct the head.

"And therefore, this is my mind and answer, which I would have to be showed in the two Houses; and for the doing thereof, you, my lord chief justice,[15] are meetest to do it in the Upper House and you, Cecil, in the Nether House." And therewith speaking of the speaker, that the Lower House would have had their speaker there, wherein they did not consider that he was not there to speak, she said he was a speaker indeed, and there ended.[16]

The Aftermath of a Speech

SPEECH 9, ADDITIONAL DOCUMENT A   CECIL'S REPORT TO THE FULL HOUSE OF COMMONS NOVEMBER 6, 1566, ON ELIZABETH'S SPEECH OF NOVEMBER 5[1]

[Endorsed] 5 November 1566. The report made to the Commons House of the queen's majesty's answer by the mouth of me the secretary, William Cecil, with the consent of thirty Lords and twenty-nine Commons.

[Headed] 5 November. The sum of the queen's majesty's speech to the Lords and Commons assembled to the number of sixty.

She took knowledge of the petition that was to be made to her consisting of two parts, the one for her marriage, the other for the limitation of

15. **lord chief justice** probably Sir Robert Catlin, who was one of the two lord chief justices in attendance and was assigned the duties of Sir Nicholas Bacon, who was ill during November.

16. In this final sentence the diarist reverts to the third person. Elizabeth's quip about the speaker speaking refers to the new speaker of the Commons appointed at the beginning of the parliamentary session. He was Sir Richard Onslowe—the queen's solicitor general, who, she suggests, spoke more than a speaker should—that is, took a rather more active part in the creation of the joint delegation than was appropriate. At least one later MS (BL, Stowe 354), albeit substantially similar to the version recorded here, reads instead "she was a speaker indeed." Most modern versions have emended the line accordingly, thereby losing Elizabeth's wry conclusion.

1. *Source*: PRO, State Papers Domestic, Elizabeth 12/41/9, fol. 14; all in Cecil's hand. At the end of her speech on November 5, Elizabeth had called upon Cecil to report it to the

the succession of the crown. Wherein she allowed not the manner of the proceeding in respect of the weight of the matters, but imputed that which she thought therein amiss to lack of foresight than[2] any evil meaning in any person.

And as to her marriage, she said she thought she had so satisfied by her answer thereto that she looked rather for thanks than for request. But for further satisfaction of any person that might thereof doubt because she had in her former speeches expressed her contrary disposition or mind, she said that ought not to move any person, considering she hath certainly declared her mind to be now otherwise and that she is fully determined to marry. And that should be proved by her deeds as soon as time and occasion would serve, if almighty God should not take away either her own person or the person of him with whom she meant to marry. And at this present she could use no other mean to satisfy the doubtful but with the word of a prince, which being in so public a place ought not to be mistrusted. And in the matter of marriage, she trusted in God's goodness to have children, for otherwise she protested that she would never marry. Except the person were present she could not now otherwise proceed, nor in this matter could use any other words for the purpose than she had, and so in the end required to be believed.

The other matter for limitation of the succession: she said as it was necessary, which she would not deny, so did she know therein such perils to enter into the decision thereof at this present time—as she was fully persuaded in her mind, considering the competitors on all sides and for other causes to her known not meet for this present to be divulged abroad—that it was neither for herself nor for her people void of great peril. For she said she knew many causes and some of her own experience, having been a second person to a sister (the late queen meant) how perilous it was for her own person. But yet if she did not also see how perilous it was for her subjects at this time, she would not forbear for her own peril to deal therein. And yet meant she not so to neglect it nor to be careless thereof, but whensoever she should find it less per-

---

"Nether House." He clearly struggled to palliate Elizabeth's angry language in the speech as she had delivered it. There are no fewer than three drafts of Cecil's report in the PRO, of which this is the last and probably the version presented to the full House on November 6. After Cecil finished, ominously, "all the House was silent." See Neale's account (1:145–50) and Hartley (1:119–65).

2. **than** rather than.

ilous for her realm than it is now, she would show herself to have regard thereof before they should require it, and would be thereof the beginner as was convenient for a prince to be towards her people. For she would be loath to live to be forced to do that which by justice and reason she ought to do, and concluded with a request not to misinterpret her words but to report of her meaning to both the Houses.

SPEECH 9, ADDITIONAL DOCUMENT B PETER WENTWORTH'S QUESTIONS ON PARLIAMENTARY PRIVILEGE, NOVEMBER 11, 1566[1]

[Endorsed] Questions about the liberty of the House in freedom of speech for succession.

[Headed in a later hand] Motions, 9 November, 11 November.

Whether her highness' commandment forbidding the Lower House to speak or treat any more of the succession, and of any their excuses in that behalf, is a breach of the liberty of the free speech of the House or not?

Whether Mr. Comptroller, the vice chamberlain, and Mr. Secretary,[2] pronouncing in the House the said commandment in her highness' name, are of authority sufficient to bind the House to silence in that behalf, or to bind the House to acknowledge the same to be a direct and sufficient commandment or not?

If her highness' said commandment be no breach of the liberty of the House; or if the commandment pronounced as afore is said be a sufficient commandment to bind the House to take knowledge thereof, then what offense is it for any of the House to err in declaring his opinion to be otherwise?

---

1. *Source*: PRO, State Papers Domestic, Elizabeth 12/41/16, fol. 33r; copy. On November 9, the queen sent a verbal "gag order" to Parliament, forbidding them to debate matters of the succession. On November 9 and 11, the House angrily debated whether or not her order was a violation of the liberties of the House. On the liberty of speech in the House of Commons as confirmed from Parliament to Parliament by the monarch, see Sir Thomas Smith, *De Republica Anglorum: The Manner of Government of England* (London: for Gregory Seton, 1583), bk. 2, chap. 2, pp. 35–43.

2. **Comptroller** Sir Edward Rogers; **vice chamberlain** Sir Francis Knollys, the queen's cousin; **Secretary** Sir William Cecil. They had been the officials charged with delivering the queen's "gag order."

SPEECH 9, ADDITIONAL DOCUMENT C QUEEN ELIZABETH'S
DIRECTIONS TO CECIL FOR LIFTING HER PREVIOUS ORDER
FORBIDDING THE HOUSE TO DEBATE MATTERS CONCERNING THE
SUCCESSION, NOVEMBER 24, 1566[1]

*[Endorsed] 24 November 1566, anno 9. The report of the queen majesty's
message to the Common House for delivering of the same from a tumult.*

*[Headed] 24 November. To be declared to the Commons House by the
speaker.*

The queen's majesty hath commanded me to let you understand that
whereas shortly after she had given her answer to certain of the Lords
and certain of this House in the matters intended to have been required
of her majesty, as the necessity of the time and other weighty considerations presently moved her, upon the sight of certain matters which
some persons intended (under pretense of dealing in the former suit)
to propound in this House touching the crown of this realm, very unmeet for the time and place and certainly dangerous to the common
quietness of her subjects now assembled, did by her majesty's commandment will you all to stay your proceeding any further in the said
matter at this time. And now being informed by such of this House as
she hath come to credit that there is not now any determination of this
House to receive or allow any such dangerous matter as she before did
doubt, is therefore pleased to deliver you at this time her former commandments, not doubting but you will be answerable in your whole doings to the good opinion which her majesty is induced to conceive of
you in this behalf. And thinketh it good that you have regard to the expedition of the matters of most moment remaining amongst you, considering the expense of the time past and the shortness of that which is
now to come, the term ending also so shortly as it shall.

1. *Source*: PRO, State Papers Domestic, Elizabeth 12/41/30, fol. 61; in Cecil's hand with corrections that appear to be in Elizabeth's hand. (For these corrections, see *ACFLO*, part 1.)
Here the queen retreats from her former order forbidding debate on the succession on the
pretext that the House had already come into conformity with her wishes. The speaker
who was to deliver the message was Richard Onslowe, the queen's solicitor general. In a
later, more general order to the same end (PRO, State Papers Domestic, Elizabeth 12/27/45,
fol. 220r), she refers to this one as having been delivered to the House by Onslowe and re-
moves its attached contingencies on the grounds that, despite the discussion by the Commons of the prohibited matters, "there followed no general report nor resolution of the
whole House."

An addition.

If any person after this message shall either presently or at any time later during this session in the Common House begin any speech tending directly or indirectly to make any declaration of any particular title to the succession of the crown of this realm, the speaker shall forthwith in her majesty's name command the party to cease off from any such further speaking and shall declare to the whole House that so is her majesty's express commandment.

This manner of answer her majesty hath thought best, without any further answer to your request that hath been made to have leave to confer upon the liberties of the House, forasmuch as thereof must needs have ensued more inconvenience presently than were meet.

SPEECH 9, ADDITIONAL DOCUMENT D PART OF A SUBSIDY BILL SENT BY PARLIAMENT TO QUEEN ELIZABETH, WITH HER ANGRY ANNOTATIONS, NOVEMBER 29, 1566[1]

Thirdly, we cannot but also thankfully remember to your majesty that it pleased the same to signify unto us that you ∧ did not mislike of us for our desire in this Parliament to have the succession of the crown declared, for that you rightly conceived the same our desire to proceed from us (as indeed it did) of mere duty and love towards your highness, your realms and countries, and not of any other disposition or pretensed purpose.[2] And signified further of your godly disposition and natural love towards us, to our great comfort, that ∧ rather than your realm should threat ruin for lack of declaration of succession, which you trusted almighty God would show of your own body in due time

1. *Source*: BL, MS Lansdowne 1236, art. 27, fol. 42; annotations in Elizabeth's hand. (For original-spelling version, see *ACFLO,* part 1.) The queen begins merely by adding emphasis marks, dark carets inserted in the text addressed to her and reproduced here by carets in boldface. The carets turn to commentary at the foot of the sheet, continuing onto the back. Parliament hoped to coerce the queen into a written commitment to settle the order of the succession as a condition for receiving a subsidy to fund her government. For an account of Elizabeth's reaction in the words of the Spanish ambassador, see *Calendar of State Papers Spanish,* vol. 1 (London: Her Majesty's Stationers' Office, 1864), pp. 589–90.

2. **pretensed** [pretended] **purpose** here and below, the document refers to the parliamentary petitions and her answering speeches (Speeches 5 and 6, pp. 70–86), as well as to her more recent address of November 5 as reported by Cecil to the House of Commons. The 1563 session and the present session of 1566–67, despite the lapse of time between them, were formally part of the same political entity, Elizabeth's second Parliament.

after your marriage, ∧ you would by God's help, though it should appear some peril to yourself (which God defend) declare the succession in such convenient time as your highness, with th'advice of your Council and assent of your realm, should think most meet, in such person as in whom the right thereof, according to law and justice, ought to be settled and renewed to the joyful comfort of us all. And so having, with your majesty's favor, presented to the same in the forefront of our small but a most free and willing gift,[3] these our most humble recognitions, we do likewise beseech your majesty to receive the rest that followeth as the fruits of our faithfulness and bounden love that we bear to your majesty, and that it may be enacted in form following:

[There follow two half lines of marks like letters, but which are not letters, ending in "*Anno*. 1566." This is the mock-up of the signed writ that the Commons wants from the queen in return for the subsidy: she is to commit herself on paper to specifying the order of the succession to the throne. The remaining four inches of the page had been left blank. In this space Elizabeth scrawls roughly:]

Set these two concernings into one meaning, and my counsel is all given. Let not other regard themselves so wholly as I have no corner left for me. Let them know that I knew, though I followed not, that some of them would my pure conscience better served me that their lewd practices could avail with me. I know no reason why any my private answers to the realm should be made for prologue to a subsidies. But neither yet do I understand why such audacity should be used to make, without my license, an act of my words.[4] Are my words like lawyers' books, which nowadays go to the wire-drawers to make subtle doings more plain? Is there no hold of my speech without[5] a act compel me to confirm? Shall my princely consent be turned to strengthen my words that be not of themselves substantives? Say no more at this time, but if these fellows were well answered and paid with lawful coin, there would be fewer counterfeits among them.

---

3. **gift** the parliamentary subsidy.

4. Elizabeth complains that members of Parliament, using the doctrine articulated in their petitions that the prince's word is *lex animata* (a living law), have attempted to give her speeches the status of a parliamentary act. Before an act attained the status of law, the queen had to accept it officially at the end of a parliamentary session by having it declared *viva voce* in her name "*La royne le veult*" (law French for "The queen wills it").

5. **without** except.

10 ➳ QUEEN ELIZABETH'S SPEECH DISSOLVING PARLIAMENT,
JANUARY 2, 1567

SPEECH 10, VERSION 1[1] *[Headed] 1563, 5th Elizabeth [error for 1567]. A
letter in Queen Elizabeth*[2] *hand to the Commons in Parliament about
their petitions concerning marriage and liberties.*

I love so evil counterfeiting and hate so much dissimulation that I may
not suffer you depart without that my admonitions may show your
harms and cause you shun unseen peril. Two visors have blinded the
eyes of the lookers-on in this present session, so far forth as under pretense of saving all they have done none good. And these they be: succession and liberties. As to the first, the prince's opinion and goodwill
ought in good order have been felt in other sort than in so public a place
be uttered. It had been convenient that so weighty a cause had had his
original from a zealous prince's consideration, not from so lip-labored
orations out of such subjects' mouths. Which what they be, time may
teach you know, and their demerits will make them acknowledge how
they have done their lewd endeavor to make all my realm suppose that
their care was much when mine was none at all. Their handling of this
doth well show, they being wholly ignorant, how fit my grant at this
time should be to such a demand. In this one thing their imperfect dealings are to be excused: for I think this be the first time that so weighty a
cause passed from so simple men's mouths as began this cause.

As to liberties, who is so simple that doubts whether a prince that is
head of all the body may not command the feet not to stray when they
would slip? God forbid that your liberty should make my bondage or
that your lawful liberties should any ways have been infringed. No,
no—my commandment tended no whit to that end. You were sore seduced. You have met with a gentle prince, else your needless scruple
might perchance have bred your caused blame (if I had not more pitied

1. *Source*: Version 1 is BL, MS Cotton Charter IV.38 (2), formerly Cotton Titus F.1, fol. 92;
a much-revised manuscript all in the queen's hand. (For original-spelling version, see Figure 7 and *ACFLO*, part 1.) This is annotated as a "letter" to the Commons: presumably Elizabeth intended for Lord Keeper Bacon to read it aloud to them. The Huntington Library
copy (HM 1340, fol. 84) may well be a copy closely associated with Bacon himself: its hand
is similar to that of BL, MS Additional 32379, "Discourses of Sir N. Bacon," and it heads the
speech "A bill delivered by her majesty unto my Lady Bacon to be delivered by her highness' commandment unto my lord keeper."
2. **Elizabeth** Elizabeth's.

you than blamed you); the lawfulness of which commandment might easily by good right be showed you, perchance to their shame that bred you that colored doubt. And albeit the soothing[3] of such be reprovable in all, yet I would not you should think my simplicity such as I cannot make distinctions among you: as of some that broached the vessel not well fined[4] and began these attempts not foreseeing well the end; others that respected the necessary facts of the matters and no whit understood circumstances expedient not to have been forgotten therein; others whose ears were deluded by pleasing persuasions of common good when the very yielding to their own inventions might have bred all your woes; others whose capacities, I suppose, yielded their judgment to their friends' will; some other that served an echo's place. Well, among all these sundry effects I assure you there be none, the beginners only except, whom I either condemn for evil minded to me or do suspect not to be my most loyal subjects.

Therefore I conclude with this opinion, which I will you to think unfainedly true: that as I have tried[5] that you may be deceive,[6] so am I persuaded you will not beguile the assured joy that ever I took to see my subjects' love to me, more staunch than ever I felt the care in myself for myself to be great. Which alone hath made my heavy burden light and a kingdom's care but easy carriage for me. Let this my displaying[7] stand you in stead of sorer strokes, never to tempt too far a prince's patience. And let my comfort pluck up your dismayed sprites and cause you think that, in hope that your following behaviors shall make amends for part of this, you return with your prince's graces. Whose care for you doubt you not to be such as she shall not need a remembrancer[8] for your weal.

[Memorandum at bottom of page] All this letter was the queen's own hand and the draft she framed herself.

---

3. **soothing** proving or verifying.

4. **fined** finished, brought to an end.

5. **tried** tested, found out.

6. **deceive** deceived (final letter of word may be hidden under binding).

7. **displaying** making examples (of you).

8. **remembrancer** one engaged or appointed for the purpose of reminding another; Elizabeth may be punning as well on "Remembrancer" as the title of an official of the Court of the Exchequer who was responsible for the collection of debts due to the sovereign. The pun would then turn on who would not engage the remembrancer, Elizabeth or the Commons.

SPEECH 10, VERSION 2[1]

Then the queen standing said, "My lords and others, the Commons of this assembly, although the lord keeper hath, according to order, very well answered in my name, yet as a periphrasis I have a few words further to speak unto you. Notwithstanding that I have not been used, nor love to do it, in such open assemblies, yet now, not to the end to amend his talk, but remembering that commonly princes' own words be better printed in the hearers' memory than those spoken by her commandment, I mean to say thus much unto you. I have in this assembly found so much dissimulation, having always professed plainness, that I marvel thereat—yea, two faces under one hood and the body rotten,[2] being covered with two visors: succession and liberty. Which they determined must be either presently granted, denied, or referred. In granting whereof, they had their desires, and denying or deferring thereof (three things being so plaudable as indeed to all men they are) they thought to work that mischief which never foreign enemy could bring to pass, which is the hatred of my Commons. But alack! They began to pierce the vessel before the wine was fined, and began a thing not foreseeing the end: how by this means I have seen my well-willers from mine enemies and can, as me seemeth, very well divide the House into four.

"First the broachers and workers thereof, who are in the greatest fault. Secondly, the speakers, who by eloquent tales persuaded others, are in the next degree. Thirdly, the agreers, who being so light of credit that the eloquence of the tales so overcame them, that they gave more credit thereunto than unto their own wits. And lastly are those which sat still mute and meddled not therewith, but rather wondered, disallowing the matter; who in my opinion are most to be excused.

1. *Source*: BL, MS Cotton Titus F.I, fols. 121v–122r; a copy. Version 2 is Elizabeth's freely revised version of the "letter," delivered by herself as a speech in the House of Lords at the end of the parliamentary session. D'Ewes's printed version is similar (116–17). For later copies, see Hartley (1:172–73).

2. **two faces under one hood** (proverbial: two-faced) **and the body rotten** In this impromptu reprise of some of the topics of her previous letter, Elizabeth elaborates upon a figure from Speaker Onslowe's lengthy oration slightly earlier the same day. He had said, "First, as the body if it should want a head were a great monster, so is it likewise if it have many heads, as if upon every several member were a head. And to speak of one head, although in the body be divers members which be made of flesh, bones, sinews and joints, yet the one head thereof governeth wisely the same, which if it should want we should be

"But do you think that either I am unmindful of your surety by succession, wherein is all my care, considering I know myself to be mortal? No, I warrant you. Or that I went about to break your liberties? No, it was never my meaning, but to stay you before you fall into the ditch. For all things hath his time.[3] For although perhaps you may have after me one better learned or wiser, yet I assure you, none more careful over you. And therefore, henceforth, whether I live to see the like assembly or no, or whosoever it be, yet beware however you prove your prince's patience, as you have now done mine. And now to conclude, all this notwithstanding (not meaning to make a Lent of Christmas), the most part may assure you to depart in your prince's grace."

Then she said openly to the lord keeper, saying, "My lord, you will do as I bade you."

Who then said aloud, "The queen's majesty hath agreed to dissolve this Parliament; therefore every man may take his ease and depart at his pleasure."

11 ❧ QUEEN ELIZABETH'S SPEECH OPENING THE 1571 PARLIAMENT, APRIL 2, 1571[1]

worse than wild beasts without a head and so worthily called a monstrous beast. Again, if the body should be governed by many heads, then the same would soon come to destruction by reason of the controversy among them, who would never agree but be destroyed without any foreign invasion. Therefore God saith it is needful that the people have a king. . . ." Cited from Hartley (1:168–69); the final words are an allusion to 1 Samuel 8:6–9.

3. Cf. Ecclesiastes 3:1 (English rendition of Vulgate phrasing).

1. *Source*: BL, MS Cotton Titus F.I, fol. 129v. For other versions, all of which are similar in wording, see D'Ewes (137) and Hartley (1:195). It was unusual for Elizabeth to speak at the beginning of a parliamentary session; however this brief speech may be taken as characteristic of many short speeches and responses she regularly made that were not recorded by her auditors. For example, at the end of the same parliamentary session, according to one of its diarists, the queen spoke as follows about a treason bill: "In this Parliament it was showed us of a bill devised of for our savity [safety] against treasons, whereof, when we had the sight, it liked us not. Nevertheless, being persuaded by our Council of the necessity thereof, and that it was for our safety, we were contented the same should proceed. This bill being brought into the Lower House, some one learned man did put to the same one other bill additional, which stretched so far that others might unwares be entrapped full much against our goodwill and pleasure. And this being brought unto us, we misliked it very much, being not of the mind to offer extremity or injury to any person; for as we mind no harm to others, so we hope none will mind unto us. And therefore, reserving to every his right, we thought it not good to deal so hardly with anybody as by that bill was meant" (Hartley, 1:257).

The judges and her highness' learned Council, being at the woolsacks[2] in the midst of the Chamber and at her highness' feet, on each side of her kneeling one of the Grooms or Gentlemen of the Chamber, their faces towards her, the knights, citizens, burgesses standing all below the bar,[3] her majesty then stood up in her regal throne; and with a princely grace and singular good countenance, after a long stay, she spake in few words to this effect:

"My right loving lords and you all, our right faithful and obedient subjects, we in the name of God, for His service, and for the safety of this state, are here now assembled to His glory I hope, and pray that it may be to your comfort and the common quiet of us, yours, and all ours forever."

12 ᘒ QUEEN ELIZABETH'S SPEECHES AND RESPONSES DURING HER VISIT TO WARWICK, AUGUST 12, 1572[1]

[The queen's response to a speech by the town recorder, Edward Aglionby[2]] This oration ended, Robert Phillips, bailiff, rising out of the place where he kneeled, approached near to the coach or chariot wherein her majesty sat, and coming to the side thereof, kneeling down, offered unto her majesty a purse, very fair wrought, and in the purse twenty pounds all in sovereigns, which her majesty, putting forth her hand received, showing withal a very benign and gracious countenance and smiling, said to th'earl of Leicester, "My lord, this is contrary to your promise," and turning toward the bailiff, recorder, and burgesses, said:

Bailiff, I thank you, and you all, with all my heart, for your goodwills; and I am very loath to take anything at your hands now because you at the last time of my being here presented to us, to our great liking and contentation,

2. **woolsacks** seats made of large bags of wool, without backs or arms, for the use of judges when summoned to attend the House of Lords at the opening of Parliament; also the usual seat of the lord chancellor in the House of Lords.

3. **bar** rail or barrier dividing off from the central space of the House of Lords a space near the door, to which nonmembers could be admitted for business purposes.

1. *Source*: Nichols's printed copy (1:315–16) of the record of the queen's visit in the Black Book of the Warwick Corporation, fols. 65–70. The queen's brief speeches here may be regarded as typical of the impromptu remarks, most of them unrecorded, that she made every year while she was on progress.

2. **Edward Aglionby** (1520–1587?), MP for Warwick in the 1571 Parliament and elected recorder of Warwick on the day of Elizabeth's visit.

and it is not the manner to be always presented with gifts. And I am the more unwilling to take anything of you because I know that a mite of their hands is as much as a thousand pounds of some others.[3] Nevertheless, because you shall not think that I mislike of your goodwills, I will accept it with most hearty thanks to you all, praying God that I may perform, as Mr. Recorder saith, such benefit as is hoped.

And therewithal offered her hand to the bailiff to kiss, who kissed it. And then she delivered to him again his mace, which before the oration he had delivered to her majesty, which she kept in her lap all the time of the oration. And after the mace delivered, she called Mr. Aglionby to her and offered her hand to him to kiss, withal smiling said:

Come hither, little recorder. It was told me that you would be afraid to look upon me or to speak boldly; but you were not so fraid[4] of me as I was of you. And now I thank you for putting me in mind of my duty, and that should be in me.[5]

And so, thereupon showing a most gracious and favorable countenance to all the burgesses and company, said again, "I most heartily thank you all, my good people."

3. Cf. Mark 12:41–44.
4. **fraid** afraid.
5. The recorder's speech had made the point that one purpose of panegyric in ancient Greece and Rome was to make good princes even more so: "by the pleasant remembrance of their known and true virtues made better, being put in mind of their office and government" (Nichols, 1:311).

LETTERS 24–33

24 ❧ QUEEN ELIZABETH TO EDWARD STANLEY, EARL OF DERBY,
JUNE 4, 1560[1]

*[Endorsed] 4 Junii, 1560. From the queen's majesty to th'earl of Derby, in
favor of his wife.*

We greet you well. Hearing sundry wise of some unkindness or
strangeness of late of your part towards your wife, whereof for both
your parts we were sorry, and being informed that no matter can be understand[2] by her friends and kinfolks of her desert, but that upon some
misliking conceived against her by your children, you should by them
be occasioned to deal strangely with her and in other sort than you
were accustomed or than is convenient, we, being very sorry to hear of
this alteration (considering we know how well you esteemed her and we
ourselves having always had very good estimation of her, both for her
good parentage and for her own discreet behavior), cannot, for the
favor and goodwill we have to you both, but require you either to re-

---

1. *Source*: BL, MS Lansdowne 94, art. 20, fol. 39; draft and corrections in Cecil's hand. Edward Stanley (1508–1572), third earl of Derby, known for Catholic sympathies, was one of
the most powerful magnates of the north of England (Lancashire and Cheshire). He
served on the Privy Councils of three successive monarchs: Edward VI, Mary I, and Elizabeth. Derby had already had nine children by two previous wives when he married Mary,
daughter of Sir George Cotton, shortly after his second wife's death in 1559. The date of this
letter indicates how quickly Derby's third marriage proved unhappy; it was also without
issue.

2. **understand** understood.

ceive her to such favor as heretofore you did bear her, without inclining
to credit such as of evil will and without just cause shall be disposed to
maintain variation betwixt you; or if you shall think her otherwise to
have defied, that we or some of our Council may be duly and particularly thereof advertised, to the end her friends may understand how to
deal for the answering thereof. Who justly think her to be rather by evil
will of others than by yourself touched in her fame, and the fault in
them by slandering her to you with obscure speeches and not in her
at all by any kind of deserving. And hereof we require you to give us a
letter.

25 ☙ ELIZABETH TO PHILIP II OF SPAIN, SEPTEMBER 30, 1562[1]

*[Endorsed by Cecil's secretary] 30 Sept. 1562. Copy of the queen's majesty's
letter to the king of Spain in English.*

Although your ambassador[2] here resident with us hath of late times in
your name dealt with us to understand our disposition touching these
troubles in France, and the rather because he perceived that we did put
a number of our subjects in order of defense both for the sea and land,
to whom we made such reasonable answer as ought to satisfy him; yet
because we have been in mind now of a long time to impart to you our
concept and judgment hereof, wherein we have been occasioned to forbear only by the mutability of the proceedings of our neighbors in
France and for that also we have some cause to doubt of the manner of
the report of your ambassador, having found him in his negotiations
divers times to have more respect towards the weal of others than of us
and our country; we have thought not only to give special charge to our

1. *Source*: PRO, State Papers Foreign, Elizabeth 70/41/503, fols. 239r–241r; draft or copy by
Cecil's secretary, with corrections in Cecil's hand. Although this important letter is printed
by Harrison as Elizabeth's and was certainly "authored" by her in the broad sense that it
represents her policy, its orotund style may be entirely or in large part Cecil's. The context
is the wars of religion in France. The House of Guise, from which Mary, Queen of Scots,
was descended through her mother, Mary of Guise, had agreed by the terms of the Treaty
of Cateau-Cambrésis (1559) to return Calais to the English within eight years. The English
government was attempting to aid beleaguered French Protestants while at the same time
securing Calais, defending itself, and maintaining cordial relations with Philip II of Spain.
2. **your ambassador** the second Spanish ambassador to England during Elizabeth's
reign, Alvaro de la Quadra, bishop of Avila, appointed January 1561.

ambassador[3] there resident with you to declare plainly and sincerely our disposition and meaning, but also by these our own letters to impart what we think of these troubles in France for our particular, and secondly what we are advised upon good considerations, not doubting but, both for your sincere and brotherly friendship and for your wisdom, ye will interpret and allow of our actions with such equity as the causes do require.

Surely we have been much troubled and perplexed from the beginning of these divisions in France, and upon divers causes. First because we had a great compassion to see the young king[4] our brother so abused by his subjects as his authority could not direct them to accord. Next thereto, we feared that hereof might follow an universal trouble to the rest of Christendom, considering the quarrel was discovered and published to be for the matter of religion. Lastly, which toucheth us most nearly and properly, we perceived that the duke of Guise and his House was the principal head of one part, and that they daily so increased their force as in the end they became commanders of all things in France, and thereupon such manner of hostile dealing used in divers sorts against our subjects and merchants in sundry parts of France as we were constrained to look about us what peril might ensue to our own estate and country.

And thereupon could we not forget how they were the very parties that evicted Callice[5] from this crown, a matter of continual grief to this realm and of glory to them, and unjustly observed also the first capitulations for the redition[6] thereof into their hands. Neither could we forget how hardly by their means we were dealt withal at the conclusion of the peace at Casteau in Cambresy, where you, the duke of Savoy,[7] and others having restitution in possession,[8] our right (notwithstanding your goodwill to the contrary) was deferred to the end of certain years without restitution of anything. And then, how immediately, notwithstanding a show of peace made with us, they privately for their own

---

3. **our ambassador** Dr. Thomas Man, sometime bishop of Gloucester and a strong Protestant. After Philip II expelled Man in 1568, there would be no subsequent English ambassador to Spain during Elizabeth's reign.

4. **king** Charles IX, then twelve years old.

5. **Callice** Calais.   6. **redition** return.

7. **duke of Savoy** Emmanuel Philibert, prince of Piedmont, a Habsburg client and political menace to France.

8. **restitution in possession** having the capability of making restitution.

particular estates by practices, by counsels, by labors, by writing both public and private, by publishing of arms and such like, and lastly even by force and arms conveyed into Scotland for our offense, they invaded the title of our crown. And finally being disappointed of all their purposes and constrained to come to a peace with us,[9] which was concluded by authority of the French king and the queen their niece,[10] whom they only had then in governance, by their direction and counsel the confirmation thereof was unjustly and unhonorably denied, and so remaineth until this day, contrary to the several promises and solemn covenants of the said French king and the queen their niece, remaining with us in writing under the great seals both of France and Scotland. Upon fresh remembrance and good consideration of which things, we seeing no small peril towards us and our realm growing by their proceedings, for the remedy thereof and for the procuring of quietness and peace in France by cessing[11] of this division, did first seek by all manner of good means that we could to bring them and the parties at controversy with them to some accord. And seeing we find plainly them of the House of Guise who hath both the power and authority of the king at their direction, utterly unwilling hereunto and the only stay thereof, we are constrained contrary to our own nature and disposition towards quietness, for the surety of us and our crown and realm to put a reasonable number of our subjects in defensible force, and by that means to preserve such ports as be next unto us from their possession without intent of offense to the king, until we may see these divisions compounded (or at the least them of Guise, whom only we have cause to doubt) out of arms in the parts of Normandy next to us.

And so we mean to direct our actions as, without any injury or violence to the French king or any of his subjects, we intend to live in good peace with the said French king, and to save to our realm in this convenient time our right to Callice with surety. Which manifestly we see by their proceeding they mean not to deliver, although in very deed we can prove that they ought presently to restore it to us. And now, our good brother, seeing this is our disposition and intent, wherein it may appear that we mean to do to no person wrong but to provide and foresee how

---

9. **peace with us** the Treaty of Edinburgh, a current nub of contention between England and Scotland (see Speech 4, p. 61n).

10. **French king and the queen their niece** Francis II and Mary, Queen of Scots.

11. **cessing** ceasing.

apparent dangers to our estate may be diverted, and that we might not remain in this kind of unsurety to have our Callice restored to us—whereof we be assured you for divers good causes will have special regard—we trust you will not only allow of our intent but also, as ye may conveniently, further us as far forth as our purpose to have Callice and peace with our neighbors doth extend.

[The rest is wholly in Cecil's hand.] And in so doing we assure you that we shall be found most ready to revoke our forces and to live as we did before these troubles, in full and perfect rest, to the recovery whereof we do heartily require you to be such a mean as may stand with the indifferency of your friendship and with the opinion that the world hath conceived, how ready you ought to be to procure the restitution of the town of Callice to this our crown of England.

26 &ᴥ QUEEN ELIZABETH TO WILLIAM CECIL, PRINCIPAL
MINISTER, SEPTEMBER 23, 1564[1]

[Endorsed in Cecil's hand] 23 September, 1564, at Saint James'. The queen writing to me being sick—Scotland.

In such a manner of labyrinth am I placed by the answer that I am to give to the queen of Scotland that I do not know in what way I will be able to satisfy her, since I will not have given her any answer for all this time, nor do I know what I now should say. Therefore let there be found something good that I will be able to put into Randol's[2] written instructions and show me your opinion in this matter.

1. *Source*: PRO, State Papers Scotland, Elizabeth 52/9/48, fol. 113r; Latin note in Elizabeth's hand. (For original-spelling version, see *ACFLO,* part 1.) The occasion of this note was probably some negotiation relating to the marriage of Mary, Queen of Scots. Elizabeth had offered Mary the hand of her own favorite, Robert Dudley, earl of Leicester. Mary was considering a marriage with Don Carlos, son of Philip II of Spain. Also entering the picture was the eighteen-year-old Henry Stewart (1545–1567), Lord Darnley, a grandson of Queen Margaret of Scotland, Henry VIII's sister; Darnley would gain Elizabeth's permission to visit Mary in Scotland in February 1565.

2. **Randol** Thomas Randolph, one of two special representatives whom Elizabeth dispatched to Scotland to negotiate regarding the marriage of Mary, Queen of Scots.

27 ⏵ QUEEN ELIZABETH TO MARY, QUEEN OF SCOTS, FEBRUARY 24, 1567[1]

[Endorsed by Cecil's clerk] Copy of the queen's majesty's letter to the queen of Scotland.

Madame:

My ears have been so deafened and my understanding so grieved and my heart so affrighted to hear the dreadful news of the abominable murder of your mad husband and my killed cousin[2] that I scarcely yet have the wits to write about it. And inasmuch as my nature compels me to take his death in the extreme, he being so close in blood, so it is that I will boldly tell you what I think of it. I cannot dissemble that I am more sorrowful for you than for him. O madame, I would not do the office of faithful cousin or affectionate friend if I studied rather to please your ears than employed myself in preserving your honor. However, I will not at all dissemble what most people are talking about: which is that you will look through your fingers[3] at the revenging of this deed, and that you do not take measures that touch those who have done as you wished, as if the thing had been entrusted in a way that the murderers felt assurance in doing it. Among the thoughts in my heart I beseech you to want no such thought to stick at this point. Through all the dealings of the world I never was in such miserable haste to lodge and have in my heart such a miserable opinion of any prince as this would cause me do. Much less will I have such of her to whom I wish as much good as my heart is able to imagine or as you were able a short while ago to wish. However I exhort you, I counsel you, and I beseech you to take this thing so much to heart that you will not fear to touch even him whom you have nearest to you[4] if the thing touches him, and that no persuasion will prevent you from making an example out of this to the world: that you are both a noble princess and a loyal wife. I do not write so vehemently out of doubt that I have, but out of the affection that I

1. *Source*: PRO, State Papers Scotland, Elizabeth 52/13/17, fol. 30r; copy, in French. (For original, see *ACFLO*, part 2.)

2. The twenty-one-year-old earl of Darnley, who had married Mary, Queen of Scots, in July 1565, was murdered February 10, 1567. Both Darnley and Mary were Elizabeth's second cousins once removed and potential claimants to her throne.

3. **look through your fingers** pretend to ignore (proverbial).

4. **nearest to you** James Hepburn (1536?–1578), fourth earl of Bothwell, whom Mary later married despite the fact that he was revealed to have been one of the chief conspirators in Darnley's murder.

bear you in particular. For I am not ignorant that you have no wiser counselors than myself. Thus it is that, when I remember that our Lord had one Judas out of twelve, and I assure myself that there could be no one more loyal than myself, I offer you my affection in place of this prudence.

As for the three things that have been communicated to me by Melvin,[5] I understand by all these instructions that you continue to desire greatly to satisfy me and that it will content you to grant the request that my Lord Bedford[6] made you in my name for the ratification of your treaty,[7] which has gone undone for six or seven years. I promise you that I demand it as much for your good as for whatever profit would result to me. About other matters I will not trouble you with a longer letter except to put you in contact with this gentleman and to thank you by this messenger for your good letters, which were and are very agreeable coming from your hands. Praying the Creator to give you the grace to recognize this traitor and protect yourself from him as from the ministers of Satan, with my very heartfelt recommendations to you, very dear sister. From Westminster February 24.

28 ଛ QUEEN ELIZABETH TO MARY, QUEEN OF SCOTS, JUNE 23, 1567[1]

[Endorsed by Cecil's clerk] 23 Junii, 1567. Copy of the queen majesty's letter to the queen of Scots by Robert Melville.[2]

Madame:

It hath been always held for a special principle in friendship that prosperity provideth but adversity proveth friends,[3] whereof at this time,

---

5. **Melvin** Robert, Lord Melville (1527–1621), then Scottish ambassador to England.

6. **Lord Bedford** Francis Russell (1527–1585), second earl of Bedford, a member of Elizabeth's Privy Council and, after February 1564, governor of Berwick. In November 1564, Bedford and Thomas Randolph had been named special representatives charged with the marriage negotiations involving Mary, Queen of Scots; Bedford had brought Elizabeth the news of the Darnley marriage.

7. Another reference to that perennial irritant, the Treaty of Edinburgh.

1. *Source:* PRO, State Papers Scotland, Elizabeth 52/13/71, fols. 137r–138v; draft, much corrected, in Cecil's hand. Mary had suddenly married James Hepburn, fourth earl of Bothwell, shortly after Bothwell acted as one of the murderers of Lord Darnley.

2. that is, to be delivered by Ambassador Melville.

3. Latin proverb: "*amicos res opimae pariunt, adversae probant.*"

finding occasion to verify the same with our actions, we have thought meet, both for our profession and your comfort, in these few words to testify our friendship, not only by admonishing you of the worst but to comfort you for the best. We have understand[4] by your trusty servant Robert Melville such things as you gave him in charge to declare on your behalf concerning your estate, and specially of as much as could be said for the allowance of your marriage. Madame, to be plain with you, our grief hath not been small that in this your marriage so slender consideration hath been had that, as we perceive manifestly, no good friend you have in the whole world can like thereof, and if we should otherwise write or say we should abuse you. For how could a worse choice be made for your honor than in such haste to marry such a subject, who besides other and notorious lacks, public fame hath charged with the murder of your late husband, beside the touching of yourself also in some part, though we trust that in that behalf falsely. And with what peril have you married him that hath another lawful wife alive,[5] whereby neither by God's law nor man's yourself can be his leeful[6] wife, nor any children betwixt you legitimate. This you see plainly, what we think of the marriage, whereof we are heartily sorry that we can conceive no better, what colorable[7] reasons soever we have heard of your servant to induce us. We wish, upon the death of your husband, your first care had been to have searched out and punished the murderers of our near cousin, your husband, which having been done effectually, as easily it might have been in a matter so notorious, there might have been many more things tolerated better in your marriage than now can be suffered to be spoken of. And surely we cannot but for friendship to yourself, besides the natural instinction that we have of blood to your late husband, profess ourselves earnestly bent to do anything in our power to procure the due punishment of that murder against any subject that you have, how dear soever you should hold him. And next thereto, to be careful how your son the prince[8] may be preserved, for

4. **understand** understood.

5. **wife alive** Lady Jean Gordon, sister of the earl of Huntly, from whom Bothwell obtained a divorce at the behest of Archbishop Hamilton on May 7, 1567. Bothwell and Mary's marriage contract was reportedly dated April 6, 1567; their marriage took place on May 15, 1567.

6. **leeful** just, lawful.

7. **colorable** plausible, fair seeming.

8. **prince** the infant James, later James VI of Scotland and James I of England.

the comfort of yours and your realm, which two things we have from the beginning always taken to heart, and therein do mean to continue. And would be very sorry but you should allow us therein, what dangerous persuasions soever be made to you for the contrary.

Now for your estate in such adversity as we hear you should be—whereof we could not tell what to think to be true, having a great part of your nobility (as we hear) separated from you[9]—we assure you that whatsoever we can imagine meet for your honor and safety that shall lie in our power, we will perform the same that it shall well appear you have a good neighbor, a dear sister, and a faithful friend, and so shall you undoubtedly always find and prove us to be indeed towards you. For which purpose we are determined to send with all speed one of our own trusty servants, not only to understand your state but also thereupon so to deal with your nobility and people as they shall find you not to lack our friendship and power for the preservation of your honor in quietness. And upon knowledge had what shall be further requisite to be done for your comfort and for the tranquility of your realm, we will omit no time to further the same, as you shall well see. And so we recommend ourselves to you, good sister, in as affectuous[10] a manner as heretofore we were accustomed. At our manor of Richmond, the 23rd of June, 1567.

9. **separated from you** After Mary's marriage to Bothwell on May 15, the outraged Scots nobles, Catholics as well as Protestants, met on June 1. They resolved to capture the queen and Bothwell as a means of restoring the liberty of the queen, preserving the life of the prince, and bringing Darnley's murderers to justice.

10. **affectuous** ardent, affectionate.

29 ❧ QUEEN ELIZABETH TO MARY, QUEEN OF SCOTS,
FEBRUARY 20, 1570[1]

[Headings inserted by Cecil's clerk] 20 Feb. 1569.[2] *Queen of England's letter to the queen of Scots. 20 February 1569. To the queen of Scots drawn by
Mr. Secretary Cecil.*

Madame:

I have well considered of your earnest, long letter d[elivered] to me
by the bishop of Ross,[3] who in the principal matters [of] the said letter
was able by reason of his sundry conferen[ces] heretofore had with me
to have either stayed you before [your] writing from such unquietness
of mind as your letter re[pre]senteth, or at the least upon the sending of
the same to have satis[fied] you with assurance of more goodwill and
care of you on [my] part than it seemeth by your letter you have by
bruits[4] and [by] untrue suggestions conceived of me. Wherein b[ecause]
I find myself somewhat wronged, yet for this present I set it [by], as imputing a great part thereof to others, who to ga[in] with you outwardly
make a gain of your favor to br[ing] you in doubt of me, that have in
your greatest dangers been your only approved friend and, when all
ways a[re] attempted, must be the chief pillar of your stay. And thus
bold am I at this present to declare min[e] ability to do you good above
all other your friends, see[ing] it seemeth nobody else of those whom
you trust [doth] you in remembrance thereof. But consider[ing] since
the sending of your letter I have had just cause [to] deny to the bishop

---

1. *Source:* BL, MS Cotton Caligula C.I, fols. 517r–519v; draft or copy with corrections in
Cecil's hand. The clerk's notation suggests that Cecil composed this letter. The extent of
Elizabeth's participation in its composition is uncertain. Elements supplied editorially to
repair damage to the MS are enclosed in square brackets.

By the time of this letter, Mary, Queen of Scots, had fled into England and was being held
in detention in the north. Her own preference had been for an immediate meeting with
Elizabeth, but that eventuality—if it was ever part of Elizabeth's plan—was postponed indefinitely by the revelation of Mary's proposed marriage to Thomas Howard (1536–1572),
fourth duke of Norfolk, and by the onset of the Northern Rebellion in the fall of 1569.

2. Old-style dating, by which 1570 officially began only on March 25.

3. **bishop of Ross** John Leslie (1527–1596), Mary's most trusted adviser and her principal commissioner for the conduct of her defense in England (September 1568–February
1569). Leslie numbered among the delegation who invited Mary to return from France
after the death of Francis II and take the throne of Scotland. In 1565 he became a member
of Mary's Privy Council, steering her ecclesiastical policy during her marriage to Darnley,
and in 1569 he was appointed ambassador to England.

4. **bruits** public rumors (from French).

of Ross such freedom of access ei[ther] to me or to others as he hath had,[5] whereby you may [get] advice from him, I have thought good with this mine own letter to impart somewhat to you whereby you may deliver yourself of such vain fears as others w[ish] you in, and not be bitten with sharper griefs th[an] your own doings hath or may nourish within your hea[rt]. Wishing nevertheless, howsoever your conscience may here[in] trouble you for your unkindness towards me and my state, yet that God may instruct you to consider your former dealings and direct you sincerely and unfainedly either to make me and my realm amends for things past, or if that cannot be in your power, yet to make your intentions manifestly appear to me how I and my states of my realm may be hereafter assured, that for my goodwill both past and to come no cause may ensue on the part of you and yours to the just offense of me and my realm. And in so doing or intending you may surely quiet your mind and conscience and be free from all suspicions that either flatterers or evil-disposed persons seek to nourish in you.

In your letter I note a heap of confused, troubled thoughts, earnestly and curiously uttered to express your great fear and to require of me comfort, concerning both which many kinds of speeches are diversly expressed and dispersed in your letter, that if I had not consideration that the same did proceed from a troubled mind, I might rather take occasion to be offended with you than to relent to your desires. For what can be said more unworthy of my former goodwill than in express words to doubt, without cause given by me, that any inventions of such whom you call your enemies with the aid of any whom you name your secret evil-willers about me (of which sort truly I know none) should be able to induce me to consent to anything that might touch your life, or for what respect of any of my doings past to you, madame, or to any other of meaner estate—yea, to any of mine own subjects? Need you to press me with the remembrance that I should not violate my w[ord] nor the laws of amity, of hospitality and parentage and such like, neither recompense your affections and fiance[6] put in [me], with any cruel conclusion? Or what example is t[here] extant of my actions to move you to remember unto me that th[ose] to whom favor hath been promised ought not to be treated [as] an enemy if the same be not first thereof ad-

5. Because of his inciting role in the Northern Rebellion against Elizabeth in the fall of 1569, Leslie, who had been Mary's staunch defender and personal agent at Elizabeth's court, was put in the custody of Edmund Grindal, bishop of London, in January 1570.

6. **fiance** affiance, trust.

vertised? For as you al[so] write, a mortal enemy will not assail his contrary without defiance before he strike him, and so forth you pass with divers speeches, which because they are through your whole letter so f[ull] of passions, I of compassion will leave to represent th[em] to your eyes. And will rather by some short remembrance [of] my former actions, full of goodwill, induce you t[o] believe and trust rather to me in all your difficulties than lightly to credit either bruits of the brainless vulgar or the viperous backbiters of the sowers of discord.

Good madame, what wrong did I ever s[eek] to you or yours in the former part of my reign, when y[ou] know what was sought against me, even to the sp[oil] of my crown from me? Did I invade your country and take or detain any part thereof, as all the wo[rld] knoweth I might, and as any king or queen of my condition, being so wronged, might with justice and ho[nor] have done? But therein my natural inclination to you overcame myself. Did I, when I might have, se[ll] or put to ransom the whole army of the French that were sent into Scotland on your behalf[7] to invade my realm and to oppress my crown? Did I not, I say, friendly send them home into France in my own ships? Yea, did I not victual them and lend them money? Was I not content to accord with your ambassadors (authorized by you and your husband) to remit all injuries past, to my great damage and charges? And what moved me thereto but my natural inclination towards you, with whom I desired to live as a neighbor and a good sister? After this, how patiently did I bear with many vain delays in not ratifying the treaty accorded by your own commission? Whereby I received no small unkindness, beside that manifest cause of suspicion that I might not hereafter trust to any[8] your treaties.

Then followed a hard manner of dealing with me, to entice my subject and near kinsman the Lord Darnley, under color of private suits for lands, to come into your realm, to proceed in treaty of marriage with him without my knowledge, yea to conclude the same without my assent or liking. And how many unkind parts accompanied that fact[9] by receiving of my subjects that were base renegades and offenders at home and enhancing them to places of credit against my will, with many such

---

7. During the so-called War of Insignia of 1559, when Mary was married to Francis II of France, both English and French troops had intervened in Scottish affairs—the English to shore up Scottish Protestants, the French to defend the Scottish monarchy against the zeal of the reformers.

8. **any** any of.   9. **fact** deed, action.

like, I will leave, for that the remembrance of them cannot but be noisome unto you. And yet all these did I (as it were) suppress and overcome with my natural inclination of love towards you, and did afterward gladly, as you know, christen your son,[10] the child of my said kinsman that had before so unloyally offended me both in marriage with you and in other undutiful usages towards me, his sovereign. How friendly dealt I also by messages to reconcile him (being your husband) and you when others nourished discord betwixt you, who (as it seemed) had more power to work their purposes, being evil to you both, than I to do you good without respect of the evil I had received.

Well I will overpass your hard accidents that followed for lack of following of my counsels. And in your most extremity—when you were a prisoner indeed,[11] not as you have [at] times noted yourself to be here in my realm, and then s[ought] notoriously by your evil-willers to the danger of your life—how far from my mind was the remembrance of any former unkin[dness] showed to me? Nay, how void was I of respect to the [hurt] that the world had seen attempted by you to my crow[n] and the security that might have ensued to my state [by] your death, when I, finding your calamity so great as you w[ere] at the pit's brink to have miserably lost your life, did not only entreat for your life but so threatened such as were irritated against you that (I only may say it) even I was the principal cause [to] save your life. And now, madame, if these my actio[ns] were at any time laid before your eyes or in your ears wh[en] malicious persons incense you with mistrust of me, I kn[ow yo]u would reject their whispering tales or false writings [and] messages and deal plainly with me, and not only [be] thankful for my good deeds, but would discover to me s[uch] pernicious persons as, to advance their own evil, seek to m[ake] you the instrument of inward troubles and rebellions in my realm. Whereof you see how frustrate their purpos[es] be by the goodness of almighty God, who rewardeth my sinc[ere] and good meaning with His blessings of peace, notwithstanding the vehement labors both of foreigners and domestics to trouble my state with wars.

If I should now enter into the accidents happened since flying for your succor out of Scotland into my realm, as well of your manner of

10. **christen your son** Elizabeth was James's godmother by proxy; the earl of Bedford had represented her at the christening in November 1566.

11. In 1567 Mary had been imprisoned on an island in Lochleven by her own Scottish subjects.

coming and your usages sithen that time, as of my benefits towards you, being [that] you have been charged with such heinous facts offensive to God and to the world, I should exceed the length of [a] letter and per-case[12] overmuch oppress you with remembrance of m[y] goodwill, an argument that I delight not to touch where so little hath been deserved. It m[ust] suffice to remember you how favorably I dealt in the trial of your great cause to stay from any open publication of the facts, how I have forborne to fortify your son's title by open act,[13] being by the states of your realm according to the laws of the same a crowned king, other-wise than for the conservation of the mutual peace betwixt the people of both the realms hath been thought very necessary and could not be avoided. But if I should remember to you your contrary late dealings by your ministers to engender and nourish troubles in my realm, to bolden my subjects to become rebels, to instruct and aid them how to continue in the same, and in the end to make invasions into my realm, I should percase move you to continue in your fear. From the which at this time of compassion I seek to deliver you, and indeed do earnestly wish you not only to be free from the fear expressed in your letters, but that you would minister to me hereafter a plain probation[14] and a demonstra-tion how I may be assured of some contrary course, both by yourself and your ministers, in answering with some like fruits of goodwill as mine hath been abundant. For otherwise surely both in honor and rea-son, not only for myself but for my people and my countries, I must be forced to change my course and, not with such remissness as I have used towards offenders, endanger myself, my state, and my realm.

And so for this time I think good, though the matter of your letter might have ministered to me occasion of more writing, to end. And to conclude, I have thought good to assure you that the restraining of the

12. **percase** perchance.

13. After Mary had escaped from Lochleven Castle and suffered a decisive defeat with her forces at Langside, she took flight and entered England on May 16, 1568. At the urging of the Privy Council, led by Cecil, Elizabeth convened a conference to investigate criminal charges against Mary, which climaxed in Elizabeth's being shown the notorious "casket letters" from Mary to Bothwell, which, if genuine, overtly implicated Mary in Darnley's murder. But Eliz-abeth adjourned the conference before a verdict had been reached. Moreover, after James Stewart (1531?–1570)—earl of Moray, regent of Scotland, and the infant James's uncle—was assassinated on January 23, 1570, leaving the Protestant cause in Scotland effectually leader-less, Elizabeth refused the urging of her Privy Council to recognize the proclamation of the young James as king, instead vowing to continue efforts to restore Mary.

14. **probation** proof.

bishop of Ross, your minister at this time, hath proceeded of many reasonable and necessary causes, as hereafter you shall understand, and not of any mind particularly to offend you, as the proof shall well follow, requiring you not to conceive hereby otherwise of me but that very necessity hath thereto urged me. And though he may not come to me, yet may you use your former manner in writing to me as you shall find meet. To the which you shall receive answers as the causes shall require, though he be not at the liberty which heretofore he had, otherwise than my favorable usage did provoke him. And so, madame, with my very hearty commendations, I wish you continuance of health, quietness of mind, and your heart's desire, to the honor of almighty God and contentation of your best friends, amongst whom in good right I may compare with any howsoever.

30 &ε· QUEEN ELIZABETH TO HENRY CAREY, LORD HUNSDON, FEBRUARY 26, 1570[1]

[Endorsed] 26 February, 1569[70]. Minute of the queen's majesty's letter to the lord of Hunsdon—Leonard Dacres.

By the queen.

Right trusty and well-beloved cousin, we greet you well. And right glad we are that it hath pleased God to assist you in this your late service against that cankered, subtle traitor Leonard Dacres,[2] whose force, being far greater in number than yours, we perceive you have overthrown, and how he thereupon was the first that fled, having as it seemeth a heart readier to show his unloyal falsehood and malice than to abide the fight. And though the best we could have desired was to have had him taken, yet we thank God that he is in this sort overthrown and

---

1. *Source*: PRO, State Papers, Addenda 1566–79, 15/17/113; secretarial copy with postscript that, in the original, was doubtless in Elizabeth's hand. Henry Carey (1524?–1596), Lord Hunsdon, a cousin of the queen, was lord warden of the Eastern Marches and governor of Berwick at the time this letter was written. The context is the Northern Rebellion: on February 20, 1570, as Hunsdon was marching toward Carlisle to link up with the main English forces, he and his party were ambushed by the rebel Leonard Dacres and three thousand men. Although outnumbered two to one, Hunsdon and his men carried the day, killing four hundred and taking three hundred prisoner.

2. **Leonard Dacres** or Dacre (died 1573), a relative of the duke of Norfolk who was deeply involved in the plot to free Mary, Queen of Scots.

forced to flee our realm to his like company of rebels, whom we doubt not but God of His favorable justice will confound with such ends as are meet for them. We will not now by words express how inwardly glad we are that you have had such success, whereby both your courage in such an inequal match, your faithfulness towards us, and your wisdom is seen to the world, this your act being the very first that ever was executed by fight in field in our time against any rebels. But we mean also in deeds by just reward to let the world see how much we esteem and can consider such a service as this is. And so we would have yourself also thank God heartly,[3] as we doubt not but you do (from whom all victories do proceed), and comfort yourself with that assurance of our most favorable acceptation. We have also herewith sent our letter of thanks to Sir John Forster,[4] and would have you namely thank our good, faithful soldiers of Berwick, in whose worthy service we do repose no small trust. 26 February 1569[70]

[Postscript] I doubt much, my Harry, whether that the victory were given me more joyed me or that you were by God appointed the instrument of my glory, and I assure you for my country's good the first might suffice, but for my heart's contentation[5] the second more pleased me. It likes me not a little that with a good testimony of your faith, there is seen a stout courage of your mind that more trusted to the goodness of your quarrel than to the weakness of your number. Well I can say no more. *Beatus est ille servus quem cum Dominus venerit invenerit faciendo sua mandata.*[6] And that you may not think that you have done nothing for your profit, though you have done much for your honor, I intend to make this journey somewhat to increase your livehood,[7] that you may not say to yourself, *Perditur quod factum est ingrato.*[8]

Your loving kinswoman, *Elizabeth R*

3. **heartly** heartily.
4. **Sir John Forster** a trusted border official in the north since 1559.
5. **contentation** contentment.
6. "Blessed is that servant whom, when the Lord comes, He will discover doing His commands" (an allusion to the parable of the vigilant servant, Matthew 24:45–47).
7. **livehood** livelihood.
8. "It [my service] is lost because it was done for an ingrate."

31 ᶜᵉ QUEEN ELIZABETH'S WARRANT TO PROCEED, IF NECESSARY,
TO TORTURE TWO OF THE DUKE OF NORFOLK'S MEN, SEPTEMBER
15, 1571[1]

*[Addressed] To our trusty and right well-beloved councillor Sir Thomas
Smith, knight, and to our trusty and well-beloved Doctor [Wil]son,[2] one
of the Masters of our Requests*

*[Endorsed] Received at the Tower the sixteenth day of September at
eleven of the clock in the forenoon, 1571*

Elizabeth R   By the queen.

Right trusty and well beloved, we greet you well, and finding in traitorous attempts lately discovered that neither Barker nor Bannister, the
duke of Norfolk's men, have uttered their knowledge in the under[3] proceeding of their master and of themselves, neither will discover the
same without torture; forasmuch as the knowledge hereof concerneth
our surety and estate, and that they have untruly already answered, we
will and by warrant hereof authorize you to proceed to the further examination of them upon all points that you can think by your discretions meet for knowledge of the truth. And if they shall not seem to you
to confess plainly their knowledge, then we warrant you to cause them
both, or either of them, to be brought to the rack, and first to move
them with fear thereof to deal plainly in their answers. And if that shall
not move them, then you shall cause them to be put to the rack, and to
fe[el][4] the taste thereof until they shall deal more plainly, or until you
shall think meet. And so we remit the whole proceeding to your further
discretion, requiring you to use speed herein, and to require the assistance of our lieutenant of the Tower. Given under our signet the 15th of
September 1571.

1. *Source*: BL, MS Cotton Caligula C.III, fol. 242r; text is in Cecil's hand, with Elizabeth's
outsized official signature, her "sign manual," in the upper left corner and seal still attached. The information wanted from Norfolk's men was evidence of his intriguing with
Mary, Queen of Scots, to marry her and seat her upon Elizabeth's throne.

2. **Sir Thomas Smith** (1513–1577) a member of the Privy Council commissioned to inquire into Norfolk's conspiracy. **Doctor Wilson** presumably Dr. Thomas Wilson, another
Protestant humanist and civil servant, better known as the author of *The Art of Rhetoric*
(1553) and *The Rule of Reason* (1552); he conveyed Norfolk to the Tower on September 7,
1571, and conducted interrogations for the next several weeks. Bracketed letters in Wilson's
name were covered up when MS was repaired.

3. **under** underhanded.

4. Bracketed letters have been lost at the worn page edge.

LETTER 31, ADDITIONAL DOCUMENT A LETTER OF THOMAS
HOWARD, DUKE OF NORFOLK, TO QUEEN ELIZABETH, SEPTEMBER
10, 1571[1]

*[Headed] A letter of submission written by the duke of Norfolk to the
queen's majesty after his last committing to the Tower.*

O my dread, dear, and sovereign lady and queen, and my most gracious
mistress,

When I consider with myself how far I have transgressed my duty to
your most excellent majesty, I dare not presume to look up or hope for
your gracious favor, I confess myself so far unworthy thereof. But again,
when I look of[2] your highness' manifold, merciful,[3] and most pitiful nature, of which so many have abundantly[4] since your majesty's most
prosperous reign, I am emboldened with a most penitent and sorrowful heart to make this, my trembling hand, to offer to your highness my
most humble and lowly submission, having no other means to ease my
oppressed mind.

I have for my sins and disobedience to ask pardon: that is, of almighty
God and of your most excellent majesty. The first I have done unto my
God, and so by the grace of Him I will continue with a new heart and
full mind of amendment, not doubting but asking mercy to receive it:
according to the Scripture, he that knocked[5] at the door shall have it
opened unto him. Now do I prostrate at your highness' gracious feet
myself, my poor children, and all that I have, hoping more on your most
gracious clemency than in any unadvised desert. I seek to excuse myself
no way, but wholly submit myself to what shall best please your most
merciful heart.

O most gracious sovereign lady, how many have run astray, who,
finding mercy, have afterward with good service redoubled their former follies? O noble queen, it is in your most gracious power to make of
my wretched mold what it pleaseth you. My faith and religion reserved
to my Savior, my body being already your highness' subject and pris-

---

1. *Source*: BL, MS Additional 32379 ("Discourses of Sir N. Bacon"), fols. 63r–64r; copy.
Another copy—Folger Library, MS V.b.214, fols. 93v–94r—offers some superior readings,
which we have indicated in the notes.

2. **of** Folger MS reads "into."

3. **merciful** Folger MS reads "mercies."

4. **abundantly** Folger MS reads "abundantly tasted."

5. **knocked** Folger MS reads "knocketh"; reference is to Matthew 7:8 and Luke 11:10.

oner by my desert, I dedicate my mind and heart to you forever, to be as it shall please your majesty to direct it. I do not seek favor at your majesty's hands for my former true service—I confess my undutifulness more now hath blotted the same. Nor I dare remember which heretofore was my greatest comfort, because I deserve not that honor, which was that it hath pleased your highness to account me your indeed unworthy kinsman.[6]

Woe worth the day that I entered into that matter which hath made such alteration of your most gracious favor unto me, and hath heaped upon myself these intolerable troubles! O unworthy wretch that I am, that in all the days of my life I have coveted nothing but a quiet life—I take God to witness—whatsoever (and if it please your highness) some have judged therein of me—and was unhappy to give ear to that which hath done[7] and ever was like to bring me to the contrary. O I dare not presume too long to trouble your excellent majesty with hearty, repentable, and pitiful lamentations, but shall not cease to make my most humble prayers to almighty God, that it will please Him of His merciful goodness to put in your highness' heart a mind to extend[8] your most gracious clemency. And then I doubt not but my service in time coming shall be such as your highness shall have no cause to repent your mercy extended upon me. And so, most humbly praying to God to continue your majesty long to reign over us here—if it be His will, to Nestor's years,[9] with all felicity and prosperity—with an overwhelmed heart and watery cheeks, even most lowly upon my knees I most humbly take my leave. From your highness' woeful Tower, the 10th of September, 1571.

> By the hand of your majesty's most humble
> subject, servant, and sorrowful prisoner,
> *Thomas Norfolk*

6. **kinsman** William Howard (1510?–1573)—first baron of Effingham, lord chamberlain until 1572—was a great-uncle of both Elizabeth and Norfolk, making them second cousins.

7. **done** Folger MS reads "undone me."

8. **to extend** written twice in MS.

9. Nestor, the white-haired king of Pylos, joined Agamemnon in the expedition against Troy although he was two generations older than the other commanders (Homer *Iliad* I:250).

32 ❧ DIGEST OF A LETTER FROM QUEEN ELIZABETH TO MARY, QUEEN OF SCOTS, FEBRUARY 1, 1572[1]

[Headed] 1 February 1571[2]. Minute of a letter from the queen's majesty to the queen of Scots, primo Februarii.

Madame:

Of late time I have received divers letters from you, to the which you may well guess by the accidents of the time why I have not made any answer, but specially because I saw no matter in them that required any such answer as could have contented you. And to have discontented you had been but an increase of your impatience, which I thought time would have mitigated as it doth commonly where the cause thereof is not truly grounded and that it be so understand.[2] But now, finding by your last letter the 27th of the last, an increase of your impatience tending also to many uncomely, passionate, and vindictive speeches, I thought to change my former opinion and by patient and advised words to move you to stay or else to qualify your passions, and to consider that it is not the manner to obtain good things with evil speeches, nor benefits with injurious challenges, nor to get good to yourself with doing evil to another.

And yet, to avoid the fault which I note you have committed in filling a long letter with multitude of sharp and injurious words, I will not by way of letter write any more of the matter, but have rather chosen to commit to my cousin the earl of Shrewsbury[3] the things which I have thought meet upon the reading of your letter to be imparted unto you, as in a memorial in writing he hath to show you. Wherewith, I think, if reason may be present with you and passion absent, at the reading you will follow hereafter rather the course of the last part of your letter than the first, the latter being written as in a calm and the former in a storm. Wishing to you the same grace of God that I wish to myself, and that He

1. *Source*: BL, MS Cotton Caligula C.III, fol. 145r; copy in a clerk's hand. A "minute" might be a copy or might be a digest of the fuller text of a letter for the purpose of retaining the gist only. The letter was written in the aftermath of the Northern Rebellion and the discovery of the Ridolfi Plot, which aimed to put Mary, Queen of Scots, on the English throne with the duke of Norfolk as her consort.

2. **understand** understood.

3. George Talbot (1528?–1590), sixth earl of Shrewsbury, was then and for many years Mary's host/jailer, as well as a member of the panel of judges who condemned the duke of Norfolk to death for high treason in January 1572.

may direct you to desire and attain to that which is meet for His honor and your quietness with contentation both of body and mind. Given at my palace of Westminster the first day of February, 1571[2].

> Your cousin that wisheth you a better mind.

33 ❧ QUEEN ELIZABETH TO WILLIAM CECIL, LORD BURGHLEY, APRIL 11, 1572[1]

[Endorsed by Burghley] 11 April 1572. The queen's majesty's with her own hand for staying of the execution of the D. O. [N.][2] Received at 2 in the morning.

My lord:

Methinks that I am more beholding to the hinder part of my head than well dare trust the forwards side of the same, and therefore sent to the lieutenant and the sergeant, as you know best, the order to defer this execution till they hear further. And that this may be done I doubt nothing without curiosity[3] of my further warrant, for that their rash determination upon a very unfit day was countermanded by your considerate admonition. The causes that move me to this are not now to be expressed, lest an irrevocable deed be in meanwhile committed. If they will needs a warrant, let this suffice, all written with mine own hand.

> Your most loving sovereign, *Elizabeth*

---

1. *Source*: Bodleian Library, University of Oxford, MS Ashmole 1729, art. 7, fol. 13; in Elizabeth's hand. (For original-spelling version, see *ACFLO,* part 1.) Elizabeth's middle-of-the-night dispatch to her secretary (created Lord Burghley in 1571) stayed the execution of the duke of Norfolk; he was put to death on June 2, 1572. See also Poem 5, "The Doubt of Future Foes," (p. 133), which was almost certainly composed about this time and within the context of the Northern Rebellion and the Ridolfi Plot.

2. **N** is absent from this MS and supplied from an eighteenth-century copy, Bodleian, MS Smith 68, art. 54, fol. 54.

3. **I doubt nothing without curiosity** I do not doubt at all, unless there is impertinent inquiry.

POEMS 4-5

4 ❧ NO CROOKED LEG, CIRCA 1565[1]

No crooked leg, no blearèd eye,
No part deformèd out of kind,
Nor yet so ugly half can be
As is the inward, suspicious mind.

Your loving mistress, *Elizabeth R*

---

1. *Source*: Windsor Castle, Royal Library, inscribed on the last leaf of Elizabeth's French psalter, an edition that cannot be readily identified because of missing front leaves; in Elizabeth's hand. (For her original-spelling version, see *ACFLO*, part 1.) In the original, the line breaks do not correspond with rhyme words. The lightly embellished, readily legible italic script suggests a date in the 1560s or 1570s. This may be the "obscure sentence" referred to by Burghley as written by the queen in "a book at Windsor" when she was "much offended with the earl of Leicester" in August 1565, hence our dating; see William Murdin, ed., *A Collection of State Papers Relating to Affairs in the Reign of Queen Elizabeth from the Year 1571 to 1596*, vol. 2 (London: William Bowyer, 1759), p. 760.

5 ❧ THE DOUBT OF FUTURE FOES, CIRCA 1571[1]

[Headed] Verses made by the queen's majesty

The doubt[2] of future foes
Exiles my present joy
And wit me warns to shun such snares
As threatens mine annoy.

For falsehood now doth flow   5
And subjects' faith doth ebb,
Which should not be if reason ruled
Or wisdom weaved the web.

But clouds of joys[3] untried
Do cloak aspiring minds   10

1. *Source:* Folger Library, MS V.b.317, fol. 20v; copy in a collection of historical materials, some of them relating to Mary, Queen of Scots, dated circa 1577. This poem first appears in miscellanies in the early 1570s and was doubtless written by Elizabeth in response to the threat posed by the Catholic queen's flight into Protestant England in 1568 and its aftermath. Although many of Elizabeth's subjects demanded that Mary be executed then, she was beheaded only in 1587, after which the poem took on new life as referring to that event. This was the most frequently anthologized of all Elizabeth's verses. It received honored place in George Puttenham's *Art of English Poesie* (London: R. Field, 1589) as an example of the "gorgious," the "last and principal figure of our poetical ornament," which attires language "with copious and pleasant amplifications and much variety of sentences all running upon one point and to one intent" (207).

   In the 1769 edition of Sir John Harington's *Nugae Antiquae,* the poem is introduced by the fragment of a letter that offers an interesting although possibly apocryphal account of how the poem entered circulation: "My Lady Willoughby did covertly get it on her majesty's tablet and had much hazard in so doing, for the queen did find out the thief and chid for spreading evil bruit of her writing such toys when other matters did so occupy her employment at this time, and was fearful of being thought too lightly of for so doing" (58).

   This poem exists in numerous MSS with many small variants, the most important of which are listed below. For a fuller list of variants, see Bradner (72–73) and Ruth Hughey, ed., *The Arundel Harington [sic] Manuscript of Tudor Poetry* (Columbus: Ohio State University Press, 1960), 1:276—the Harington family's version of the poem, cited below as Arundel. Other MSS cited below include Folger (our copy text); Bodleian, MS Rawlinson Poetical 108, fol. 44v, a copy from circa 1570; and a somewhat later MS, London, Inner Temple Library, MS Petyt 538, vol. 10, fol. 3v, where the poem is identified as "*per reginam* (by the queen)."

2. **doubt** Arundel reads "dread."

3. **joys** Puttenham reads "toys," as do later MSS that may well have been copied from his printed version.

Which turns to rage of late repent
By changèd course of winds.[4]

The top of hope supposed
The root of rue shall be[5]
And fruitless all their grafted guile,   15
As shortly you shall see.

Their dazzled eyes with pride,
Which great ambition blinds,
Shall be unsealed by worthy wights
Whose foresight falsehood finds.   20

The daughter of debate
That discord aye doth sow
Shall reap no gain where former rule
Still peace hath taught to know.[6]

No foreign banished wight   25
Shall anchor in this port:
Our realm brooks no seditious sects—[7]
Let them elsewhere resort.

My rusty sword through rest
Shall first his edge employ   30
To pull[8] their tops who seek such change
Or[9] gape for future joy.
                    Vivat Regina[10]

---

4. Lines 11–12 vary significantly among MSS. Arundel has "Which turn to rage of late report, by changèd course of minds." Puttenham has "Which turn to reign of late repent, by course of changèd winds." Petyt has "Which turn to rain of late repent by changèd course of winds."

5. Lines 13–14 vary significantly: Rawlinson has "The top of hope suppressed, the root upreared shall be." Arundel has "The tops of hope suppose, the root of rue shall be." Puttenham and Petyt have "The top of hope supposed, the root of ruth will [Petyt 'shall'] be."

6. **Still peace hath taught to know** Puttenham reads "Hath taught still peace to grow."

7. **Our realm brooks no seditious sects** Puttenham reads "Our realm it brooks no stranger's force."

8. **pull** all other MSS read "poll," cut off. Cf. the gardener's scene in Shakespeare's *Richard II* 3.4.

9. **Or** spelling in MS reads "our."   10. "Long live the Queen."

PRAYERS 3 – 28
POEM 6

❦

PRAYERS 3–9
Private Prayers of Queen Elizabeth at Court, 1563[1]

3 ❧ A COLLECT[2]

Sovereign Lord, omnipotent God, Father of mercies, God of all grace,
who hast made me according to Thine image so that I might praise

---

1. *Source: Precationes privatae. Regiae E. R.* (London: T. Purfoot, 1563) (*STC* 7576.7), sigs.
Aii r–Fi r. This small volume (sextodecimo gathered in eights) is entirely in Latin and intersperses collections of scriptural verses and prayers by Elizabeth in its first section. The
next section is occupied by her commonplace book (sigs. Fii r–Kvi r). The final section
(sigs. Kvii r–Mviii v) comprises lists of the civil and ecclesiastical offices of the realm. Here
we include only the prayers from the first section. (For the original Latin of the materials
translated here and transcriptions of the versicles and other materials not included here,
see *ACFLO*, part 2, where biblical references are noted and evidence for Elizabeth's authorship is discussed.)

The publication of this volume may well have been motivated by Elizabeth's desire to
make a public demonstration of gratitude to God for her recovery from a near-fatal case of
smallpox in October 1562. A near prototype is Queen Katherine Parr's highly psalmic
Prayers or Meditations (London: Thomas Berthelet, 1545), which the twelve-year-old Elizabeth translated into Latin, French, and Italian as a New Year's gift for Henry VIII. Another
relevant prototype is the English translation of a Latin collection by Bishop John Fisher,
which Henry VIII authorized for publication in a series of editions (*STC* 3001.7ff.). The
collection quickly became known as *The King's Psalms.*

2. **Collect** a comparatively short prayer, condensed in form and aiming at one or two
closely related points; used in Western Christianity from an early date in worship connected with a specific occasion or season.

Thee, even I whom Thou hast redeemed by Thy Son Jesus Christ, so that I might acknowledge Thee: Pour out upon me the bowels of Thy mercies, that Thy handmaid may acquire a heart for praying to Thee and a mouth for sounding forth Thy praises. Indue me with Thy Holy Spirit, so that when my desires are spurned, I may humbly seek the things that please Thee and may serve Thy glory. From the dwelling place which Thou hast prepared, look upon me, Thy handmaid, and hear my prayer. Illumine Thy holy face that, as I serve Thee, I may learn Thy way on earth, which may lead me to Thee. Ignite my heart with desire for Thee, so that I seek Thee above all things and in all things. May I love Thee who art my Strength, my Refuge, and my Deliverer; may I fear Thy majesty, who alone art powerful; and, as Thou dost wonders, may Thy wisdom be fixed in my soul, that it may teach me Thy will; and write Thy law into the center of my heart, which may direct me in all Thy ways. Thou art the King of heaven and earth, King of kings. O King, may I Thy handmaid and Thy universal people committed to me be readied by Thy grace in all things to proclaim Thy glory and to acknowledge Thy supreme sovereignty, through Jesus Christ, amen.

4 ॐ A COLLECT[3]

Merciful God and most kind Father, long-suffering and of great compassion, and true to Thy Word, who dost not wish the death of a sinner, but rather that he be converted and live: Create in me a clean heart, O God, which may truly declare Thy mercy and my misery. For Thou art my God and my King; I am Thy handmaid and the work of Thy hands. To Thee therefore I bend the knees of my heart; against myself I confess my impiety. I have sinned, I have sinned, Father, against heaven and in

---

3. The "versicles" (short scriptural phrases) preceding this prayer are of particular interest:

Enter not into judgment with Thy handmaid,
For in Thy sight no man living shall be justified.
If Thou wilt mark iniquities, O Lord,
Lord, who will be able to stand?
From my secret ones cleanse me;
From those of others spare Thy handmaid.
Many sins have been forgiven her.
She has loved much.

Thy sight; I am unworthy the whole of Thy compassion. I have not kept Thy covenant, nor have I walked in Thy law. I have abandoned Thee, O God, my Maker; I have withdrawn from Thee, my Savior. I have strayed from Thy counsels. Deal not with me in proportion to my sins, nor requite me according to my iniquities. Turn away Thy anger from me, I pray, and make me find grace in Thy sight according to the greatness of Thy mercies. May Thy goodness conquer my badness; may Thy patience overcome my sins.

For Thou art the God of compassion, and long-suffering. Justice is Thine, O Lord, and mercy, and propitiation; but mine is confusion upon my face on account of my iniquities. Restore Thou my entire love for Thy holy name. Grant me a penitent heart, O Thou who dost disregard the sins of men on account of their penitence. Say unto my soul, "I am thy health." Be propitious, most merciful Father, to me and to Thy people committed to me; when we confess that mercy is in Thee alone, vouchsafe that we do not thereafter offend Thy majesty, but live to Thee in holiness and justice all the days of our life, through Thy mercy in Christ Jesus, amen.

5 ❧ A COLLECT

Lord God of mercy, my and my people's King, I acknowledge Thy great name, for Thou hast made Thyself a helper and a protector to me. I will extol Thee highly, God of my salvation, who hast freed my body from perdition and rescued me from the hands of those who sought my soul. Thy hand, O God, hath preserved me in an evil time; Thy grace hath looked with favor upon me since my youth and from that time has miraculously set me up in this Thy kingdom.

What am I, Lord God, or what is the house of my fathers, that Thou shouldst do this great mercy unto us? Thou makest peace in my days; Thy arm in strength has fought for me and my people against all our enemies. Thou hast given Thy holy law that we may fear Thee, and Thou hast led us from our straying ways into the right ways. Thy divine benefits are infinite. Fill us with Thy grace, most kind Father, that we may not forget these many things that Thou hast done for us, but that we may magnify Thy holy name in all things, that my mouth may ever speak Thy praise, and my people may bless Thee forever; that all may know that Thou alone art God, nor is there any other before Thee, who, one with the Son and the Holy Spirit, reigneth God, immortal and glorious forever, amen.

6 &❧ A COLLECT

Almighty, eternal God, Lord of lords, King of kings, to whom is all power, who hast constituted me prince of Thy people and by Thy mercy alone hast made me sit on the throne of my father, I Thy handmaid am slight of age, and inferior in understanding of Thy law. Give me, I pray, a teachable heart, that I may know what is acceptable before Thee at all times, that I may be able to judge Thy people justly, and discern between good and evil. Send from heaven the Spirit of Thy wisdom, that He may lead me in all my doings. Fill my heart with a sense of this; may Thy true wisdom give knowledge and counsel and understanding from Thy mouth.

May Thy grace (by which I may set in order these Thy many people in equity and justice) attend upon those appointed as Thy ministers to be pious, upright, and prudent. Impart Thy Spirit to them that I may administer justice in Thy fear without acceptation of persons.[4] Grant me faithful councillors, who by Thy counsel will advise me about my kingdom. Grant good shepherds, who may feed diligently from Thy Word Thy sheep committed to them, and that all ministers in zeal for justice may discharge their office for Thee. O my God, God of all power and mercy, govern all Thy people by Thy most holy Spirit, so that they may religiously worship Thee, excellent Prince and only Power, with true service; and may quietly be subject unto me, their queen on earth by Thy ordinance; and may in obedience to Thee live together in mutual peace and concord.

Grant, most loving Father, for the glory of Thy name, to all ranks of this Thy kingdom the fulness and continuation of Thy peace, that they by turns may devote themselves to one another in charity, that they may love each other and do each other kindnesses, that they each may walk in their vocation, piously, justly, and soberly. That I myself may rule over each one of them by Thy Word in care and diligence, infuse the spirit of Thy love, by which both they to me may be joined together very straitly, and among themselves also, as members of one body. Do this, God of all charity, so that not with the fear of severity or the sword,

---

4. **acceptation of persons** favoritism based on a person's rank.

but with royal passion and divine fear I may administer this Thy kingdom. Be present also, God most high, Governor and Ruler of every prince, by whom kings rule, to whom belongs all strength and an arm stretched out everywhere. God of peace and concord, who hast chosen me Thy handmaid to be over Thy people that I may preserve them in Thy peace, be present and rule me with the Spirit of Thy wisdom, that according to Thy will I may defend a Christian peace with all peoples. In Christ Thy Son (who is our peace) make us all be of one accord, so that Thy enemies may be ruled by Thy hand, and confound them with Thy outstretched arm. Thou Thyself give us Thy peace, because there is no other who fights for us if not Thou, our God, who alone art strong, maintaining Thy covenant and mercy towards those who walk before Thee with their whole heart. Incline our hearts to Thee, that we may walk in all Thy ways and keep Thy commandments. Under Thy sovereignty, princes reign and all the people obey. Since Thou art the supreme King and Protector, may we all serve Thee in unity of spirit to Thy eternal glory. Through Jesus Christ Thy Son, our Lord, to whom with the Father and Holy Spirit be all honor and power in every age.

7 ❧ THANKSGIVING FOR RECOVERED HEALTH

Most good and most great Savior Jesus Christ, Son of the living God, who hast come to earth among mortals, by Thee all sicknesses having been dispelled and sins of the faithful remitted, Thou hast declared Thyself to be, in the world, that sole heavenly and truly perfect Physician, as of souls, so also of bodies. And Thou wert the same when one was turning from vice to Thee: when Thou wast consorting with sinful men, Thou hast witnessed in clear words, saying, "A physician was needful not to those who were well, but to those who were sick."

Behold here, most merciful Jesus, a subject not unworthy of Thee with respect to Thy power and likewise Thy mercy. Behold me, Thy handmaid, whom Thou hast heaped with immense and infinite benefits from my beginning years onwards; who, descended from a king, raised to the dignity of a kingdom, Thou hast placed in the highest rank of honor among mortals, not by any means because of my merit, but rather because of Thy freely bestowed goodness and kindness toward me. Yet now, regarding the selfsame me, whether lest (after the saying) the too abundant success of worldly things might seize my soul athwart and draw me from myself into forgetfulness of my duty to Thee, or whether, supplied with the highest favors by Thy divine liberality and made queen of Thy people, I never acknowledge from my soul what I owe, and never confess fully enough what it is to be subject to Thy majesty, and Thy handmaid; nor show myself pleasing to Thee as my most beneficent Savior, nor compliant enough to Thee as my most merciful Lord; or whether for other reasons Thou thinkest it best in Thy divine wisdom, I say now, as Thy handmaid of late, whether by being healthfully warned or justly punished and, thus corrected and amended by grace, Thou hast affected me in this body with a most dangerous and nearly mortal illness.[5] But Thou hast likewise gravely pierced my soul with many torments; and besides, all the English people, whose peace and safety is grounded in my sound condition as Thy handmaid nearest after Thee, Thou hast strongly disregarded in my danger, and left the people stunned. Nevertheless and truly, by Thy judgment, most mild Savior, having remembered Thy handmaid in the accustomed goodness of Thy mercy, beyond all hope and all human power, freeing her from present danger of death, hast appeared both in my sudden and dire illness, and more, in my sudden and unexpected remedy by Thy mercy in a matter wholly despaired of. Thou hast shown and declared Thy divine power conjoined with ineffable mercy to the eyes of men.

Complete, most merciful Savior, the work of health upon Thy handmaid that Thou hast compassionately begun; finish, O perfect Physician, the cure that Thou hast mildly undertaken. Heal my soul; I having been pardoned for my ingratitude towards Thee, my forgetfulness of Thee, and all my other offenses against Thy majesty, may my sins be wholly obliterated and destroyed. Heal my mind, forming and framing me by Thy heavenly grace that I may bear patiently and with an equable spirit this sickness sent upon me by Thee; and furthermore at the same time heal my body, so that it may straightway be without any remains of sickness, if it should seem thus to Thy mercy. Impart purity and restore soundness throughout, so that Thy handmaid, by medicine made by Thee Thyself, may recover from all sickness equally of body and soul; and following the perfect health of both, by Thy favor, that she herself, together with all of Thy English peoples, by this danger may teach the reverence and due obedience that must be shown to Thy majesty; and, for freedom from such danger and perfect health by Thy supreme favor, may honor and celebrate Thy mildness, goodness, and kindness with

---

5. Reference is to Elizabeth's near-fatal case of smallpox in October 1562.

continual praise and perpetual thanksgiving. To whom, one with Thy heavenly Father and the Holy Spirit, as One, livest immortal, infinite, glorious God, to whom is all sovereignty, power, and majesty through everlasting ages, amen.

8 ❧ THANKSGIVING FOR BENEFITS CONFERRED

Eternal God, Creator and Accomplisher of all things, and the same most merciful Father to those who are faithful to Thee, when I think how of late I was altogether nothing—without body, without soul, without life, without sense or any understanding—and when I think that at this point I was as clay in the hand of the potter, so that by Thy will Thou mightst make me a vessel of honor or of disgrace, Thou hast willed me to be not some wretched girl from the meanest rank of the common people, who would pass her life miserably in poverty and squalor, but to a kingdom Thou hast destined me, born of royal parents and nurtured and educated at court. When I was surrounded and thrown about by various snares of enemies, Thou hast preserved me with Thy constant protection from prison and the most extreme danger; and though I was freed only at the very last moment,[6] Thou hast entrusted me on earth with royal sovereignty and majesty.

Beyond this, indeed, when I consider how many—not only from among the common people but also from the nobility as well as royal blood, by Thy hidden but just judgment—some are miserably deformed in body, others (more miserably by far) destitute of wit and intelligence, still others (by far the most miserable) disordered in their mind and reason, and finally how many were and are, even today, insane and raging. Indeed, I am unimpaired in body, with a good form, a healthy and substantial wit, prudence even beyond other women, and beyond this, distinguished and superior in the knowledge and use of literature and languages, which is highly esteemed because unusual in my sex. Finally I have been endowed with all royal qualities and with gifts worthy of a kingdom, and have been given these freely by Thee. I perceive how much I owe to Thy goodness, most merciful Father, for other things that are from Thee, even though of these other things I have not at all been deserving beforehand.

6. **last moment** on one level, an autobiographical reference to her extreme danger in the final months of her sister Mary's reign.

What truly can I first have deserved of Thee, who had my being before, and began to be, and am thus, by Thee and Thy free gift? O Thou who hast presented, adorned, and honored me with so many and so great benefits, grant me the divine grace of Thy Spirit, that I may understand the immensity of Thy kindness to me, that I may frankly acknowledge Thee as my Author, that I may be perpetually pleasing to Thee, not by any gift as if proud that it is mine, for I have received all things from Thee; not as if I first have deserved, when I have received all things freely beyond my deserts and beyond my prayers. Grant, I say, that I may understand this Thy immense generosity to me to be equally a burden and an honor, and that I may remember that it will be required—for much is, from those to whom Thou hast given much[7]— that I may rightly and perpetually use upright governance towards Thy people, and sound administration of the kingdom and Thy commonwealth, and indeed principally and above all, use Thy gifts to Thy illustrious glory as the Author of the gifts. To whom, One with Thy Son Jesus Christ, our Savior, and with the Holy Spirit, one immortal God, all thanks, honor, and glory is due from all for everlasting ages, amen.

9 ❧ PRAYER FOR WISDOM IN THE ADMINISTRATION OF THE KINGDOM

Almighty God and King of all kings, Lord of heaven and earth, by whose leave earthly princes rule over mortals, when the most prudent of kings who administered a kingdom, Solomon, frankly confessed that he was not capable enough unless Thou broughtst him power and help, how much less am I, Thy handmaid, in my unwarlike sex and feminine nature, adequate to administer these Thy kingdoms of England and of Ireland, and to govern an innumerable and warlike people, or able to bear the immense magnitude of such a burden, if Thou, most merciful Father, didst not provide for me (undeserving of a kingdom) freely and against the opinion of many men. Instruct me from heaven, and give help so that I reign by Thy grace, without which even the wisest among the sons of men can think nothing rightly.

Send therefore, O inexhaustible Fount of all wisdom, from Thy holy heaven and the most high throne of Thy majesty, Thy wisdom to be ever with me, that it may keep watch with me in governing the com-

7. Cf. Luke 12:48.

monwealth, and that it may take pains, that it may teach me, Thy handmaid, and may train me that I may be able to distinguish between good
and evil, equity and iniquity, so as rightly to judge Thy people, justly to
impose deserved punishments on those who do harm, mercifully to
protect the innocent, freely to encourage those who are industrious and
useful to the commonwealth. And besides, that I may know what is acceptable to Thee alone, vouchsafe that I wish, dare, and can perform it
without paying respect to any earthly persons or things. So that when
Thou Thyself, the just Judge, who askest many and great things from
those to whom many and great things are entrusted, when Thou requirest an exact accounting, charge me not with badly administering my
commonwealth and kingdom. But if by human thoughtlessness or infirmity Thy handmaid strays from the right in some thing, absolve me of it
by Thy mercy, most high King and most mild Father, for the sake of Thy
Son Jesus Christ; and at the same time grant that after this worldly kingdom has been exacted of me, I may enjoy with Thee an eternity in Thy
heavenly and unending kingdom, through the same Jesus Christ, Thy
Son and the Assessor of Thy kingdom, our Lord and Mediator. To whom
with Thee and with the Holy Spirit, one everlasting King, immortal, invisible, only-wise God, be all honor and glory forever and ever, amen.

PRAYERS 10–28 · POEM 6
Queen Elizabeth's Prayers and Poems, 1569[1]

———•———

The French Prayers and Poems
A SHORT FORMULARY FOR PRAYER

10 ࣮ PREFACE

O Lord, good God and Father, may Thy name be blessed forever. Dispose my heart, open my lips, and lead me by Thy Holy Spirit to a true

---

1. *Source: Christian Prayers and Meditations in English, French, Italian, Spanish, Greek, and*
Latin (London: J. Day, 1569) (*STC* 6428), sigs. Hh.i r–Ll.i v. Despite references to the "queen"
in various languages in the closing section of the volume reproduced here, Elizabeth's
name nowhere appears. Her authorship of these prayers, and perhaps one of the verses, is
indicated, however, by a variety of strong evidence. Elizabeth's royal arms supply the orna-

acknowledgment of all my faults, so that my prayer may be heard by Thee in the name of Thy Son Jesus Christ, amen.

CONFESSION OF SINS

O Lord my God, eternal and almighty God, I acknowledge and confess before Thy holy and high majesty that I, being conceived and born in iniquity and corruption, have never ceased since my birth and every day do not cease from transgressing Thy commandments. Doing this, I cannot, according to Thy just judgment, avoid ruin and perdition: being displeased nevertheless at having offended Thee, and condemning both myself and my sin; since it hath pleased Thee to love us even when we were Thy enemies. In witness thereof Thou hast given Thy only and well-beloved Son, our Lord Jesus Christ, as a Mediator and Advocate between Thee and us, with the promise of obtaining in His name all that we shall ask of Thee. Vouchsafe therefore, most kind God and merciful Father, in His name and in His favor to give me pardon and mercy. And in purifying my heart of every vanity and defilement, direct and lead me by Thy Holy Spirit in all my ways, in order that I may walk according to Thy holy and divine commandments all the days of my life, to the glory of Thy name, by Thy same well-beloved Son, amen.

11 ࣳ⁊ MORNING PRAYER

My God, my Father, and my Savior, as Thou now sendest Thy sun upon the earth to give corporeal light to Thy creatures, vouchsafe also to illumine my heart and understanding by the heavenly light of Thy Holy Spirit, that I neither think nor say nor do anything unless to serve and please Thee. During this whole day may my principal purpose be to

---

ments on its first and last leaves, and the frontispiece shows her kneeling in prayer before a private altar on which she has placed her crown; the illustration is captioned *Elizabeth Regina.* It would have been impossible to publish such a volume without Elizabeth's knowledge and approval. Moreover, within the volume, gendered self-references are feminine throughout, and the frequent anglicisms are characteristic of Elizabeth's habitual practice. (See *ACFLO,* part 2, where the foreign language originals of these compositions are transcribed and the frontispiece is reproduced.) In its sixteenth-century printed form, the octavo volume also had elaborate pictorial borders, many with scriptural commentary—though often unrelated to the text and reused from a previous printing project. The book may well have been intended as a Tudor Protestant substitute for the illuminated Books of Hours that had been so popular as an aid to lay piety in England under Catholicism.

walk in Thy fear, to serve Thee and honor Thee, expecting all luck and prosperity from Thy blessing alone. As for my body and my soul, mayst Thou be my Protector, strengthening me against all the temptations of the devil and of the flesh, preserving me from the encroachments and conspiracies of all my enemies, their accomplices, and adherents. And, good God, inasmuch as there is nothing well begun if one does not persevere, may it please Thee not only to receive me under Thy guidance and protection for this day, but for the whole course of my life, continuing and increasing from day to day the gifts and graces of Thy Holy Spirit in me until I, being united and conjoined with Thy only Son my Savior, may enjoy that blessed life which Thou hast promised to all Thy elect, through Thy same Son, our Lord Jesus Christ, amen.

12 ❧ THANKSGIVING

O all-good and all-wise God, heavenly Father, full of mercy and mildness, in compacting into memory the works of Thy hands I cannot but admire Thy great wisdom and infinite goodness, which Thou hast declared towards all Thy creatures, and singularly in regard to me, as in having given me being, movement, and life; but also, besides these infinite benefits that Thou distributest commonly to all men on earth, Thou hast given me so many special graces that it is impossible for me to rehearse them or even be able to comprehend them. It has pleased Thee by the light of Thy Gospel to deliver me from the shadows of error and ignorance—truly, to pull me back from the abyss of death and from the horrible confounding for which I was destined according to the corruption of my nature—and so Thou hast transported me to the kingdom of Thy well-beloved Son, who according to Thy pleasure and eternal decree gave Himself for my sins. There is this also, O Lord: that having received me into Thy Church among the number of Thy children, Thou hast raised me and chosen me by Thy wonderful providence to confer on me under the majesty of Thy greatness a state of honor and excellence, to wit, royal dignity for the government and preservation of Thy people.

But now, according to the word of David, what shall I render unto the Lord for all His benefits towards me?[2] I know that my whole life

2. Psalm 116:12.

ought to be devoted to a perpetual thanksgiving, to proclaim with the holy flock and redeemed people the goodness of Him who has called us from the shadows to His marvelous light. The cup of deliverance should never leave my hands, nor should the new songs ever leave my mouth. But O Lord, give me grace as formerly Thou didst to David, a man according to Thy heart, who treating this same subject and reciting the testimonies of Thy goodness, said: "Thus it is, Lord, I am Thy manservant, I am Thy manservant, the son of Thy chambermaid; Thou hast broken my bonds. I will offer unto Thee an offering of thanksgiving and entreat the name of the Lord."[3] Thus I say, Lord, of myself, and say it by Thy grace: I am Thy maidservant, I am Thy maidservant. Thou hast broken my bonds, and hast preserved me in the midst of mortal dangers; Thou hast set me at large and in safety. To the everlasting King, immortal and invisible, to God, who alone is good and alone is wise, be honor and glory forever and ever, through Jesus Christ His Son our Savior, amen.

13 ⟪ PRAYER FOR THE WHOLE KINGDOM AND BODY OF THE CHURCH ACCORDING TO THEIR ESTATES AND MEMBERS

O God almighty, heavenly Father, Thou hast given commandment to Thy faithful ones to pray one for another with the promise to hear them in the name of the Mediator, Thy well-beloved Son. I, therefore, Thy humble maidservant, in the confidence of Thy promises and in consideration of such great and urgent necessities that present themselves on every side—Satan making every effort to put the earth into confusion and especially to hinder the course of Thy Gospel—Lord, good God, who art my refuge and my hope, I beseech Thee and beg Thee, as Thou art the Father of lights,[4] that it may please Thee to illumine the hearts and understandings of all men, inasmuch as Thou desirest all peoples to be saved and to come to the knowledge of truth, and as Thou hast specially ordained that kings and all those who are placed in dignity are to be prayed for, so that human society might live in peace and tranquility with all piety and honesty. I, therefore, knowing how weighty crowns and scepters are, and that the managing of them is difficult to discharge well—whether with regard to Thee, my God, or to my sub-

3. Psalm 116:16–17.   4. James 1:17.

jects—I beg Thee with all my heart, as much for me as for all others
whom Thou hast constituted in the same degree of preeminence, to
give us that which a Solomon once asked of Thee, whose prayer Thou
approvedst as having been put into his heart and his mouth by Thy
Holy Spirit, which teaches us to pray that Thou wilt help our infirmities.

O Lord, good God, Thou hast made me to reign in the midst of Thy
people; Thou wilt give to Thy maidservant and to Thy menservants an
understanding heart to judge Thy people and to distinguish good from
evil, so that we may not be unprofitable or, worse, pernicious in a vocation so holy as this. Give us also prudent, wise, and virtuous councillors,
driving far from us all ambitious, malignant, wily, and hypocritical ones.
Give us for judges true men who hate greediness and who shun acceptation of persons, so that my people may be governed in all equity and
righteousness, the virtuous sustained in their justice and innocence, the
wicked punished and chastised according to their faults. Also, O Lord,
make that all those whose charge Thou hast committed into my hand
render to me the duty of a just obedience, so that there will be a good and
holy union between the head and the members, and that by this means all
may know that on Thee alone depends the state of kingdoms and the
government of nations. And may I therefore ever sing in Thy praise the
song of David, where he claims to do the duty of a good prince:

PSALM 101[5]
A wish seized me to sit and write
A psalm that told of good and right;
If Thou willst, my God, I'll sing it Thee
And bring it Thee.

I will not walk my path amiss.   5
When wilt Thou make me king of peace?
I'll rule my house with heart all pure,
With reason sure.

Of no bad thing will I wish sight,
I hate their lives who do no right;   10

5. The following stanzas are the work of the French Protestant poet Clément Marot
(1496–1544) and were first published in his *Trente-deux Pseaulmes de David* . . . (Paris: E.
Roffet, [1543]).

To have e'en one attached to me
Shall never be.

Every heart with thought disloyal
Will I dislodge from my court royal;
The bad will find no welcome here,   15
And no good cheer.

Who loads his neighbor with slanders sly,
Who's crass of heart and haughty of eye,
I'll abase the one; hold th'other for true
I cannot do.   20

My eyes will be most sharp to find
Dwellers on earth of faithful mind
To me; for he who has true sight
Will serve me right.

He who takes pains to use deceit   25
Within my house will find no seat;
Never from me will liar or babbler
Get gift or favor.

In good time I'll banish from this place
All wicked ones, keeping none of such race;   30
Fear of the Lord will cleanse the city
From iniquity.

I also pray Thee, true Father and Savior, for all those whom Thou hast ordained true pastors of Thy faithful, and to whom Thou hast entrusted the cure of souls and the dispensation of Thy holy Gospel, that Thou mayst lead them by Thy Holy Spirit so that they may be found faithful and diligent in their holy vocation. And furthermore I pray Thee to drive out false shepherds, men corrupt in their understanding, fell wolves, ambitious and avaricious, who only serve to destroy and lead astray Thy Churches. And inasmuch as Thou requirest in all Thy children the zeal of Thy house,[6] give me the grace to cleanse my people

6. Psalm 69:9; John 2:17.

of all sects, heresies, and superstitions, so that Thy Churches under my charge may thrive and grow from day to day in the truth of Thy Gospel to all justice and sanctity.

May it generally please Thee to make deliverance and restoration of Thy Churches throughout the earth, to send workmen to Thy harvest —able men and sufficient to gather in the poor lost sheep with the crook of that great Shepherd of souls, Thy Son Jesus Christ. As for those hearers who already profess Thy name, grant them true perseverance in faith, in charity, and in all good works for the glory of Thy name and to their salvation. As for others who still walk in the vanity of their senses, touch Thou their hearts and give them illumined eyes, so that all may order themselves to serve and please Thee.

Finally, O God of all consolation, I pray Thee to have pity on the calamities and afflictions of all Thy creatures in general: the peoples whom Thou visitest with sickness, wars, or famines; the persons whom Thou afflictest with poverty, prison, illness, banishment, or other of Thy rods, whether in body or in spirit. And especially mayst Thou have pity on Thy elect who suffer and endure for the witness of Thy holy Gospel.

And as it hath pleased Thee to do me this goodness and this honor—to give repose to my land, other kingdoms being in horrible confusion—and that Thou hast sent to me the bowels of Thy Son Jesus Christ to give them refuge in their afflictions, give me the grace to be a true nourisher and nurse of Thy people according to the word of Thy prophet Isaiah, to have true compassion, as much on those who are here as on all others, to the end that at the accomplishing of Thy promises, when the word will be said: "Come you blessed of my Father, possess the kingdom that has been prepared for you since the foundation of the world,"[7] that Thou mayst receive me, O heavenly Father, into the number of Thy children, for the love of Thy Son, my Savior Jesus Christ, to whom with Thee and the Holy Spirit be honor and glory everlasting, amen.

14 ❧ EVENING PRAYER

Lord my God, my Father and my Savior, prostrating myself in all humility before Thy holy majesty I beseech Thee very lovingly, as Thou hast given me the grace to come to the end of this day, more especially

7. Matthew 25:34.

as Thou hast created the night for man's rest, that Thou mayst do me this favor along with Thy other infinite benefits—to let me so rest this night for the relieving of my infirmity, that my heart being always raised to Thee, my soul may also have its spiritual rest as the body takes its own rest. May my sleep be in no way excessive, gratifying my flesh with ease beyond measure, but only for the necessity of my nature, so that tomorrow I may be better disposed to Thy service.

Preserve me also from all defilement of body and spirit, and keep me from the temptations of the enemy and from all dangers that could befall me. And because this day has not passed by without my having offended Thee in several ways and kinds, as Thou sendest now darkness in the absence of the sun to hide all things, even so mayst Thou blot out all my offenses by Thy infinite mercy, so that they will never come into reckoning before Thy judgment. All these things I beseech and ask in the name and in the favor of Thy only Son, my Lord and Savior Jesus Christ, as He himself has given us the rule for praying to Thee:

Our Father who art in heaven, hallowed be Thy name. Thy kingdom come. Thy will be done, on earth as it is in heaven. Give us this day our daily bread, and forgive us our offenses as we forgive those who have offended against us. And lead us not into temptation, but deliver us from evil. For Thine is the kingdom, the power, and the glory forever and ever, amen.

15 ৶ PRAYER TO MAKE BEFORE CONSULTING ABOUT THE BUSINESS OF THE KINGDOM

O Lord our good God, who dost contemplate from on high all that there is in heaven and on earth, whose throne is wonderful and whose glory is incomprehensible, before whom the company of angels stand in fear, we Thy humble maidservant and Thy menservants, being assembled here in Thy presence to treat and advise about the business which concerns the holy vocation to which Thou hast called us by Thy grace, acknowledging that Thou sustainest and preservest under the guidance of Thy providence the state and government of all the kingdoms of the earth, and that to Thee it belongs to preside in the midst of princes in their councils; on the other hand, acknowledging that we are surrounded with darkness, full of errors and ignorance, and are indeed unworthy of Thy assistance if Thou lookest upon our iniquities: for these reasons, good God, we pray Thee in the name of Thy only Son, our Savior Jesus Christ, to pardon us all our offenses, and for the love of Him to impart to us the gifts and graces of Thy Holy Spirit, so that, being impelled by a true zeal for Thy glory and by a paternal love towards the people whom Thou hast given into our charge, we may with prudence and wisdom treat of the things that now will be propounded.

Dispose, therefore, Lord, our mouths, our hearts, and our understandings, making us to know the things that Thou approvest so that we embrace them, and to discern the bad things in order to deny and dismiss them. Furthermore, keep Thou Thy hand in all our deliberations, so that Thou mayst make us see a happy issue from them, to the glory of Thy name, to the good and profit of our people, and to the discharging of our consciences. This we ask Thee humbly in the favor of Thy well beloved Son, as by Him we are taught to pray to Thee, Our Father, who art, etc.

POEM 6 ❧ PRAYER[8]

O Governor of all the spheres in motion
O Thou who hast set down the world's foundation
And parceled it out, by Thy good intent,
Amongst all men, without asking consent,
Thou raisest one, another castest low;   5
To one in pain Thou dost Thy comfort show
And makst him king, if so Thou willst him be;
Thus, God and Master, hast Thou dealt with me
By pulling me out from a prison cruel,
The prison of flesh, and suffering eternal.   10
I dwelt in one for sins that I committed
From youthful years, and these Thou hast remitted;
The other was mine because the truth I took
Unto myself in love, and lies forsook
To follow Christ; therefore Thou pulledst me   15

8. The authorship of this poem, which we have numbered Poem 6 despite its title "Prayer," is uncertain. Its content correlates closely with the events of Elizabeth's life; on the other hand, it is written in a more polished style than Elizabeth's other French verses and may be the work of an as yet unidentified French poet of the period.

By Thy strong hand from being withdrawn from Thee
In giving this great royalty to me.
Align me then with what Thou dost decree:
Strength, counsel, doctrine sound to me provide
That well I may Thy people rule and guide;   20
And in Thy goodness, vouchsafe not to see
Or heed at all my own iniquity.

End of the Prayers in French.

———•———

The Italian Versicles and Prayers

16 ੨❧ CONFESSION OF SINS UNTO THE LORD

I have made known unto Thee my sin, and I have not covered my iniquity; I
have said I will confess my transgressions unto the Lord, and Thou hast
taken away the iniquity of my sin. (Solomon 32)[9]

My God and my Lord, humbly and with a soul full of infinite displeasure at having offended Thee and at offending Thee all day long, I, Thy
humble handmaid and sinner, present myself before Thy divine majesty
to confess my sins candidly and freely and to ask pardon of Thee. I was,
as Thou knowest, conceived and born in sin; I have come out of the
same mass of corruption from which the whole lineage of mankind is
taken. I find myself always full of evil affections, and I know nothing
good to which Thy Holy Spirit might guide me, but every hour I bend
lower towards the earth and towards evil, whither the heavy weight of
this flesh draws me. The occasions for offending Thee through the
height of the place where Thou hast set me—through riches, through
actions, through honors—are many; and the temptations are infinitely
many, continual, and most urgent. My flesh is so frail that I am not able
to do otherwise than err and sin heavily before Thee, my God, for
which I feel over me Thy just wrath leading to final condemnation.

9. The citation is Psalm 32:5.

On the other side Thou hast planted, by Thy infinite mercy, a lively faith in my heart that Christ is my true and certain Salvation, and that through Him every soul washed in His blood will be received of Thy mercy. Behold, I come with assurance and certain faith to find pardon at the judgment seat of Thy mercy through the same Jesus Christ. Receive then, I pray Thee, merciful Father, this Thy daughter who comes in obedience to Thee; gather in, O loving Shepherd, this straying lamb who returns to Thy sheepfold; and heal, O heavenly Physician, all the wounds of my soul with the medicine of Thy grace, assuring me first in my conscience that, all sin being remitted unto me, I may be reconciled with Thee, and then, with Thy Spirit renewing me and sanctifying me every day, I may lead this life that remains to me in sanctity and justice in the sight of Thee and Thy Church, until Thou callest me to the glory of eternal life, which I await and expect assuredly through Jesus Christ my Lord, to whom be honor and glory everlasting, amen.

17 ৬ FIRST PRAYER AS A CREATURE OF GOD

Whosoever adores God with delight will be received, and his prayer will ascend up into the clouds. The prayer of one who humbles himself will pierce the clouds. (Ecclesiasticus 32)

Acknowledging, Lord, how I am Thy creature, created in Thy image and likeness, an excellent work of Thy hands above all the other creatures, I render Thee infinite thanks for this, and I pray Thee humbly that it may please Thee so to grant that I may continually have care and regard not to sully nor to abase this Thy holy image restored in me through Jesus Christ, but instead keeping it pure and untainted by any carnal affection, may it reflect in the eyes of everyone the splendor of Thy face, which Thou hast bestowed upon me from above to Thy glory, through Jesus Christ, amen.

18 ৬ SECOND PRAYER, AS A CHRISTIAN AND A QUEEN

God, my Father and Protector, greatly do I feel myself a debtor to Thy mercy for having called me early by the preaching of the Gospel of Jesus Christ to the true worship and sincerity of Thy religion, to the end that with the authority which Thou hast given me and with the zeal for which I am indebted to Thee, I might be made Thy instrument for replanting and establishing in this part of the world, where it hath pleased Thee that I reign in the name of Thy kingdom, Thy worship, and most holy religion. I pray Thee, my God and good Father, that as in part by Thy grace I have served Thee in this according to Thy holy will, so may it please Thee to remove all impediment and resistance of unbelief from my people, and to inspire me from well to better yet, goodwill and ardent zeal; giving me efficacious means, apt and sufficient instruments, so that I may be able to do as I desire, uprooting every wicked seed of impiety, to spread, plant, and root Thy holy Gospel in every heart, increasing thoughout this Thy earthly kingdom, that heavenly one of Jesus Christ, to whom be evermore honor and glory, amen.

19 ಎ THIRD PRAYER, FOR THE ADMINISTRATION OF JUSTICE

Finally, O God, supreme King and my Lord, I confess that very great among worldly greatness is the honor and dignity in which Thou hast placed me—both placed me and maintained me miraculously, preserving me and freeing me from many evils and dangers of mischievous men. I acknowledge that until now, if I have administered with prudence, vigilance, justice, equity, mercy, and peace the office in which Thou hast placed me, all has been a gift of Thy fatherly goodness to me. Now I pray Thee dearly that it may please Thee to continue, holding Thy hands above me, humbling me under Thy dominion, to which I am a handmaid, and grant that this crown, which Thou hast placed on my head, I may always put beneath Thy feet, and the regal scepter placed in my hand may serve Thy glory, and the justice and equity of Thy people, the peace and concord of the kingdom. May the mind of Thy handmaid be clear and just, her will sincere, her judgments fair and pious. Grant me, O Lord, help, counsels, and sufficient ministers, just and capable, full of piety and of Thy most holy fear; may the people be faithful and governable, so that I and all my flock, living in quietness and peace, may have the occasion and time to serve Thy majesty, praying and supplicating Thee for all this through Jesus Christ my Lord and Thy only begotten Son, to whom with Thee and the Holy Spirit be honor and glory everlasting, amen.

——•——

The Spanish Versicles and Prayers[10]

20 ?❧ FIRST PRAYER

Great are the tribulations of the just, but the Lord will free them from all these. (Psalm 34)

My God and my most sweet Father, whose goodness is infinite, whose mercy never can be exhausted, and whose mouth always speaks truth because Thou art the same Truth which Thou hast promised to those who believe in Thee, to those who trust and put their hope in Thee, free them, protect them, and be a Father to them in all their necessities both temporal and spiritual. And this Thou hast performed with Thy act, neither more nor less than Thou hast promised by Thy Word, as witness so many testimonies of Thy holy Scripture. Thus Thou hast freed Noah from the flood, Abraham from the Chaldeans, Lot from Sodom, and Jacob from the bloody hands of his own brother Esau, Daniel from the den of lions, and Susanna from the false testimony of those two accursed men and unjust judges.

I, Thy humble maidservant, prostrate myself, O my God, O my Father, before the throne of Thy divine Majesty and give Thee infinite thanks, thanks as great as I am able, because Thou hast made me one of the number of those whom Thou freest from great afflictions. Thou freest me from the cruel hands of my enemies—they who like ravenous wolves attempt to suck my blood and devour me alive. They hate me so because I put all my hope in Thee alone, because I am not ashamed of the Gospel of Thy most loving Son; much rather, I have been honored as one who surely holds the Gospel to be Thy power for giving salvation to all those who believe. I pray, O my God, give me grace that I forget not such a notable benefit and mercy; suffer not the good herb of gratitude and acknowledgment which Thy Majesty hast planted in the garden of my soul to be choked out by thorns, which are anxiety and care for temporal things and the deceit of riches. Vouchsafe, Lord, that I possess them in such manner that I may be the mistress of them, and not they

---

10. These prayers constitute Elizabeth's only known composition in the Spanish language, which she had learned but deliberately avoided later in her reign for political reasons.

of me; that I always may be ready to employ them in Thy service. All
this I ask of Thee in the name of Thy Son Jesus Christ, He who is my
God, my Lord, and my Redeemer, amen.

21 ⮞ SECOND PRAYER

> Give to thy maidservant a wise heart to pass judgment on Thy people and to
> discern the good from the bad, for who is able to judge Thy people that are
> so great a multitude? (1 Kings 3)

Omnipotent Lord God and my most loving Father, who by Thy admirable goodness and immense mercy hast wished to make of me, poor,
sinning daughter of Adam, an instrument of Thy glory, an instrument
with which Thou mayst be glorified in constituting me as head and governess of Thy wealthiest kingdom in these most unhappy times in which
Thy Church, Thy only spouse, is in so great a manner oppressed by the
tyranny of Satan and his ministers, be willing to assist me with Thy Holy
Spirit, He who is the Spirit of wisdom and of understanding, the Spirit of
counsel and of fortitude, the Spirit of knowledge and of Thy fear, by
whom I, Thy maidservant, may have a wise heart that can discern between the good and the bad. And in this manner may justice be administered in this Thy kingdom and the good approved and rewarded; and on
the contrary the evil condemned and castigated. Since for this Thou hast
constituted magistrates and hast put the weapon of authority in their
hand, vouchsafe it, O Lord and my God, in the name of Thy only-begotten Son Jesus Christ, my Redeemer and Intercessor, amen.

22 ⮞ THIRD PRAYER

> The unjust shall perish without any resting place, and the stopping place of
> the wicked is perdition. (Psalm 37)

O Lord, my God and my Father, I render undying thanks unto Thy divine Majesty with my mouth, with my heart, and with all that I am, for
the infinite mercies which Thou hast used toward me—that not only
hast made me Thy creature, made me by Thy hands to be formed in
Thy image and similitude; and hast by the death and passion of Thy
only Son Jesus Christ reconciled me with Thee, adopted me, and made

me Thy daughter, sister of Jesus Christ Thy firstborn and of all those who believe in Thee, who hope and trust in Thee; more yet because Thou hast done me so special and so rare a mercy that, being a woman by my nature weak, timid, and delicate, as are all women, Thou hast caused me to be vigorous, brave, and strong in order to resist such a multitude of Idumeneans, Ishmaelites, Moabites, Muhammadans, and other infinity of peoples and nations who have conjoined, plotted, conspired, and made league against Thee, against Thy Son, and against all those who confess Thy name and hold to Thy holy Word as the only rule of salvation.

O my God, O my Father, whose goodness is infinite and whose power is immense, who art accustomed to choose the weak things of this world in order to confound and destroy the strong, persist—persist for the glory of Thy name, for the honor of Thy Son, for the repose and quietude of Thine afflicted Church—in giving me strength so that I, like another Deborah, like another Judith, like another Esther, may free Thy people of Israel from the hands of Thy enemies. Lord, rise up and judge Thy cause. Pour out Thy wrath upon the peoples who do not acknowledge Thee and upon the kingdoms that do not call upon Thy name. Before our eyes let the case between the nations be judged; let the blood of Thy servants, which has been poured out, be avenged. Let the groaning of the afflicted come into Thy presence and, according to Thy great power, exempt those who were appointed to die. Lord, may those who persecute Thy Church be ashamed and disquieted perpetually, and may they be confounded and perish. May they acknowledge that Thou, whose name is Jehovah, art alone the Highest over all the earth. O Lord, grant this to Thy Church for the sake of Him who is our only Intercessor and Advocate, He who is always in the presence of Thy Majesty interceding for her, who is Jesus Christ Thy eternal Son, He who with Thee and the Holy Spirit is one God and our Lord, amen.

The Latin Prayers

23 ❧ THE QUEEN'S PRAYER

O most good and most great God, wonderful in the depth of Thy judgments, Thou art King of kings and Lord of lords; Thou by whose command it is seen Thou removest and transposest, rootest out and plantest, destroyest and buildest up; Thou, for it is Thy singular kindness, hast freed Thy handmaid who was almost the daughter of death—me, me once imprisoned in my native land, Thou hast set on a royal throne. Therefore to Thee I give thanks, to Thee I sing praises and hymns; I will celebrate Thy name day and night. By Thee the freedom of my native land, the truth of doctrine, and the tranquility of the Church have been restored. It was Thy kindness, Thine alone, and my enthroned office—a heavy weight, surely, for a woman's shoulder, but light with Thee making it light. Assist me, I pray, most merciful Father, and regard neither my wickedness nor the deserts of my forebears or my people, for they are evil and infinite; but remember Thou Thy mercy, for it is ancient and eternal and open to all the unfortunate. Preserve the realm, protect religion, defend Thy cause, Thy queen, and Thy and my people. Let enemies who want war with Thee be scattered; let those who adore idols be ashamed and convert. Let us not be the spoil of peoples who do not acknowledge Thee and do not invoke Thy name. Confirm, O God, the work that Thou hast begun; breathe Thy ruling Spirit into Thy maidservant and Thy little flock, that we may join pure religion with purity of living, that we may bring forth grapes and no wild grapes, fruits worthy of repentance and of the Gospel, in which immortal treasure may we delight immortally, by which we here, the living and the dead, may witness hereafter the inheritance of Thy heavenly kingdom, through Jesus Christ our Lord. For Thine is the kingdom, the power, and the glory in all perpetuity, amen.

24 ❧ PRAYER TO GOD FOR THE AUSPICIOUS ADMINISTRATION OF THE KINGDOM AND THE SAFETY OF THE PEOPLE

Great Framer and Preserver of things, God, before whom here at the feet of Thy Majesty I humbly lie prostrate, I consider seriously with myself how unworthy I am, to whom Thou kindly offerest Thine ear. Suffused all over with shame, I scarcely dare to lift up mine eyes to Thee. For formerly when I was in my mother's womb, a fall into sin stained me, on account of which, like the rest of the descendants of Adam, I was most worthy of miscarriage; yet Thy fatherly hand led me out from thence and allowed me to be born into the light—born to die with Christ and, dead, be reborn to enjoy eternal life. And yet (unhappy me) my youth—indeed my cradle—breathed forth nothing but the dung of that prior life, whence yet again I have had to await your coming as a Judge angry with me. But Thou through Thy infinite goodness hast called me, most unworthy, from courtly pleasures to the delights of Thy kingdom, even by the communion of saints and the voice of the Gospel. And when I have not given ear attentively or diligently enough to Thy words, although Thou hast struck with Thy rod me along with other ingrates of this kingdom, nevertheless Thy goodness here also has conquered innate evil. Behold me truly, then, in the place of a daughter whom Thou hast adopted in Christ (such as Thy justice was bound to drive away) walking in infinite mercy and heaped with new favor, released from prison and custody, also indeed from the maws of lions. Thou hast led me forth into a kingdom, enclosing my unworthy head with a golden diadem and furnishing my right hand with a royal scepter. I add to this (which I value not the least of all) that Thou hast granted that Christ, banished from the realm of England, be returned and restored to His rights and privileges by my ministry.

These are, most merciful Father, the principal heads of Thy favors to me, which how much more excellent they are, so much the more unworthily have I borne myself towards Thee, when I corrupt my life with new faults immediately thereafter—whence it has been that, by consideration of these, I have despaired completely of my salvation. But contrariwise, when I bring back to memory Thy shining holy promise in the blood of Christ, altogether remade and recreated and recovered in my former hope I approach Thy throne more fearlessly, not indeed because any offering could expiate my sins, but rather in that the offering of Thy Christ, by which He at once makes perfect those who are sanctified, opens up sanctification and expiation for me when I pray humbly and Thou sustainest me in Thy protection; as when Thou hast secured the compliance of Thy sheep, Thou preferrest the virtues of the lips to the flesh and blood of cattle,[11] so in proclaiming Thy praises and performing Thy commandments may I complete the remaining course of life. Expressly, in truth, since I am feminine and feeble, and only Thou art worthy to sit in governance of this kingdom and this administration (which in all things appears very difficult) it befits me to give an accounting in the presence of Christ before Thy judgment seat. Extend, O Father, extend, I say, to Thy daughter from Thy sublime throne those

11. **flesh ... cattle** animal sacrifice under Judaic law.

things Thou judgest to be necessary for her in such an arduous and unending office.

Thou hast granted councillors; grant unto them to use counsel rightly. Grant them, moreover, a pious, fair, sound mind and truly industrious diligence, that these may be employed for the people placed under me, and that they may be willing and able both to make provision under Thy direction and to give counsel. Thou hast granted besides that the same people reborn by Thy Word, they and I, be well pleased to be cherished and fed; grant, therefore, that faithful pastors and pious and sound men of learning feed them. For the rest, keep hirelings and every kind of wolves away from this flock of ours, however little it be, promised to Thee and Christ. Wherefore furnish Thou the same flock with Thy new favors, that to Thee and Thy supreme honor, doing obeisance to us standing in Thy place, they one to another may deny themselves mutual charity in nothing. Preserve henceforth by Thy goodness my share of peace, and free the country and kingdom most especially from all assault of war; keep us exempt from the internal and domestic tumults by which a good part of the Christian world is now disturbed. And since affliction belongs to us who are Thine, who are most poor and whose condition is most abject, even all the afflicted who are seen to be ready to perform Thy works, I humbly pray and beseech that Thou mayst have mercy, and this through the merits and name of Thy Son our Lord Jesus Christ, who lives and reigns with Thee to all eternity. May it be done.

25 ॐ ANOTHER PRAYER

God most high, who hast preserved me from a youthful age and even before that, when I was housed in light, with wonderful power and incredible providence safe and sound from the mortal enemy of humankind and his wicked ministers, grant in like manner that, trusting to Thy singular goodness, I may be snatched away from all secretly faithless persons as well as from domestic and foreign enemies, and remain steadfast in freedom of mind and in a quiet and tranquil state so that Thou mayst preserve from all dangers the people and kingdom committed to my trust and care, and that when I shall be unburdened from this life I shall enjoy everlasting blessedness with Thee for an eternity of ages, amen.

———•———

The Greek Prayers

26 ❧ THE PRAYER OF THE SUBJECTS ON BEHALF OF THE QUEEN[12]

God most high, most great, who hast founded all things and observest all things in heaven and on earth, direct Thy handmaid, Elizabeth our queen, and illumine her soul with the light of Thine unbounded wisdom, that she may honor Thy name through her whole life with true service and piety, and that day by day she may continue faithfully to teach us, the people who are subject to her, remembering always that sovereign rule is not hers, but that the governance of the whole kingdom has been given to her as heir to the kingdom, or rather as servant, by Thee as sovereign, on condition that she revere Thee absolutely, defend the virtuous, and seek vengeance on the wicked and lawless. Grant at the same time to us who are her subjects, mindful that she holds power from Thee, that we may be subjects not only in outward servitude, but in the inward service of our hearts, and may receive all her commands with zeal and with humility. And may she progress ever further in all virtue, reverence, and care for this country. Give her long life with health of the body, peace, prosperity, and magnificence, and provide her with power against enemies so that she may conquer them and prevail, and may turn away all harm from the realm. So that, even though she lives in an unstable world, yet in the end, after the end of the life that is common to all humans, she may obtain eternal life and blessedness in accordance with Thy boundless mercy, through the blood of Thy only-begotten Son, the undefiled Lamb who died upon the cross to redeem us, amen.

12. The first Greek prayer is the only one in this collection not composed in Elizabeth's first person; it may not be her work. But she could well have composed devotionally for other voices. "A prayer for men to say entering into battle" in Katherine Parr's *Prayers or Meditations* would have furnished a precedent.

27 ❧ THE PRAYER OF THE QUEEN ON BEHALF OF HERSELF AND
HER SUBJECTS

O Lord God, high throned, invisible, who hast made all things from
nothing, with Thy indescribable wisdom and providence and kindness
Thou orderest the things in heaven, earth, and sea. And for us humans,
with no strength at all in ourselves, Thou hast set under our feet the cattle of the plain, the birds of the heaven, and the fish of the sea. And
Thou hast given to me the people of this realm as subjects, although I
am weak and unworthy. Implant, I beseech Thee, humility in my soul,
so that I may acknowledge every day that I do not hold royal rule by my
own merit, but received it from Thee as a handmaid or servant. May I
serve Thee in fear and rejoice in trembling, performing all things not
for my reward or honor or gratification but for Thy glory and praise,
and for the safekeeping of the people over whom I have been set up in
this rank. And since there is no private wisdom in me, trusting in which
I might continue to govern well such a realm, fill my breast with the intelligence and wisdom of the Holy Spirit, and put forth Thy light so that
by seeing light in Thy far-shining light[13] I may know Thy way upon the
earth, and through all of life may welcome Thy holy and true worship
and convey this to the people who are my subjects so that we all with
one voice and in harmony of hearts may hymn Thy most holy name.
Make my soul always obedient to Thy holy will and, in the same fashion, make the people obey me. So grant vigor and health to this body
that it will be more competent in its daily tasks and never cease being
Thy holy and sacred Temple. Grant me to use mildness towards the virtuous, to encourage them still more to their duty and to chastise the
wicked and lawless, so that I may turn them from evil and, truly in the
manner of a physician, may bring this body of the realm from sickness
to health and safety. And convert the souls of our enemies so as to tame
their hatred towards us, or provide me the strength to be victorious
against my enemies and those of my people, to overturn them in every
attempt and conquer all, that we may live in most longed-for peace. Finally, save Thy people now in this life and bless Thine inheritance.[14] Be
with them after the departure of the soul, expelled from the body.
Crown me myself with a crown of heavenly blessedness, secure and

13. Cf. Psalm 36:9: "In Thy light shall we see light."
14. Except for the addition "now in this life," a verbatim quotation from Psalm 28:9.

imperishable through Christ Jesus, Thy only-begotten Son and our
Savior, amen.

28 ࣘ PRAYER OF THE QUEEN TO GOD

Father most high, who hast laid out the universe with Thy Word and
adorned it with the Holy Spirit, and who hast appointed me as monarch
of the British kingdom, favor me by Thy goodness to implant piety and
root out impiety, to protect freely willed religion, to destroy supersti-
tious fear by working freely to promote divine service, and to spy out
the worship of idols; and further, to gain release from the enemies of religion as well as those who hate me—Antichrists, Pope lovers, atheists,
and all persons who fail to obey Thee and me. With all these things,
omnipotent Lord, favor me, and after death my kingdom will be the
kingdom of heaven, amen.

III

SPEECHES, LETTERS,

POEMS, AND PRAYERS OF

QUEEN ELIZABETH I

1572–1587

FIGURE 8   Queen Elizabeth sitting in state, title page of Christopher Saxton, *Atlas of England and Wales*, 1579. Copyright © The British Museum.

SPEECHES 13–18

13 &ᵉ QUEEN ELIZABETH'S SPEECH AT THE CLOSE OF THE PARLIAMENTARY SESSION, MARCH 15, 1576[1]

1. *Source:* The Syndics of Cambridge University Library, MS Dd.V.75, fols. 28r–29r; copy from the miscellany of Henry Stanford, a member of the household of Henry Carey, first Lord Hunsdon. Although this speech was delivered in Parliament, it appears to have been little heard and is not recorded in D'Ewes. Thomas Cromwell's Commons journal records of the end of this parliamentary session, "Hereupon the greatest company went forth, and after, her majesty made an oration, but I could not hear the same, scant one word of twenty, no one perfect sentence" (Hartley, 1:495). Francis and Gilbert Talbot, sons of the earl of Shrewsbury, wrote their father that the queen made "a very eloquent and grave oration, which was as well uttered and pronounced as it was possible for any creature" (Lambeth Palace Library, MS 3197, fol. 125; letter of March 16, 1575[6]).

Among numerous other copies, most of them later, are BL, MS Additional 32379 ("Discourses of Sir N. Bacon"), fols. 22r–24r; BL, MS Additional 15891, fols. 198r–199r; and the printed version in *Nugae Antiquae,* which probably derives from the copy given by Elizabeth to Sir John Harington (her godson and favorite). Harington wrote the following on his copy: "These good words were given unto me by my most honored lady and princess, and did bring with them these good advices: 'Boy Jack, I have made a clerk write fair my poor words for thine use, as it cannot be such striplings have entrance into Parliament assembly as yet. Ponder them in thy hours of leisure and play with them till they enter thine understanding; so shalt thou hereafter, perchance, find some good fruits hereof when thy godmother is out of remembrance; and I do this because thy father was ready to serve and love us in trouble and thrall" (Henry Harington and Thomas Park, eds., vol. 1 [London: for Vernor and Hood, etc., 1804], pp. 127–28). The most important variants among copies of the speech listed here are recorded in the notes.

[Headed] Oratio Elizabethae reginae habita in regni conventu convocato ad diem 15 Martii anno 1575[6].[2]

Do I see God's most sacred, holy Word and text of holy Writ drawn to so divers senses, being never so precisely taught, and shall I hope that my speech can pass forth through so many ears without mistaking, where so many ripe and divers wits do ofter bend themselves to conster[3] than attain the perfect understanding? If any look for eloquence, I shall deceive their hope; if some think I can match their gift which spake before, they hold an open heresy. I cannot satisfy their longing thirst that watch for these delights, unless I should afford them what myself had never yet in my possession. If I should say the sweetest tongue or eloquentest speech that ever was in man were able to express that restless care which I have ever bent to govern for the greatest wealth, I should wrong mine intent and greatly bate the merit of mine own endeavor. I cannot attribute this hap and good success to my device without detracting much from the divine Providence, nor challenge to my own commendation what is only due to His eternal glory. My sex permits it not, or if it might be in this kind, yet find I no impeachment why to persons of more base estate the like proportion should not be allotted. One special favor yet I must confess I have just cause to vaunt of: that whereas variety and love of change is ever so rife in servants to their masters, in children to their parents, and in private friends one to another (as that though for one year or perhaps for two they can content themselves to hold their course upright, yet after, by mistrust or doubt of worse, they are dissevered and in time wax weary of their wonted liking), yet still I find that assured zeal amongst my faithful subjects, to my special comfort, which was first declared to my great encouragement. Can a prince which of necessity must discontent a number to delight and please a few[4] continue so long time without great offense, much mislike, or common grudge? Or haps it often that princes' actions are conceived in so good part and favorably interpreted? No, no, my lords, how great my fortune is in this respect I were ingrate if I should not acknowledge.

2. "The speech of Queen Elizabeth, vested in majesty, in the Parliament assembled on the fifteenth day of March 1575[6]."

3. **conster** construe, determine the meaning of.

4. BL, MS Additional 32379 adds the following parenthetical phrase "(because the greatest part is oft not the best inclined)" and makes the sentence a statement beginning with "And" instead of **Can.**

And as for those rare and special benefits which many years have followed and accompanied my happy reign, I attribute to God alone, the Prince of rule, and count myself no better than His handmaid, rather brought up in a school to bide the *ferula*[5] than traded in a kingdom to support the scepter. If policy had been preferred before truth, would I, trow you, even at the first beginning of my reign, have turned upside down so great affairs or entered into tossing of the greatest waves and billows of the world, that might (if I had sought mine ease) have harbored and cast anchor in more seeming security? It cannot be denied but worldly wisdom rather bade me link myself in league and fast alliance with great princes to purchase friends on every side by worldly means, and there repose the trust of my assured strength where force could never want to give assistance. Was I to seek it, to man's outward judgment this must needs be thought the safest course. No, I can never grant myself so simple as not to see what all men's eyes discovered. But all those means of leagues, alliances, and foreign strengths I quite forsook and gave myself to seek for truth without respect, reposing my assured stay in God's most mighty grace with full assurance. Thus I began, thus I proceed, and thus I hope to end. These seventeen years[6] God hath both prospered and protected you with good success under my direction, and I nothing doubt but the same maintaining hand will guide you still and bring you to the ripeness of perfection. Consider with yourselves the bitter storms and troubles of your neighbors, the true cause whereof I will not attribute to princes (God forbid I should) since these misfortunes may proceed as well from sins among the people. For want of plagues declare not always want of guilt, but rather prove God's mercy. I know beside that private persons may find rather fault than mend a prince's state. And for my part, I grant myself too guilty to increase the burden or mislike of any. Let all men therefore bear their private faults; mine own have weight enough for me to answer for. The best way, I suppose, for you and me were by humble prayers to require of God that not in weighing but in perfect weight, in being not in seeming, we may wish the best and further it with our abilities. Not the finest wit, the judgment that can rake most deeply or take up captious ears with pleasing tales, hath greater care to guide you to the safest state,[7] or would be

---

5. *ferula* rod for punishment in grammar schools.   6. Other MSS add "and more."
7. BL, MS Additional 15891 reads, "Not the finest wit nor the sharpest judgment that can sound most deeply and take up captious cares with pleasing tales hath greater care to guide

gladder to establish you where men ought to think themselves most sure and happy, than she that speaks these words.

And touching dangers chiefly feared: first, to rehearse my meaning lately unfolded to you by the lord keeper, it shall not be needful, though I must confess mine own mislike so much to strive against the matter as, if I were a milkmaid with a pail on mine arm, whereby my private person might be little set by, I would not forsake that single state to match myself with the greatest monarch. Not that I condemn the double knot or judge amiss of such as, forced by necessity, cannot dispose themselves to another life, but wish that none were driven to change save such as cannot keep honest limits. Yet for your behoof there is no way so difficile[8] that may touch my private, which I could not well content myself to take, and in this case as willingly to spoil myself quite of myself as if I should put off my upper garment when it wearies me, if the present state might not thereby be encumbered. I speak not this for my behoof; I know I am but mortal, which good lesson Mr. Speaker[9] in his third division of a virtuous prince's properties required me with reason to remember, and so the whilst prepare myself to welcome death whensoever it shall please almighty God to send it, as if others would endeavor to perform the like it could not be so bitter unto many as it hath been counted. Mine experience teacheth me to be no fonder of these vain delights than reason would, nor further to delight in things uncertain than may seem convenient. But let good heed be taken lest in reaching too far after future good, you peril not the present, or begin to quarrel and fall by dispute together by the ears before it be decided who shall wear my crown. I will not deny but I might be thought the indifferentest judge in this respect, that shall not be at all when these things be fulfilled: which none beside myself can speak in all this company. Misdeem not of my words as though I sought what heretofore to others hath been granted.[10] I intend it not. My brains be too thin to carry so

---

you to the safest state"; BL, MS Additional 32379 reads, "Not the finest wit or exactest judgment that can search most deeply, or most fill up men's captious ears with pleasing tales hath greater care to guide you to the safest state . . ."

8. **difficile** difficult (the reading in other MSS).

9. **Speaker** Mr. Bell, who had spoken earlier and "humbly and earnestly petitioned her majesty to marriage"; see Hartley (1:462, 467).

10. **to others hath been granted** These mysterious words have puzzled most commentators. Elizabeth may refer to bodily translation into heaven without having to experience death, as granted by God to the holy man Enoch (Genesis 5:24, Hebrews 11:5), the prophet Elijah (2 Kings 2:1–11), and, according to Roman Catholic tradition, to the Virgin Mary.

tough a matter, although I trust God will not in such haste cut off my days but that, according to your own desert and my desire, I may provide some good way for your security.

And thus as one which yieldeth you more thanks—both for your zeal unto myself and service in this Parliament—than my tongue can utter, I recommend you to the assured guard and best keeping of the Almighty, who will preserve you safe, I trust, in all felicity. And wish withal that each of you had tasted some drops of Lethe's[11] flood to deface and cancel these my speeches out of your remembrance.

SPEECH 13, ADDITIONAL DOCUMENT A THE LORDS' AND COMMONS' PETITION TO THE QUEEN, MARCH 2, 1576, AND THE QUEEN'S ANSWER TO THE COMMONS BY DEPUTY[1]

[Headed] A petition of the Lower House unto the queen's majesty, secundo Martii 1575[6].

The first reading.

	The Lord Treasurer		
Upper	The Lord Steward	*Lower*	Mr. Treasurer
House	The Lord Chamberlain	*House*	Mr. Controller
	The earl of Leicester		Mr. Chancellor of th'Exchequer

To the queen's most excellent majesty, our most sovereign lady:

In most humble wise beseeching your highness, your majesty's most loving, faithful, and obedient subjects, the Commons in this present Parliament assembled. That whereas by the lack of the true discipline of the Church, amongst other abuses, a great number of men are admitted *unlearned* to occupy the place of ministers in the Church of England who are not *ministers,* only altogether unfurnished of such gifts as are by the word of God *infamous* necessarily and inseparably required to be incident to their calling, but *ministers,* also are infamous in their lives and conversations. And also many of the *pluralities,* ministry whom God hath induced with ability to teach, are by means of *dispensations* nonresidence, pluralities, and suchlike dispensations so withdrawn from

---

11. **Lethe** river of the classical underworld that induced forgetfulness.

1. *Source:* BL, Additional MS 33271, fols. 13v–14r; an early copy with marginal headings reproduced here. There is a notable disparity between this petition and the queen's answer (Speech 13), in tone, perspective, and content.

their flocks that their gifts are almost altogether become unprofitable, whereby an infinite number of your majesty's subjects, for want of the preaching of the Word—the only ordinary mean of salvation of souls and th'only good means to teach your majesty's subjects to know their true obedience to your majesty and to the magistrates under you, and without the which the Lord God hath pronounced that the people must needs perish[2]—have already run headlong into destruction, and many thousand of the residue yet remain in great peril (if speedy remedy be not provided) daily to fall into the ditch[3] and to die in their sins, to the

abuse of
excommunication,
commutation
of penance,
the number
of atheists,
schismatics,
and obstinate
papists

great danger and charge of those to whom the Lord God hath committed the care of provision for them in this behalf. And by means whereof the common blaspheming of the Lord's name, the most licentiousness of life, the abuse of excommunication, the great number of schismatics and heretics daily springing up, and to conclude, hindrance and increase of obstinate papists, which ever since your majesty's sworn enemy the Pope did by his bull[4] pronounce definitive sentence against your highness' person and proceedings, have given evident testimony of their corrupt affection to him and of their willful disobedience to your majesty, in that they forbear to participate with your majesty's faithful subjects in prayer and administration of sacraments, wherein they most manifestly declare that they carry very unsound and undutiful hearts unto your majesty. In consideration, therefore, of the premises, having regard first and principally to the advancement of the glory of God, next to the long and most blessed continuance of your majesty's reign and safety (which we most instantly beseech almighty God long to preserve), then to the discharge of our most bounden obedience which in all duty and reverence we bear unto your majesty, besides being moved to pitiful consideration of the most lamentable estate of so many thousands of your majesty's subjects daily in danger to be lost for want of the food of the Word and true discipline; and lastly, respecting the peace of our consciences and the salvation of our souls, being at this present assembled by your majesty's authority, to open the griefs and to seek the salving of the fears of our country. And these before remembered,

2. Cf. Proverbs 29:18: "Where there is no vision, the people perish."

3. Cf. Elizabeth's speech to the Commons, January 28, 1563 (Speech 5, p. 72): "I trust you likewise do not forget that by me you were delivered whilst you were hanging on the bough ready to fall into the mud, yea to be drowned in the dung."

4. For William Camden's English translation of "*Regnans in excelsis*," the 1570 papal bull excommunicating Elizabeth, see Tanner (144–46).

beyond measure exceeding in greatness all the residue which can be disclosed in your majesty's commonwealth, we are met humbly to beseech your highness, seeing the same is of so great importance, if the plaint at this present may not be so long continued as that, by good and godly laws established, in the same provision may be made for supply and reformation of these great wants and grievous abuses, that yet by such other good means as to your majesty's most godly wisdom shall seem best, a perfect redress may be had of the same. Which doing, you shall do such acceptable service to the Lord God, which cannot but procure at His hands the sure establishment of your seat and scepter. And the number of your majesty's most faithful subjects (the bond of conscience being of all other most straitest) by mean of preaching and discipline be so multiplied, and the great swarms of malefactors, schismatics, atheists, Anabaptists, and papists, your most dangerous enemies, so weakened and diminished that by the help and assistance of almighty God, if all popish treasons and traitorous practices should conspire together in one against your majesty, they should not be able to shake the estate. And we, your majesty's most loving and obedient subjects, together with the remembrance of those inestimable and innumerable benefits which by your majesty's means the Lord God hath already blessed us withal, far beyond any other of our neighbors round about us, shall not only be more and more stirred up to dutiful thankfulness unto your majesty and continual and earnest prayer unto almighty God (which we will nevertheless) for the long and prosperous continuance of your majesty's reign; but also both we and the residue of your majesty's most faithful subjects and our posterity shall be most bounden to continue in that obedient duty which we owe to your most royal majesty. And to conclude, your majesty shall be recommended to all posterity for such a pattern to be followed that nothing may seem to be added to the perfection of your renown.

An answer to the petition of the Common House exhibited to her majesty, delivered by her commandment by the lord treasurer and other lords and uttered in the House by Sir Walter Mildmay, anno 1575[6].

The queen's majesty had of these things consideration before in such sort as, though this motion had not been, their reformation thereof nevertheless should have followed. And yet she alloweth well that her subjects, being aggrieved therewith, have in such sort and discreet manner both opened their griefs and remitted them to be reformed by her majesty. And considering that reformation hereof is to be principally sought in the clergy, and namely in the bishops and ordinaries, her majesty did in the beginning of her convocation confer with some of the principals of them, and such as she thought were best disposed to reform[5] these errors in the Church. From whom, if she shall not find some direct dealings for the reformation, then she will by her supreme authority, as with th'advice of her Council, direct them herself to amend; whereof her majesty doubteth not but her people shall see that her majesty will use that authority which she hath, to the increase of th'honor of God and to the reformation of th'abuses in the Church.

14 &❧ QUEEN ELIZABETH'S SPEECHES AND RESPONSES DURING HER VISIT TO NORWICH, AUGUST 16–22, 1578[1]

[Sig. Aiii v; the queen's greeting by the mayor, Robert Wood, and other dignitaries who awaited her coming outside the city on Saturday, August 16] Her majesty . . . within one hour or little more after their attendance, came in such gracious and princely wise as ravished the hearts of all her loving subjects, and might have terrified the stoutest heart of any enemy to behold. Whether the majesty of the prince, which is incomparable, or joy of her subjects, which exceeded measure, were the greater, I think would have appalled the judgment of Apollo to define. The acclamations and cries of the people to the almighty God for the preservation of her majesty rattled so loud as hardly for a great time could anything be heard. But at last, as everything hath an end, the noise appeased and Master Mayor saluted her highness with the oration following, and yielded to her majesty therewith the sword of the city and a fair standing cup of silver and gilt with a cover, and in the cup one hundreth pounds in gold. The oration was in these words:

[Sig. Bi v–Bii v; the mayor's Latin speech in English] "If our wish should be granted unto us by the Almighty, what human thing we would chiefly desire, we would account nothing more precious, most royal

---

5. **to reform** written twice in MS.

1. *Source:* Excerpts from [Bernard Garter], *The Joyful Receiving of the Queen's Most Excellent Majesty into Her Highness' City of Norwich* . . . (London: Henry Bynneman, [1578]) (*STC* 11627). Latin speech is given here as translated in the source.

prince, than that the bright beam of your most chaste eye, which doth so cheer us, might penetrate the secret, strait corners of our hearts. Then surely should you see how great joys are dispersed there, and how the spirit and lively blood tickle in our arteries and small veins in beholding thee, the light of this realm (as David was of Israel[2]) now at length, after long hope and earnest petitions, to appear in these coasts. Truly on mine own part, which by your highness' authority and clemency (with humble thanks be it spoken) do govern this famous city, and on the part of these my brethren and all these people which by your authority we rule (speaking as they mean and as I myself do think), this only with all our hearts and humble prayers we desire—that we may so find your majesty gracious and favorable unto us as you for your part never came to any subjects better welcome than to us your poor subjects here. For most manifest token whereof, we present unto your majesty here these signs of honor and office, which we received of the most mighty Prince Henry the Fourth in the fifth year of his reign, then to us granted in the name of mayor, aldermen, and sheriffs—whereas before, time out of mind or mention, we were governed by bailiffs (as they term them)— which ever since have been both established and increased with continual privileges of kings, and which by your only clemency, which with immortal thanks we shall never cease to declare, we have now these twenty years enjoyed. And together with those signs, this treasure is a pledge of our goodwills and ability, which all, how great or little soever they be, we pour down at your pleasure, that if we have neglected anything in all this course of your most happy reign which becometh most loving, obedient, and well-willing subjects to perform for the preservation of your crown and advancement of your highness, you may then determine of us and all ours at your most gracious pleasure.

"But if we have (God being our guide) so ordered the governance of this city that we have kept the same in safety to your majesty's use and made the people therein (as much as in us lieth) first, most studious of God's glory and true religion, and next, of your majesty's health, honor, and pleasure, then ask we nothing of you, for that the singular clemency engraft in your highness will easily of itself grant that which is requisite for us to obtain. We only therefore desire that God would abundantly bless your highness with all good gifts of mind and body."

2. Cf. 2 Samuel 21:17.

Which oration ended, her majesty, accepting in good part everything delivered by the mayor, did thankfully answer him in these words or very like in effect:

"We heartily thank you, Master Mayor and all the rest, for these tokens of goodwill. Nevertheless, princes have no need of money; God hath endowed us abundantly. We come not therefore, but for that which in right is our own: the hearts and true allegiance of our subjects, which are the greatest riches of a kingdom. Whereof as we assure ourselves in you, so do you assure yourselves in us of a loving and gracious sovereign."

[Sig. Dii r; the queen's interaction with another orator, Stephen Limbert, master of Norwich Grammar School, who was preparing to speak in the late afternoon of Wednesday, August 20]

Her majesty drew near unto him and, thinking him fearful, said graciously unto him, "Be not afeared."

He answered her again in English, "I thank your majesty for your good encouragement," and then with good courage entered into this oration.

[Sig. Ei r] Immediately after the beginning of the oration, her majesty called to her the French ambassadors,[3] whereof there were three, and divers English lords, and willed them to hearken; and she herself was very attentive, even until the end thereof. And the oration ended, after she had given great thanks therefor to Master Limbert, she said to him, "It is the best that ever I heard. You shall have my hand," and pulled off her glove and gave him her hand to kiss.

[Sig. Eiv v–Fi r; the queen's leave-taking from Norwich, Friday, August 22] Her majesty in princely manner marched towards the confines of the liberties of the city of Norwich, which I suppose almost two miles. Before she came there, Master Mayor brake[4] to my lord chamberlain[5] that he was to utter to her majesty another oration, whereof my lord seemed to have good liking; but before they came to the said confines Master Mayor was willed to forbear the utterance of the same his oration because it was about seven of the clock and her majesty had then five miles to ride. Nevertheless, he gave to her majesty both his orations in writing, which she thanked him for. She also thanked the

---

3. **French ambassadors** sieurs de Bacqueville and de Quincy had been dispatched by the queen's suitor, the duke of Alençon, to intercept her on her late summer progress through the eastern counties and press his suit for marriage.

4. **brake** broke.

5. **lord chamberlain** Thomas Radcliffe (1526?–1583), third earl of Sussex.

mayor, every alderman, and the commoners, not only for the great cheer they had made her, but also for the open households they kept to her highness' servants and all other. Then she called Master Mayor and made him knight, and so departing said, "I have laid up in my breast such goodwill as I shall never forget Norwich," and proceeding onward did shake her riding rod and said, "Farewell, Norwich!" with the water standing in her eyes. In which great goodwill towards us all I beseech God to continue her majesty with long and triumphant reign over us all, amen.

15 ॐ QUEEN ELIZABETH'S SPEECH TO BISHOPS AND OTHER CLERGY AT SOMERSET PLACE, FEBRUARY 27, 1585, WHILE PARLIAMENT WAS IN SESSION[1]

[Headed] A brief effect of her majesty's speech unto the bishops and other of the clergy offering unto her their subsidy in her Privy Chamber at Somerset Place, 27 February 1584[5], at what time there were of the clergy my lord archbishop of Canterbury, the bishops of Worcester, Sarum,[2] and Rochester, Mr. Archdeacon of Canterbury prolocutor,[3] the deans of Paul's,[4] Westminster, and Ely, Doctor Bell and Doctor Bound, and in the presence of my lords chancellor, treasurer, Leicester, Bedford, Chamberlain, and Hampton, Mr. Secretary Walsingham and Mr. Solicitor.

1. *Imprimis.* The subsidy being delivered by the archbishop of Canterbury[5] in the name of the whole clergy, her majesty answered that she did accept of it thankfully, and the rather for that it came voluntarily and frankly, whereas the laity must be entreated and moved thereunto. My lord treasurer,[6] standing by, said, "Madam, these men come with mites, but we will come with pounds."

---

1. *Source:* PRO, State Papers Domestic, Elizabeth 12/176/68, fol. 215; condensed version of the conversation.

2. **Sarum** Salisbury.

3. **prolocutor** presider over the Lower House of Convocation (the clergy of the Church of England) and spokesman for the Lower House in the Upper House.

4. **Paul's** Saint Paul's Cathedral.

5. **archbishop of Canterbury** John Whitgift.

6. **treasurer** William Cecil, Lord Burghley.

Her majesty answered, "I esteem more of their mites than of your pounds,[7] for that they come of themselves not moved, but you tarry till you be urged thereunto," and then gave the clergy thanks, saying, "Whatsoever you have bestowed upon me, I am to bestow it upon you again. God grant I may bestow it to His glory and the benefit of this realm."

[2.][8] Then she said unto the bishop, "We understand that some of the Nether House have used divers reproachful speeches against you, tending greatly to your dishonor, which we will not suffer; and that they meddle with matters above their capacity not appertaining unto them, for the which we will call some of them to an account. And we understand they be countenanced by some of our Council,[9] which we will redress or else uncouncil some of them. But," saith she, "we will not charge the whole House with this disorder, for although there be some intemperate and rash heads in that House, yet there be many wise and discreet men who do find just cause of grievance against some of you: first, in that you have not greater care in making ministers, whereof some be of such lewd life and corrupt behavior whereof we know of some such that be not worthy to come into any honest company.

3. "Again, you suffer many ministers to preach what they list, and to minister the sacraments according to their own fancies—some one way, some another—to the breach of unity; yea, and some of them so curious in searching matters above their capacity as they preach they wot not what: that there is no hell, but a torment of conscience; nay, I have heard of there be six preachers in one diocese the which do preach six sundry ways. I wish such men to be brought to conformity and unity, that they minister the sacraments according to the order of this realm and preach all one truth; and that such as be found not worthy to preach, to be compelled to read homilies such as were set forth in our brother King Edward his time and since. For there is more of learning in one of those than in twenty of some of their sermons. And we require you that you do not fav[or] such men being carried away with pity, hoping of their conformity and inclining to noblemen's letters and

7. Cf. Mark 12:41–44.

8. Here and below, square brackets enclose item numbers and other elements lost when the manuscript was damaged or bound.

9. **some of our Council** Puritan sympathizers on the Privy Council included, preeminently, Robert Dudley, earl of Leicester; Sir Francis Walsingham; Sir Francis Knollys; and Sir Walter Mildmay.

gentlemen's letters[10]; for they will be hanged before they will be re-formed."

[4.] Then she told how she had received a letter from beyond the sea written by one that bare her no goodwill. "Would ye know who it were?" *quod*[11] she, "for I saw and read the letter, who wrote that the papists were [in] hope to prevail again in England, for that her Protestants themselves misliked her, and indeed so [they] do," *quod* she, "for I have heard that some of them of late have said that I was of no religion, neither hot [nor] cold, but such a one as one day would give God the vomit.[12] I pray you look unto such men. I doubt not but you will look unto the papists, for that they not only have spite at me, and that very nearly, but at the whole realm and the state of religion. There is an Italian proverb which sayeth, 'From mine enemy let me defend myself, but from a pretensed friend, good Lord deliver me.' Both these join together in one opinion against me for neither of them would have me to be queen of England. And as for their curious and busy fellows, their preaching tendeth only to popularity."[13]

[5.] After this, she wished the bishops to look unto private conventicles.[14] "And now," *quod* she, "I miss my lord of London,[15] who looketh no better unto the city, where every merchant must have his schoolmaster and nightly conventicles expounding Scriptures and catechizing their servants and maids, in so much that I have heard how some of their maids have not sticked to control learned preachers, and say that such a man taught otherwise in our house."

[6.] Last of all she came to the High Commission,[16] and showed how it was abused by the commissioners, in that they dealt with matters not

10. **letters** a means by which men of rank used their influence to get like-minded clergy appointed to curacies in the parishes of their country or London residences; or, more specifically, the letters and petitions that had recently flowed into Parliament on the subject of ecclesiastical reform (see Speech 13, Additional Document A, p. 171).

11. *quod* said.

12. Cf. God's curse upon the insufficiently zealous Church of Laodicea in Revelation 3:16: "Because thou art neither hot nor cold I will spew thee out of my mouth."

13. **popularity** courting popular favor.

14. **conventicles** private meetings of religious dissidents to pray and expound Scripture; these were illegal when they infringed on the clergy's prerogatives to say divine service and preach.

15. **lord of London** John Aylmer, bishop of London.

16. **High Commission** the highest ecclesiastical court, created during the reign of Henry VIII to deal with matters of canon law. At this period it was widely perceived as high-handed in the enforcement of religious conformity.

incident to their commission, as with tithes, legacies, debts, etc., affirming that if they kept not themselves within their commission, she would call them to an account for it and take it from them.

[7.] Then spake my lord of Canterbury, saying, "Madam, for mine own part, I will look unto these things as well as I can, and I will take such order with my brethren as I trust they will look better unto such things. But, madam, let me use the best means I can, some things will escape and be amiss; and when it is so, I would every man were charged with his own fault and not the fault of one or two to be laid unto all."

8. Then spake my lord treasurer, saying, "Truly, my lord, her majesty hath declared unto you a marvelous great fault in that you make in this time of light so many lewd and unlearned ministers."

My lord of Canterbury said, "Well."

Quod her majesty, "Draw articles and charge them with it that have offended."

"I do not burden," *quod* my lord treasurer, "them that be here, but it is the bishop of Lichfield and Coventry[17] that I mean, who made seventy ministers in one day for money: some tailors, some shoemakers, and other crass men. I am sure the greatest part of them are not worthy to keep horses."

9. Then said the bishop of Rochester,[18] "It may be so, for I know one that made seven in one day. I would every man might bear his own burden; some of us have the greatest wrongs can be offered. For mine own part, I am sure I never made above three in one day, but, my lord, if you would have none but learned preachers to be admitted into the ministry you must provide better livings for them."

10. Then said my lord of Canterbury, "We complain, in these days, of darkness in time of light, of ignorance in time of learning, of want of preachers in time of plenty. I dare avouch, let all records be sought, and there was never that number of learned preachers that is in these days, and do and will increase daily more and more."

11. "You cannot choose," *quod* my lord treasurer, "in this time of light there should be so many unlearned ministers as were in the time of darkness."

12. "To have learned ministers in every parish is, in my judgment, impossible," *quod* my lord of Canterbury. "Thirteen thousand parishes

---

17. **bishop of Lichfield and Coventry** William Overton.
18. **bishop of Rochester** John Young.

in England—I know not how this realm should yield so many learned preachers."

13. "Jesus!" *quod* the queen, "thirteen thousand! It is not to be looked for. I think the time hath been there hath not been four preachers in a diocese. My meaning is not you should make choice of learned ministers only, for they are not to be found, but of honest, sober, and wise men, and such as can read the Scriptures and Homilies well unto the people." And so she rose, thanked the bishops, and bade them farewell.

16 ཙ QUEEN ELIZABETH'S SPEECH AT THE CLOSING OF PARLIAMENT, MARCH 29, 1585[1]

[Headed] Her majesty's speech in the Parliament House at the prorogation of the last session, 29 Martii, 1585.

My lords and you of the Lower House: My silence must not injure the owner[2] so much as to suppose a substitute sufficient to render you the thanks my heart yields you; not so much for the safekeeping of my life, for which your care appears so manifest, as for your neglecting of your private future perils, not regarding other way than my present state.[3] No

1. *Source:* BL, MS Additional 15891, fol. 148; miscellany of the royal favorite, Sir Christopher Hatton (1540–1591), vice chamberlain and member of the Privy Council since 1577. There are many other good contemporary copies, among them BL, MS Additional 38823, fol. 25, Sir Edward Hoby's miscellany; BL, MS Harley 540, fol. 115, in the hand of the antiquarian John Stow and later printed in Stow's *Annals . . . of England* (London, 1615); and Simonds D'Ewes's printed version, which he states he copied from John Stow's own hand (328–29).

A copy dating from the 1620s—Cambridge University Library, MS Ee.V.23, p. 460—is of particular interest because it demonstrates how the royal speeches could alter in political meaning as they circulated in MS. It bends the queen's language at several crucial junctures to make her more critical of episcopacy. Important variants among the Hatton, Hoby, Stow, and Cambridge versions are recorded in the notes.

Stow's heading for this speech describes it more accurately than Hatton's as "The queen's majesty's oration, made in the Parliament House at the breaking up thereof," since the 1584–85 Parliament was not prorogued but closed and new elections held for the Parliament of 1586–87.

2. **the owner** the queen herself; Stow reads "owner"; Hoby and Cambridge read "your honors."

3. Cf. Additional Document A, one of several extant texts of "The Bond of Association for the Defense of Queen Elizabeth," 1584, by which many of her subjects swore to defend her life personally with their own.

prince herein, I confess, can be surer tied or faster bound than I am
with links of your goodwills, and can for that but yield a heart and head
forever to seek all your best. Yet one matter toucheth me so near as I
may not overslip: religion, the ground on which all actions ought to
take root and, being corrupted, may mar all the tree; and that there be
some fault-finders with the order of clergy, which so may make a slander of [4] myself and the Church, whose overruler God hath made me,
whose negligence cannot be excused if any schism or errors heretical
were suffered. Thus much I must say: that some faults and negligences
may grow and be, as in all other great charges it happeneth—and what
vocation without? All which if you, my lords of the clergy,[5] do not mend,
I mind to depose you. Look you well, therefore, to your charges. This
may be amended without heedless or open exclamations.

I am supposed to have many studies, but most philosophical. I must
yield this to be true: that I suppose few (that be no professors) have read
more. And I need not tell you that I am so simple that I understand not,
nor so forgetful that I remember not. And amid my many volumes, I
hope God's Book hath not been my seldomest lectures. In which we
find that which by reason[6] (for my part) we ought to believe: that seeing
so great wickedness and griefs in this world in which we live as way-
faring pilgrims, we must suppose that God would never have made us,
but for a better place and for more comfort than we find here. I know no
creature that breatheth whose life standeth hourly in more peril for it
than mine own, who entered not into my state without sight of manifold dangers of life and crown, as one that had the mightiest and greatest to wrestle with. Then it followeth that I regarded it so much as I left
myself behind my care. And so, you see that you wrong me too much (if
any such there be) that doubt my coldness in that behalf. For if I were
not persuaded that mine were the true way of God's will, God forbid
that I should live to prescribe it to you. Take you heed that Ecclesiastes
said not too true: "They that fear the hoary frost, the snow shall fall
upon them."[7] I see many overbold with God almighty, making too

4. **slander of** Stow, Hoby, and Cambridge read "slander to."

5. **lords of the clergy** the bishops in attendance as members of the House of Lords. The
later Cambridge version of this sentence leaves out the conditional: "All which you my
lords of the clergy do not amend; I mean to depose you."

6. **by reason** omitted in Hoby.

7. The quotation is not from Ecclesiastes but is an exact English rendering of the Latin
Vulgate reading of Job 6:16: "*Qui timent pruinam, irruet super eos nix.*"

many subtle scannings of His blessed will, as lawyers do with human testaments. The presumption is so great as I may not suffer it. Yet mind I not herein to animate Romanists[8]—which, what adversaries they be to mine estate is sufficiently known—nor tolerate newfangleness. I mind to guide them both by God's holy true rule; in both sorts be perils. And of this latter, I must pronounce them dangerous to a kingly ruler to have every man according to his own censure to make a doom[9] of the validity and piety of his prince's government with a common veil and cover of God's Word, whose followers must not be adjudged but by private men's expositions. God defend you from a ruler that so evil will guide you! But now I conclude that your love and care neither is, nor shall be, bestowed on a careless prince, but such as but for your good passeth[10] as little for this world as who careth least, with thanks for your free subsidy, a manifest show of the abundance of your goodwills. Which, I assure you, but[11] to be employed to your weals, I would be better pleased to return than receive.

SPEECH 16, ADDITIONAL DOCUMENT A   THE BOND OF ASSOCIATION FOR THE DEFENSE OF QUEEN ELIZABETH, 1584[1]

Forasmuch as almighty God hath ordained kings, queens, and princes to have dominion and rule over all their subjects, and to preserve them in the profession and observation of the true Christian religion according to His holy Word and commandment; and in like sort that all subjects should love, fear, and obey their sovereign princes, being kings or queens, and to the uttermost of their powers at all times to withstand, pursue, and suppress all manner of persons that shall by any means intend and attempt anything dangerous or hurtful to the honor, estate, or

---

8. **Romanists** Roman Catholics; for **animate**, Cambridge alone reads "imitate."

9. **doom** judgment; further along in same sentence, for **piety** Stow and Cambridge read "privity"; against the other MSS, Cambridge's version of the final clause is "whose followers must not be judged by private men's exposition."

10. **good passeth** (**passeth** cares, is concerned for); Stow and Cambridge read "goodwill passeth."

11. **but** except, unless.

1. *Source:* BL, MS Cotton Caligula C.IX, art. 41, fol. 122. This particular copy of the Bond (or Oath) does not specify the signers, but another copy—MS Cotton Caligula C.IX, art. 54, fols. 156v–157r—is endorsed "Protested, sworn, and subscribed by the doctors and proctors of the Arches, the 7th of November, 1584." There are several other similarly signed copies of the Bond in the PRO.

persons of their sovereigns; therefore we whose names have or shall be subscribed to this writing, being natural-born subjects of this realm of England and having so gracious a lady our sovereign, Elizabeth, by the ordinance of God our most rightful queen reigning over us these many years with great felicity to our most enviable comfort; and finding of late by divers depositions, confessions, and sundry advertisements out of foreign parts from credible persons well known to her majesty's Council and to divers others, that for the furtherance and advertisement of some pretended titles to the crown of this realm it hath been manifest that the life of our gracious sovereign Lady, Queen Elizabeth, hath been most traitorously and devilishly sought, and the same followed most dangerously to the peril of her person if almighty God, her perpetual Defender, of His mercy had not revealed and withstood the same, by whose life we and all other her majesty's loyal and true subjects do enjoy an inestimable benefit of peace in this land; do for the reasons and causes before alleged not only acknowledge ourselves most justly bound with our bodies, lives, lands, and goods in her defense and for her safety to withstand, pursue, and suppress all such mischievous persons and all other her enemies, of what nation, condition, or degree soever they shall be, or by what color[2] or title they shall pretend to be her enemies or to attempt any harm to her person.

But we do also think it our most bounden duties, for the great benefits of peace, wealth, and godly government, which we have more plentifully received these many years under her majesty's government than our forefathers have done in any longer time of any other her progenitors, kings of this realm, do[3] declare and by this writing make manifest our loyal and bounden duties to our said sovereign lady for her safety. And to that end we and every of us, first calling to witness the holy name of almighty God, do voluntarily and most willingly bind ourselves every one of us to the other jointly and severally in the bond of one firm and loyal society. And do hereby vow and promise before the majesty of almighty God that with our whole powers, bodies, lives, lands, and goods, and with our children and servants, we and every of us will faithfully serve and humbly obey our said sovereign Lady, Queen Elizabeth, against all estates, dignities, and earthly powers whatsoever, and will as well with our joint as particular forces during our lives withstand, offend, and pursue—as well by force of arms as by all other

2. **color** aspect, show.   3. **do** that is, to.

means of revenge—all manner of persons of what estate soever they shall be and their abettors that shall attempt by any act, counsel, or consent to anything that shall tend to the harm of her majesty's royal person; and we shall never desist from all manner of forcible pursuit against such persons to the uttermost extermination of them, their consorts, aiders, and abettors.

And if any such wicked attempt against her most royal person shall be taken in hand or procured, whereby any that have, may, or shall pretend title to the crown of this realm by the untimely death of her majesty so wickedly procured—which God for his mercy' sake forbid may be advanced—we do not only vow and bind ourselves both jointly and severally never to allow, accept, or favor any such pretended successors by whom or for whom any such detestable act shall be attempted or committed, as unworthy of all government in any Christian realm or civil society, but do also further vow and protest, as we are most bounden, and that in the presence of the eternal and ever living God, to prosecute such person or persons to the death with our joint and particular forces and to take the uttermost revenge on them that by any possible means we or any of us can devise or do or cause to be devised or done for their utter overthrow and extirpation.

And to the better corroboration of this, our loyal Bond and Association, we do also testify by this writing that we do confirm the contents hereof by our oaths corporally taken upon the holy Evangelists with this express condition: that none of us shall for any respect of persons or causes or for fear or reward separate ourselves from this Association or fail in the prosecution hereof during our lives, upon pain to be by the rest of us prosecuted and suppressed as perjured persons and as public enemies to God, our queen, and our native country, to which punishments and pains we do voluntarily submit ourselves and every of us without benefit of any exception to be hereafter challenged by any of us by any color or pretext. In witness of all which premises to be inviolably kept, we do to this writing put to our hands and seals and shall be most ready to accept and admit any others hereafter to this, our society and Association.

17 ⮞ QUEEN ELIZABETH'S FIRST REPLY TO THE PARLIAMENTARY PETITIONS URGING THE EXECUTION OF MARY, QUEEN OF SCOTS, NOVEMBER 12, 1586

SPEECH 17, VERSION 1[1] *[Headed] The queen's speech to the committees of both Houses.*

At the day appointed all the said commissioners came to the court at Richmond and there the lord chancellor, in the name of the Lords and Commons of the Parliament, exhibited to her majesty the said petition engrossed[2] in Parliament alleging divers authorities and other arguments to move her highness to assent thereunto. And amongst other speeches said that she was sworn at her coronation to do justice, so that it were hard to deny justice to anyone, but much more to deny justice to all her people humbly craving the same upon their knees at her majesty's hand.

Afterwards, the said speaker pursued the same with very great and weighty reasons to move her majesty to assent to the said petition, to both which speeches her highness answered as hereafter ensueth:

"When I remember the bottomless depth of God's great benefits towards me, I find them to be so many or rather so infinite in themselves as that they exceed the capacity of all men, much more of any one, to be comprehended. And considering the manifold dangers intended and practiced against me, which through the goodness of almighty God I have always escaped, I must needs say it is admirable and miraculous (if that be a miracle which is beyond and above the reason of man) that now I live. Yet do I not thank God for that nor for all the rest so much as for this: that after twenty-eight years' reign I do not perceive any diminition[3] of my subjects' good love and affection towards me. This is the thing I most joy in and that wherein I take my greatest comfort, and without which I would not desire to live; for then life should be a death unto me, who do not think it life to breathe, but to live with that comfort and joy of life which is fit for me to have.

"But together with this, my greatest joy, I conceive no small grief that there should be some within my realm, of mine own subjects, found so

---

1. *Source:* The Syndics of Cambridge University Library, MS Gg.III.34, pp. 304–308; a copy of a contemporary report of the speech and probably close to the speech as the queen delivered it to the parliamentary delegates who waited on her with their petition at Richmond. Since she spoke impromptu, all MSS were created after the fact. For other reported texts of the speech, see Hartley (2:254–61).

2. **engrossed** put into official form.   3. **diminition** diminution.

wicked and disloyal as that they should seek to take away my life, and most of all that one of mine own sex, state, and kin should be consenting thereunto, and guilty thereof; wherein, notwithstanding, I must needs say they would have done no worse to me than to themselves, for that in seeking to destroy my body they sought the destruction of their own souls. I thank God such disloyal subjects are but few: I am sure I have the hearts and goodwills of the greater part. For these horrible treasons and practices, to tell you truly, I must protest that I am not grieved in respect of myself or of mine own life—which for itself I do not regard, knowing that the less life the less sin. And I assure you for mine own part I am so far from desiring to live as that I think that that person to be most happy which is already dead.[4] Wherefore the regard of life which I have is in respect of you and the rest of my good subjects, knowing that my blood could not have been shed but yours and theirs should have been spilt likewise. Whose happy and good estate if I were sure might be redeemed and preserved with my death, I protest before almighty God I would not desire to live.

"And now, as touching that person which with so foul treasons hath stained her estate and blood as that I cannot think of her but to my grief, I may seem peradventure to bear her malice and to be desirous of revenge. And malice I know bringeth forth rash judgment and hasty proceeding oftentimes; but I take God to witness, from whom no secrets of hearts can be hidden, I bear her no malice nor seek other revenge but this: that I wish with all my heart that she may be repentant for this and all other her crimes. And that you may the better perceive how maliciously I have proceeded against her, I will declare a matter unto you wherein I shall become a blab: after these last conspiracies and treasons were discovered unto me, of myself I sent and wrote unto her, giving her so to understand that if she would confess the truth and by her letters advertise me for what cause and by whose means she was induced to consent thereunto, and withal discover the conspirators in this action, assuring her that I dealt not cautelously[5] with her to draw from her the knowledge of anything whereof I was already ignorant, I would cover her shame and save her from reproach. Which offer of mine she utterly refused and steadfastly denied her guiltiness therein.

---

4. Cf. the chorus's closing line in Sophocles' *Oedipus the King,* which Princess Elizabeth had read in Greek with her tutor, Roger Ascham: "Count no man happy until he is dead."

5. **cautelously** craftily, deceitfully.

"Notwithstanding, I assure you, if the case stood between her and myself only, if it had pleased God to have made us both milkmaids with pails on our arms, so that the matter should have rested between us two; and that I knew she did and would seek my destruction still, yet could I not consent to her death. Nay, to say further, the case standing as it doth, if I were assured that she would repent and desist from further attempts, which perhaps may be promised (but it were hard to trust words where such deeds hath gone before)—yea, if I could perceive how besides the practices of the Scottish queen herself, I might be freed from the conspiracies and treasons of her favorers in this action—by your leaves she should not die. This is the malice I bear unto this woman, and so should I deal with her if the case were only mine own, and did concern my life alone. Which again, for itself, I must plainly tell you I little esteem, considering that I have lived many years, that I have lived as a subject and in place of rule, and that I have tasted of those sorrows and troubles whereunto each kind of life is subject, and have felt more grief and fewer joys than haply to the world I may seem to have done. And yet must I needs confess that the benefits of God to me have been and are so manifold, so folded and embroidered one upon another, so doubled and redoubled towards me, as that no creature living hath more cause to thank God for all things than I have.

"But to return to the matter: I will tell you the cause of the manner of my proceedings with the Scottish queen and why I did not deal by the course of the common law of the realm. I know very well the same to be sufficient, for God forbid that the ancient law should be defective to punish a person which should offend in so high a degree. But you, my masters of the law, are so fine—you regard so much the words, syllables, and letters thereof more than the true sense and meaning indeed—that oftentimes you make the same to seem absurd. For if I should have followed that course of the common law, forsooth, she must have been indicted by a jury of twelve men in Staffordshire. She must have held up her hand and openly been arraigned at a bar, which had been a proper manner of proceeding with a woman of her quality! (I mean her quality by birth and not by conditions.) Yet this way I might have used according to the common course of the law, as I was assured by the judges of the realm who showed it me written in their books. I mean not the pettifoggers of the law, who look more on the outside of their books than study them within. But I thought it much better and more fit to have her tried by the most honorable and ancient nobility of the realm, against whom and whose proceedings no exceptions might or can be taken.

"And now, to come to the matter in hand, and first to speak of your Oath of Association: of all other things I take it most thankfully at your hands, and note therein your singular zeal and affection towards me, in that it was done and offered by you not being required by me. Nay, which is more, I assure you I never knew of it until three thousand hands with seals thereof were brought and showed unto me at Hampton Court. And besides I must needs say that you showed great conscience and considerate dealing therein, in that you would swear to pursue to death all and every person which should seek my life and the place which I hold, and not anyone (though some of you might intend her above others) which now is in question. And further yet, by law the party offending is first to be tried and convicted, wherefore I must thank you specially for this above all the rest. And yet, by your leaves, you have laid a hard and heavy burden upon me in this case, for now all is to be done by the direction of the queen—a course not common in like cases. But for answer unto you, you shall understand the case is rare and of great weight, wherefore I must take such advice as the gravity thereof doth require. And yet I know delays are dangerous; and I have small reason to use much delay at this time. For I will tell you a secret which is most true. There are yet some living who within fourteen days have undertaken to take away my life, and have offered to be hanged if within a month it be not performed. There are some here present which I am sure know this to be true. Yet truly, I am afraid neither of them nor of death; though perchance, seeing death to all flesh is dreadful, I might be at the very moment fearful thereof. But I think they would provide my death should be so sudden and so violent that if their purposes should take place I should have small time or respite to be afraid.

"To your petition I must pause and take respite before I give answer. Princes, you know, stand upon stages so that their actions are viewed and beheld of all men; and I am sure my doings will come to the scanning of many fine wits, not only within the realm, but in foreign countries. And we must look to persons as well abroad as at home. But this be you assured of: I will be most careful to consider and to do that which shall be best for the safety of my people and most for the good of the realm."

Then, her majesty having ended her speech and being gone from her seat of estate a little towards her Privy Chamber, she returned again and said:

"I will not leave you in an error, for that perchance you may think the cause of my not coming to the Parliament amongst you to be the fear I have of myself, which is not so, but the grief which I should have continually to hear of these causes."

The said speeches of her majesty was delivered by the speaker unto the Lower House the Monday following.

SPEECH 17, VERSION 2[1] *[Headed] A report of her majesty's most gracious answer, delivered by herself verbally to the first petitions of the Lords and Commons, being the Estates of Parliament, in her Chamber of Presence at Richmond the 12 day of November, 1586, at the full almost of twenty-eight years of her reign, whereof the reporter requireth of all that were hearers a favorable interpretation of his intent, because he findeth that he cannot express the same answerable to the original, which the learned call prototypon.*

The bottomless graces and immeasurable benefits bestowed upon me by the Almighty are and have been such as I must not only acknowledge them, but admire them—accounting them as well miracles as benefits, not so much in respect of His divine majesty, with whom nothing is more common than to do things rare and singular, as in regard of our weakness, who cannot sufficiently set forth His wonderful works and graces, which to me have been so many, so diversely folded and embroidered one upon another, as in no sort I am[2] able to express them.

---

1. *Source:* R[obert] C[ecil], *The Copy of a Letter to the Earl of Leicester . . . with a Report of Certain Petitions and Declarations Made to the Queen's Majesty at Two Several Times . . . and Her Majesty's Answers Thereunto by Herself Delivered* (London: C. Barker, 1586), sigs. Ci r–Civ v; (*STC* 6052); the same volume was issued in French in 1587. This published version of the speech, issued with the royal arms as its frontispiece, closely follows Elizabeth's own working copy created after the speech's formal delivery (BL, MS Lansdowne 94, art. 35A, fols. 84r–85r; a damaged transcript in a formal italic hand, probably Robert Cecil's, with Elizabeth's corrections. The Lansdowne version shows the queen in the process of turning the original oral "prototype" into a reading text for public dissemination. (For the original-spelling version, see Figure 9 and *ACFLO,* part 1.) MS Lansdowne without the queen's corrections also circulated separately; Inner Temple Library, MS Petyt 538, vol. 10, fols. 6v–7r, is almost identical to it. The printed version of the speech is the one that circulated most widely. Sir Edward Hoby's copy—BL, MS Additional 38823, fols. 76r–77r—is very close to the 1586 printed text, as is the version in Holinshed (3:1582–83). The most important differences between the MS containing Elizabeth's corrections and Cecil's printed version are recorded in the notes. However, the notes do not record differences derived from our conjectural restoration of damaged portions of the MS.

2. **I am** Elizabeth's MS reads "am I."

[Copy] of her Ma:ties most gracious Answer deliuered by his self
...ly to the Petition of the Ll: and Commons of ...
Parliament. ...

...ottonles graces and immeasurable benefitts bestowed vpon mee by Almightie God
and haue bin such, as I must not only acknowledg them but ... admire them, accoun
...ing them as well miracles as benefitts, not so much in respect of his diuine Ma:tie
with whome nothing is more comon then to do thinges rare & singuler, as in regard
of oure weaknes, who cannot sufficiently sett forth his wonderfull woorkes ...
... to mee ... haue bene so many, so diuerslie folded and imbrodered one ...
another as in no sort I am able to expresse them.

And although there liueth not any that may more iustly acknowledg themselues
...ly bound vnto God then I ... whose life he hath ... preserued
at sondrie tymes beyond my merit ... from a multitude of perills and daungers
Yet is not that the ... for ... I account my self deepliest bound to giue him the
... thanckes, or to yeld him the greatest recognition, but this ... I shall
... you hereafter w:ch will deserue the name of wonder. At each things and
some seene be worthie ... namely that as I came to the Crowne
with the willing harts of ... subiects so do I now after xxviij yeres migne
perceaue in you ... no deminution of ... goodwilles w:ch if happelie I
should wante, well mowght I breath, but ... thincke I liued ...
...

And now not w:thstanding if I finde apparauntlie my life hath byn ... daunge-
rouslie sought, and ... death ... contriued, Yet am I ... therof so cleare
frome malice, which hath the propertie to make ... of ... ... as ...
falls and faultes of theire enimies and make them seeme to do ... for other
cawses, when as with vancor they ... ... to pursue there ... I ...
... it is to mee and hath bene a thing most greuious to thinke that one
not different in sex, of like estate and my neare kinne, shold be ... of grace
or false in faith as now to seeke my death by whome so long her life hath bene
preserued w:th th' intollerable perill of my owne. Yea I had so litle purpose
to pursue her w:th any colour of malice, y:t as it is not vnknowne to some of my
Ll: here (for now I will play the blabb) I secretlie wrote her a l:re vpon the
discouerie of her treasons that if she w:ld ... thoroughlie of her will confesse it and priuatlie acknowledge it by her l:res vnto mee, shee neuer should be
called for it into publike question. Neither did I it of any minde to circumuent her,
for then I knew as much as she cold confesse and so did I write.

And ... now the matter is made so apparant, I thought she trulie
were repentant as perhapps she wolde easilie appeare ... sheowe) and that
for her none other wolde take the matter vppon them, or that we were but as two
milke maides, w:th pailes vpon oure armes, or that there were no more dependency
vpon us, but ... myne owne life were onlie in perill, and not the whole estate
of youre religion and well doings, I protest (wherein you may beleeue mee) for
although I may haue many vices, I hope I haue nor accustomed my tongue
to be an Instrument of vntruth ... I wolde most willinglie pardon and remit
... offense.

FIGURE 9 Speech 17, version 2, first page of transcript with Queen Elizabeth's corrections;
BL, MS Lansdowne 94, fol. 84r. Reproduced by permission of the British Library.

And although there liveth not any that may more justly acknowledge themselves infinitely bound unto God than I, whose life He hath miraculously preserved at sundry times (beyond my merit) from a multitude of perils and dangers; yet is not that the cause for which I count myself the deepliest bound to give Him my humblest thanks, or to yield Him[3] greatest recognition, but this which I shall tell you hereafter, which will deserve the name of wonder if rare things and seldom seen be worthy of account. Even this it is: that as I came to the crown with the willing hearts of my[4] subjects, so do I now after twenty-eight years' reign perceive in you no diminution of goodwills, which if haply I should want, well might I breathe but never think I lived.

And now, albeit I find my life hath been full dangerously sought and death contrived by such as no desert procured,[5] yet am I therein[6] so clear from malice (which hath the property to make men glad at the falls and faults of their foes, and make them seem to do for other causes when rancor is the ground) as I protest[7] it is and hath been my grievous thought that one not different in sex, of like estate, and my near kin, should fall[8] into so great a crime. Yea, I had so little purpose to pursue her with any color of malice that as it is not unknown to some of my lords here (for now I will play the blab), I secretly wrote her a letter upon the discovery of sundry treasons, that if she would confess them and privately acknowledge them by her letters to myself, she never should need be called for them into so public question. Neither did I it of mind to circumvent her, for then I knew as much as she could confess, and so did I write. And if even yet, now that the matter is made but too apparent, I thought she truly would repent (as perhaps she would easily appear in outward show to do) and that for her none other would take the matter upon them; or that we were but as two milkmaids with pails upon our arms; or that there were no more dependency upon us but mine own life were only in danger and not the whole estate of your religion and well-doings; I protest (wherein you may believe me, for though I may have many vices, I hope I have not accustomed my tongue to be an instrument of untruth) I would most willingly pardon and remit this offense. Or if by my death, other nations and kingdoms might

3. **Him** struck through in Elizabeth's MS.
4. **my** struck through in Elizabeth's MS.
5. **procured** Elizabeth's MS adds "it."
6. **therein** Elizabeth's MS reads "hereof."
7. **as I protest** Elizabeth's MS reads "yet protest."
8. **fall** Elizabeth's MS reads "be fallen."

truly say that this realm had attained an ever prosperous and flourishing estate, I would (I assure you) not desire to live, but gladly give my life to the end my death might procure you a better prince.

And for your sakes it is that I desire to live, to keep you from a worse. For[9] as for me, I assure you I find no great cause I should be fond to live;[10] I take no such pleasure in it that I should much wish it, nor conceive such terror in death that I should greatly fear it. And yet I say not but if the stroke were coming, perchance flesh and blood would be moved with it and seek to shun it.

I have had good experience and trial of this world: I know what it is to be a subject, what to be a sovereign; what to have good neighbors, and sometime meet evil willers. I have found treason in trust, seen great benefits little regarded, and instead of gratefulness, courses of purpose to cross.

These former remembrances, present feeling, and future expectation of evils, I say, have made me think an evil is much the better the less while it endureth, and so, them happiest that are soonest[11] hence; and taught me to bear with a better mind these treasons than is common to my sex—yea, with a better heart, perhaps, than is in some men. Which I hope you will not merely impute to my simplicity or want of understanding, but rather that I thus conceived: that had their purposes taken effect, I should not have found the blow before I had felt it, and though my peril should have been great, my pain should have been but small and short. Wherein as I would be loath to die so bloody a death, so doubt I not but God would have given me grace to be prepared for such an event, chance when it shall, which I refer to His good pleasure.

And now, as touching their treasons and conspiracies, together with the contriver of them, I will not so prejudicate myself and this my realm as to say or think that I might not without the last statute, by the ancient laws of this land, have proceeded against her; which was not made particularly to prejudice her, though perhaps it might then be suspected, in respect of the disposition of such as depend that way. It was so far from being intended to entrap her, that it was rather an admonition to warn the danger thereof; but sith it is made, and in the force of a law,[12] I thought

9. **For** omitted in Elizabeth's MS, but page tear affects the text at this point.

10. **to live** Elizabeth's MS reads "of life."   11. **soonest** omitted in Elizabeth's MS.

12. According to the Act for the Queen's Safety (1585), Mary, Queen of Scots, would incur the death penalty if others made a plot on her behalf even if she did not participate in the plot.

good in that which might concern her to proceed according thereunto, rather than by course of common law. Wherein if you, the judges, have not deceived me, or that the books you brought me were not false (which God forbid), I might as justly have tried her by the ancient laws of the land.

But you lawyers are so nice[13] in sifting and scanning every word and letter that many times you stand more upon form than matter, upon syllables than sense of the law. For in the strictness and exact following of common form, she must have been indicted in Staffordshire, have holden up her hand at the bar and been tried[14] by a jury—a proper course forsooth, to deal in that manner with one of her estate! I thought it better, therefore, for avoiding of these and more absurdities, to commit the cause to the inquisition of a good number of the greatest and most noble personages of this realm, of the judges and others of good account, whose sentence I must approve. And all little enough, for we princes, I tell you, are set on stages in the sight and view of all the world duly observed. The eyes of many behold our actions; a spot is soon spied in our garments; a blemish quickly noted in our doings. It behooveth us therefore to be careful that our proceedings be just and honorable.

But I must tell you one thing more: that in this last act of Parliament you have brought me to a narrow strait,[15] that I must give direction for her death, which cannot be to me[16] but a most grievous and irksome burden. And lest you might mistake mine absence from this Parliament (which I had almost forgotten), although there be no cause why I should willingly come amongst multitudes—for that amongst many, some may be evil—yet hath it not been the doubt of any such danger or occasion that kept me from thence, but only the great grief to hear this cause spoken of; especially that such a one of state and kin should need so open a declaration, and that this[17] nation should be so spotted with blots of disloyalty. Wherein the less is my grief, for that I hope the better part is mine; and those of the worse not much to be accounted of; for that in seeking my destruction, they might have spoiled their own souls.

13. **nice** picky; Elizabeth's MS reads "so nice and so precise."
14. **Staffordshire . . . tried** Elizabeth's version reads "Staffordshire and have been arraigned at the bar, holden up her hand, been tried."
15. **brought me to a narrow strait** Elizabeth's MS reads "laid an hard hand on me."
16. **to me** moved to end of sentence in Elizabeth's MS.
17. **and that this** Elizabeth's MS reads "as a."

And even now could I tell you that which would make you sorry. It is a secret, and yet I will tell it you, although it is known I have the property to keep counsel but too well, oftentimes to mine own peril. It is not long since mine eyes did see it written that an oath was taken within few days either to kill me or to be hanged themselves; and that to be performed ere one month were ended.[18] Hereby I see your danger in me, and neither can nor will be so unthankful or careless of your consciences as not provide[19] for your safety.

I am not unmindful of your Oath made in the Association manifesting your great goodwills and affections taken and entered into upon good conscience and true knowledge of the guilt,[20] for safety of my person and conservation of my life: done (I protest to God) before I heard it or ever thought of such a matter, until a great number of hands with many obligations[21] were showed me at Hampton Court, signed and subscribed with the names and seals of the greatest of this land. Which as I do acknowledge as a perfect argument of your true hearts and great zeal to my safety, so shall my bond be stronger tied to greater care for all your good.[22]

But forasmuch as this matter is rare, weighty, and of great consequence, I think you do not look for any present resolution; the rather for that, as it is not my manner in matters of far less moment to give speedy answer without due consideration, so in this of such importance I think it very requisite with earnest prayer to beseech His divine Majesty so to illuminate my understanding and inspire me with His grace, as I may do and determine that which shall serve to the establishment of His Church, preservation of your estates, and prosperity of this commonwealth under my charge. Wherein for that I know delay is dangerous, you shall have with all conveniency our resolution delivered by our message. And whatever any prince may merit of their subjects, for

18. Elizabeth's MS includes a marginal note (not in her hand) at this point: "Her majesty referred the further knowledge hereof to some of the lords there present, whereof the lord treasurer seemed to be one for that he stood up to verify it."

19. **not provide** Elizabeth's MS reads "to take no care."

20. **true knowledge of the guilt** added in Elizabeth's MS but struck through; in the same sentence **and conservation of my life** is not in Elizabeth's MS.

21. **a great number of ... obligations** Elizabeth's MS reads "3 [struck through and replaced by] a thousand hands' obligations."

22. Elizabeth's much-revised version of this sentence is "Which as I do acknowledge the greatest argument of your hearts to me and great zeal to my safety, so shall my bond be stronger tied to greater care for all good."

their approved testimony of their unfained sincerity—either by governing justly, void of all partiality, or sufferance of any injuries done even to the poorest—that do I assuredly promise inviolably to perform for requital of your so many deserts.

18 ɞ QUEEN ELIZABETH'S SECOND REPLY TO THE PARLIAMENTARY PETITIONS URGING THE EXECUTION OF MARY, QUEEN OF SCOTS, NOVEMBER 24, 1586

SPEECH 18, VERSION 1[1] *[Headed] Another speech of the queen's.*

Then her majesty turned to the lords and said that she never had a greater strife within herself than she had that day, whether she should speak or be silent, lest if she should speak, in showing her affection she might seem to dissemble, and if she should be silent she might do them wrong in not answering their expectations. And then with a low voice she spake unto them of the complaint, which afterwards she spake unto the Commons as ensueth:

"I perceive you have well considered of my last message sent unto you, proceeding from an earnest desire and a hungry will in me that some way might be by you for my safety devised without the execution of that Act whereunto by your petition I was moved. But nothing being found for my satisfaction in that behalf, I must needs make a great complaint, not of you for I make it unto you, nor of myself but of my case, which at this present is such, by reason of the many practices against me and the great mischief intended towards me, that now the bane of the injurer must be the only cure of my danger. Whereof to think it grieveth me not a little, considering that there be some which will not stick to shed their own blood for the sake and defense of their kin, and that by

1. *Source:* The Syndics of Cambridge University Library, MS Gg.III.34, pp. 312–16; a version that may be close to Queen Elizabeth's actual delivery of the speech, although it is likely that some of her specific topical references have been toned down. The textual situation for this speech is similar to Speech 17, p. 186, and the two speeches circulated together in manuscript.

At the time of this speech, Parliament and the Privy Council were poised for Mary's execution, but Elizabeth continued to delay. Mary, Queen of Scots, was finally beheaded at Fotheringay Castle, Northamptonshire, on February 8, 1587. See also Elizabeth's letter to Sir Amyas Paulet and her final letters to and about Mary, Letters 68, 71, and 72, pp. 284, and 287–89.

me it should be said hereafter, a maiden queen hath been the death of a prince, her kinswoman. A thing in no sort deserved by me, howsoever by the despite of malice it may be reported of me.

"I have cause to think how narrowly mine actions are like to be sifted and finely scanned by some good fellows abroad, who spare not to publish pamphlets, libels, and books against me with detestation of me and my government,[2] giving me for an alms[3] (I thank them for it) to be a tyrant—that from which always my nature above all things hath most abhorred; but I think they meant to send it me for news, for that I never knew or heard that ever I was suspected thereof before. I would their wickedness were like news unto me, and that the same were no more true of them than this is of me, but I trust both I and they shall lie in our graves ere that it shall be proved true by me. Such rebels there are beyond the seas; I hope there are no such within the realm. I pray God there be not, but I will not swear it. But to clear myself of that fault, this I may justly say: I have pardoned many traitors and rebels, and besides I well remember half a score treasons which have been either covered or slightly examined or let slip and passed over, so that mine actions have not been such as should procure me the name of a tyrant. Yet this of myself must I needs confess: though for that crime I am not justly to be touched, I am a wretched sinner and humbly desire pardon at His hands against whom I have offended for the same.

"And now to say more unto you of myself, when I first came to the scepter and crown of this realm I did think more of God who gave it me than of the title. And therefore my first care was to set in order those things which did concern the Church of God and this religion in which I was born, in which I was bred, and in which I trust to die, not being ignorant how dangerous a thing it was to work in a kingdom a sudden alteration of religion, and that it was like to be a foundation and a ground for such great kings and princes as were mine enemies to build and

2. As an example of the libels that circulated after the execution of Mary, Queen of Scots, Neale offers the following ditty, displayed in the open streets of Edinburgh "with a little cord of hemp tied halter-wise" (2:135):

To Jezebel, that English whore:
  Receive this Scottish chain
As presages of her great malheur [misfortune]
  For murdering of our queen.

3. **alms** charitable gifts, usually to the poor.

work their devices upon, ill intended against me. But I committed my cause unto Him for whose sake I did it, knowing He could defend me, as I must confess He hath done unto this time, and doubt not but He will do unto the end. After that I did put myself to the school of experience, where I sought to learn what things were most fit for a king to have, and I found them to be four: namely, justice, temper,[4] magnanimity, and judgment.[5] Of the two last, I will say little, because I will not challenge nor arrogate to myself more than I know there is cause. Yet this may I say, and truly: that as Solomon,[6] so I above all things have desired wisdom at the hands of God. And I thank Him He hath given me so much judgment and wit as that I perceive mine own imperfections many ways and mine ignorance in most things. As for magnanimity, I will pass it over. And for the course of justice, I protest that I never knew difference of persons—that I never set one before another but upon just cause, neither have preferred any to office or other place of ruling for the preferrer's sake, but that I knew or was made believe he was worthy and fit for it. Neither did I ever lend mine ear to any person contrary to order of law to pervert my verdict. And for temper, I have had always care to do as Augustus Caesar, who being moved to offense, before he attempted anything was willed to say over the alphabet.[7] And I trust such hath been my actions and the carriage of myself as that my subjects have no cause in that respect to repent themself for their prince. And that I am staunch enough in mine actions I am sure there are sufficient witnesses here present.

"And now, as touching you, I must needs say and confess that there was never prince more bound to his people than I am to you all. I can but acknowledge your great love and exceeding care of me to be such as I shall never be able to requite, having but one life, except I had as many lives as you all. But I will never forget it while I shall breathe. And though I may want the means and the wit, yet surely I shall never want

---

4. **temper** temperance.

5. Cf. book 4 of Plato's *Republic*, where it is agreed that a state that is good in the full sense of the word will be wise, courageous, temperate, and just (427c); and where the same virtues are specified as the attributes of the fully good man (441e–442e). For Platonic courage, however, Elizabeth substitutes **magnanimity**, defined by Aristotle as a lofty pride and self-esteem that reach moral nobility through concern for one's honor (*Nicomachean Ethics*, 1123b).

6. Cf. 1 Kings 3:9.

7. For the same story in Plutarch, see Speech 5 n. 2, p. 71.

the will to requite it. And so I pray you tell them all I do but acknowledge I cannot requite. And as for your proceedings in this cause, I assure you I do not mislike your judgments, for they are grounded upon sure grounds—upon the Word of God and great reason. Neither do I misconster[8] your petition. I know it did proceed from earnest and dutiful affection towards me. But peradventure it may seem strange unto you that I should cherish a sword in mine own realm to shed mine own blood. I do not say I will do so. And yet I know there are many which venture their lives oftentimes for a less matter than the safety of a kingdom. And haply in this case I might adventure much more, were it with danger of mine own life, which I protest before God I chiefly regard in regard of yours.

"But it seemeth most strange unto me that everyone, both of you, my lords, and the rest, should all agree in one that it should be a thing most hard, or rather impossible, for me to live in safety without execution of your demand. And here I must say unto you, if any person be so wicked to think that the last message which I sent unto you was a thing done *pro forma tantum*[9] and that I meant it not indeed, or that it proceeded from a vainglorious mind, as that I sought thereby the more to be commended for clemency and gentleness of nature, or that I meant to make the lords wire-drawers to draw the matter still into length without cause, he doth me greater wrong than ever he can be able to recompense. I did it, I protest before God, as being most desirous to understand every man's opinion whereby to perceive what was fittest for me to do, wherein my mind was that every one of my lords should frankly utter his conceit either publicly in the House or privately to myself, lest some of them, being suspected, might for that cause be silent. And this I willed, my lords, my commissioners to signify, which if they did not, they did me the more wrong. For I am not so unwise but that I know that although by calling I go before a great many, yet many particular persons for wisdom and other respects are to be preferred before me.

"But now for answer unto you, you must take an answer without answer at my hands. For if I should say I would not do it, I should peradventure say that which I did not think, and otherwise than it might be. If I should say I would do it, it were not fit in this place and at this

---

8. **misconster** misconstrue.

9. "only *pro forma.*"

time, although I did mean it. Wherefore I must desire you to hold your-selves satisfied with this answer answerless. I know there is none of you but is wise and well affected towards me and therefore will consider what is most fit for me to do. There must be deeds and not words which must satisfice[10] your demand. I pray you therefore, let this answer an-swerless content you for this present, assuring yourselves that I am now and ever will be most careful to do that which shall be best for your preservation. And be not too earnest to move me to do that which may tend to the loss of that which you are all most desirous to keep."

SPEECH 18, VERSION 2[1] *[Headed] The second answer made by the queen's majesty, delivered by her own mouth to the second speech uttered in the names of the Lords and Commons of the Parliament in her Chamber of Presence at Richmond, the 24th day of November, 1586.*

Full grievous is the way whose going on and end breed cumber[2] for the hire of a laborious journey.

I have strived more this day than ever in my life, whether I should speak or use silence. If I speak and not complain, I shall dissemble; if I hold my peace, your labor taken were full vain. For me to make my moan were strange and rare; for I suppose you shall find few that for their own particular will cumber you with such a care. Yet such, I protest, hath been my greedy desire and hungry will that of your con-sultation might have fallen out some other means to work my safety joined with your assurance than that for which you are become such earnest suitors as I protest I must needs,[3] though not of you, but unto

10. **satisfice** satisfy/suffice.

1. *Source:* Robert Cecil's 1586 printed *Copy,* sigs. Div v–Eiii r. The textual complexities surrounding Speech 18 are very similar to those surrounding Speech 17, and the two fre-quently circulated together. For fuller citation and a more detailed discussion see Speech 17, Version 2, n. 1, p. 190. Queen Elizabeth's revised, published version reproduced here is very close to Sir Edward Hoby's copy—BL, MS Additional 38823, fols. 77r–78r—and to Holinshed's printed text (3:1585–86). Elizabeth's own revisions appear in BL, MS Lans-downe 94, art. 35B, fols. 86r–88r, a continuation of the MS containing her first speech on Mary, Queen of Scots. (For original-spelling version, see *ACFLO,* part 1.) The most signifi-cant differences between Elizabeth's manuscript and the printed version are recorded in the notes below.

2. **cumber** encumbrance; in Elizabeth's MS and here, the maxim is set off as though it were the scriptural text for a sermon. Instead of **breed,** Elizabeth's MS reads "breeds."

3. **must needs** Elizabeth's MS reads "must needs use complaint."

you, and of the cause. For that I do perceive by your advices, prayers, and desires, there falleth out this accident, that only my injurer's bane must be my life's surety.

But if any there live so wicked of nature to suppose that I prolonged this time only *pro forma,* to the intent to make a show of clemency, thereby to set my praises to the wire-drawers to lengthen them the more: they do me so great a wrong as they can hardly recompense. Or if any person there be that think or imagine that the least vainglorious thought hath drawn me further herein, they do me as open injury as ever was done to any living creature, as He that is the Maker of all thoughts knoweth best to be true. Or if there be any that think that the lords appointed in commission durst do no other, as fearing thereby to displease or else to be suspected to be of a contrary opinion to my safety, they do but heap upon me injurious conceits. For either those put in trust by me to supply my place have not performed their duties towards me, or else they have signified unto you all that my desire was that everyone should do according to his conscience, and in the course of his[4] proceedings should enjoy both freedom of voice and liberty of opinion. And what they would not openly declare, they might privately to myself have revealed.[5] It was of a willing mind and great desire I had that some other means might be found out, wherein I should have taken more comfort than in any other thing under the sun.

And since now it is resolved that my surety cannot be established without a princess's end,[6] I have just cause to complain that I, who have in my time pardoned so many rebels, winked at so many treasons, and either not produced them or altogether slipped them over with silence, should now be forced to this proceeding against such a person. I have besides, during my reign, seen and heard many opprobrious books and pamphlets against me, my realm, and state, accusing me to be a tyrant. I thank them for their alms: I believe therein their meaning was to tell me news, and news it is to me indeed. I would it were as strange to hear of their impiety! What will they not now say when it shall be spread that for the safety of her life, a maiden queen could be content to spill the blood even of her own kinswoman? I may therefore full well complain

---

4. **his** Elizabeth's MS reads "these."

5. Elizabeth's version of this sentence reads "And what they would not openly they might privately to myself declare."

6. **end** Elizabeth's MS reads "head."

that any man should think me given to cruelty, whereof I am so guiltless and innocent as I should slander God if I should say He gave me so vile a mind. Yea, I protest I am so far from it that for mine own life, I would not touch her. Neither hath my care been so much bent how to prolong mine, as how to preserve both, which I am right sorry is made so hard—yea, so impossible. I am not so void of judgment as not to see mine own peril; nor yet so ignorant as not to know it were in nature a foolish course to cherish a sword to cut mine own throat; nor so careless as not to weigh that my life daily is in hazard. But this I do consider: that many a man would put his life in danger for the safeguard of a king. I do not say that so will I, but I pray you think that I have thought upon it.

But sith so many have both written and spoken against me, I pray you give me leave to say somewhat for myself and, before you return to your countries, let you know for what a one you have passed so careful thoughts.[7] Wherein as I think myself infinitely beholding unto you all that seek to preserve my life by all the means you may, so I protest unto you[8] that there liveth no prince that ever shall be more mindful to requite so good deserts. And[9] as I perceive you have kept your old wonts in a general seeking of the lengthening of my days, so am I sure that I shall never[10] requite it, unless I had as many lives as you all; but forever I will acknowledge it while there is any[11] breath left me. Although I may not justify, but may justly condemn my sundry faults and sins to God, yet for my care in this government let me acquaint you with my intents.

When first I took the scepter, my title made me not forget the Giver: and therefore began as it became me with such religion as both I was born in, bred in, and I trust shall die in. Although I was not so simple as not to know what danger and peril so great an alteration might procure me, how many great princes of the contrary opinion[12] would attempt all they might against me; and generally, what enmity I should thereby breed unto myself. Which all I regarded not, knowing that He for whose sake I did it might and would defend me; for which it is that ever since I have been so dangerously prosecuted as I[13] rather marvel that I am than

---

7. **careful thoughts** Elizabeth's MS adds "that will never be forgetful of your exceeding cares for my safety" and begins the next sentence with "And" instead of **Wherein**.

8. **unto you** not in Elizabeth's MS.   9. **And** Elizabeth's MS reads "Wherein."

10. **I shall never** Elizabeth's MS reads "never shall I."

11. **any** Elizabeth's MS reads "any my."

12. **opinion** In Elizabeth's MS the immediately following phrase, "that term themselves Catholic," is struck through.

13. **for which … I** struck through in Elizabeth's MS.

that mame a man wold put his life in danger, for the safegard of a kinge, I
doe not say that I meane to doe so, but I praie you thinke that I haue
thought vpon it.   But sith so mame hath both writen and spoken

against me I praie you giue me leaue to say somewhat for my self, and
before you retorne to your contries fett your knowe ___ that will neuer be forgetfull of youre exceeding cares, for my safetie   And

as I thinke my selfe beholdinge vnto youe, that you seeke to preserue
my life by all meanes yoe cann, so I protest, that there is no Prince that
nor euer halfe more ___ to require so good
mee hath ___ than ___ for it: wherein as I
perceaue yoge haue kept your old wont in a generall seeking of the ___
my ___ so doe I conceaue that I am neuer ___ requite it, vnles I had
as many liues as yoe all, but for euer I will acknowledge it whill there is
any ___ left ___

___ Next I will make my confession ___ and say before you
all, that I am a ___ full of faults, a wretch that haue bone ___
forgetfull of my dutie towards God, for if I shold say otherwise I shold
___ offend both God and youe, and most of all forget my self   And seeing so
mame ___ haue bene vsed to discourse the actions of youer gouernours, I
will say somewhat for my self.

When I first tooke the sceptre my titel made me not forget
the giuer and therfor began as hit became me with
that gaue it, and therfore sought to establish in this kingdome, his church
and that Religion, wherein I was borne and bred, and wherein I hope to
die, although I was not so simple as not to know what danger and
___ so great an alteration might procure me, how mame great princes of
the contrare, ___ wold attempt all they might

FIGURE 10 Speech 18, version 2, middle section of transcript with Queen Elizabeth's corrections; BL, MS Lansdowne 94, fol. 87v. Reproduced by permission of the British Library.

muse that I should not be, if it were not God's holy hand that continueth me beyond all other expectation.[14] Then entered I further into the school of experience, bethinking what it fitted a king to do; and there I saw he scant was well furnished if either he lacked justice, temperance, magnanimity, or judgment. As for the two latter, I will not boast; my sex doth not permit it. But for the two first, this dare I say: amongst my subjects I never knew a difference of person where right was one, nor never to my knowledge preferred for favor whom I thought not fit for worth; nor bent my ears to credit a tale that first was told me; nor was so rash to corrupt my judgment with my censure before I heard the cause. I will not say but many reports might fortune be brought me by such as might hear the case whose partiality might mar sometime the matter, for we princes may not hear all ourselves. But this dare I boldly affirm: my verdict went ever with the truth of my knowledge. As full well wished Alcibiades[15] his friend that he should not give any answer till he had recited the letters of the alphabet, so have I not used over-sudden resolutions in matters that have touched me full near. You will say that with me, I think. And therefore, as touching your counsels and consultations, I conceive them to be wise, honest, and conscionable: so provident and careful for the safety of my life (which I wish no longer than may be for your good) that though I never can yield you of recompense your due, yet shall I endeavor myself to give you cause to think your goodwill not ill bestowed, and strive to make myself worthy for such subjects.

And now for your petition. I shall pray you for this present to content yourselves with an answer without answer. Your judgment I condemn not, neither do I mistake your reasons, but pray you to accept my thankfulness, excuse my doubtfulness, and take in good part my answer answerless. Wherein I attribute not so much to mine own judgment, but that I think many particular persons may go before me, though by my degree I go before them. Therefore if I should say I would not do what you request, it might peradventure be more than I thought; and to say I would do it might perhaps breed peril of that you labor to preserve, being more than in your own wisdoms and discretions would seem convenient, circumstances of place and time being duly considered.

14. From here on, Elizabeth's MS is so different from the printed version that the reader is referred to *ACFLO,* part 1.

15. For the origin of this anecdote, see Speech 5 n. 2, p. 71.

LETTERS 34-77

34 ❧ QUEEN ELIZABETH TO SIR FRANCIS WALSINGHAM,
AMBASSADOR TO FRANCE, JULY 23, 1572[1]

*[Headed] To our right trusty and well-beloved Francis Walsingham,
Esquire, our ambassador resident with our good brother, the French king.*

Elizabeth Regina　　　　　　　　　　　　　By the queen.

Trusty and well beloved, we greet you well. Where at the being here with
us of the duke of Montmorency, he and de Foix, after other their ordinary matter of ratification of the treaty passed over,[2] did many times
very earnestly deal with us, and in like manner with sundry of our Council, to move us to incline to an offer of marriage which the French king
and queen mother willed them to make to us for the duke of Alençon;
and that we found the matter somewhat strange, considering some

---

1. *Source*: BL, MS Additional 30156, fols. 326r–329v; copy in a seventeenth-century collection entitled "Sir Dudley Digges. The Complete Ambassador," which was published in London in 1655. Sir Francis Walsingham (1530?–1590) was a member of the Privy Council and
ambassador to France in 1570–76 and 1579–82. The French dukes in question were Anjou,
later Henry III of France, and his younger brother François Hercule (1554–1584), duke of
Alençon, later duke of Anjou. François Hercule, uniformly identified in our notes as
Alençon or Monsieur, became the subject of protracted marriage negotiations later in the
decade and in the early 1580s. At the time of this letter he was seventeen and Elizabeth,
thirty-eight.

2. François, **duke of Montmorency**, headed the French delegation sent to England to
ratify the Treaty of Blois in April 1572. Paul **de Foix**, formerly French ambassador to England, was another member of the delegation.

things past not in good order, as you know, in the matter of like offer for Monsieur d'Anjou, wherein the said Montmorency and his colleagues labored much to satisfy us, but especially considering the youngness of the years of the duke of Alençon being compared to ours; so for those respects, although we could give them no answer of comfort to content them, yet such was their importunacy in reciting of many reasons and arguments to move us not to mislike thereof, in respect as well of the strength of the amity which this amity should give to the continuance of this last league,[3] and consideration as also of the worthiness of the said duke of Alençon for his excellent virtues and good conditions which they allege to be in him, with sundry other arguments tending to remove the difficulties and to gain our contentation and liking of the said duke.

And in the end after their many conferences had both with us as with our Council, when we perceived them very much perplexed to see our strangeness[4] from assenting to their desires and how loath they were to have any flat denial, we were advised to forbear from making of a plain refusal and to expect the return of my lord admiral,[5] by whom and by others of his company we might understand what might be further conceived of the personage and conditions of the said duke. And so our answer to them at their departure was this: that we found such difficulties in this matter, especially for the difference of his age, as presently we could not disgest[6] the same; yet such was the importunacy of our own subjects of all estates to have us to marry as we would forbear to give any such resolute answer as might miscontent the said ambassadors and as we know would much grieve our people at this time. And so we would take some further time to be advertised[7] upon the matter, and after one month space we would make a direct answer to the French king, which also we would first communicate to the said duke of Montmorency to be by him, if he would, delivered over to the said king.

And so with this answer they departed, whereupon after the return of the lord admiral, we have considered with him and with some other

---

3. The Treaty of Blois, ratified in April 1572, which altered the previous direction of English policy by creating a defensive alliance between England and France.

4. **strangeness** absence of friendly feeling, aloofness.

5. **lord admiral** Edward Fiennes de Clinton (1512–1585), recently created earl of Lincoln, who had headed the English delegation to Paris for ratification of the Treaty of Blois.

6. **disgest** digest, get used to.

7. **advertised** informed, notified.

that were there, by whom we find that indeed the conditions and qualities of the said duke, as far forth as they could by their observation gather or by report of others understand, were nothing inferior to Monsieur d'Anjou, but rather better to be liked. But as to his visage and favor,[8] everybody doth declare the same to be far inferior, and that especially for the blemishes that the smallpox hath wrought therein, so as his young years considered and the doubtfulness of the liking of his favor joined therewith, wherein nobody that hath seen him can otherwise report, although otherwise to all other purposes he is commended before his brother, we cannot indeed bring our mind to like of this offer, specially finding no other greater commodity offered to us with him whereby the absurdity that the general opinion of the world might grow to concerning this our choice, after so many refusals of others of great worthiness,[9] might be counterpoised or in some manner recompensed.

Wherefore, according to our answer made to the said ambassadors, we have determination that you shall in our name say as followeth to Montmorency, or if he shall desire that you yourself (considering the answer is not plausible) shall make it to the king, then you shall so do, requiring him to be present and to move the king and his mother[10] to interpret the same to the best, as indeed we mean it plainly and friendly. And then you shall say that we have considered of the matter of the king's offer unto us of Monsieur d'Alençon in marriage, and for the same we do most heartily thank the king and the queen mother, knowing manifestly that the same proceedeth of very great goodwill to make a very perfect continuance of the amity lately contracted between us by this last treaty. And considering we have as great desire to have the same amity continued and strengthened, we are very sorry to find so great difficulties in this matter, that should be a principal bond thereof, as we cannot disgest the inconveniences of the same (by reason of the differences of our ages) to assent thereunto. Praying the king and his mother to assure themselves that there is no lack of desire in us to continue—yea, if it might be, to increase—this amity, that maketh us to think of the difficulties in this offer otherwise than we think all others that doth

8. **favor** face, countenance.

9. **others of great worthiness** Elizabeth had declined to marry Emmanuel Philibert, duke of Savoy; King Erik XIV of Sweden; his brother Duke John of Finland; and, preeminently, King Philip II of Spain.

10. **the king and his mother** Charles IX of France and the powerful Catherine de Médicis.

consider thereof and must conceive (which proceedeth almost only of the difference of the age of Monsieur d'Alençon and ourself) a matter that cannot be remedied either by the king his brother that desireth the match, or by us. So as the lack of not perfecting this manner of bond of amity cannot be justly imputed to either of us, nor to the party himself, of whose conditions and virtues (truly you may say), we hear so well as we cannot but esteem him very much, and think him well worthy to have as good fortune by marriage as he or any other might have by us.

And you may say, if so you see cause, although we might have known thus much as concerning his age when the ambassadors were here, and therefore might at that time have given them answer and not thus to have deferred it until this time; yet to satisfy the king therein you shall say that true it is that although we ourselves were of this mind from the beginning, to think the match inconvenient for his age, yet at the being here of the ambassadors we continually labored by our Council and also by our estates then assembled in Parliament, in laying before us the necessity of our marriage, both for our own comfort and also for the weal of the realm. And some of them alleging unto us that there could be no such difficulty in this matter of years, but the evil opinion that might be conceived thereof in the world to our lack might percase[11] be recompensed with some other matter of advantage to us in our realm, in the sight also of the world, as being overcome with the importunity of their reasons, we did yield to take some further consideration of the matter and to prove[12] whether in some time we could work our mind in the mean season to some other purpose, or whether any such further matter might be offered to which this match as might counterpoise in the judgment of the world the inconvenience of the difference of the age. But so it is that in all this time we can neither find our mind altered nor yet hear of any other thing that might countervail the inconvenience. But so for observing of our promise, and especially because we mean to deal plainly with our good brother and the queen his mother, we do make them this answer: that surely we cannot find ourselves void of doubt and misliking to accept this offer, which is principally for the difference of years, allowing nevertheless of his worthiness for his virtuous and honorable conditions, as much as we can require in any prince to be our husband. And so we pray the king and his mother that the duke himself may understand our judgment to be of his worthiness.

11. **percase** perchance.   12. **prove** test.

And for the great goodwill we understand that he hath borne to us, who do assure him that we shall for the same esteem and to him at all times hereafter as well as any other prince of his estate, reserving only the band of love that ought to accompany marriage. Given under our signet at Theobalds[13] the 23 of July, 1572, in the fourteenth year of our reign.

35 ❧ QUEEN ELIZABETH TO SIR FRANCIS WALSINGHAM, AMBASSADOR TO FRANCE, JULY 25, 1572[1]

[Headed] To our trusty and well-beloved Francis Walsingham, Esquire, our ambassador resident with our good brother the French king.

By the queen.

Right trusty and well beloved, we greet you well. After we finished our other letters and determined to have sent them away, in such sort as you might have had them in convenient time to have delivered our answer according to our promise made to the duke of Montmorency, the French ambassador[2] here gave knowledge that he had received letters from thence, whereupon he required to have audience before we should send to you, which we did accord. And thereby our former letters were stayed[3] contrary to our determination. And so we would give out, should it be known, where you shall find it requisite for answering to their expectation for the time limited for our answer. And therefore at the delivery of our former letters of credit, both to the king and to Montmorency, you shall say that you are to show them our answer as we did conceive it to be given when those letters were written. And upon the ambassador's access after that time and the delivery of letters from the king and the queen mother and from Monsieur d'Alençon, all full of purposes to further the matter of marriage, besides the private, earnest dealing also with us of the French ambassador to the same end, we were occasioned thereby to do some further matter to our former answer, not being anywise so different as it doth alter our said answer, but in respect of the earnestness of the desire we see to be in the king

13. **Theobalds** Burghley's sumptuous estate near London, where Elizabeth frequently stayed on progress.

1. *Source:* BL, MS Additional 30156, fols. 329v–332v; seventeenth-century copy.

2. **ambassador** Bertrand de Salignac, sieur de La Mothe-Fénélon.

3. **stayed** held back.

and queen mother, and specially in the duke of Alençon himself, not only by their letters to ourselves, but by the duke's letters to the French ambassador, we have thought convenient to enlarge our answer in some part, to lay open before the king our conceit in the matter. Which you shall say we do of very sincerity of goodwill, to be answerable to their earnest dealing with us, to be nevertheless considered and ordered by them as they shall think best.

After you have used this kind of speech to them, you shall say that when we think of this matter we find no other principal impediment but in the difference of the ages and the cause of religion. And as to this latter, which is the difficulty about religion, we do not think that such but, the form and substance of our religion being well made known to the duke, there is no such cause to doubt but by God's goodness the same may be removed to the satisfaction of us both. But as to the other which concerneth the person of the duke—of his age and otherwise—forasmuch as the difficulties thereof may seem to consist rather in opinion than in matter indeed, we do thereto thus yield to think that in marriages, when the persons are to think one of the other, nothing doth so much rule both parties as to have their own opinions satisfied. And seeing that in respect thereof, nothing can make so full a satisfaction to us for our opinion nor percase in him of us in respect of the opinion he may conceive of the excess of our years above his, as that either of us might by some convenient means with our own eyes satisfy our own conceits,[4] a matter we know somewhat difficult, but such as in like cases hath been yielded to us, though by other impediments not perfected.[5] And nevertheless how this may be granted, allowed by the king and the queen to be done without offense, we do leave it to them in whom we perceive (by their ambassador's speech) the stay hath consisted, when the duke himself both by his letters to the ambassador as otherwise hath showed himself disposed, that is, to come hither in person. For the which we cannot but greatly esteem his love and affection that he beareth to us. This you shall say is as much as we can conceive of the matter. And if it were not for the desire we have to deal plainly in this matter, being so much provoked by the great goodwill we find in them there, we would not in that sort propound such a matter. Neither yet do we otherwise propound it but that it may be friendly interpreted, and

4. **conceits** personal opinions or judgments.
5. **perfected** carried out.

not to conceive that thereby we mean any abuse to the disgrace of the duke, whom we have great cause to love and esteem; but that surely in this sort our opinion by sight may be satisfied, which otherwise, we perceive, cannot be by report of any other,[6] for that none of our own dare adventure to deliver their advice for our own liking of him. As the case is, we plainly affirm that, so as the difficulty of the matter of religion be provided for, and that all other points concerning the marriage may be performed as was communed upon in the person of Monsieur d'Anjou, we find no cause of doubt but that the king and queen mother shall obtain their desires.

And after that you have declared thus much, because it is likely they will object that either this purpose of his coming over to us cannot be granted for respect of the honor of the king, in that heretofore no like usage hath been in the marriages of the children of France with any strange prince; or that they shall doubt that this is by us in this sort propounded as thereby to increase our own reputation without intent to marry with him,[7] though his person might not mislike us, to such objections you may answer. As to the first you may say as of yourself that you are not so acquainted with their own stays and with the marriage of the children of France, yet you dare affirm that you know there can be no example showed us of the like of this: that is, that either the elder son of France or any younger was at any time to be matched in marriage with such a prince having such kingdoms as we have, by whom such an advancement might have grown as may by marriage with us, both to the duke himself and to the king and crown of France. And therefore this special cause can have no former example answerable to rule this, but this all ought to be followed with all manner of means and all respect set aside.

6. Elizabeth reportedly told the Spanish ambassador Count Feria that she had "taken a vow to marry no man whom she has not seen, and will not trust portrait painters" (Anne Somerset, *Elizabeth I* [New York: St. Martin's Press, 1991], p. 92).

7. On this widely held perception of the queen's motives, the duke of Parma wrote somewhat later to the Spanish ambassador in London: "The marriage of that queen seems to me like the weaving of Penelope, undoing every night what was done the day before and then reweaving it anew the next, advancing in these negotiations neither more nor less than has been done and undone countless times without reaching a conclusion one way or the other. And in this way the years will pass her by, so that there will be very little to desire in her." Cited from the Parma State Archives in Charles Wilson, *Queen Elizabeth and the Revolt of the Netherlands* (London: Macmillan, 1970), pp. 74–75.

And as to the second part that may be objected, you shall affirm certainly in our name that we have no meaning hereby to gain any particular estimation to ourselves, but do plainly and simply seek hereby to procure the satisfaction of our own mind in this difficulty as touching his person, wherein no other of our own dare deal with us, nor we can otherwise be satisfied. And for the preservation of the duke's estimation and honor, we shall be as careful as his own brother the king shall be. And therefore you shall conclude that, howsoever we have thus propounded our own conceit in the matter, we desire not that the king or the queen mother should do or consent to anything that might anyways seem to them dishonorable for the duke.

Finally, if you shall perceive that they shall stick only upon the reputation of his honor that is to come and not to be allowed for his person, you may as of yourself propound it as you see cause that the matter of religion may utterly be so left in suspense as the breaking off, if any so should follow either on his part or on ours, may to the world be thereto imputed. And besides that his coming may be secret and privately, without any outward pomp or show, whereof we leave the consideration to themselves. Given under our signet at Gorhambury[8] the twenty-fifth of July, 1572, and in the fourteenth year of our reign.

36 ⤳ QUEEN ELIZABETH TO GEORGE TALBOT, EARL OF SHREWSBURY, OCTOBER 22, 1572[1]

[Addressed] To our right trusty and right well-beloved cousin[2] and councillor the earl of Shrewsbury and earl marshal of England

By the queen.

Right trusty and right well-beloved cousin and councillor, we greet you well. By your letters sent to us we perceive that you had heard of some

8. **Gorhambury** location of an elaborate residence, built by Sir Nicholas Bacon, where he frequently entertained the queen.

1. *Source:* Lambeth Palace Library, MS 3197, fols. 41–43; body of letter in a secretary's hand, postscript in Elizabeth's hand, and remnants of seal attached. (For the queen's postscript in original spelling, see *ACFLO,* part 1.) There is also a draft of this letter in the PRO, State Papers Domestic, Elizabeth 12/89/39, fol. 128, with corrections in Burghley's hand.

According to Burghley's note for October 4, 1572, "The queen's majesty appeared to have the smallpoxes at Hampton Court, but she recovered speedily" (William Murdin, ed., *A Collection of State Papers . . . Left by William Cecil, Lord Burghley,* vol. 2 [London: William

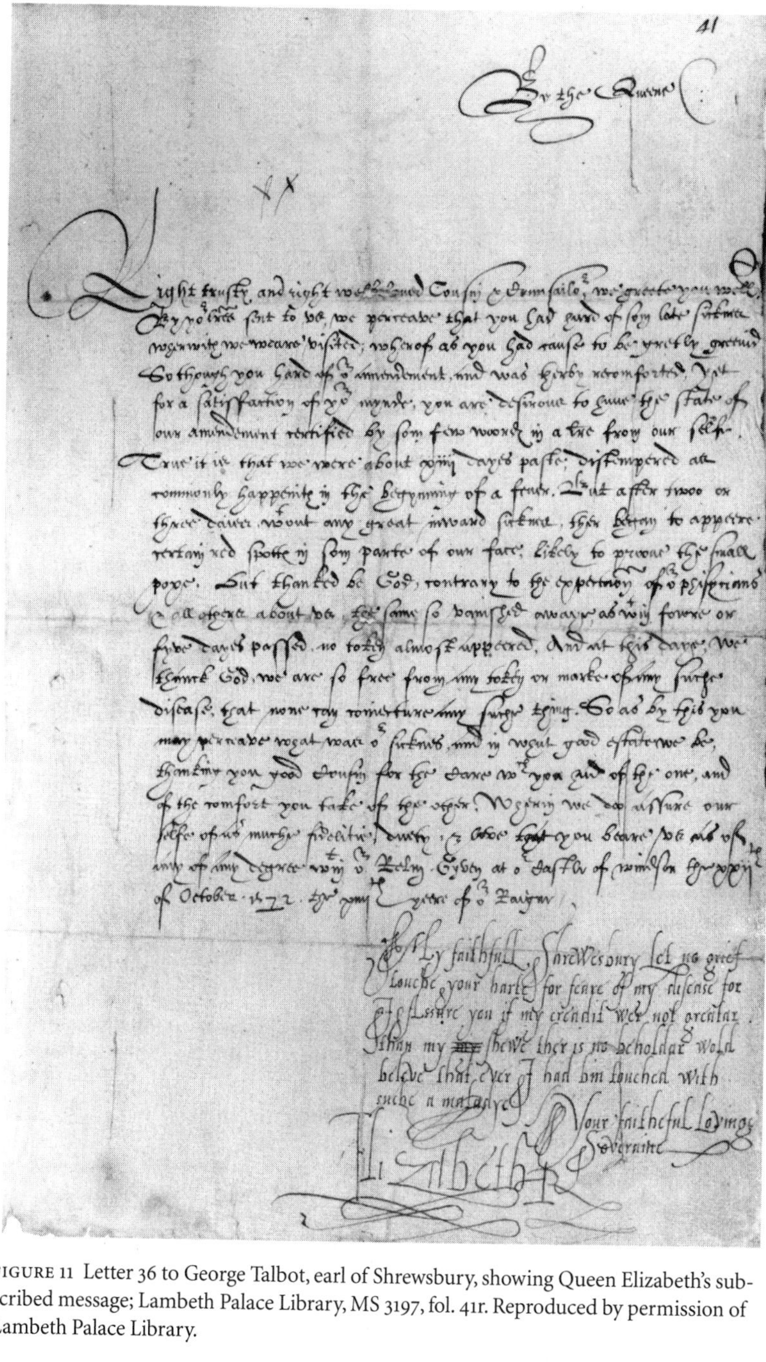
41

By the Quene

My faithfull Shrewsbury let no grief touche your harte for feare of my disease for I assure you if my creddit wer not greater than my shewe ther is no beholdar wold beleve that ever I had bin touched with suche a malady.

Your faithful Lovinge Soveraine

Elizabeth R

FIGURE 11 Letter 36 to George Talbot, earl of Shrewsbury, showing Queen Elizabeth's subscribed message; Lambeth Palace Library, MS 3197, fol. 41r. Reproduced by permission of Lambeth Palace Library.

late sickness wherewith we were visited, whereof as you had cause to be greatly grieved, so though you heard of our amendment and was thereby recomforted, yet for a satisfaction of your mind you are desirous to have the state of our amendment certified by some few words in a letter from ourself. True it is that we were about fourteen days past distempered, as commonly happeneth in the beginning of a fever, but after two or three days without any great inward sickness there began to appear certain red spots in some part of our face likely to prove the smallpox. But thanked be God, contrary to the expectation of our physicians and all others about us, the same so vanished away, as within four or five days past no token almost appeared, and at this day we thank God we are so free from any token or mark of any such disease that none can conjecture any such thing. So as by this you may perceive what was our sickness and in what good estate we be, thanking you, good cousin, for the care which you had of the one and of the comfort you take of the other, wherein we do assure ourself of as much fidelity, duty, and love that you bear us as of any of any degree within our realm. Given at our castle of Windsor the twenty-second of October, 1572, the fourteenth year of our reign.

[Postscript in Elizabeth's hand] My faithful Shrewsbury, let no grief touch your heart for fear of my disease, for I assure you if my credit were not greater than my show, there is no beholder would believe that ever I had been touched with such a malady.

Your faithful, loving sovereign, *Elizabeth R*

Bowyer, 1759], p. 773). Since she had already suffered a severe attack of smallpox in 1562, this malady was presumably a less serious disorder.

2. **cousin** here, as frequently during the period, the term is used as an honorific rather than to indicate blood relation.

37 ❧ QUEEN ELIZABETH TO SIR FRANCIS WALSINGHAM, AMBASSADOR TO FRANCE, DECEMBER 1572[1]

[Headed] To our trusty and well-beloved Francis Walsingham, Esquire, our ambassador resident in France.

[Endorsed] Received 19 December, 1572.

Elizabeth R

Trusty and well beloved, we greet you well. There hath been with us Monsieur de Mauvissière[2] with letters from the king, the queen mother, and the duke of Alençon. His credence was in three points: the continuance of the amity, that we should be godmother to the infant,[3] and pursue still to the request of marriage with the duke of Alençon. To whom we answered: first, that as for amity, having it of late by league so straitly[4] made betwixt us, on our behalf we never attempted or minded to attempt anything that should impair it, but rather do study and wish to increase the same if we could.

And therefore, you may say, it is that and the goodwill appertaining to that amity that made us, by you before and now de Mauvissière, to declare what we have heard of our good brother. We are sorry to hear, first, the great slaughter made in France of noblemen and gentlemen, unconvicted and untried, so suddenly (as it is said at his commandment), did seem with us so much to touch the honor of our good brother as we could not but with lamentation and with tears of our heart hear it of a prince so well allied unto us, and in a chain of undissoluble love knit unto us by league and oath. That being after excused by a conspiracy and treason wrought against our good brother's own person, which whether it was true or false, in another prince's kingdom and jurisdiction where we have nothing to do, we minded not to be curious. Yet that we[5] were not brought to answer by law and to judgment before they were executed (those who were found guilty) we do hear it marvelously evil taken and as a thing of a terrible and dangerous exam-

---

1. *Source:* BL, MS Additional 30156, fols. 437r–440r; seventeenth-century copy. This letter offers Queen Elizabeth's retrospective analysis of the Saint Bartholomew's Day Massacre of French Protestants, August 23–24, 1572.

2. **Mauvissière** Michael de Castelnau, sieur de Mauvissière, the French ambassador.

3. **infant** newborn daughter of Charles IX.

4. **straitly** tightly.

5. **we** possibly miscopied for "they."

ple; and are sorry that our good brother was so ready to condescend to any such counsel, whose nature we took to be more humane and noble.

But when more was added unto it—that women, children, maids, young infants, and sucking babes were at the same time murdered and cast into the river,[6] and that liberty of execution was given to the vilest and basest sort of the popular, without punishment or revenge of such cruelties done afterwards by law upon those cruel murderers of such innocents—this increased our grief and sorrow in our good brother's behalf, that he should suffer himself to be led by such inhumane counselors. And now sithence it doth appear by all doings, both by the edicts and otherwise, that the rigor is used only against them of the religion reformed, whether they were of any conspiracy or no, and that contrary to the edict of pacification[7] so oftentimes repeated, they of the reformed religion are driven either to fly or to die, or to recant or lose their offices, whereby it doth appear by all actions now used by our good brother that his stop and intent doth tend[8] only to subvert that religion that we do profess and to root it out of this realm. At the least, all the strangers of all nations and religions so doth interpret it, as may appear by the triumphs and rejoicing set out as well in the realm of France and other.

Which maketh that it must needs seem very strange, both to us and to all other, that our good brother should require us to be godmother to his dear child, we being of that religion which he doth now persecute and cannot abide within his realm. And if we should believe the persuasions of others and the opinions of all strangers, our friends who be not our subjects, we should not in no wise condescend to any association in that or any other matter. But as we have always hitherto had a special love to our good brother in his younger age and a desire to the conservation of his good estate and quietness, which we have indeed manifestly showed, never seeking any advantage of time against him as peradventure other princes would have done, but ever sought to preserve his estate and his subjects of what quality or condition in religion so-

---

6. **river** the Seine.

7. By the **edict of pacification** or Edict of Saint Germain (January 17, 1562), the Huguenots had been granted religious toleration and virtual self-government in specified towns and districts.

8. **tend** MS could read either "tend" or "bend."

ever they were, exhorting them to unity and concord[9] and with loyal
heart to live together in quiet under our good brother without offering
injury the one to the other, glad of their agreement, and sorry of the division and discord; so the late league of straiter amity made betwixt our
good brother and us, to the which he did so frankly and lovingly condescend, or rather procure it at our hands, is so fresh in our memory
that we cannot suffer that by us in any jot it should be diminished, but
rather increased daily so long as our good brother do show the like unto
us. And that maketh us to interpret all things in better part than otherwise by any means they can appear, such is our love to our good
brother; and so can we be content to persuade ourselves for the love
that we do bear unto him and for the hope of the continuance in our
begun amity without faintness or dissimulation. And this, for the matter of amity, we said to Mauvissière: we would not be slack in any good
office-doing at the request of our good brother. And so, notwithstanding the doubts and impediments before mentioned, we intend to send a
worthy personage—a nobleman of our realm—to repair to his court
and to visit the king our good brother, the queen, and the queen
mother, and the rest that hath written in our behalf, and to do what office which is required of us as appertaineth, wishing that these spiritual
alliances may be to our comforts and conservation of the amity begun
betwixt us.

To the motion of the marriage with the duke of Alençon, wherein
Mauvissière seemed somewhat earnest, after declaration of inconveniences that might come in that marriage by the diversity of age and religion, which we termed in our talk extreme and in true impediments,
we made this final resolution and answer: that forasmuch that we had
given to our ambassador resident there charge to demand and make relation of certain things touching the matter to the king and queen
mother, to the which you have had no answer but of the queen mother
in a certain generality, before that we shall have a special answer to
them we cannot well resolve. The which once being done, we shall the
better understand what to answer for any other proceedings in that
request.

9. Here Elizabeth echoes the prayer for the state of Christ's Church militant in the Order
for Holy Communion in the *Book of Common Prayer*, 1559 (Booty, 254): "beseeching Thee
to inspire continually the universal Church with the spirit of truth, unity, and concord."

38 ⟨❧⟩ QUEEN ELIZABETH TO SIR WILLIAM FITZWILLIAM, LORD
DEPUTY, AND TO THE COUNCIL OF IRELAND, JUNE 29, 1573[1]

Right trusty and well beloved, and trusty and well beloved, we greet you
well. We have received your letter of the 12 of June, in the which, for the
matter of pardon granted and also touching Sir Edward Fitton,[2] having
read and considered the whole that you have written and likewise that
he hath written of that matter unto us, we cannot but mislike that you,
the deputy, should be so hasty to give such and so general a pardon
upon the slaying of a gentleman.[3] For where the corrupt jury of the
coroner's quest did find it but *se defendendo,*[4] it may easily appear that
was no true verdict and that it was a murder, or else you would not in
that case have made out a general pardon but a particular pardon upon
the indictment and of course, as in like cases are wont. But this pardon
is so general that all treasons, murders, and other enormities and transgressions of laws be pardoned, and from the friend of the man murdered, all prosecution of law taken away: such a one as we ourself (for
we have seen the copy of it) would be afraid to grant nor have not
granted (to our knowledge) at any time sithence the first day of our
reign. For it is not unknown to our Council here and to all that have any
doings with us, how seldom and with what difficulty and conscience we
be brought to pardon any man where suspicion of murder and malice

1. *Source:* BL, MS Additional 15891, fols. 25r–26r; copy from the miscellany of the royal favorite Sir Christopher Hatton, who was at this time one of Elizabeth's gentlemen of the
Privy Chamber. The recipient was Sir William Fitzwilliam (1526–1599), who, after substantial service to the crown in Ireland, was named its lord deputy in 1572 and its lord chief justice in 1573.

2. **Sir Edward Fitton** the elder (1527–1579) was lord president of Connaught and vice
treasurer of Ireland. Ill health and chronic shortages of Elizabeth's monetary support led
Fitzwilliam to a series of quarrels with Fitton.

3. In April 1573, a brawl broke out between Fitton's servant Roden and one Burnell, a
friend of Fitzwilliam's nephew. Roden, having broken Burnell's head with a dagger, was run
through the body by Meade, a servant of Fitzwilliam's nephew, a day or two later. Meade
was acquitted on grounds of self-defense by the coroner's jury (**quest**) but indicted for
manslaughter by the Queen's Bench. At this point Lord Deputy Fitzwilliam stepped in with
a general pardon. When this document came into Fitton's hands, he refused to relinquish
it. Fitzwilliam clapped Fitton into jail for contempt, but on second thought released Fitton
the next day and invited him to resume his place on the Council of Ireland. Fitton complained to the queen about this treatment; she sided with him and his story, writing this
letter of reproof to Fitzwilliam and the Council.

4. "in self-defense."

pretensed is, and how curious we be to be informed of the matter, when any of our subjects be slain, before we will condescend to discharge any man of it. That discretion we looked for in you, our deputy, and therefore we put you in that place—lest the blood of the man slain should cry vengeance upon us[5] and our realm, not doing justice for it—and that the punishment of the murder should be a terror to others to adventure upon the like.

But if you, our deputy, should overslip yourself in this, either by hastiness or temerity; yet as it appeareth, you the rest of our Council there, have done as little your duties to God and us in that you would put your hands unto it as whatsoever the deputy therein for the time should do and allow, you would straight run into the same rashness and affirm it, with subscription of your hands as applauders of our deputy. You be put there to be grave and sage advisers to temper such sudden affections either the one way or the other—of love or of hatred—as may chance to our deputy, being but a man made of flesh and blood who cannot lightly be without them; and to have regard to God first and then to our honor and the surety and good government of our realm.

Sir Edward Fitton seemeth to us a true and good councillor, who seeing so unreasonable a pardon so unadvisedly granted, made stay of it to bring it unto you, our deputy, to be better advised of it—not resisting, but discreetly requiring more mature consultation. And for this, you will agree to put him to that shame as to commit him for a contemner of your doings, imputing rashness unto him in that behalf; where in truth he honored us in requiring more deliberation and regard than was had, to be had in justice, the which is clean taken away by that rash and unjust pardon. He refused to sit with you and he had cause so to do: for it appeareth you are all rather followers of the deputy's affections than careful ministers of justice or of our honor. If you had done well, you should have done as he did, requiring the deputy to stay to take better advisement. So should you have showed more care of justice, of our honor, and of the good government of that our realm, than of following the hasty affection of our deputy. You are adjoined to him from us as councillors and in one commission, not to follow one head or whatsoever the deputy willeth, but to consider what is just and reason to be

---

5. Cf. Genesis 4:10, where God declares, after Cain had murdered his brother Abel: "The voice of thy brother's blood crieth unto me from the ground."

done, and so agree with him and set to your hands, and no otherwise. And therefore be you more than one: that if need be, one may temper the other.

Nicholas White,[6] as appeareth by your letter, not daring to dissent against so running a consent, yet showed his conscience not to consent to affection and would prescribe no punishment to that fact: which in his conscience he thought to be the duty of a good councillor to do. If this had been in our father's time—who removed a deputy thence for calling of one of the Council dissenting from his opinion, "Churl"— you may soon conceive how it would have been taken. Our moderate reign and government can be contented to bear this, so you will take this for a warning, and hereafter have before your eyes not the will or pleasure of our deputy or any other councillor, but first God's honor and then justice and our service, which is always joined to the good government of the realm, not following in any respect any private quarrels or affections.

And as to you, our deputy, we shall hereafter write our mind more at large; so will we not forget to give thanks to our good cousin the earl of Kildare[7] for his good service. And we could be content that the earl of Ormond[8] were at home. We have written to Sir Edward Fitton, willing him to join with you in Council and take his place again; and do wish that, all sinister affections laid apart, you do join all in one to do that which may be to the honor of God and of our service, to the execution of justice and to the good government of that realm. Given under our signet at our manor of Greenwich,[9] the 29 of June 1573, the fifteenth year of our reign.

6. Sir **Nicholas White** (d. 1593), a descendant of one of the early Pale settlers, served as Master of the Rolls in Ireland; he had alienated the English Lords of the Council in the autumn of 1572 in a dispute over the custody of the Great Seal.

7. **earl of Kildare** Gerald FitzGerald (1525–1585), also baron of Offaly; he had served on various commissions in Ireland entrusted with enforcing martial law and had incurred repeated suspicions of disloyalty, but was considered during this period an ally of the English crown.

8. **earl of Ormond** Thomas Butler (1532–1614), earl of Ormond, who professed strong Irish sympathies while usually aligning himself firmly with the English crown. At the time of this letter, he was organizing his own military bid for power.

9. **Greenwich** Greenwich Palace, one of Elizabeth's favorite residences, located on the south bank of the Thames, downriver from London.

39 ❧ QUEEN ELIZABETH TO VALENTINE DALE, AMBASSADOR
RESIDENT IN FRANCE, FEBRUARY 1, 1574[1]

[Addressed] To our trusty and well-beloved Doctor Dale,[2] our ambassador resident in France

Elizabeth R   By the queen.

Right trusty and well beloved, we greet you well. Whereas the French ambassador sithence the return of our servant Randolph[3] hath sundry times had access unto us, requiring our answer whether we could allow of the coming over of the duke of Alençon upon the view of his portraiture brought over by our said servant, you shall therefore at the time of your audience with the king and his mother show them that the cause of our stay in answering them hath proceeded upon two respects. Th'one, for that we have had sundry conferences with our Council to know their opinions what inconvenience might follow if upon a public and open entrevue[4] there should not grow satisfaction of our persons; for that we would be loath that the king our good brother, seeking to enter into straiter amity with us by this offer of marriage, there should fall out such discontentment by this occasion through not satisfaction as might impair the good amity already between us. And therefore we thought it a matter worthy of good deliberation.

Th'other for that as well upon the discovery of a late enterprise intended against those of Rochelle,[5] as other advertisements from that country, there is conceived in the hearts of our good subjects a new jealousy and misliking of this match. And therefore we, desiring nothing more than the conservation and continuance of their good devotion

---

1. *Source:* University of Texas at Austin, Harry Ransom Humanities Research Center, MS Pforzheimer 17; in the hand of a secretary, signed with the queen's sign manual, with seal still affixed and slits for ribbons. In all likelihood, this letter was composed by Burghley rather than Elizabeth herself: several draft copies in his hand are preserved in the PRO among the *State Papers Foreign* (1572–74), calendared as nos. 1309–12. A transcription of this letter along with five others in the same series is printed in *The Carl H. Pforzheimer Library: English Literature 1475–1700* (New York: privately printed, 1940), 3:1195–97.

2. **Doctor Dale** Valentine Dale (1520?–1589), a scholar of civil law who took up the ambassadorship to France in March 1573.

3. **Randolph** Sir Thomas Randolph (1523–1590), Burghley's agent, who had been sent to France to compare the miniature of Monsieur, duke of Alençon, with the living subject.

4. **entrevue** (French) interview or, more literally, mutual viewing.

5. [La] **Rochelle** principal French port on the Atlantic; it was an embattled refuge for Huguenots.

towards us, know not what to resolve. Notwithstanding, being pressed
by their ambassador to yield our answer, he received the same from us
as followeth. We showed him that whereas he used divers reasons to
persuade us to give our consent to an open and public entrevue, we
could in no case be led to yield thereto, for that we can be put in no
comfort by those that desire most our marriage and are well affected to
that crown who have also seen the young gentleman, that there will
grow any satisfaction of our persons. And therefore you may say that if
it were not more to satisfy the earnest request of our good brother the
king and the queen his mother (whose honorable dealings towards us,
as well in seeking us himself as in offering unto us both his brethren,[6]
we cannot but esteem as an infallible argument of their great goodwills
towards us), we could in no case be induced to allow of his coming neither publicly nor privately; for that we fear (notwithstanding the great
protestations that he and his mother make to the contrary) that if upon
the entrevue satisfaction follow not, there is like to ensue thereby instead of straiter amity, disdain, unkindness, and a gall and wound of
that good friendship that is already between us. The doubt whereof
maketh us very much perplexed to yield to a thing that we in our own
conceit greatly fear will not have that good success and issue that of either party is desired.

Notwithstanding, if you shall see that the doubts that we lay before
them shall not stay them, but that Monsieur le Duke[7] will needs come
over in some disguised sort, that then you shall tell the king from us
that we desire that the gentleman in whose company he shall come over
(as one of his followers) may be one not of so great quality as the duke
of Montmorency, nor accompanied with any great train, to avoid the
suspicion that otherwise will be of his coming, for that if there follow no
liking between us after a view taken the one of the other, the more secretly it be handled the less touch will it be to both our honors.

We are of late earnestly requested by a daughter of the duke of
Montpensier's[8] who is presently in house with the elector palatine in
Germany to recommend her reasonable request unto the king our good
brother and to queen mother. Which is, that she may enjoy by benefit of
the edict such her living as she hath in France during the time of her ab-

---

6. **brethren** the duke of Anjou (later Henry III) and the duke of Alençon.

7. **le Duke** semi-anglicized version of Monsieur's title.

8. Charlotte de Bourbon (d. 1582), who converted to Calvinism while in residence with
Frederick III, elector Palatine, and married William the Silent, prince of Orange, in 1575.

sence, being withdrawn from thence in respect of the liberty of her conscience. You shall therefore say unto queen mother from us that we desire her to join with you in the furtherance of this suit unto the king her son, our good brother, who, we hope—as well for our sakes as that the gentlewoman is so near of blood unto her children, and that it is a natural virtue incident to our sex to be pitiful of those that are afflicted—will so tender her case as by her good means the gentlewoman shall be relieved and we gratified, which we shall be ready to requite as occasion shall serve us. Given under our signet at our honor of Hampton Court the first day of February 1573[4], the sixteenth year of our reign.

40 ♃ QUEEN ELIZABETH TO VALENTINE DALE, AMBASSADOR RESIDENT IN FRANCE, MARCH 15, 1574[1]

[Addressed] To our trusty and well-beloved Doctor Dale, our ambassador resident with our good brother the French king

Elizabeth R   By the queen.

Trusty and well beloved, we greet you well. Of late the French ambassador presented to us letters from the king his master, the queen mother, and the duke of Alençon, all which were almost of one argument: signifying that both by a depeach[2] of their ambassador and also by conference with you, they did understand our affection to be very great towards this marriage and that we have sought out the means how the interviews should be made. Whereof we had much marvel. And namely that by your speech any such thing hath been there collected, which all their letters do affirm, considering that neither to this ambassador here, nor to you there, anything hath passed to give occasion of such concepts. Wherefore you shall desire audience and declare to the king and his mother that we have advertised you how their ambassador of late delivered to us letters by which we found it strange that they should conceive by the sight of a depeach of their ambassador here resident, and also by conference with you, our ambassador there attending upon them, that we have lately given great demonstrations of a singular

1. *Source:* Huntington Library, MS HM 359; original with seal attached; body of letter in a secretarial hand, signed with Elizabeth's sign manual. Reproduced with permission of The Huntington Library, San Marino, California.

2. **depeach** dispatch (anglicized form of the French *depêche*).

affection which we bear to effectuate the negotiation of marriage betwixt us and Monsieur the duke of Alençon. Yea, it is written by the letters of Monsieur le Duc that we have sought out means how the interview shall succeed. For the which they do give us to understand how great pleasure they take thereof, with assurance on their part that they do therein proceed with all sincerity.

In this matter you shall say howsoever our dealings or demonstrations have been by their ambassador in his last dispatch notified to them, or by conference with you our ambassador conceived on their part, we cannot tell. But meet it is that by this our letter we deliver the truth of our answer made to their ambassador. Whereof there could not ensue occasion for them or any others to write that we had now lately sought out the means how the interview shall be, or make any other great demonstrations of our affection to this marriage than by all other former answers had appeared. But rather we might have thought that our answer last given to their ambassador might have given them there some cause to have doubted of diminution of our affection, for that we did not then yield to that which their ambassador so earnestly pressed: both for the hastening of the duke's coming to us and also for the manner thereof, in open sort according to his estate. And though we have hereof admonished their ambassador, as that our answers to him could not give occasion of that which is written to us, which he cannot deny; yet you shall say that we have (as briefly as the matter will suffer it) advertised you of the substance of our last answer to his requests, to be reported unto them there.

First, the sum of their ambassador's request was that we would make and deliver to him our safe-conduct for the king's brother to come to us. Whereunto our answer was (as in our former dealings with him before that time we always had made the like) that it was to be doubted whether if he should come and not obtain that which he desired, the same might not make some great alteration of the mutual amity betwixt the king and us. Whereunto the ambassador answered that it could not so do, putting us in remembrance of sundry letters and messages, both from the king and the queen mother, by which he said we were certified that whatever succeeded in the cause of marriage, there should be no cause of doubt but that the amity should continue firm and stable. Whereupon, being continually pressed to grant the safe-conduct—and perceiving that the same being had, the duke would come in some such sort as his voyage should be notorious to the world

—we resolved with ourselves that if we should deny his coming, it might be interpreted that we had a determination either not to marry at all, or not to marry with the duke, though he were comparable with any other prince to be allowed. To both which we had made sufficient answers beforetime, to the satisfaction of the ambassador, and do still continue in that mind. And on the other part, if we should deliver our safe-conduct as it was required, and the duke's coming should thereupon be so notorious to the world as we saw it was intended, then might that happen that we still feared if there should not be a mutual liking on both our parts. And therefore we determined, and so gave our resolute answer, that if the coming of the duke should be absolutely agreed upon by the king and the queen his mother, notwithstanding the doubts by us so often alleged and in our answer renewed, we were content that he should come in some private sort, and yet not in company of so great a personage as had been named, but of some of mean quality, of purpose to make his coming either covert or less notorious to the world. And that this was the substance of our answer, without any argument of other, greater affection to effectuate this marriage or other device for the interview as in their several letters is notified, the proof is extant and very demonstrative.

For when the ambassador had moved in speech our cousin the count of Leicester[3] to procure our answer for this matter, we did deliver it to the said count by speech. And he, having such just impediment as he could not make his repair to the ambassador, addressed by writing a letter in Italian to him[4] containing our answer, the true copy of which letter remaineth to be seen. And we doubt not but if the ambassador did send the same letter (or the true double thereof) to the king, as we heard say he did, and that they will peruse the same letter, then shall it manifestly appear what kind of demonstration is to be seen therein of any affection to this marriage (other than beforetime we had showed, wherein we do continue); or whether we did seek the means how the interview should succeed. And for your own purgation, you shall also do well to say that which in truth you ought to say in respect of any our letters or messages to you. And in conclusion you shall in our name require our good brother to accept in good part his necessary deduction

3. **count of Leicester** Robert Dudley, earl of Leicester, who was deeply involved in the intrigue surrounding the Alençon match.

4. **him** Gondi, count de Retz, a Florentine in the service of Catherine de Médicis; he had been sent to England in late summer 1573 to work out conditions for Alençon's visit.

of this matter to such a length as to make it plain we could not do it in fewer words.

And to conclude, for our answer that now we have made to a later motion moved to us by the French ambassador at the time he brought unto us these letters that seemed so strange—which was that the king's intention was to make a voyage himself into Picardy, under color to take the air after his late sickness, to carry the duke his brother with him, and so, coming to Boulogne, the duke his brother might suddenly pass over hither, as of a meaning to see us, being so near to our realm, without any open note of his coming beforehand.[5] And for the more speed of the interview, it was required, or at the least moved by the ambassador, that we would repair from the place where we now are to Dover, or to some place near thereunto, so as the interview might be sooner had. To this you shall say that we take it thankfully that the king would offer any such occasion to make so long a journey (as it seemeth) to gratify us, in covering his brother's coming with his presence; and yet we cannot conceive but that thereby will be rather a more manifestation of his journey than a coverture. And for that which is moved by the ambassador—that we would repair to Dover, being the furthest part of our realm that way and the place where we were but the last summer, and never there before in our life—we leave to express the inconveniences of such a motion.[6] Because it cannot be but manifest that, granting thereto, then not only the king and his ministers—yea, and brother—might write as they have done, that we have showed great demonstrations of our affection to this marriage and sought means for the interview; but the whole world might also take it as a thing by us published. Which for many respects we would be loath should be imagined of us, and lacking therein so much consideration of our state and calling. And therefore to these motions we cannot accord.

But yet, because the king shall not find in us any lack of answer or change of our former intentions, we are still content, if the duke's com-

---

5. Allusion is to the complex maneuverings of the queen mother and her three royal sons of the House of Valois. In October–November 1573, the ailing Charles IX went to Picardy, in the company of his mother and Alençon, to escort the duke of Anjou as far as the French border. Anjou was on his way to assume the throne of Poland, but he had delayed his departure, perhaps hoping for an imminent succession to the French throne instead.

6. Elizabeth's stay at Dover in August 1573 had been arranged to accommodate a meeting with Alençon that his mother, Catherine, refused to allow because of her suspicions of his pro-Huguenot activities.

ing shall be (as afore is said) thought there absolute to be taken in hand notwithstanding the former doubts by us alleged, that he may come in sort as is in our former answer contained in the letter written to their ambassador by our cousin of Leicester. And that also because we use in this springtime to remove from our standing houses to certain private houses with small companies, and to avoid great resort, only to take the air, we will here in Kent, being the next country to the seaside, devise journeys to certain private places with small train and without resort. So as if the duke shall come this springtime, he might more covertly come to our presence in those places than he should do, being at our own houses. And if this shall be accepted, upon knowledge thereof given there to you our ambassador, you shall say that you will deliver a safe-conduct which you have for that purpose, to be used only for the duke's satisfaction and not notoriously thereby to be known in his journey.[7]

You shall also say to the king that though the contents of his letters seemed strange to us for the reasons before alleged, yet it did much content us to receive the letter written wholly with his own hand, for the which we do heartily thank him, and pray him at this time to hold us for excused that we do not acquit him with the like. The cause thereof being in that our hand was at the time of this depeach somewhat strained, that we could not write. You shall also declare to the king that now very lately we have by his ambassador understand[8] of his affairs, which, though they be somewhat disturbed (as it seemeth) by malicious devices of such as seek their profit by troubling of his estate, yet do we accept it for an argument of great goodwill of the king, in that he is content to make us partaker thereof as communicating with us by way of friendship all his accidents, and considering the intentions of the authors of these new troubles are already seen to our good brother before their actions have any force, we doubt not but by wisdom he will prevent the increase thereof, and presently without delay withstand the beginnings and stablish in his realm that universal quietness whereof there was of late very great appearance. And so we trust the same shall soon be recovered again, whereof we shall be very glad to hear from thence. Given under our signet at our manor of Greenwich the 15th of March 1573[4] in the sixteenth year of our reign.

7. Elizabeth formally granted her safe-conduct for Alençon in April 1574.
8. **understand** understood.

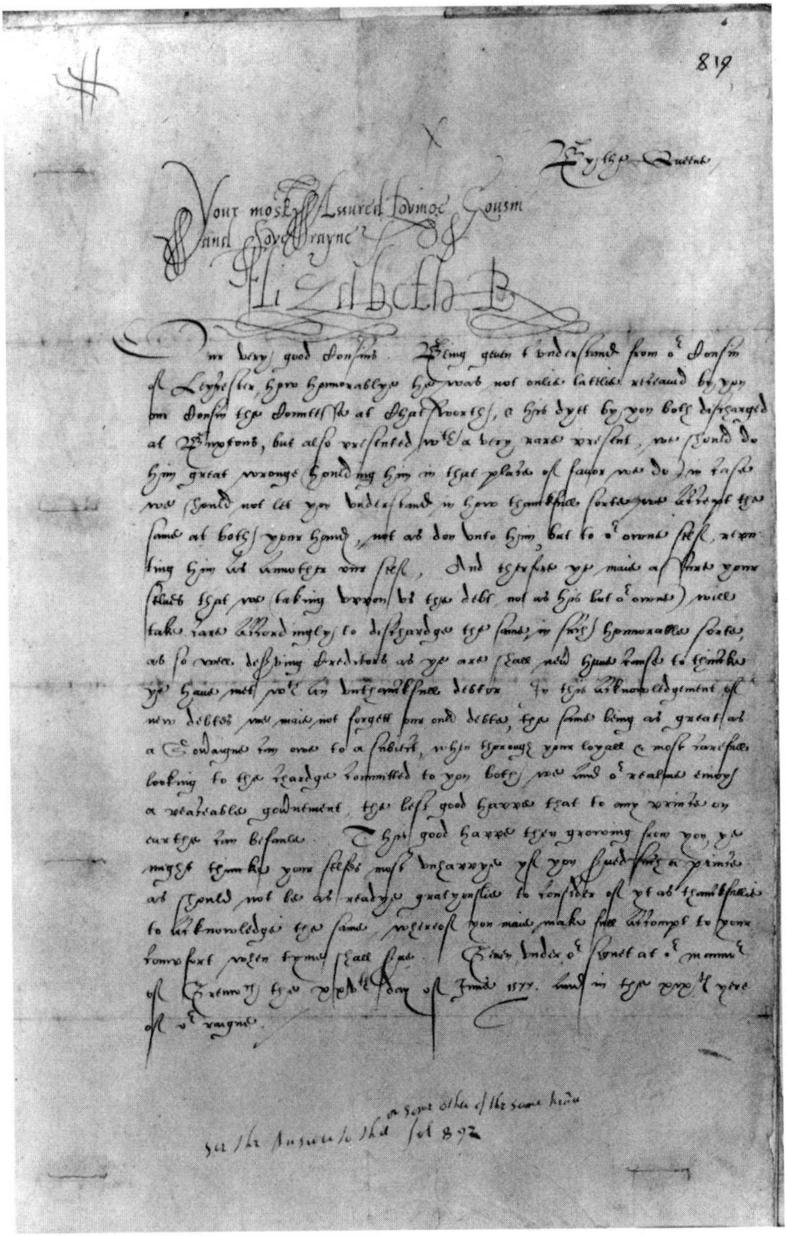

FIGURE 12 Letter 41 to the earl and countess of Shrewsbury, showing Queen Elizabeth's superscription; Lambeth Palace Library, MS 3206, fol. 819r. Reproduced by permission of Lambeth Palace Library.

41 ❧ QUEEN ELIZABETH TO THE EARL AND COUNTESS OF SHREWSBURY, JUNE 25, 1577[1]

[Addressed] To our right trusty and right well-beloved cousin and councillor the earl of Shrewsbury, and to our right dear and right well-beloved cousin the countess his wife.

By the queen.

[Superscription in Elizabeth's hand] Your most assured loving cousin and sovereign, Elizabeth R

Our very good cousins,

Being given to understand from our cousin of Leicester how honorably he was not only lately received by you, our cousin the countess, at Chatsworth,[2] and his diet by you both discharged at Buxton,[3] but also presented with a very rare present, we should do him great wrong (holding him in that place of favor we do) in case we should not let you understand in how thankful sort we accept the same at both your hands, not as done unto him but to our own self, reputing him as another ourself. And therefore ye may assure yourselves that we, taking upon us the debt not as his but our own, will take care accordingly to discharge the same in such honorable sort as so well-deserving creditors as ye are shall never have cause to think you have met with an unthankful debtor.

In this acknowledgment of new debts we may not forget our old debt—the same being as great as a sovereign can owe to a subject—when, through your loyal and most careful looking to the charge[4] committed to you, both we and our realm enjoy a peaceable government, the best good hap that to any prince on earth can befall. This good hap, then, growing from you, ye might think yourselves most unhappy if you served such a prince as should not be as ready graciously to consider of

1. *Source:* Lambeth Palace Library, MS 3206, fol. 819; in a secretary's hand with Elizabeth's superscription and signature, with remnants of seal attached and slits for ribbon. The PRO preserves another longer version of this letter that apparently was not sent but exists in the form of a "Minute." See Letter 41, Additional Document A, p. 230.

2. **countess, at Chatsworth** Shrewsbury's wife Elizabeth Talbot (1518–1608) was the celebrated "Bess of Hardwick"; at **Chatsworth** in Derbyshire, the family's principal seat, she had recently built a fine mansion (not, however, the present structure, which dates from the next century).

3. **Buxton** also in Derbyshire, another family residence.

4. **charge** custody of Mary, Queen of Scots.

it as thankfully to acknowledge the same, whereof you may make full account, to your comfort, when time shall serve. Given under our signet at our manor of Greenwich, the twenty-fifth day of June, 1577, and in the nineteenth year of our reign.

LETTER 41, ADDITIONAL DOCUMENT A QUEEN ELIZABETH TO THE EARL AND COUNTESS OF SHREWSBURY, JUNE 4, 1577[1]

[Endorsed] 4 Junii 1577. Minute of her majesty's letter to the earl and countess of Shrewsbury of thanks for the good usage of my lord of Leicester.

Right trusty etc. Being given to understand from our cousin of Leicester how honorably he was lately received and used by you our cousin the countess at Chatsworth and how his diet is by you both discharged at Buxtons, we should do a him[2] great wrong, holding him in that place of our favor as we do, in case we should not let you understand in how thankful sort we accept the same at both your hands. Which we do not acknowledge to be done unto him but to ourselves, and therefore do mean to take upon us the debt and to acknowledge you both as creditors, so you can be content to accept us for debtor, wherein is the danger unless you cut off some part of the large allowance of diet you give him, lest otherwise the debt thereby may grow to be so great as we shall not be able to discharge the same, and so become bankrout.[3]

And therefore we think it meet for the saving of our credit to prescribe unto you a proportion of diet which we mean in no case you shall exceed. And that is to allow him by the day for his meat two ounces of flesh, reserving the quality to yourselves so you exceed not the quantity, and for his drink the twentieth part of a pint of wine to comfort his stomach, and as much of Saint Anne's sacred water[4] as he lusteth to drink, as is fit for a man of his qualities. On festival days we can be content you shall enlarge his diet by allowing unto him for a fit dinner the shoulder of a wren, and for his supper a leg of the same besides his or-

---

1. *Source:* PRO, State Papers Scotland, Mary, Queen of Scots, 53/10/84; a longer and fuller draft copy of Letter 41 in the hand of a secretary and with numerous revisions, this text may be considerably closer to the letter originally planned by Elizabeth, but it was apparently never sent.

2. **a him** that is, him (much-revised text with **a** not struck through).

3. **bankrout** bankrupt.

4. **sacred water** probably May dew; early morning dew gathered during May and early June was popularly believed to have special curative powers.

dinary ounces. The like proportion we mean you shall allow unto our
brother of Warwick,[5] saving that we think it meet, in respect that his
body is more replete than his brother's, that the wren's leg allowed at
supper on festival days be abated, for that light suppers agree the best
with rules of physic. This order our meaning is you shall inviolably observe, and so may you right well assure yourselves of a most thankful
debtor to so well-deserving creditors.

42 ❧ QUEEN ELIZABETH TO SIR AMYAS PAULET, AMBASSADOR TO FRANCE, JANUARY 1579[1]

*[Headed] Queen Elizabeth to Sir Amyas Paulet upon the death of his son
in Paris.*

Trusty and right well beloved, we greet you well. Whereas we understand by your letters written to our secretaries that God of late hath
called your son[2] to His mercy, we were at the first hearing thereof inwardly sorry that God had not spared him longer life; because besides
that he was your chief comfort, we knew in him such rare gifts of nature
to do us and our realm most especial service as the like is not left behind him for his years, to our knowledge. But seeing it was the good
pleasure of God that he should no longer tarry in this world, being
meeter for heaven than earth, it is our part and yours also to refer all
things to His holy will, who as He gave him life here upon earth, may at
His good pleasure take him out of this life to a better, unto the which
state of grace and better life they that come soonest are most happy.

   Touching your revocation,[3] we have the same in especial care and do
mind very shortly to send some choice man to succeed in your place,
assuring you that your service hath been ever very acceptable unto

   5. **brother of Warwick** Leicester's brother Ambrose Dudley, whom Elizabeth had created earl of Warwick in 1561.
   1. *Source:* BL, MS Harley 787, fol. 17v; seventeenth-century copy. This late copy may show
considerable alteration from the letter as sent. We know from a contemporary report, however, that the ambassador to France Sir Amyas Paulet (1536?–1588) did receive a condolence
letter from the queen on January 31 and that it brought him "singular comfort" (PRO, State
Papers France 78/3/5, a letter of February 6, 1579).
   2. **son** Hugh Paulet (b. 1558).
   3. Paulet had evidently signified a wish to be recalled from his ambassadorship in France,
a post he held from 1576 to 1579.

us—yea, and in such sort liked that we pray God your successor (whosoever he be) may follow your steps. Unto whom we doubt not but you will give such instructions and admonitions as may be for the better advancement of our service in this most dangerous world. And considering that my lady your wife,[4] as a tender and loving mother, hath an equal portion of sorrow with you in this temporal death of your said dear son, our meaning is that she be also like partaker with you of the comfort we send you here. Finally, we do thank you heartily for the rich and rare gift[5] which you did send unto us at the beginning of this New Year, wherein you have showed both your grave judgment and also uttered your dutiful affection. Given under our signet at our manor of Richmond the   day of January 1578[9],[6] in the twenty-first year of our reign.

43 ⇀ QUEEN ELIZABETH TO MONSIEUR, FEBRUARY 14, 1579[1]

Monsieur,

If the importunate request of this bearer were not constraining me, I would not have troubled your eyes so soon after my last encumbrances. If my courage had not doubled at having the good acceptance that the others had, for the which you put me under obligation as in several other places of greater consequence, and principally because your return into France was made not least out of a desire to come to me, a thing which I would not wish, being doubtful how it would end. But I would strongly desire otherwise if by this I am to understand that you have set aside the great part of the advice laid before you in order to follow the desire that proceeds from you alone, assuring you that it infinitely displeases me that this ungrateful multitude—a true chaos—should so abuse such a prince.[2] And I think that God, if not men, will

4. **wife** Margaret (b. 1536) daughter and heir of Anthony Hervey; she and Sir Amyas had three sons and three daughters.

5. **gift** The list of New Year's gifts to the queen in 1578[9] records Sir Amyas Paulet as having presented "a piece of tissue of carnation, gold, and silver, eighteen yards in length" and Lady Paulet as having presented "five pounds in gold" (Nichols, 2:258, 256).

6. **1578** In this late copy of the letter, the date (here amended) is transposed as 1587 and the day of the month is left blank.

1. *Source:* PRO, State Papers France, Elizabeth 78/3/9, fol. 21r; copy. (For French original, see *ACFLO,* part 2.)

2. Although Monsieur's unpaid, unruly, and deserting army provided him with abundant motivation for leaving the Netherlands at the end of 1578, he wrote to Elizabeth that

take revenge for it, and am very glad that you have escaped their iniquitous hands in safety. Nor do I doubt at all that, having passed Scylla, you will take care upon entering into Charybdis,[3] as I pray Mr. Simier[4] will discourse at greater length. And also, as for the advice that it has pleased you to ask of me, while protesting that I recognize my lack of wit keen enough to instruct you; nevertheless, you will be pleased to accept it as from such a one who will never have a thought that is not dedicated to your honor, and who will not shortly betray you with her advice, but will give it as if my soul depended on it. As the Creator knows, to whom I will not cease to pray that He will protect you from those who do not esteem you and that He will do for you all that will be the best for you, Monsieur. With my most heartfelt commendations, from our palace of Westminster on the fourteenth day of February, 1578[9].

44 ﷼ QUEEN ELIZABETH TO SIR AMYAS PAULET, CIRCA MAY 1579[1]

[Headed] Her majesty's letter to Sir Amyas Paulet, then her ambassador resident in France.

Trusty, etc. Finding de Simier, at a certain late conference between him and some of our Council about the treaty of marriage between the duke his master and us, to insist very peremptorily upon certain articles that have always heretofore been denied to such princes as in former time have sought us in way of marriage, as also to the king, the said duke his brother[2] (a thing falling out far contrary to our expectation considering that before his repair hither we caused one of our secretaries to advertise him upon view of certain letters of his directed to the king's ambas-

---

he was doing so because he wanted to come to see her (*Calendar of State Papers Foreign, 1578–1579* [1903], p. 421).

3. **Scylla** and **Charybdis** were the twin female perils—one, a monster amidst murderous rocks, and the other, a whirlpool—faced by Odysseus in the *Odyssey* XII. Cf. the analogous expression "between a rock and a hard place."

4. **Mr. Simier** Jean de Simier, Alençon's personal emissary for dealing with Elizabeth.

1. *Source:* BL, MS Additional 15891, fols. 10v–12v; copy recorded in Sir Christopher Hatton's miscellany, lightly corrected in an italic hand. The MS is damaged at the outer bottom corners, and lost readings, enclosed in square brackets, have been restored by translating from the French copy of the same letter in PRO, State Papers Foreign, Elizabeth 78/3/23, fols. 49r–51r, which is endorsed "26 November 1578" and corrected in pencil to May 9, 1579.

2. **brother** Henry III of France, formerly duke of Anjou, who had briefly engaged in marriage negotiations with Elizabeth during 1570–71.

sador here, by which he signified unto him that he was to repair hither about th'interview and the concluding of th'articles), that our meaning was not to enter into any treaty of articles, being resolved not to yield to any other than were before agreed on between us and other princes that have sought [the said marriage with us] in like case; and therefore advised him to forbear to rep[air thus to us], if he were sent to any such end. Only thus (b[eing resolved] that in case any of the said articles were doubtful or obscure, to explain and make them more clear), we have therefore thought meet, for that we know not what to judge of such a strainable kind of proceeding, even at that time when to our seeming we were growing to a conclusion touching the interview, to acquaint you therewith to the end that you may let both the king and Monsieur know what we conceive thereof.

And for that you may the more substantially and fully deal therein, you shall understand that the articles upon the which he did at the said conference with certain of our Council insist, were three. The first, that the said duke might jointly have authority with us to dispose of all things donative within this our realm and other our dominions. The second, that he might be after marriage crowned king, offering certain cautions that nothing should be done thereby to the prejudice of our realm. And lastly, that he might have threescore thousand pounds' pension during his life. Touching the first, the inconveniences were laid before him by our said Council, who declared unto him that it was a matter that greatly toucheth our regality, in so much as Monsieur might have thereby *vocem negativam*.[3] And also that in the marriage between the king of Spain and our late sister, the contents of that demand was by an especial article prohibited in the treaty between them, which afterward was ratified by Parliament; yet was he not without great difficulty drawn to desist from urging us to yield our consent therein, notwithstanding he was plainly given to understand that our consenting thereto could not but breed dangerous alienation of our subjects' goodwill from us. And for the other two articles, it was showed unto him that the consideration of the said articles being committed to our whole Council, it was by them, after long deliberation had thereon, resolved that they were not presently to be granted or considered of, but by the Council of the whole realm in Parliament, without whose consent they could no wise be accorded unto, and therefore thought meet to be held in suspense until the duke's coming over.

3. "veto power."

With which answers he, not resting satisfied, did still peremptorily insist in pressing the granting of the same, plainly protesting as well to ourself as to our Council that though he had very ample and large authority to treat and deal in the cause, yet durst he not take upon him (considering what curious eyes there were bent to behold his actions and doings in this cause) to qualify the said articles. And thus [he] would no otherwise be satisfied unless he might have our private allowance and assurance that the said [two] articles should be both propo[sed and ratified] by consent [from us]. Wherein, though it was very pl[ainly] showed unto him [how] dishonorable it would be for us to give any such private assurance in a matter that rested in the allowance and consent of others, and how much the same would mislike our subjects that any such things should be yielded unto before such time as it were seen what contentment of our persons might grow by the interview, yet did he not forbear still to press us therein.

Whereupon we, finding that by no persuasion that could be used either by us or by our Council he could be induced to allow of our answers, both we and certain of our Council did plainly let him know that such a kind of insisting upon such articles as had been denied to other princes (specially having before his repair hither let him understand that our meaning was not to alter former articles, but only to clear such as were obscure and doubtful) did minister unto us just cause of suspicion either to think that they had no mind of further proceeding, by standing upon such hard points as in reason we could not yield unto; or else that they sought this match to some other end than hitherto hath been by them pretended, having always heretofore, as well by letters as by most earnest speeches and protestations, given out that not our fortune but our person was the only thing that was sought. Which upon the conclusion seeming to fall out otherwise—as manifestly appeareth by their insisting upon points chiefly incident and depending upon our fortune—giveth us just cause to suppose that the mark that is shot at is our fortune and not our person. For if the affection were so great as is pretended, neither would the duke have directed him, his minister, to have stood upon so hard conditions, nor himself made so great difficulty to have come over and seen us, without standing upon so many ceremonies—being persuaded that a duke of Anjou[4] could receive no dishonor by taking a journey to see a queen of England, whatsoever

4. **Anjou** Monsieur, formerly duke of Alençon, had been created duke of Anjou in 1576; thereafter he was next in line to the French throne.

success the end of his coming took, whenas at the least, there could not but grow thereby increase of friendship. For we are well assured that his repair unto us could not be accompanied with harder success (we will not say with so great dishonor) than his late voyage into the Low Countries. And therefore we saw no cause why the one might not be performed with as little difficulty as the other if they were both sought with like goodwill and devotion.

It was also declared unto him that if they had to deal with a princess that had either some de[ficiency] of body or some other notable defect of nature, or [lacked gi]fts of the mind fit for one of our place and [quality, then] such a kind of strainable proceeding (carrying a greater show of profit than of goodwill) might in some sort have been tolerated. But considering how other ways, our fortune laid aside, it hath pleased God to bestow His gifts upon us in good measure, which we do ascribe to the Giver and not glory in them as proceeding from ourselves (being no fit trumpet to set out our own praises) we may in true course of modesty think ourself worthy of as great a prince as Monsieur is, without yielding to such hard conditions as by persons of greater quality than himself (being denied upon just cause) hath not been stood upon.

And so we concluded with him that seeing we saw apparently by their course of proceeding that we were not sought either with that affection or to that end we looked for, that we had just cause to think ourselves in this action not so well dealt with as appertained to one of our place and quality, having not without great difficulty won in ourself a disposition to yield to the match, in case upon the interview there should grow a liking of our persons. Wherein we showed him that if the duke his master knew what advertisements were received from foreign parts, what effectual persuasions were used towards us at home to dissuade us from the same, and how carefully we travailed to win our subjects to allow thereof (who are not the best affected to a foreign match), he should then see what wrong he had done us (we will not say unto himself) to stand so much upon terms of profit and reputation. Assuring him therefore, seeing we saw we had just cause to doubt that there was not that account made of our plain and friendly dealing in this action towards him that we looked for and as we conceived that we have deserved, that the duke his master should perhaps hereafter hardly draw us to yield so far forth as we have already done, unless we should find him—and that by effects—to be otherwise affected towards us than as yet we can perceive he is; wishing him therefore, and rather advising him, to proceed in the other matches that by some of his nearest friends are (as we be not ignorant of) embraced. Whereof it should seem, by the manner of dealing, both he and they have better liking.

And as for the gentleman himself—de Simier—whom we found greatly grieved, for that he saw we could not allow of his insisting upon the said articles as a matter very offensive unto us, we do assure him that we had [no c]ause to mislike of him, who, we [know, hath] dealt in no other sort than either he was directed [or thought good, see]ing otherwise (though his authority were large) he could not, without peril to himself in respect of such as are not the best affected towards him, follow his own discretion and affection to the cause, having found in him otherwise so great fidelity towards his master, so rare a sufficiency and discretion in one of his years in the handling of the cause, and so great devotion towards the match itself, as we had both great reason to like of him, as also to wish that we had a subject so well able to serve us. And therefore, we would have you let both the king and the duke his master understand how well we conceive of the gentleman and how happy his master may think himself to have so rare a servant.

Having thus at large laid before you the whole course of our late proceedings with de Simier and th'effect of such speech as both by ourself and our Council have been delivered unto him, we nothing doubt but that you will report the same both to the king and to the duke, in that good sort as both they may be induced to see their error and we discharged of such calumniations as perhaps by such as are maliciously affected towards us in that court may be given out against us.

Your sovereign

45 &❧ QUEEN ELIZABETH TO MONSIEUR, DECEMBER 19, 1579[1]

[Addressed] To my dear Monsieur, duke of Anjou

My dearest,

If the thing long awaited had been good when it arrived, I had been better content with the long wait which it pleased Stafford[2] to afford me.

1. *Source:* Hatfield House, Cecil Papers 135/23, fol. 40; in Elizabeth's hand. (For original French, see *ACFLO*, part 1.)

2. **Stafford** Sir Edward Stafford (1552?–1605) was charged with following up marriage negotiations after Monsieur's first visit to Elizabeth in August 1579; Stafford officially became the ambassador resident in France in 1583.

But seeing that the peace seems only half made, I do not see too much reason for his delay, except that he makes me believe that this is done by your commandment, to whom I am entirely willing that he be obedient. And having just at this turn received letters from France that the king is prolonging this peace under several difficulties which will not be possible to resolve too soon, I would be very happy if people allowed themselves to be astonished at his long stay, assuring myself that some of them are making sport of him.

And for the cause of the king of Navarre[3] and his party, this I will make bold to tell you: that it will touch you very near in reputation if you should leave him in worse state than they were in at the beginning of these new troubles. For if their greatest sureties were torn from them, how could they trust to the king in this?—adding that the king himself sent to tell me by his ambassador that he would not deny them the first pacification and would ask nothing except the cities and places newly taken. You will forgive me the curiosity that holds me to your actions, to whom I wish all the honor and glory that can accrue to the perpetual renown of a prince. I assure myself that desire of greatness after this peace will not blind your eyes so as to make you omit that which will be for the safety of those that trust in your goodness.

As for the commissioners, I believe that they will resemble words which, recited too many times, make the tongue slip out of order. I see that time runs on, and I with it, which renders me unfit to please as I would wish. And I am almost in agreement with the opinion of those who do not quit reminding you of my faults. But God, I hope, will govern all for your good. Let it not displease you, Monsieur, that I ask some answer about Simier, for whom I wish some end to his unhappiness[4]— either that he may be condemned justly and you purged of a crime often imputed to princes, whose favors are said to hang by very slender threads, or that he may be employed in your service to shut the mouths of scandal-mongers who do not cease passing their time on public affairs in order to make their expoundings of them.

My dearest, I give you now a fair mirror to see there very clearly the foolishness of my understanding, which I once found so suited to hop-

---

3. **king of Navarre** Henry of Navarre (1553–1610), later Henry IV of France, leader of the Huguenot forces in the French civil wars.

4. Monsieur had evidently taken offense at some of the activities of Simier, but Elizabeth pleads for him; he had established himself so far in her graces that she gave him the nickname "Ape," a pun on his name.

ing for a good conclusion, weighing the place where you reside with the company that is there. We poor inhabitants of the barbarous isle must be careful in appearing for judgment where such ingenious judges of our knowledge hold their seat in so high a place in your favor. But in making my appeal to Monsieur alone and undivided, I will not let my suit drop. And if you would have me given over to the rack, I will not put a gloss on this text, assuring myself that you understand it only too well. Finally, my sole request consists in this: that you always hold me as the same one whom you have obliged to be dedicated to you. And that I can only be she who has lodged you in the first rank of what is dearest to me, as God can best witness, to whom I will not cease my supplications that He grant you a hundred years of life. With my very humble remembrances to be commended to my dearest. From Westminster this nineteenth of December.

Your most assured, as she is
obliged to be, *Elizabeth R*

LETTER 45, ADDITIONAL DOCUMENT A THE DUKE OF ALENÇON TO THE EARL OF SUSSEX, SEPTEMBER 13, 1579[1]

[Addressed] To Monsieur the count of Sussex,[2] my cousin

My cousin,

I do not want to let this occasion slip without assuring you of my goodwill, and praying you to continue for me all good offices in regard to the queen, my mistress, and give her on all occasions assurance of my faithful service. I am very relieved to hear, by way of Lord Ape, that her majesty was right about her rebels in Ireland. I rejoice infinitely at it. Keep me in her good grace and assure yourself of mine, as much as any friend's whom you have ever had. And believe that I will always give proof of it to you and to all those in other quarters who will be, as you are, most faithful to the queen, my mistress. Towards whom I kiss hands

1. *Source:* BL, MS Cotton Titus B. VII, fol. 360v; in French, in Monsieur's italic hand. This is one of several extant letters to English courtiers by whom Monsieur sought to advance the match. The assignment of the year is conjectural.

2. **count of Sussex** the earl of Sussex, Queen Elizabeth's grand chamberlain and a member of the Privy Council—hence strategically placed to forward the match.

a thousand times and pray God to have her in His keeping. From Paris this thirteenth of September.

> Your good cousin and very
> assured friend, *François*

LETTER 45, ADDITIONAL DOCUMENT B WILLIAM CECIL, LORD BURGHLEY, TO QUEEN ELIZABETH, 1579[1]

[Endorsed] 1579. To the queen's majesty. Advice about her match.

The clock that stond[2] so long hath now so weighty plummets[3] of favor and courage put on that it striketh still, a clock not to tell how this day passeth only, but how days and time passeth like river streams, whose waves return no more. In so great a matter it was necessary to consider well what was good with counsel and leisure, and as good reason and policy to go through with the good when it is determined, except some secret stay that is not within the level of our sights to see. But if your majesty tarry till all clocks strike and agree of one hour, or tarry till all the oars row the barge, you shall never 'point the time and you may slip the tide that yet patiently tarryeth for you.

In the beginning, the morning of your time, your majesty hath taken the sweet dew of pleasure and delight, the temperate air of a quiet and a calm, contented mind—a moisture and a breath as natural to maintain and feed a dainty nature as the most wholesome meat to strengthen and maintain the body. From the beginning, pleasure and content agrees with your nature; long custom makes it not voluntary but necessary. It is not enough then your majesty reign and to be queen still, but to reign and rule honored, pleased, and contented; and to have the morning dew all the whole day of your life. Admitting then all reasons of policy and causes removed and answered that persuade and lead you to this match, your majesty still in your old state to sit sure and rule singly as you did, could you yet then think it morning still? Have you the sweet

---

1. *Source:* BL, MS Lansdowne 94, art. 31, fols. 70r–71r; attribution is conjectural but likely: this copy is in the hand of one of Burghley's secretaries and occurs as part of a collection of Burghley's papers, others of which are written in the same secretarial hand and corrected in Burghley's hand.

2. **stond** stood.

3. **plummets** weights of a clock.

dew and the temperate air so agreeable and necessary to your nature? No, but either they be quite altered, or if they be not, yet are your senses so full that the satisfaction makes an end of pleasure.

And so in that state—the food of your mind spent and not new provided for—is it mirth, meat, or music, honor, duty, and service done by your servants, that doth satisfy, if there be not some partner of the delight, honor, and pleasure, and that your majesty may love and esteem above the rest? Or lives the man and speaks he English that you highly esteem and love at this day? I grant it is enough for some to think upon a good dinner, a supper, a soft bed, a carpet and a cushion, of coin and crowns, and to keep a reckoning. But to some others of more fine spirits, all these not seasoned with the presence of a virtuous, discoursing, and delightful friend have neither taste nor savor. Who might command the whole world, and had every necessary and every pleasure provided to her hand, without pain or care, and no companion, friend, or servant beloved on whom to bestow favors of that plenty, nor from whom to receive any sign of love and service—should that person live contented and be glad of full dishes, full coffers, and of elbow room? No, since it were no more able to content nature, at least the best natures, than an empty cup were able to slake an extreme thirst. God himself was not contented alone with perfection and height of all happiness till He made the angels and man to be witnesses and partakers of His felicity. How shall they content you then, madam—your honor, state, wealth, and delights—if you have not the friend that may content you best, and who you find desirous to content you most? For without that person you are alone though a hundred be about, as well as the person I brought for example that had never a one.

If then I have proved it as necessary your majesty have content and pleasure as rule and treasure; if I have showed where it is not, and where it is, and now prove plainly you may take it if you please, I have then ended my desire, though to no effect beside. Three sorts of people we find against this marriage: one for doubt lest a husband of contrary faith should alter and overthrow the religion; the second sort, lest it might be impediment or defeasance[4] of some plot and hope laid and had of a successor to their likings; a third kind, for loathness and doubt lest such as have had the highest credit should come down, on whom their suits and their profits have and do depend. To the first is answered

---

4. **defeasance** defeat.

that he[5] shall not have authority nor power to alter religion now used and established. He brings no preachers to persuade; and violently to do it, where shall be his force? Example shall do no hurt, since his chapel door shall be shut.[6] The second sort be unanswerable, and be for their expectation and foresight to be contemned, and for their number and small power to be contemned. The third kind will be satisfied when they see their lovers or their loves take no hurt.

Then may it please your majesty to peruse on the other side whom ye have with it, and the reckoning I think, madam, not to be disproved: first, the nobility of all your Council and all other of your Council, either warmly with it or very coldly against it, and yet I hope none against you, howsomever you please to proceed. Next, the whole nobility of England, three or four excepted, who either would come fast on if they saw your majesty resolute or sit as still as a bird in a dark winter night. All the Protestants of England that love you for yourself could not choose but desire it; the Catholics pray for it, not in hope to have their religion set at liberty, but to have a privy coat[7] against persecution; as for the sort of men that be not earnest in any religion, they follow directly what the prince commandeth and desireth. Add to this strength at home, the strength of the neighbor and alliance that be bound in honor and for their own security and better peace to war and wrestle on your side in this quarrel, and if there be a party so wicked and so hardy to disturb the marriage by tumult and by force as they did the queen your sister's[8] (if you mean to meet at home), as God knows and the reckoning plain, you are ten times so strong; your majesty might be strongly assisted from thence. But doubt not, lady, for when lions make a leap, the bears and other beasts lie down. And at least be resolute and know what you may, though you know not what you will; or so your majesty be quit and out of doubt, it is no matter though all we doubt still. I most humbly beseech your majesty that as I know you read, so you take order that none read after ye; and for the pain taken in reading and for your last favors, I vow my life and all I have to serve you. And kissing your hands with the humble and earnest affection of my heart, singly and simply yours, I take my leave and ask leave for two days' absence.

5. **he** Monsieur.

6. English negotiators regarding the match with Monsieur consistently specified that he could be permitted no public practice of the Catholic religion in England.

7. **privy coat** coat of mail worn for protection under ordinary dress.

8. For Elizabeth's expression of the fear that her Catholic marriage could arouse the same violent domestic opposition as had Mary's to Philip II of Spain, see Letter 48, p. 247.

46 ❧ QUEEN ELIZABETH TO MONSIEUR, CIRCA DECEMBER
1579–JANUARY 1580[1]

Monsieur,

When I remember that there is no more lawful debt than the word of
a just man, nor anything that more binds our actions than a promise, I
would forget myself too much in regard to you and my honor if I passed
over the term appointed for my answer to the matter that we have long
discussed. You are not unaware, my dearest, that the greatest delays consist in doing what our people should rejoice in and applaud. And in so
doing, I have used time, which ordinarily accomplishes more than reason does. And having made use of both, I have not refrained from
roundly declaring to you what I know and you will find true always. I
see well that many people go away repenting of having made rash judgments at the first stroke, without having weighed in a better balance the
depth of their opinions; I assure myself that some, upon hazard of their
own lives, wish not to be so foolishly governed. And nevertheless I
promise you on my faith, which has never yet sustained a spot, that the
public exercise of the Roman religion sticks so much in their hearts that
I will never consent to your coming among such a company of malcontents without your being pleased to consider that the commissioners
loosen the strict terms that Monsieur Simier offered us; and because I
do not want you to send them unless the cause would thereby be concluded, I entreat you to give great consideration to this, as a thing so
hard for the English to bear that you would not be able to imagine it
without knowing it.

For my part, I confess that there is no prince in the world to whom I
would more willingly yield to be his, than to yourself, nor to whom I
think myself more obliged, nor with whom I would pass the years of my
life, both for your rare virtues and sweet nature, accompanied with so
many honorable parts that I cannot recite them for their number nor
dare to make mention of them for the length of time that would take
me. Such that if it would please you to consider how sincerity accompa-
nies me in this negotiation from the beginning to the present, I do not
fear to present myself before the seat of your just judgment and acquit
myself of every wile and dissimulation. I have doubts about our agree-
ments as individuals, being uncertain as much about not complying as

1. *Source:* Hatfield House, Cecil Papers 149/24, no foliation; copy in a secretary's hand
with one local correction in Elizabeth's hand. (For French original, see *ACFLO,* part 2.)

not assured that I should consent, seeing the great questions that were then being raised about the nation from which you come, then about the manner of government and several other things which ought not to be written down. And[2] in the which, having used up so many means of making them agreeable, I do not believe I have done hard work but rather huge labor for a whole week! And at this hour I would not deceive you by not placing openly before your eyes how I find the case, and what I think of it, in which I have had so much regard to your ease and contentment as if for my own life or consideration of my state, which would otherwise have moved me to make another answer.

And for conclusion I cannot deny that I do not want this negotiation to trouble you thus any more, that we may remain faithful friends and assured in all our actions, unless it pleases you to make other resolution than the open exercise of religion, and it seems good to you to write me about it or to send some good answer; for I desire nothing that does not content you. There are still some things to be said about your allowance, which I have given in charge to this bearer for him to tell you, from well to better, like other things that it will please you with your customary goodness to hear, and to entrust yourself to him as to a faithful man, as you know him to be, and as I have well proved. For which I owe you a million thanks for the honor, favor, and liberality which you have used towards him in his place, for which you have put me under obligation long before now.

I received eight days ago a letter that it pleased you to send me, by which I see that your affection is not diminished by absence, nor cools by persuasions, for which I can only return a sincere and immovable goodwill, ready to serve you on all occasions contrary or ill, and such that I will never forsake your fortune, but take my part in it. I have never heard any news from you either of France or of the Low Countries or of any other parts since the arrival of Simier, and believe that you doubt too much of a woman's silence or otherwise I would learn less by other means and more by you. For from another place I learn more than it pleases you to communicate to me, as God knows, whom I pray to preserve you in good life and long, with my commendations to my very dear Frog.[3]

2. **And** This word (*Et* in French), inserted to begin a new sentence, appears to be in Elizabeth's hand.

3. **Frog** Elizabeth's nickname for Monsieur (*Grenouille* in French). As inventoried in BL, MSS Donation, "Book of Queen Elizabeth's Jewels," July 1587, the queen's jewelry included a frog brooch in gold with vermeil and precious stones. See Henry Ellis, ed., *Original Letters Illustrative of English History*, 1st ser., 2nd ed. (London, 1847), 3:53.

47 ?❧ QUEEN ELIZABETH TO MONSIEUR, JANUARY 17, 1580[1]

[Endorsed] The 17 of January to Monsieur

For me to delay so, my dearest, in acknowledging the infinite ways that my obligations increase in regard to you may render me with good reason unworthy of treatment so honorable. But the extreme pain in my throat continually these past two weeks will have force, I hope, to efface such a thought. And at this hour, finding myself a bit better, I present to you my most humble thanks for having shown us a bright rock from which neither the tempests of false persuasions nor the storm of evil tongues has had the force to shake the constancy of your affection, of which I confess myself very unworthy for any perfection that I possess. And because of this, it seems to me so much the more illustrious as what occasions it is more simple. At one thing I rejoice—that you are so well furnished with good friends that you will not be ignorant of some of my defects, so that I am assured of not being found worse than they have represented me. And yet, being so well admonished, you will be well resolved or you will not hazard it. And I pray God to give you the grace of clear sight to pierce the unfathomable depths of their leadings, and that I do not live to be the means of your discontent.

It is so difficult in these times to know the difference between seeming and being that I wish the wisdom of Solomon to reside in your mind to separate the false ones from the true ones and such as look further beyond[2] rather than setting you up as the target of their arrows. Those are to be most esteemed who respect us, not mixing in their own greatness and government. But at this hour I muse as do those on night watch,[3] dreaming, not having slept well. I have received news from the king that the commissioners are readying themselves, not yet knowing who they are. I did not think before that France had been so ill furnished with princes and persons of great quality that they would be constrained to send me a child or man of low descent. I believe that they do it to diminish the greatness of my honor or to throw impediments in the way, so as not to send at all. I have, however, used round-

---

1. *Source:* Hatfield House, Cecil Papers 149/25, no foliation; copy in a secretarial hand with one local correction in Elizabeth's hand. (For the original French, see *ACFLO*, part 2.)

2. **beyond** the scribe had written *"autre"* (instead of), which Elizabeth corrects to *"outre"* (beyond).

3. **those on night watch** The French reads *"vielles,"* translated by Harrison as *"vieilles"* (old women), but interpreted here as *"veilles"* (those on night watch). Either reading is possible.

ness with regard to the king, sending to tell him by his ambassador that I would not allow a thing of so great importance to be disgraced because of hatred that may be borne to me.

I am careful not to allow chronicles to say that there will be a lack of esteem for the executors of so great a celebration, promising, I believe, that the king will hold in honorable consideration both the place that you hold and the rank in which I hold myself. For your commissioners, I take it for certain that you will make selection without changing the instrument, to complete what he has so well begun. I speak of Simier, of whom having heard all that is laid against him and neither seeing reason to believe it nor proof to condemn him, I swear to you, my dearest, on my life I see no occasion for his exile. It is true that I know too much indignity used against your person by those who make the people believe that you are so presumptuous and fickle that they can easily make you withdraw your favor from your dearest ones when they have you apart. And in convenient time I will not fail to show you, to their shame, who have been the authors of this.

See where the love that I bear you carries me—to act against my nature (quite the opposite of those who fish in troubled waters), to intermeddle in someone else's doings. Notwithstanding, I cannot refrain from entreating you, with clasped hands, to remember that we who are princes, setting ourselves in high places, are solicited by showings from several heads, the greater part of whom accuse us, since our favors attach themselves by slender strings, which make them fear for their share of grace, from among whom I wish you to be exempt. See, Monsieur, the foolishness of my understanding, who write to you about this matter in hope of a good answer, weighing the place where you reside with the company that is there. We poor inhabitants of the barbarous isle have not been careful in appearing for judgment where such ingenious judges—judges of our knowledge—hold their seat in so high a place in your favor. But in making my appeal to Monsieur alone and undivided, I will not leave this my suit if you should give me over to the rack. I will not put a gloss on this text, assuring myself that you understand it only too well.

And finally I entreat you to pardon this[4] irksome letter and receive my most humble thanks for the offer that you make me to determine Simier's case as will seem best to me, assuring you that I have never

---

4. **this** French equivalent written twice in MS.

cared to give you counsel that will betray your honor. I would rather die. I am not partial to him that I forget you, and if there were for his fidelity towards you that of which I have had my share of proof, he is only a stranger to me, with whom I have nothing at all to do. As the Creator knows, whom I pray to give you a hundred years of life. With my very affectionate commendations.

[Postscript] I pray you will send me your good pleasure by this bearer, who will return in haste.

48 ❧ QUEEN ELIZABETH TO SIR EDWARD STAFFORD, AMBASSADOR TO FRANCE, CIRCA AUGUST 1580[1]

[Headed] Her majesty's letter to Sir Edward Stafford.

Stafford,

As I greatly regard your poor man's diligence, so will I not leave him unrewarded. For the charge I have written to Monsieur that I have given unto you, this it is: first for the commissioners' authorities, I have good reason to require that they may be as I desired, both for present mislikes as well as for after mishaps. It happened in Queen Mary her days that when a solemn ambassade of five or six at the least were sent from th'emperor and king of Spain, even after the articles were signed, sealed, and the matter divulged, the danger was so near the queen's chamber door that it was high time for those messengers to depart without leave-taking, and bequeathed themselves to the speed of the river stream, and by water passed with all possible haste to Gravesend[2] and so away. I speak not this that I fear the like, but when I make collection of sundry kinds of discontentments all tied in a bundle, I suppose that faggot[3] will be harder altogether to be broken.

There is even now another accident fallen out of no small consequence to this realm. I am sure the States have accorded to the demands of Monsieur, and do present him the sovereignty of all the Low Countries. Suppose now how this may make our people think well of him

---

1. *Source:* BL, MS Additional 15891, fol. 19; copy from the miscellany of Sir Christopher Hatton.

2. **Gravesend** the final substantial town on the River Thames before it emptied into the sea.

3. **faggot** bundle of sticks.

and of me—to bring them to the possession of such neighbors! O Stafford, I think not myself well used, and so tell Monsieur that I am made a stranger to myself, who he must be if this matter take place. In my name show him how impertinent it is for the season to bring to the ears of our people so untimely news. God forbid that the banns[4] of our nuptial feast should be savored with the sauce of our subjects' wealth. O what may they think of me, that for any glory of my own would procure the ruin of my land?[5] Hitherto they have thought me no fool; let me not live the longer the worse: the end crowneth all[6] the work. I am sorry that common posts of London can afford me surer news than th'inhabitants of Tours will yield me. Let it please Monsieur to suspend his answer unto them till he send some unto me of quality and of trust to communicate and concur with that I may think best for both our honors. For I assure him, it shall too much blot his fame if he deal otherwise, not only in my sight, unto whom it hath pleased him to promise more than that, but especially to all the world that be overseers of his actions. Let him never procure her harm whose love he seeks to win. My mortal [foe can][7] no ways wish me a greater loss than England's hate; neither should death be less welcome unto me than such mishap betide me.

You see how nearly this matter wringeth me: use it accordingly. If it please him, the deputies may have the charge of this matter, joined with the other two that were afore mentioned. I dare not assure Monsieur how this greater matter will end until I be assured what way he will take with the Low Countries. For rather will I never meddle with marriage than have such a bad covenant added to my part. Shall it be ever found true that Queen Elizabeth hath solemnized the perpetual harm of England under the glorious title of marriage with Francis, heir of France? No, no, it shall never be. Monsieur may fortune ask you why should not the Low Countries be governed by the indwellers of that country as they were wont, and yet under my superiority as well, as the king of

---

4. **banns** proclamation required to be made in church in advance of an intended marriage, so that anyone knowing of an impediment to the marriage has the opportunity to raise an objection.

5. The not quite expressed fear in this passage is that by marrying a French prince who was sovereign of the Netherlands, Elizabeth would court reprisal in the form of a Spanish attack on England. As her later letters make clear, she also feared the ruin of English trade with the Continent.

6. **the end crowneth all** proverbial; cf. Shakespeare's *Troilus and Cressida* 4.5.223.

7. Brackets enclose words supplied conjecturally because of a tear in the MS.

Spain did. I answer the case is too far different, since the one is far off by seas distant and the other near upon the Continent. We willingly will not repose our whole trust so far in the French nation as we will give them in pawn all our fortune and afterward stand to their discretion. I hope I shall not live to that hour. Farewell, with my assurance that you will serve with faith and diligence. In haste,

Your sovereign, Queen Elizabeth.

49 ?❧ QUEEN ELIZABETH TO MONSIEUR, MARCH 17, 1581[1]

[Addressed] To Monsieur d'Anjou, my very dear cousin

My dearest,

The honor that you do me is indeed great, sending me often of your letters; but the comfort that I conceive from them exceeds it by much. Wishing nothing so much as the continuation of your good opinion in regard to me; thanking you very humbly for the sweet flowers culled by the hand that has the little fingers that I bless a million times. And I promise you that there was never gift better carried, for the verdure stayed as fresh there as if they had been culled in the same instant, and showed me in an altogether lively fashion your verdant affection in regard to me. And I hope that I will never give just cause for it to wither at my behest. Monsieur, I have taken care not to lose a leaf or a flower, despite all the other jewels that I have. I entreat you to believe that I cannot express the contentment that this bearer bore to me. And pardon me if he did not return sooner when awaiting my courier, by whom I have received a letter from you in which you put me under infinite obligation, not least by so many honorable offers, all full of affection which, however much it is in all, I cannot satisfy it at all, unless I fail to recognize it by all the means that are in my power.

I content myself, Monsieur, that you assure yourself of me as of the most faithful friend[2] that ever prince had. And if you trust to such a rock, all the tempests of the sea will be far from shaking it, nor will any

---

1. *Source:* Hatfield House, Cecil Papers 135/21, fol. 36; in Elizabeth's hand, with remnants of two seals. (For her original French, see *ACFLO,* part 1.)

2. **friend** The French, *amie,* could also connote "beloved."

storm on the earth turn it aside from honoring and loving you. There has not been a word written in the intention of separating myself from your good affection, but for this: that you may not be ignorant of all that is done here. But what I ought to think I do not know, unless that you make me obliged to you forever. And I will never think otherwise of you than the same honor and a heap piled high with virtue. As the Creator knows, to whom with my very cordial commendations I pray to grant you all the honor and contentment in the world, entreating you always to hold me in your good graces. From Westminster this 17 of March.

Your most obliged forever, *Elizabeth R*

50 ❧ QUEEN ELIZABETH TO MONSIEUR, CIRCA JUNE 1581[1]

I cannot express, Monsieur, the contentment that I feel about nets that are broken and you so happily escaped from such bonds.[2] If I did not too much regret your troubles and make myself seem inhumane in adding more ills, I would not leave off condemning you as the source of such inconveniences, being well worthy to cull such a vintage from so evil a harvest. Set at a distance, I pray you, such evil counsels from the favor of your ears and believe that, whatever the evil deserts that others will bear you, it is for a prince always to resemble himself. I have communicated with you by Simier as much as my ignorance can impart to you.

Consider the true basis of all my writings, which tend to no other end except to preserve you in all surety and honor. God is my witness that I never use subtleties or stratagems to do myself good at your expense, as perhaps persons more sly and less faithful do very often. Prove by their fruits the variety and incertitude of such wits, and by this confirm your judgment. And so treat those who seek nothing for the good, unless all for you, in such manner that their souls utter no sighs for lack of better reward, and that you may not wish for them when

1. *Source:* Hatfield House, Cecil Papers 149/31, no foliation; copy. (For the original French, see *ACFLO*, part 2.)

2. Probable reference to Monsieur's successful evasion of his mother's and brother's efforts to prevent him from going to the aid of Cambrai, whose French garrison was under siege by forces of Philip II of Spain. However, the cool tone of the following passage reflects the queen's displeasure at Monsieur's acceptance of the sovereignty of the Netherlands: she reportedly told the French ambassador often that she "would not be married to a war" (*Calendar of State Papers Foreign, 1581–82*, p. 260).

their wits will wander instead of desiring to please you. I do not doubt in the least that the rock will at this hour be assaulted by several storms and winds that blow from divers climes. I wish you so good an astronomer that you could judge of the future and clearly know where they are tending, for fear that in avoiding Scylla you fall into Charybdis.

Monsieur, my dearest, grant pardon to the poor old woman who honors you as much (I dare say) as any young wench whom you ever will find. I thank you a million times for what you write to me from the border of our country, where she who governs desires to have the grace to be able to serve you in some manner, assuring you that England possesses nothing good that will not be dedicated to you, provided that you treat for such. Hearing that Dunkirk[3] does not afford you very good air, I wish you some place more healthy, not at all doubting the continuation of your health, which I understand by du Bex[4] to be better than several others' of your train, for which messenger I thank you very humbly, being the first since Bacqueville[5] who stayed more than half a year with me. And believe that I will not be annoyed if at each hour I were to receive a letter. They are so heartwarming that you are to have no scruple about sending them to me, because otherwise I will think myself dead in your opinion, where I will merit to preserve myself sure and spotless. As God knows, to whom I pray to preserve you from every evil and to give you one hundred years of good life, commending myself a thousand times to the little fingers.

51 ೭☙ QUEEN ELIZABETH TO MONSIEUR, MAY 14, 1582[1]

[Endorsed] Copy of the queen's letter sent to Monsieur by Bacqueville's man from Greenwich the fourteenth of May, 1572 [error for 1582]

So much, my dearest, the happy arrival of Monsieur de Bacqueville has aroused my spirit that I suppose myself to have had the melancholic

3. **Dunkirk** coastal city of the lower Netherlands on the Straits of Dover northeast of Calais. At this period Dunkirk was reported to be plague ridden; its French garrison was also threatened by Spanish forces, which finally overran the town in 1583.

4. **du Bex** Monsieur's secretary, who had accompanied the French embassy to England in May 1581.

5. **Bacqueville** Monsieur's chamberlain, dispatched in an embassy to Elizabeth in early 1579.

1. *Source:* Hatfield House, Cecil Papers 149/36, no foliation; copy. (For original French, see *ACFLO*, part 2.) Between October 1581 and February 1, 1582, Monsieur had again visited

malady that often makes some believe that they are headless, others that they are stripped of sight, and others that they are dead altogether. So I cannot hide from you the evident reasons that lead me to think myself out of this world—because assuring myself for my part since our doleful parting not to have omitted in the least syllable what I had promised you, but rather in order to accomplish it have[2] rendered myself shameless in sending and again sending so many times to the king in order to get him clear about some little difficulty. This matter came to a halt while entreating him to consider it better, as such a thing that would not inconvenience him too much if he had the desire to conclude it. To which, indeed, he answered me this last week by assuring me that he could no longer do what he promised in his letter sent by Pinard.[3]

Judge of this, my dearest—what more can I do, you having taken on such state[4] as you have? For otherwise, according to your very honorable offer, you could forgo the war and the Netherlands and conclude your pact, notwithstanding the difficulties of the agreement, as one not having need of such assurance. But at this hour what shall we do? It is for you to think what it will be. I entreat you not to think that you have made such a perilous journey in order to obtain from it a she who confesses herself so unworthy of half such a risk. If I do not dare to justify myself before everybody that it has never been owing to me that he himself did not conclude after my last promise—which I made you under such conditions as you alone know and admit as well as I myself to be very difficult ones—notwithstanding, in keeping with your contentment, I accorded myself with a very good will. And God is my witness that I

England. During this stay, Elizabeth's behavior veered from one extreme to another. On November 22, 1581, she reportedly told Leicester and Walsingham that she and Monsieur would marry, drawing a ring from her finger and putting it on his hand, while he gave her a ring in return (*Calendar of State Papers Spanish, 1580–1586* [London, 1896], p. 226). However, as Monsieur continued to press Elizabeth for money to underwrite his intervention in the Netherlands, she grew more and more disaffected. At last, on December 16, 1581, she promised Monsieur a loan of £60,000, virtually a bribe to get him to leave England. At long last he did so on February 1, accompanied by Leicester and other nobles whom the queen had commanded to escort Monsieur back to his base of operations. This was the last the two ever saw of each other, although they continued to exchange letters (of which Letters 52 and 55 are examples), and Monsieur also continued to press for the full amount of the promised loan money. As Elizabeth heard worse and worse reports of his management of his military affairs, climaxed by a disastrous attempt to take Antwerp from the duke of Parma's forces in January 1583, she stalled out her loan payments indefinitely.

2. **have** I have.

3. Claude **Pinard** (or Pinart) secretary of state to Catherine de Médicis.

4. **state** Monsieur's acceptance of the supreme governorship of the Netherlands.

have never drawn back from it since. And I swear to you that I never wish to show myself unworthy of the favor of such a prince, having no need to be put in mind again of the least grace that I have received from your goodness. And I do not at all doubt that my merits are always very good advocates of my affection and constancy in regard to you. Consider, my dearest, if I dare to say it, whether the whole universe was not astonished how the queen of England had so much forgotten England as to bring in new neighbors on the Continent near to her border. Your good judgment, not blinded by others, will be able to judge what it is that hangs on such an opinion. And then see if, for my part, I have hazarded nothing for you, the love of my nation being dearer to me than my life, and kings of little duration when that is alienated from them.

To conclude all, that which you wish me to do that will not touch my honor too much I will do, rendering you most humble thanks for your last message with the letter, which have aroused me from a very deep sleep, having never heard mention of this matter since our separation of bodies—not of souls—at which I was astonished in strange fashion. I rejoice to hear that you are so greatly honored by that people, who seem to me to have very just cause for it. But I do not doubt that you keep always in memory, of what nature the vulgar are in all countries, and will place your trust according to the occasion that I present you with, desiring nothing more than the continuation of our contentments, and cursing (my charity being very cold in this regard) all who overturn our good designs. You understand me in few words. To put an end to this letter, I pray you to believe that if the king asks my ambassador one more time what my intention is, I will charge him with singing the same song as before, while blushing myself to recite so often what has so little effect.

52 ⪾ QUEEN ELIZABETH TO MONSIEUR, MAY 24, 1582[1]

[Endorsed] Copy of the queen's letter to Monsieur sent from Greenwich by one of his lackeys,[2] twenty-fourth of May, 1582

My dearest,

You make me acknowledge that notwithstanding the great affairs and importance of your business, you fail not to console me with the

---

1. *Source:* Hatfield House, Cecil Papers 149/38, no foliation; incomplete copy in a contemporary hand with one local insertion in Elizabeth's hand. (For original French, see *ACFLO*, part 2.)

2. **lackeys** liveried footmen.

coming of your long writings, and for them, confessing myself infinitely obliged to you, I render you a million thanks. And in reading them I see a mass of affection there, containing humors of several qualities. And however much I am not a scholar in natural philosophy nor a good enough physician to make a right distinction of them, still I will take the boldness of enlightening you on the true property of some parts that I set down in the keeping of my memory.

It seems to me that in commemorating the history of the dealings between us, it pleases you to tell me at length of the hazards, losses, and machinations that you have endured for my sake. The which I cannot forget, having them engraved in my soul, where, until its separation from my body, I will not leave to recognize and be pained by them always. Only I entreat you not to forget[3] that all these postponements have not derived from me, my thoughts not having been lacking in respect of our more happy stay in this country, tending not only towards my honor but as well towards your surety. Remove, therefore, my dearest Monsieur, any thought that I stand to blame for the passion of anger that gives you offense because your constancy should be doubted. I absolve myself of such a doubt, having never said nor thought it, whatever opinion others may have had of it. I care not to offer you so much injury; only by machination do I purge myself of the calumnies imputed to me, in France and elsewhere, of having used subtleties or changefulness in what I promised you. And so much was it wrong that I was to blame that I will not cease to impute it to the person to whom it most pertained.

What I see by your letters written to Pinard has given you an argument for writing in the same fashion with our permission, which seems strange to me in making a show that I push you to proceed more urgently, as much from my doubtfulness as from my haste. O Monsieur, how that touches my honor, lady that I am! You will think about it at your good leisure; some will laugh about it at their ease. And I feel it to my regret, which lessens notwithstanding when I imagine an end leading to attaining an end to our long enmeshments that redouble so, before the fastening of my bonds, that no one will ever know how to unloose them.

You wrote me about having sent me the copies of the letters of the king and the queen, the which I have not yet seen except a letter to

---

3. **not to forget** inserted over the line in Elizabeth's hand.

Pinard, which was only written the twelfth of May, a day very distant from the time of your departure from this kingdom; by which I see that you have never mentioned it since your arrival in Flanders. Herein I can justify myself as not having delayed shamelessly, my ambassador having several times made mention of it. And I think that the king will repute me for such a one as goes a-wooing, which will always be a fine reputation for a woman! You can see, if you please, clearly and easily, the hope that I can conceive of a sincere accomplishment of the thing which is resolved with such difficulty, or rather not at all.

If you bring up the subject of money, I am so poor an orator for my profit and like so little to play the housewife that I give charge of this to such as are wiser than I. They have declared everything to Marchaumont,[4] who is of my resolution. To whom I have made request to inform you of it particularly, you being very importunate in this affair, and entreat you with hands clasped to be willing to weigh in a just balance on what foundation I go; and you will see that I do not have less consideration of your greatness and contentation in your enterprises than you yourself would be able to wish.

Receiving your last letter of news sent by the queen of Navarre,[5] I am only too bound to you by the great joy that you take from it. But for my part, I heard nothing of it by the last audience that my ambassador had with the king, which was the sixth of this month, and believe that my last information will be found too true, since I received it from a good place and am very greatly astonished that you have not yet received it, since I dispatched it to you as soon as the wind permitted. You will pardon me if I do not easily give credit to too good news, for fear that deception will redouble my anxiety. Without being assured of it, I keep myself still from answering to the name by which you conjure me. Only I can tell you that such obligation does not more tie my affection than your merits have already done, which cannot receive increase. And I will make comparison with whomever it may be in having no less affection for you than if the little priest had already performed his office. I will perform in such a sort that you will not justly be able to impute any deficiencies in your behalf.

4. **Marchaumont** Clausse de Marchaumont, count de Beaumont, Monsieur's principal envoy in England at this time.

5. **queen of Navarre** Marguerite de Valois (1553–1615), Monsieur's sister, then the wife of Henry of Navarre.

I could dilate on the answer that I sent you by Marchaumont, but I have left that work for him, entreating you to believe that if our marriage were made, I would not take away from it any good for England. If by chance God took me out of this world before having children, if ever I will have any, you are wise to think what good turn I had done them to gain them such good neighbors, if perchance Flanders changed masters and the French governed there. Pardon me this frankness. Do not forget my heart, which I risk a little for you in this matter—more than you will be able to imagine but not more than I already feel. And it rejoices me to have tasted of it, more than a fine liquor. But when I remember for whom this is, I console myself so and then am borne up by it. As for the commission that we will give you, I shall not entertain myself with it so far as to understand, if the desire to please you so much occupied the queen's mind that she understood the king's intention to resemble the sum of your desires, not at all the interpretation that perhaps can be made of it, which to understand. . . .[6]

53 ❧ QUEEN ELIZABETH TO GEORGE TALBOT, EARL OF SHREWSBURY, ON THE DEATH OF HIS SON, CIRCA SEPTEMBER 5, 1582[1]

[Headed] Letter of comfort to the earl of Shrewsbury touching the death and loss of his son.

By the queen.

Right trusty and right well-beloved cousin and councillor, we greet you well. We had thought immediately upon understanding of the death of the Lord Talbot,[2] your son, to have sent you our letters of comfort, but that we were loath that they should have been the first messengers unto you of so unpleasant matter as the loss of a son of so great hope and towardness,[3] that might have served to have been a comfortable staff unto

---

6. The copy breaks off here. We can only speculate as to the conclusion of the letter in the form that was sent to Monsieur.

1. *Source:* BL, MS Additional 15891, fols. 92v–93r; copy in the miscellany of Sir Christopher Hatton.

2. **Lord Talbot** Francis Talbot (born ca. 1551), the earl of Shrewsbury's eldest son.

3. **towardness** favorable development, promise.

you in your old years and a profitable pillar unto this our estate in time to come. Whereof he gave as great hope as anyone of his calling within this our realm, which we know, in respect of the love you bear us, cannot but greatly increase your grief.

But herein, we as his prince and sovereign and you as a loving and natural father, for that we both be interested in the loss (though for several respects), are to lay aside our particular causes of grief and to remember that God, who hath been the worker thereof and doth all things for the best, is not to be controlled. Besides, if we do duly look into the matter in true course of Christianity, we shall then see that the loss hath wrought so great a gain to the gentleman whom we now lack, as we have rather cause to rejoice than lament. For if the imperfections of this declining age we live in be truly weighed and the sundry miseries that we are daily subject unto be duly looked into, we shall then find more cause to judge them unhappy that live than to bewail those as unfortunate that are dead. But for that the weakness of frail flesh cannot so rest upon that comfort which the happy estate of his change hath wrought, but that nature will have her force; we cannot therefore but put you in mind how well God in His singular goodness hath dealt with you, in that he left you behind other sons of great hope, who through the good education that you have carefully given them and the good gifts of nature they are plentifully indued withal, are like to prove no less comfortable unto you than serviceable unto us. And therefore, for your comfort, you are to remember that of four sons that He hath given you, He hath taken only one to Himself.

These reasons, which we have thought on and used with good fruit as means to lessen our own grief, we have thought meet to impart them unto you, and do hope they shall work no less effect in you, whose case we tender as much as our own, having made as great trial of your care and fidelity towards us as ever prince hath made of servant. And therefore we do assure ourself that in this discomfort there is no earthly thing can yield you more comfort than the assurance of our gracious favor towards you. Whereof you may make full account to receive the same from us in as full measure as a well-deserving servant and subject may in true gratuity[4] look for at a gracious and thankful prince's hands. Given under our signet.

4. **gratuity** graciousness or favor.

54 ❧ QUEEN ELIZABETH TO MISTRESS TALBOT, CIRCA 1582[1]

By the queen.

Dear and well beloved, we greet you well. Upon knowledge of an earnest and great affection that our trusty and well-beloved servant Sir Robert Stapleton,[2] knight, beareth unto you, tending to a godly purpose of matching with you in marriage, we have been pleased by our special letters to commend his suit unto you to that end, and to give you such further testimony of him as we ourself know that for his worthiness he deserveth; not meaning thereby to press or vex your[3] further than your own mind can in this case suffer you to like; but that if you shall be content to yield like mutual affection towards him, you may be very well assured to bestow the same upon a gentleman of whom for his deserts by service to us we have just cause to make good account, and for his good parts and discreet government otherwise is worthy to be well thought of generally, his estate, both for livelihood and calling, being also such as doth give him credit among the best. Which respects, though they do justly commend him to win favor at your hands, yet if you shall be thereafter moved (upon our commendation and desire to do him good) so to like of him as to consent to this his honest and godly suit, we will take the same in the most thankful part and declare our gracious acceptation thereof towards you to your comfort hereafter. Adding thus much further for the present: that if we had not likewise a good opinion of yourself, being by this gentleman partly informed of your virtues and good qualities, we would not thus commend him to you to any such end. And so being in each of you good parts to deserve well of each other, there is no likelihood but of great comfort by this match, which we wish unto you both.

1. *Source:* BL, MS Additional 15891, fols. 91–92; copy from Sir Christopher Hatton's miscellany. The identity of Mistress Talbot is uncertain. The BL Catalogue identifies her by inference as Alice (or Anne) Talbot, the widow of Francis Talbot, the earl of Shrewsbury's eldest son, whom she had married in 1562. Nichols identifies her as the daughter and heir of Sir Henry Sherington, of Lacock, Wiltshire, and relict of John Talbot, Esquire, of Solway, Worcestershire.

2. **Sir Robert Stapleton** identified in Thomas Fuller's *History of the Worthies of England* (London, 1662) as a descendant of a distinguished Yorkshire family, a "comely and goodly personage, had scant an equal (except Sir Philip Sidney), no superior in England" (bk. 2, p. 223). According to Nichols, Stapleton did marry Mistress Talbot and had by her a "numerous posterity" (2:628).

3. **your** you.

55 ❧ QUEEN ELIZABETH TO MONSIEUR, SEPTEMBER 10, 1583[1]

[Endorsed in Burghley's hand] Copy of the queen's letter to Monsieur, sent by Monsieur de Reaux[2] from Oatlands[3] the 10th of September 1583

Monsieur,

After a long wait to receive some news of you and your affairs, Monsieur de Reaux came to visit me on your behalf, carrying nothing but letters entirely full of affection and assurance of the continuance of the same forever, for which I render you an infinity of thanks, for I have heard of the care that you take for fear of some bad impression that I could conceive of your actions. Then he tired me with language that seemed very strange to me: that you desired to know what will be the aid you will give for the preservation of the Netherlands, saying to me that you are assured by the king that he will aid you the same as I do. My God, Monsieur, how unfortunate you are to believe that this is the way to preserve your friends, by always debilitating them! Whoever they are who have given you the advice on this have thought to make a spot on our friendship, or to break it altogether in order by the same means to achieve their designs and reclaim you to their desire.

Do you not remember at all, Monsieur, against how many friends I have to prepare? Must I think so much of those afar while I neglect the closest? The king, our brother—is he so feeble a prince that he is not able to defend you without another neighbor who has enough on her back, or so weakened as to open a path for assailants? You will not esteem me so unworthy of reigning that I may not fortify myself, indeed, with the sinews of war[4] while waiting too long for courtesy from those who seek my ruin. I am astonished at the king our brother, who has given me the precedence in fortifying you in so great a need, I having begun before him while he is not lacking in better means by way of less inconvenience. Pardon me, I pray you, that I tell you that this answer is altogether clear: he would do nothing, thinking that I would have little reason for not giving. So much so that if the king will not speak and will not do much more than formerly, such an enterprise will break off very

---

1. *Source:* Hatfield House, Cecil Papers 149/40, no foliation; copy with one local correction in Elizabeth's hand. (For original French, see *ACFLO*, part 2.)

2. **de Reaux** the latest emissary to be sent by Monsieur in the Netherlands.

3. **Oatlands** principally a hunting lodge, situated southwest of London in Surrey.

4. Cf. Cicero's "*Nervos belli, pecuniam infinitam.*" ("The sinews of war, unlimited money.") *Fifth Philippic,* chap. 5.

soon; and if it be up to him alone, I think that such is his determination. There is my opinion.

As for you, Monsieur, I see that you are so environed with contrarious persuasions and such differing humors—doubting so much and assuring yourself of nothing—that you do not know where you should well turn, as you have sufficient reason not to. Would to God I were skilled enough in judgment to give you counsel[5]—the best and most assured counsel—and that I had the understanding, as I have the will, to do it. Then rather would I bring it to you than send it. I hope among other things that you will remember that he is well worthy of falling who enters into nets: do not only take advice, think shrewdly—that is enough.

I hear to my great regret that the king, the queen mother—even your own—put on me the fault that I have never committed, having always looked to the king to perfect that which I can no longer do more than mention, except to entreat you to do me so much right as to exculpate me even by the sentence of your ministers, who themselves know my innocence in this matter. For I cannot bear such an injury—that they bite and weep at my affection with regard to you. I appeal to the king's ambassador, to Monsieur La Mothe, Marchaumont, and Bacqueville; and as long as God does not permit such a pact, so long will I never cease honoring, loving and esteeming you like the dog who, often beaten, returns to his master. God keep you from glozing counsels and permit you to follow those who respect you more than themselves.

56 &❧ QUEEN ELIZABETH TO CATHERINE DE MÉDICIS, QUEEN MOTHER OF FRANCE, ON MONSIEUR'S DEATH, CIRCA JULY 1584[1]

[Addressed] To Madame, my good sister the queen mother

Madame,

If the extremity of my unhappiness had not equaled my grief for his sake and had not rendered me inadequate to touch with pen the wound that my heart suffers, it would not be possible that I would have so forgotten myself as not to have visited you in the company that I make

5. **counsel** supplied over the line, apparently in Elizabeth's hand.
1. *Source:* BL, MS Cotton Galba E.VI, fol. 255; in Elizabeth's hand, loosely formed and paper badly worn. (For original French, see *ACFLO*, part 1.)

with you in your sorrow, which I am sure cannot be greater than my own. For inasmuch as you are his mother, so it is that there remain to you several other children. But for me, I find no consolation except death, which I hope will soon reunite us. Madame, if you were able to see the image of my heart, you would see the portrait of a body without a soul. But I will trouble you no longer with my plaints, since you have too many of your own. It remains to me at this point to avow and swear to you that I will turn a good part of my love for him towards the king my good brother and you, assuring you that you will find me the most faithful daughter and sister that ever princes had. And this for the principal reason that he belonged to you so nearly, he to whom I was entirely dedicated. He to whom, if he had had the divine favor of a longer life, you would have sent more help.[2] Madame, I pray you to give firm credit to this gentleman who will tell you more amply in my stead my thoughts on your behalf. And believe that I will fulfil them faithfully as if I were your daughter born. As God knows, to whom I pray to give you long life and every consolation.

Your very affectionate sister and cousin,
Elizabeth R

57 ⁊ QUEEN ELIZABETH TO JAMES VI OF SCOTLAND, CIRCA JUNE OR JULY 1585[1]

[Addressed] To my good brother the king of Scots

Right dear brother,

Your gladsome acceptance of my offered amity, together with the desire you seem to have engraven in your mind to make merits correspondent, makes me in full opinion that some enemies to our goodwill shall lose much travail with making frustrate their baiting stratagems,

---

2. The implication is that the king of France and his mother had sent Monsieur inadequate aid in his failed military efforts in the Netherlands.

1. *Source:* BL, MS Additional 23240, fols. 15v–16v; MS volume entitled "Autograph Correspondence of Q. Elizabeth with James VI of Scotland, 1582–1596"; in Elizabeth's hand. (For original-spelling version, see *ACFLO,* part 1.) Here, as in many of the letters to James in Elizabeth's hand, the address in the original is in French.

which I know to be many and by sundry means to be explored.[2] I cannot halt with you so much as to deny that I have seen such evident shows of your contrarious dealings that if I made not my reckoning the better of the months,[3] I might condemn you as unworthy of such as I mind to show myself toward you; and therefore I am well pleased to take any color[4] to defend your honor, and hope that you will remember that who seeketh two strings to one bow, they may shoot strong but never straight. And if you suppose that princes' causes be veiled so covertly that no intelligence may bewray[5] them, deceive not yourself: we old foxes can find shifts to save ourselves by others' malice, and come by knowledge of greatest secret, specially if it touch our freehold. It becometh therefore all of our rank to deal sincerely; lest if we use it not, when we do it we be hardly believed. I write not this, my dear brother, for doubt but for remembrances.

My ambassador[6] writes so much of your honorable treatment of him and of Alexander[7] that I believe they be converted Scots. You oblige me for them, for which I render you a million of most entire thanks, as she that meaneth to deserve many a good thought in your breast through good desert. And for that your request is so honorable, retaining so much reason, I were out of senses if I should not suspend of any hearsay till the answer of your own action, which the actor ought best to know. And so assure yourself I mean and vow to do with this request, that you will afford me the reciproque.[8] And thus with my many petitions to the Almighty for your long life and preservation, I end these scribbled lines.

Your very assured, loving sister
and cousin, *Elizabeth R*

2. The cryptic phrasing of this letter is occasioned in part by the difficult political situation in early 1585: after Dr. William Parry's plot to assassinate Elizabeth had been exposed, James's mother, Mary, Queen of Scots, was transferred from the relatively permissive custody of Shrewsbury into much stricter imprisonment under Sir Amyas Paulet.

3. **if ... months** if I had calculated the months better.

4. **color** excuse; also official insignia, as in heraldry.

5. **bewray** reveal.

6. **my ambassador** Sir Edward Wotton (1548–1626), who had been sent to James in April 1585.

7. **Alexander** Robert Alexander, a member of Wotton's entourage.

8. **afford me the reciproque** reciprocate in kind; in MS **the** is written twice.

LETTER 57, ADDITIONAL DOCUMENT A JAMES TO ELIZABETH, CIRCA JULY 31, 1585[1]

Madame and mother,

Since haste, anger, and extraordinary sorrow will not permit any long letter, this present shall only serve to assure you of my honest innocence in this late mischief[2] and of my constancy in that course mentionate[3] in my last letter unto you, not doubting but your ambassador hath written to you at large both of the one and the other. I have also directed expressly the bearer hereof unto you to know your mind and desire for the repairing of this foresaid mischief, whom praying you firmly to credit and to esteem still of my truth, I commit you, madame and mother, to God's holy protection. From Saint Andrews the 3 day[4] of July, 1585.

Your most loving and devoted brother and son,

James R.

[Postscript] I doubt not, madame, but ye have kept one ear for me, notwithstanding of many malicious tongues that now do boldly speak.

58 ⪧ ELIZABETH TO JAMES, AUGUST 1585[1]

[Addressed] To my good brother and cousin the king of Scots

Right dear brother,

I find too true the French adage "Qu'un mal ne vient jamais seul,"[2] for as the horrible and sudden murder of my most faithful subject and most valiant baron was unto me a heartsore and grievous tidings, so was it tenfold redoubled with knowledge that a Scot should dare violate

---

1. *Source:* Bruce, no. 11, pp. 18–19 (reported there as from "Thompson MS, p. 9").

2. The occasion of this letter was the murder of Francis Lord Russell, eldest surviving son of Francis, second earl of Bedford, in a July 28, 1585, border quarrel that the English alleged to have been premeditated by James's favorite, the earl of Arran.

3. **mentionate** mentioned.

4. **3 day** emended by Bruce to "31 day."

1. *Source:* BL, MS Additional 23240, art. 6, fol. 19; in Elizabeth's hand. (For original-spelling version, see *ACFLO,* part 1.)

2. Also proverbial in English: "Misfortunes never come singly."

his hands on any of our noble blood in a peaceable concord, when our friendship should have sent out his hottest beams to the kindling of the entire affection of both realms. That any of that nation should once dare have had a thought to maculate[3] such a contract of amity, I perceive by my ambassador that your grief is little less than such a hap deserveth, and do perceive that you have not spared your well favored[4] to cause him answer such a suspicion. I think myself therefore greatly obliged unto your care for my satisfaction, and therein I thank you for being so considerate of your own honor, which I assure you lieth a-bleeding in the bowels of many an Englishman until full reason be made for such a treachery. God send us better luck after our league be finished than this bloody beginning may give Calends[5] of, else many a red side will follow such demerits.

But I hope you will spare no man that may be doubted of such a meaning: I mean not only of the murder, but of the breaking out upon our borderers,[6] which commonly are the beginnings of our quarrels. I doubt nothing of your curious care in this behalf. And for that the warden of that March[7] hath been the open and common fosterer and companion of the traitor Westmoreland[8] and his complices[9] in France and Scotland, I hope you will agree easily to send him to my hands, where he shall never receive injury nor evil measure. And thus, desiring[10] to credit my ambassador in certain particularities that he shall impart unto you as to myself, I recommend you to God's safe tuition, who grant you many gladsome years.

Your most affectionate sister
and cousin, *Elizabeth R*

3. **maculate** spot, stain (cf. Latin *maculatus*).

4. **well favored** James Stewart, earl of Arran (d. 1595), the first of James's known minions; after his death James burned their correspondence.

5. **Calends** the first day of the ancient Roman month; also, foretaste, prelude.

6. **borderers** those dwelling near the border between England and Scotland.

7. **warden of that March** the Scotsman Sir Thomas Ker of Fernihurst.

8. **Westmoreland** Charles Neville (1543–1601), earl of Westmoreland, a major conspirator in the Northern Rebellion, who was formally attainted for treason in 1571. When the rebellion failed, he at first took refuge with the Kers at Fernihurst Castle in Scotland but was residing in Louvain by 1572.

9. **complices** accomplices.

10. **desiring** desiring you.

LETTER 58, ADDITIONAL DOCUMENT A JAMES TO ELIZABETH,
AUGUST 13, 1585[1]

Madame and dearest sister,

The receipt of your three favorable letters, whereof two be of your
own hand, hath moved me to give you by this present the most hearty
thanks therefor of him who is most devoted to you of any prince in
Christendom; but specially I think myself more beholden unto you
than I can ever acquit for the promise and vow ye make in one of your
letters not to trust any evil of me while[2] ye hear my own declaration of
my part. Madame, since ye have so honorably dealt with me in this case
I think it my part, as it was always, to sift out the trial of this last mishap
with all possible speed, and on the other part I will earnestly require
you to suspend your judgment while ye hear from me what success my
travails have taken, whereof ye shall be with God's grace advertised in
very few days. So shall my honest part be cleared, the guilty known and
punished, ye resolved what to crave for your satisfaction and repara-
tions of the fact, and the conclusion of the amity and league go forward,
whereunto I do already fully assent. Whereof since your ambassador
doth more largely write, I will end here with promise of my utter diligence in the foresaid trial and committing to the holy protection of the
Almighty. From Stirling the 13 day of August 1585.

> Your most loving and devoted
> brother and son, *James R.*

LETTER 58, ADDITIONAL DOCUMENT B JAMES TO ELIZABETH,
AUGUST 19, 1585[1]

Madame and mother,

In great haste ready to ride. Your ambassador's present dispatch hath
moved me to write this few words to assure you that, although my articles that the ambassador sends you desires the league to concern only
religion, yet my plain intention is that the league shall be offensive and

---

1. *Source:* Bruce, no. 13, pp. 20–21 (reported there as from "Copy in Thompson MS, p. 9").
2. **while** (Scots *quhill*) until (used again in the next sentence).
1. *Source:* Bruce, no. 14, pp. 21–22 (from "Copy in Thompson MS, p. 10").

defensive for all invasions upon whatsomever pretext. And therefore I will pray you to keep this present in token and testimonial of my plain assent thereunto, and that I will employ my crown and country to resist to whatsomever invasions upon yours. Thus praying to appardon[2] this scribbling in haste and to continue still my loving mother, as I shall be your devoted son, I commit you, madame and mother, to God's holy protection. The 19 day of August from Stirling, 1585.

Your most loving and devoted
brother and son, *James R.*

59 ❧ ELIZABETH TO JAMES, NOVEMBER 1585[1]

[Addressed] To my very dear brother the king of Scots

Right dear brother,

The strangeness of hard accidents that are arrived here of unlooked-for or unsuspected attempts in Scotland, even by some such as lately issued out of our land,[2] constraineth me as well for the care we have of your person as of the discharge of our own honor and conscience to send you immediately this gentleman, one that appertaineth to us in blood,[3] both to offer you all assistance of help as all good endeavor of counsel, and to make it plain that we dealt plainly. These lords making great outcries that I would not or could help them to be restored, I by their great importunity yielded that if I might be freed of my assurance given unto you for their safekeeping, I would consent unto their departure. And so, after your answer, as my thought[4] most honorable, that they might take their way to Germany with your gracious grant of some live-

2. **praying to appardon** praying you to pardon.

1. *Source:* BL, MS Additional 23240, art. 7, fol. 23; in Elizabeth's hand. (For original-spelling version, see *ACFLO*, part 1.)

2. This letter was occasioned by actions of the earls of Angus, Mar, Glammis, and other banished Scots lords. They had remained in England until October 1585, but they now crossed back into Scotland and mounted a successful coup against the influence of the royal favorite, Arran, on the king and the government.

3. **one ... blood** William Knollys, eldest son of Sir Francis Knollys and his wife Katherine, daughter of William Carey by Elizabeth's aunt Mary Boleyn.

4. **my thought** alternative reading could be "methought."

hood,[5] after a week's space I gave them my passport and so dismissed them without, I swear unto you, once the sight of any one of them.

Now when I weigh how suddenly beyond my expectations this sudden stir ariseth, and fearing lest some evil and wicked person might surmise that this was not without my foresight, I beseech you trust my actions according[6] the measure of my former dealings for your safety and answerable to the rule of reason, and you shall find that few princes will agree to constraint of their equals, much less with compulsion of their subjects. Judge of me therefore as of a king that carries no abject nature and think this of me, that rather than your danger I will venture mine. And albeit I must confess that it is dangerous for a prince to irritate too much through evil advice the generality of great subjects, so might you or[7] now have followed my advice, that would never betray you with unsound counsel. And now to conclude, making haste, I pray you be plain with this bearer that I may know what you would that I should do, without excuse hereafter that constrained you did it, for I dare assure you of his secrecy and thereof be you bold. For the Lord Russell's death and other things, I refer me to this gentleman, who I dare promise is of no faction beside my will. God bless you in all safety, as I wish myself

Your true, assured cousin and sister, *Elizabeth R*

[Postscript] Fear not, for your life must be theirs or else they shall smart well, every mother's son of them.

60 ❧ ELIZABETH TO JAMES, CIRCA JANUARY 1586[1]

[Addressed] To my dearest brother and cousin the king of Scots

Right dear brother,

I am not a little satisfait[2] of many a careful thought that my mind tossed up and down with doubts what care might do to a king's breast

5. **livehood** livelihood.
6. **according** according to.   7. **or** ere.
    1. *Source:* BL, MS Additional 23240, art. 10, fols. 30r–31r; in Elizabeth's hand, with remnants of seal attached. (For original-spelling version, see *ACFLO*, part 1.)
    2. **satisfait** satisfied.

environed of a sudden with so unlooked-for an accident. My thanks, therefore, may scace³ be contained in this paper for your most acceptable messenger,⁴ whom it pleased you to command my satisfaction of your good estate, together with your good liking of the lords and their action, whom I beseech God no longer preserve in life than they be ready for your preservation to spend all theirs—so far were ever my intents from any treachery toward you. And whereas your desire seemeth great that the league in hand might come to end, I am addressing a gentleman⁵ unto you for the same purpose, and will delay no time for so good a intent, trusting then that no whispering treason shall have credit in your ear to retard or cut off so needful an action. Suppose such, I pray you, to resemble a golden hook that oft deceives the unwary fish and makes him receive his worst in lieu of better hope. Amidst all these kind dealings of yours, let me not forget how little care the world shall think you prize me at if in midst of greatest friendship my loss of honor be no whit repaired for the shameful murder of the Baron Russell. Ponder it deeply, I beseech you, for it striketh near me, so public an injury to have no redress. Without we show the thought which God alone reserves His part,⁶ the like answer was never yet given, and hope for better payment.

For your Church matters, I do both admire and rejoice to see your wise paraphrase, which far exceedeth their text. Since God hath made kings, let them not unmake their authority and let brooks and small rivers acknowledge their springs and flow no further than their banks. I praise God that you uphold ever a regal rule.

For all other matters which this gentleman hath told me, I will hope still that your faithful profession of constancy in my behalf shall far surmount the devilish practices and subtle iniquity of those which under pretense of your advancement will scant your best fortune. And albeit I am advertised, even from among themselves, that your assurance to them doth show that all my fair offers from you be *ad EΦesios*⁷ and ridiculous, meaning wholly to follow them and temporize with me; yet

3. **scace** scarce.

4. **messenger** Sir William Keith.

5. **gentleman** the veteran diplomat Sir Thomas Randolph.

6. **thought . . . part** "To me belongeth vengeance, and recompense" (Deuteronomy 32:35).

7. "to Ephesians"; that is, to companions in merrymaking (Latin phrase with Greek Φ instead of *ph*). Cf. Shakespeare's 2 *Henry IV* 2.2.164 and *Merry Wives* 4.5.19.

I mind to *peccare in meliorem*[8] if I must needs be beguiled and mind not to trust them till I see you fail me, and then *deceptis ad decipientem digne vertitur.*[9] Till then I will trust your word, and dare assure you shall never on my behalf have cause to repent your vows, meaning you no less good than I pray God ever to afford me, praying Him long to conserve you. And to end this letter, let me not forget to recommend this gentleman's good behavior in this his charge, having used it to your honor and his great praise. Thus I finish to trouble you but do rest

> Your most assuredst, loving sister
> and cousin, *Elizabeth R*

61 ᑌ QUEEN ELIZABETH TO SIR THOMAS HENEAGE, HER EMISSARY TO THE EARL OF LEICESTER IN THE NETHERLANDS, FEBRUARY 10, 1586[1]

[Headed] Belgia, 10 February, 1585[6]. Instructions for Sir Thomas Heneage.[2] *February 10.*

You shall let the earl understand how highly upon just cause we are offended with his last late acceptation of the government of those provinces,[3] being done contrary to our commandment delivered unto him both by ourself in speech and by particular letters from certain of our Council written unto him in that behalf by our express direction, which we do repute to be a very great and strange contempt least looked for at his hands, being he is a creature of our own. Wherewith we have

---

8. "sin by doing the better thing."

9. "by his own deceits, [the deception is] deservedly turned back upon the deceiver."

1. *Source*: BL, MS Cotton Galba, C.VIII, fols. 22r–26r; copy containing a few scribal underlinings not reproduced here. The original was probably in the hand of a secretary and signed by the queen.

2. **Sir Thomas Heneage** (d. 1595) a gentleman of the Privy Chamber and one of Elizabeth's most trusted courtiers. In 1589 she would make him a privy councillor and vice chamberlain of her household.

3. In 1585 Elizabeth had decided to intervene militarily in the Netherlands and sent a large army with Leicester at its head. The Dutch received him with magnificent feasts and public entertainments; on January 14, 1586, they offered him the absolute government of the United Provinces. After an initial refusal, he capitulated, was installed as absolute governor on January 25, and his title announced publicly on February 6.

so much the greater cause to be offended for that he hath not had that regard that became him, to have (at the least) by his letters acquainted us with the causes that moved him so contemptuously to break our said commandment; nor used that diligence that appertained in sending our servant Davison[4] unto us with instructions how to answer the said contempt, which hath greatly aggravated the fault. Though for our own part we cannot imagine that anything can be alleged by him to excuse so manifest a contempt, at the least to make it appear that there was any such necessity in the matter (as we doubt not that will be greatly prevented) but that th'acceptation might have been stayed until our pleasure had been first known.

You shall let him understand that we hold our honor greatly touched by the said acceptation of that government, and least as we may not with our honor endure, or that it carryeth a manifest appearance of repugnancy to our protestation set out in print, by the which we declare that our only intent in sending him over into those parts was to direct and govern th'English troops that we had granted to the States for their aid and to assist them with his advice and counsel for the better ordering both of their civil and martial courses, as is contained in the late contract passed between us and their commissioners that were here, so as the world may justly thereby conceive. You shall say unto him that men of judgment will conceive another course taken by him, that the declaration published by us was but to abuse the world, for that they cannot in reason persuade themselves that a creature of our own, having for that purpose given him express commandment upon pain of his allegiance[5] to proceed, all delays and excuses laid apart, to the present demission[6] thereof, considering the great obedience that ever from the beginning of our reign hath been generally yielded us by our subjects, would ever have presumed to have accepted of the said government contrary to our commandment without some secret assent of ours, or at least they will think that there is not now that reverent regard carried to our commandment as for[7] hath been and as in due course of obedience ought to be.

4. **Davison** William Davison (1541?–1608), Elizabeth's newly appointed agent in the Netherlands.

5. Disobedience to a royal command given "on pain of allegiance" constituted treason.

6. **demission** resignation, abdication.

7. **for** heretofore (probably copyist's error).

For the removing of which hard conceit that the world may justly take upon consideration either of the said abuse or contempt, you shall let him understand that our express pleasure and commandment is, upon pain of his allegiance, that—all delays and excuses set apart, without attending any further assembly of the States than such as shall be provided present with him at the time of their access there or in some other convenient place—he shall make an open and public resignation in the place where he accepted the same, the absolute government, as a thing done without our privity[8] and consent, contrary to the contract passed between us and their commissioners. Letting them notwithstanding understand that this direction of ours given unto the said earl for the demission of his absolute authority proceedeth not of any decay or alteration of our own goodwill or favor towards them, whose well doing we do no less tender than our own natural subjects', as it hath manifestly appeared unto them by our former actions, having for their sakes opposed ourselves to one of the mightiest princes of Europe, assuring them hereafter, therefore, that we do mean the continuance thereof of the same towards them, and our intent is that the said earl should hold that form of government. Both likely to touch us greatly in honor, we see (you may tell him) no other way but the said election must be revoked with some such solemnity as the same was publicly published, and the States and people let understand that our meaning is not he shall hold or exercise any other sort of government during the time of his abode there, as is expressed in the said contract which we do purpose inviolably to observe according to our promise, not doubting but that th'assistance they shall receive that way will be as effectual for their safety and benefit or rather more (for some causes best known to ourself) as th'other course.

[Horizontal space for the insertion of the copy of Letter 62, after which the text of Letter 61 continues:]

After the delivery of which message to th'earl, we think meet to th'end the States or such as shall assist the earl at the time of your access may know the cause that moveth us to dislike of the said acceptance and to have the same revoked, that you shall advertise yourself to them and let them understand that we find yet strange that a nobleman—a minister ours[9] sent thither to execute and hold such a course of govern-

8. **privity** private knowledge.
9. **ours** of ours.

ment as was contained in the said contract—should without our assent
be pressed to assent to accept of more large and absolute authority over
the said countries than was accorded on by virtue of the said contract,
especially seeing that we ourself, being oftentimes pressed by their
commissioners to accept of th'absolute government, did always refuse
the same.[10] And therefore by this manner of proceeding we hold ourself
two sundry ways wronged by them, greatly to our dishonor. Th'one by
provoking a minister of ours to commit so notorious a contempt against
us. Th'other in that they show themselves to have a very slender and a
weak conceit of our judgment by pressing a minister of ours to accept
of that which we refused, as though our long experience in government
had not yet taught us to discover what were fit for us to do in matters of
our state. And though we cannot think but that this offer of theirs proceeded of the great goodwill they bear us, and so consequently acknowledge the same with all thankfulness, yet may it minister cause of
suspicion to such as are apt to judge the worst of things best meant that
the said offer under color of goodwill to us was made by favor, some
(though not by the generality) of a malicious purpose, supposing the
same would have been refused; and that there would thereby have followed a change and alienation of the hearts of the common sort when
they shall see a plain refusal of an offer that contained so evident and
manifest a stayed argument of their goodwill and devotion towards us.
You shall further let them understand that forasmuch as we cannot
conceive that the said acceptation hath greatly wounded our honor for
the causes above specified, we have resolved to have the said earl's authority revoked, requiring them therefore in our name to see the same
executed out of hand. And to th'end they may not enter into any hard or
jealous conceit upon knowledge of this our purpose, you shall on our
behalf assure them that the promised assistance according to the contents of the contract shall be faithfully performed, and that the said earl
during his abode there shall second and assist them with his best advice
and counsel accordingly as is above expressed, as is also at large contained in our own letters directed to them.

You shall also let the said earl understand that whereas by his instructions he hath specially direction upon his first arrival to inform

10. Elizabeth had declined the sovereignty of the United Provinces, which Dutch commissioners had offered to her in late July 1585, after the 1584 assassination of William of Orange had left Dutch Protestants leaderless.

himself of the particular state of their forces there, both by sea and land, as also of their means and ability to maintain the same and of the likelihood of their continuance of the said means, we find it very strange that in all this time of his abode there we hear yet nothing thereof, considering how often he hath otherwise written hither since his arrival there, and that he cannot be ignorant how much it importeth us to have knowledge of these things, which maketh the fault of his slackness therein so much the greater. And whereas in the late government in those countries there hath been great abuse committed as well in the collection of the contributions as in the distribution of the same, which hath bred no little offense and mislike in the people, then hindrance in the public service, you shall in our name, showing both the earl and such as by the States are appointed to assist him, to have an especial care the said abuses redressed[11] and the offenders punished, for the better performance whereof it shall be necessary that the earl do press the States to grant him extraordinary power and authority in their name, as well to displace such officers as shall be found to have committed the said abuses as to take charge of the distribution of the said contributions, which we know be well enough performed without carrying the title of an absolute governor.

62 ào QUEEN ELIZABETH TO ROBERT DUDLEY, EARL OF LEICESTER, BY SIR THOMAS HENEAGE, FEBRUARY 10, 1586[1]

[Headed] To my lord of Leicester from the queen, by Sir Thomas Heneage

How contemptuously we conceive ourselves to have been used by you, you shall by this bearer understand: whom we have expressly sent unto you to charge you withal. We could never have imagined (had we not seen it fall out in experience) that a man raised up by ourself and extraordinarily favored by us, above any other subject of this land, would have in so contemptible a sort broken our commandment in a cause that so greatly toucheth us in honor. Whereof although you have showed yourself to make but little account in so most undutiful a sort, you may

---

11. **redressed** be redressed.

1. *Source:* BL, MS Cotton Galba C.VIII, fol. 27v; copy. The original of this letter was inserted in Letter 61, p. 271.

not therefore think that we have so little care of the reparation thereof as we mind to pass so great a wrong in silence unredressed. And therefore our express pleasure and commandment is that, all delays and excuses laid apart, you do presently upon the duty of your allegiance obey and fulfill whatsoever the bearer hereof shall direct you to do in our name. Whereof fail you not, as you will answer the contrary at your uttermost peril.

63 ৯ ELIZABETH TO JAMES, MARCH 1586[1]

The expertest seamen, my dear brother, makes vaunt of their best ships when they pass the highest billows without yielding and brook nimblest the roughest storms. The like proof I suppose may best be made, and surest boast of friends, when greatest persuasions and mightiest enemies oppose themselves for parties. If then a constant, irremovable goodwill appear, there is best trial made. And for that I know there is no worse orator for truth than malice, nor shrewder inveigher than envy, and that I am sure you have wanted neither to assail your mind to win it from our friendship if, not availing all these miners,[2] you keep the hold of your promised inward affection, as Randol[3] at length have told me and your own letters assure me, I dare thus boldly affirm that you shall have the better part in this bargain; for when you weigh in equal balance with no palsy hand the very ground of their desires that would withdraw you, it is but root of mischief to peril yourself with hope to harm her who ever hath preserved you. And since you may be sure that Scotland nor yourself be so potent as for your greatness they[4] seek you, nor never did but to injure a third; and if you read the histories, there is no great cause of boast for many conquest,[5] though your country served their malice: this, you see, the beginning why ever Scotland hath been sought.

1. *Source:* BL, MS Additional 23240, art. 12, fols. 38r–39v; in Elizabeth's hand. (For original-spelling version, see *ACFLO*, part 1.)

2. **miners** underminers; that is, all these underminers being unavailing.

3. **Randol** Sir Thomas Randolph, Elizabeth's longtime ambassador to Scotland.

4. **they** the French, who were attempting to influence James with promises of money to fill his almost empty coffers to the injury of Elizabeth and England (the "third" mentioned in the same sentence).

5. **conquest** conquests.

Now to come to my groundwork, only natural affection *ab incunab-ulis*[6] stirred me to save you from the murderers of your father and the peril that their complices might breed you. Thus, as in no counterfeit mirror you may behold without mask the faces of both beginners, it is for you to judge what are like to be the best event of both; and thereafter I pray God you may use your best choice to your surest good, no semblant false to beguile. And as I rejoice to have had even in this hammering world such present proof of your sincerity, so shall you be sure to employ it upon no guileful person nor such as will not take as much regard of your good as of her own.

Touching an instrument[7] (as your secretary terms it) that you desire to have me sign, I assure you though I can play of some and have been brought up to know music, yet this discord would be so gross as were not fit for so well-tuned music. Must so great doubt be made of free goodwill, and gift be so mistrusted that our sign Emmanuel[8] must assure? No, my dear brother, teach your new, raw councillors better manner than to advise you such a paring of ample meaning. Who should doubt performance of a king's offer? What dishonor may that be deemed? Follow next your own nature, for this never came out of your shop.

But for your full satisfaction, and to pluck from the wicked the weapon they would use to breed your doubt of my meanings, these they be. First, I will, as long as you with evil desert alter not your course, take care for your safety, help your need, and shun all acts that may damnify[9] you in any sort either in present or future time. And for the portion of relief, I mind never to lessen, though as I see cause I will rather augment. And this I hope may stand you in as much assurance as my name in parchment, and no less for both our honors. I cannot omit also to request you, of all amity between us, to have good regard of the long-waiting expectation that all our subjects looks after, that some persons be delivered into my hands for some repair of my honor, though no redress for his death,[10] according as my Ambassador Randol shall signify.

---

6. "from the cradle."

7. **instrument** allusion to her agreement to supply James with an allowance, which Elizabeth refuses to put in the form of a signed and sealed grant of financial assistance and other rights, among them James's title to the English crown.

8. **sign Emmanuel** sign manual, but with a pun on Emmanuel, "God with us."

9. **damnify** damage, injure.

10. She requests that the earl of Ker of Fernihurst, accused of plotting the death of Lord Russell, be transferred into her jurisdiction for trial.

And that there be no more delays, which have been over-many already. And thus I end my troubling you, committing you to the tuition of the living God, who grant you many years of prosperous reign.

Your most assured, loving sister
and cousin, *Elizabeth R*

LETTER 63, ADDITIONAL DOCUMENT A JAMES TO ELIZABETH, CIRCA APRIL 1, 1586[1]

I doubt not, madame and dearest sister, but ye have there[2] times past accused and condemned me in your own mind of forgetfulness or great sloth in having been so long unvisiting you with any letter; and yet I must most heartily crave your pardon in respect I did it upon good intention. For upon consideration of your ambassador's negotiating with me upon the accomplishing of the league, I thought it much better (though I should have stayed the longer) to write you the performance than excuse the delay thereof. And therefore I would not finish my letter while[3] the same had also been finished in like manner. As indeed I have now at last (though not without crossing) subscribed and delivered the same to your ambassador, whom according to your recommendation I have lovingly used, as I will whomsoever ye can send, for the sender's sake.

And as for the instrument whereunto I desire your seal to be affixed, think not, I pray you, that I desire it for any mistrust; for I protest before God that your simple promise would be more than sufficient to me, if it were not that I would have the whole world to understand how it pleaseth you to honor me above my demerits. Which favor and innumerable others, if my evil hap will not permit by action to acquit, yet shall I contend by good meaning to countervail the same at her hands, whom, committing to the Almighty's protection, I pray ever to esteem me

Her most beholden and loving
friend and cousin, *James R.*

1. *Source:* BL, MS Additional 23240, art. 13, fol. 41r; draft in James's hand.
2. **there** MS reads "thir"; reading should probably be "other."
3. **while** (Scots *quhill*) until.

[Postscript] Madame, I must earnestly request you, by your favorable and speedy dispatch of the true servant and faithful subject to you and to me, James Hudson, to let him know that my mediation has availed at your hands.

64 ᨀ QUEEN ELIZABETH TO ROBERT DUDLEY, EARL OF LEICESTER, IN THE NETHERLANDS, APRIL 1586[1]

[Headed] Belgia, 1586, April.

By the queen.

Right trusty and right well-beloved cousin and councillor, we greet you well. It is always thought in the opinion of the world a hard bargain when both parties are leasoned,[2] and so doth fall out in the case between us two. You, as we hear, are greatly grieved in respect of the great displeasure you find we have conceived against you; and we, no less grieved that a subject of ours of what quality that you are, a creature of our own and one that hath always received an extraordinary portion of our favor above all our subjects even from the beginning of our reign, should deal so carelessly—we will not say contemptuously—as to give the world just cause to think that we are had in contempt by him that ought most to respect and reverence us, from whom we would never have looked to receive any such measure. Which, we do assure you, hath wrought as great grief in us as any one thing that ever happened unto us.

We are persuaded that you that have so long known us cannot think that ever we could have been drawn to have taken so hard a course herein, had we not been provoked by an extraordinary cause. But for that your grieved and wounded mind hath more need of comfort than reproof, whom we are persuaded (though the act in respect of the contempt can no way be excused) had no other meaning and intent than to advance our service, we think meet to forbear to dwell upon a matter wherein we ourselves do find so little comfort, assuring you that whosoever professeth to love you best taketh not more comfort of your well-doing or discomfort of your evildoing than ourself.

1. *Source:* BL, MS Cotton Galba C.IX, fol. 171; copy.
2. **leasoned** belied, slandered.

Now to come to the breach itself, which we would be glad to repair in such sort as may be for our honor without the peril and danger of that country, we do think meet that you shall, upon conference with Sir Thomas Heneage and such others whose advice you shall think meet to be used therein, think of some way how the point concerning the absolute title may be qualified in such sort as the authority may notwithstanding remain, which we think most needful to continue for the redress of th'abuses and avoiding of confusion that otherwise is likely to ensure. Which as we conceive may be performed if the States may be induced to yield that authority unto you, carrying the title of lieutenant general of our forces, that they do now yield unto you under the title of an absolute governor. And for that we are persuaded that you may be best able, knowing the dispositions of all sorts of people there as well of the inferior as the superior, to judge what is fit to be done to bring such a qualification as we desire to pass, we think meet that the whole of proceeding should be referred to the good consideration and extraordinary care of you and Sir Thomas Heneage, and such others whose advice you shall use in the matter. For we must needs confess that it is a thing that we do greatly desire and affect. And therefore we do look that you should use all the best endeavor that possibly you may to bring the same presently to pass. And yet notwithstanding, if by conference with Sir Thomas Heneage and others whose advice you shall like to use therein, you shall find that any such motion for the present may work any peril of consequence to that State, then do we think meet it be forborne and are content to yield that the government shall be continued as it now doth under you for a time until we shall hear from you how the said qualification we so greatly desire touching the title may be brought to pass without breeding any alteration in those countries. For our meaning is not that the absolute governance shall continue, though we can be content (if necessity shall so require) to tolerate the same for a time. And so, we think, must the Council of State be given to understand, for that they may be the rather drawn thereby to devise some way to yield us contentment in this our desire.

And whereas by our letters directed to our servant Sir Thomas Heneage we have appointed that the answer to the requests of the Council of Estate there contained in their letters directed unto us for the stay of the revocation of your authority should be delivered by him unto the Council of State there according to such resolution as should be taken between you, wishing it shall fall out to be such as you shall think meet that our assent be yielded for the continuance of your government as it now standeth for a time, then would we have the said Sir Thomas in the delivery thereof let the said Council of State understand how we are drawn, for the love we bear towards them and the care we have that nothing should proceed from us that might any way work their peril, to leave all respects unto our own hands, hoping that the consideration thereof will draw them the rather to devise some way how to satisfy us in the point of qualification, as also to be more ready from time to time to carry that respect and regard to you, our minister during the time of your employments there, as may be both for our honor, your comfort, and the particular benefit of themselves. Given under our signet at our manor of Greenwich the   day[3] of   in the twenty-eighth year of our reign.

65 ૭► QUEEN ELIZABETH TO WILLIAM DAVISON, APRIL 27, 1586[1]

[Headed] Belgia, 1586, 27 April. Copy of her majesty's letter.

Trusty and well beloved, we greet you well. Upon perusal of your late letters and of the copy of the speech delivered in our name unto the States, we find it very strange that in that matter that doth so greatly touch us in honor as the continuance of the title of absolute governor, there is nothing yet done for the qualification thereof, for anything we have yet received from you; for we did look, accordingly as we directed, that there would have been some resolution taken in that behalf between the Council of Estates, our cousin of Leicester, and you. Which being not performed falleth out far contrary to our expectation and the regard we looked you would have both had to our honor and contentment, being a thing by us so much asserted. And therefore our pleasure is, wheresoever this our letter shall find you, you shall with all convenient speed return to our cousin of Leicester and to join with him in conference, and with the Council of Estates there, how the said qualification in point of title may be performed accordingly as we desire, and

3. In this copy the date is left blank.
1. *Source:* BL, MS Cotton Galba C.IX, fol. 200; copy. In the original letter, Elizabeth's postscript was probably in her own hand, as the survival of several of her characteristic spellings suggests. William Davison was at this period commander of Flushing.

yet the authority reserved unto our cousin the earl under the title of our lieutenant general, which we see no cause to doubt but that the same will work as good effect for the avoiding of the confusion of government there as the other title of absolute governor.

We are further to let you understand that we have cause greatly to mislike of two points in your proceeding there. The one, that there was stay made in the delivery of our letters unto the States, for the doing whereof we gave no special direction neither to our cousin of Leicester nor unto you, nor yet do see any cause to allow thereof for anything contained in your letters. The other is the assurance given by your speech unto the States that we would make no peace with the king of Spain without their privity and assent, wherein we either think that you have far exceeded your commission, or else our secretary had greatly mistaken our direction given unto him in that behalf; for that our meaning was that they should only have been assured that in any treaty that might fall out between us and Spain, we would have no less care of their safety than of our own. And whereas by your letters unto us you do let us understand that you received a short answer from the Council of Estates to the points by you propounded, we marvel greatly why you forbear to send the same unto us, importing us so much as it doth to have some speedy resolution in the said point of qualification, wherein we do assure you we shall receive no satisfaction until the same be performed as we desire. And therefore our meaning is not that you shall return unto us before the same be accomplished. And in the meantime we do look to hear often from you touching your proceeding therein. Given under our signet at our manor of Greenwich the twenty-seventh day of April, 1586, in the twenty-eighth year of our reign.

[Elizabeth's postscript] What phlegmatical reasons soever were made you, how happeneth it that you will not remember that when a man hath faulted, and counseled by abetters thereto, that neither the one nor the other will willingly make their own retreat? Jesus, what availeth wit when it fails the owner at greatest need! Do that you are bidden, and leave your considerations for your own affairs; for in some things you had clear commandment, which you did not, and in other none and did—yea, to the use of those speeches from me that might oblige me to more than I was bound or mind ever to yield. We princes be wary enough of our bargains: think you I will be bound by your speech to make no peace for mine own matters without their consent?

It is enough that I injury[2] not their country nor themselves in making peace for them without their consent. I am assured of your dutiful thoughts, but I am utterly at square[3] with this childish dealing.

[Annotated at bottom] The above is the copy of her majesty's letter written with her own hand to me.

66 ⮞ ELIZABETH TO JAMES, LATE MAY 1586[1]

[Addressed] To my good brother and cousin, the king of Scots

I muse much, right dear brother, how possibly my well-meant letter, proceeding from so faultless a heart, could be either misliked or misconstered. And first, for my promise made of reciproque[2] usage in all amicable manner, I trust I neither have nor never shall make fraction of[3] in the least scruple.[4] And as for doubt of your performance of your vow made me, I assure you if I did not trust your words I should esteem but at small value your writings. And if you please to read again my last letter, you shall perceive how much I prize your tried constancy, for all the many assaults that I am sure your ears have been assailed with. And therefore I am far from doubt, when such proof is made me, you might worthily forethink you to have bestowed so much faithful dealing upon one that either had small judgment or much ingratitude. And thereof I may clearly purge me from such crime, for I have more just cause to acknowledge thankfulness manifold than in any part to overrun my own wit to leave it behind me.

And for the sum that you suppose my many affairs made me forget, together with the manner of the instrument or letter *quocumque nomine datur*,[5] for the first, I assure you I never gave commission for

---

2. **injury** injure.   3. **at square** in disagreement.

1. *Source:* BL, MS Additional 23240, fol. 45; in Elizabeth's hand, with remnants of seal attached. (For original spelling, see *ACFLO*, part 1.) According to Patrick Fraser Tytler in *History of Scotland 1149–1603* ([Edinburgh: W. Tait, 1845], 7:282), Elizabeth had responded to an earlier letter from James with a rejection of the "instrument" and a decrease in the promised pension from £5,000 to £4,000, to which he wrote an angry letter in reply.

2. **reciproque** reciprocal (form common circa 1570–1620).

3. **make fraction of** break.   4. **scruple** doubt, but also small weight or measure.

5. "whatever it is to be called."

more. Some other might mistake, as Randol will tell you. And for the
letter, some words and form was such as fitted not our two friendships,
as Randol also can show you. But I have sent you a letter that I am sure
contains all you desired in special words, which I trust shall content
you, although I must say for myself this much—that the pith and effect
of all, you received afore. And beseech you think that I find it my greatest fault that I remember but too well—yea, many times more than I
would—but never aught that may be for your behalf either in honor or
contenta[tion][6] shall ever slip out of my mind, but will take so good regard into it as it that ever shall nearly touch myself. As knoweth God,
who ever preserve you from deceit[ful] counsel and grant you true
knowledge of your assured, with long and many years to reign.

Your most affectionate and assured, loving sister
and cousin, *Elizabeth R*

67 ❧ QUEEN ELIZABETH TO LEICESTER, JULY 19, 1586[1]

*[Endorsed] 19 July, 1586. Copy of her majesty's letter sent by W.[2] to the earl
of Leicester, her highness' lieutenant general in the Low Countries.*

19 July, 1586. Rob, I am afraid you will suppose by my wandering writings that a midsummer moon hath taken large possession of my brains
this month, but you must needs take things as they come in my head,
though order be left behind me. When I remember your request to have
a discreet and honest man that may carry my mind and see how all goes
there, I have chosen this bearer, whom you know and have made good
trial of. I have fraught him full of my conceits of those country matters,
and imparted what way I mind to take and what is fit for you to use. I
am sure you can credit him, and so I will be short with these few notes.

---

6. Here and below, missing letters at worn edge of page are supplied from the later transcription that follows on fol. 47 of the same MS collection.
   1. *Source:* PRO, State Papers Holland and Flanders, Elizabeth 84/9/38, fols. 85r–86v; copy.
Judging by the letter's personal tone, the original may well have been in Elizabeth's hand.
   2. **W.** Thomas Wilkes, who was dispatched by Elizabeth to help Leicester with the difficulties in administering the English expeditionary force that the queen's letter addresses in
some detail.

First, that Count Maurice and Count Hollock[3] find themselves trusted of you, esteemed of me, and to be carefully regarded if ever peace should happen; and of that assure them on my word, that yet never deceived any. And for Norris[4] and other captains that voluntarily without commandment have many years ventured their lives and won our nation honor and themselves fame, be not discouraged by any means, neither by new-come men nor by old trained soldiers elsewhere. If there be fault in using of soldiers or making of profit by them, let them hear of it without open shame, and doubt not but I will well chasten them therefor. It frets me not a little that the poor soldier that hourly ventures life should want their due that well deserve rather reward; and look in whom the fault may duly be proved—let them smart therefor. And if the treasurer be found untrue or negligent, according to desert he shall be used, though you know my old wont, that love not to discharge from office without desert. God forbid! I pray you let this bearer know what may be learned herein; and for this treasure I have joined Sir Thomas Shirley[5] to see all this money discharged in due sort where it needeth and behooveth. Now will I end, that do imagine I talk still with you, and therefore loathly say farewell, ộ ộ,[6] though ever I pray God bless you from all harm, and save you from all foes with my million and legion of thanks for all your pains and cares.

As you know, ever the same,[7] *E. R.*

[Postscript] Let Wilkes see that he is acceptable to you. If anything there be, that Wilkes shall desire answer of, be such as you would have but me to know, write it to myself. You know I can keep both others' counsel and mine own. Mistrust not that anything you would have kept shall be disclosed by me; for although this bearer ask many things, yet may you answer him such as you shall think meet, and write to me the rest.

---

3. **Count Maurice and Count Hollock** commanders of the Dutch resistance against Spain.

4. **Norris** Sir John Norris (1547?–1597) had fought successfully with an army of English volunteers in the Netherlands from 1577 to 1584 and again in 1585–86. Leicester was said to be openly jealous of Norris's military prowess.

5. **Sir Thomas Shirley** (1542–1612) one of Leicester's adherents, officially appointed treasurer-at-war to the English army in the Netherlands in 1587.

6. ộ ộ "Eyes," Elizabeth's pet name for Leicester.

7. **ever the same** Elizabeth's motto (in Latin, *semper eadem*).

68 ⁀⬧ QUEEN ELIZABETH TO SIR AMYAS PAULET, AUGUST 1586[1]

[Addressed] To my faithful Amyas

Amyas, my most careful and faithful servant,

God reward thee treblefold in the double for thy most troublesome charge so well discharged.[2] If you knew, my Amyas, how kindly besides dutifully my careful heart accepts your double labors and faithful actions, your wise orders and safe regards performed in so dangerous and crafty a charge, it would ease your troubles' travail and rejoice your heart. In which I charge you to carry this most nighest thought: that I cannot balance in any weight of my judgment the value I prize you at. And suppose no treasure to countervail such a faith, and condemn me in that behalf which I never committed if I reward not such deserts. Yea, let me lack when I have most need if I acknowledge not such a merit with a reward *non omnibus datum.*[3]

But let your wicked mistress know how with hearty sorrow her vile deserts compels these orders, and bid her from me ask God forgiveness for her treacherous dealing towards the saver of her life many years, to the intolerable peril of her own. And yet not content with so many forgivenesses, must fall again so horribly, far passing a woman's thought, much more a princess', instead of excusing, whereof not one can serve, it being so plainly confessed by the actors of my guiltless death. Let repentance take place; and let not the fiend possess her so as her best part be lost, which I pray with hands lifted up to Him that may both save and spill, with my loving adieu and prayer for thy long life.

> Your assured and loving sovereign in heart, by
> good desert induced, *Elizabeth Regina*

---

1. *Source:* BL, MS Lansdowne 1236, art. 28, fol. 44; copy. This was Elizabeth's most famous letter in the eyes of her contemporaries. There are many other copies, among them BL, MS Cotton Caligula C.IX, fol. 654; BL, MS Additional 15226, fol. 34B; BL, MS Additional 22587, fol. 18D; Cambridge University Library, MS Gg.III.34, fols. 318–19; and Huntington Library, MS HM 1340.

2. Elizabeth commends and thanks Paulet for his secure keeping of Mary, Queen of Scots, at Fotheringay Castle during the sensational revelations of the Babington Plot of 1586, for which Mary was finally judged guilty of treason against Elizabeth and beheaded.

3. "not given to all."

69 ⮸ QUEEN ELIZABETH TO THE COMMONERS OF LONDON, AUGUST 18, 1586[1]

[Headed] Her majesty's letter to the lord mayor and citizens of London.

Right trusty and well beloved, we greet you well. Being given to understand how greatly our good and most loving subjects of that City did rejoice at the apprehension of certain devilish and wicked-minded subjects of ours[2] that through the great goodness of God have been of late detected to have most wickedly and unnaturally conspired not only the taking away of our life, but also to have stirred up, as much as in them lay, a general rebellion through our whole realm, we could not but by our letters witness unto you the great and singular contentment we received upon the knowledge thereof, assuring you that we did not so much rejoice at the escape of the intended attempt against our person, as to see the great joy our most loving subjects took at the apprehension of the contrivers thereof, which to make their love more apparent they have (as we are to our great comfort informed) omitted no outward show that by any external means might witness to the world the inward love and dutiful affection they bear towards us. And as we have as great cause with all thankfulness to acknowledge God's great goodness towards us by the infinite blessings He layeth upon us—as many as ever prince, yea, rather, as ever creature had—yet do we not for any worldly blessing received from His divine Majesty so greatly acknowledge the same, as in that it hath pleased Him to incline the hearts of our subjects from the first beginning of our reign to carry as great love towards us as ever subjects carried towards prince, which ought to move us, as it doth in very deed, to seek with all care and by all good means that appertaineth to a Christian prince the conservation of so loving and dutiful-affected subjects. Assuring you that we desire no longer to live than while we may in the whole course of our government carry ourself in such sort as may not only nourish and continue their love and goodwill towards us, but also increase the same, we think meet that these our letters should be communicated in some general assembly to our most

1. *Source:* Reproduced by permission of the Masters of the Bench of the Inner Temple Library, MS Petyt 538, vol. 10, fol. 6r; copy.

2. On August 14 Anthony Babington had been arrested; on August 18 he confessed to a plot to murder the queen along with all her principal ministers and implicated Mary, Queen of Scots, in the conspiracy.

loving subjects the commoners of that City. Given under our signet at
our castle of Windsor the 18 of August, 1586, *annoque regni nostri 28°*.[3]

70 ❧ ELIZABETH TO JAMES, OCTOBER 4, 1586[1]

[Addressed] To Monsieur, my good brother and cousin the king of Scots

[Endorsed] Of the 4 of October, 1586

I hope, my dear brother, that my many weighty affairs in present may
make my lawful excuse for the retardance of the answer to your ambassador's charge, but I doubt not but you shall be honorably satisfait in all
the points of his commission. And next after my own errand done, I
must render you my innumerable thanks for such amicable offers as it
hath pleased you make, making you assured that with God's grace you
shall never have cause to regret your good thoughts of my meaning to
deserve as much goodwill and affection as ever one prince owed another. Wishing all means that may maintain your faithful trust in me,
that never will seek aught but the increase of your honor and safety.

I was in mind to have sent you such accidents[2] as this late month
brought forth, but the sufficiency of Master Archibald[3] made me retain
him. And do[4] render you many loving thanks for the joy you took of my
narrow escape from the chaws[5] of death, to which I might easily have
fallen but that the hand of the Highest saved me from that snare.[6] And
for that the curse of that design rose up from the wicked suggestion of
the Jesuits,[7] which make it an acceptable sacrifice to God and meritori-

---

3. "and in the twenty-eighth year of our reign."

1. *Source:* BL, MS Additional 23240, art. 16, fol. 49; in Elizabeth's hand, with remnants of
seal attached. (For original-spelling version, see *ACFLO*, part 1.)

2. **accidents** the Babington Plot, whose chief conspirators were executed on September
20 and 21. Within a few days thereafter, it was determined that Mary, Queen of Scots,
should be tried for treason.

3. **Master Archibald** Archibald Douglas, James's current representative in England.

4. **do** I do.   5. **chaws** jaws.

6. **Highest ... snare** "The most High shall ... deliver thee from the snare of the fowler"
(Psalm 91:1, 3).

7. Cf. Lord Burghley's *Execution of Justice in England* (1583), which claimed that the illegal
Jesuit mission launched by Robert Parsons and Edmund Campion in 1580 aimed at inciting English Catholics with their "religious obligation to rise in revolt against Elizabeth at
the earliest feasible moment," since the papal bull of 1570 had deposed her and absolved

ous to themself[8] that a king not of their profession should be murdered, therefore I could keep my pen no longer from discharging my care of your person, that you suffer not such vipers to inhabit your land. They say you gave leave under your hand that they might safely come and go. For God's love, regard your surety above all persuasions, and account him no subject that entertains them! Make not edicts for scorn, but to be observed. Let them be rebels, and so pronounced, that preserve them. For my part I am sorrier that they cast away so many goodly gentlemen than that they sought my ruin. I thank God I have taken more dolor for some that are guilty of this murder than bear them malice that they sought my death; I protest it before God, but such iniquity woll[9] not be hid, be it never so craftily handled. And yet when you shall hear all, you will wonder that one accounted wise will use such matter so fondly. But no marvel, for when they are given to a reprobate sense,[10] they often make such slip. I have been so tedious that I take pity of your pain and so will end this scribbling, praying you believe that you could never have chosen a more sure trust that will never beguile than myself, who daily prays to God for your long prosperity.

Your most assured, loving sister
and cousin, *Elizabeth R*

71 ⪻ DIGEST OF ELIZABETH'S LETTER TO MARY, QUEEN OF SCOTS, OCTOBER 6, 1586[1]

[Headed] 6 October 1586. A minute of her majesty's letter written to the Scottish queen to prepare herself to her arraignment.

Whereas we are given to understand that you, to our great and inestimable grief, as one void of all remorse of conscience, pretend with

English Catholics of all allegiance to her. See Robert M. Kingdon, ed., *The Execution of Justice in England by William Cecil, and A True, Sincere, and Modest Defense of English Catholics by William Allen* (Ithaca: Cornell University Press, 1965), p. xx.
    8. **themself** themselves.   9. **woll** will.
    10. A reference to the doctrine of reprobation—the state of being already damned in this life, invoked by militant Protestants and Catholics alike against those of the opposite persuasion.
    1. *Source:* BL, MS Cotton Caligula C.IX, fol. 459r; copy.

great protestation not to be in any sort privy or assenting to any attempt either against our state or person; forasmuch as we find by most clear and evident proof that the contrary will be verified and maintained against you, we have found it therefore expedient to send unto you divers of our chief and most ancient noblemen of this our realm, together with certain of our Privy Council, as also some of our principal judges, to charge you both with the privity and assent to that most horrible and unnatural attempt. And to the end you may have no just cause (lying as you do within our protection, and thereby subject to the laws of our realm and to such a trial as by us shall be thought meet, agreeable to our laws) to take exception to the manner of our proceeding, we have made choice of the these[2] honorable personages to be used in this service, having for that purpose authorized them by our commissions under our great seal to proceed therein. And therefore do both advise and require you to give credit and make answer to that which the said honorable personages so authorized by us shall from time to time during their abode there object or deliver unto you in our name, as if it were to ourself. Given at our castle of Windsor the 6th day of October, 1586.

72 ❧ DIGEST OF QUEEN ELIZABETH'S LETTER TO WILLIAM CECIL, LORD BURGHLEY, OCTOBER 12, 1586[1]

[Headed] A minute of a letter from her majesty to the Lord Treasurer Burghley at Fotheringay for staying the sentence till their return to her presence, 12 October, 1586.

By the queen.

Right trusty and right well-beloved councillor, we greet you well. Whereas by your letters received this evening we find that the Scottish queen doth absolutely refuse to submit herself to trial or make any answer as by you and the rest of the commissioners there she is to be charged with, and that notwithstanding you are determined to proceed to sentence against her according to our commission given you in that behalf, we have thought good hereby to let you understand that albeit upon the examination and trial of the cause you shall by verdict find the

2. **the these** these (copying error).
1. *Source:* BL, MS Cotton Caligula C.IX, fol. 467r; copy.

same queen guilty of the crimes wherewith she standeth charged, and that you might accordingly proceed to your sentence against her, yet do we find it meet and such is our pleasure that you nevertheless forbear the pronouncing thereof until such time as you shall have made your personal return to our presence and report to us of your proceedings and opinions in that behalf, or otherwise (if you find it may prejudice your principal commission or hinder our service) to advertise us thereof accordingly and abide there our further answer. And thus our letters shall herein be to you and the rest of our said commissioners there our sufficient warrant and discharge given herein.

73 ᕒᕒ ELIZABETH TO JAMES, OCTOBER 15, 1586[1]

[Addressed] To my good brother and cousin the king of Scots

[Endorsed] Of the 15 of October, 1586

My dear brother,

It hath sufficiently informed me of your singular care of my estate and breathing that you have sent one in such diligence to understand the circumstances of the treasons which lately were lewdly[2] attempted and miraculously uttered, of which I had made participant your ambassador afore your letters came. And now am I to show you that as I have received many writings from you of great kindness, yet this last was fraughted with so careful passion and so effectual utterance of all best wishes for my safety, and offer of as much as I could have desired, that I confess if I should not seek to deserve it and by merits tie you to continuance, I were evil worthy such a friend. And as the thanks my heart yields, my pen may scant render you, so shall the owner ever deserve to show it not evil employed, but on such a prince as shall requite your goodwill and keep a watchful eye to all doings that may concern you.

And whereas you offer to send me any traitor of mine residing in your land, I shall not fail but expect th'accomplishment of the same in case any such shall be, and require you in the meantime that speedy delivery may be made of the Kers,[3] which toucheth both my conscience

---

1. *Source:* BL, MS Additional 23240, art. 17, fol. 53; in Elizabeth's hand. (For original-spelling version, see *ACFLO*, part 1.) Date assigned to the letter may be the date of its receipt by James.

2. **lewdly** basely.   3. **Kers** See Letter 58 nn. 7–8 and Letter 63 n. 10, pp. 264, 275.

and honor. I thank God that you beware so soon of Jesuits that have been the source of all these treacheries in this realm and will spread like an evil weed if at the first they be not weeded out. I would I had had Prometheus for companion, for Epimetheus[4] had like have been mine too soon. What religion is this that they pay—the way to salvation is to kill the prince for a merit meritorious? This is that they have all confessed without torture or menace—I swear it on my word. Far be it from Scotland to harbor any such! And therefore I wish your good providence may be duly executed, for else laws resemble cobwebs whence great bees get out by breaking and small flies sticks fast for weakness. As concerning the retarding of your answers to all points of your ambassador's charge, you had received them or[5] now but that matters of that weight, that I am sure you would willingly know, cannot as yet receive an conclusion. And till then Master Douglas[6] doth tarry, and with his return I hope you shall receive honorable requital of his amicable embassade, so as you shall have no cause to regret his arrival. As knoweth the Lord, whom ever I beseech to bring you many joyful days of reign and life.

> Your most assured, loving, and faithful sister
> and cousin, *Elizabeth R*

[Postscript] I must give you many thanks for this poor subject of mine, for whom I will not stick to do all pleasure for your request, and would wish him under the ground if he should not serve you with greatest faith that any servant may. I have willed him tell you some things from me. I beseech you hear them favorably.

---

4. **Prometheus . . . Epimetheus** Prometheus ("Forethought") and Epimetheus ("Afterthought") were Greek demigods, sons of Zeus, who played decisive roles in determining what the lot of mortals would be; cf. Hesiod's *Theogony*, lines 511ff; and Pindar *Pythian 5,* line 27.

5. **or** ere.

6. **Master Douglas** See Letter 70 n. 3, p. 286.

LETTER 73, ADDITIONAL DOCUMENT A JAMES TO ELIZABETH,
JANUARY 26, 1587[1]

*[Addressed] To madame my very dear sister and cousin, the queen of
England.*

Madame and dearest sister,

If ye could have known what divers thoughts have agitate[2] my mind
since my directing of William Keith unto you for the soliciting of this
matter whereto nature and honor so greatly and unfeignedly binds and
obliges me—if, I say, ye knew what divers thoughts I have been in and
what just grief I had, weighing deeply the thing itself,[3] if so it should
proceed (as God forbid), what events might follow thereupon, what
number of straits I would be driven unto, and amongst the rest, how it
might peril my reputation among my subjects—if these things, I yet say
again, were known unto you, then doubt I not but ye would so far pity
my case as it would easily make you at the first to resolve your own best
into it. I doubt greatly in what façon[4] to write in this purpose, for ye
have already taken so evil with my plainness as I fear if I shall persist in
that course ye shall rather be exasperated to passions in reading the
words than by the plainness thereof be persuaded to consider rightly
the simple truth.

Yet, justly preferring the duty of an honest friend to the sudden passions of one who (how soon they be past) can wiselier[5] weigh the reasons than I can set them down, I have resolved in few words and plain
to give you my friendly and best advice, appealing to your ripest judgment to discern thereupon. What thing, madame, can greatlier touch
me in honor that is a king and a son than that my nearest neighbor,
being in straitest friendship with me, shall rigorously put to death a free
sovereign prince and my natural mother, alike in estate and sex to her
that so uses her, albeit subject (I grant) to a harder fortune, and touching her nearly in proximity of blood? What law of God can permit that

1. *Source:* BL, MS Cotton Caligula C.IX, art. 72, fols. 192r–93r; in James's hand, with seals
and ribbon still attached. A few damaged letters are supplied from a later copy in the same
volume, fols. 190r–91r.

2. **agitate** agitated.

3. **thing itself** his mother's pending execution.

4. **façon** fashion (French).

5. **wiselier** more wisely.

justice shall strike upon them whom He has appointed supreme dispensators of the same under Him, whom He hath called gods[6] and therefore subjected to the censure of none in earth, whose anointing by God cannot be defiled by man, unrevenged by the author thereof, who being supreme and immediate lieutenants of God in heaven cannot therefore be judged by their equals in earth. What monstrous thing is it that sovereign princes themselves should be the example-givers of their own sacred diadems' profaning! Then what should move you to this form of proceeding, supponing[7] the worst, which in good faith I look not for at your hands—honor or profit? Honor were it to you to spare when it is least looked for; honor were it to you (which is not only my friendly advice, but my earnest suit) to take me and all other princes in Europe eternally beholden unto you in granting this my so reasonable request, and not (appardon, I pray you, my free speaking) to put princes to straits of honor wherethrough your general reputation and the universal (almost) misliking of you may dangerously peril both in honor and utility your person and estate. Ye know, madame, well enough how small difference Cicero concludes to be betwixt *utile* and *honestum*[8] in his discourse thereof, and which of them ought to be framed to the other. And now, madame, to conclude, I pray you so to weigh their few arguments that as I ever presumed of your nature, so the whole world may praise your subjects for their dutiful care for your preservation, and yourself, for your princely pity, the doing whereof only belongs unto you, the performing whereof only appertains unto you, and the praise thereof only will ever be yours.

Respect, then, good sister, this my first, so long continued, and so earnest request, dispatching my ambassadors with such a comfortable answer as may become your person to give and as my loving and honest heart unto you merits to receive. But in case any do vaunt themselves to know further of my mind in this matter than my ambassadors do, who indeed are fully acquainted therewith, I pray you not to take me to be a chameleon, but by the contrary to be malicious imposters as surely they are. And thus praying you heartily to excuse my too rude and longsome[9] letter I commit you, madame and dearest sister, to the blessed

6. **called gods** allusion to Psalm 82:6.

7. **supponing** supposing.

8. "useful" and "virtuous"; the central categories in Cicero's *De officiis*.

9. **longsome** tedious.

protection of the Most High, who mot[10] give you grace so to resolve in this matter as may be honorable for you and most acceptable to Him. From my palace of Holyrood, the 26 day of January, 1586[7].

Your most loving and affectionate
brother and cousin, *James R.*

74 ⟨⟩ ELIZABETH TO JAMES, JANUARY–FEBRUARY 1587[1]

[Addressed] To my very good brother and cousin, the king of Scots

[Endorsed] Received 17 February, 1586[7] by post

I find myself so troubled lest sinister tales might delude you, my good brother, that I have willingly found out this messenger, whom I know most sincere to you and a true subject to me, to carry unto you my most sincere meaning toward you and to request this just desire: that you never doubt my entire goodwill in your behalf. And do protest that if you knew even since the arrival of your commissioners (which if they list they may tell you) the extreme danger my life was in by an ambassador's honest silence—if not invention[2] and such good complices[3] as have themselves (by God's permission) unfolded the whole conspiracy and have avouched it before his face, though it be the peril of their own lives—yet voluntarily one of them, never being suspected, brake it with a councillor to make me acquainted therewith.[4] You may see whether I keep the serpent that poisons me when they confess to have reward. By saving of her life they would have had mine.

Do I not make myself, trow ye, a goodly prey for every wretch to devour? Transfigure yourself into my state and suppose what you ought to

---

10. **mot** may.

1. *Source:* BL, MS Additional 23240, art. 18, fols. 57v–58r; in Elizabeth's hand, with seal and ribbon attached. (For original-spelling version, see *ACFLO*, part 1.)

2. **invention** discovery.

3. **complices** accomplices.

4. William Stafford (1554–1612), brother of Sir Edward Stafford, the queen's ambassador in France, charged Guillaume de l'Aubespine, baron de Chateauneuf, the French ambassador in England, with involvement in yet another plot against the life of Elizabeth. Chateauneuf denied the charge, and Stafford himself was eventually imprisoned for concocting it.

do, and thereafter weigh my life and reject the care of murder[5] and shun all baits that may untie our amities, and let all men know that princes know best their own laws, and misjudge not that you know not. For my part I will not live to wrong the meanest. And so I conclude you with your own words: you will prosecute or mislike as much those that seek my ruin as if they sought your heart blood, and would I had none in mine if I would not do the like. As God knoweth, to whom I make my humble prayers to inspire you with best desires.

Your most affectionated sister and cousin,
Elizabeth R

[Postscript] I am sending you a gentleman forwith,[6] the other being fallen sick, who I trust shall yield you good reason of my actions.

75 ❧ ELIZABETH TO JAMES, CIRCA FEBRUARY 1, 1587[1]

[Addressed] To my dear brother and cousin the king of Scots

[Endorsed] Received 8 February 1586[7] by post.

Be not carried away, my dear brother, with the lewd persuasions of such as instead of informing you of my too, too needful and helpless cause of defending the breath that God hath given me, to be better spent than spilt by the bloody invention of traitors' hands, may perhaps make you believe that either the offense was not so great, or if that cannot serve them for the over-manifest trial which in public and by the greatest and most in this land hath been manifestly proved, yet they will make that her life may be saved and mine safe. Which would God were true! For when you make view of my long danger endured these four, well nigh five months' time, to make a taste of the greatest wits amongst my own, and then of French, and last of you, you will grant with me that if need were not more than my malice, she should not have her merit.

---

5. **care of murder** concern that his mother's execution would be a murder.
6. **forwith** forthwith.
1. *Source:* BL, MS Additional 23240, art. 19, fols. 61r–62r; in Elizabeth's hand. (For original spelling, see *ACFLO*, part 1.) The endorsement is as reported by Bruce but is no longer visible on the MS because it has since been repaired.

And now, for a good conclusion of my long-tarried-for answer, your commissioners tells me that I may trust her in the hands of some indifferent prince, and have all her cousins and allies promise she will no more seek my ruin. Dear brother and cousin, weigh in true and equal balance whether they lack not much good ground when such stuff serves for their building! Suppose you I am so mad to trust my life in another's hand and send it out of my own? If the young master of Grey[2] (for currying favor with you) might fortune[3] say it, yet old Master Melvin[4] hath years enough to teach him more wisdom than tell a prince of my judgment such a contrarious, frivolous, maimed reason. Let your councillors for your honor discharge their duty so much to you as to declare the absurdity of such an offer. And for my part I do assure myself too much of your wisdom, as though, like a most natural good son, you charged them to seek all means they could devise with wit or judgment to save her life. Yet I cannot nor do not allege any fault to you of these persuasions, for I take it that you will remember that advice or desires ought ever agree with the surety of the party sent to, and honor of the sender. Which when both you weigh, I doubt not but your wisdom will excuse my need and weight[5] my necessity, and not accuse me either of malice or of hate.

And now to conclude, make account, I pray you, of my firm friendship, love, and care—of which you may make sure account as one that never minds to fail from my word nor swerve from our league, but will increase by all good means any action that may make true show of my stable amity. From which, my dear brother, let no sinister whisperers nor busy troublers of princes' states persuade you to leave your surest and stick to unstable stays. Suppose them to be but the echoes to such whose stipendiaries they be, and will do more for their gain than your good. And so God hold you ever in His blessed keeping, and make you

---

2. **master of Grey** Patrick (d. 1612), sixth Baron Grey, an aspiring Scottish courtier who was closely connected with the duke of Guise and Mary, Queen of Scots, and who played complicated double games with Mary, the French, James, and Elizabeth.

3. **fortune** happen to.

4. **Melvin** probably Sir Robert Melville; "Melvin" and another emissary from James received Elizabeth's letter from the hand of her messenger on the road outside Berwick. The messenger would have endangered his life if he had delivered the letter personally at the Scottish court.

5. **weight** possibly "wait"; MS reads "waite."

see your true friends. Excuse my not writing sooner, for pain in one of
my eyes was only the cause.

Your most assured, loving sister and cousin,
Elizabeth R

76 ❧ ELIZABETH TO JAMES, FEBRUARY 14, 1587[1]

*[Endorsed] A minute of a letter from her majesty to the king of Scots, 14
February, 1586[7], disavowing her privity to the execution of his mother*

My dear brother,

I would you knew though not felt the extreme dolor that over-
whelms my mind for that miserable accident,[2] which far contrary to my
meaning hath befallen. I have now sent this kinsman of mine,[3] whom
ere now it hath pleased you to favor, to instruct you truly of that which
is too irksome for my pen to tell you. I beseech you that—as God and
many more know—how innocent I am in this case, so you will believe
me that if I had bid aught I would have bid by it.[4] I am not so base
minded that fear of any living creature or prince should make me afraid
to do that were just or, done, to deny the same. I am not of so base a lineage nor carry so vile a mind; but as not to disguise fits most a king, so
will I never dissemble my actions but cause them show even as I meant
them. Thus assuring yourself of me that, as I know this was deserved,
yet if I had meant it I would never lay it on others' shoulders, no more
will I not damnify[5] myself that thought it not. The circumstance it may
please you to have of this bearer. And for your part, think you have not
in the world a more loving kinswoman nor a more dear friend than myself, nor any that will watch more carefully to preserve you and your estate. And who shall otherwise persuade you, judge them more partial to

1. *Source:* BL, MS Cotton Caligula C.IX, fol. 212r; copy.

2. **accident** event; Mary, Queen of Scots, had finally been executed on February 8, 1587.

3. **kinsman of mine** Sir Robert Carey (1560?–1639), seventh son of Henry Carey, Lord
Hunsdon, and grandson of Sir William Carey and Mary Boleyn; he was a skilled diplomat
and a favorite with James.

4. **if I had bid ... it** if I had commanded her death, I would have abided by my decision;
bid could mean either requested or commanded.

5. **damnify** damage.

others than you. And thus in haste, I leave to trouble you, beseeching God to send you a long reign. The 14 of February, 1586[7].

Your most assured, loving sister and cousin,
Elizabeth R.

LETTER 76, ADDITIONAL DOCUMENT A JAMES TO ELIZABETH, MARCH 1587[1]

Madame and dearest sister,

Whereas by your letter and bearer, Robert Carey,[2] your servant and ambassador, ye purge yourself of your unhappy fact,[3] as on the one part —considering your rank and sex, consanguinity, and long-professed goodwill to the defunct, together with your many and solemn attestations of your innocency—I dare not wrong you so far as not to judge honorably of your unspotted part therein; so on the other side, I wish that your honorable behavior in all times hereafter may fully persuade the whole world of the same. And as for my part I look that ye will give me at this time such a full satisfaction in all respects as shall be a mean to strengthen and unite this isle, establish and maintain the true religion, and oblige me to be as of before I was, your most loving ...

[Postscript] This bearer hath somewhat to inform you of in my name, whom I need not desire you to credit, for ye know I love him.

1. *Source:* BL, MS Additional 23240, art. 20, fol. 65r; unsigned and incomplete draft or copy in James's hand.

2. Carey's memoirs recount his experiences on this journey: "The next year, which was 1586[7], was the queen of Scots' beheading. I lived in court ... at which time (few or none in the court being willing to undertake that journey) her majesty sent me to the king of Scots, to make known her innocence of her sister's death, with letters of credence from herself to assure all that I should affirm. I was waylaid in Scotland, if I had gone in, to have been murdered; but the king's majesty, knowing the disposition of his people and the fury they were in, sent to me to Berwick to let me know that no power of his could warrant my life at that time; therefore, to prevent further mischief, he would send me no convoy but would send two of his Council to the bound road to receive my letters or what other message I had to deliver" (*Memoirs of Robert Carey, Written by Himself,* ed. Sir Walter Scott [Edinburgh: R. Constable; London: John Murray, 1808], p. 12).

3. **fact** deed.

77 ❧ ELIZABETH TO HENRY III OF FRANCE, MAY 1587[1]

[Addressed] To my good brother the most Christian king

[Endorsed] . . . us, etc. May, 1587[2]

Monsieur, my good brother,

Is it possible that I, meriting so much in your regard by the entire affection and solid friendship which for a long time I have always held out towards you—beyond the honor that I hold in the rank of king—that I should be treated so strangely, indeed, rather as a true enemy, having written to you by my ambassador[3] a thing of great importance most suitable for your quarrel? As for me, what touches me as closely as anything in this world is that it has not pleased you to deign him an audience these past two months—this is a thing never denied to a prince of my standing—and also to have stopped all the ships of our subjects,[4] a true act of hostility which I figured not to be from your quarrel nor at your commandment. And notwithstanding, they answer me only that this is by your order, which makes me very astonished what the cause of it might be. Wherefore for this, being a thing so intolerable to endure, so bad, so perfidious, from one from whom I have deserved better treatment, I entreat you that by writing or word of mouth I may be given satisfaction concerning it. For from one day to the next I get so many complaints and disputes from my afflicted subjects, to whom unless you remedy everything very soon it is not at all possible that I will deny them the justice of avenging it. As God knows, to whom I pray to grant you a good and long life, commending myself very strongly to your good graces.

Your well-affectioned sister
and cousin, *Elizabeth R*

1. *Source:* Bodleian Library, University of Oxford, MS Arch. F.c.8, fol. 26; in Elizabeth's hand. (For original, see *ACFLO*, part 1.) The French coolness about which Elizabeth complains in this letter was adopted in reaction to the execution of Mary, Queen of Scots, Henry III's fellow Catholic and his sister-in-law during her marriage to Francis II of France.

2. Most of the endorsement is missing because of a large tear in the MS.

3. **ambassador** Sir Francis Walsingham.

4. In reprisal for English piracy against French ships, several English merchantmen had been arrested at Rouen, a port on the Seine, and held there for months.

POEMS 7-12

7 ❧ VERSE EXCHANGE BETWEEN QUEEN ELIZABETH AND SIR
THOMAS HENEAGE, GENTLEMAN OF THE PRIVY CHAMBER,
CIRCA 1572[1]

[Elizabeth's elegaics and her translation]

> *Genus infoelix vitae*
> *Multum vigilavi, laboravi, presto multis fui,*
> *Stultitiam multorum perpessa sum,*
> *Arrogantiam pertuli, Difficultates exorbui,*
> *Vixi ad aliorum arbitrium, non ad meum.*   5
> A hapless kind of life is this I wear:[2]
> Much watch I dure, and weary, toiling days

---

1. *Source:* The Pierpont Morgan Library, New York, PML 7768; first flyleaf recto and second flyleaf recto of a copy of Henry Bull's *Christian Prayers and Holy Meditations* (London: for Henry Middleton, 1570) (*STC* 4028), on which an unknown hand inscribed both of the following poems. Initial letters of Heneage's poem now obliterated in the original volume are transcribed from Curt F. Bühler, "Libri Impressi Cum Notis Manuscriptis," *Modern Language Notes* 53 (1938): 245–49. The Heneage poem may bear Heneage's own signature, although the transcribing hand may be another's. For discussion of this exchange and of the close relationship between the queen and Heneage, see Steven W. May, *The Elizabethan Courtier Poets: The Poems and Their Contexts* (Columbia: University of Missouri Press, 1991), pp. 338–39.

2. **wear** tolerate, accept, endure.

I serve the rout and all their follies bear;
I suffer pride and sup full hard assays;
To others' will my life is all addressed,   10
And no way so as might content me best.

This above was written in a book by the queen's majesty.

[Heneage's sonnet to Elizabeth]

Madam, but mark the labors of our life,
And therewithal what errors we be in:
We sue and seek with prayers, stir, and strife
Upon this earth, a happy state to win,
And whilst with cares we travail to content us   5
[In]³ vain desires, and set no certain scope,
[We] reap but things whereof we oft repent us,
[And f]eed our wills with much beguiling hope.
[We] pray for honors, lapped in danger's hands;
We strive for riches, which we straight forego;   10
We seek delight that all in poison stands,
And set with pains but seeds of sin and woe.
Then, noble lady, need we not to pray
The Lord of all for better state and stay?

Your Ladyship's much bound, *T. Heneage*

3. Square brackets enclose restoration of elements lost when MS was repaired.

8 ⮞ VERSE EXCHANGE BETWEEN QUEEN ELIZABETH AND PAUL
MELISSUS, POET LAUREATE OF THE COURT OF EMPEROR
MAXIMILIAN II, CIRCA 1577[1]

[Melissus' epigram][2]

To Elizabeth, queen of England, France, and Ireland
O Queen, not only do I consecrate
    My books to you, now that they are polished—
Whether verse or song or I know not what lyrics,
    Assuredly all is yours. To you, I say,
Not books alone I give and consecrate: 5
    Myself I offer, goddess, to your genius.
Known as a German man of Frankish stock,
    I place myself beneath your royal yoke.
Make me your bondsman, lady, and be mistress
    To a freeborn slave who ever sings your praises.   10
Could freedom be of such great worth to any
    That he'd refuse such patron's noble chains?

---

1. *Source: P. Melissi Mele sive Odae . . . Epigrammata* (Nuremberg, 1580), p. 72. (For Latin
originals, see *ACFLO*, part 2.) In "Elizabeth I as a Latin Poet: An Epigram on Paul Melissus," *Renaissance News* 16 (1963): 289–98, James E. Phillips places this verse exchange
within the context of negotiations between England and the German Protestant princes
during the late 1570s and makes a strong case for Elizabeth's authorship of the response to
Melissus' poem, although Melissus may have altered her verses before publishing them.

Bradner judges Elizabeth's authorship of this epigram dubious on grounds that no other
Latin verse by the queen is known to survive, but Poem 7, p. 299, provides such an instance.
Given that Puttenham describes Elizabeth as prolific in ode, elegy, epigram, heroic, and
lyric poetry (*Art of English Poesie* [London, 1589], p. 51), it is possible that she wrote Latin
(as well as French and English) poetry that either has not survived or has not been attributed to her.

2. Paul Melissus, born Paul Schede (1539–1602), was a German Protestant humanist with
a considerable reputation as a Greek and Latin poet, musician, and negotiator on behalf of
a German Protestant league against the Catholic powers of Europe. Melissus expressed
great admiration of Elizabeth in two Latin poems published in a 1575 volume of his verse,
then in six more in a volume of 1580 (to one of which Elizabeth's epigram responds), and
finally in his elaborate *Ode Pindarica ad serenissimam Elizabetham* (Augsburg, 1582?). In
1585 Melissus journeyed to England with a delegation of German princes seeking support
for their military efforts on behalf of Henry of Navarre. Elizabeth promised aid and met
Melissus personally.

[Queen Elizabeth's epigram]

The Queen's Answer
Welcome your song, most welcome your gift, Melissus—
    More welcome its sweet image of your spirit.
But what cause moves you so, what urge impels you,
    That you, a free man, wish to be a slave?
'Tis not our custom poets to mure up,   5
    Or cause them suffer the least loss of rights.
Rather you would be freed, your patroness
    Loosing the bonds that held you as a servant.
But you are prince of poets, I, a subject
    To a poet when you choose me as the theme   10
Of your high song. What king would shame to cherish
    A poet who, from demigods, makes us gods?

9 ἐ❧ ON MONSIEUR'S DEPARTURE, CIRCA 1582[1]

I grieve and dare not show my discontent;
I love, and yet am forced to seem to hate;
I do, yet dare not say I ever meant;
I seem stark mute, but inwardly do prate.

---

1. *Source:* Bodleian Library, University of Oxford, MS Tanner 76, fol. 94r. This is a late seventeenth-century copy in the hand of the amanuensis of Archbishop William Sancroft (1617–1693), who was strongly interested in antiquarian matters and placed the poem erroneously among Essex materials in a volume of original and copied documents relating to the year 1601. Sancroft's version was almost certainly copied from an early seventeenth-century manuscript of the poem (Bodleian, MS Ashmole 781*), which is now illegible because of water damage. Nichols's version of the poem is worded similarly to Sancroft's and is described by Nichols as a "parting sonnet by her majesty" preserved "in the Ashmolean Museum" (2:346). There is also a later and metrically rougher copy in BL, MS Stowe 962, fol. 231v, which probably dates from the 1630s and which titles the poem "Elizabeth: On Monsieur's Departure." The most significant variants in Nichols's version are recorded in the notes.

    Although this poem does not exist in any known manuscript version dating to the lifetime of Elizabeth, it is almost certainly hers, written in connection with Monsieur's final leave-taking in 1582 after a long and perplexing visit with the queen (see Letter 51 and notes, pp. 251–53).

I am, and not; I freeze and yet am burned,   5
Since from myself another self[2] I turned.

My care is like my shadow in the sun—
Follows me flying, flies when I pursue it,
Stands, and lies by me, doth what I have done;
His too familiar care doth make me rue it.   10
    No means I find to rid him from my breast,
    Till by the end of things it be suppressed.

Some gentler passion[3] slide into my mind,
For I am soft, and made of melting snow;
Or be more cruel, Love, and so be kind.   15
Let me or float or sink, be high or low;
    Or let me live with some more sweet content,
    Or die, and so forget what love e'er meant.
           Elizabetha Regina.

10 ⧫ WHEN I WAS FAIR AND YOUNG, CIRCA 1580S

VERSION 1[1]

When I was fair and young, and favor graced me,
Of many was I sought unto, their mistress for to be.

---

2. **another self** Nichols reads "my other self."
3. **passion** Nichols reads "passions."
1. *Source:* The Syndics of Cambridge University Library, MS Dd.V.75, fol. 38v; an unattributed copy in a volume bound as "Commonplace Book, 1575" and discussed in Steven W. May, ed., as *Henry Stanford's Anthology: An Edition of Cambridge University MS Dd.5.75* (New York: Garland, 1988). Henry Stanford had very good access to court lyrics: he belonged to the household of Henry Carey, first Lord Hunsdon, who served as lord chamberlain between 1585 and 1596.
Bradner doubts Elizabeth's authorship of this poem on grounds that one manuscript (Folger, MS V.a.89) attributes the poem to the earl of Oxford and that Elizabeth was incapable of verse of this quality (pp. 75–76n). But the poem is also attributed to Elizabeth in BL, MS Harley 7392, fol. 21v, which closes "Finis. Ely. [abbreviation of 'Elizabeth']"; moreover, Bodleian, MS Rawlinson Poetical 85—which also attributes the poem to Elizabeth—attributes several other poems in the same collection to Oxford. Both Puttenham's praise of Elizabeth as a lyric poet and her reply to Ralegh (Poem 12, p. 308), which was unknown to Bradner, offer evidence that counters his view of Elizabeth's poetic range.

But I did scorn them all, and said to them therefore,
"Go, go, go seek some otherwhere; importune me no more."

But there fair Venus' son, that brave, victorious boy,   5
Said, "What, thou scornful dame, sith that thou art so coy,
I will so wound thy heart, that thou shalt learn therefore:
Go, go, go seek some otherwhere; importune me no more."[2]

But then I felt straightway a change within my breast:
The day unquiet was; the night I could not rest,   10
For I did sore repent that I had said before,
"Go, go, go seek some otherwhere; importune me no more."

VERSION 2[1]

When I was fair and young, and[2] favor graced me,
Of many was I sought their mistress for to be.
But I did scorn them all, and answered them therefore,
        "Go, go, go seek some otherwhere,
                        Importune me no more."   5

How many weeping eyes I made to pine with woe;
How many sighing hearts I have no[3] skill to show.
Yet I the prouder grew, and answered them therefore,[4]
        "Go, go, go seek some otherwhere,
                        Importune me no more."   10

Then spake fair Venus' son, that proud victorious boy,
And said: "Fine dame, since[5] that you be so coy,

---

2. This line could be the queen's or Cupid's. We have punctuated it as Cupid's.

1. *Source:* Bodleian Library, University of Oxford, MS Rawlinson Poetical 85, fol. 1r, the miscellany of the courtier John Finet; this is a possibly later copy in which the poem is attributed to Elizabeth and headed "Verses made by the queen when she was supposed to be in love with Monsieur." This heading is struck through, which could mean that Finet came to question the attribution but is more likely to mean that he thought better of reporting its occasion so directly. The most significant variants in another good copy, BL, MS Harley 7392, fol. 21, are recorded in the notes.

2. **and** Harley reads "then."   3. **no** Harley reads "not."

4. Harley version of this line is "But I the prouder grew, and still this spake therefore."

5. **And said ... since** Harley reads "Saying, 'You dainty dame, for.'"

I will so pluck your plumes that[6] you shall say no more
  'Go, go, go seek some otherwhere,
                    Importune me no more.'"   15

When he had spake these words,[7] such change grew in my breast
That neither night nor day since that,[8] I could take any rest.
Then lo,[9] I did repent that I had said before,
  Go, go, go seek some otherwhere,
                    Importune me no more.   20
                    Finis
              Elizabetha Regina.

---

11 ❧ NOW LEAVE AND LET ME REST, CIRCA 1580S[1]

1. Now leave and let me rest. Dame Pleasure, be content—
Go choose among the best; my doting days be spent.
By sundry signs I see thy proffers are but vain,
And wisdom warneth me that pleasure asketh pain;
And Nature that doth know how[2] time her steps doth try,   5
Gives place to painful woe, and bids me learn to die.

6. **pluck ... that** Harley reads "pull ... as."
7. **When he had spake these words** Harley reads "As soon as he had said."
8. **since that** omitted in Harley.
9. **Then lo** Harley reads "Wherefore."
1. *Source:* The Syndics of Cambridge University Library, MS Dd.V.75, fol. 44v (cf. note on this MS, Poem 10, Version 1, p. 303). In Henry Stanford's anthology, this poem, like most of the others, is unattributed. It is, however, attributed to Elizabeth in another, possibly later MS—BL, Harley 7392, fol. 49v—which uses some spellings that are idiosyncratically characteristic of Elizabeth (*ar* are; *oldar* older).
Bradner disputes the attribution to Elizabeth on grounds that the Harington family's version, as reproduced in Hughey's edition of the Arundel MS (1:180–81), fails to identify the poem as Elizabeth's, despite the Haringtons' close ties to the court. But that reasoning is unpersuasive: given the private, even secret, nature of Elizabeth's poetic production at court, manuscript attribution was not to be expected from her intimates. Significant variations between the Cambridge, Harley, and Arundel versions are recorded in the notes. The Arundel and Harley versions arrange the poem's rhyming couplets as trimeter quatrains, rather than hexameters with internal rhyme, as here. Moreover, in Arundel, the poem's resulting forty-eight lines are arranged as six eight-line stanzas rather than four six-line stanzas, as here.
2. **how** Arundel reads "her."

2. Since all fair earthly[3] things, soon ripe, will soon be rot
And all that pleasant springs, soon withered, soon forgot,
And youth that yields men[4] joys that wanton lust desires[5]
In age repents the toys that reckless youth requires.   10
All which delights I leave to such as folly trains[6]
By pleasures to deceive, till they do feel the pains.

3. And from vain pleasures past I fly, and fain would know
The happy life at last whereto[7] I hope to go.
For words or wise reports ne yet[8] examples gone   15
'Gan bridle youthful[9] sports, till age came stealing[10] on.
The pleasant courtly games that I do pleasure[11] in,
My elder years[12] now shames such folly to begin.

4. And all the fancies strange that fond[13] delight brought forth
I do intend to change, and count them nothing worth.   20
For I by proffers vain am taught to know the skill[14]
What might have been forborne in my young reckless will;
By which good proof[15] I fleet from will to wit again,
In hope to set my feet in surety to remain.

---

3. **earthly** Harley reads "youthful" and has "rotten" and "forgotten" as rhyme words for this and the next lines.

4. **men** Harley reads "all"; Arundel reads "new."

5. **lust desires** Harley reads "youth requires."

6. Harley version of this line is "All such desire I leave / To such as follow trains"; that is, to would-be courtiers.

7. **whereto** Arundel reads "wherein"; Harley's version of the line is "The happy place at last whereto I hope to go."

8. **ne yet** Harley reads "nor all."

9. **youthful** Harley reads "wilful."

10. **came stealing** Harley reads "come creeping"; Arundel's reading of this line is "Can bridle youthful sports, till age comes stealing on."

11. **do pleasure** Harley reads "delighted"; Arundel reads "did pleasure."

12. **elder years** Harley reads "older years," corrected to "older age."

13. **the … fond** Harley reads "those fancies strange that vain."

14. Harley's reading of this line is "For I by proofs am ['warned' corrected to] worn, / And taught to know the skill"; Arundel's reading is "For I by process worn, / Am taught to know the skill."

15. **proof** Harley reads "words"; Arundel reads "will."

12 ʃ·VERSE EXCHANGE BETWEEN QUEEN ELIZABETH AND SIR WALTER RALEGH, CIRCA 1587[1]

[Ralegh to Elizabeth]

Fortune hath taken away my love,
My life's joy and my soul's heaven above.
Fortune hath taken thee away, my princess,
My world's joy and my true fantasy's[2] mistress.

Fortune hath taken thee away from me;   5
Fortune hath taken all by taking thee.
Dead to all joys, I only live to woe:
So is Fortune become my fantasy's foe.

1. *Source:* Ralegh's poem to Elizabeth is transcribed by permission of the British Library from BL, MS Additional 63742, fol. 116r; a volume bound in limp vellum and described as "Letters of Henry, fourth Earl of Derby" (1531–1593). Other MS copies are listed in Peter Beal, *Index of English Literary Manuscripts,* vol. 1, pt. 2 (London: Mansell, 1980), pp. 388–89. For discussion of the verse exchange, which was occasioned by the earl of Essex's rapid rise to favor in 1587 and Ralegh's consequent loss of status (at least in his own eyes), see L. G. Black, "A Lost Poem by Queen Elizabeth I," *TLS* (May 23, 1968): 535. Black transcribes another MS of Ralegh's poem from a verse miscellany in Archbishop Marsh's Library, Dublin (MS Z. 3. 5.21, fol. 30v). Our text of Elizabeth's answer is transcribed from Inner Temple Library, MS Petyt 538, vol. 10, fol. 3r, which identifies the poem in the margin as "*per reginam* / Walter Rawley,*" but strikes through both the identification and the poem itself. George Puttenham also quotes lines 11 and 12 as Elizabeth's in his *Art of English Poesie* as an example of "Sententia" or the "Sage Sayer." As has been noted by several scholars, both poems can be sung to the ballad tune "Fortune My Foe"; indeed, the verses circulated together anonymously and were eventually printed in somewhat altered form (perhaps as early as the 1590s, as Peter Beal conjectures, but certainly by the 1640s) as a broadside ballad that titles the exchange simply "The Lover's Complaint for the Loss of His Love" and "The Lady's Comfortable and Pleasant Answer."

This verse conversation between Elizabeth and Ralegh is, like the Elizabeth-Heneage exchange in Poem 7, p. 299, a surviving instance of the sophisticated poetic banter that took place between the queen and her favorites. In *The History of the Worthies of England* (London, 1662), Sir Thomas Fuller reports an earlier and briefer exchange between Ralegh and Elizabeth in a rather more public medium (261). When Ralegh had newly come to court, desire for the queen's favor "made him write in a glass window, obvious to the queen's eye, 'Fain would I climb, yet fear I to fall.' Her majesty, either espying or being shown it, did underwrite, 'If thy heart fails thee, climb not at all.'"

2. **fantasy's** here and in line 8, MS reads "fantasies," with "ta" struck through in a hand identified in a modern note as that of the eighteenth-century antiquarian William Oldys, who underlined key words and made several corrections, as he explains, to improve the "uneven measure." However, "fantasy" and "fancy" were frequently interchanged in verse of the period and probably pronounced similarly.

In vain, my eyes, in vain ye waste your tears;
In vain, my sights[3], the smoke of my despairs,   10
In vain you search the earth and heaven above.
In vain you search, for Fortune keeps my love.

Then will I leave my love in Fortune's hand;
Then will I leave my love in worldlings' band,
And only love the sorrows due to me—   15
Sorrow, henceforth, that shall my princess be—

And only joy that Fortune conquers kings.
Fortune, that rules the earth and earthly things,
Hath taken my love in spite of virtue's might:
So blind a goddess did never virtue right.   20

With wisdom's eyes had but blind Fortune seen,
Then had my love, my love forever been.
But love, farewell—though Fortune conquer thee,
No fortune base nor frail shall alter me.

[Elizabeth to Ralegh]

Ah, silly Pug,[4] wert thou so sore afraid?
Mourn not, my Wat, nor be thou so dismayed.
It passeth fickle Fortune's power and skill
To force my heart to think thee any ill.
No Fortune base, thou sayest, shall alter thee?   5
And may so blind a witch so conquer me?
No, no, my Pug, though Fortune were not blind,
Assure thyself she could not rule my mind.
Fortune, I know, sometimes doth conquer kings,
And rules and reigns on earth and earthly things,   10
But never think Fortune can bear the sway
If virtue watch, and will her not obey.

3. **sights** possibly an idiosyncratic spelling for "sighs."
4. **Pug** general term of endearment but also Elizabeth's pet name for Ralegh, who is referred to in the next line by the nickname **Wat**, a diminutive form of Walter.

Ne chose I thee by fickle Fortune's rede,[5]
Ne she shall force me alter with such speed
But if to try this mistress' jest with thee.[6]   15
Pull up thy heart, suppress thy brackish tears,
Torment thee not, but put away thy fears.
Dead to all joys and living unto woe,
Slain quite by her that ne'er gave wise men blow,
Revive again and live without all dread,   20
The less afraid, the better thou shalt speed.

5. **rede** judgment, decree.
6. There may be a missing line after this one, designed to rhyme with "thee," since in this copy a line is left blank; alternatively, the queen may have intended lines 13–15 as a triplet of near-rhymes, followed by a new turning of the argument in lines 16–21.

PRAYERS 29-35

29 ·❧· QUEEN ELIZABETH'S PRAYER AT BRISTOL, AUGUST 15, 1574[1]

[Endorsed] A prayer made by Queen Elizabeth

[Headed] A prayer made by the queen's majesty the 15 of August, being then in Bristow

I render unto Thee, O merciful and heavenly Father, most humble and hearty thanks for Thy manifold mercies, so abundantly bestowed upon me as well for my creation, preservation, regeneration, and all other Thy benefits and great mercies exhibited in Christ Jesus. But specially for Thy mighty protection and defense over me in preserving me in this long and dangerous journey, as also from the beginning of my life unto this present hour, from all such perils as I should most justly have fallen into for mine offenses, hadst not Thou, Lord God, of Thy great goodness and mercy, preserved and kept me. Continue this Thy favorable goodness towards me; and I beseech Thee that I may still likewise be

---

1. *Source:* BL, MS Lansdowne 115, art. 45, fol. 108r; copy. Elizabeth journeyed to Bristol to ratify in person the Treaty of Bristol (August 28, 1574) between England and Spain. The issues requiring resolution included the breaking off of all normal trade relations, the practice by both sides of piracy or in-port confiscations of ships and their cargoes, and the mutual harboring of rebels against one another's governments. England had been provided with a motive to make peace with Catholic Spain by the upsurge of militant Catholicism in France symptomatized in the Saint Bartholomew's Day Massacre (August 24, 1572). See J. B. Black, *The Reign of Elizabeth 1558–1603,* 2nd ed. (Oxford, 1959), pp. 163–64.

defended from all adversities both bodily and ghostly. But specially, O
Lord, keep me in the soundness of Thy faith, fear, and love, that I never
fall away from Thee, but continue in Thy service all the days of my life.
Stretch forth, O Lord most mighty, Thy right hand over me, and defend
me against mine enemies that they never prevail against me. Give me, O
Lord, the assistance of Thy Spirit and comfort of Thy grace, truly to
know Thee, entirely to love Thee, and assuredly to trust in Thee. And
that as I do acknowledge to have received the government of this Church
and kingdom of Thy hand, and to hold the same of Thee, so grant me
grace, O Lord, that in the end I may render up and present the same
again unto Thee a peaceable, quiet, and well-ordered state and kingdom, as also a perfect reformed Church, to the furtherance of Thy glory.
And to my subjects, O Lord God, grant, I beseech Thee, faithful and
obedient hearts willing to submit themselves to the obedience of Thy
Word and commandments, that we all together, being thankful unto
Thee for Thy benefits received, may laud and magnify Thy holy name,
world without end. Grant this, O merciful Father, for Jesus Christ's sake,
our only Mediator and Advocate,[2] amen.

PRAYERS 30–35
Queen Elizabeth's Prayer Book, circa 1579–82[1]

30 ﷽ THE FIRST ENGLISH PRAYER

O most glorious King and Creator of the whole world, to whom all
things be subject both in heaven and earth, and all best princes most
gladly obey, hear the most humble voice of Thy handmaid, in this only

2. Except for **merciful,** this sentence is a verbatim echo of the close of the prayer for the
state of the Church Militant in the Order for Holy Communion; see Booty (254).

1. *Source:* BL, MS Facsimile 218, sigs. 3r–36r; in Elizabeth's own hand. (For original-
spelling versions, see *ACFLO,* part 1.) Facsimile 218 is a photostatic copy of the original,
which was lost at the beginning of this century. It is described in the prefatory note to the
copy by "J. W." from Southwood, June 3, 1893, as follows: "This tiny volume, measuring 2
inches wide by 3 inches long, has 38 vellum leaves. It is bound in shagreen with gold enam-
eled clasps; in the center of each is a small ruby. Two miniatures on gold backgrounds with
fleurs de lis are by Nicholas Hilliard: the one represents Queen Elizabeth, the other
François Hercule de Valois, successively Duc d'Alençon and Duc d'Anjou (1554–1584), her
'Monsieur,' twenty years her junior, and the last seriously entertained suitor for her hand

FIGURE 13 Miniature of the duke of Alençon from Queen Elizabeth's Prayer Book, BL, MS Facsimile 218, sig. 1v. Reproduced by permission of the British Library.

happy—to be so accepted. How exceeding is Thy goodness and how great mine offenses! Of nothing hast Thou made me not a worm, but a creature according to Thine own image:[2] heaping all the blessings upon me that men on earth hold most happy; drawing my blood from kings and my bringing up in virtue; giving me that more is, even in my youth knowledge of Thy truth, and in times of most danger, most gracious deliverance; pulling me from the prison to the palace; and placing me a

---

(in 1579–82). These years are the probable date of this text, penned by the queen in her best calligraphic italic handwriting, apparently for her own use as a girdle prayer-book. The ruled margins and capital letters are gilded, while the opening word or words of each prayer are in outsize lettering." In size, page format, and autograph text, this little volume strongly resembles the Kendal Town autograph that Queen Katherine Parr made of her own *Prayers or Meditations* as a gift for her friend Mistress Tuke circa 1545.

The following comprises what is known of the history of *Queen Elizabeth's Prayer Book*. James II gave it to the duke of Berwick, whence it passed to Horace Walpole and then to the duchess of Portland, who sold it on May 24, 1786. Queen Charlotte bought it for £106 1s. and gave it to one of her ladies-in-waiting, the dowager duchess of Leeds. Its last recorded owner went unnamed when it was exhibited by J. W. Whitehead at the "Fine Art Society" in 1902; it disappeared sometime thereafter. Roy Strong listed it as still missing in his *Portraits of Queen Elizabeth I* (Oxford: Clarendon Press, 1963), p. 102.

2. An inversion of Psalm 22:6: "I am a worm and no man." This and the following prayers contain so many deep liturgical and scriptural echoes, particularly of the Psalms, that we have not attempted to note them all. Further identifications are provided in *ACFLO*, part 2.

sovereign princess over Thy people of England. And above all this, making me (though a weak woman) yet Thy instrument to set forth the glorious Gospel of Thy dear Son Christ Jesus. Thus in these last and worst days of the world, when wars and seditions with grievous persecutions have vexed almost all kings and countries round about me, my reign hath been peaceable and my realm a receptacle to Thy afflicted Church. The love of my people hath appeared firm and the devices of mine enemies frustrate.

Now for these and other Thy benefits, O Lord of all goodness, what have I rendered to Thee? Forgetfulness, unthankfulness, and great disobedience. I should have magnified Thee; I have neglected Thee. I should have prayed unto Thee; I have forgotten Thee. I should have served Thee; I have sinned against Thee. This is my case. Then where is my hope? If Thou, Lord, wilt be extreme to mark what is done amiss, who may abide it? But Thou art gracious and merciful, long suffering, and of great goodness, not delighting in the death of a sinner. Thou seest whereof I came, of corrupt seed; what I am, a most frail substance; where I live, in the world full of wickedness, where delights be snares, where dangers be imminent, where sin reigneth and death abideth. This is my state. Now where is my comfort?

In the depth of my misery I know no help, O Lord, but the height of Thy mercy, who hast sent Thine only Son into the world to save sinners. This, God of my life and Life of my soul, the King of all comfort, is my only refuge. For His sake therefore, to whom Thou hast given all power and wilt deny no petition, hear my prayers. Turn Thy face from my sins, O Lord, and Thine eyes to Thy handiwork. Create a clean heart, and renew a right spirit within me. Order my steps in Thy Word, that no wickedness have dominion over me; make me obedient to Thy will, and delight in Thy law. Grant me grace to live godly and to govern justly, that so living to please Thee and reigning to serve Thee, I may ever glorify Thee, the Father of all goodness and mercy, to whom, with Thy dear Son, my only Savior, and the Holy Ghost my Sanctifier, three Persons and one God, be all praise, dominion, and power, world without end, amen.

31 ❧ THE FRENCH PRAYER

My God and my Father, since it has pleased Thee to extend the treasures of Thy great mercy towards me, Thy most humble servant, having early in the day drawn me back from the deep abysses of natural ignorance

and damnable superstitions to make me enjoy this great sun of righteousness which brings in its rays life and salvation, even while Thou
leavest still many kings, princes, and princesses in ignorance under the
power of Satan; for which I will praise Thee, magnifying Thy name, O
my Father, and will sing psalms with those who fear Thy majesty, and
shall do so for as long as I live. For Thou art my Lord and my King; I will
recount to posterity with rejoicing the effects of Thy singular goodness.
It is Thou who hast raised and exalted me by Thy providence to the
throne, and hast crowned me with peace, to this end: that I may govern
my people and nourish Thy Church. I thank Thee, my good God, for
the honor that Thou hast done me, and I entreat Thee to give me grace
that I may acquit myself of my duty of well governing the state and
faithfully administering justice, without making exception for any persons. And thus I shall feel, with my subjects, Thy most holy benediction, from the which I know peace to have come, accompanied with
many good things, which until now, to Thy honor and the comforting
of Thy Church, I have enjoyed while my nearest neighbors have felt the
evils of bloody war and the poor, persecuted children have found an assured dwelling with rest.[3] Therefore, my God and Father, I render Thee
everlasting thanks that Thou hast given me the honor of being mother
and nurse of Thy dear children. Surely it is Thou, O my Savior, who hast
given me, with the power, the will to do the things by which Thou hast
confirmed Thy holy promises and hast made the effects of Thy singular
goodness felt by Thy servants and Thy people. Therefore continue, Lord,
to make use of me, rendering me willing to advance Thy kingdom.

And because I know for a truth that I have not entirely acquitted
myself of my charge nor esteemed the gifts with which Thou hast
adorned me, making every effort to serve and honor Thee according to
Thy holy Word, I confess without hypocrisy that I do not deserve to be
served and honored thus, but to be forever covered with ignominy and
abandoned by all. Nevertheless, Thou knowest that I am grieved by it
and very sorrowful: that has been human infirmity. Alas, my God, do
not judge me according to my works, for they are unclean; therefore
look on me with the eyes of Thy fatherly mercy. I know, and confess as
the truth, that I have offended Thee in several ways; have therefore
mercy on me and pardon me according to Thy promises. For Thou art

---

3. Apparently a reference to the numerous Huguenots who had emigrated to England,
particularly after the Saint Bartholomew's Day Massacre of 1572.

my Father; I know my transgressions and my black and bloody sins are habitually before me to terrify me, but Thou reassurest me by Thy Word and the goodness of Thy Spirit. It is against Thee, it is against Thee only that I have sinned—doing wrong and by negligence permitting wrong to be done against Thy laws, so that if Thou wert to punish me most harshly along with all of my people, I confess to have well deserved it. Assuredly I confess to have well deserved it; it would be very right; Thy judgments would be found just. Nevertheless, mayest Thou remember Thy kindnesses of old, and give me grace according to Thy mercy and Thy great compassion.

Continue, therefore, my good God, for the love of Thee and of Thy dear Son to make me feel Thy benedictions, governing and defending me and my people from all my enemies, who are adversaries to Thy truth and who rise up against Thy Christ, always plotting treason like workers of iniquity. Preserve therefore the mother and the children whom Thou hast given her; thus shall we serve Thee better still to the good of Thy poor Church. Show, O my Lord and Father, Thy power to the enemies of Thy truth, and make them know that Thou alone reignest, garbed with magnificence, who surroundest Thy Church as with high mountains of virtue, with which Thou art girded about. Vouchsafe therefore by Thy mercy to make firm and stable the throne to which Thou hast raised me, sustaining it by Thy great power, and give good advice and counsels to my councillors, and fidelity to all my servants, and to me, care, love, constancy, and discretion to receive the counsels of my faithful servants. And that this may be done, give us more abundantly of the graces of Thy Spirit, to the end, O my King, that we may throw ourselves into Thy arms, letting ourselves be guided by Thee; and living without fear of our enemies, we may serve Thee all the days of our life, renouncing the world and all the vanities of the same, bending ourselves towards the goal of our heavenly calling. Give ear to me, my God and Father, through Jesus Christ Thy dear Son, amen.

32 ཁ THE ITALIAN PRAYER

Acknowledging truly, sincerely, I confess to having received from Thee alone, O supreme Emperor and my most merciful Father, the scepter and the crown; and because of that, as humbly as I can I now present myself before the sacred throne of Thy most high majesty, in whose presence there in Thy high heaven, bending my knees here on earth, I open my humble and contrite heart, which I feel pierced by a true sense of such and so many of my deeds, errors, and sins that I confess render me unworthy of eternal life and the day of royal dignity. But because I feel and recognize myself having been truly called to the certain knowledge of Thy beloved Son and of Thee, Fountain of life, I make bold, sustained by His sole merits, to consecrate to Thee my scepter, and supplicate Thee as my most kindly Father not to hold it against me in judgment. Ah me, who will ever be able to stand in Thy presence, if his offenses are not freely pardoned and the perfect and entire righteousness of Thy Christ imputed to him? Deign, therefore, to open the ample treasures of Thy mercy so that I may be freed from so much misery; and therewith disclose to me the living fountains where I may be purified and made clean of all my stains of sin, through the virtue of the pure and cleansing waters that are in Thy sacred fountains. And thus made clean I shall at last be received into Thy everlasting courts, wherein dwelling with Thee, O my sweet Lord, I with the holy kings will perpetually contemplate Thy serene face, most happy and content to be enjoying everlasting life.

And so long as it shall please Thee, O my highest Emperor, to let me live on earth, I entreat Thee to keep me under the shadow of the wings of Thy divine power, as Thou hast done with a powerful hand since my girlhood, freeing me from a thousand mortal dangers, governing me always with Thy Holy Spirit, for only he is secure whose dwelling is in the secret place of the Most High and whose lodging is in the shadow of the Almighty, and has holy truth for a shield. Now Thou art the most high and almighty God; therefore in Thee only have I put my trust. Lord, let me not be confounded. Since I am weak and subject to human ignorance, in this my vocation I feel the need of good advice, of wise counsel and ready help at all times, and most when I might come to be attacked by impetuous winds and wild storms to which Christian kings are subject, having as their enemy the world subjected to that roaring lion who goes about ever seeking prey.[4] And although I yet enjoy the peace that Thou hast given me as my most merciful Father and I am not distressed, nevertheless I know that grave and mortal dangers hang over me, threatened by many enemies who are the adversaries of Thy truth

---

4. Cf. 1 Peter 5:8–9: "Your adversary the devil, as a roaring lion walketh about, seeking whom he may devour; whom resist, steadfast in the faith."

which I have received in this my reign. Therefore, my greatest Shepherd, defend me: Thou art the most mighty God of hosts such that Thou alone canst defend me, even as Thou, being most wise, canst counsel me in my every difficulty. Thou dost as Thou willst in heaven and on earth, and Thy counsels are firm and stable, and they render flawed human ones vain. Therefore, my Lord, make me feel Thy grace and divine favors more than ever; so that, as I await the day of my going from hence, by serving Thee I may glorify Thy holy name, and so finally receive the incorruptible crown. Grant this, my most sweet and almighty Father, through Thy dear Son my Savior, amen.

33 ﴾ THE LATIN PRAYER

Lord God, everlasting Father, whose is the power, the kingdom, and the glory; who art above all things, through all things, and in all things; by whom kings reign and princes rule on earth; who hast subjected all things to the dominion and power of man, so that man may subject himself in everything to the power of the Word and of Thy will; give me, a queen, Thy judgments so that I may judge Thy people in righteousness and Thy poor in justice. The frail body presses down upon the soul, and its earthly dwelling much hinders the thinking mind; nor does anyone born among men know Thy counsel or understand Thy mind, unless Thou hast first given him wisdom and breathed upon him with Thy divine Spirit. Give me, Thy handmaid, a teachable heart, so that I may know what is acceptable in Thy sight; send from heaven the Spirit of Thy wisdom and rule my heart with its guidance. O blessed is he whom Thou dost teach, Lord, and make knowledgeable in Thy will, without which I can neither desire good for myself nor do good to others, nor obey Thee as is my duty; nor can I rule the people with equity. Wherefore, most mighty King and most merciful Father, I come as a suppliant to the throne of Thy grace, I bend my knees before the footstool of Thy feet; I lift my hand, I direct my eyes, I pour out words, I beat my breast, I prostrate myself body and soul; from my soul asking most humbly that Thy Spirit may teach me and instruct me in all Thy ways, that Thy wisdom may please me more than thousands in gold and silver. Impart, Lord, Thy Holy Spirit who ever and everywhere may be with me and guide me, and direct and impel me to those things alone that are to be meditated, treated, established, and determined, for they regard the praise of Thy name, the good of the Church, and the benefit of the commonwealth.

Thus instructed with the help of Thy wisdom, may I so assist others that I not harm myself, so rule others with the scepter that I may rule myself by Thy Word; managing the commonwealth so that the soul may rule the flesh, reason the soul, faith the reason, and Thy grace faith, that nothing may please me which displeases Thee, and nothing be to my taste which is not favorable to Thy Word. May Thy Word, Lord, be a light to my eyes, a lamp to my feet, honey in my mouth, a song to my ears, a joy to my heart; may it be a girdle of truth for my loins, a corselet of righteousness for my breast, a helmet of salvation for my head, a sword of the Spirit for my right hand, a shield of faith for my left, and for my whole body the armor of God.[5] May it be salvation to my soul, protection for my life, hope in fear, delight in love, nourishment in food, rest in sleep, meditation while waking, peace in my conscience, prudence in my counsels, moderation in severity, equity in mercy, and impartiality in both; straightness in the court of justice, prophecy in deliberation, courage in war, glory in peace, in strife victory, in victory triumph. In my hand may it be a scepter; on my head, a diadem; for my throne, majesty; and in all my empire, my glory, my blessedness.

With love for Thee alone before all else, good Jesus, may my heart be aflame, may my memory flourish, may my reason be comprehending, may my mind be wise; may my whole soul be impassioned and my spirit exultant with joy, that I may follow Thee in Thy law as my Leader; hear Thee in Thy Word as my Teacher; love Thee as a Father for Thy promises; honor Thee as my King for Thy kindnesses; worship Thee in Thy works as my Creator; fear Thee in Thy threatenings as my Lord; embrace Thee in things well done as Thy servant; in all words, deeds, and thoughts glorify Thee as God. To whom with the Father and the Holy Spirit be all honor, glory, and majesty for evermore, amen.

34 ⧽ THE GREEK PRAYER

Whenever I reflect upon the evils of this world, the doings of the wicked, the hatred of enemies, and the dangers and contrivances of the ungodly, I perceive the besetting snares in which we, Thy servants, continually risk danger. Yet the more, whenever I remember the stumblings

5. **armor of God** cf. the "whole armor of God" in Ephesians 6:14, 16, 17, which includes many of the same attributes.

and offenses of my own life from my youth as it presents itself to me, I am afraid, I am ashamed, and I am full of faintheartedness. But whenever I consider again Thy mighty hand, the magnitude and the continuance of Thy help given unto me, I again take up my meditations and in these I become more lighthearted—they make me hope. On account of this, drawing near to Thee now with a broken spirit, first I thank Thee, Lord Jesus Christ, my Savior, for all the good things Thou hast bestowed on me, who hast kept me safe from so many dangers, and hast raised me to the royal throne of this sovereignty and dost not cease to preserve me in it. And then I entreat Thee, my Christ, and I confess. For I know my transgressions and my acts that I have committed; but this, again, I know: that the magnitude of my sins cannot surpass the great patience of my Savior. For Thou didst not slip away from the woman, hardened in sin, who approached Thee in tears; nor didst Thou cast out a tax collector who repented; nor didst Thou chase away a thief who acknowledged Thy kingdom; nor didst Thou abandon him who had been a persecutor and repented;[6] but after their repentances Thou wentest to meet them and didst change their standing into that of Thy friends. Thus, emboldened by Thy unspeakable goodness, I draw near unto Thee and I ask: Christ my Lord, my Master, my Redeemer, everlasting King, send me up, send me forth; reconcile me to Thee and make allowance for me as a sinner and an unworthy servant of Thine, for sin committed in youthful rashness, whether in knowledge or in ignorance, whether in word or in deed. Thou alone being the Holy of Holies, make me holy, soul and body, mind and heart; and renew me entirely. And be Thou an ally and partaker with me, directing in peace the life of my people and myself, Thou alone to whom praise at all times belongs, now and in unending ages, amen.

35 ❧ THE SECOND ENGLISH PRAYER

O Lord God, Father everlasting, which reignest over the kingdoms of men and givest them at Thy pleasure, which of Thy great mercy hast chosen me Thy servant and handmaid to feed Thy people and Thine inheritance; so teach me, I humbly beseech Thee, Thy Word and so strengthen me with Thy grace that I may feed Thy people with a faithful and a true heart, and rule them prudently with power. O Lord, Thou

6. The biblical allusions in this passage are, successively, to Luke 7:37–38, 48, 19:2–11, 23:42–43; and to Acts 9:4–5, 22:7–15, and 26:14–18.

hast set me on high; my flesh is frail and weak. If I therefore at any time forget Thee, touch my heart, O Lord, that I may again remember Thee. If I swell against Thee, pluck me down in my own conceit, that Thou mayest raise me in Thy sight. Grant me, O Lord, a listening ear to hear Thee and a hungry soul to long after Thy Word. Endue me with Thy heavenly Spirit. Give me Thy Spirit of wisdom that I may understand Thee. Give me Thy Spirit of truth, that I may know Thee, Thy feeling Spirit that I may fear Thee, Thy Spirit of grace that I may love Thee, Thy Spirit of zeal that I may hunger and thirst after Thee, Thy persevering Spirit that I may live and dwell and reign with Thee.

I acknowledge, O my King, without Thee my throne is unstable, my seat unsure, my kingdom tottering, my life uncertain. I see all things in this life subject to mutability, nothing to continue still at one stay; but fear and trembling, hunger and thirst, cold and heat, weakness and faintness, sorrow and sickness, doth evermore oppress mankind. I hear how ofttimes untimely death doth carry away the mightiest and greatest personages. I have learned out of Thy holy Word that horrible judgment is nigh unto them which walk not after Thy will, and the mighty, swerving from Thy law, shall be mightily tormented. Therefore sith all things in this world, both heaven and earth, shall pass and perish and Thy Word alone endureth forever, engraft, O most gracious Lord

FIGURE 14 Miniature of Queen Elizabeth from her Prayer Book, BL, MS Facsimile 218, sig. 38r. Reproduced by permission of the British Library.

Christ, this Thy Word of grace and life so in my heart that from henceforth I neither follow after feigned comforts in worldly power, neither
distract my mind to transitory pleasures, nor occupy my thoughts in
vain delights, but that carefully seeking Thee where Thou showest Thyself in Thy Word, I may surely find Thee to my comfort and everlast-
ingly enjoy Thee to my salvation.

Create therefore in me, O Lord, a new heart and so renew my spirit
within me that Thy law may be my study, Thy truth my delight, Thy
Church my care, Thy people my crown, Thy righteousness my pleasure,
Thy service my government, Thy fear my honor, Thy grace my strength,
Thy favor my life, Thy Gospel my kingdom, and Thy salvation my bliss
and my glory. So shall this my kingdom through Thee be established
with peace; so shall Thy Church be edified with power; so shall Thy
Gospel be published with zeal; so shall my reign be continued with
prosperity; so shall my life be prolonged with happiness; and so shall
myself at Thy good pleasure be translated into immortality. Which, O
merciful Father, grant for the merit of Thy Son Jesus Christ, to whom
with the Holy Ghost be rendered all praise and glory forever, amen.

IV

SPEECHES, LETTERS,
POEMS, AND PRAYERS OF
QUEEN ELIZABETH I

1588–1603

FIGURE 15 The Armada Portrait of Queen Elizabeth, by George Gower. Reproduced by kind permission of the Marquess of Tavistock and Trustees of the Bedford Estate.

SPEECHES 19–24

***

19 ⇨ QUEEN ELIZABETH'S ARMADA SPEECH TO THE TROOPS AT TILBURY, AUGUST 9, 1588[1]

[Subscribed] Gathered by one that heard it and was commanded to utter it to the whole army the next day, to send it gathered to the queen herself.

My loving people, I[2] have been persuaded by some that are careful of my safety to take heed how I committed myself to armed multitudes, for

---

1. *Source:* BL, MS Harley 6798, art. 18, fol. 87; late sixteenth- or early seventeenth-century copy written on a single 6-by-8-inch leaf. There is a printed version of the Armada Speech in *Cabala, Mysteries of State, in Letters of the Great Ministers of K. James and K. Charles* (London: for M. M. G. Bedell and T. Collins, 1654), pp. 259–60, which describes its occasion in a letter by Dr. Lionel Sharp, who had been attached to the earl of Leicester at Tilbury camp and decades later became chaplain to the duke of Buckingham: "The queen the next morning rode through all the squadrons of her army as armed Pallas attended by noble footmen, Leicester, Essex, and Norris, then lord marshal, and divers other great lords. Where she made an excellent oration to her army, which the next day after her departure, I was commanded to redeliver all the army together, to keep a public fast." Sharp comments further of this speech, "No man hath it but myself, and such as I have given it to." Important variants in the *Cabala* version are indicated below in the notes.

At the time of the queen's speech, the main body of the Spanish Armada had been deflected, but no one yet knew that it would not regroup and that the chief Spanish peril was already past. The duke of Parma's independent fleet was still expected to launch an invasion up the Thames estuary, on whose banks, across from Gravesend, the Tilbury camp was strategically placed. Although there has been much speculation about Elizabeth's warlike garb and demeanor on this famous occasion, there can be little doubt that her speech was actually delivered, and in language reasonably close to that reproduced here.

2. **I** here and in the rest of the sentence, *Cabala* version uses "we" and "our."

fear of treachery. But I tell you that I would not desire to live to distrust my faithful and loving people. Let tyrants fear: I have[3] so behaved myself that under God I have placed my chiefest strength and safeguard in the loyal hearts and goodwill of my subjects. Wherefore I am come among you at this time but for my recreation and pleasure, being resolved in the midst and heat of the battle to live and die amongst you all,[4] to lay down for my God and for my kingdom and for my people mine honor and my blood even in the dust. I know I have the body but of a weak and feeble woman, but I have the heart and stomach of a king and of a king of England too—and take foul scorn that Parma[5] or any prince of Europe should dare to invade the borders of my realm. To the which rather than any dishonor shall grow by me, I myself will venter[6] my royal blood; I myself will be your general, judge, and rewarder of your virtue[7] in the field. I know that already for your forwardness you have deserved rewards and crowns, and I assure you in the word of a prince you shall not fail of them.[8] In the meantime, my lieutenant general[9] shall be in my stead, than whom never prince commanded a more noble or worthy subject. Not doubting but by your concord in the camp and valor in the field and your obedience to myself and my general, we shall shortly have a famous victory over these enemies of my God and of my kingdom.[10]

---

3. **have** *Cabala* version reads "have always."

4. *Cabala* version of sentence to this point is markedly different: "And therefore I am come amongst you, as you see at this time, not for my recreation and disport, but being resolved in the midst and heat of the battle to live or die amongst you all."

5. **take foul scorn that Parma** *Cabala* version reads "think foul scorn that Parma or Spain"; Alessandro Farnese, duke of Parma, was regent of the Spanish Netherlands under Philip II.

6. **venter** venture, but possibly also "vent"; *Cabala* version reads instead "take up arms."

7. **your virtue** *Cabala* version reads "every one of your virtues."

8. **I assure you ... them** *Cabala* version of this clause is "we do assure you in the word of a prince, they shall be duly paid you."

9. **lieutenant general** Leicester, whose death came only shortly afterward, in September.

10. *Cabala* version of final sentence is "Not doubting but by your obedience to my general, by your concord in the camp, and your valor in the field, we shall shortly have a famous victory over those enemies of my God, of my kingdoms, and of my people."

20 &ℯ QUEEN ELIZABETH'S LATIN SPEECH TO THE HEADS OF
OXFORD UNIVERSITY, SEPTEMBER 28, 1592[1]

Merits and gratitude have so captured my reason that they compel me to do what reason itself prohibits; for the cares of kingdoms have such great weight that they are wont rather to blunt the wit than to sharpen the memory. Let there be added besides a disuse of this language, which has been such and so constant that in thirty-six years I scarcely remember using it thirty times. But now the ice is broken: I have either to stick with it or to get off of it. Your merits are not the exceptional and notable praises (unmerited by me) that you have given me; nor declarations, narrations, and explications in many kinds of learning; nor orations of many and various kinds eruditely and notably expressed; but another thing which is much more precious and more excellent: namely, a love that has never been heard nor written nor known in the memory of man. Of this, parents lack any example; neither does it happen among familiar friends; no, nor among lovers, in whose fate faithfulness is not always included, as experience itself teaches. It is such that neither persuasions nor threats nor curses can destroy. On the contrary, time has no power over it—time that eats away iron, that wears away rocks, cannot disjoin it. Such are your merits, of such a kind that I would think them to be everlasting if I also were eternal. For which, if I had a thousand rather than one tongue, I would not be able to express due thanks, so much is the mind able to conceive that it knows not how to express.

In gratitude for which, accept thus much of prayer and advice. From the beginning of my reign, my greatest and special concern, care, and watchfulness has been that the realm be kept free as much from external enemies as from internal tumults, that it, long flourishing for many ages, might not be enfeebled under my hand. Truly, after the guardian-

1. *Source:* Bodleian Library, University of Oxford, MS Bodley 900. (For original Latin, see *ACFLO,* part 2.) Of the many extant manuscript and printed copies of Elizabeth's 1592 speech, this copy is the one most closely associated with the court: it is written in an elegant italic hand of the period and bound in a fine gilt and tooled limp vellum cover along with Queen Elizabeth's autograph English translation of Cicero's *Pro Marcello,* dating from the same era, and (on smaller sheets) Latin and English versions of "The Blessed Virgin Mary to the Messanians," a text that may be related to one of the Oxford debates or entertainments offered to the queen in 1592. This volume may have been presented as a gift to one of the Oxford heads during or after the royal visit. The italic hand recording Elizabeth's speech shows many close similarities to the secretary hand recording her 1593 speech before Parliament (Speech 21, Version 2, p. 330) in Bodleian, MS Eng. hist. C.319, and may be the work of the same copyist.

ship of my own soul, I have centered my single, perpetual care in that which, if I have always been watchful for the whole, this university may be thought not the least part. How is my providing not extended also to her? For her I shall always use such diligence that there will be no need of a goad to spur me; for of itself my diligence is ready to advance, preserve, and adorn her.

Now for my advice, attend to this, which if you follow, I doubt not that it will be to God's glory, your advantage, and my special joy: that this university may be long enduring, let its care be especially to worship God—not in the manner of the opinion of all nor according to over-curious and too-searching wits, but as the divine law commands and our law teaches. For indeed, you do not have a prince who teaches you anything that ought to be contrary to a true Christian conscience. Know that I would be dead before I command you to do anything that is forbidden by the Holy Scriptures. If, indeed, I have always taken care for your bodies, shall I abandon the care of your souls? God forbid! Shall I neglect the care of souls, for the neglect of which my own soul will be judged? Far from it. I admonish you, therefore, not to go before the laws but to follow them, nor dispute whether better ones could be prescribed but observe what the divine law commands and ours compels. And henceforth, remember that each and every person is to obey his superior in rank, not by prescribing what things ought to be, but by following what has been prescribed, bearing this in mind: that if superiors begin to do that which is unfitting, they will have another superior by whom they are ruled, who both ought and is willing to punish them. Finally, be of one mind, for you know that unity is the stronger, disunity the weaker and quick to fall into ruin.

21 ❧ QUEEN ELIZABETH'S SPEECH AT THE CLOSING OF
PARLIAMENT, APRIL 10, 1593

SPEECH 21, VERSION 1[1]

The lord keeper's[2] speech ended, after some time of intermission, the queen being settled in her chair of state, the queen herself used a most

1. *Source:* BL, MS Cotton Titus F.II, fols. 98v–99v; Parliament roll headed "Matters propounded in the Parliament amongst the assembly of the Lower House which were called the 35th year of the reign of Queen Elizabeth, February 19, *Anno Domini* 1592[3]."

2. **lord keeper** Sir John Puckering (1544–1596), who held this office from May 28, 1592.

princely speech to the House, but ill fortune was I stood so as I could not hear but little of it. Of that I heard this was the sum; and as I learned by others, this was the chief substance of her oration. The first words I heard not at all, till it came to this saying:

"This kingdom hath had many noble and victorious princes. I will not compare with any of them in wisdom, fortitude, and other virtues; but (saving the duty of a child that is not to compare with her father) in love, care, sincerity, and justice, I will compare with any prince that ever you had or ever shall have. It may be thought simplicity in me that all this time of my reign have not sought to advance my territories and enlarged my dominions, for both opportunity hath served me to do it, and my strength was able to have done it. I acknowledge my womanhood and weakness in that respect, but it hath not been fear to obtain or doubt how to keep the things so obtained that hath withholden me from these attempts; only, my mind was never to invade my neighbors, nor to usurp upon any, only contented to reign over my own and to rule as a just prince. Yet the king of Spain doth challenge me to be the beginning of this quarrel and the causer of all the wars—that I have sought to injury[3] him in many actions. But in saying that I have wronged him, that I have caused these wars, he doth me the greatest wars that may be. For my own conscience cannot accuse my thought wherein I have done him the least injury; but I am persuade[4] in my conscience if he knew what I know, he himself would be sorry for the wrongs he hath done me. I fear not all his threatenings; his great preparations and mighty forts do not scare me.[5] For though he come against me with a greater force than ever was his invincible navy, I doubt not (God assisting me, upon whom I always trust) but I shall be able to defeat him and utterly overthrow him. I have a great advantage of him, for my cause is just. I heard say that when he attempted his last invasion, some inhabiting upon the coasts forsook the towns and fled up higher into the country, leaving all naked and exposed to his entrance. But I swear unto you if I knew those persons or may know of any that shall so do hereafter, I will make them know and feel what it is to be so fearful in so urgent a cause.

Before the queen's speech, he had, as was customary, spoken for her and delivered her final directions to the Parliament.

3. **injury** injure.

4. **persuade** persuaded.

5. Despite the great victory over the Spanish Armada in 1588, at the time of this speech and at several other critical junctures during the 1590s, the English fully expected Spain to launch a new invasion.

"The subsidy which you offer me I accept thankfully if you give me your goodwills with it, but if the necessity of the time and your preservations did not require it, I would refuse it. But yet let me tell you the sum is not such but that it is needful for the prince to have so much always lying in our coffers for your defense in time of need, and not to be driven to get it when we should use it. You that be lieutenants and gentlemen of command in your countries, I would require to take care and special order that the people be well and thoroughly armed, and that in readiness upon all present occasions. You that be judges and justices of peace, I command and straitly charge that you see the laws to be made, and those already made, to be duly executed; and that you make them living laws when we have put life into them."[6]

And thus, with most gracious thanks unto the House, her princely speech ended.

SPEECH 21, VERSION 2[1]   *[Endorsed] April, 1593. A report of her majesty's speech in the Parliament House at the dissolving of the Parliament.*

My Lords and you, my Commons of the Lower House, were it not that I know no speeches presented by any other nor words delivered by any substitute can be so deeply imprinted into your minds as spoken by myself (whose order and direction was but followed and delivered by

6. According to parliamentary custom, the laws it enacted did not come into force and "life" until they were orally endorsed at the close of Parliament by the monarch, who was styled *lex animata*, "a living law," or *anima legis*, "the soul of law." That ceremony followed Elizabeth's speech. Her remarks about "living law" respond to an earlier speech by the speaker of the House (recorded as part of the same parliamentary roll as the present version of Elizabeth's speech), which had asserted: "Our laws we have conferred upon this session of so honorable a Parliament are of two natures: the ones that had life but are ready to die except your majesty breathe into them life again, the other are laws that never had life but are capable of life, and come to seek life of your majesty. Of the first sort are those laws that had continuance but unto this Parliament and now are to receive new life or to die forever; the other that I term capable of life are those that are newly made but have no essence in being until your majesty give them life." For a printed version of the full speech and others from the same MS, see Hartley (3:61–175, esp. 172–75).

1. *Source:* Bodleian Library, University of Oxford, MS Eng. hist. C.319; an early copy on a single folded sheet in a hand that may be closely associated with the court if it is by the same copyist as Speech 20. This version of the speech is fuller but considerably less vivid and explicit than Version 1 and may represent the speech as revised by the queen and/or others after its delivery for promulgation to a wider public. It is quite similar to John Stow's version, printed in *The Annals of England*, ed. E. Howes (London, 1615) (*STC* 23338), p. 765; the most significant variants in Stow's version are indicated in the notes.

the lord keeper), I could be content to spare speech, whom silence better pleaseth than to speak. And because much hath been spoken, much less shall I now need to speak of mine own indisposition in nature and small desire for any private respect to be enriched by your present[2]— which words shall not witness but deeds, by your former experience, having expended what I have received to the preservation and defense of yourselves. And thus much I dare assure you: that the care you have taken for myself, yourselves, and the commonweal, that you do it for a prince that neither careth for any particular—no, not for life—but so to live that you may flourish. For before God and in my conscience, I protest (whereunto many that know me can witness) that the greatest expense of my time, the labor of my studies, and the travail of my thoughts chiefly tendeth to God's service and the government of you, to live and continue[3] in a flourishing and happy estate. God forbid you should ever know any change thereof! Many wiser princes than myself you have had, but one only excepted, none more careful over you[4] (whom in the duty of a child I must regard and to whom I must acknowledge myself far shallow); I may truly say none whose love and care can be greater or whose desire can be more to fathom deeper for prevention of danger to come or resisting of dangers, if attempted towards you, shall ever be found to exceed myself in love (I say) towards you and care over you.

You have heard at the beginning of this Parliament some doubt of danger—more than I would have you to fear. Doubt only should be if not prevented; and fear, if not provided for. For mine own part, I protest I never feared; nor what fear was, my heart never knew. For I knew that my cause was ever just, and that standing upon a sure foundation, I should not fail, God assisting the quarrel of the righteous, and such as arm[5] but to defend. Glad might that king, my greatest enemy, be to have the like advantage against me, if in truth for his own actions he might truly so say. For in th'ambition of glory I have never sought to enlarge the territories of my land, nor thereby to advance you. If I have used my forces to keep the wars[6] from you, I have thereby thought your safety the greater and your danger the less. If you suppose I have done it for

2. **your present** Stow reads "you present."

3. **and continue** not in Stow.

4. **none more careful over you** not in Stow; the phrase is added over the line in another hand and could easily have been missed (or not yet present) when the MS was copied.

5. **arm** Stow reads "are."   6. **wars** Stow reads "enemy far."

fear of the enemy or in doubt of his revenge, I know his power is not to prevail, nor his force to fear[7] me, having so mighty a Protector on my side. I would not have you returning into the country to strike fear into the minds of any of my people, as some, upon the arrival of the late navy, dwelling in a maritane[8] shire fled for fear farther into the middle of the land; but if I had been by him, I would sure have taught him to have showed so base and cowardly a courage. For even our enemies hold our nation resolute and valiant, which though they will not outwardly show, they inwardly know. And whensoever the malice of our enemies should cause them to make any attempt against us, I doubt not but we shall have the greatest glory, God fighting for those that truly serve Him with the justness of their quarrel. Only let them know to be wary, and not to be found sleeping. So shall they show their own valor and frustrate the hopes of their enemies. And thus far let me charge you that be lieutenants and you that in shires have the leading of the most choice and serviceable men under your bands: that you see them sufficiently exercised and trained so often as need shall require, that the wants of any of them be supplied by others to be placed in their rooms, and that all decays of armor be presently repaired and made sufficient. The enemy, finding your care such and so great,[9] will with the less courage think of your disturbance.

To conclude, that I may show my thankful mind, in my conscience never having been willing to draw from you but what you should contentedly give (and that for yourselves), and having my head by years and experience better stayed (whatsoever any shall suppose to the contrary) than that you may easily believe I will enter into any idle expenses, now must I give you all as great thanks as ever prince gave to loving subjects, assuring you that my care for you hath and shall exceed all my other cares of worldly causes whatsoever.

22 ﷼ QUEEN ELIZABETH'S LATIN REBUKE TO THE POLISH AMBASSADOR, PAUL DE JALINE, JULY 25, 1597[1]

O how have I been deceived! I expected an embassage, but you have brought to me a complaint; I was certified by letters that you were an

---

7. **fear** scare.   8. **maritane** maritime; bordering the sea.

9. **great** Stow adds "to provide for him."

1. *Source:* Folger Library, MS V.a.321, fol. 36r; a seventeenth-century translation. This much-celebrated speech demonstrates Elizabeth's skill as an impromptu orator; it exists in

ambassador, but I have found you an herald.[2] Never in my lifetime have I heard such an oration. I marvel much at so great and insolent a boldness in open Presence; neither do I believe if your king[3] were present that he himself would deliver such speeches. But if you have been commanded to use suchlike speeches (whereof I greatly doubt) it is hereunto to be attributed: that seeing your king is a young man and newly chosen, not so fully by right of blood as by right of election, that he doth not so perfectly know the course of managing affairs of this nature with other princes as his elders have observed with us, or perhaps others will observe which shall succeed him in his place hereafter.

And as concerning yourself, you seem to have read many books, but the books of princes you have not so much as touched, but show yourself utterly ignorant what is convenient between kings. And where you make mention so often of the law of nature and the laws of nations, know you that this is the law of nature and of nations: that when hostility interposeth herself between princes, it is lawful for either party to cease on either's provisions for war, from whence soever derived, and to foresee that they be not converted to their own hurts. This, I say, is the law of nature and of nations.

And where you recite the new affinity with the House of Austria,[4] what account soever you make thereof, you are not ignorant that some one of that House would have had the kingdom of Polonia[5] from your king. For other matters, for which time and place serve not, seeing they are many and must be considered by themselves, this you shall expect: to be certified of them by some of our councillors that shall be ap-

---

several contemporary or near-contemporary translations of which this version is the most vigorous and closest to Elizabeth's own style. (Earlier translations include Folger MS V.b.214; BL, MS Harley 6798, fol. 90r; a copy at Hatfield House recorded in Historical Manuscripts Commission Reports No. 9, pt. 7, pp. 315–16; and Sir Robert Cecil's partial translation in his letter to Essex, from which we have excerpted his account of the circumstances of Elizabeth's response—see Speech 22, Additional Document A, p. 334).

2. **herald** one lower in status than an ambassador and also more potentially menacing; the herald's duty was to announce an action (such as a declaration of war) rather than to negotiate.

3. **king** Zygmunt (Sigismund III) Vasa, third son of Duke John of Finland, later king of Sweden.

4. **new affinity . . . Austria** Earlier in 1592 Zygmunt had married Anna, daughter of Archduke Charles of Styria (lower Austria).

5. **Polonia** Poland.

pointed to those matters. In the meantime, fare you well and repose yourself.[6]

SPEECH 22, ADDITIONAL DOCUMENTS A, B LETTER EXCHANGE BETWEEN SIR ROBERT CECIL AND ROBERT DEVEREUX, EARL OF ESSEX, ON THE SUBJECT OF ELIZABETH'S RESPONSE TO THE POLISH AMBASSADOR[1]

[Cecil to Essex] There arrived three days since in the city an ambassador out of Poland, a gentleman of excellent fashion, wit, discourse, language, and person. The queen was possessed by some of our new councillors, that are as cunning in intelligence as in deciphering, that his negotiation tendeth to a proposition of peace. Her majesty, in respect that his father the duke of Finland had so much honored her,[2] besides the liking she had of this gentleman's comeliness and qualities, brought to her by report, did resolve to receive him publicly in the Chamber of Presence, where most of the earls and noblemen about the court attended, and made it a great day. He was brought in attired in a long robe of black velvet, well jeweled and brodered,[3] and came to kiss her majesty's hands where she stood under the state; from whence he straight retired three yards off and then began his oration aloud in Latin with such a countenance as in my life I never beheld. The effect of it was this, that the king hath sent him to put her majesty in mind of the ancient confederacies between the king of Poland and England, that never a monarch in Europe did willingly neglect their friendship, that he had ever friendly received her merchants and subjects of all qualities, that she had suffered his to be spoiled without restitution, not for lack of knowledge of the violencies but out of mere injustice, not caring to minister remedy notwithstanding many particular petitions and letters received, but to confirm her own disposition to avow these courses vio-

6. **repose yourself** The Latin *quiescas* can also carry the stronger meaning of "be quiet," as it is translated in some other MSS.

1. *Source:* Cecil's letter of July 26, 1597, to the earl of Essex is excerpted from a secretarial copy, PRO, State Papers Domestic, Elizabeth 12/264/57, fols. 82r–83v; Essex's response is excerpted from an autograph letter to Cecil dated July 28, 1597, PRO, State Papers Domestic, Elizabeth 12/264/57, fol. 84r. Sir Robert Cecil (1563?–1612), son of Lord Burghley, was at this time a privy councillor and secretary of state; Robert Devereux (1565–1601), earl of Essex, was a leading magnate and the great favorite of Elizabeth's final years.

2. Duke John, younger brother of King Eric XIV of Sweden, had brought Eric's marriage proposal to Elizabeth in December 1559.

3. **brodered** embroidered.

lating both the law of nature and nations. Because there was quarrels between her and the king of Spain, she therefore took upon her by mandate to prohibit him and his countries, assuming thereby to herself a superiority not tolerable over other princes, nor he determined to endure, but rather wished her to know that if there were no more than the ancient amity between Spain and him, it were no reason to look that his subjects should be impeded, much less none when strait obligation of blood had so conjoined him with the illustrious House of Austria, concluding that if her majesty would not reform it, he would. To this, I swear by the living God that her majesty made one of the best answers *extempore* in Latin that ever I heard, being much moved to be so challenged in public, especially so much against her expectation.

[Essex to Cecil] I have this bark received your packet wherein you send me the news of her majesty's encounter with that braving[4] Polack, and what a princely triumph she had of him by her magnanimous, wise, and eloquent answer! It was happy for her majesty that she was stirred and had so worthy an occasion to show herself. The heroes would be but as other men if they had not unusual and unlooked-for encounters. And sure her majesty is made of the same stuff of which the ancients believed their heroes to be formed: that is, her mind of gold, her body of brass. O foolish man that I am, that can compare La Jupe Blanche[5] to the hardest metal. But in that wherein I mean to compare it, it holds proportion, for when other metals break and rust and lose both form and color, she holds her own—her own pure colors which no other of nature can match or of art imitate. But how dares my melancholy, dulled spirit praise her whose truest praise is silent admiration?

23 ❧ ELIZABETH'S GOLDEN SPEECH, NOVEMBER 30, 1601

SPEECH 23, VERSION 1[1] *[Commons journal of Hayward Townshend, MP for Bishopscastle, Shropshire]*

30 November, Monday. . . . In the afternoon the Commons attended the queen at Whitehall about three of the clock to the number of seven-

4. **braving** insolent, swaggering.   5. "The White Skirt" (French).

1. *Source:* Bodleian Library, University of Oxford, MS Rawlinson A 100, fols. 97v–101r; a full transcription by one of the members of Parliament in attendance. What became known

score.[2] At length the queen came into the Council Chamber, where sitting under the cloth of estate at the upper end, the speaker[3] with all the Commons came in and after three low reverences made, he spake to this effect: "Most sacred and more than most gracious sovereign, we your faithful, loyal, and obedient subjects and Commons here present, vouchsafed of your special goodness to our unspeakable comfort, access to your sacred presence, do in all duty and humbleness come to present that which no words can express: our most humble and thankful acknowledgment of your most gracious message, and most bounden and humble thanks for your majesty's most abundant goodness extended and performed to us. We cannot say, most gracious sovereign, we have called and have been heard, we have complained and have been helped; though in all duty and thankfulness we acknowledge your sacred ears are ever open and ever bowed down to hear us,[4] and your blessed hands ever stretched out to relieve us. We acknowledge, sacred sovereign, in all duty and thankfulness we acknowledge that before we call, your preventing grace[5] and all-deserving goodness doth watch over us for our good, and more ready to give than we can desire, much less deserve. That attribute which is most proper unto God—to perform all He promiseth—most gracious sovereign queen, of all truth, of all constancy, of all goodness, never wearied in doing good unto us, the deeds themselves do speak that we must render unto you, most zealous, most careful to provide all good things for us, most gracious, most tender to remove all grievances from us, which all your princely actions

---

as the Golden Speech was the queen's most celebrated parliamentary speech, copied, recopied, and reprinted many times in the course of the seventeenth century as an example of royal assent to the redress of public grievances, most particularly, the royal grants of monopolies that had created economic hardship for many of her subjects. For particulars, see Speech 23, Additional Document A.

Nearly every copy of this speech differs from the rest in some of its wordings, and all appear ultimately based on reports by members of Parliament in attendance. We offer three distinct early versions, each of which became a prototype for further copies later on. BL, MS Stowe 362, fols. 168r–172r, and D'Ewes's 1682 printed version (659–60), closely follow Townshend's diary (our Version 1).

2. **sevenscore** amended in Stowe to "fourscore."

3. **speaker** Sir John Croke (1553–1620), recorder of London, first elected to Parliament in 1585.

4. **ears . . . hear us** an echo of the opening words of Psalm 86; cf. Poem 14, p. 410.

5. **preventing grace** prevenient grace, a theological term for the grace sent by God that softens human hearts to the point that they are able to accept Him.

have ever showed. And even now your most gracious published proclamation,[6] of your own only mere motion and special grace for the good of all your people, doth witness to us we came not, sacred sovereign, one of the ten to render thanks and the rest to go away unthankful, but all of all, in all duty and thankfulness do throw down ourselves at the feet of your majesty. Neither dare we present thanks in words or any outward thing, which can be no sufficient retribution for so great goodness; but in all duty and thankfulness, prostrate at your feet we present our most loyal and thankful hearts, even the last drop of blood in our hearts and the last spirit of breath in our nostrils to be poured out to be breathed up for your safety."

After three low reverences made, he with the rest kneeled down, and her majesty began thus to answer herself, viz.: "Mr. Speaker, we have heard your declaration and perceive your care of our estate by falling into the consideration of a grateful acknowledgment of such benefits as you have received, and that your coming is to present thanks unto us, which I accept with no less joy than your loves can have desire to offer such a present. I do assure you there is no prince that loveth his subjects better, or whose love can countervail our love. There is no jewel, be it of never so rich a price, which I set before this jewel—I mean your loves. For I do more esteem it than any treasure or riches, for that we know how to prize. But love and thanks I count unvaluable,[7] and though God hath raised me high, yet this I count the glory of my crown: that I have reigned with your loves. This makes me that I do not so much rejoice that God hath made me to be a queen, as to be a queen over so thankful a people. Therefore I have cause to wish nothing more than to content the subjects, and that is a duty which I owe. Neither do I desire to live longer days than that I may see your prosperity, and that is my only desire. And as I am that person which still yet under God hath delivered you, so I trust by the almighty power of God that I shall be His instrument to preserve you from envy, peril, dishonor, shame, tyranny, and oppression, partly by means of your intended helps, which we take very acceptable because it manifesteth the largeness of your loves and loyalties unto your sovereign. Of myself I must say this: I never was any

6. **proclamation** the proclamation "Reforming Patent Abuses" issued by the queen in response to Parliament's protest against royal monopolies, November 28, 1601; no. 812 in Hughes and Larkin (3:235–38).

7. **unvaluable** invaluable.

greedy, scraping grasper, nor a strait, fast-holding prince, nor yet a waster. My heart was never set on worldly goods, but only for my subjects' good. What you bestow on me, I will not hoard it up, but receive it to bestow on you again. Yea, my own properties I account yours to be expended for your good, and your eyes shall see the bestowing of all for your good. Therefore render unto them from me, I beseech you, Mr. Speaker, such thanks as you imagine my heart yieldeth but my tongue cannot express."

Note that all this while we kneeled,[8] whereupon her majesty said, "Mr. Speaker, I would wish you and the rest to stand up, for I shall yet trouble you with longer speech." So we all stood up and she went on in her speech, saying, "Mr. Speaker, you give me thanks, but I doubt me that I have more cause to thank you all than you me; and I charge you to thank them of the Lower House from me. For had I not received a knowledge from you, I might have fallen into the lapse of an error only for lack of true information. Since I was queen yet did I never put my pen to any grant but that upon pretext and semblance made unto me, it was both good and beneficial to the subject in general, though a private profit to some of my ancient servants who had deserved well. But the contrary being found by experience, I am exceedingly beholding to such subjects[9] as would move the same at the first. And I am not so simple to suppose but that there be some of the Lower House whom these grievances never touched; and for them I think they speak out of zeal to their countries and not out of spleen or malevolent affection, as being parties grieved. And I take it exceedingly gratefully from them, because it gives us to know that no respects or interests had moved them other than the minds they bear to suffer no diminution of our honor and our subjects' love unto us, the zeal of which affection tending to ease my people and knit their hearts unto me, I embrace with a princely care.

8. Another variant version of the speech—preserved as BL, MS Harley 787, fols. 127r–128v, which dates from later in the seventeenth century—offers further particulars about the occasion, noting, "Many things through want of memory I have omitted, without setting down many her majesty's gestures of honor and princely demeanor used by her. As when the speaker spake any effectual or moving speech from the Commons to her majesty, she rose up and bowed herself. As also in her own speech, when the Commons, apprehending any extraordinary words of favor from her, did any reverence to her majesty, she likewise rose up and bowed herself, etc."

9. **such subjects** members who had frankly debated the abuses of royal monopolies and patents in recent sessions of the Commons (see Speech 23, Additional Document A, p. 344).

For above all earthly treasures I esteem my people's love, more than which I desire not to merit. That my grants should be grievous unto my people and oppressions to be privileged under color of our patents, our kingly dignity shall not suffer it. Yea, when I heard it I could give no rest unto my thoughts until I had reformed it. Shall they (think you) escape unpunished that have thus oppressed you, and have been respectless of their duty and regardless of our honor? No, no, Mr. Speaker, I assure you, were it not more for conscience' sake than for any glory or increase of love that I desire, these errors, troubles, vexations, and oppressions done by these varlets and low persons (not worthy the name of subjects) should not escape without condign punishment.

"But I perceive they dealt with me like physicians who, ministering a drug, make it more acceptable by giving it a good aromatical savor; or when they give pills, do gild them all over. I have ever used to set the Last Judgment Day before my eyes and so to rule as I shall be judged, to answer before a higher Judge. To whose judgment seat I do appeal that never thought was cherished in my heart that tended not unto my people's good. And now if my kingly bounties have been abused and my grants turned to the hurts of my people, contrary to my will and meaning, or if any in authority under me have neglected or perverted what I have committed to them, I hope God will not lay their culps[10] and offenses to my charge. Who, though there were danger in repealing our grants, yet what danger would I not rather incur for your good than I would suffer them still to continue? I know the title of a king is a glorious title, but assure yourself that the shining glory of princely authority hath not so dazzled the eyes of our understanding but that we well know and remember that we also are to yield an account of our actions before the great Judge.

"To be a king and wear a crown is a thing more glorious to them that see it than it is pleasant to them that bear it. For myself, I was never so much enticed with the glorious name of a king or royal authority of a queen as delighted that God hath made me His instrument to maintain His truth and glory, and to defend this kingdom (as I said) from peril, dishonor, tyranny, and oppression. There will never queen sit in my seat with more zeal to my country, care to my subjects, and that will sooner with willingness venture her life for your good and safety, than myself. For it is not my desire to live nor reign longer than my life and reign

10. **culps** sins, guilt.

shall be for your good. And though you have had and may have many princes more mighty and wise sitting in this seat, yet you never had or shall have any that will be more careful and loving. Shall I ascribe anything to myself and my sexly weakness? I were not worthy to live then, and of all most unworthy of the mercies I have had from God, who hath ever yet given me a heart which yet never feared any foreign or home enemy. I speak it to give God the praise as a testimony before you, and not to attribute anything unto myself. For I, O Lord, what am I, whom practices and perils past should not fear? Or what can I do"—these words she spake with a great emphasis—"that I should speak for any glory? God forbid. This, Mr. Speaker, I pray you deliver unto the House, to whom heartily recommend me, and so I commit you all to your best fortunes and further counsels; and I pray you, Mr. Comptroller, Mr. Secretary, and you of my Council, that before these gentlemen depart into their countries, you bring them all to kiss my hand."

SPEECH 23, VERSION 2[1] COPY OF THE GOLDEN SPEECH FROM THE PAPERS OF SIR THOMAS EGERTON

[Headed] Queen Elizabeth's speech

Mr. Speaker, we perceive your coming is to present thanks unto me; know it I accept with no less joy than your loves can desire to offer such a present, and more esteem it than any treasure or riches (for that we know to prize), but loyalty, love, and thanks I count invaluable. And though God hath raised me high, yet this I count the glory of my crown —that I have reigned with your loves. This makes I do not so much rejoice that God hath made me to be a queen, as to be a queen over so thankful a people, and to be the mean under God to conserve you in safety and preserve you from danger—yea, to be the instrument to de-

---

1. *Source:* Huntington Library, MS EL 2571. Reproduced by permission of The Huntington Library, San Marino, California. Copy in a contemporary hand (not that of Egerton himself) preserved among the papers of **Sir Thomas Egerton** (1540?–1607), privy councillor, lord keeper of the Great Seal, and Master of the Rolls from 1596 until the end of the reign. This version is quite different from Townshend's and evidently based on an independent report of the speech. It is followed in most particulars by a number of later seventeenth-century copies, among them Bodleian, MS Additional C.304b, fol. 16; and Cambridge University Library, MS Additional 335, fol. 39. For further discussion of MSS containing this version, see Hartley (3:294). Although neither Version 1 nor Version 2 can be considered the authoritative text of Elizabeth's speech, between them they allow us a vivid sense of the setting and language of her most famous utterance before Parliament.

liver you from dishonor, from shame, from infamy, from out of servitude and slavery under our enemies, to keep you from cruel tyranny and vile oppression intended against us. For better withstanding whereof we take very acceptably your intended helps, chiefly in that it manifesteth your loves and largeness of hearts unto your sovereign. Of myself, I must say this: I never was any greedy, scraping grasper, nor a strait fast-holding prince, nor yet a waster; my heart was never set on any worldly goods, but only for my subjects' goods. What you do bestow on me I will not hoard it up, but receive it to bestow on you again. Yea, mine own properties I account yours to be expended for your good. And your eyes shall see the bestowing of all for your good.

Mr. Speaker, I would wish you and the rest to stand up, for I shall yet trouble you with longer speech.

Mr. Speaker, you give me thanks, but I am more to thank you, and I charge you thank them of the Lower House from me. For had I not received a knowledge from you, I might have fallen into the lapse of an error, only for lack of true information. For since I was queen, yet did I never put pen to any grant but upon pretext and semblance made to me that it was for the good and avail of my subjects generally, though a private profit to some of my ancient servants who had deserved well. But that my grants should be made grievances to my people and oppressions to be privileged under color of our patents, our kingly dignity shall not suffer it. And when I heard it, I could give no rest unto my thoughts until I had reformed it. And those varlets, lewd persons, abusers of my bounty, shall know I will not suffer it. And Mr. Speaker, tell the House from me I take it exceeding gratefully that the knowledge of these things is come to me from them. And though amongst them the principal members are such as are not touched in their private, therefore need not speak from any feeling of the grief; yet we have heard that other gentlemen also of the House who stand as free have spoken freely in it, which gives us to know that no respects or interests have moved them other than the minds they bear to suffer no diminution of our honor and our subjects' love unto us. The zeal of which affection tending to ease my people and knit their hearts unto us, I embrace with a princely care. For above all earthly treasure, I esteem my people's love, more than which I desire not to merit. And God that gave me here to sit, and set me over you, knows that I never respected myself, but as your good was concerned in me. Yet what dangers, what practices, what perils I have passed! Some (if not all) of you know. But it is God that hath delivered. And in my governing, this I have ever had the grace to use—

to set the Last Judgment Day before mine eyes and so to rule as I shall be judged, and to answer before a higher Judge, to whose judgment seat I do appeal that never thought was cherished in my heart that tended not to my people's good. And if my kingly bounty have been abused and my grants turned to the hurt of my people, contrary to my will and meaning; or if any in authority under me have neglected or perverted what I have committed to them, I hope God will not lay their culps unto my charge.

To be a king and wear a crown is a thing more glorious to them that see it than it is pleasant to them that bear it. For myself, I was never so much enticed with the glorious name of a king or royal authority of a queen as delighted that God had made me His instrument to maintain His truth and glory, and to defend this kingdom from dishonor, damage, tyranny, and oppression. But should I ascribe anything of this to myself, or my sexly weakness, I were not worthy to live, and of all, most unworthy of the mercies I have had from God. But to God only and wholly, all is to be given and ascribed. The cares and troubles of a crown I cannot resemble more fitly than to the confections of a learned physician, perfumed with some aromatical savor, or to bitter pills gilded over, by which it is made acceptable or less offensive which indeed is bitter and unpleasant to take. And for my part, were it not for conscience' sake to discharge the duty which God hath laid upon me, and to maintain His glory and keep you in safety, in mine own disposition, I should willingly resign the place I hold to any other, and glad to be free of the glory with the labors. For it is not my desire to be or reign longer than my life and reign shall be for your good. And though you have had and may have many mightier and wiser princes sitting in this seat, yet you never had nor shall have any that will love you better. Thus, Mr. Speaker, I commend me to your loyal love, and you to my best care and your further counsels. And I pray you, Mr. Comptroller and you of my Councils, that before these gentlemen depart into their countries, you bring them all to kiss my hand.

SPEECH 23, VERSION 3[1] THE GOLDEN SPEECH AS PRINTED IN 1601

[Title page] Her majesty's most princely answer, delivered by herself at the court at Whitehall, on the last day of November, 1601, when the speaker of the Lower House of Parliament, assisted with the greatest part of the

1. *Source:* PRO, State Papers Domestic, Elizabeth 12/282/67, fols. 137r–141v; a contemporary printed text (London: Robert Barker, 1601) (*STC* 7578). This version, though appar-

knights and burgesses, had presented their humble thanks for her free and
gracious favor in preventing and reforming of sundry grievances by abuse
of many grants commonly called monopolies. The same being taken ver-
batim in writing by A. B.,[2] *as near as he could possibly set it down. Im-*
printed at London, anno 1601.

Mr. Speaker, we perceive by you, whom we did constitute the mouth of
our Lower House, how with even consent they are fallen into the due
consideration of the precious gift of thankfulness, most usually least esteemed where it is best deserved. And therefore we charge you tell them
how acceptable such sacrifice is, worthily received of a loving king who
doubteth much whether the given thanks can be of more poise[3] than
the owed is to them. And suppose that they have done more for us than
they themselves believe. And this is our reason: who keeps their sovereign from the lapse of error, in which, by ignorance and not by intent
they might have fallen, what thank they deserve, we know, though you
may guess. And as nothing is more dear to us than the loving conservation of our subjects' hearts, what an undeserved doubt might we have
incurred if the abusers of our liberality, the thrallers of our people, the
wringers of the poor, had not been told us! Which, ere our heart or
hand should agree unto, we wish we had neither, and do thank you the
more, supposing that such griefs touch not some amongst you in particular. We trust there resides in their conceits of us no such simple care
of their good, whom we so dearly prize, that our hand should pass
aught that might injure any, though they doubt not it is lawful for our
kingly state to grant gifts of sundry sorts of whom we make election, either for service done or merit to be deserved, as being for a king to
make choice on whom to bestow benefits, more to one than another.

  You must not beguile yourselves nor wrong us to think that the glos-
ing luster of a glittering glory of a king's title may so extol us that we
think all is lawful what we list, not caring what we do. Lord, how far

---

ently prepared by one in attendance during the queen's delivery of the speech and printed
with the royal arms as its frontispiece, is better described as summary than transcription.
If, indeed, this version of the speech was published under the auspices of the court, the
publication itself may have stimulated some who had been in attendance to produce their
own more detailed accounts of the speech. This imprint served as the basis for a number of
later MS copies, among them BL, MS Lansdowne 94, art. 52, fol. 123; PRO, State Papers Domestic, Elizabeth 12/282/65, fol. 134, and 12/282/66, fol. 136.

  2. **A. B.** possibly Anthony Blagrave, who was, according to Neale, the only MP in 1601
with these initials.   3. **poise** weight.

should you be off from our conceits! For our part we vow unto you that we suppose physicians' aromatical savors, which in the top of their potion they deceive the patient with, or gilded drugs that they cover their bitter sweet with, are not more beguilers of senses than the vaunting boast of a kingly name may deceive the ignorant of such an office. I grant that such a prince as cares but for the dignity, nor passes[4] not how the reins be guided, so he rule—to such a one it may seem an easy business. But you are cumbered (I dare assure) with no such prince, but such a one as looks how to give account afore another tribunal seat than this world affords, and that hopes that if we discharge with conscience what He bids, will not lay to our charge the fault that our substitutes (not being our crime) fall in.

We think ourselves most fortunately born under such a star as we have been enabled by God's power to have saved you under our reign from foreign foes, from tyrants' rule, and from your own ruin; and do confess that we pass not so much to be a queen as to be a queen of such subjects, for whom (God is witness, without boast or vaunt) we would willingly lose our life ere see such to perish. I bless God, He hath given me never this fault of fear; for He knows best whether ever fear possessed me, for all my dangers. I know it is His gift, and not to hide His glory, I say it. For were it not for conscience' and for your sake, I would willingly yield another my place, so great is my pride in reigning as she that wisheth no longer to be than best and most would have me so. You know our presence cannot assist each action, but must distribute in sundry sorts to divers kinds our commands. If they (as the greatest number be commonly the worst) should (as I doubt not but some do) abuse their charge, annoy whom they should help, and dishonor their king whom they should serve, yet we verily believe that all you will (in your best judgment) discharge us from such guilts. Thus we commend us to your constant faith, and yourselves to your best fortunes.

SPEECH 23, ADDITIONAL DOCUMENT A EXCERPTS FROM THE 1601 PARLIAMENTARY DEBATES CONCERNING MONOPOLIES[1]

21 November, 1601, Saturday . . . Mr. Solicitor Fleming said, "I will briefly give you account of all things touching those monopolies. Her majesty

---

4. **passes** cares.

1. *Source:* Bodleian Library, University of Oxford, MS Rawlinson A 100, fols. 67v–75r, passim; the parliamentary journal of Hayward Townshend.

in her provident care gave charge to Mr. Attorney and myself that speedy and special order may be taken for those patents; this was in the beginning of Hilary Term[2] last. But you all know the danger of that time, and what great affairs of importance happened to prevent these businesses;[3] since that, that naught could be done therein for want of leisure, etc."

Sir Robert Wroth said, "I would but note, Mr. Solicitor, that you were charged to take order in Hilary Term last: why not before? There was time enough ever since the last Parliament. I speak it and I speak it boldly: these patents are worse than ever they were; and I have heard a gentleman affirm in this House that there is a clause of revocation in these patents. If so, what need this stir of *scire facias, quo warranto,*[4] and I know not what, when it is but to send for the patentees and cause a redelivery? There hath been divers patents granted since the last Parliament. These are now in being, viz.: the patents for currants, iron, powder, cards, horn, ox shinbones, train oil,[5] lists of cloth, ashes, bottles, glasses, bags, shreds of gloves, aniseed, vinegar, sea coals,[6] steel, *aqua vitae,*[7] brushes, pots, salt, saltpeter, lead, accidences,[8] oil, transportation of leather, calamite stone, oil of blubber, fumaths or dried pilchers[9] in the smoke, and divers others."

Upon reading of the patents aforesaid, Mr. Hackwell of Lincoln's Inn stood up and asked this: "Is not bread there?"

"Bread?" quoth one.

"Bread," quoth another.

"This voice seems strange!" quoth a third.

"No," quoth Mr. Hackwell, "for if order be not taken for these, bread will be there before the next Parliament."

23 November, Monday . . . There was a gentleman which sat by me which showed me a paper in which was contained the discommodities

2. **Hilary Term** the winter legal term, that is, winter 1601.

3. The earl of Essex's rebellion, trial, and execution in February 1601 had cast a dark shadow over the 1601 Parliament and made the issue of love between monarch and subjects a matter of particular concern.

4. a judicial writ founded on some matter of record that required the party proceeded against to show cause why the record should be disregarded (Latin for "you should cause to know by what warrant").

5. **train oil** oil from fish or seals.

6. **sea coals** coal from the earth or seashore, so termed to distinguish it from charcoal.

7. *aqua vitae* ginlike liquor made from juniper berries.

8. **accidences** by-products from manufacturing (?).

9. **fumaths or dried pilchers** small smoked fish similar to herring.

of divers patents called monopolies. First of steel, where it hath been sold to Mr. Rowland Hayward of London in former time for twelve pounds ten shillings, the barrel is sold for nineteen pounds and the faggot for forty shillings; besides it is mixed and worse than the steel in former times; and where it hath been but at two pence halfpenny a pound before the patent, it is now at five pence the pound. And where two thousand poor people were maintained by working of steel and edge tools,[10] and might well live by working thereof at two pence halfpenny the pound, they are not now able by reason thereof to work, but now many go a-begging because it hath also less weight, to the utter undoing of all edge-tool makers.

20 November, Friday . . . Mr. Francis Moore said, "Mr. Speaker, I know the queen's prerogative is a thing curious to be dealt withal, yet all grievances are not comparable. I cannot utter with my tongue or conceive with my heart the great grievances that the town and country for which I serve sustaineth by some of these monopolies. It bringeth the general profit into a private hand and the end of all is beggary and bondage to the subject. We have a law for the true and faithful currying[11] of leather. There is a patent that sets all at liberty notwithstanding that statute. And to what purpose is it to do anything by act of Parliament when the queen will undo the same by her prerogative? Out of the spirit of humility, Mr. Speaker, I do speak it: there is no act of her that hath been or is more derogatory to her own majesty and more odious to the subject or more dangerous to the commonwealth than the granting of these monopolies."

24 ❧ QUEEN ELIZABETH'S FINAL SPEECH BEFORE PARLIAMENT, DECEMBER 19, 1601

SPEECH 24, VERSION 1[1] *[Headed] The queen's last speech. Queen Elizabeth's speech in Parliament.*

Before your going down at the end of the Parliament, I thought good to deliver unto you certain notes for your observation that serve aptly for the present time, to be imparted afterward where you shall come abroad,

10. **edge tools** implements with a sharp cutting edge, like knives or swords.

11. **currying** dressing, curing.

1. *Source:* BL, MS Cotton Titus C.VI, fols. 410r–411v; from a bound volume entitled *Original Letters and Papers of Henry Howard, Earl of Northampton* (1540–1614). This version

to this end: that you by me, and other by you, may understand to what prince, and how affected to the good of this estate, you have declared yourselves so loving subjects and so fully and effectually devoted your unchangeable affection. For by looking into the course which I have ever holden since I began to reign, in governing both concerning civil and foreign causes, you may more easily discern in what a kind of sympathy my care to benefit hath corresponded with your inclination to obey, and my caution with your merit.

First civilly: yourselves can witness that I never entered into the examination of any cause without advisement, carrying ever a single eye to justice and truth. For though I were content to hear matters argued and debated *pro* and *contra,* as all princes must that will understand what is right, yet I look ever (as it were) upon a plain table[2] wherein is written neither partiality nor prejudice. My care was ever by proceeding justly and uprightly to conserve my people's love, which I account a gift of God not to be marshaled in the lowest part of my mind, but written in the deepest of my heart, because without that above all, other favors were of little price with me, though they were infinite. Beside your dutiful supplies for defense of the public—which, as the philosophers affirm of rivers coming from the ocean, return to the ocean again—I have diminished my own revenue that I might add to your security, and been content to be a taper of true virgin wax, to waste myself and spend my life that I might give light and comfort to those that live under me.

The strange devices, practices, and stratagems (never heard nor written of before) that have been attempted not only against my own person, in which so many as acknowledge themselves beholding to my care and happy in my government have a interest, but by invasion of the state itself by those that did not only threaten to come, but came at the last in very deed with their whole fleet, have been in number many and by preparation dangerous. Though it hath pleased God, to whose honor it is spoken without arrogation of any praise or merit to myself, by many hard escapes and hazards both of divers and strange natures, to

---

may have been based on Northampton's own recollection, and offers the fullest known contemporary copy of Elizabeth's final speech, which was delivered at the closing of Parliament when most of the MPs had already left and therefore had but a small auditory. Sir Dudley Carleton described its delivery in a letter to John Chamberlain: "The queen concluded all with a long speech which was very much commended by those which heard her, and the bishop of Durham told me he never heard her in a better vein" (PRO, State Papers Domestic, Elizabeth 12/283/48, fol. 140r).

2. **plain table** blank tablet or notebook.

make me an instrument of His holy will in delivering the state from danger and myself from dishonor, all that I challenge to myself is that I have been studious and industrious, in confidence of His grace and goodness, as a careful head to defend the body, which I would have you receive from my own mouth for the better acknowledging and recognizing of so great a benefit.

Now touching foreign courses, which do chiefly consist in the maintenance of war, I take God to witness that I never gave just cause of war to any prince (which the subjects of other states can testify) nor had any greater ambition than to maintain my own state in security and peace without being guilty to myself of offering or intending injury to any man, though no prince have been more unthankfully requited whose intention hath been so harmless and whose actions so moderate. For to let you know what is not perhaps understood by any other than such as are conversant in state matters and keep true records of dealings past, even that potent prince the king of Spain (whose soul I trust be now in heaven[3]), that hath so many ways assailed both my realm and me, had as many provocations of kindness by my just proceedings as by hard measure he hath such returned effects of ingratitude. It is neither my manner nor my nature to speak ill of those that are dead, but that in this case it is not possible without some touch to the author to tax the injury. For when the color of dissension began first to kindle between his subjects of the Netherlands and him—I mean not Holland and Zealand only, but of Brabant and the other provinces which are now in the Archdukes'[4] possession—about the bringing in of the Inquisition (a burden untolerable), increase of impositions,[5] planting foreigners in the chiefest offices and places of government, then I gave them counsel to contain their passions and rather by humble petition than by violence or arms to seek ease of their aggrievances; nay (which is more) I disbursed great sums of money out of my own purse[6] to stay them from revolt till a softer hand might reduce these discords to harmony.[7]

---

3. Philip II had died in 1598.

4. **Archdukes** Archduke Albert of Austria and his wife Isabella, daughter of Philip II of Spain, who jointly ruled the Spanish Netherlands beginning in 1598.

5. **impositions** taxes.

6. Elizabeth had sent the Dutch a loan of £20,000 after the Pacification of Ghent (November 1576), which formalized the resolve of the United Provinces to work together to expel the occupying Spanish armies. In September 1577 she had sent a further loan of £100,000 and a military force to assist the Dutch.

7. At this point the following passage is struck through: "After this, again at such time as many malcontents finding very small compassion or regard of their complaints, much less

After this again, at such time as these malcontents, finding very small compassion of their complaints, much less abatement of the burdens which they purposed no longer to endure, made an offer of their state and service to myself upon a condition that I would secure their conscience and protect their liberties. I was so far from forgetting that old league that had lasted long between the race of Burgundy and my progenitors and the danger that might grow to many states by giving countenance or encouragement to opposition against the prince in one, as I dissuaded them. And though they sought to clear this scandal by vouching books and records of an oath taken to the States by Charles the emperor,[8] for maintenance of their liberties with this condition: that it should be for them to revolt from obedience whensoever he should any way infringe or impugn their liberties (a very strange oath, I confess, but such a one as they[9] produced for the warrant of their opposition), yet I advertised the king of Spain at sundry times and by sundry messengers of this intent, advising him to be wary lest his grieved subjects, being brought to despair, did not closely put the state into the protection of some other prince that might turn this[10] advantage to his prejudice in another sort than one of conscience and care to conserve the league, I, meant to do. If my endeavor only tended to this scope—that the prince's indignation and the subjects' opposition might be kept by mild and gentle lenitives from festering any deeper till time might cure the corrosive of either part—I doubt not but you will imagine that it was an office of a true friend and a kind ally, considering in what sort the king of Spain had dealt with me. I know that some other prince that had been wise according to the manner of the world, of high conceit and apt to fish in waters troubled, would have cast this matter in another mold, but I proceeded thus out of simplicity, remembering

---

abatement of the burdens which they had endured long, and resolving to endure no longer, made an offer of their country and themselves, upon condition that I would only guard and protect them from extremity. I was so tender of that old league that had been long between the House of Burgundy and my progenitors, and so careful to conserve the loyalty of subjects to their prince (a case that may concern all princes in their own estates, and so desirous to deal as I would be dealt withal) as I did discourage their intention as much as lay in me."

8. **Charles the emperor** Holy Roman Emperor Charles V (1500–1558).

9. **they** alternative reading could be "there"; "they," their," and "there" are often indistinguishable in this hand.

10. **this** alternative reading could be "the." Here and at several other points in the manuscript, particularly in its second half, "the" and "this," final "e" and final "es" and "is," are indistinguishable.

who it was[11] that said that the wisdom of the world was folly unto God, and hope in that respect that I shall not suffer the worse for it.

But to go on with the matter once again, after the coming of the duke of Alva,[12] when there was less hope of moderation than before, I still persisted in my proposition[13] advising them to hold so good a temper in their motion as might not altogether quench that life spark of expectation that the king, by looking better into the true state of the cause, might in time grow more compassionate of their calamity. In recompense of this kind care and faithful dealing on my part, he first begins to stir rebellion within the body of my realm by encouraging the earls of Northumberland and Westmoreland to take arms against myself,[14] though by the providence of God I cut off the best means of their maintenance and by the victory which I had over my own rebels made him see how hard a matter it was to prevail against a prince[15] confident in the protection of God and constant to the grounds of honor. Not content with this bad motion, he sent his whole fleet afterward with a proud conceit that nothing could withstand his attempt, and a purpose to invade her kingdom that had holden others from invading his. But it pleased God again to make him more unfortunate by this second enterprise, as the carcasses both of his subjects and his ships, floating upon all the seas between this and Spain, could testify.[16] Now that the father is at rest, the son, whom I did never in my life offend, assails me in another parallel, seeking to take away one of two crowns,[17] but very simply induced and as simply persuaded by his Council, the grounds considered

11. **who it was** Saint Paul in I Corinthians 1:21–25.

12. **duke of Alva** Ferdinand de Toledo, duke of Alva, sent to the Netherlands by Philip II in 1567 to purge the territories of religious and political disaffection. His methods were so harsh that the Council of Troubles he established to conduct the purge quickly became known as the "Council of Blood."

13. **proposition** alternative reading could be "**pre-position**," meaning her earlier position.

14. in the Northern Rebellion, 1569; see Letters 29–33, pp. 120–31.

15. **prince** the immediately following phrase, "grounded upon the rock of justice," is struck through.

16. When the remnants of the 1588 armada had attempted to retreat to Spain, many of the vessels were dashed on the rocks or otherwise lost in storms along the English and Scottish coasts.

17. Philip III of Spain sought to sever Catholic Ireland from the English crown. In 1601 the Spanish had actually attempted to land in Ireland and enlist local Catholics against Queen Elizabeth. At the time of this speech and for several years afterward until James I made peace in 1604, England remained at war with Spain.

whereon they build. And therefore take this with you for an encouragement, and assure all those who in you doubt, that such a quarrel thus unworthily begun and unjustly prosecuted without provocation by the least offense since the death of his father from hence can never prosper in this world, since both his conscience must acknowledge it and God will punish it.

At this time it will be sufficient to let you know the grounds and motives of the war to which you contribute, the merit of the princess for whose sake you contribute: that my care is neither to continue war nor conclude a peace but for your good, and that you may perceive how free your queen is from giving any cause of these attempts that have been made on her, unless to save her people or defend her state be to be censured. This testimony I would have you carry hence for the world to know: that your sovereign is more careful of your conservation than of herself, and will daily crave of God that they that wish you best may never wish in vain.

SPEECH 24, VERSION 2[1]

The Parliament being dissolved and each one ready to depart without further expectation, as the manner is, the queen's majesty raised herself out of her royal seat and made a short, pithy, eloquent, and comfortable speech somewhat to this effect. For besides I could not well hear all she spake, the grace of pronunciation and of her apt and refined words, so learnedly composed, did ravish the sense of the hearers with such admiration as every new sentence made me half forget the precedents.[2]

"My lords, we have thought it expedient in this general assembly to let you know out of our own mouth the unfained attestation of our heart. First, we humbly acknowledge the innumerable and unspeakable

---

1. *Source:* Journal of Sir Roger Wilbraham, the queen's solicitor general for Ireland, as reproduced in *The Camden Miscellany,* Publications of the Camden Historical Society, 3rd series, vol. 10, ed. Harold Spencer Scott (London: Royal Historical Society, 1902), pp. 44–47. We have not located the original MS, which Scott describes as follows: "The notebook or occasional journal . . . was kept by Sir Roger Wilbraham during the years 1593–1616 in a duodecimo volume, bound in vellum, of about 300 pages, closely written in a small hand, and described by him as a 'book of observations for my age or children.' . . . This book is in the possession of the earl of Latham, who traces his descent through Sir Roger's father, Richard Wilbraham of Nantwich" (v).

2. **precedents** those that went before.

benefits of almighty God for our miraculous preservation from the traitorous practices of miscreant subjects who, designed thereto by foreign enemies, have sought by taking away our life (which we are ever most willing to render up to Him that gave it), have sought thereby to bring our people and kingdom—being far more dear to us than our own life—into perpetual thralldom and foreign tyranny. And to say the truth, there have been so many and divers stratagems and malicious practices and devices to surprise us of our life as in recording thereof I am forced to recognize the mercies and omnipotency of the eternal God, by whose providence I have escaped all their snares, and some of the malefactors sentenced to perpetual shame and deserved punishment. The number of these wicked complotters, the several manners of undertaking thereof, and how some of them were discovered before they came to their ripeness, other brought forth abortive, some others even in their full maturity extinguished, it were to small purpose particularly now to recount. There be divers gentlemen, our ministers, that can readily testify the truth and circumstances hereof. Our purpose only is to acknowledge our constant and irremovable dependency upon His mercies, by whose goodness we that trust ever in Him have ever been preserved.

"Next, you shall understand that touching our civil government, sithence the beginning of our reign, in all causes we have undertaken to hear and determine, our heart hath been as a plain table ready to receive any impression—so most willing to hear the allegations of each party, yet evermore inclining our sentence to the sincerity of proof and soundness of reason. Touching our affairs with foreign princes, I must discover some things not known to many, and those of our Council in the secrecy of our state. In the beginning of our reign those of the Low Countries presented many petitions to us and our neighbor princes to be protected against inquisitioners of Spain and other oppressions not sufferable, wherein we, remembering the ancient amity between our predecessors and the House of Burgundy, and knowing how far Spain was remote from the Low Countries, and fearing his soldiers' revolt there for want, sent pay to them to contain them, and advertised the king of Spain by twelve persons severally at the least that if he did not loose the rein in easing the Low Countries from their over-heavy burdens, they were ready and likely to seek their protection from other foreign princes to his harm and dishonor. But this potent prince (whose soul I trust is with God, howsoever his demerits have been towards us) not regarding our advice, continued still in extremities, which forced those people to seek and sue for our protection by many petitions; and in their own wisdom finding our inclination inseparably knit to continue the former amity with Spain, they showed us the several instruments whereby the king and the emperor his father were sworn (a strange oath for kings!) that if these subjects did not enjoy the immunities therein promised them, they might lawfully seek protection of any other prince—exciting us, out of our compassionate disposition, to relieve their known extremities. Upon which we granted them some defense, only till by our mediation or process of time some moderation might be found, which we thought was required in Christianity, and yet no breach of amity. But the late king (before this), in recompense of our princely kindness towards him in our former advertisement and loves, excited a dangerous rebellion in the north by the earls of Northumberland and Westmoreland, which being quickly and happily extinguished, he still continued all malicious courses—I need not say of attempts of invasion, but the invasion itself, which by God's potency was defeated.

"And now the young king, following his father in malice, will begin, it seems, war upon us, when it is well known that we have often refused the resignation of the Low Countries, which the archduke hath, into our protection (a great temptation to any prince to be sovereign over so rich a people!) being led thereto by a desire not to infringe in any point that former amity, and especially desiring an established prosperity and peace to our people rather than any enlargement to our own honor. This we speak to let you and all others know this war is causeless, not drawn upon us by any provocation of ours, but a rash enterprise proceeding of malice or vainglory. Whereby as we nothing fear, so let no man doubt but that the justice and omnipotence of God is such that in every war He giveth victory to the innocent and fighteth evermore for those that sincerely serve Him, upon which confidence we may repose ourselves in courage and alacrity, whatsoever be practiced against us.

"Concerning our affection to our people, it is our happiest felicity and most inward joy that no prince ever governed a more faithful, valiant, and loving people, whose peace and prosperity we evermore prefer before all temporal blessings. And be you well assured, whether we make peace or war, the good of our people shall be evermore preferred therein. We never attempted anything to damage or dishonor our people, and though we may not attribute merits to our own wit in choosing out the safest harbor for us all to anchor at, yet the finger of God, directing the actions of all princes that sincerely serve Him, and our long-lived experience (though in a mean wit), shall make us able to discern and embrace that which shall tend to the prosperity of our people, to whom I wish that they that wish them best may never wish in vain."

LETTERS 78-103

78 &❧ ELIZABETH TO JAMES, CIRCA JULY 1, 1588[1]

[Addressed] To our right dear brother, the king of Scotland

[Endorsed] 9 July 1588

I am greatly satisfied, my dear brother, that I find by your own grant that you believe the truth[2] of my actions so manifestly, openly proved, and thank you infinitely that you profess so constant defense of your country, together mine,[3] from all Spaniards or strangers. A matter far otherwise given out by both our enemies, which blotting your fame with assurance of double dealing, as though you assured them underhand to betake you to their course, which what a stain it were in a prince's honor you yourself in judgment can well deem. For my part, I will ever trust your word till I be too sure of the contrary. Right well am I persuaded that your greatest danger should chance you by crossing your straight paths, for he that hath two strings to his bow may shoot stronger, but never straight, and he that hath no sure foundation cannot but ruin. God keep you ever, therefore, in your well-begun path. I have sent you this gentleman[4] as well to declare my good agreement to send

1. *Source:* BL, MS Additional 23240, art. 22, fol. 71; in Elizabeth's hand. (For original-spelling version, see *ACFLO*, part 1.)

2. **truth** Elizabeth writes "troth," which suggests both truth and trust.

3. **together mine** along with mine.

4. **gentleman** probably Sir Robert Carey, the consummate courtier and favorite with James. Robert was the son of Henry Carey, Lord Hunsdon, Elizabeth's first cousin, who had also served as an emissary to the Scottish court in 1587.

some finishers of our league as other matters which he hath to communicate unto you, if it please you to hear him: as my desire of answering your good friendship and amity in as ample sort as with honor I may, as one that never seeks more of you than that which shall be best for yourself. Assure yourself of me, therefore, and show by deeds ever to maintain it, and never was there in Christendom between two princes surer amity nor sounder dealing. I vow it and will perform it.

And for that you speak oft of satisfaction,[5] I have much urged, as now again I do, to know what thereby is meant, since I both mind and also do whatsoever may honorably be required of such as I profess myself. And therefore I require you therein to answer me, and so—trusting that all your protestations lately made me by Carey shall be readily performed, together with your constant, resolute course of late professed—I end[6] to molest you longer, but with my thanks to God that any your offenders be entered to your hands, and not the less not having been done without some of our help. Which glads me no less than happened to ourself, whose force shall never fail you in all leeful[7] causes. As knoweth God, who ever bless you from all malignant spirits and increase your happy years.

Your most assurest sister
and cousin, *Elizabeth R*

LETTER 78, ADDITIONAL DOCUMENT A JAMES TO ELIZABETH, AUGUST 1, 1588[1]

Madame and dearest sister,

In times of straits, true friends are best tried.[2] Now merits he thanks of you and your country who kiths[3] himself a friend to your country and estate. And so this time must move me to utter my zeal to the religion, and how near a kinsman and neighbor I find myself to you and

---

5. **satisfaction** for his mother's death.   6. **end** cease.
7. **leeful** permissible, lawful.

1. *Source:* BL, MS Additional 23240, art. 23, fol. 75r; copy. At the time of this letter, the English had succeeded in beating back the Spanish Armada, and some of its retreating ships were approaching the Scottish coast.
2. **tried** tested.   3. **kiths** makes known.

your country. For this effect, then, have I sent you this present[4] hereby to offer unto you my forces, my person, and all that I may command, to be employed against yon strangers in whatsomever façon[5] and by whatsomever mean as may best serve for the defense of your country. Wherein I promise to behave myself not as a stranger and foreign prince, but as your natural son and compatriot of your country in all respects. Now, madame, to conclude: as on the one part I must heartily thank you for your honorable beginning by your ambassador[6] in offers for my satisfaction, so on the other part I pray you to send presently down commissioners for the perfiting[7] of the same. Which I protest I desire not for that I would have the reward to precede the deserts, but only that I with honor, and all my good subjects with a fervent goodwill, may embrace this, your godly and honest cause, whereby your adversaries may have ado not with England but with the whole isle of Britain. Thus praying you to dispatch all your matters with all possible speed, and wishing you a success convenient to those that are invaded by God's professed enemies, I commit, madame and dearest sister, your person, estate, and country to the blessed protection of the Almighty. From Edinburgh the first of August, 1588.

> Your most loving and affectionate brother and
> cousin, as time shall now try, *James R*

79 ⇨ ELIZABETH TO JAMES, AUGUST 1588[1]

[Addressed] To my very good brother, the king of Scots.

Now may appear, my dear brother, how malice joined with might strikest to make a shameful end to a villainous beginning, for by God's singular favor, having their fleet well beaten in our narrow seas and pressing with all violence to achieve some watering place to continue their pretended invasion, the winds have carried them to your coasts, where

---

4. **this present** this letter.
5. **whatsomever façon** whatsoever fashion.
6. **ambassador** probably Robert Carey.
7. **perfiting** perfecting.
1. *Source:* BL, MS Additional 23240, art. 24, fol. 77; in Elizabeth's hand, with remnants of seal and ribbon attached. (For original-spelling version, see *ACFLO*, part 1.)

I doubt not they shall receive small succor and less welcome, unless those lords[2]—that so traitors-like would belie their own prince and promise another king relief in your name—be suffered to live at liberty to dishonor you, peril you, and advance some other (which God forbid you suffer them live to do). Therefore I send you this gentleman,[3] a rare young man and a wise, to declare unto you my full opinion in this great cause as one that never will abuse you to serve my own turn, nor will you do aught that myself would not perform if I were in your place. You may assure yourself that for my part, I doubt no whit but that all this tyrannical, proud, and brainsick attempt will be the beginning, though not the end, of the ruin of that king that most unkingly, even in midst of treating peace, begins this wrongful war. He hath procured my greatest glory that meant my sorest wrack, and hath so dimmed the light of his sunshine that who hath a will to obtain shame, let them keep his forces company. But for all this, for yourself's sake let not the friends of Spain be suffered to yield them force, for though I fear not in the end the sequel, yet if by having them unhelped you may increase the English hearts unto you, you shall not do the worst deed for your behalf. For if aught should be done, your excuse will play the boiteux[4] if you make not sure work with the likely men to do it. Look well unto it, I beseech you. The necessity of this matter makes my scribbling the more speedy, hoping that you will measure my good affection with the right balance of my actions, which to you shall be ever such as I have professed, not doubting of the reciproque of your behalf, according as my last messenger unto you hath at length signified, for the which I render you a million of grateful thanks together for the last general prohibition to your subjects not to foster nor aid our general foe. Of which I doubt not the observation if the ringleaders be safe in your hands. As knoweth God, who ever have you in His blessed keeping with many happy years of reign.

Your most assured, loving sister

and cousin, *Elizabeth R*

2. **lords** the Scottish Catholic earls, who were continually intriguing with Spain.

3. Sir Robert Sidney, elder brother of Sir Philip Sidney and nephew of the earl of Leicester.

4. **boiteux** lame man (French).

LETTER 79, ADDITIONAL DOCUMENT A JAMES TO ELIZABETH,
SEPTEMBER 1588[1]

Madame and dearest sister,

The sudden parting of this honorable gentleman your ambassador upon these unfortunate and displeasant news of his uncle[2] has moved me with the more haste to trace these few lines unto you: first to thank you as well for the sending so rare a gentleman unto me, to whose brother I was so far beholden, as also for the [late][3] sending me such sums of money, which according to the league I shall thankfully repay with forces of men whensoever your estate shall so require, according as my last letter hath made you certified. Not doubting but as ye have honorably begun, so ye will follow forth your course towards me, which thereby I shall so procure the concurrence of all my good subjects with me in this course as shall make my friendship the more steadable[4] unto you. The next is to pray you most heartily that in anything concerning this gentleman fallen out by the death of his uncle, ye will have a favorable consideration of him for my sake, that he may not have occasion to repent him of his absence at such a time. All other things I remit to his credit, praying you to think of me as of one who constantly shall continue his professed course and remain

Your most loving and affectionate
brother and cousin, *James R.*

Postscrip:[5] I thought good in case of sinister reports, madame, hereby to assure you that the Spanish fleet never entered within any road or haven within my dominion, nor never came within a kenning[6] near to any of my coasts.

---

1. *Source:* Bruce, 54–55, which transcribes a "Copy in Thompson MS, p. 50."

2. The earl of Leicester's death in September 1588 required his nephew Sir Robert Sidney, then serving as Elizabeth's ambassador in Scotland, to return to England.

3. **late** word conjecturally supplied for Bruce's "tayce."

4. **steadable** serviceable, helpful.

5. **Postscrip** postscript.

6. **within a kenning** anywhere near.

80 ❧ QUEEN ELIZABETH TO PEREGRINE BERTIE, LORD
WILOUGHBY, IN FRANCE, DECEMBER 6, 1589[1]

[Superscription] My good Peregrine, I bless God that your old prosperous success followeth your valiant acts, and joy not a little that safety ac-
companieth your luck.

Your loving sovereign, *Elizabeth*

Right trusty and well beloved, we greet you well. Albeit your abode and
of our troops in that realm hath been longer than was first required and
by us meant; whereof, as it seemeth, your yielding to divers services
there hath been partly a cause, contrary to our expectation, to the king's
purpose at the first declared, and to your own writing also hither, whose
advertisements moved us to give order for certain ships of ours to be
sent for the safe conducting of you and our subjects with you; yet now
perceiving the great contentment and satisfaction the king, our good
brother, hath received by your good service, and of our companies
under your charge, whereby also such as heretofore might have conceived an opinion either of our weakness or of the decay and want of
courage or other defects of our English nation may see themselves
much deceived, in that the contrary hath now well appeared in that
country by so small a troop as is with you, to the great honor and reputation of us and of our nation, and to the disappointing and (as we
hope) the daunting of our enemies.

   We have, upon request of our said good brother that king, declared
by his ambassador here,[2] accorded unto them, and hereby we signify
unto you, that we are pleased you shall continue your abode there with
the numbers under you for this month longer, hoping the king will then
be content to dismiss you with liberty and his good favor to return into

---

1. *Source:* PRO, State Papers France, 70/20/119, fol. 228; copy with superscription that, in
the original, was doubtless in Elizabeth's hand. Peregrine Bertie (1555–1601), Lord Wiloughby
de Eresby, was the leader of an expeditionary force of four thousand English Protestants,
many of them volunteers, sent to aid the new French king—the Protestant Henry IV, who
had succeeded Henry III that same year—against the ultra-papist forces of the Guise. The
English fought valiantly amidst enormous hardships and remained in France from early
October until the next January. See also the queen's letter of December 1, 1589 (*Historical
Manuscripts Commission Reports*, Ancaster MSS, p. 297), which is superscribed by Elizabeth "Good Peregrine, suppose not that your travail and labors are not graciously accepted, and shall be ever kept in good memory."
   2. **ambassador here** Philippe Canaye, sieur de Fresnes.

this our realm, in case he shall not be able to keep them in pay and sat-isfy them for any longer time; and that in the meantime he will be care-ful for the well using of you and them, so as ye may neither want pay nor suffer otherwise too many wants. And for that it is to our no small comfort to perceive the forward endeavors and valor, both of yourself and of those under you, we are pleased not only to let you understand the same by these our own letters, with our thankful acceptation to yourself in particular; but also we will and require you to signify so much, both to the whole company of our soldiers there, and to such captains and gentlemen particularly as you shall think most worthy thereof, who we trust we show the continuance of their valiant and will-ing minds, rather more than less, knowing the same shall be an increase of our comfort, and of the honor of the whole realm and nation, and to their own more reputation.

You shall also say unto the king that although we have cause, in re-spect of the wants which we heard our men endured sundry ways there, to be unwilling that they should remain there any longer time, yet when we understood that he hoped to do himself the more good by the use of them than otherwise he might look for, wanting them, we were—we know not how—overcome and enchanted by the king to yield there-unto. Given under our signet at Richmond, the sixth day of December, 1589, in the thirty-second year of our reign.

81 ❧ LETTER EXCHANGE BETWEEN QUEEN ELIZABETH AND LADY ELIZABETH DRURY, 1589[1]

[Endorsed] 1589. The copy of the letter her majesty writ to the Lady Drury upon the death of her husband and her answer thereto.

Be well ware, my Bess, you strive not with divine ordinance nor grudge at irremediable harms, lest you offend the Highest and no whit amend the married hap.[2] Heap not your harms where help there is none, but since you may not that you would, wish that you can enjoy with com-

1. *Source:* BL, MS Harley 6986, art. 36, fol. 59; secretarial copy, with postscript by Lady Drury in her own hand. Since the queen's letter and its answer constitute a single docu-ment, they are so printed here, contrary to our usual pattern of supplying answers to Eliz-abeth as additional documents.

2. **married hap** what has befallen your marriage (that is, your husband's death).

fort a king for his power and a queen for her love, who leaves not now to protect you when your case requires care; and minds not to omit whatever may be best for you and yours.

Your most loving, careful sovereign, *E. R.*

[Lady Drury's reply]

Most royal and my most dear sovereign,

Your sweet lines of comfort received by your poorest, humblest, and most distressed servant did eftsoons reclaim herself from her former conceived thoughts of being the person whom all sorrows had taken lodging in, and all comforts had taken wings to fly away from her, and began to despise to be overgoverned by such despairing thoughts, and fed myself with the sight of the fruit of God's great mercy, showed to me in stirring up such a princess to regard me with pity. What can I say to my sweet Savior for this His second redemption, which was of my body from the intolerable burthen of grief, but as I said, for the greatest and the first, which was the redemption of my soul from hellfire: that His mercy showed was unmeasurable and His power infinite. To which mercy unmeasurable and which power infinite I present my heart at your majesty's feet to pour forth my continual prayers with all mine,[3] that you may be continued a monarch of happiness above all other princes in this world and after be possessed of the unspeakable and endless bliss of the world to come.

Your majesty's most humble subject and poor
bondwoman, *E. D.*

[Postscript in Lady Drury's hand] I have sent you this because of my promise—to assure you, as I said, to keep my word I hold it religion. The other promise I made you is as a law inviolable in my heart, yet will I keep the show of a sword, although in secret it be a wooden weapon. With this name I will make good my wound, *E. Drury.*

---

3. **with all mine** the prayers of all those close to her.

82 ❧ ELIZABETH TO HENRY IV OF FRANCE, CIRCA 1590[1]

[Addressed] To my dearest good brother and cousin the most Christian king

If by chance in a vision Monsieur de Beauvoir[2] astonishes you, my dearest brother, do not be displeased that the desire he has to live and die at your feet has constrained him to offend you, not having the authority to do so; and he has begged me with great earnestness to interpose my credit for the absolution of this offense. He would be ashamed to reside at his ease while his dear master dwells so near his enemies. The which I find so reasonable that I have instead become desirous to use him in this respect, for I lack so faithful a servant, and indeed you yourself do, to whom I wish the number redoubled of such as he is to you, both for fidelity, experience, and valor. However, I assure myself so much of your goodness that you will not deny me so honorable a request, and also because, for my part, I have charged him with a task without which he would not have had his leave.

It is for you to reflect, with a reminder from me, how much you will show yourself in greater need of a bridle than a spur. For the honor of God, consider how much it matters to the whole cause—the preservation of your person! You will pardon me for telling you that what is called valor in another, in you is imputed to temerity and feebleness of such judgment as should be greatest in a great prince. If at this very hour, proof were to be made of your courage, I would rather wish you a thousand dangers than such a doubt. For as to my son, if I had had one, I would rather have seen him dead than a coward. But with too much experience in having made exemplary assurance of your invincible magnanimity, I conjure you by everything that you love most that you esteem yourself not as a private soldier but as a great prince.

It may be that you will disdain this advice as coming from the fearful heart of a woman, but when you remember how many times I have not showed my breast too much afraid of pistols and swords that were prepared against me, this thought will pass, being a fault of which I do not

1. *Source:* Folger Library, MS V.b.131; in Elizabeth's hand, with remnants of seal still attached. (For original-spelling version, see *ACFLO,* part 1.) Dating of the letter is conjectural, based on apparent references to the English expedition of 1589 (see Letter 80, p. 360).

2. **Monsieur de Beauvoir** Beauvoir la Nocle, Henry's emissary, had persuaded Elizabeth to aid the Huguenots with four thousand troops, powder, munitions, and a loan of £20,000 in September 1589; hence the expedition of Lord Willoughby and his men.

acknowledge myself guilty. Attribute it, however, to my singular affection towards you, and believe that you cannot receive harm from it which I have no share of. This writing cannot pass from my hands without imparting to you the great diligence and extreme care of this gentleman, who does not cease to plead your causes like a most faithful servant. May God send you more men like him, praying Him also to give you good instruction and to grant you the grace always to take the best path in all your enterprises, and to preserve you as the darling of His eye.

> Your very assured, faithful, good sister
> and cousin, *Elizabeth R*

[Postscript] For the honor of God, assemble those outlying inhabitants together. What use is it for Paris and the king to perish? O how angry I am, as this gentleman will tell you for my [part].[3]

83 ⪧ ELIZABETH TO JAMES, JULY 6, 1590[1]

[Addressed] To my dear brother the king of Scotland

Greater promises, more affection, and grants of more acknowledgings of received good turns, my dear brother, none can better remember than this gentleman[2] by your charge hath made me understand, whereby I think all my endeavors well recompensed that see them so well acknowledged, and do trust that my counsels, if they so much content you, will serve for memorials to turn your actions to serve the turn of your safe government and make the lookers-on honor your worth and reverence such a ruler. And lest fair semblance, that easily may beguile, do not breed your ignorance of such persons as either pretend religion or dissemble devotion, let me warn you that there is risen both in your realm and mine a sect of perilous consequence—such as would have no kings but a presbytery,[3] and take our place while they enjoy our privi-

---

3. **part** word supplied conjecturally; it is very faded in the MS.

1. *Source:* BL, MS Additional 23240, art. 28, fol. 94; in Elizabeth's hand, with seals and ribbon attached. (For original-spelling version, see *ACFLO,* part 1.)

2. **gentleman** James's emissary to Elizabeth, Sir John Carmichael.

3. **sect . . . presbytery** Scotch Presbyterians, who refused to accept the monarch's headship of the Kirk, were a constant thorn in James's side during this period.

lege with a shade of God's Word, which none is judged to follow right without by their censure they be so deemed. Yea, look we well unto them. When they have made in our people's hearts a doubt of our religion and that we err if they say so, what perilous issue this may make I rather think than mind to write. *Sapienti pauca.*[4] I pray you stop the mouths or make shorter the tongues of such ministers as dare presume to make orison in their pulpits for the persecuted in England for the Gospel.

Suppose you, my dear brother, that I can tolerate such scandals of my sincere government? No. I hope, howsoever you be pleased to bear with their audacity towards yourself, yet you will not suffer a strange king[5] receive that indignity at such caterpillars' hand that instead of fruit I am afraid will stuff your realm with venom. Of this I have particularized more to this bearer, together with other answers to his charge, beseeching you to hear them and not to give more harbor room to vagabond traitors and seditious inventors but to return them to me or banish them your land. And thus with my many thanks for your honorable entertainments of my late embassade,[6] I commit you to God, who ever preserve you from all evil counsel and send you grace to follow the best.

Your most assured, loving sister
and cousin, *Elizabeth R*

84 ❧ ELIZABETH TO JAMES, JANUARY 1593[1]

[Addressed] For our dear brother the king of Scotland

[Endorsed] Delivered by Mr. Bowes, Ambassador, 21 January, 1593

My most dear brother,

Wonders and marvels do so assail my conceits as that the long expecting of your needful answer to matters of such weight as my late letters carried needs not seem strange, though I know they ought be more

---

4. "To a wise man, few words." (Cf. "A word to the wise is sufficient.")

5. **strange king** Elizabeth herself, who was **strange** (a foreigner) to the Scots.

6. Earlier in 1590, the earl of Worcester had been dispatched to Scotland to invest James with the Order of the Garter.

1. *Source:* BL, MS Additional 23240, art. 32, fols. 108r–109r; in Elizabeth's hand. (For original-spelling version, see *ACFLO*, part 1.)

regarded and speedily performed. Yet such I see the imminent danger and well-nigh ready approach of your state's ruin, your lives' peril, and neighbors' wrong,[2] as I may not (to keep you company) neglect what I should, though you forget that you ought. I am sorry I am driven from warning to heed, and from too much trust to seek a true way how your deeds, not your words, may make me assurance that you be no way guilty of your own decay and other danger. Receive therefore in short what course I mind to hold, and how you may make bold of my unfained love and ever-constant regard.

You know, my dear brother, that since you first breathed I regarded always to conserve it as mine own it had been you bare.[3] Yea, I withstood the hands and helps of a mighty king to make you safe, even gained by the blood of many my dear subjects' lives. I made myself the bulwark betwixt you and your harms when many a wile was invented to steal you from your land and making other possess your soil. When your best holds were in my hands, did I retain them? Nay, I both conserved them and rendered them to you. Could I endure (though to my great expense) that foreigners should have footing in your kingdom, albeit there was then some lawful semblance to make other suppose (that cared not as I did) that there was no danger meant? No, I never left till all the French that kept their life parted from your soil, and so it pleased the Highest to bless me in that action as you have ever since reigned void of other nation than your own.

Now to preserve this you have overslipped so many sundry and dangerous attempts in neither uniting with them when you knew them, nor cutting them off when you had them, that if you haste no better now than heretofore, it will be too late to help when none shall avail you. Let me remember you how well I was thanked or he rewarded that once brought all the letters of all those wicked conspirators of the Spanish faction—even the selfsame that yet still you have to your eminent

2. **wrong** reference to the recently discovered plot of the "Spanish blanks," a Catholic plan initiated by Scottish Jesuits to land thirty thousand Spanish troops from the Netherlands, of whom four thousand were to establish Catholic control in Scotland while the rest proceeded south against England. Several of James's Catholic earls had signed blank letters (apparently giving carte blanche to the Spaniards), and those "blanks" had been found in the possession of a captured messenger.

3. **as mine own it had been you bare** as if you bore my own breath; or, alternatively, as if I had borne you.

peril conserved in their estates.[4] Was I not so much doubted as it was thought an Italian invention to make you hold me dearer, and contrived of malice, not done by cause? And in that respect the poor man that knew no other of his taking but as if thieves had assailed him, he most cruelly suffered so guiltless a martyrdom as his tormentors doubted his life, so sore had he the boots[5] when they were evil worthy life that bade it. See what good encouragement I received for many watchful cares for your best safety! Well did this so discomfort my goodwill as, for all this, did I not ever serve for your true espial, even when you left your land and yours ready well nigh to receive such foreign forces as they required and were promised, which if you had pleased to know was and is too evident to be proved. But what of all this, if he who most ought did naught to assure him or to requite them?

Now of late by a fortunate good hap a lewd[6] fellow hath been apprehended with letters and instructions: I pray God he be so well handled as he may confess all his knowledge in the Spanish conspiracy and that you use not this man as slightly as you have done the ringleaders of this treason. I vow if you do not rake it to the bottom you will verify what many a wise man hath (viewing your proceedings) judged of your guiltiness of your own wrack, with a whining that they will you no harm in enabling you with so rich a protector that will prove in the end a destroyer. I have beheld of late a strange, dishonorable, and dangerous pardon, which, if it be true, you have not only neglected yourself but wronged me, that have too much procured your good to be so evil guerdoned with such a wrong as to have a free forgiveness of aught conspired against my person and estate. Suppose you, my dear brother, that these be not rather ensigns of an enemy than the tact of a friend?

I require therefore to all this a resolute answer, which I challenge of right, that may be deeds both by speedy apprehension with heedy regard and not in sort as public rumor may precede present action, but

---

4. Reference is to Catholic highland earls like Huntly, Crawford, Angus, and Errol, whom James continued to tolerate despite their rebelliousness because they served as a check upon the equally ungovernable Protestant border earl, Bothwell (identified in Letter 85 n. 6, p. 369).

5. **the boots** an instrument of torture shaped like a boot that encased the victim's leg, lacerating the flesh and sometimes crushing the bone. The identity of the tortured man is uncertain.

6. **lewd** low; a reference to George Ker, the captured messenger in the affair of the "Spanish blanks."

rather that they be entrapped or they do look therefor; for I may make doom[7] you would not have taken, and what will follow then, you shall see when least you look. Think me, I pray you, not ignorant what becometh a king to do, and that will I never omit, praying you to trust Bowes[8] in the rest as myself. I am ashamed that so disordered courses makes my pen exceed a letter, and so drives me to molest your eyes with my too long scribbling, and therefore end with my earnest prayers to God that He will inspire you to do in best time all for your best.

Your loving, affectionate sister, *Elizabeth R*

85 ⪺ ELIZABETH TO JAMES, MARCH 1593[1]

[Addressed] To our dear brother the king of Scots

[Endorsed] Delivered by the Lord Borto . . . gh,[2] 16 March, 1592[3]

My dear brother,

The care of your estate with fear of your neglect so afflicts my mind as I may not overslip the sending you a nobleman to serve you for a memorial of my readiness and desire of your speed. The sliding dame,[3] who when she is turned leaves no afterstep to witness her arrival save repentance that beareth too sour a record of her short abode, may make you so far awake that you have never cause through too long discoursing to lose the better knowledge of hideousest treason. One hour breeds a day's gain to guileful spirits, and guilty conscience skills more to shift than ten wiser heads knows how to win. Let the anvil be stricken while it is warm, for if it grow cold the goldsmith mars his work, and the owner his jewel.

It vexeth me to see that those of whom the very fields of Scotland could (if they might speak truly) tell how their banners were displayed

7. **doom** judgment.

8. **Bowes** Sir Robert Bowes, Elizabeth's emissary charged with delivery of the letter.

1. *Source:* Folger Library, MS X.d.397; in Elizabeth's hand with address cut away and supplied in a later hand. (For original-spelling version, see *ACFLO,* part 1.) The second half of this letter is reproduced in facsimile in Jean F. Preston and Laetitia Yeandle, *English Handwriting 1400–1650* (Binghamton, N.Y.: MRTS, 1992), p. 65.

2. The name of Elizabeth's emissary is only partially legible because the ink has faded.

3. **dame** probably Opportunity, whose head was depicted as bald in back so that none could grasp her once she had passed.

again[4] your person, who divers nights did sentinel their acts. Those self-same be but now bid to a ward[5] who long ago, God wot, ought so have smarted as you need not now examine their treachery. All this I say not for my gaping for any man's blood, God is witness, but wish you saved wherever the rest go. And this I must tell you: that if the lands of them that do deserve no breath were made but yours (as their own acts have caused), you should be a richer prince, and then abler of your own to defend a king's honor and your own life.

Methinks I frame this letter like to a lamentation, which you will pardon when the matter bids it so. I cannot but bewail that any lewd, unadvised, headsick fellow,[6] a subject of mine, should make his sovereign be supposed of less government than mistress of her word. I have never yet dishonored my tongue with a leasing[7]—not to a meaner person than a king, and would be ashamed to deserve so foul an infamy. I vow I never knew, but did forbid, that ever he should enter my territory that so boldly attainted your doors. You know best what I writ for that, and he (as I hear) hath heard it so much as hardly he will trust my hands to be his safe refuge. Yet you know best what was offered and why he was not made more desperate. If your long-expected and never-had-as-yet answer had not lingered, I think he would have gone far enough or[8] now. Let this suffice: be your doings as sound as my profession staunch, and I warrant no Spaniard nor their king shall have ever footing so near to you or me. Trust, I pray you, never a conqueror with trust of his kindness, nor never reign *precario more* when you may rule *regis regula*.[9] Now do I remember your cumber[10] to read such scribbled lines, and pray the Almighty to cover you safely under His blessed wings.

Your most loving sister, *Elizabeth R*

---

4. **again** against.   5. **bid to a ward** sent to a prison.

6. **fellow** probably Francis Stewart Hepburn (d. 1624), fifth earl of Bothwell and nephew of the Bothwell who had married Mary, Queen of Scots. During the 1590s, this rebel leader of the ultra-Protestant faction in Scotland made a series of increasingly humiliating raids against James. At Christmas 1591 he had broken into James's Edinburgh palace, Holyrood House, and come close to seizing the king. In June 1592 he staged a siege against James that lasted seven hours before help arrived. When Bothwell needed to elude Scottish forces defending James, he slipped across the border into England.

7. **leasing** falsehood.   8. **or** ere.

9. *precario more* "by way of entreaty"; *regis regula* "in the manner of a king."

10. **cumber** difficulty.

86 ᵱ⊷ QUEEN ELIZABETH TO WILLIAM CECIL, LORD BURGHLEY,
APRIL 22, 1593[1]

*[Addressed] To our right trusty and right well-beloved councillor the Lord
Burghley, our high treasurer of England.*

*[Endorsed] 22 April, 1593. Her majesty's letter of dispensation for my lord's
absence from Saint George's Feast, signed by the queen.*

Elizabeth R   By the queen.
Right trusty and right well-beloved councillor, we greet you well. Forasmuch as by reason of the indisposition of your person, you cannot conveniently be present with us upon this even or vigil,[2] and tomorrow, being
the Day of Saint George, to solemnize that feast of our most noble Order
of the Garter, we let you understand that we are pleased to accept your reasonable excuse in this behalf, and by these presents do pardon you for
your absence from the said feast at this time, any statute of our said order
to the contrary notwithstanding. Given under our signet at our palace of
Westminster the 22th of April, 1593, in the thirty-fifth year of our reign.

87 ᵱ⊷ ELIZABETH TO HENRY IV OF FRANCE, JULY 1593[1]

Ah what griefs, O what regrets, O what groanings felt I in my soul at the
sound of such news as Morlains[2] has told me! My God, is it possible that

1. *Source:* BL, MS Lansdowne 94, art. 47, fol. 112r; text in a secretary's hand with Elizabeth's sign manual and remnants of seal attached. This MS is a mock writ resembling in all
its features an actual legal document. To compound the air of officialese, the scribe added
indecipherable jottings with elaborate flourishes in the lower right corner of the sheet.

2. **vigil** the night before a feast day.

1. *Source:* Hatfield House, Cecil Papers 133/101, fol. 157r; copy. (For two versions of the
original French letter, see *ACFLO*, part 2.) According to William Camden, Henry IV's
politic conversion to Catholicism (as legend has it, with the remark "Paris is well worth a
mass") so troubled Elizabeth that "in her grief she sought comfort out of the holy Scriptures, the writings of the holy Fathers, and frequent conferences with the archbishop, and
whether out of the philosophers also I know not. Sure I am that at this time she daily
turned over Boethius his books *De Consolatio* [*The Consolation of Philosophy*] and translated them handsomely into the English tongue" (*History of ... Princess Elizabeth ... Composed by Way of Annals*, trans. Thomas Norton [London: for Benjamin Fisher, 1630] [*STC*
4500], bk. 4, p. 51).

2. **Morlains** Jean de Morlans or Morlaix, the emissary charged by the French king to
convey the news of his conversion to the English court (in July) and to the States-General
of the Netherlands (in November).

any worldly respect should efface the terror with which the fear of God threatens us? Can we with any reason expect a good sequel from an act so iniquitous? He who has preserved you many years by His hand—can you imagine that He would permit you to walk alone in your greatest need? Ah, it is dangerous to do evil to make good out of it; I still hope that a sounder inspiration will come to you. However, I will not cease to place you in the forefront of my devotions, that the hands of Esau may not spoil the blessing of Jacob.[3] And where you promise me all friendship and fidelity, I confess I have dearly merited it, and I will not repent it, provided you do not change your Father. Otherwise I will be only a bastard sister, at least not your sister by the Father. For I will always prefer the natural to the adopted, as God best knows. May He guide you in the right path of the best way.

> Your most assured sister, if it be after the old
> fashion; with the new I have nothing to do.

88 ॐ QUEEN ELIZABETH TO HENRY HASTINGS, EARL OF HUNTINGDON, APRIL 8, 1594[1]

[Addressed] To our right trusty and well-beloved cousin the earl of Huntingdon, lord president of our Council established in the north parts

Elizabeth R

Right trusty and well-beloved cousin, we greet you well. Although we doubt not but you have understood from divers of our Council in what good part we have taken your exceeding care and pain in divers things greatly importing our service (even according to your old custom, whereof we have had good trial); yet can we not forbear at this time to

---

3. See Genesis 27. In Protestant circles, the story of Esau's lost birthright was frequently applied to Reformation history, in which the younger brother (Jacob, identified with Protestantism) takes away the birthright of the elder (Esau and Catholicism). With Henry's conversion and other setbacks to the international Protestant cause, the gains of the younger brother, Elizabeth suggests, are in danger of being recaptured by the elder.

1. *Source:* Huntington Library, MS HA 2540; in a secretarial hand with seal and with Elizabeth's sign manual. Reproduced by permission of The Huntington Library, San Marino, California. Henry Hastings (1535–1595), third earl of Huntingdon, served as lord president of the Council of the North; he was charged with furthering policies of the central government and generally keeping order.

let you know it by our own hand—the rather for that these new occasions of disorders in Scotland[2] and on our borders have crossed our purpose to have had you come up in regard of your health, whereof we have great care and consideration. It was strange unto you to hear of your new guest[3]—but to us more than most strange, as a matter incredible, but that we found you so seriously to assure it. For as that presumption in any such person should have been contrary to our liking, so in him (of all others) it was beyond our expectation, having sent so many cautions in that behalf.

But now that things are as they be (whereof the issues are yet uncertain) and that the looseness of those northern parts is fit to be guided by wise and sound directions, though we know your own vigilance and watchful care is such as you would be loath to be absent in this tickle time, yet do we require you there (even seriously from ourself) to have care of your health and state of body, in such sort as you may neither prove wearisome to yourself (which is the fruit of sickness) or be less able to continue so serviceable unto us as we have ever found you, and for such a one both do and will esteem you. And when we may understand that the troubles are anything overpassed, we shall be glad to license you to repair hither for your health before the year be too far spent. Given under our privy signet at our manor of Greenwich the eighth of April, 1594.

89 ⅊ ELIZABETH TO JAMES, DECEMBER 22, 1593[1]

[Endorsed] 22 December 1593. Copy of her majesty's letter to the king of Scots, of her own hand. By the Lord Zouche.

My dear brother,

To see so much, I rue my sight that views the evident spectacle of a seduced king, abusing Council, and wry-guided kingdom. My love to your good and hate of your ruin breeds my heedful regard of your

2. **disorders in Scotland** continuing struggles for dominance among the Catholic highland lords on the one hand, and Bothwell and the Presbyterians on the other.

3. **guest** presumably the earl of Bothwell, who had crossed over into England to rally support for his revolt against James (see Letter 85, pp. 368–69).

1. *Source:* PRO, State Papers Scotland 52/51/75; copy. Edward la Zouch (1556?–1625), Baron Zouche of Harringsworth, was Elizabeth's latest emissary to James and received au-

surest safety. If I neglected you, I could wink at your worst and yet with-stand my enemies' drifts. But be you persuaded by beguilers, I will ad-vise you void of all guile, and will not stick to tell you that if you tread the path you go in, I will pray for you but leave you to your harms.

I doubt whether shame or sorrow have had the upper hand when I read your last lines to me. Who of judgment that deemed me not simple could suppose that any answers you have writ me should satisfy, nay, enter into the opinion of one not void of four senses, leaving out the fifth? Those of whom you have had so evident proof by their actual re-bellion in the field you present,[2] whose offers you knew then so large to foreign princes—and now at last when, plainest of all, was taken about the carrier[3] himself, confessing all afore many commissioners and divers councillors—because you slacked the time till he was escaped and now must seem deny it (though all men knew it); therefore, for-sooth, no jury can be found for them. May this blind me that knows what a king's office were to do? Abuse not yourself so far. Indeed, when a weak bowing and a slack seat in government shall appear, then bold spirits will stir the stern, and guide the ship to greatest wrack, and will take heart to supply the failure. Assure yourself—no greater peril can ever befall you, nor any king else, than to take for payment evil ac-counts; for they deride such and make their prey of their neglect. There is no prince alive but, if he show fear or yielding, but he shall have tutors enough, though he be out of minority.

And when I remember what sore punishment those so lewd traitors shall have, then I read again, lest at first I mistook your mind. But when the re-viewing granted my lecture[4] true, Lord, what wonder grew in me that you should correct them with benefits who deserve much severer correction! Could you please them more than save their lives and make them shun the place they hate, where they are sure that their just-deserved haters dwell, and yet enjoy as much their honors and liveli-

---

dience on January 15, 1594, which is presumably when the original letter was delivered. We have moved this letter slightly out of sequence (since it is dated earlier than Letter 88) in order to preserve intact the sequence of the queen's correspondence with James between December 1593 and July 1594 (Letters 89–91, pp. 372–84).

2. **present** possibly miscopied for "preserve"; Elizabeth complains of James's leniency toward the earls of Huntly, Errol, and Angus, who were known to be in league with Spain and were implicated in the affair of the "Spanish blanks" (see Letter 84, p. 366).

3. **carrier** George Ker, the messenger in the affair of the "Spanish blanks."

4. **lecture** reading.

hoods as if for sporting travel they were licensed to visit other countries? Call you this a banishment[5]—to be rid from whom they fear and go to such they love? Now, when my eyes read more, then smiled I to see how childish, foolish, and witless an excuse the best of either three made you, turning their treasons' bills to artificers' reckonings with items for many expenses, and lacked but one billet which they best deserved—an item for so much for the cord whose office they best merited. Is it possible that you can swallow the taste of so bitter a drug, more meet to purge you of them than worthy for your kingly acceptance? I never heard a more deriding scorn, and vow that, if but this alone, were I you, they should learn a short lesson.

The best that I commend in your letter is that I see your judgment too good to affirm a troth of their speech, but that alone they so say. Howbeit, I muse how you can want a law to such as whose denial, if it were ever, could serve to save their lives whose treasons are so plain as the messenger who would for his own sake not devise it, if for troth's cause he had it not in his charge. For who should ever be tried false if his own denial might save his life? In princes' causes many circumstances yield a sufficient plea for such a king as will have it known; and ministers they shall lack none that will not themselves gainsay it. Leave off such cloaks, therefore, I pray you—they will be found too thin to save you from wetting. For your own sake play the king, and let your subjects see you respect yourself, and neither to hide or to suffer danger and dishonor. And that you may know my opinion, judgment, and advice, I have chosen this nobleman, whom I know wise, religious, and honest, to whom I pray you give full credit, as if myself were with you; and bear with all my plainness, whose affection, if it were not more worth than so oft not followed, I would not have gone so far. But blame my love if it exceed any limits. Beseeching God to bless you from the advices of them that more prize themselves than care for you, to whom I wish many years of reign.

Your most assured, loving sister and cousin,
Elizabeth

---

5. **banishment** James had offered the implicated Catholic earls a choice between converting to Protestantism or forfeiting their estates and honors and going into exile.

LETTER 89, ADDITIONAL DOCUMENT A JAMES TO ELIZABETH,
APRIL 13, 1594[1]

So many unexpected wonders, madame and dearest sister, have of late
so overshadowed my eyes and mind and dazzled so all my senses as in
truth I neither know what I should say nor where at first to begin. But
thinking it best to take a pattern of yourself since I deal with you, I
must, repeating the first words of your last letter, only the sex changed,
say "I rue my sight that views the evident spectacle of a seduced queen."
For when I enter betwixt two extremities in judging of you I had far
rathest[2] interpret it to the least dishonor on your part—which is ignorant error. Appardon me, madame, for so long-approved friendship requires a round plainness.

For when first I consider what strange effects have late appeared in
your country—how my avowed traitor hath not only been openly reset[3]
in your realm, but plainly made his residence in your proper houses,
ever plainliest kitheth[4] himself where greatest confluence of people was,
and which is most of all, how he hath received English money in a reasonable quantity, waged[5] both English and Scottish men therewith,
proclaimed his pay at divers parish churches in England, convened his
forces within England in the sight of all that border, and therefrom contemptuously comed[6] and camped within a mile of my principal city and
present abode, all his trumpeters and divers waged men being English,
and being by myself in person repulsed from that place, returned back
in England with displayed banners, and since that time with sound of
trumpet making his troops to muster within English ground—when
first, I say, I consider these strange effects and then again I call to mind
upon the one part what number of solemn promises not only by your
ambassadors but by many letters of your own hand ye have both made
and reiterate unto me that he should have no harbor within your country—yea, rather stirring me further up against him than seeming to
pity him yourself; and upon the other part weighing my deserts, you
know for being a friend to you I have ever been an enemy to all your en-

---

1. *Source:* Bruce, 100–102, who cites as his source a "Copy in Thompson MS, p. 27." In his
much-delayed reply, James parodies the wording of Elizabeth's previous letter and also her
practice of beginning missives to him in a highly indignant, exclamatory mode.

2. **far rathest** very much rather.

3. **reset** received.   4. **kitheth** makes known.

5. **waged** paid wages to.   6. **comed** came.

emies, and the only point I can be challenged in, that I take not such form of order and at such time with some particular men of my subjects as peradventure ye could do if ye were in my room; when thus I enter in consideration with myself I cannot surely satisfy myself with wondering enough upon these above-mentioned effects.

For to affirm that these things are by your direction or privity, it is so far against all princely honor as I protest I abhor the least thought thereof. And again that so wise and provident a prince, having so long and happily governed, should be so sullied and contemned by a great number of her own subjects, it is hardly to be believed, if I knew it not to be a maxim in the state of princes that we see and hear all with the eyes and ears of others, and if these be deceivers we cannot shun deceit. Now, madame, I have refuge to you at this time, as my only pilot to guide me safely betwixt their Charybdis and Scylla.[7] Solve their doubts and let it be seen ye will not be abused by your own subjects who prefers the satisfying of their base-minded affections to your princely honor.

That I wrote not the answer of your last letters with your late ambassador and that I returned not a letter with him, blame only, I pray you, his own behavior, who although it pleased you to term him wise, religious, and honest, had been fitter in my opinion to carry the message a herald[8] than any friendly commission betwixt two neighbor princes. For as no reason could satisfy him, so scarcely could he have patience ever to hear it offered. But if ye gave him a large commission I dare answer for it: he took it als[9] well upon him and therefore have I rather choosed to send you my answer by my own messengers.[10] Suffer me not, I pray you, to be abused with your abusers nor grant no oversight to oversee your own honor. Remember what ye promised by your letter of thanks for the delivery of O'Rourke.[11] I trust ye will not put me in

---

7. twinned hazards from the *Odyssey;* see Letter 43 n. 3, p. 233.

8. **message [of] a herald** that is, to proclaim like a herald rather than come for peaceful negotiation; evidently Zouche offended James with the warmth of his objection to the treatment of the highland lords.

9. **als** as.

10. **messengers** identified by Bruce as Colvill, laird of Wemyss, and Edward Bruce, the titular abbot of Kinloss.

11. Sir Brian O'Rourke, an Irish rebel chieftain who had taken refuge in Scotland. Among many other offenses while in Ireland, he had displayed an effigy of Queen Elizabeth upon which he showered verbal abuse; his followers hacked the image with axes and had horses drag it with a halter around its neck through the dirt. James had delivered O'Rourke over to the English, and he had been executed for treason in 1591.

balance with such a traitorous counterpoise, nor wilfully reject me, constraining me to say with Virgil, *Flectere si nequeo superos, Acheronta movebo.*[12] And to give you a proof of the continuance of my honest affection, I have directed these two gentlemen unto you, whom I will heartily pray you to credit as myself in all that they have in charge to deliver unto you; and because the principal of them goes to France, to return the other back with a good answer with all convenient speed. And thus assuring you that friendship shall never fail upon my part, I commit you, madame and dearest sister, to the holy protection of the Almighty. From Edinburgh the 13 of April, 1594.

> Your most loving and affectionate brother and
> cousin, *James R.*

90 ⮞ ELIZABETH TO JAMES, MAY 1594[1]

[Addressed] To our good brother the king of Scots

[Endorsed] 18 May 1594.

Though by the effects I seld[2] see, my good brother, that ever my advices be followed, yet you have witsafed[3] to give them the reading, I well understand, having made some of them the theme of your last, though God knows applied far awry[4] from their true sense or right desert. For if I sin in abuse, I claim you the author of my deceit, in believing[5] more good than sequel hath told me. For I have great wrong if you suppose that any persuasion from whomsoever can make me have one evil opinion of your actions if themselves be not the cause. I confess[6] that divers be the affections of many men, some to one,[7] some to another,

---

12. "If I am unable to sway the gods above, I will stir up Acheron [a river of the underworld]" (*Aeneid* VII.312; wrathful Juno vows redoubled effort to hinder Aeneas).

1. *Source:* BL, MS Additional 23240, fol. 132; in Elizabeth's hand. This is the letter that was sent; atypically, a draft of this letter also exists in Elizabeth's hand (Hatfield House, Cecil Papers 133/80, fol. 120). (For original-spelling versions of both, see *ACFLO*, part 1.) The most significant variants between the two versions are recorded in the notes.

2. **seld** seldom.   3. **witsafed** vouchsafed.

4. **far awry** Hatfield reads "far away."

5. **believing** Hatfield reads "having believed."

6. **confess** Hatfield reads "admit."   7. **one** Hatfield reads "one part."

but my rule of trust shall never fail me when it is grounded not on the sands of every[8] man's humor, but on the steady rock of approved[9] fact. I should condemn my wicked disposition to found any amity[10] promised upon so tickle ground that others' hate might break the bounds[11] of my love, and upon others' judgments to build my confidence.

For Bothwell's bold and[12] unruly entrance into my borders,[13] I am so far from guilt of such a fault as I protest if I had received an answer in seventeen weeks' space of my letter that contained his offer to reveal unto you the treason of the lords[14] with foreigners,[15] I could soon have banished him from thence. And next he came with your own hand to warrant that no offense was imputed,[16] which made the borderers readier to receive him. But after I had not left unpunished some of his receipters[17] I could not have believed they durst have procured[18] the pain due for such desert, and mind to make them afraid to venture[19] such a crime again. And if order given now to all the wardens do not suffice, I vow their bodies and purses shall well suffer[20] therefor. I will not trouble you with recital of what this gentleman hath heard in all the other points, but this toucheth me so near as I must answer that my deserts to you have been so sincere as shall never need a threat of hell to her that hath ever procured your bliss.[21] And that you may know I am that prince that never can endure a menace at my enemy's hand, much less

8. **sands of every** Hatfield reads "slippery sands of each."

9. **approved** Hatfield reads "undenied."

10. **any amity** Hatfield reads "my friendship."

11. **that others' hate might break the bounds** Hatfield reads "that the rage of others' hate might break the bands."

12. **bold and** omitted in Hatfield.

13. Bothwell had rallied support on the English borders, marched upon Edinburgh at the head of several hundred men, been successfully held off by King James, dispersed his men, and retired back beyond the English border, all of which caused James to suspect Elizabeth's collusion.

14. **lords** the Catholic northern lords, who were conspiring with Spain.

15. **if … foreigners** Hatfield version of this clause is "if in seventeen weeks I had received your answer to my letter that contained his offer to utter to you all the treasons that the northern lords had with foreigners."

16. **that no offense was imputed** Hatfield reads "your favor toward him."

17. **receipters** harborers of criminals (in this instance, Bothwell).

18. **have procured** Hatfield reads "adventure."

19. **venture** Hatfield reads "commit."

20. **suffer** Hatfield reads "pay."

21. Cf. James's quotation of Virgil in the letter to which this responds, Letter 89, Additional Document A, p. 377.

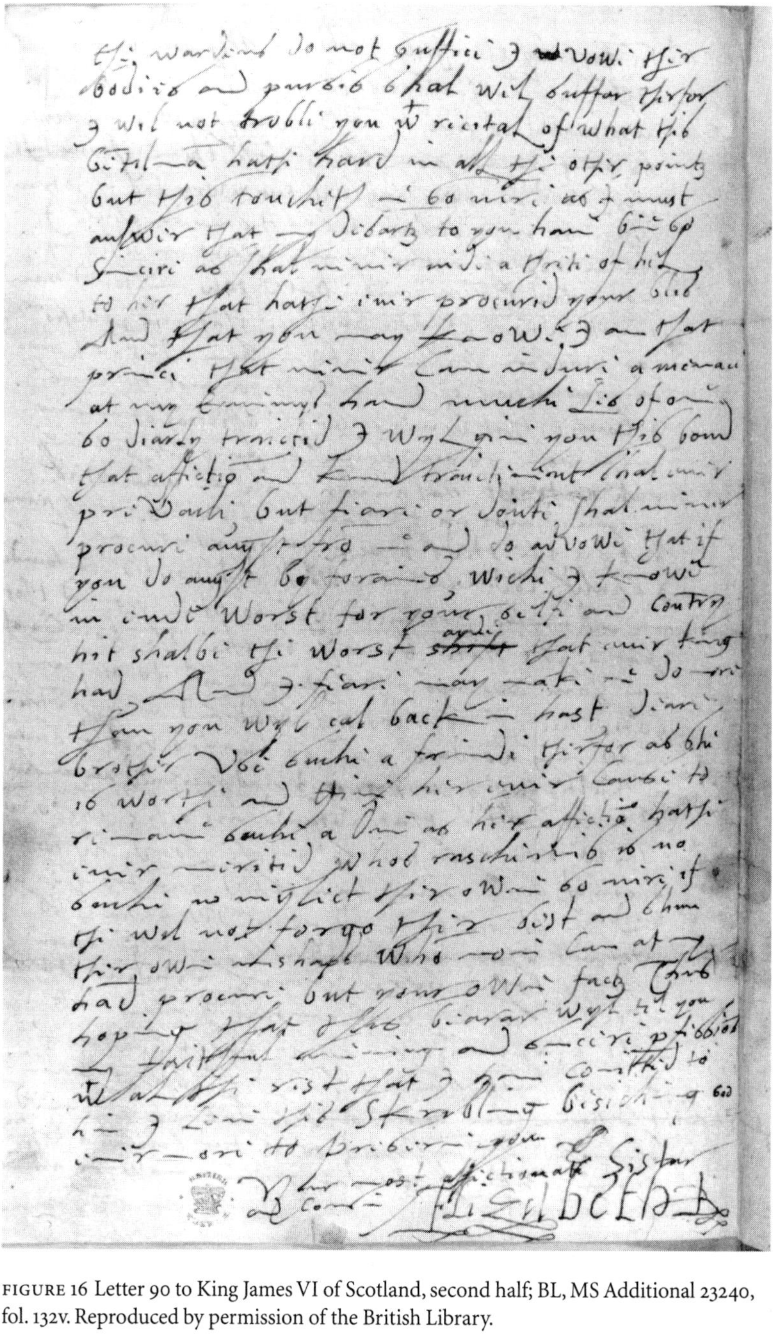

FIGURE 16 Letter 90 to King James VI of Scotland, second half; BL, MS Additional 23240, fol. 132v. Reproduced by permission of the British Library.

of one so dearly treated, I will give you this bond: that affection and kind treatment shall ever prevail, but fear or doubt shall never procure aught from me; and do avow that if you do aught by foreigners,[22] which I know in end worst for yourself and country, it shall be the worst aid that ever king had, and I fear may[23] make me do more than you will call back in haste.[24]

Dear brother, use such a friend, therefore, as she is worth, and give her ever cause to remain such a one as her affection hath ever merited.[25] Whose rashness is no such as neglect their own so near, if they will not forgo their best and shun their own mishaps (whom none can at my hand procure but your own facts). Thus hoping that this bearer will tell you my faithful meaning and sincere professions, with all the rest that I have committed to him, I leave this scribbling, beseeching God evermore to preserve you.

Your most affectionate sister
and cousin, *Elizabeth R*

LETTER 90, ADDITIONAL DOCUMENT A JAMES TO ELIZABETH, JUNE 5, 1594[1]

Because I perceive by your last letter and the report of my ambassador, madame and dearest sister, that ye have far mistaken the meaning of my last letter, I am forced to let this present serve for a short apology thereof, for in two principal points I perceive ye have mistaken me. And first, whereas ye interpret my imitation of your words in the beginning of my letter to mean that ye are seduced by trusting false reports made of me, if ye please to consider the following discourse of my letter, ye will find I meaned[2] by some of your own subjects, who in resetting[3] and assisting my avowed traitor in divers parts of your kingdom without

22. **foreigners** Hatfield reads "foreigners to help" and omits the following phrase.

23. **and I fear may** Hatfield reads "and shall."

24. **will call back in haste** Hatfield reads "shall ever undo."

25. **Dear ... merited** this is the letter's final sentence in Hatfield, which reads "Use such a friend, therefore, as she is worth, and give her ever cause to remain such one as her loving affection hath ever merited: so shall you work your own best and shun your own mishaps, whom none can at my hand procure, but your own acts."

1. *Source:* Bruce, 105–108, citing as his source a "Copy in Thompson MS, p. 30."

2. **meaned** meant.   3. **resetting** receiving.

your allowance or privity, seduced you in abusing your princely honor and will—which appears to be but over-true, since by your own letter ye grant and avows to make them to be duly punished for the same. And surely, madame, it appears your subjects do not yet weary to abuse you, since notwithstanding your late proclamations he is still reset within your own country. But in this I trust I need not to move you since the hurting of your princely honor by the contempt of your laws will, I doubt not, stir you up to take order therewith.

Now the other point of mistaking is of yon Latin verse in the hinder end of my letter, which I perceive ye interpret to be a threatening of you. But I doubt not ye will conceive far otherways of my meaning thereby if ye will pleased[4] to weigh first the meaning of the author that first wrote it, and since consider what precedes and follows in my letter that alleges it. For Virgil feigneth that Juno—being in a rage that the rest of the gods through Venus' persuasion nold[5] consent to the wrack of Aeneas, whom against she bare inveterate hatred as against all Troy—she not only pronounceth these words of my letter but immediately goes to Alecto, one of the hellish Furies, and persuades her to stir up Turnus in Italy to war against Aeneas, thereby to hinder his conquests there. Now, to make the allusion then: suppose (*Omnis comparatio claudicat uno pede*[6]) I am Juno, ye are the rest of the gods, Bothwell is Aeneas, and other foreign princes are Acheron. Juno's seeking aid of Acheron, then, was only for the wrack of Aeneas, and no ways either for the invading or threatening of the rest of the gods. On the other part, where this verse is set down in my letter, I say not that I am of mind so to do, but by the contrary I say I trust you will not constrain me so to do. And the very next words I subjoin are "and to give you a proof of my honest affection."

And thus, madame, my intention was to complain unto you, not to threaten you, thereby seeking your aid and neither seeking nor leaning to the aid of others. So in a word my prayer was to you as we all pray to God, "Lead us not into temptation." But as ever it be suppose[7] in this I interpret my intention, yet I ever bare that reverence to all virtuous ladies, but above all to you, whose blood, long and trusty friendship, and manifold virtues requires such loving and kind reverence of me as I am not so to stand in my defense. But if ye think it a fault, I will crave pardon for it, and only claim to my homely rudeness which I hope ye will

---

4. **pleased** be pleased.   5. **nold** would not.
6. "Every comparison is lame in one foot."   7. **suppose** supposed.

accept in the better part since what I wrote of you I wrote only to you. And therefore, madame, I trust never to deserve the least thought of your suspicion of any dealing of mine with your enemies, for I protest before God I never to this hour had dealing directly or indirectly with any of them, either to the prejudice of you or your state or the state of religion—and am content besides my many by-past promises, that this letter remain a pledge of my faith herein als well for times to come as by-past, aye and while (as God forbid) I discharge myself honestly unto you—which shall never be except ye constrain me unto it, but *absit omen*.[8]

I also trust that before this time your ambassador has informed you of some of my proceedings at this Parliament, to your satisfaction. As to the dispatch given to my ambassadors, whereas ye are general in time of payment and quantity of the support craved by them, yet I doubt not ye will consider my present ados,[9] having now begun and entered in action, wherein I crave an answer according to the proverb *Qui cito dat bis dat*.[10] That of one thing I will heartily pray you that what is done to me in this turn ye do it only of yourself, that my thanks may only be for you, for I desire never to be in the common[11] of any subjects in such cases. And now to end, I cannot omit to show you that the only comfort I received of your answers at the return of the one of my ambassadors was the prime conference ye had with Bruce[12] concerning me, who hath made such discourse thereof to me as in my opinion he might pass master in the art of chirurgie[13] for descriving[14] so well the anatomy of your kind and constant affection towards me. But assuring you that I shall never forget to pay it with all thankfulness on my part, I commit you, madame and dearest sister, to God's most holy protection. From my palace of Holyrood House the fifth of June, 1594.

> Your most loving and affectionate brother
> and cousin, *James R.*

8. "let the omen be absent" (equivalent to "God forbid").
9. **ados** affairs, troubles.
10. "Who gives quickly gives twice."
11. **common** common fund, stock, or purse (cf. French *commun*).
12. **Bruce** Edward Bruce, one of James's emissaries to Elizabeth.
13. **chirurgie** surgery.
14. **descriving** describing, discerning.

91 ☙ ELIZABETH TO JAMES, JUNE OR JULY 1594[1]

[Endorsed] June 1594. Minute of her majesty's letter with her own hand to the king of Scots

My good brother,

You have so well repaired the hard lines of menacing speech that I like much better the gloss than the text, and do assure you that the last far graceth you better, and fitteth best our two amities. You may make sure account that what counsel, advice, or mislike my writing can make you, receiveth ever ground of what is best for you, though my interest be least in them. And therefore having so good foundation, I hope you will make your profit of my plainness, and remember that others may have many ends in their advices, and I but you for principal of mine.

I render you many thanks for your bond of firm and constant amity, with most assurance of never entering with my foes in treaty or good-will until constraint of my behalf cause the breach. It pleaseth me well that this addition may assure me a perpetuity, for never shall my act deserve so foul an imputation. But I muse what such an Horace his "but"[2] should need to me, whose solid deeds have never merited such a halved suspicion. Put out of your breast, therefore, my sincere heart entreats you, so unfit a thought for a royal mind, and set in such place the unfeigned love that my deserts have craved, and make a great distance betwixt others not tried and mine so long approved.

It gladdeth me much that you now have falsified such bruits as forepast deeds have bred you, for tongues of men are never bridled by kings' greatness, but by their goodness; nor is it enough to say they will do well, when present acts gainsay their belief. We princes are set on highest stage, where looks of all beholders verdicts our works; neither can we easily dance in nets so thick as may dim their sight. Such, therefore, our works should be as may praise our Maker and grace ourselves. Among the which I trust you will make one whose facts shall tend to strengthen yourself, whoso you feeble, and count it best-spent time to

1. *Source:* PRO, State Papers Scotland 52/53/69, fol. 247; copy, possibly somewhat condensed since it is termed a "Minute" in the endorsement. Dated July 3 in the *Calendar of State Papers Scotland,* but June in a modern hand on the MS itself.

2. **Horace his "but"** "But if you think to retain as friends those retainers whom nature gives you without taking any effort, wretched man! You lose your pains" (Horace *Satires* I.l.88–90).

govern your own and not be tuted.[3] And since no government last where duly pain and grace be not inflicted where best they be deserved, I hope no depending humors of partial respects shall banish from you that right. And as you have, I may so justly say, almost alone, stand[4] princely to your own estate, without prizing others' lewdness that scarcely could afford a grant to a true request or an yea to well-tried crimes; so, I beseech you, comfort yourself with this laud: that so much the more shineth your clearness through the foil of dim clouds as their spot will hardly be blotted out when your glory remains. And by this dealing, you shall ever so bind me to be your faithful watch and staunch sister that nothing shall, I hope, pass my knowledge that any way may touch you but I will both warn and ward in such sort as your surety shall be respected and your state held up, as God, that best is witness, knoweth, whom ever I implore to counsel you the best and preserve your days.

Your affectionate sister and cousin, *E. R.*

[Postscript] Such remembrance of my affection as I send, take in good part as being—such my affairs as now they be—more than millions sent from a richer prince, and fraughted with fewer foes; which I doubt not but in wisdom you can consider and as, in some part, I have at length dilated to this gentleman.[5]

92 ❧ ELIZABETH TO HENRY IV OF FRANCE, CIRCA SEPTEMBER 4, 1596[1]

[Endorsed in Burghley's hand] Her majesty to the French king, September 1596

My dearest brother,

Inasmuch as I have always reckoned that voluntary good wishes, not tied by any other ligature than sincere affection, were sufficient enough for a sure foundation of long duration, so it is that, understanding the

---

3. **tuted** tutored.   4. **stand** stood.

5. **gentleman** Robert Bowes, the English ambassador to Scotland.

1. *Source:* Hatfield House, Cecil Papers 133/153, fol. 236r; copy, in French. (For original-language version, see *ACFLO*, part 2.)

very great desire you had that a league[2] be made public between us two, I have consented to it, and according to the customs between great princes have added thereto my faith and word, which, as they have never received spot, so (if it pleases God) my soul is sincere to keep them in the same manner. And inasmuch as I have advanced the old custom of kings by being the first to begin the match, so I hope that you will not hold me for impudent, being of my sex, for beginning the dance of love, not fearing that you will mock me for such haste, but rather will measure thereby that I will never be slothful to act in honoring you.

I have received by the duc de Bouillon[3] your letters, all filled with protestations of faithful love towards me, with an ardent desire to honor me with your presence, a thing that would remove all your trust in your ministers, who have abused you, I fear, by so much praise of that which, when you shall be the ocular judge, you will not find at all to answer to the half of what they make you believe, who disgrace me in thinking thus to advance my respect. But one thing they will be found never to have falsified, if they represent to you the purity of my assured friendship and the lively feeling for any honorable chance that befalls you, with a promptitude to help you as my opportunity will permit me, as I do not doubt that the sieur de Bouillon will represent to you, to whose sufficiency I commit myself, praying the Creator to preserve you in good and long life, as desires

Your very affectionate good sister.

93 &❧ ELIZABETH TO HENRY IV OF FRANCE, SEPTEMBER 13, 1596[1]

[Addressed] To my good brother the most Christian king

Monsieur, my good brother,

Having carried through for my part the final conclusion of our league with the ceremonies suitable to such an act, having anticipated

2. By this league, discussed further in the next letter, Elizabeth committed herself publicly to a triple offensive and defensive alliance with France and the Dutch United Provinces against Spain.

3. **duc de Bouillon** Henry de la Tour d'Auvergne, duke of Bouillon, a powerful Huguenot magnate and court official under Henry IV.

1. *Source:* BL, MS Additional 24023, fol. 1; in French, in Elizabeth's hand, with seals and

with my precedence the sequel which urged me to such haste, I do not doubt at all that you will deign to second this act with your faith given to this count,[2] whom I have ordered to receive it as if given to me. And by this means you will shade if not cover my error, if such I may call it, who was the first to present to you my faith, assuring you that if all pacts were as inviolate as this one will be on my side, everyone would be astonished to see such constant friendship in this century. As for you, I imagine that there will never lodge in a heart so generous a single ungrateful thought; thus I persuade myself that I will have no reason to repent of having honored, favored, and helped such a prince, who not only will think of what is fitting for him but will take care of what belongs to me, regarding justice as a true end of reciprocal affection. To whom I wish all the prosperity and victory that a great king may desire, as God knows, to whom I pray to preserve you from all enemies.

As desires your very affectionate
sister, *Elizabeth R*

94   QUEEN ELIZABETH TO ROBERT DEVEREUX, EARL OF ESSEX, JULY 1597[1]

[Headed] Queen Elizabeth to the earl of Essex

[Endorsed in Burghley's hand] Her majesty's letters.

Eyes of youth have sharp sights, but commonly not so deep as those of elder age, which makes me marvel less at rash attempts and headstrong counsels which give not leisure to judgment's warning, nor heeds advice, but makes a laughter at the one and despises with scorn the last.

---

ribbon attached. (For original-spelling version, see *ACFLO*, part 1.) Date is supplied from a copy of this letter, BL, MS Additional 48212, fol. 13.

    2. **count** Gilbert Talbot (1552–1616), seventh earl of Shrewsbury, sent by Elizabeth to get Henry's oath to observe the conditions of the league and also to invest him with the Order of the Garter.

    1. *Source:* PRO, State Papers Domestic, Elizabeth 12/264/14, fol. 19; copy. This letter was prompted by Essex's bad luck in his 1597 expedition against the Spanish fleet in Ferrol and the Azores (see also Prayer 39, p. 426). The English fleet set out July 10 but encountered violent winds that did considerable damage to the ships, although no ships were lost.

This have I not heard but seen, and thereof can witness bear. Yet I cannot be so lewd[2] of nature to suppose that the scope was not good, howso the race was run, and do more condemn the granters than the offerer. For when I see the admirable work of the eastern wind so long to last beyond the custom of nature, I see as in a crystal[3] the right figure of my folly, that ventured supernatural haps upon the point of frenetical imputation. But it pleaseth His goodness to strengthen our weakness, and warns us to use wit when we have it hereafter. Foreseen haps breeds no wonder; no more doth your short-returned post before his time.

But for answer, if your full-fed men were not more than fitted by your desired rate, that purse should not be thinned at the bottom that daily by lightness is made too thin already. But if more heed were taken how, than haste what, we needed not such by-reckonings. Kings have the honor to be titled earthly gods,[4] and therefore breeds our shame if we disgrace so much our name as though too, too far short. Yet some piece of properties were not in us not ever to reward desert by the rule of their merit, but bear with weakness and help to lift from ground the well-nigh falling man. This at this present makes me like the lunatic man that keeps a smacker[5] of the remain of his frenzy's freak, helped well thereto by the influence of *sol in leone*,[6] that makes me yield for company to a longer proportion than a wiser in my place would ever grant unto with this caveat: that this lunatic goodness make you not bold to keep too many that you have, and much less take in more to heap more errors to over-many. Also, that you trust not to the grace of your crazed[7] vessel, that to the ocean may fortune be[8] too humble. Foresee and prevent it now in time, afore too late you vex me too much with small regard of what I scrape or bid. Admit that by miracle it would do well, yet venture not such wonders where such approachful mischief might betide you.

There remains that you, after your perilous first attempt, do not aggravate that danger with another in a farther-off climate, which must cost blows of good store. Let characters serve your turn and be contented when you are well, which hath not ever been your property. Of

---

2. **lewd** ignorant, doltish.   3. **crystal** mirror.
4. Cf. Psalm 82:6.   5. **smacker** taste.
6. "the sun in the lion," that is, the constellation Leo, during the hottest part of summer.
7. **crazed** cracked.
8. **fortune be** happen to be.

this no more; but for all my moods, I forget not my tenses,[9] in which I see no leisure for aught but petitions to fortify with best forwardness the wants of this army, and in the same include your safe return. And grant you wisdom to discern betwixt *verisimile* and *potest fieri.*[10] Forget not to salute with my great favor good Thomas and faithful Mountjoy.[11] I am too like the common faction that forget to give thanks for what I received, but I was so loath to take that I had well nigh forgot to thank; but receive them now with millions, and yet the rest[12] keeps the dearest.

95 ᏋᏮ QUEEN ELIZABETH TO ESSEX, JULY 24, 1597[1]

[Headed] Minute of a letter to Essex from the queen.

How irksome long toil, much danger, and heart's care may seem to the feeler's part when they that only hears report of what might be full of evil chance or danger's stroke are so filled with doubts of unfortunate sequel! You may well suppose the weight of these balances, but remember that who doth their best shall never receive the blame that accidents may bring; neither shall you find us so rigorous a judge as to verdict enterprises by events. So the root be sound, what blasts soever wither the fruits, no condemnation shall light on their share. Make of this fleet, I charge you, a match, which being a fire runs *in extremum,*[2] with good caution of such points as my signed letter gives you. Adieu with many good wishes to yourself, not forgetting good Thomas, Mountjoy, with your joined Council, and tell them that no orison shall be made by us of whence they have not part.

                                                                                 E. R.

9. **tenses** times (pun upon *moods* and *tenses* in the grammatical sense).

10. *verisimile* probably; *potest fieri* it can be done.

11. **Thomas and faithful Mountjoy** Sir Thomas Baskerville and Charles Blount, Lord Mountjoy, both of whom were serving under Essex.

12. **yet the rest** inserted in a blank space in the text in Burghley's hand.

1. *Source:* Hatfield House, Cecil Papers 56/46; copy of an original that may have been a personal note in Elizabeth's hand that was sent to Essex along with the more formal signed letter of instructions referred to in the penultimate sentence.

2. "to the very end."

96 ᭓᭣ QUEEN ELIZABETH TO MARGERY, LADY NORRIS, ON THE
DEATH OF HER SON, SEPTEMBER 22, 1597[1]

[Headed] The queen to the Lady Norris

[Elizabeth's jotted superscription] Mine own Crow,[2] harm not yourself
for bootless help, but show a good example to comfort your dolorous
yokefellow.

Although we have deferred long to represent to you our grieved
thoughts, because we liked full ill to yield you the first reflection of misfortunes, whom we have always rather sought to cherish and comfort,
yet knowing now that necessity must bring it to your ears and nature
consequently must move both grief and passions in you, we resolved no
longer to smother either our care for your sorrow or the sympathy of
our grief for his loss. Wherein, if it be true that society in sorrow work-
eth diminution, we do assure you by this true messenger of our mind
that nature can have stirred no more dolorous affection in you, as a
mother for a dear son, than gratefulness and memory of his service past
hath wrought in us, his sovereign, apprehension of our miss of so worthy a servant. But now that nature's common work is done, and he that
was born to die hath paid his tribute, let that Christian discretion stay
the flux of your immoderate grieving, which hath instructed you both
by example and knowledge that nothing of this kind hath happened but
by God's divine providence.

   And let these lines from your loving and gracious sovereign serve to
assure you that there shall ever appear the lively characters of you, and
yours that are left, in valuing all their faithful and honest endeavors.
More at this time we will not write of this unpleasant subject, but have
dispatched this gentleman to visit both your lord and you to condole
with you in the true sense of your love and to pray you that the world
may see that what time cureth in weak minds, that discretion and mod-

---

1. *Source:* Folger Library, MS V.b.214, fol. 68r; copy. This famous letter exists in numerous
manuscript copies from the period, most of which do not include the queen's intimate su-
perscript. Lady Norris (d. 1599) was the wife of Sir Henry Norris, baron of Rycote. Their
son Sir John Norris—a distinguished soldier who had commanded troops in the Netherlands and Brittany in 1591 and 1594 and had served as commander of troops in Ireland
since 1595—had died there earlier in 1597. In 1599 Lady Norris would lose two more sons to
military service in Ireland.
   2. **Crow** Elizabeth's nickname for the dark-complexioned Lady Norris.

eration helpeth in you in this accident, where there is so just cause to demonstrate true patience and moderation. Given at our manor of Richmond, September 22, *Anno Domini* 1597, and in the thirty-ninth year of our reign.

97 🙦 QUEEN ELIZABETH TO THE EARL OF ESSEX IN IRELAND, JULY 19, 1599[1]

[Headed] 19mo Julii. From her majesty to the lord lieutenant.

We have perceived by your letters to our Council brought by Henry Carey[2] that you are arrived at Dublin after your journey into Munster, where though it seemeth by the words of your letter that you had spent divers days in taking an account of all[3] that have passed since you left that place, yet have you in this dispatch given us small light either when or in what order you intend particularly to proceed to the northern action.[4] Wherein if you compare the time that is run on and the excessive charges that is spent with the effects of anything wrought by this voyage (howsoever we may remain satisfied with your own particular cares and travails of body and mind), yet you must needs think that we that have the eyes of foreign princes upon our actions and have the hearts of people to comfort and cherish—who groan under the burden of continual levies and impositions which are occasioned by these late actions—can little please ourself hitherto with anything that hath been effected.

For what can be more true (if things be rightly examined) than that your two months' journey hath brought in never a capital rebel against whom it had been worthy to have adventured one thousand men; for of their two coming-in that were brought unto you by Ormond (namely

1. *Source:* Folger Library, MS V.b.214, fols. 229v–230v; early seventeenth-century copy. There is another, possibly later copy in PRO, State Papers Ireland, Elizabeth 63/205/114, fols. 219r–221r. The most significant variants in that text are indicated in the notes. Essex had arrived in Ireland in April 1599, charged with restoring order.

2. **Henry Carey** the son of Lord Hunsdon, Elizabeth's first cousin.

3. **all** PRO reads "all things."

4. **northern action** that is, in Ulster, home territory for Hugh O'Neill (1540?–1616), second earl of Tyrone, who had spearheaded a powerful rebellion against English rule and was openly courting Spanish aid.

Mountgarrett and Cahir), whereupon ensued the taking of Cahir Castle,[5] full well do we know that you would long since have scorned to have allowed it for any great matter in others to have taken an Irish hold from a rabble of rogues with such force as you had and with the help of the cannon, which were always able in Ireland to make his passage where it pleased. And therefore, more than that, you have now learned upon our expenses, by knowledge of the country, that those things are true which we have heretofore told you. If you would have believed us, how far different things would prove from your expectation! There is little public benefit made to us of any things happened in this action which the president[6] with any convenient addition to his numbers by you might not have effected either now or hereafter in a time more seasonable, when it should less have hindered the other enterprise on which depends our greatest expectation.

Whereas[7] we will add this one thing that doth more displease us than any charge or expense that happens: which is that it must be the queen of England's fortune (who hath holden down the greatest enemy she had) to make a base bush kern[8] to be accounted so famous a rebel as to be a person against whom so many thousands of foot and horse, besides the force of all the nobility of that kingdom, must be thought too little to be employed. For we must now remember unto you that our cousin of Ormond, by his own relation when you arrived, assured us that he had delivered you a charge of a kingdom without either town maritime, or island, or hold[9] possessed by the traitors. But we did ever think that Tyrone would please himself to see such a portion of our fair army, and led by the person of our general, to be harrassed out and adventured in encountering those base rogues who were no way strengthened by foreign armies, but only by such of his offal as he was content to spare and let slip from himself, whiles he hath lived at his pleasure, hath

5. **Ormond** the Anglo-Irish Thomas Butler (1532–1614), tenth earl of Ormond, lord deputy of Ireland from 1597 to 1599; **Mountgarret** Richard Butler, third Viscount Mountgarret, married to Tyrone's eldest daughter; **Cahir** (or Cahirs) Thomas Butler, baron of Cahir, married to Mountgarret's sister. Both men were kinsmen to Ormond. After they had made their submission, Cahir's younger brother unsuccessfully sought to defend **Cahir Castle**, the family stronghold in Leinster, against Essex's forces.

6. **president** Sir Thomas Norris, brother of Sir John Norris and lord president of Munster after his brother's death. Sir Thomas Norris himself died in Ireland in 1599.

7. **Whereas** PRO reads "Whereunto."

8. **kern** peasant, rascal.

9. **town … hold** PRO reads "town of ours, maritime or inland, or wold."

spoiled all where our army should come, and preserved for himself what he thought necessary. Little do you know how he hath blazed[10] in foreign parts the defeats of regiments, the death of captains, and loss of men of quality in every corner; and how little he seemeth to value their power who use it so as it is like to spend itself!

It is therefore apparent that all places require not one and the self-same knowledge, and that drafts and surprises would have found better successes than public and notorious marches, though where the rebel attends you with greater forces, it is necessary that you carry our army in the form you use. But it doth sound hardly[11] in the ears of the world that in a time when there is a question to save a kingdom, and in a country where experience giveth so great advantage to all enterprises, regiments should be committed to young gentlemen that rather desire to do well than know how to perform it. A matter wherein we must note that you have made both us and our Council so great strangers as to this day we know but by reports who they be that spend our treasure and carry places of note in our army. Wherein you know we did by our instructions direct you as soon as you should be arrived, seeing you used reasons why it could not be done so conveniently beforehand.

These things we would pass over but that we see your pen flatters you with phrases—that here you are deceived,[12] that you are disgraced from hence in your friends' fortune, that poor Ireland suffers in you—still exclaiming against the effects of your own causes. For if it be not enough that you have all and more than that which was agreed on before you went concerning public service, but that you must by your voluntary actions there in particular things (which you know full well are contrary to our will and liking) raise an opinion that there is any person that dare displease us, either by experience of our former toleration or with a conceit to avoid blame by distinctions, then[13] must we not hide from you, how much soever we do esteem you for those good things which are in you, but that our honor hath dwelt too long with us to leave the point now uncleared that whosoever it be that you do clad with any honor or place (wherein the world may read the least suspicion of neglect or contempt of our commands) we will never make dainty to set on such shadows as shall quickly eclipse any of these lusters.

---

10. **blazed** boasted, advertised (with a hint of the incendiary nature of such activities).
11. **hardly** harshly.
12. **deceived** PRO reads "defeated."
13. **then** PRO reads "then this."

And therefore, although by your letter we found your purpose to go northward, on which depends the main good of our service and which we expected long since should have been performed, yet because we do hear it bruited (besides the words of your letter written with your own hand, which carries some such sense) that you who allege such weakness in our army by being traveled with you, and find so great and importunate affairs to digest at Dublin, will yet engage yourself personally in Offaly,[14] being our lieutenant, when you have there so many inferiors able enough to victual a fort or seek revenge of these that have lately prospered against our forces. And when we call to mind how far the sun hath run his course, what dependeth upon the timely plantation of garrisons in the north, and how great a scandal it would be to our honor to leave that proud rebel unassaulted[15] when we have with so great an expectation of our enemies engaged ourself so far in this action, so as without that be done, all these former courses will prove like *via navis in mare*,[16] besides that our power, which hitherto hath been dreaded by potent enemies, will now even be held contemptible amongst our rebels, we must now plainly charge you, according to the duty you owe us, so to unite soundness of judgment to the zeal you have to do us service, and with all speed to pass thither in such order as the axe may be put to the root of that tree which hath been the treasonable stock from whence so many poisoned plants and grafts have been derived. By which proceedings of yours we may neither have cause to repent our employment of yourself for omitting these opportunities to shorten the war, nor receive in the eye of the world imputation of too much weakness in ourself to begin a work without better foresight.

What would be the end of our excessive charge, the adventure of our people's lives, and the holding-up of our own greatness against a wretch whom we have raised from the dust[17] and who could never prosper if the charges we have been put to were orderly employed? For the matter of Southampton,[18] it is strange to us that his continuance or displacing should work so great an alteration either in yourself (valuing our com-

---

14. **Offaly** a county in Leinster, in central Ireland.

15. **unassaulted** PRO reads "unassailed."

16. "a ship's path in the sea"; that is, quickly effaced.

17. In 1562 Elizabeth had offered the young Hugh O'Neill protection and education in England after the murder of his father. Before assuming the earldom of Tyrone, he had served under Sir Henry Sidney in Ireland.

18. Against the queen's explicit wishes, Essex had attempted to make Henry Wriothesley, earl of Southampton, his Master of Horse. Southampton had been in disfavor with the

mandments as you ought) or in the disposition of our army, where all
the commanders cannot be ignorant that we not only not allowed of
your desire for him, but did expressly forbid it. And being such a one
whose counsel can be of so little and experience of less use, yea, such a
one as, were he not lately fastened to yourself by an accident wherein for
our usage of yours we deserve thanks, you would have used many of
your old, lively arguments against him for any such ability or commandment. It is therefore strange to us that, we knowing his worth by
your report and you our disposition from ourself in this point, will dare
thus to value your own pleasing in things unnecessary, and think by
your private arguments to carry for your own glory a matter wherein
our pleasure to the contrary is made notorious. And where you say further that divers or the most of the voluntary gentlemen are so discouraged thereby as they begin to desire passports and prepare to return, we
cannot as yet be persuaded but that the love of our service and the duty
which they owe us have been as strong motives to these their travails
and hazards as any affection to the earl of Southampton or any other. If
it prove otherwise, which we will not so much wrong[19] as to suspect, we
shall have the less cause either to acknowledge or reward it. At the court
at Greenwich the nineteenth of July, 1599.

98 ≋ QUEEN ELIZABETH TO THE EARL OF ESSEX IN IRELAND,
SEPTEMBER 14, 1599[1]

*[Headed] A copy of a letter sent by the queen's majesty into Ireland but
never deliver[2] because the earl of Essex was come from thence before messenger was arrived*

Elizabeth Regina.
Right trusty and right well-beloved cousin and councillor, and trusty

---

queen since his secret marriage with Essex's cousin, Elizabeth Vernon, one of the queen's
maids of honor, in 1598.

    19. **wrong** PRO reads "wrong ourself."

    1. *Source:* Folger Library, MS V.b.214, fols. 205v–207r; early seventeenth-century copy.
There is another, possibly later copy in PRO, State Papers Ireland, Elizabeth 63/206/170,
fols. 317r–318v. The most significant variants in that text are indicated in the notes.

    2. **deliver** delivered.

and well beloved,[3] we greet you well. Having sufficiently declared unto you before this time how little the manner of your proceeding hath answered either our directions or the world's expectation, and finding now by your letters by Cuffe[4] a course more strange (if strange[5] may be), we are doubtful what to prescribe you at any time or what to build upon by your own writing to us in anything. For we have clearly discerned of late that you have ever to this hour possessed us with expectation that you would proceed as we directed you, but your actions always show the contrary, though carried in such sort as you were sure we had no time to countermand them.

Before your departure, no man's counsel was held sound which persuaded not presently the main prosecution in Ulster. All was nothing without that, and nothing was too much for that. This drew on the sudden transportation of so many thousands to be carried with you as when you arrived we were charged with more than the list on which we resolved. The number of three hundred horses, also above the[6] which was assented to, which were only to be in pay during the service in Ulster, have been put[7] in charge ever since the first journey—the pretense of which journey, as appeared by your letters, was to do some service in the interim whilst the season grew more commodious for the main prosecution. For the which purpose you did importune with great earnestness that all manner of provisions might be hastened to Dublin against your return. Of this resolution to defer your going into Ulster, you may think that we would have made stay if you had given us more time by warning or if we could have imagined by the contents of your own writing that you would have spent nine weeks abroad. At your return[8] a third part of July was past, and that you had understood our mislike of your former courses, and making your excuse of undertaking it only in respect of your conformity to the Council's opinions, with great protestations of haste into the north, we[9] received another letter and new reasons to suspense[10] that journey yet awhile and to draw the army into Offaly, the fruits whereof was no other at your coming home

---

3. This second salutation is for the queen's council in Ireland, to whom the letter was also addressed.

4. **Cuffe** Henry Cuffe, Essex's secretary.   5. **strange** PRO reads "more strange."

6. **horses...the** PRO reads "horsemen above the thousand."

7. **have been put** PRO reads "we have been also put."

8. **return** PRO reads "return when."   9. **we** PRO reads "we then."

10. **suspense** suspend (the PRO reading).

but more relations of farther miseries of your army and greater difficulties to perform your Ulster war. Then followed from you and the Council a new demand of two thousand men, to which if we would assent you would speedily undertake what we had[11] commanded. When that was granted and your going onward promised by divers letters, we received by this bearer new, fresh advice[12] that all that you can do is to go to the frontiers, and that you have provided only for twenty days' victual.

In which time[13] of proceeding we must deal[14] with you and that Council that it were more proper for them to leave troubling themselves with instructing us by what rules our power and their obedience are limited and to bethink them, if the courses had been only derived from their Council, how to answer this part of theirs—to train us into a new expense for one end and employ it upon another, to which we would never have assented if we could have suspected it should have been undertaken before we heard it was in action. And therefore we do wonder how it can be answered, seeing your attempt is not in the capital traitor's country, that you have increased your list. But it is true (as we have often said) that we are drawn on to expenses[15] by little and little, and by protestations of great resolutions in generalities till they come to particular executions. Of all which courses, whosoever shall examine the arguments used for excuse shall find that your own proceedings beget the difficulties, and that no just cause doth breed the alteration. If lack of numbers, if sickness of the armies be the reasons, why was not the action undertaken when the army was in better state? If winter's approach, why were the summer months of July and August lost? If the spring was too soon and the summer that followed otherwise spent, if the harvest that succeeded was so neglected as nothing hath been done, then surely we must conclude that none of the four quarters in the year will be in season for you and that Council to agree of Tyrone's prosecution, for which all our charge was intended.

Further we require you to consider whether we have not great cause to think that the purpose is not to end the war, when yourself have so often told us that all the petty undertakings in Leinster, Munster, and Connaught are but loss of time, consumption of treasure, and waste of

11. **had** PRO reads "had so often."

12. **advice** PRO reads "advertisement."

13. **time** PRO reads "kind."

14. **deal** PRO reads "deal plainly."

15. **are ... expenses** PRO reads "were ever won to expense."

our people until Tyrone himself be beaten, on whom the rest depended. Do you not see how he maketh the war with us in all parts by his ministers' seconding all places where any attempt be offered? Who doth not see that, if this course be continued, the wars are like to spend us and our kingdom beyond all moderation, as well as the report of the success in all parts hath blemished our honor and encouraged others to no small proportion?[16] We know you cannot fail so much in judgment as not to understand that all the world seeth how time is dallied, though you think the allowance of that Council (whose superscriptions are yours)[17] shall serve and satisfy us. How would you have derided any man else that should have followed your steps? How oft have you told us that others which preceded you had no intent to end the wars? How oft have you resolved that until Loughfoyle and Ballyshannon[18] were planted, there could be no hope of doing service upon the capital rebel? We must therefore let you know that, as it cannot be ignorance, so it cannot be want of means, for you had your asking: you had choice of times, you had power and authority more ample than ever any had or ever shall have. It may well be judged with how little contentment we search out these and other errors, for who doth willingly seek for that they are so loath to find? But how should that be hidden which is so palpable? And therefore, to leave that which is past, and that you may prepare to remedy matters of weight hereafter rather than to fill your papers with impertinent arguments, being in your general letters savoring still in mean points of humors that concern the private[19] of your lord lieutenantship,[20] we do tell you plainly that are of that Council that we wonder at your indiscretion to subscribe to letters which concern our public service when they are mixed with any man's private and directed to our Council table, which is not wont to have things of so small importance.

To conclude, if you will say, though the army be in list nineteen thousand, that you have them not, we answer then to our treasurer[21]

16. **proportion** PRO reads "presumption."

17. **superscriptions are yours** PRO reads "subscriptions are but your echoes."

18. **Loughfoyle** the broad, marshy estuary of the Lough River in northern Londonderry, which contained an English garrison; **Ballyshannon** (or Bealshannon) a castle at the mouth of the Erne River in Donegal.

19. **private** personal concern or interest.

20. **your lord lieutenantship** PRO reads "you, our lord lieutenant."

21. **treasurer** George Carey (or Carew) of Cockington, Devonshire, appointed the queen's treasurer-at-war for Ireland in March 1599.

that we are ill served and that there need not so frequent demands of full pay. If you will say that the Muster Master is to blame, we much must marvel,[22] then, why he is not punished, though say we might to you, our general (if we would *ex ore proprio judicare*[23]) that all defects by musters, yea though in never so remote garrisons, have been affirmed to us to deserve to be imputed to the want of care in the general. For the small proportion you say you carry with you of three thousand five hundred foot, when lately we augmented you two thousand more, it is to us past comprehension, except it be that you have left still too great numbers in unnecessary garrisons which do increase our charge and diminish our army. Which we command you to reform, especially since you by your continual reports of the state of every province describe them all to be in worse condition than ever they were before you set foot in that kingdom, so that whosoever shall write the story of this year's action must say that we were at great charges to hazard our kingdom, and you have taken great pains to prepare for many purposes which perish without undertaking.

And therefore, because we see by your own word that the hope is spent of this year's service upon Tyrone and O'Donnell,[24] we do command you and our Council jointly to fall in present deliberation and thereupon to send us over in writing with all expedition (you shall then understand our pleasure in all things fit for our service) a true declaration of the state to which you have brought our kingdom, and what be the effects which this your lordship's journey hath produced, and why these garrisons which you will plant as far within the land in the Breanie and Monaghan,[25] as others whereof we have writ, shall not have the same difficulties? Secondly we look to hear from you and them jointly how you think the remain of this year shall be employed: in what kind of war, and where, and with what numbers, which being done and sent us hither in writing with all expedition, you shall then understand our pleasure in all things fit for our service. Until which time we command you to be very careful to meet with all inconvenience that may arise in that kingdom, where the ill-affected will grow so insolent upon our ill

22. **much must marvel** PRO reads "must muse."

23. "offer judgment from our own mouth."

24. **O'Donnell** Hugh Roe O'Donnell, powerful rebel chieftain allied with Tyrone.

25. **Breanie** possibly Brefne, which included much of what is now Cavan County, and **Monaghan**, adjacent territories with recent English plantations; Monaghan bordered on Ulster to the south.

success, and the good subjects grow in despair when they see the best of our preserving them.

We have received a letter in form of a cautel,[26] full of challenges[27] and of comparisons that are needless, such as hath not been before this time presented to a state, except it hath been done with hope to terrify all men from censuring your proceedings. Had it not been enough to have sent us the testimony of the Council, but that you must call so many of those that are of slender experience, and none of our Council, to such a form of subscription? Surely howsoever you may have warranted them, we doubt not but to let them know what belongs to us, to you, and to themselves. And thus, expecting your answer, we end, at our manor at Nonsuch[28] this fourteenth of September, in forty-first year of reign, 1599.

99 ⁊ QUEEN ELIZABETH TO CHARLES BLOUNT, LORD MOUNTJOY, LORD DEPUTY OF IRELAND, DECEMBER 3, 1600[1]

Mistress Kitchenmaid,[2]

I had not thought that precedency had been ever in question but among the higher and greater sort; but now I find by good proof that some of more dignity and greater calling may by good desert and faithful care give the upper hand to one of your faculty, that with your frying pan and other kitchen stuff have brought to their last home more rebels, and passed greater breakneck places than those that promised more and did less. Comfort yourself, therefore, in this: that neither your careful endeavors, nor dangerous travails, nor heedful regards to our service, without your own by-respects, could ever have been bestowed upon a prince that more esteems them, considers and regards them, than

26. **cautel** crafty trick.

27. **challenges** PRO reads "challenges that are impertinent."

28. **Nonsuch** a royal house in Surrey (no longer extant), erected as a hunting lodge by Henry VIII.

1. *Source:* Lambeth Palace Library, MS 604, fol. 242 (Carew Papers); copy in the hand of Sir Robert Cecil's clerk. Charles Blount (1563–1606)—earl of Devonshire, eighth Lord Mountjoy, whom Elizabeth had reportedly passed over in favor of Essex in 1599—was appointed lord deputy of Ireland to succeed Essex and was slowly but surely accomplishing the subjugation of Ireland. One of his successful tactics was to burn the crops of adherents of the rebel chieftains.

2. In a previous dispatch to Elizabeth, Mountjoy had compared his task in pacifying Ireland to that of a kitchen wench.

she for whom chiefly, I know, all this hath been done, and who keeps this verdict ever in store for you—that no vainglory nor popular fawning can ever advance you forward, but true vow of duty and reverence of prince, which two afore your life I see you do prefer.

And though you lodge near papists and doubt you not for their infection, yet I fear you may fall in an heresy, which I hereby do conjure you from—that you suppose you be backbited by some to make me think you faulty of many oversights and evil defaults in your government. I would have you know for certain that as there is no man can rule so great a charge without some errors, yet you may assure yourself I have never heard of any had fewer; and such is your good luck that I have not known them, though you were warned of them. And learn this of me, that you must make difference betwixt admonitions and charges, and like of faithful advices as your most necessariest weapons to save you from blows of princes' mislike. And so I absolve you *a poena et culpa*[3] if this you observe. And so God bless you and prosper you as if ourself were where you are.

Your sovereign that dearly regards you.

100 ?❧ QUEEN ELIZABETH TO THE OTTOMAN SULTAN MAHUMET CHAM, JANUARY 20, 1601[1]

[Addressed] The direction of the letter: To the most high and most mighty prince, Sultan Mahumet Cham[2] of the Ottomanical Empire and dominion of the east parts, most puissant, sole, and supreme lord and monarch.

Elizabeth (by the grace of God almighty, Creator of the world) of England, France, and Ireland queen, and of the true Christian faith against idolators falsely professing the name of Christ the constant, perpetual, and victorious Defender;[3] to the most high and most mighty prince, Sultan Mahumet Cham of the Ottomanical Empire and dominion of

3. "from punishment and guilt."

1. *Source:* Folger Library, MS V.a.321, fols. 33v–34r; copy.

2. **Mahumet Cham** Mehmed III, Ottoman sultan from 1595 to 1603.

3. **Defender** Elizabeth newly emphasized her title "Defender of the Faith" after Henry IV of France—who styled himself "the most Christian king"—converted to Catholicism.

the east parts, most puissant, sole, and supreme lord and monarch, greeting.

Most high and most puissant prince:

It is no small contentment to us that the amity we have with so high and renowned a prince as you, is by our neighbor princes and their subjects so well known that when they have need to seek any favor or kindness from you, they implore our mediation as the readiest way to obtain their desires. Which as at other times we have been importuned to use towards you, and received therein great satisfaction, so are we pressed at this time by the earnest suit of the friends of certain distressed gentlemen to entreat your princely favor and relief of their extremities; whose names are Lawrence Oliphant, master of Oliphant, and Robert Douglas, master of Morton, two sons and heirs of two noblemen, subjects of our neighbor and good brother the king of Scotland, who having been many years since taken prisoners casually at sea by pirates, and by them sold in Barbary for bondmen, have ever since remained in that state of captivity, and so much the more miserable because none of their friends knew of their being, until that of late it hath been understood (though not of certainty) that they are prisoners in Argier[4] under the viceroy there, your tributary.

Upon knowledge whereof, their friends and kinsfolk have sent and authorized this bearer, Robert Oliphant, one of their kinred,[5] to seek and inquire of their estate and to procure their redemption from that servitude; who knowing no other way of address to you, because they are of a nation that have little trade in those quarters of the world, have humbly besought our letters and furtherance to you; which we as willingly have yielded, for that the said persons were not taken in action of war by sea or land against you or your people, whereby you might have cause of just indignation against them, but only by mere casualty of fortune, deserving the compassion of all princes. Whereof our earnest desire is that you interpose your authority towards the said viceroy of Argier, that he will set the said Lawrence Oliphant and Robert Douglas at liberty, if they be found under him or any other of your dominions, to return home into their native country, whereby you shall increase in us the kind remembrance we have of your former friendships, and oblige us to requite it in any like manner you may require at our hands,

4. **Argier** Algiers.   5. **kinred** kindred.

as more at large shall declare to you our ambassador[6] there, to whom we pray you to give credit and favor in this matter. Given under our privy seal at our palace of Westminster the 20 day of January, in the year of our Lord God, 1600[1], and of our reign the 43.

Elizabeth

101 ⪽ ELIZABETH TO JAMES, JULY 4, 1602[1]

[Endorsed] 4 July 1602. Copy of her majesty's letter to the king of Scots, sent by Mr. Roger Ashton.

My good brother,

Who longest draws the thread of life and views the strange accidents that time makes doth not find out a rarer gift than thankfulness is, that is most precious and seldomest found. Which makes me well gladded that you, methinks, begin to feel how necessary a treasure this is, to be employed where best it is deserved, as may appear in those lines that your last letters express, in which your thanks be great for the sundry cares that of your state and honor my dear friendship hath afforded you, being ever ready to give you ever such subjects for your writing, and think myself happy when either my warnings or counsels may in fittest time avail you.

Whereas it hath pleased you to impart the offer[2] that the French king hath made you, with a desire of secrecy, believe that request includes a trust that never shall deceive, for though many exceeds me in many things, yet I dare profess that I can ever keep taciturnity for myself and my friends. My head may fail, but my tongue shall never, as I will not say but yourself can in yourself, though not to me, witness. But of that no more: *Praetererunt illi dies.*[3] Now to the French: in plain dealing, without fraud or guile, if he will do as he pretends, you shall be more beholding to him than he is to himself, who within one year hath winked

6. **ambassador** John Wroth, appointed in 1598.

1. *Source:* PRO, State Papers Scotland 52/68/75; copy.

2. Henry IV proposed a league of France, Scotland, and England against Spain, sending an ambassador to James to broach the matter in the summer of 1602.

3. "Those days will be past."

at such injuries and affronts as or[4] I would have endured, that am of the weakest sex, I should condemn my judgment.[5] I will not enter into his. And therefore, if his *verba* come *ad actionem*[6] I more shall wonder than do suspect; but if you will needs have my single advice, try him if he continue in that mind. And as I know that you would none of such a league as myself should not be one, so do I see by his overture that himself doth; or if for my assistance you should have need of all help, he would give it, so as since he hath so good consideration of me, you will allow him therein. And doubt nothing but that he will have me willingly for company; for as I may not forget how their league with Scotland was reciproque when we had wars with them, so is it good reason that our friendships should be mutual.

Now to confess my kind taking of all your loving offers and vows of most assured oaths that naught shall be concealed from me that either prince or subject shall, to your knowledge, work against me or my estate; surely, dear brother, you right me much if so you do. And this I vow, that without you list, I will not willingly call you in question for such warnings if the greatness of the cause may not compel me thereunto. And do entreat you to think that if any accident so befall you as either secrecy or speed shall be necessary, suppose yourself to be sure of such a one as shall neglect neither to perform so good a work. Let others promise, and I will do as much with truth as others with wiles. And thus I leave to molest your eyes with my scribbling, with my perpetual prayers for your good estate,

> As desireth your most loving
> and affectionate sister

[Postscript] As for your good considerations of border causes, I answer them by my agent, and infinitely thank you therefor.

.

4. **or** ere.

5. Henry IV is reported to have remarked of Elizabeth's superior skill in suppressing rebels against the crown, "She only is a king! She only knows how to rule."

6. "words [*verba*] come to action [*ad actionem*]."

102 ᙏ QUEEN ELIZABETH TO CHARLES BLOUNT, LORD MOUNTJOY,
FEBRUARY 16, 1603[1]

*[Addressed] To our right trusty and well beloved, the Lord Mountjoy, our
deputy of our realm of Ireland*

Elizabeth R   By the queen.
Right trusty and well beloved, we greet you well. We have seen the submission made by Tyrone which you have sent us, and perceive the course
which you have taken thereupon, which hath been to give no such credit
to his words, either in deed or appearance, as upon those fair pretexts to
give over any other good means of his prosecution. Which if you should
have done upon this overture, the same effect might follow which hath
done before, when in the instant of his submission he hath been deepest
in practice. In which respects, we acknowledge that you have proceeded
very discreetly. And now to speak of the course he holdeth, we conceive
the world hath seen sufficiently how dear the conservation of that kingdom and people hath been unto us, and how precious we have been of
our honor that have of late rejected so many of those offers of his, only
because we were sorry to make a precedent of facility to show grace or
favor to him that hath been the author of so much misery to our loving
subjects.

Nevertheless, because it seemeth that there is a general conceit that
this reduction may prove profitable to the state by sparing the effusion
of Christian blood (the prevention whereof Christian piety teacheth
us), and because the manner of the submission maketh the best amends
that penitency can yield to offenses against sovereignty (if amends
there can be after so horrible treasons), we are content to lay aside anything that may herein contrary[2] our own private affections, and will
consider that clemency hath as eminent a place in supreme authority as
justice and severity.

And therefore, to the intent that either the effect may fall out which
is expected by his submission or the engrafted falsehood and corruption of his nature may declare itself, we are content, and so we give you
authority hereby, to assign him a day with all expedition to make his

1. *Source:* Bodleian Library, University of Oxford, MS Tanner 76, fol. 167r; in the hand of
a secretary, with Elizabeth's sign manual and seal attached. This and the following letters
were among the last of Elizabeth's reign. During the second week in March, she became ill
and died March 24, 1603.

2. **contrary** run contrary to.

personal repair to you. Where we require you to be careful to preserve our dignity in all circumstances, assuring him that, seeing he referreth all absolutely to our grace and mercy, where we would never have yielded that if he had kept his former courses of presumption, to indent[3] with us beforehand, we are now contented that you do let him know he shall have his life and receive upon his coming-in such other conditions as shall be honorable and reasonable for us to grant him. And thus much for that which he shall need to know before his coming-in. Which if he do accept without any other particular promise procured from you beforehand, then could we like it very well that you should make stay of him in safe custody until you hear our further pleasure, whose meaning is not to break our word in the point of his life, for which it is only given, but only to suspend his liberty till we see whether any conditions which shall leave him free again to return as he came can make us in better state than we are now, when we shall have nothing to trust to but the ordinary assurances which can be had from traitors. And these our letters shall be your sufficient warrant and discharge in this behalf. Given under our signet at our manor of Richmond the 16th of February, 1602[3], in the five-and-fourtieth year of our reign.

103 ई QUEEN ELIZABETH TO CHARLES BLOUNT, LORD MOUNTJOY, FEBRUARY 17, 1603[1]

[Addressed] To our right trusty and well-beloved Lord Mountjoy, our deputy of our realm of Ireland

Elizabeth R

Right trusty and right well beloved, we greet you well. Forasmuch as we in our former letter have made you see that we do not retain so deep an impression of the heinous offenses committed by Tyrone (for which he hath made himself unworthy to live) but that we can be content to yield him a life to save so many of our subjects', and although we would take it for an acceptable service if he might be taken in so (by the words of

---

3. **indent** make a formal agreement or indentures.

1. *Source:* Bodleian Library, University of Oxford, MS Tanner 76, fols. 171r–172r; in the hand of a secretary, with the queen's sign manual and seal. By the time of Tyrone's formal submission to Elizabeth on March 30, 1603, the queen was already dead. The news was concealed from the Irish until April 5.

his late submission) as we might have him in our power without violating of public faith, yet rather than we would for our own satisfaction let go any such opportunity as his personal submission (whereof universality of opinions concur that good use might be made), we can be content if he shall come in upon such humble terms as are formally contained in his submission that you shall not only receive him, as is expressed in the other letter, but forasmuch as it may be when the time comes to perform what he hath promised he may particularly stand upon assurance of liberty also as well as life before he will come to you, we are then contented that you do in that case give him your word for his coming and going safe though you should in other things not agree.

And for your better judgment and knowledge how in such case we mean to dispose, we do give you warrant hereby to pass him our pardon upon these conditions. First, our pleasure is upon no consideration to give him our pardon except he do come personally where you shall assign him to receive it. Secondly, that in the point of religion he presume not to indent,[2] seeing it savors but of presumption when he knows so little fear of prosecution. Thirdly, he shall publicly abjure all manner of dependency upon Spain and other potentates, and shall promise to you to reveal all he knows of our enemy's purposes, and refuse the name of O'Neill.[3] Fourthly, he shall not presume to treat for any but himself and his own natural followers of Tyrone, but shall leave all others (over whom he injustly usurps either as uriaths[4] or as dependents, and over whom he can challenge no superiority, but as a chosen head of rebellion) absolutely to make their own suits for themselves. He shall yield to such places for garrisons, and such portions of lands and composition be of us to be reserved, as you shall think fit for our service, with this condition: to banish all strangers from him and call home all his followers that do maintain the rebellion in any other province, together with such a subjection to sheriffs and execution of justice as you shall think fit for our service and the present time. And as heretofore he offered to send over his eldest son—if you can get it—to be disposed at our pleasure, either in Ireland or in England.

All which being done, we leave the rest of your proceedings to your own best judgment so to dispose of him in one kind or other as shall be

2. **indent** make formal agreement.

3. **O'Neill** the legendary name of Irish monarchs and hence associated with a denial of English sovereignty.

4. **uriaths** the "urraghs," or vassal chieftains, whom Tyrone was accustomed to dominate.

fittest for our service. This being our end in the writing of both these
letters: first to let you see what we wish to be done if it may be in the first
kind, as is contained in our other letter; next to let it appear to you and
the world that seeing there is so general a conceit that good may happen
thereby, that we will not leave any course untried which can be expected
of any prince to take in commiseration of her distressed and loving
subjects of both her realms, whose conservation she preferreth before
any other worldly thing; lastly because we do consider that his living
nearer with you for some time (if it could be procured) would be a
good security from those practices which may be doubted he may fall
into when he returneth (seeing how common it is to them to neglect either faith or pledges when the breach of any conditions may serve their
turn), we do only recommend unto you that the longer he doth remain
under your wing, it were the better.

But because we do confess that we remain assured of your affection
to use all things to the best for us, and see that you have extraordinary
foresight and judgment in the government of that realm, we do attribute so much to you in the handling of this matter as we leave it and
the rest of the particular conditions (mentioned in the former letter or
in this) to your discretion, who may see ca[use]⁵ to vary in some circumstances which are not worthy the sending to know our pleasure in,
but to be altered as you shall see cause. Only in these two letters we
show you two things. In the first, of [the] sixteenth of February, our desire appears to have him stayed if he [come] in without asking more
than yet he doth; and in this other, our resolution (rather than he
should not come in at all) to give you authority to secure him both of
life and liberty, and comi[ng] in upon those terms, both to maintain
your word really ([which] is given in our behalf and which shall never
be violated) and rather than to send him back unpardoned (to be a
head still of rebellion), to afford him these above-mentioned or other
reasonable conditions, considering the long work you find it to extir-
pate him and the difficulty our estate findeth to maintain that acti[on]
which must finish it.

For the rest, concerning some enlargement of your authority in case
you see occasion to increase at any time some numbers, we minded not
to tie you to such strictness in petty things, having committed so much

---

5. Square brackets enclose elements conjecturally supplied because a worn page edge in
the original makes them illegible.

trust to you in greater; and therefore we have given order to our Council to direct our letters to the treasurer[6] for the same, and hereby do give you authority to do it and to use the advice of as ma[ny] or as few of the Council in this as you shall think fit to do in this service, requiring you (above all things) to drive him to some issue presently, because contrariety of successes there or change of accidents in other parts may turn very much to our disadvantage. For which we are still apt to believe that he lieth in advantage, and will spin out all things further than were requisite with delays and shifts if you do not abridge him. Given at our manor of Richmond this 17 of February, 1602[3], and of our reign the forty-fifth.

6. **treasurer** Sir George Carey, Elizabeth's treasurer-at-war for Ireland.

POEMS 13–15

13 ❧ VERSE EXCHANGE BETWEEN QUEEN ELIZABETH AND KING
PHILIP OF SPAIN, CIRCA SPRING 1588[1]

The king of Spain to her majesty:

1. *Te veto ne pergas armis defendere Belgas,*
2. *Quas Dracus eripuit Gazae reddantur oportet.*

1. *Source:* Bodleian Library, University of Oxford, MS Rawlinson Poetical 148, fol. 3v; "*Liber Lilliati,*" the miscellany of the cathedral musician John Lilliat (1555?–1629). Elizabeth's part in this exchange of epigrams is also attributed to her in at least two later MSS: Bodleian, MS Douce 280, fols. 199v–200r (written by John Ramsey before 1618); and BL, MS Additional 15227, fol. 81v, where the author of the opening quatrain is said to be the pope rather than Philip of Spain.

If this exchange indeed took place, the most likely time, as specified in Ramsey's version, was the early months of 1588, when the English and Spaniards had sent ambassadors to the Netherlands to negotiate a peace. But it seems unlikely that Philip would have delivered such an ultimatum on that occasion; rather, his envoys were instructed to stall negotiations as long as possible in order to give his armada time to set sail undetected by the English. If, as seems likely, Philip's verses were constructed by some other party and circulated as his, perhaps after the armada victory, Elizabeth's response could still have been composed by the queen, and it certainly circulated as hers during the 1590s. Lilliat's copy dates from the period 1589–1600, during which he entered most or all of the initial section of his miscellany; see Edward Doughtie, ed., *Liber Lilliati: Elizabethan Verse and Song* (Bodleian, MS Rawlinson Poetry 148) (Newark: University of Delaware Press; London: Associated University Presses, 1985).

3. *Quas pater evertit jubeo te condere cellas,*
4. *Religioque Papae fac restituatur ad unguem.*[2]

Responsio Elizabethae:

1. *Ad Grecas fient isthaec mandata calendas.*[3]
When Greeks do measure months[4] by the moon
Then, Spanish Philip, thy will shall be done.

Finis.

14 ♆ SONG ON THE ARMADA VICTORY, DECEMBER 1588[1]

[Headed] A song made by her majesty and sung before her at her coming from Whitehall to Paul's through Fleet Street in Anno Domini 1588.

[Headed] Sung in December after the scattering of the Spanish navy.

Look and bow down Thine ear, O Lord.[2]
From Thy bright sphere behold and see

2.   I bid you, make no armed defense of Belgians;
       Drake's plundered treasures see that you give back;
       The cells your father emptied, reconstruct;
       Restore the Pope's religion perfectly.
Sir Francis Drake (line 2) had conducted a number of humiliating raids against Spanish towns and ships in the years before the armada. The "cells" in line 3 are the monastic cells "emptied" by Henry VIII and his ministers through the dissolution of the religious houses.

3. Response of Elizabeth: 1. On the Greek calends these things shall be done [that is, never, since the Greeks didn't have calends, which established the first day of each Roman month. The phrase was proverbial, based on Suetonius' *Life of Caesar* 87.1: when Augustus wanted to avoid paying a debt, he would promise payment "on the Greek calends"].

4. **months** spelled "monthes" in the original and probably pronounced as disyllabic.

1. *Source:* Caird Library, National Maritime Museum, Greenwich, MS SNG/4; copy on a quarto sheet numbered 160, formerly bound as part of a volume of papers belonging to Sir Henry Spelman, the seventeenth-century antiquarian. Reproduced here by permission of the Trustees of the National Maritime Museum. The volume was broken up for sale in 1936. See the Sotheby Sale Catalogue, 1936, *Catalogue of a Selected Portion of the Valuable Library and Collection of Manuscripts, the Property of Major Q. E. Gurney, D.L., of Bawdeswell Hall, Norfolk,* Second Day's Sale, Tuesday, March 31, 1936, Lot 109, item 111, p. [23].

2. This first line closely echoes the opening of Psalm 86.

Thy handmaid and Thy handiwork,
Amongst Thy priests, offering to Thee
Zeal for incense, reaching the skies;   5
Myself and scepter, sacrifice.

My soul, ascend His holy place.
Ascribe Him strength and sing Him praise,
For He refraineth princes' sprites
And hath done wonders in my days.   10
He made the winds and waters rise
To scatter all mine enemies—[3]

This Joseph's Lord and Israel's God,
The fiery Pillar and day's Cloud,[4]
That saved his saints from wicked men   15
 And drenched the honor of the proud;
And hath preserved in tender love
The spirit of his turtle dove.[5]
Finis.

3. Cf. Exodus 14:16; Elizabeth draws an analogy between the armada's fate and that of
Pharaoh and his men who were drowned in the Red Sea when they pursued the Israelites.
   4. Cf. Exodus 13:21: In a pillar of cloud by day and a pillar of fire by night, God led the Israelites out of Egypt into the Promised Land.
   5. **turtle dove** term of endearment for the beloved in the Song of Songs.

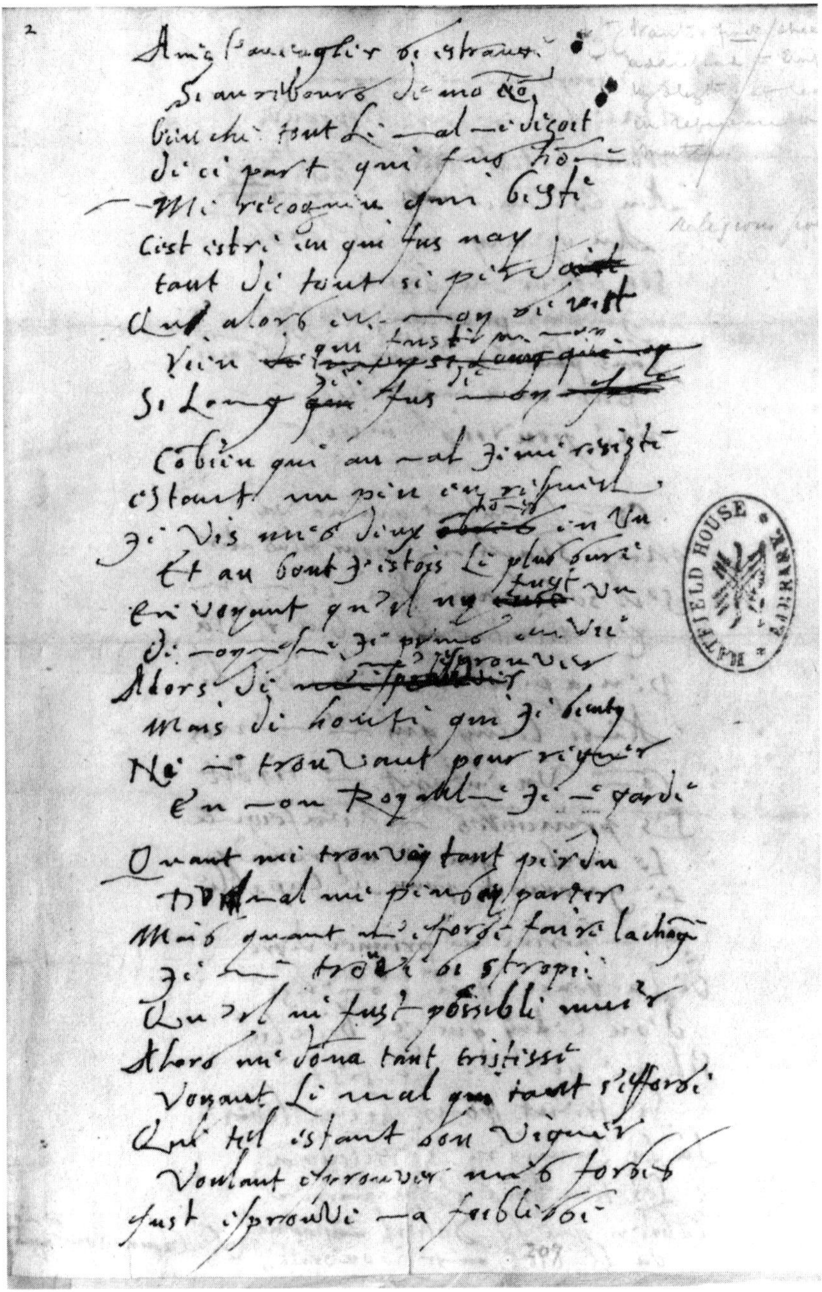

FIGURE 17 Poem 15, opening stanzas; Hatfield House, Cecil Papers 147, fol. 207r. Reproduced courtesy of The Marquess of Salisbury.

15 ☙ TWENTY-SEVEN STANZAS IN FRENCH, COMPOSED
CIRCA 1590[1]

With the blinding so strange,
    So contrary to my name,[2]
Although every evil deceives me
By this share in being man,
I recognized how foolish   5
This being in which I was born—
    So much was it lost from all
That appeared in me then—
    Nothing that was mine
So far was I from me.   10

    However much I resist evil,
Being a little awakened,
I saw my two men[3] in one
    And in the end I was most sure,
In seeing that it was one there.   15
    Of myself I had a wish

1. *Source:* Hatfield House, Cecil Papers 147, fols. 207r–213r. An untitled and mostly un-
rhymed stanzaic poem in Elizabeth's late, loosely cursive italic hand. (For the French original of this much-revised and enigmatic poem, see *ACFLO,* part 1.) Elizabeth's Armada
Prayer, in her hand of the same period, immediately follows the poem in the Hatfield manuscript volume (although the prayer is written on different paper). Steven W. May announced his discovery of this poem in *The Elizabethan Courtier Poets: The Poems and
Their Contexts* (Columbia: University of Missouri Press, 1991), pp. 41–68, and character-
ized it as an original composition by Elizabeth. Subsequently, May and Anne Lake Prescott
published a transcription of the poem and a prose translation in "The French Verses of
Elizabeth I," *English Literary Renaissance* 24 (no. 1, winter 1994): 9–43. While May and
Prescott now are of the opinion that this poem is a fragmentary translation into French
from some unknown original, barring the discovery of such an original we find no features of the manuscript to invalidate our assumption that this poem is a complete, original
composition by Elizabeth. The fact that Elizabeth arranges the stanzas in her pages in
groups of three (perhaps to suggest the tripartite nature of the soul) need not imply, as it
does for May and Prescott, that she was working from a foreign original; she could simply
have been copying from her own initial draft.

2. **my name** according to William Camden, *Elizabeth* means "Peace of the Lord or quiet
rest of the Lord, the which England hath found verified in the most honored name of our
late sovereign" (*Remains of a Greater Work concerning Britain* [London: G. E. for Simon
Waterson, 1605] [*STC* 4521], p. 79).

3. **men** see Ephesians 4:22, 24, and Colossians 3:9–10: Christ remakes the "old man" of
sin into the "new man" of grace

Then to put myself to the proof,
    But for shame that I felt,
Not finding myself to reign
    In my kingdom, I hold back.   20

When I found myself so lost,
    I thought to depart from evil,
But when I strive to make the change
    I find myself so crippled
That it was not possible to change.   25
Then it gave me so much sorrow—
    Seeing evil strive so much
And its vigor being such
    That I, wanting to prove my strength—
It made proof of my weakness.   30

    Help was not lacking to me
As I tried to stand up alone,
But He who helped me
At the beginning would hold me up;
    Halfway, He let go of me,   35
He did not let up on his pains,
    Ever, in holding me up,
Without otherwise giving His help,
    Whereby I myself could help
My own weakness.   40

    Like the child who does not walk
But leans forward to go further,
If he who leads it is wise
    And takes care where it goes,
Little by little he will hurry it along—   45
    Just so, He who led me
Drew me along like a child;
He taught me fundamentals;
    The remainder that I did not learn
He was keeping for one who was capable.[4]   50

4. **keeping . . . capable** An alternative reading might be "keeping for when I was

I arrive at the first degree
Of grace, which begins
    Where he is who is well bound
(If he does not lose his head)
    Thinks himself well placed.   55
There the light shone brightly;
    The shadows vanished away.
Although the sun did not appear,
    Where the heaven opened wide
    The clear day dawned.   60

Seeing myself, who at dawn
    Begin to understand myself,
It was time then for me to depart,
    But not in such sort
That I did not know how to govern well.   65
    Little by little I remembered
(For I was so sad)
    That the dream that grieved me—
The dream that was past—
    Seemed to torment me.   70

    As a shepherd who has slept
The night in his hut
    When the morning comes,
Gets up, half asleep,
    And goes to the mountain,   75
And blowing on his hands
    Staggers about and wakes up,
So the soul that was dead
    In desires only too futile
Found that it was watchful.   80

As far as the abyss of heaven
    I saw the air serene
And remembering my baptism,

---

capable"; cf. 2 Corinthians 3:1–2, which compares the newly converted to "babes in Christ"
fed with milk and not yet with the meat of the Word.

I acknowledged that so far
I was always from myself;   85
   I saw the sun, in its appearance
So lovely and so shining,
   That like what it was in the East,
So much light in one instant
   It showed in the West.   90

Now the Second Help
   Began to uphold me,
From whom I knew how to prevail
   Over the evils of this world
Without danger of destroying myself.   95
   From my evil I thought myself cured
But not so much without pain
   That this much was in my power:
To tread as well by the crooked path
   As by the level one.   100

Remembering God in dream,
   Looking on high
I found myself so advanced
   That in me only the habit
Of sin remained;   105
   And I turned myself from sin,
And my soul was ready to flee
   The evil that I apprehended,
But it was killed so soon—
   Just as soon as the evil appeared.[5]   110

Thus newly made,
   I saw the state of my heart,
Which was so ruinous
   That reason, seated in my soul,
Was most scornful of it.   115

---

5. An alternative reading of the reversible correlative conjunction in these two lines (*tôt* ... *tantôt* in French) would be, following May and Prescott, "But as soon as this was killed / Just so soon the evil reappeared." We have preferred the more positive reading because of its better fit with the opening line of the next stanza.

Created as from nothing,
I saw my inner man[6]
    So reduced from thence into its center[7]
That his life, being past,
    Rid him of a bad encounter.   120

Ceasing to be a stranger;
    I was remade in a moment
With all well conjoined.
    For Him who is the best
I raised up the sword;   125
For He who created me,
    Who is well pleased with all,
Furnished me in divers sorts:
    To begin with, He made me,
And then He converted me.   130

Being advanced so high,
    As I said, and transformed
Into my ordained rank,
    I saw my realm well governed
By reason and not by degree.   135
    I saw three similar souls
Set in operation,
    Each in his office:
One to command,
And two to serve.[8]   140

Soon I saw Fantasy
    Panting like a child,
But Reason did not allow it
    For the good of the other part,
Which bypassed the dispute.   145

6. **inner man** literally in French the "man within," but we use the typically Pauline vocabulary; see, for example, Ephesians 3:6, "His Spirit in the inner man."

7. **center** center of the heart; an alternative reading, adopted by May and Prescott, would interpret it as the center of the man.

8. The "three similar souls" are, as the following stanzas indicate, the tripartite soul of Reason, Will, and Fantasy or Imagination.

I saw the same dull feelings
Without wanting to have them,
And found that, according to their habits,
   They were seeking only
   Their first motions.   150

I saw the highest sphere
   Of the soul that governed
And, as it seemed to me,
   Inside it burned,
And outside was shadowed.   155
There I saw the Understanding,
   Having Truth for its object,
And I saw the whole government
   So very near to perfect,
That it brought me contentment.   160

I saw the Will give responsibility,
   Absolute and ordinary,
By which her retinue increased
   To something extraordinary;
She went along very gently.   165
I saw the part that is the spur
   Of Salvation, and the bridle;
I saw Love, who hoisted his sail
   Of desire, who for a farthing
Went his way, well paid for his canvas.[9]   170

I saw, besides, exalted Memory,
   The treasury of human good,
Where I found the extended story
   Of my being, which was so vain
That it existed only to give glory.   175
   That sufficed to make me remember
My iniquitous evil, sent away

---

9. The imagery in lines 166–70 takes the same sequence as James 3:2–4, a series of reflections on sins of the tongue: "If any man offend not in word, the same is a perfect man, and able also to bridle the whole body. Behold we put bits in the horses' mouths, that they may obey us, and we turn about their whole body. . . . Behold also the ships, . . . driven of fierce winds, yet turned about . . . whithersoever the governor listeth."

Since my soul has agreed
That, remembering its past,
It would correct its present,   180

Its past, and what is to come—
   All laid out before it.
And of having been inconstant
   I have just given it an account,
Whom it did not make constant.   185
   There returns to my awareness
What it is and what it was.
   All of this, in my presence, put
On me, who retained the handling;
   It put itself in its dwelling place.   190

Regret for my fault
Delivered me from sin,
   For it afflicted me so
That this alone was my care—
   That I did not have care enough;   195
Knowing better, that in joy
   I had to suffer,
I turned myself to so many tears
   That a thousand times my comfort
Renewed my pains.   200

To increase the grief
Of my foolish past,
   Contemplating my Creator,
I remembered the making
   Of me, a sad sinner;   205
I saw that God redeemed me,
   Being cruel against Him,
And considering well who He was,
   I saw how He made Himself me,
   So that I would make myself Him.   210

I saw that when He formed me
   He gave me no state at all,
But placed in my hand

What I myself took,
What contented me most—   215
    Which could be bestial,
Or otherwise human,
    Or which was angelical—
And that it was in my hands
    To take the divine.   220

I saw His high providence
    Where all is done that happens,
Who never gave me counsel
    That was not for the good.
From my own knowledge   225
    I saw the cause why He wished
To make the fire everlasting—
    And it was to exhort me,
To keep me from hell
    That I might gain paradise.   230

I saw that when Justice
    Went away, compelled by Discord,
That compelled by my Malice,
    Seeking Mercy,
I made her ask for Justice.   235
    Seeing this, I perceived such an intent
Of penitence in me
    That one moment of this pain
Would alleviate eternal torment.

I fled so high to convert,   240
    And was so much helped by God,
That soon to the highest degree
    In my firm deliberation
I saw that I was exalted
    Such that, inside the door, I find myself—   245
So much in peace and so exalted,
    The war so far given over,
That the flesh fell dead
    That the soul might keep itself alive.

The last of graces   250
    Is the same that confirms all,
After the second and the first.
    And there soon putting its seal[10]
Left me in this sort:
    Left me in such salvation,   255
Placed me in such state,
    And within me made accord—
Virtue with nature,
    And custom with virtue.[11]

Like the blind man who in all that happens   260
    Maintains such equilibrium
And comports himself such
    And his being so equal,
Neither stirs itself up nor grieves,
    Just so the soul in its substance   265
Has placed these temperings
    With such equal accord
That in herself she neither has nor could
    Wear inconstancy for a garment.[12]

---

10. **seal** cf. the "seal" of salvation, 2 Corinthians 1:22, Ephesians 1:14 and 4:20, and Revelation 7:3–8.

11. This inward accord in the state of salvation is markedly Stoic in its triple conjunction of virtue, nature, and custom (or law). According to Diogenes Laertius, Zeno taught that virtue was life in agreement with nature, and Chrysippus further held that such life in agreement with nature was lived "by the law common to all things, that is to say, the right reason which pervades all things, and is identical with God, Lord and ruler of all that is" (*Lives of Eminent Philosophers*, trans. R. D. Hickes [Cambridge: Harvard University Press, 1925], 2:195, 197).

12. Immediately below the last line of this stanza, at the bottom of a recto page, Elizabeth has written two capital *S*'s with transverse strokes through them: this notation pointedly signals the end of her text. If Elizabeth was using "habit" in the English rather than the French sense, an alternative translation of the final two lines might be "That in herself she neither has nor could have inconstancy as her habit."

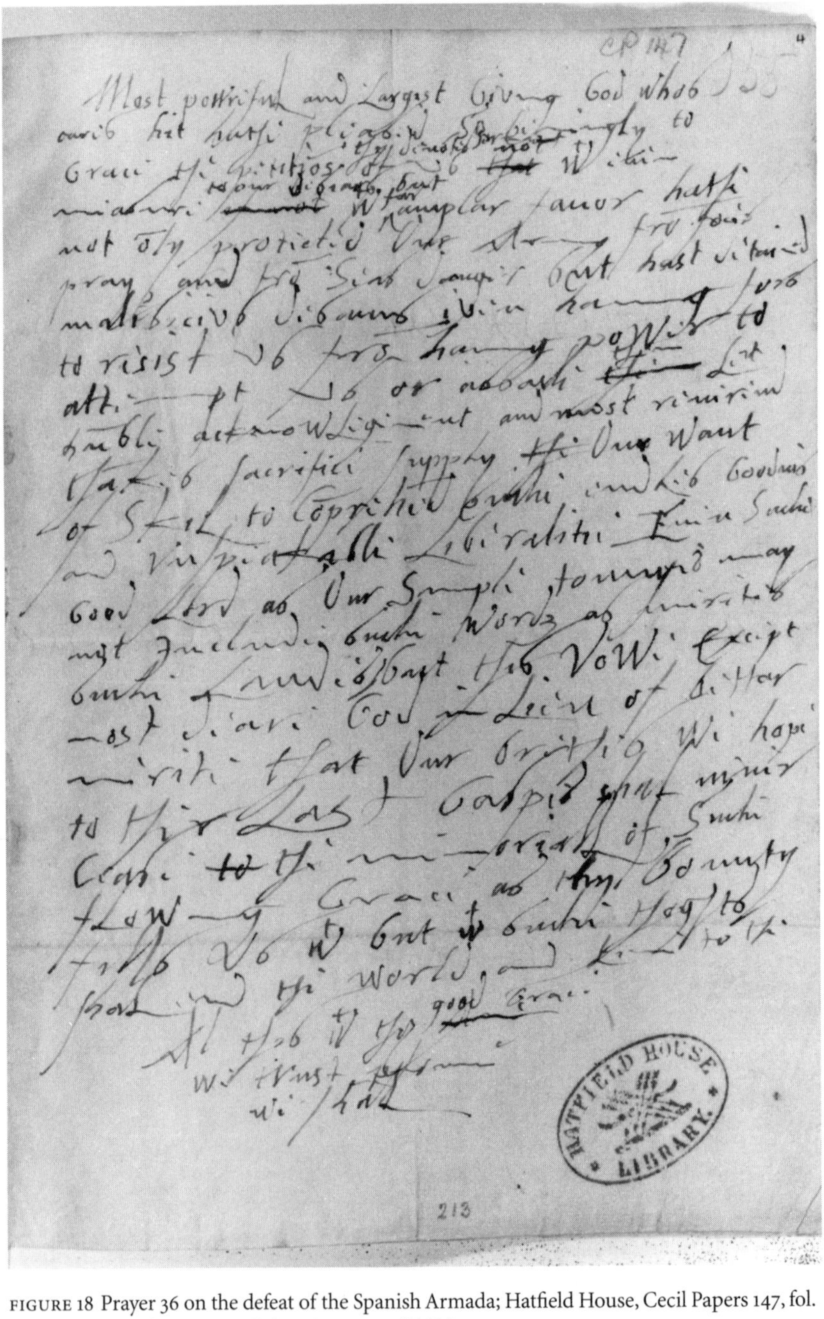

FIGURE 18 Prayer 36 on the defeat of the Spanish Armada; Hatfield House, Cecil Papers 147, fol. 214r. Reproduced courtesy of The Marquess of Salisbury.

PRAYERS 36–39

36 ➤ ON THE DEFEAT OF THE SPANISH ARMADA, 1588[1]

Most powerful and largest-giving God, whose ears it hath pleased so benignly to grace the petitions of us Thy devoted servant, not with even measure to our desires but with far ampler favor hath not only protected our army from foes' prey and from sea's danger, but hast detained malicious dishonors (even having force to resist us) from having power to attempt us or assail them.[2] Let humble acknowledgment and most reverend thanks' sacrifice supply our want of skill to comprehend such endless goodness and unspeakable liberality—even such, good Lord, as our simple tongues may not include such words as merits such lauds. But this vow accept, most dear God, in lieu of better merit: that our breaths, we hope to their last gasps, shall never cease the memorial of such flowing grace as Thy bounty fills us with, but with such thoughts shall end the world and live to Thee. All these with Thy good grace, we trust perform we shall.

---

1. *Source:* Hatfield House, Cecil Papers 147, fol. 214r; draft in Elizabeth's hand, immediately following the French stanzaic verses (Poem 15, p. 413) but an independent composition on different, smaller paper. (For original-spelling version, see *ACFLO,* part 1.) Dating is conjectural, based on the prayer's subject and the appearance of the hand. The possibility cannot be excluded that the prayer was composed even later and records the queen's thanks for delivery from one of the several threatened invasions by a reconstituted Spanish Armada during the 1590s.
2. **them** the English army.

37 ❧ ON THE DEFEAT OF THE SPANISH ARMADA, SEPTEMBER 1588[1]

[Headed] A godly prayer and thanksgiving, worthy the Christian Deborah and Theodosia[2] of our days.

Everlasting and omnipotent Creator, Redeemer, and Conserver, when it seemed most fit time to Thy worthy providence to bestow the workmanship of this world or globe, with Thy rare judgment Thou didst divide into four singular parts the form of all this mold, which aftertime hath termed elements, they all serving to continue in orderly government the whole of all the mass; which all, when of Thy most singular bounty and never-earst-seen[3] care Thou hast this year made serve for instruments both to daunt our foes and to confound their malice,[4] I most humbly, with bowed heart and bended knees, do render my humblest acknowledgments and lowliest thanks; and not the least for that the weakest sex hath been so fortified by Thy strongest help that neither my people might find lack by my weakness nor foreigners triumph at my ruin. Such hath been Thy unwonted grace in my days, although Satan hath never made holiday[5] in busy practices both for my life and state, yet that Thy mighty hand hath overspread both with shade of Thy blessed wings so that both neither hath been overthrown nor received shame but obtained victory to Thy most great glory and their greatest ignomy;[6] for which, Lord, of Thy mere goodness grant us grace to be hourly thankful and ever mindful. And if it may please Thee to pardon my request, give us the continuance in my days of like goodness, that

1. *Source:* Huntington Library, MS EL 2072, fol. 2a; copy in a late sixteenth-century hand among the papers of Sir Thomas Egerton, who was probably responsible for the heading. Reproduced by permission of The Huntington Library, San Marino, California.

2. **Deborah** the only female judge (political, religious, and military leader) of Israel (Judges 4–5); **Theodosia** of the several saints with this name, the most relevant is the eighth-century virgin martyr whom the iconoclast Emperor Constantine Copronymus tortured and left to die in prison because she had prevented his soldiers from destroying the great image of Christ over the entry to the monastery of Saint Anastasia in Constantinople. The name was associated generally during the Byzantine period with the protection of religion from its persecutors.

3. **never-earst-seen** never before seen.

4. The conceit here is that all four elements combined to destroy the Spanish fleet: air in the form of gale-force winds, earth in the form of coastal rocks on which many fleeing vessels foundered; fire in the form of English fire ships that destroyed Spanish vessels and sent them into retreat, and water in the form of heavy seas.

5. **made holiday** taken a rest.

6. **ignomy** ignominy.

mine eyes never see change of such grace to me, but specially to this my kingdom, which, Lord, grant to flourish many ages after my end, amen.

38 ᏋᎾ ON THE SAILING OF THE CADIZ EXPEDITION, MAY 1596[1]

[Headed] Anno 1596. A prayer made by her majesty herself on the behalf of her army sent into Spain under the conduct of the right honorable Robert, earl of Essex, and th'earls Lord Howard, lord high admiral of England, and lords generally of the same.

Most omnipotent Maker and Guider of all our world's mass, that only searchest and fathomest the bottom of all our hearts' conceits[2] and in

---

1. *Source:* BL, MS Additional 38823, fol. 96r; copy preserved in "Sir Edward Hoby's Commonplace Book." There are at least three other important early texts of this prayer: Bodleian, MS Rawlinson B.259, fols. 53v–54r, where the prayer is headed "A most brief, pithy, and profound private prayer for the prosperous good success and happy return of this her majesty's navy and army royal. Made and composed by the queen's majesty" and embedded in a narrative titled "An English quid for a Spanish quo . . . or a true relation of the late honorable expedition and memorable exploit (GOD so assisting) performed by her majesty's most royal navy and army at Cadiz on the coast of Spain in the months of June and July last, this year of CHRIST our Savior, 1596. Diligently collected, advisedly corrected, and out of most credible advertisements newly and truly written out by Richard Robinson, citizen of London"; Huntington Library, MS EL 1205c, where the prayer occupies the bottom of the same sheet as the Armada Prayer (our Prayer 37) under the heading "Her majesty's privy addition upon this present expedition, when my lord of Essex was general at the winning of Calse [Cadiz]"; and Masters of the Bench of the Inner Temple Library, MS Petyt 538, vol. 10, fol. 6. The most significant variants among the Bodleian and Huntington versions are recorded in the notes.

The original of this prayer was evidently sent to the earl of Essex on the eve of his departure on the highly successful expedition against Cadiz, along with a brief note from the queen that read as follows: "I make this humble bill of requests to Him that all makes and does, that with His benign hand He will shadow you so as all harm may light beside you, and all that may be best hap to your share, that your return may make you better and me gladder. Let your companion, my most faithful Charles [Lord Howard of Effingham, the lord high admiral] be sure that his name is not left out in this petition. God bless you both, as I would be if I were there, which, whether I wish or not, He alone doth know." Cited from W. B. Devereux, *Lives and Letters of the Earls of Essex* (London, 1853), 1:345. According to Camden and Stow, Elizabeth ordered this prayer to be distributed among the departing fleet; it was also apparently issued in a printed version for use in parish churches, perhaps against the queen's wishes, since in 1597 she ordered it to be removed from a printed collection of prayers prepared by Archbishop Whitgift. See Tucker Brooke, "Queen Elizabeth's Prayers," *The Huntington Library Quarterly* 2 (no. 1, October 1938): 69–77; and a letter from Cecil to Whitgift (July 11, 1597) in Lambeth Palace Library, MS Fairhurst 3740, fol. 195.

2. **all . . . conceits** Huntington reads "all hearts, consciences, and conceits."

them seest the true original of all our actions intended, Thou that by Thy foresight dost truly discern how no malice of revenge nor quittance of injury,[3] nor desire of bloodshed, nor greediness of lucre hath bred[4] the resolution of our now-set-out army, but a heedful care and wary watch that no neglect of foes nor our surety of harm might breed either harm[5] to us or glory to them. These being grounds, Thou that didst inspire the mind, we humbly beseech[6] (with bended knees), prosper the work and with best forewinds guide the journey, speed the victory, and make the return the advancement of Thy glory, the triumph of their[7] fame, and surety to the realm, with the least loss of English blood. To these devout petitions, Lord, give Thy blessed grant, amen.[8]

39 ❧ ON THE SAILING OF THE AZORES EXPEDITION, JULY 1597[1]

O God, All-maker, Keeper, and Guider, inurement[2] of Thy rare-seen, unused[3] and seld-heard-of goodness, poured in so plentiful sort upon us full oft, breeds now this boldness—to crave with bowed knees and hearts of humility Thy large hand of helping power to assist with wonder our just cause, not founded on pride's motion nor begun on malice-stock but, as Thou best knowest to whom naught is hid, grounded on just defense from wrongs, hate, and bloody desire of conquest. For since means Thou hast imparted to save that Thou hast given by enjoying such a people as scorns their bloodshed where surety ours is won;[4] for-

---

3. **discern . . . injury** Bodleian reads "discern that we are not in malice of revenge nor seek aquittance of injury."

4. **Thou . . . bred** Bodleian reads "But Thou which knowest that a heedful care and wary watch moveth us that no neglect of foes, nor over-surety of harm might breed."

5. **harm** other MSS read "danger."

6. **beseech** other MSS read "beseech Thee."

7. **their** Huntington reads "Thy."

8. **give . . . amen** Bodleian reads "give Thou Thy blessed grant, so be it."

1. *Source:* BL, MS Harley 6986, art. 35, fol. 58r; in Elizabeth's hand. (For original-spelling version, see *ACFLO,* part 1.) This prayer also exists in several MS copies (e.g., BL, MS Additional 38823, fol. 96r; and on the endpaper of the Newberry Library copy of Katherine Parr's *Prayers or Meditations*). These copies offer minor variations in wording not recorded in our notes.

The Azores or "Islands" expedition of 1597, also commanded by Essex, was far less successful than the Cadiz expedition. See Letters 94–95, pp. 386–88.

2. **inurement** habituation.   3. **unused** unusual.

4. **won** alternative reading of "one" is also possible.

tify, dear God, such hearts in such sort as their best part may be worst that to the truest part meant worst, with least loss to such a nation as despise their lives for their country's good, that all foreign lands may laud and admire the omnipotency of Thy work—a fact alone for Thee only to perform. So shall Thy name be spread for wonders wrought; and the faithful encouraged to repose in Thy unfellowed grace; and we that minded naught but right, enchained in Thy bonds for perpetual slavery, and live and die the sacrificers of our souls for such obtained favor. Warrant, dear Lord, all this with Thy command, amen.

LIST OF
SPEECHES, LETTERS,
POEMS, PRAYERS

SECTION I: 1533–1558

LETTER 1: Princess Elizabeth to Queen Katherine, July 31, 1544 / 5

LETTER 2: Princess Elizabeth to Queen Katherine, Prefacing Her New Year's Gift of an English Translation of Marguerite of Navarre's *Miroir de l'âme pécheresse*, December 31, 1544 / 6

LETTER 3: Princess Elizabeth to King Henry VIII, Prefacing Her Trilingual Translation of Queen Katherine's *Prayers or Meditations*, December 30, 1545 / 9

LETTER 4: Princess Elizabeth to Queen Katherine, Prefacing Her English Translation of Chapter 1 of John Calvin's *Institution de la Religion Chrestienne* (Geneva, 1541), December 30, 1545 / 10

LETTER 5: Princess Elizabeth to King Edward VI, February 14, 1547 / 13

LETTER 6: Princess Elizabeth to King Edward VI upon His Recovery from Sickness, September 20, 1547 / 14

LETTER 7: Princess Elizabeth to King Edward VI, February 2, 1548 / 15

LETTER 8: Princess Elizabeth to Dowager Queen Katherine, circa June 1548 / 17

LETTER 9: Princess Elizabeth to Thomas Seymour, Lord High Admiral, Summer 1548 / 19

LETTER 10: Princess Elizabeth to Dowager Queen Katherine, July 31, 1548 / 20

LETTER 11: Princess Elizabeth to King Edward VI, Summer or Fall 1548 / 21

LETTER 12: Princess Elizabeth to Edward Seymour, Duke of Somerset, Lord Protector, September 1548 / 22

LETTER 13: Princess Elizabeth to Edward Seymour, Lord Protector, January 28, 1549 / 22

LETTER 13, Additional Documents A–D: Examinations and Depositions of Katherine Ashley, Governess to Princess Elizabeth, Regarding Possibly Questionable Dealings with Thomas Seymour, Lord High Admiral, February 1549 / 25

LETTER 14: Princess Elizabeth to Edward Seymour, Lord Protector, February 6, 1549 / 31

LETTER 15: Princess Elizabeth to Edward Seymour, Lord Protector, February 21, 1549 / 31

LETTER 16: Princess Elizabeth to Edward Seymour, Lord Protector, March 7, 1549 / 33

LETTER 17: Princess Elizabeth to King Edward VI, with a Present of Her Portrait, May 15, 1549 / 35

LETTER 18: Princess Elizabeth to King Edward VI, April 21, 1552 / 36

LETTER 19: Princess Elizabeth to Princess Mary, October 27, 1552 / 37

LETTER 20: Princess Elizabeth to King Edward VI, circa Spring 1553 / 38

LETTER 21: Princess Elizabeth to the Lords of the Privy Council, May 31, 1553 / 39

LETTER 22: Princess Elizabeth to Queen Mary, March 16, 1554 / 41

LETTER 23: Princess Elizabeth to Queen Mary, August 2, 1556 / 43

POEM 1: Written on a Window Frame at Woodstock / 45

POEM 2: Written with a Diamond / 46

POEM 3: 'Twas Christ the Word / 47

PRAYERS 1 and 2: Princess Elizabeth's Prayers in the Tower of London / 48

SECTION II: 1558–1572

SPEECH 1: Queen Elizabeth's First Speech, Hatfield, November 20, 1558 / 51

SPEECH 2: Richard Mulcaster's Account of Queen Elizabeth's Speech and Prayer during Her Passage through London to Westminster the Day Before Her Coronation, January 14, 1559 / 53

SPEECH 3: Queen Elizabeth's First Speech before Parliament, February 10, 1559,
    Versions 1 and 2 / 56, 58

SPEECH 4: Queen Elizabeth's Conversations with the Scottish Ambassador,
    William Maitland, Laird of Lethington, September and October 1561 / 60

SPEECH 5: Queen Elizabeth's Answer to the Commons' Petition that She Marry,
    January 28, 1563 / 70

SPEECH 5, Additional Document A: The Commons' Petition to the Queen at
    Whitehall, January 28, 1563 / 72

SPEECH 6: Queen Elizabeth's Answer to the Lords' Petition that She Marry,
    April 10, 1563, Delivered by Lord Keeper Nicholas Bacon / 79

SPEECH 6, Additional Document A: The Lords' Petition to the Queen, circa
    February 1, 1563 / 81

SPEECH 7: Queen Elizabeth's Latin Oration at Cambridge University, August 7,
    1564 / 87

SPEECH 8: Queen Elizabeth's Latin Oration at Oxford University, September 5,
    1566 / 89

SPEECH 9: Queen Elizabeth's Speech to a Joint Delegation of Lords and
    Commons, November 5, 1566, Versions 1 and 2 / 93, 94

SPEECH 9, Additional Document A: Cecil's Report to the Full House of
    Commons November 6, 1566, on Elizabeth's Speech of November 5 / 98

SPEECH 9, Additional Document B: Peter Wentworth's Questions on
    Parliamentary Privilege, November 11, 1566 / 100

SPEECH 9, Additional Document C: Queen Elizabeth's Directions to Cecil for
    Lifting Her Previous Order Forbidding the House to Debate Matters
    Concerning the Succession, November 24, 1566 / 101

SPEECH 9, Additional Document D: Part of a Subsidy Bill Sent by Parliament to
    Queen Elizabeth, with Her Angry Annotations, November 29, 1566 / 102

SPEECH 10: Queen Elizabeth's Speech Dissolving Parliament, January 2, 1567,
    Versions 1 and 2 / 105, 107

SPEECH 11: Queen Elizabeth's Speech Opening the 1571 Parliament, April 2,
    1571 / 108

SPEECH 12: Queen Elizabeth's Speeches and Responses during Her Visit to
    Warwick, August 12, 1572 / 109

LETTER 24: Queen Elizabeth to Edward Stanley, Earl of Derby, June 4,
    1560 / 111

LETTER 25: Elizabeth to Philip II of Spain, September 30, 1562 / 112

LETTER 26: Queen Elizabeth to William Cecil, Principal Minister,
    September 23, 1564 / 115

LETTER 27: Queen Elizabeth to Mary, Queen of Scots, February 24, 1567 / 116

LETTER 28: Queen Elizabeth to Mary, Queen of Scots, June 23, 1567 / 117

LETTER 29: Queen Elizabeth to Mary, Queen of Scots, February 20, 1570 / 120

LETTER 30: Queen Elizabeth to Henry Carey, Lord Hunsdon, February 26, 1570 / 125

LETTER 31: Queen Elizabeth's Warrant to Proceed, if Necessary, to Torture Two of the Duke of Norfolk's Men, September 15, 1571 / 127

LETTER 31, Additional Document A: Letter of Thomas Howard, Duke of Norfolk, to Queen Elizabeth, September 10, 1571 / 128

LETTER 32: Digest of a Letter from Queen Elizabeth to Mary, Queen of Scots, February 1, 1572 / 130

LETTER 33: Queen Elizabeth to William Cecil, Lord Burghley, April 11, 1572 / 131

POEM 4: No Crooked Leg, circa 1565 / 132

POEM 5: The Doubt of Future Foes, circa 1571 / 133

POEM 6: Prayer / 151

PRAYERS 3–9: Private Prayers of Queen Elizabeth at Court, 1563 / 135

PRAYERS 10–28: Queen Elizabeth's Prayers and Poems, 1569 / 143

SECTION III: 1572–1587

SPEECH 13: Queen Elizabeth's Speech at the Close of the Parliamentary Session, March 15, 1576 / 167

SPEECH 13, Additional Document A: The Lords' and Commons' Petition to the Queen, March 2, 1576, and the Queen's Answer to the Commons by Deputy / 171

SPEECH 14: Queen Elizabeth's Speeches and Responses during Her Visit to Norwich, August 16–22, 1578 / 174

SPEECH 15: Queen Elizabeth's Speech to Bishops and Other Clergy at Somerset Place, February 27, 1585, while Parliament Was in Session / 177

SPEECH 16: Queen Elizabeth's Speech at the Closing of Parliament, March 29, 1585 / 181

SPEECH 16, Additional Document A: The Bond of Association for the Defense of Queen Elizabeth, 1584 / 183

SPEECH 17: Queen Elizabeth's First Reply to the Parliamentary Petitions Urging the Execution of Mary, Queen of Scots, November 12, 1586, Versions 1 and 2 / 186, 190

SPEECH 18: Queen Elizabeth's Second Reply to the Parliamentary Petitions Urging the Execution of Mary, Queen of Scots, November 24, 1586, Versions 1 and 2 / 196, 200

LETTER 34: Queen Elizabeth to Sir Francis Walsingham, Ambassador to France, July 23, 1572 / 205

LETTER 35: Queen Elizabeth to Sir Francis Walsingham, Ambassador to France, July 25, 1572 / 209

LETTER 36: Queen Elizabeth to George Talbot, Earl of Shrewsbury, October 22, 1572 / 212

LETTER 37: Queen Elizabeth to Sir Francis Walsingham, Ambassador to France, December 1572 / 215

LETTER 38: Queen Elizabeth to Sir William Fitzwilliam, Lord Deputy, and to the Council of Ireland, June 29, 1573 / 218

LETTER 39: Queen Elizabeth to Valentine Dale, Ambassador Resident in France, February 1, 1574 / 221

LETTER 40: Queen Elizabeth to Valentine Dale, Ambassador Resident in France, March 15, 1574 / 223

LETTER 41: Queen Elizabeth to the Earl and Countess of Shrewsbury, June 25, 1577 / 229

LETTER 41, Additional Document A: Queen Elizabeth to the Earl and Countess of Shrewsbury, June 4, 1577 / 230

LETTER 42: Queen Elizabeth to Sir Amyas Paulet, Ambassador to France, January 1579 / 231

LETTER 43: Queen Elizabeth to Monsieur, February 14, 1579 / 232

LETTER 44: Queen Elizabeth to Sir Amyas Paulet, circa May 1579 / 233

LETTER 45: Queen Elizabeth to Monsieur, December 19, 1579 / 237

LETTER 45, Additional Document A: The Duke of Alençon to the Earl of Sussex, September 13, 1579 / 239

LETTER 45, Additional Document B: William Cecil, Lord Burghley, to Queen Elizabeth, 1579 / 240

LETTER 46: Queen Elizabeth to Monsieur, circa December 1579–January 1580 / 243

LETTER 47: Queen Elizabeth to Monsieur, January 17, 1580 / 245

LETTER 48: Queen Elizabeth to Sir Edward Stafford, Ambassador to France, circa August 1580 / 247

LETTER 49: Queen Elizabeth to Monsieur, March 17, 1581 / 249

LETTER 50: Queen Elizabeth to Monsieur, circa June 1581 / 250

LETTER 51: Queen Elizabeth to Monsieur, May 14, 1582 / 251

LETTER 52: Queen Elizabeth to Monsieur, May 24, 1582 / 253

LETTER 53: Queen Elizabeth to George Talbot, Earl of Shrewsbury, on the Death of His Son, circa September 5, 1582 / 256

LETTER 54: Queen Elizabeth to Mistress Talbot, circa 1582 / 258

LETTER 55: Queen Elizabeth to Monsieur, September 10, 1583 / 259

LETTER 56: Queen Elizabeth to Catherine de Médicis, Queen Mother of France, on Monsieur's Death, circa July 1584 / 260

LETTER 57: Queen Elizabeth to James VI of Scotland, circa June or July 1585 / 261

LETTER 57, Additional Document A: James to Elizabeth, circa July 31, 1585 / 263

LETTER 58: Elizabeth to James, August 1585 / 263

LETTER 58, Additional Document A: James to Elizabeth, August 13, 1585 / 265

LETTER 58, Additional Document B: James to Elizabeth, August 19, 1585 / 265

LETTER 59: Elizabeth to James, November 1585 / 266

LETTER 60: Elizabeth to James, circa January 1586 / 267

LETTER 61: Queen Elizabeth to Sir Thomas Heneage, Her Emissary to the Earl of Leicester in the Netherlands, February 10, 1586 / 269

LETTER 62: Queen Elizabeth to Robert Dudley, Earl of Leicester, by Sir Thomas Heneage, February 10, 1586 / 273

LETTER 63: Elizabeth to James, March 1586 / 274

LETTER 63, Additional Document A: James to Elizabeth, circa April 1, 1586 / 276

LETTER 64: Queen Elizabeth to Robert Dudley, Earl of Leicester, in the Netherlands, April 1586 / 277

LETTER 65: Queen Elizabeth to William Davison, April 27, 1586 / 279

LETTER 66: Elizabeth to James, Late May 1586 / 281

LETTER 67: Queen Elizabeth to Leicester, July 19, 1586 / 282

LETTER 68: Queen Elizabeth to Sir Amyas Paulet, August 1586 / 284

LETTER 69: Queen Elizabeth to the Commoners of London, August 18, 1586 / 285

LETTER 70: Elizabeth to James, October 4, 1586 / 286

LETTER 71: Digest of Elizabeth's letter to Mary, Queen of Scots, October 6, 1586 / 287

LETTER 72: Digest of Queen Elizabeth's Letter to William Cecil, Lord Burghley, October 12, 1586 / 288

LETTER 73: Elizabeth to James, October 15, 1586 / 289

LETTER 73, Additional Document A: James to Elizabeth, January 26, 1587 / 291

LETTER 74: Elizabeth to James, January–February 1587 / 293

LETTER 75: Elizabeth to James, circa February 1, 1587 / 294

LETTER 76: Elizabeth to James, February 14, 1587 / 296

LETTER 76, Additional Document A: James to Elizabeth, March 1587 / 297

LETTER 77: Elizabeth to Henry III of France, May 1587 / 298

POEM 7: Verse Exchange between Queen Elizabeth and Sir Thomas Heneage, Gentleman of the Privy Chamber, circa 1572 / 299

POEM 8: Verse Exchange between Queen Elizabeth and Paul Melissus, Poet Laureate of the Court of Emperor Maximilian II, circa 1577 / 301

POEM 9: On Monsieur's Departure, circa 1582 / 302

POEM 10: When I Was Fair and Young, circa 1580s, Versions 1 and 2 / 303, 304

POEM 11: Now Leave and Let Me Rest, circa 1580s / 305

POEM 12: Verse Exchange between Queen Elizabeth and Sir Walter Ralegh, circa 1587 / 307

PRAYER 29: Queen Elizabeth's Prayer at Bristol, August 15, 1574 / 310

PRAYERS 30–35: Queen Elizabeth's Prayer Book, circa 1579–82 / 311

SECTION IV: 1588–1603

SPEECH 19: Queen Elizabeth's Armada Speech to the Troops at Tilbury, August 9, 1588 / 325

SPEECH 20: Queen Elizabeth's Latin Speech to the Heads of Oxford University, September 28, 1592 / 327

SPEECH 21: Queen Elizabeth's Speech at the Closing of Parliament, April 10, 1593, Versions 1 and 2 / 328, 330

SPEECH 22: Queen Elizabeth's Latin Rebuke to the Polish Ambassador, Paul de Jaline, July 25, 1597 / 332

SPEECH 22, Additional Documents A and B: Letter Exchange between Sir Robert Cecil and Robert Devereux, Earl of Essex, on the Subject of Elizabeth's Response to the Polish Ambassador / 334

SPEECH 23: Elizabeth's Golden Speech, November 30, 1601, Versions 1, 2, and 3 / 335, 340, 342

SPEECH 23, Additional Document A: Excerpts from the 1601 Parliamentary Debates Concerning Monopolies / 344

SPEECH 24: Queen Elizabeth's Final Speech before Parliament, December 19, 1601, Versions 1 and 2 / 346, 351

LETTER 78: Elizabeth to James, circa July 1, 1588 / 355

LETTER 78, Additional Document A: James to Elizabeth, August 1, 1588 / 356

LETTER 79: Elizabeth to James, August 1588 / 357

LETTER 79, Additional Document A: James to Elizabeth, September 1588 / 359

LETTER 80: Queen Elizabeth to Peregrine Bertie, Lord Wiloughby, in France, December 6, 1589 / 360

LETTER 81: Letter Exchange between Queen Elizabeth and Lady Elizabeth Drury, 1589 / 361

LETTER 82: Elizabeth to Henry IV of France, circa 1590 / 363

LETTER 83: Elizabeth to James, July 6, 1590 / 364

LETTER 84: Elizabeth to James, January 1593 / 365

LETTER 85: Elizabeth to James, March 1593 / 368

LETTER 86: Queen Elizabeth to William Cecil, Lord Burghley, April 22, 1593 / 370

LETTER 87: Elizabeth to Henry IV of France, July 1593 / 370

LETTER 88: Queen Elizabeth to Henry Hastings, Earl of Huntingdon, April 8, 1594 / 371

LETTER 89: Elizabeth to James, December 22, 1593 / 372

LETTER 89, Additional Document A: James to Elizabeth, April 13, 1594 / 375

LETTER 90: Elizabeth to James, May 1594 / 377

LETTER 90, Additional Document A: James to Elizabeth, June 5, 1594 / 379

LETTER 91: Elizabeth to James, June or July 1594 / 383

LETTER 92: Elizabeth to Henry IV of France, circa September 4, 1596 / 384

LETTER 93: Elizabeth to Henry IV of France, September 13, 1596 / 385

LETTER 94: Queen Elizabeth to Robert Devereux, Earl of Essex, July 1597 / 386

LETTER 95: Queen Elizabeth to Essex, July 24, 1597 / 388

LETTER 96: Queen Elizabeth to Margery, Lady Norris, on the Death of Her Son, September 22, 1597 / 389

LETTER 97: Queen Elizabeth to the Earl of Essex in Ireland, July 19, 1599 / 390

LETTER 98: Queen Elizabeth to the Earl of Essex in Ireland, September 14, 1599 / 394

LETTER 99: Queen Elizabeth to Charles Blount, Lord Mountjoy, Lord Deputy of Ireland, December 3, 1600 / 399

LETTER 100: Queen Elizabeth to the Ottoman Sultan Mahumet Cham, January 20, 1601 / 400

LETTER 101: Elizabeth to James, July 4, 1602 / 402

LETTER 102: Queen Elizabeth to Charles Blount, Lord Mountjoy, February 16, 1603 / 404

LETTER 103: Queen Elizabeth to Charles Blount, Lord Mountjoy, February 17, 1603 / 405

POEM 13: Verse Exchange between Queen Elizabeth and King Philip of Spain, circa spring 1588 / 409

POEM 14: Song on the Armada Victory, December 1588 / 410

POEM 15: Twenty-seven Stanzas in French, Composed circa 1590 / 413

PRAYER 36: On the Defeat of the Spanish Armada, 1588 / 423
PRAYER 37: On the Defeat of the Spanish Armada, September 1588 / 424
PRAYER 38: On the Sailing of the Cadiz Expedition, May 1596 / 425
PRAYER 39: On the Sailing of the Azores Expedition, July 1597 / 426

INDEX OF NAMES

Note: Includes only names pre-1700

Abel (biblical figure), 219n
Abraham (biblical figure), 84, 155
Adam (biblical figure), 156, 158
Adonijah (biblical figure), 85
Aeneas, 377n, 381
Agamemnon, 129n
Aglionby, Edward, 109–10
Albert, archduke of Austria, 348, 353
Alcibiades, 71n, 204
Alecto, 381
Alençon, François Hercule, duke of (later
    duke of Anjou), 205–12, 215–17, 221–27,
    233–56, 259–61, 302–3, 304n, 311n, 312
Alexander III (of Scotland), 75
Alexander the Great, 74, 83, 88
Alexander, Robert, 262
Allen, William, 287n
Alva. *See* Toledo, Ferdinand de
Angus, earl of, 266n, 367n, 373
Anjou. *See* Alençon, François Hercule;
    Henry III
Anna (biblical mother of Samuel), 84
Anna of Styria, 333n
Anne, Saint, 230
Antoninus Pius, 83
Apollo, 174

Aristotle, 6n, 198n
Arran. *See* Stewart, James
Ascham, Roger, 15n, 187
Ashley, Katherine, 17n, 20, 24, 33n, 34;
    testimony of, 25–30
Ashley, Thomas, 26–27, 35
Ashton, Sir Robert, 402
Athenodorus, 71n
Atropos, 71n, 88
Aubespine, Guillaume de l', baron de
    Chateauneuf, 293n
Augustine, Saint (St. Austin), 36
Augustus Caesar, 71n, 86, 198, 410n
Aylmer, John, 179

Babington, Anthony, 285
Bacon, Lady, 105n
Bacon, Sir Nicholas, 73, 79–80, 98n, 105n,
    107–8, 128n, 167n, 170
Bacqueville, sieur de, 176, 251, 260
Baker, Sir Richard, 47n
Bale, John, 6n
Basil the Great, Saint, 34
Baskerville, Sir Thomas, 388
Beauvoir. *See* Nocle, Beauvoir la
Bedford. *See* Russell, Francis

Bell, Doctor, 177
Bell, Robert, 94, 170
Bentley, Thomas, 48n
Bereblock, John, 89n
Berkeley, Lady, 26, 27
Bertie, Peregrine, Lord Wiloughby, 360–61, 363n
Berwick, duke of, 312n
Bill, Dr. Thomas, 22
Blagrave, Anthony, 343n
Blount, Charles, Lord Mountjoy, 388, 399–400, 404–8
Boethius, 370n
Boleyn, Anne, 6n
Boleyn, Mary, 266n, 296n
Bothwell. See Hepburn, Francis Stewart; Hepburn, James
Bouillon. See Tour d'Auvergne, Henry de la
Bound, Doctor, 177
Bourbon, Charlotte de, 222–23
Bowes, Sir Robert, 365, 368, 384
Brandon, Katherine Willoughby, duchess of Suffolk, 25, 133
Bruce, Edward, 376–77, 382
Buckingham, duke of, 325n
Bull, Henry, 299n
Burghley. See Cecil, William
Butler, Richard, third Viscount Mountgarret, 391
Butler, Thomas, baron of Cahir, 391
Butler, Thomas, tenth earl of Ormond, 220, 390–91

Caesar, Julius, 88n
Cain (biblical figure), 219n
Calvin, John, 10, 96n
Camden, William, 58n, 172n, 370n, 413n, 425n
Campion, Edmund, 286n
Canaye, Philippe, sieur de Fresnes, 360n
Carey, Sir George, 397, 408
Carey, Henry, first Lord Hunsdon, 125–26, 167n, 296n, 303n, 355n
Carey, Henry (son of Hunsdon), 390
Carey, Sir Robert, 296–97, 355–56, 357

Carey, William, 266n, 296n
Carleton, Sir Dudley, 347n
Carlos, Don (prince of Spain), 115n
Carmichael, Sir John, 364
Castelnau, Michael de, sieur de Mauvissière, 215, 217
Catherine. See Katherine
Catherine of Aragon (queen, wife of Henry VIII), 24n
Catherine de Médicis, 205–12, 215–17, 221–27, 250n, 252n, 259–61
Catlin, Sir Robert, 98
Cecil, Sir Robert, 190n, 200n, 334–35, 399n, 425n
Cecil, William, Lord Burghley, 51, 67, 73n, 87n–88n, 98, 100–2, 124n, 177–78, 180, 195n, 209, 370; arguments in favor of marriage to Alençon, 240–42; documents in hand of, 98–100, 101–2, 111–12, 117–19, 127, 221; and execution of Mary, Queen of Scots, 286n, 287–89; marginal notes and corrections by, 70n, 72–76, 81–86, 93, 112–15, 120–25, 131, 212n, 259, 384, 386
Chamberlain, John, 347n
Charles V (Holy Roman Emperor), 349, 353
Charles VII (of France), 65–66
Charles VIII (of France), 65
Charles IX (of France), 113–14, 205–12, 215–17, 221–27
Charles, archduke of Austria, 95n
Charles, archduke of Styria, 333n
Charybdis, 233, 251, 376
Cheke, Sir John, 29n
Cheke, Mary, 29
Cholmley, Ranulph, 54
Cicero, 16, 259n, 292, 327n
Clinton, Edward Fiennes de, earl of Lincoln, 206
Clotho, 71
Colville, laird of Wemyss, 378–77
Constance I (of Sicily), 83
Constantine Copronymus (Byzantine emperor), 424n
Cotton, Sir George, 111n
Cotton, Sir Robert, 5n

Cox, Richard, bishop of Ely, 88n

Cranmer, Thomas, 6n

Crawford, earl of, 367

Croke, Sir John, 336–43, 346

Cromwell, Thomas, 167n

Cuffe, Henry, 395

Cupid, 304–6

Dacres, Leonard, 125–26

Dale, Dr. Valentine, 221–27

Daniel (biblical figure), 55, 155

Darnley. *See* Stewart, Henry

David (biblical figure), 85, 145–47, 175

Davison, William, 270, 279–81

Deborah (biblical figure), 157, 424

Democritus, 88n

Demosthenes, 88

Denny, Lady, 20, 32n

Denny, Sir Anthony, 20, 26

Derby, Henry, fourth earl of, 307 n. *See also* Stanley, Edward

Devereux, Henry, earl of Essex, 307n, 325n, 334–35, 386–88; execution of, 345 n; in Ireland, 390–99, 425–27

D'Ewes, Sir Simonds, 56n, 79n, 97n, 107n, 167n, 181n, 336n

Digges, Sir Dudley, xv, 205n

Diogenes Laertius, 421n

Donne, John, xiii, 47n

Douglas, Archibald, 286, 290

Douglas, Robert, of Morton, 401

Drake, Sir Francis, 409–10

Drury, Lady Elizabeth, 361–62

du Bex (secretary), 251

Dudley, Ambrose, earl of Warwick, 231

Dudley, Guilford, 38n, 67n

Dudley, John, duke of Northumberland, 38n, 67n, 350, 353

Dudley, Robert, earl of Leicester, xiii, 67, 87, 89n–91n, 109, 115, 132n, 171, 177–78n, 358n; death of, 326n, 359; entertainment at Chatsworth, 229–31; and marriage negotiations, 225, 227, 252; in the Netherlands, 269–74, 277–80, 282–83; and the Spanish Armada, 325n, 326n

Durham, bishop of, 347n

Edward VI (of England), 13–17, 21, 24, 29n, 30, 35–40, 63; later recollections of, 52, 76n, 97, 178

Egerton, Sir Thomas, 340, 424n

Eleazar (biblical figure), 84

Elijah (biblical figure), 170

Elizabeth (biblical mother of John the Baptist), 84–85

Elizabeth I of England: accession as queen, 50–55; aid to Henry IV, 360–64; on the armada victory and its aftermath, 325–26, 328–35, 346–59, 409–27; and Babington Plot, 284–87; controversy with Scotland over Bothwell and the Affair of the Spanish Blanks, 364–69, 371–84; as courtier-poet, 299–309; and crisis over monopolies, 335–46; and Darnley affair, 115–25; departure from Seymour household, 17–19; early humanist education, 5–17; and ecclesiastical reform, 167–74, 177–83; entertainments on progress, 109–10, 174–77; and Irish rebellion, 389–400, 404–7; and Leicester's governorship of the Netherlands, 269–74, 277–83; maneuvers against Spain in late 1590s, 384–88, 402–3; negotiations over Alençon marriage, 205–61 passim, 302–3, 311–21; and Northern Rebellion, 125–34; peril under Mary I, 41–48; publication of prayer books, 135–63; reaction to conversion of Henry IV, 370–71; struggles over marriage and succession, 56–108; suspected collusion with Thomas Seymour, 22–35; and trial and execution of Mary, Queen of Scots, 183–204, 287–98. *See also individual names and itemized contents of the edition,* 429–37

Elizabeth of York (queen, wife of Henry VII), 74

Ely, bishop of, xiv. *See also* Cox, Richard

Ennius, 16

Enoch (biblical figure), 170n

Epimetheus, 290

Eric XIV (king of Sweden), 207n, 334n

Errol, earl of, 367, 373

Esau (biblical figure), 155, 371
Essex. *See* Devereux, Henry
Esther (biblical figure), 157
Evesham, Alex, 56n
Ezekiel (biblical figure), 85

Farnese, Allesandro, duke of Parma, 211n, 252n, 325n, 326n
Faustina (daughter of Roman emperor), 83n
Feria, Count, 211n
Finet, John, 304n
Fisher, Bishop John, 135n
Fitton, Sir Edward, 218–20
FitzGerald, Gerald, earl of Kildare, 220
Fitzwilliam, Sir William, 218–20
Fleming, Mr. (solicitor), 344–45
Foix, Paul de, 205
Forster, Sir John, 126
Fortescue, Lady. *See* Parry, Anne
Foxe, John, 46n, 55n
Francis I (of France), 6n, 65
Francis II (of France), 60n, 61n, 68–69, 114, 120n, 122, 298n
Frederick II (Holy Roman Emperor), 83
Frederick III (elector Palatine), 222n
Fuller, Thomas, 258n, 307n

Gage, Sir John, 28n
Gage, Philippa, 28
Galileo Galilei, 12n
Garter, Bernard, 174
Glammis, earl of, 266n
Godwin, Dr. Thomas, 89n
Gordon, Lady Jean (wife of James Hepburn, fourth earl of Bothwell), 118
Gregory of Nazianzus, Saint, 34
Grey, Henry, duke of Suffolk, third marquis of Dorset, 38, 63
Grey, Lady Jane, 38n, 39n, 63n, 67n
Grey, Lady Katherine, 63, 66
Grey, Patrick, sixth baron, 295
Grindal, Edmund, bishop of London, 97n, 121n
Guise, dukes of, 60n, 113–14
Guise, Mary of (queen regent of Scotland), 60n, 75n

Hackwell, Mr., of Lincoln's Inn, 345
Hadrian (Roman emperor), 85n
Hamilton, Archbishop, 118n
Harington, Sir John, 133n, 167n
Hastings, Henry, third earl of Huntingdon, 371–72
Hatton, Sir Christopher, 181n, 218n, 233n, 247n, 256n, 258n
Hayward, Sir John, 55n, 60n
Heneage, Sir Thomas, 269–73, 278–79, 299–300
Henry III (of France; formerly duke of Anjou), 205n, 205–6, 207, 211, 212, 226, 233–39, 245–46, 250n, 252–56, 259–61, 298, 360n
Henry IV (of England), 175n
Henry IV (of France, formerly king of Navarre), 238, 255, 301n, 360–61, 363–64, 384–86, 400n, 402–3; conversion of, 370–71
Henry VII (of England), 74, 77
Henry VIII (of England), 4, 5n, 8–10, 11, 56n, 135n, 138, 139; death of, 13n, 25, 29; later recollections of, 52, 76, 220, 410; will of, 23n
Henry (Hohenstaufen, king of Germany and Sicily), 83
Henry (prince of France), 65
Hentzner, Paul, 45n
Hepburn, Francis Stewart, fifth earl of Bothwell, 367n, 369, 372, 375–81
Hepburn, James, fourth earl of Bothwell, 116, 118–19, 124, 369n
Hervey, Anthony, 232n
Hesiod, 290n
Hill, Richard, 29n
Hilliard, Nicholas, 311n
Hoby, Sir Edward, 181n, 200n, 425n
Holinshed, Raphael, 46n, 53n, 190, 200n
Hollock, Count, 283
Homer, 15, 129n
Horace, 36, 383
Howard, Charles, lord of Effingham, 425
Howard, Henry, earl of Northampton, 346–51

Howard, Thomas, fourth duke of Norfolk, 87n, 94, 120n, 125n, 127–31
Howard, William, first baron of Effingham, 129n
Hudson, James, 277
Huish, Alexander, 47n
Humphreys, Dr. Lawrence, 89n–90n
Huntly, earl of, 367, 373

Innocent II (Pope), 83n
Isabella of Spain, "Archduke" of the Netherlands, 348
Isaiah (biblical figure), 149

Jacob (biblical figure), 155, 371
Jaline, Paul de, 332–35
James I (of England). See James VI
James II (of England), 312n
James V (of Scotland), 75
James VI (of Scotland; later James I of England), xv; birth and early years of, 93n, 118, 123–24; correspondence with Elizabeth, 261–69, 274–77, 281–82, 286–87, 289–97, 355–59, 364–69, 372–84; peace with Spain, 350n
Jezebel (biblical figure), 197n
John the Baptist, Saint, 85
John, duke of Finland, 207n, 333n, 334
John, Saint, 85
Joseph (biblical figure), 411
Joshua (biblical figure), 85
Judas (biblical figure), 117
Judith (biblical figure), 157
Julius Capitolinus, 83n
Juno, 377n, 381

Katherine (queen, wife of Henry VIII), 5, 9–11, 17–20, 28, 30, 96n; as author and translator, 9, 135n, 161n, 312n, 426n; death of, 21n, 23n, 25
Keith, Sir William, 268, 291
Kempis, Thomas à, 9n
Kennal, Dr. John, 89n
Ker, earl of (of Fernihurst), 275n, 289n
Ker, George, 367, 373
Ker, Sir Thomas, 264, 289n

Kingsmill, Mr., 90n
Knollys, Sir Francis, 100, 178, 266n
Knollys, Katherine, 266n
Knollys, William, 266

Lawrence, Giles, 90n
Leicester. See Dudley, Robert
Leo X (Pope), 9
Leslie, John, bishop of Ross, 120–21, 125
Lilliat, John, 409n
Limbert, Stephen, 176
Lincoln. See Clinton, Edward Fiennes de
Lot (biblical figure), 155
Louis XI (of France), 65, 66n
Louis XII (of France), 66

Maitland, William, laird of Lethington, 60–70
Man, Dr. Thomas, 113
Mar, earl of, 266n
Marbeck, Roger, 89n, 91n
Marchaumont, Clausse de, count de Beaumont, 255–56, 260
Marcus Aurelius (Roman emperor), 83n
Margaret (queen of Scotland), 75n
Margaret (queen of Scotland, sister of Henry VIII), 115n
Marguerite d'Angoulême (queen of Navarre), 6, 96n
Marguerite de Valois (queen of Navarre), 255
Marot, Clément, 147n
Mary (Virgin, mother of Christ), 170n, 327n
Mary I (of England), 24n, 37–38, 41–44, 46n, 56n, 61n, 63n, 72n; later recollections of, 51, 76n, 96, 97, 99, 141, 234, 242, 247
Mary, Queen of Scots, 60–70, 74, 75, 93, 130–31, 133n, 229n, 262, 284, 298n, 369n; and Darnley affair, 114–25, 127; trial and execution of, 186–204, 286n, 287–89, 291–97
Master, William, 87
Maurice, Count, 283
Mauvissière. See Castelnau, Michael de

Maximillian II (Holy Roman Emperor), 301

Mehmed III (Ottoman Emperor Mahumet Cham), 400–2

Melissus (Paul Schede), 301–2

Melville, Robert, Lord, 117–18, 295

Mewtas, Sir Peter, 69

Mildmay, Sir Walter, 173, 178n

Miltiades, 88n

Monsieur. See Alençon, François Hercule

Montmorency, François, duke of, 205–12 passim, 222

Montpensier, duke of, 222

Moore, Francis, 346

Morlans, Jean de, 370

Moses (biblical figure), 85

Mountjoy. See Blount, Charles

Mulcaster, Richard, 53

Navarre. See Henry IV (of France); Marguerite d'Angoulême; Marguerite de Valois

Nestor, 129

Neville, Charles, earl of Westmoreland, 264, 350, 353

Noah (biblical figure), 155

Noailles, François de, 42n

Nocle, Beauvoir la, 363, 364

Norfolk. See Howard, Thomas

Norris, Sir Henry, 389

Norris, Sir John, 283–84, 325n, 389–90

Norris, Lady Margery, 389–90

Norris, Sir Thomas, 391

Northumberland. See Dudley, John

Norton, Thomas, 370n

Ochino, 96n

O'Donnell, Hugh Roe, 398

Odysseus, 233n

Oliphant, Lawrence, 401

Oliphant, Robert, 401

O'Neill, Hugh, second earl of Tyrone, 390–99, 404–8

Onslowe, Sir Richard, 98, 101, 107n

Ormond. See Butler, Thomas, tenth earl of

O'Rourke, Sir Brian, 376

Overton, William, 180

Ovid, 6n

Oxford, earl of, 303n

Pallas, 325n

Parker, Matthew, Archbishop, 90n

Parma. See Farnese, Allesandro

Parr. See Katherine (queen, wife of Henry VIII)

Parry, Anne, Lady Fortescue, 28

Parry, Thomas, 17n, 23n, 24, 26–30

Parry, Dr. William, 262n

Parsons, Robert, 286n

Paul, Saint, 12, 85

Paulet, Sir Amyas, 196n, 231–32, 233–37; as jailor of Mary, Queen of Scots, 262n, 284

Paulet, Hugh, 231

Paulet, Margaret, 232

Paulet, William, marquis of Winchester, 27, 56, 81–86

Peter (king of Aragon), 83

Philibert Emmanuel (prince of Piedmont and duke of Savoy), 56n, 113, 207n

Philip II (of Spain), 56n, 112–15, 207n, 234, 242, 247–49, 250n, 329–32, 335, 369, 409–10; later recollections of, 348–53

Philip III (of Spain), 350

Phillips, Robert, 109–10

Pilkington, James, bishop of Durham, 97n

Pinard, Claude, 252, 254–55

Pindar, 15, 290n

Plato, 198n

Platter, Thomas, 45n

Plutarch, 66n, 71n, 83n, 88n, 198n

Pompey, 66n

Portland, duke of, 56

Prometheus, 290

Publilius Syrus, 36n

Puckering, Sir John, 328

Puttenham, George, 133n, 301n, 303n, 307n

Pyrrhus (of Epirus, king of the Molossians), 83

Quadra, Alvaro de la, 102n, 112

Quincy, sieur de, 176

Radcliffe, Thomas, third earl of Sussex, 176–77, 239

Ralegh, Sir Walter, 303n, 307–9

Ramsey, John, 409n
Randolph, Sir Thomas, 115, 117, 221, 268, 274–75, 282
Reaux, Monsieur de, 259
Retz, Gondi de, count, 225
Richard III (of England), 74n
Robinson, Richard, 425n
Roger II (of Sicily), 83n
Rogers, Sir Edward, 100
Ross. See Leslie, John
Russell, Anne, 37n
Russell, Francis, Lord, 263, 267, 275n
Russell, Francis, second earl of Bedford, 117, 123n, 177, 263n
Russell, Jane, 37
Russell, John, first earl of Bedford, 37n, 39–40
Russell, William, 26–27

Salignac, Bertrand de, sieur de La Mothe-Fénélon, 209–10, 260
Samuel (biblical figure), 84
Sancroft, William, 302n
Scylla, 233, 251, 376
Seymour, Anne Stanhope, 22, 27, 29n
Seymour, Edward, duke of Somerset, 22–24, 25, 29–35, 41–42
Seymour, Edward, earl of Hertford, 63n
Seymour, John, 29
Seymour, Mary, 17n
Seymour, Thomas, lord high admiral, 17n, 19–25 passim, 29–35, 41–42; plans for marriage with Elizabeth, 25–30
Shakespeare, William, xiii, 268n
Sharp, Dr. Lionel, 325n
Sherington, Sir Henry, 258n
Shirley, Sir Thomas, 283
Shrewsbury. See Talbot, Elizabeth; Talbot, George; Talbot, Gilbert
Sidney, Sir Henry, 393n
Sidney, Sir Philip, 258n, 358n
Sidney, Sir Robert, 358, 359
Sigismund III (king of Poland), 333–34
Simeon (biblical figure), 80n
Simier, Jean de, 233–37, 238, 239, 243–44, 246–47
Smith, Sir Thomas, 25n, 28, 100n, 127

Solomon (biblical figure), 85, 142, 147, 198, 245
Somerset. See Seymour, Edward
Sophocles, 187n
Spelman, Sir Henry, 410
Stafford, Lady, 56n
Stafford, Sir Edward, 237, 247–49, 293n
Stafford, William, 293
Stanford, Henry, 167n, 303n, 305n
Stanley, Edward, third earl of Derby, 111–12
Stanley, Mary, 111–112
Stapleton, Sir Robert, 258
Stewart, Henry, Lord Darnley, 115–16, 118, 122, 123, 275
Stewart, James, earl of Arran, 263n–264
Stewart, James, earl of Moray, 124n
Stow, John, 181n, 330n, 425n
Suetonius, 86, 410
Suffolk. See Brandon, Katherine Willoughby; Grey, Henry
Susanna (biblical figure), 155
Sussex. See Radcliffe, Thomas

Talbot, Elizabeth, countess of Shrewsbury, 229–31
Talbot, Francis, 167n, 256–57, 258
Talbot, George, sixth earl of Shrewsbury, xiii, 130, 167n, 212–13, 229–31, 262; son's death, 256–57, 258
Talbot, Gilbert, seventh earl of Shrewsbury, 167n, 386
Talbot, John, 258n
Talbot, Mistress, 258
Themistocles, 88n
Theodosia, 424
Timothy (biblical figure), 85
Toledo, Ferdinand de, duke of Alva, 350n
Tour d'Auvergne, Henry de la, duke of Bouillon, 385
Townshend, Hayward, 335–40, 344–46
Tudor. See under names of individual monarchs
Tuke, Mistress, 312n
Turnus, 381
Tyrone. See O'Neill, Hugh
Tyrwhit, Sir Robert, 22–24, 31

Valerius Maximus, 99n

Venus, 304

Vernon, Elizabeth, 394n

Virgil, 377, 378n, 381

Waldstein, Baron (Zdeněk Brtnický z
    Valdštejina), 45n, 46n

Walsingham, Sir Francis, xv, 178n, 205–12,
    215–17, 252, 298

Wemys, Colvill, laird of, 376

Wentworth, Peter, 100

Westmoreland. See Neville, Charles

White, Sir Nicholas, 220

White, Dr. Thomas, 89n

Whitford, Richard, 9

Whitgift, John, 177, 180, 189, 425n

Wilbraham, Richard, of Nantwich, 351n

Wilbraham, Sir Roger, 351–54

Wilkes, Thomas, 282–83

Wilkinson, Rudolph, 87n

William the Silent, prince of Orange, 222n,
    272n

Williams, Thomas, 70, 72n, 76

Wiloughby. See Bertie, Peregrine

Willoughby. See Brandon, Katherine

Wilson, Dr. Thomas, 127

Wood, Anthony à, 89n

Wood, Robert, 174–77

Worcester, earl of, 365n

Wotton, Sir Edward, 262

Wriothesley, Henry, earl of Southampton,
    393–94

Wroth, John, 402

Wroth, Sir Robert, 345

Wyatt, Sir Thomas, the younger, 42,
    56n

York, archbishops of, 94; See also Young,
    Dr. Thomas

Young, John, 180

Young, Dr. Thomas, 97

Zeno, 421n

Zeus, 290n

Zouch, Edward, Baron Zouche of
    Harringsworth, 372, 376